Democracy in the European Union

It is widely believed that the European Union (EU) suffers from a democratic deficit. This raises a fundamental question: can democracy ever be applied to decision-making bodies beyond the nation-state? Today, the EU is a highly complex entity undergoing profound changes. This book asks how the type of co-operation upon which the EU is based can be best explained, what the integrative forces in the EU are and how integration at a supranational level can come about.

The book is premised on the notion that precisely how we conceive of democracy is essential to how we understand the nature of the democratic deficit. Furthermore, the question of the democratic deficit cannot be considered as separate from the question of what type of entity the EU is. To address these issues, this book revisits the field of political theory and adopts a theoretical approach to democracy that allows us to assess the prospects for democracy at a supranational level.

The key thinkers represented in this volume stress that in order to understand integration beyond the nation-state, we need new explanatory categories associated with deliberation because a supranational entity such as the EU possesses far weaker and less well-developed means of coercion – bargaining resources – than do states. The most appropriate term to denote this is the notion of 'deliberative supranationalism'. This pioneering work, headed by major writers such as Bellamy, Habermas, Joerges and Schlesinger, brings a new perspective to this key issue in contemporary politics and political theory.

The editors: Erik Oddvar Eriksen is Professor at ARENA, University of Oslo, and Senior Researcher at LOS Centre, the University of Bergen, Norway. He has written in the fields of public policy and social and political theory. **John Erik Fossum** is Associate Professor in the Department of Administration and Organisation Theory, the University of Bergen, Norway. He has written in the fields of comparative public policy, political theory and international relations.

Democracy in the European Union

Integration through deliberation?

Edited by Erik Oddvar Eriksen and John Erik Fossum

London and New York

First published 2000
by Routledge
11 New Fetter Lane, London EC4P 4EE

Simultaneously published in the USA and Canada
by Routledge
29 West 35th Street, New York, NY 10001

Routledge is an imprint of the Taylor & Francis Group

Typeset in Baskerville by Taylor & Francis Books Ltd
Printed and bound in Great Britain by St Edmundsbury Press, Bury St
Edmunds, Suffolk

British Library Cataloguing in Publication Data
A catalogue record for this book is available from the British Library

Library of Congress Cataloging in Publication Data
Democracy in the European Union: Integration through deliberation? /
edited by Erik Oddvar Eriksen and John Erik Fossum.
  Includes bibliographical references and index.
  1. European Union.   2. Democracy.
  I. Eriksen, Erik Oddvar, 1955– .   II. Fossum, John Erik.
  JN40.D47   2000   99-39942
  341.242'2–dc21   CIP

ISBN 0–415–22591–4 (hbk)
ISBN 0–415–22592–2 (pbk)

Contents

Contributors

Richard Bellamy is Professor of Politics and International Relations at the University of Reading. Recent publications include *Liberalism and Modern Society* (1992) and (with Darrow Schecter) *Gramsci and the Italian State* (1993). He is the editor of *Constitutionalism, Democracy and Sovereignty* and (with Dario Castiglione) *Constitutionalism in Transformation* (1996). He has most recently published *Liberalism and Pluralism: Towards a Politics of Compromise* (1999), and is currently directing a project on European citizenship.

Lars Chr. Blichner is Associate Professor in the Department of Administration and Organisation Theory, University of Bergen, Norway. Relevant publications include *Spørsmål i Stortinget. Sikkerhetsventil i petroleumspolitikken* (with Johan P. Olsen), and (both with Linda Sangolt) 'Internasjonalisering av offentlig forvaltning' (1993) and 'The concept of subsidiarity and the debate on European operations: pitfalls and possibilities' (1994). His current work is on communication and the role of the state in promoting justice.

Else Grete Broderstad is a Research Fellow and Ph.D. candidate in Political Science at the University of Tromsø, Norway. During the period 1992–97 she was director of the Centre for Saami Studies, at the University of Tromsø. Recent publications include 'Samepolitikk i et deliberativt perspektiv' (1995), 'Saami identity in cultural and political communities' (1997) and 'Samepolitikk: selvbestemmelse og medbestemmelse' (1999). The focus of her current research is on indigenous politics in a new European context.

Dario Castiglione is Senior Lecturer in Political Theory at the University of Exeter. He has written on eighteenth-century political theory, and on the history of civil society and constitutionalism. He has edited (with R. Bellamy) the 1996 Political Studies special issue on *Constitutionalism in Transformation: European and Theoretical Perspectives*, and has written several articles on constitutionalism and Europe. He is currently working on a monograph on David Hume's political philosophy.

Erik Oddvar Eriksen is Professor at ARENA, the University of Oslo, and Adjunct Professor at the LOS Centre, University of Bergen, Norway. Recent publications include *Grenser for staten* (1993) and *Kommunikativ ledelse* (1999). He has edited *Den politiske orden* (1993), *Deliberativ politikk* (1995) and (with Jørn Loftager) *The Rationality of the Welfare State* (1996). He is the co-author, with Jarle Weigård, of *Kommunikativ handling og deliberativt demokrati* (1999). His research interest is in social and political theory, with particular emphasis on the EU.

Michelle Everson is Jean Monnet Fellow and Managing Editor of the European Law Journal at the European University Institute, Florence, Italy. Recent publications include 'Administering Europe?' (1998), 'Beyond the *Bundesverfassungsgericht* – on the necessary cunning of constitutional reasoning' (1998) and 'Constitutionalising European administrative law' (1999). Her major research interests lie in the fields of European economic regulation and an increasingly internationalized body of administrative law.

Andreas Føllesdal is Senior Researcher at ARENA, and Associate Professor in the Department of Philosophy, the University of Oslo. His work on the political theory of the EU includes articles on distributive justice, federalism, democracy, subsidiarity and European citizenship. Recent publications include 'Democracy, legitimacy and majority rule in the EU' (1998) and 'Subsidiarity' (1998). He is co-editor of *Democracy and the European Union* (1997) and *Restructuring the Welfare State* (1997), both with P. Koslowski.

John Erik Fossum is Associate Professor in the Department of Administration and Organisation Theory, University of Bergen, and is affiliated with ARENA. Recent publications include *Oil, the State, and Federalism* (1997), 'Citizenship, diversity and pluralism: the case of the European Union' (1999) and (with Stuart Robinson) 'A phoenix arises: the social reconstruction of Europe' (1999). His current research is on constitutionalism, citizenship and democratic legitimacy in the EU and Canada.

Roberto Gargarella is Associate Professor in the Department of Law and Political Science, at the Universidad di Tella, Buenos Aires, Argentina. He teaches constitutional law and political philosophy at the Universidad Torcuato Di Tella (Buenos Aires) and Pompeu Fabra (Barcelona). He is the author of *Public Discussion and Political Radicalism in the Origins of Constitutionalism* (forthcoming), as well as several articles, including 'Full representation, deliberation, and impartiality', and two other books on political philosophy.

Jürgen Habermas is Professor Emeritus of Philosophy and Sociology at the University of Frankfurt, Germany. A brief selection of some of his recent books includes *The Theory of Communicative Action* (2 vols) (1981), *Moral Consciousness and Communicative Action* (1983), *The Philosophical Discourse of Modernity - Twelve Lectures* (1985), *Postmetaphysical Thinking* (1988), *Justification and Application* (1991); *Between Facts and Norms* (1996), *The Inclusion of the Other* (1998) and *Die postnationale Konstellation* (1998).

Christian Joerges is Professor of European Economic Law at the European University Institute in Florence. He is co-editor of *Critical Legal Thought: An*

American-German Debate (1989), *Das Recht des Franchising: Konzeptionelle, Rechtsvergleichende und Europarechtliche Analysen* (1991), *Integrating Scientific Expertise into Regulatory Decision-Making: National Traditions and European Innovations* (1997), *Private Governance, Democratic Constitutionalism and Supranationalism* (1998) and *European Committees: Social Regulation, Law and Politics* (1999).

Deirdre Kevin (BA, MA) is Researcher at the European Institute for the Media, Duesseldorf, Germany. She previously worked as a researcher at the Stirling Media Research Institute at the University of Stirling, Scotland, on the project 'Political Communication and Democracy' funded by the UK Economic and Social Research Council. She is currently managing the eight-country 'Building Bridges between Cultures' project, which is researching news media and collective identities in the EU.

Philip Schlesinger is Professor of Film and Media Studies at the University of Stirling, Director of Stirling Media Research Institute, and Adjunct Professor at the University of Oslo. His publications on European questions include the co-edited volumes *European Transformations* (1994) and *Exploring the Limits: Europe's Changing Communication Environment* (1997). The author of *Media, State and Nation* (1991) and co-editor of *Media, Culture and Society* journal, he recently completed research on 'Political Communication and Democracy' and is concluding a study of 'The Scottish Parliament and Political Communication'.

Preface

The collapse of the Berlin Wall – an event which Archibugi, Held and Köhler find 'now rivals the storming of the Bastille as a symbol of historical change' – marked the end of the Cold War and reinvigorated people's faith in the merits of democracy. It also underlined the need for democracy and democratization across the world. It had repercussions of a more theoretical character, as well. It sparked renewed interest in the very concept of democracy and in how different kinds of decision-making processes can be organized democratically. An important contribution to theorizing has been labelled *deliberative democracy*, a mode of thinking which seeks to reconstruct democracy as governance based upon the public use of reason.

The optimism that was sparked in 1989 was not borne out in practice, in particular in the new democracies in Eastern Europe and the former Soviet Union, which have faced numerous setbacks and hardships since then. Further, the process of economic globalization has led many to seriously question the room for and the role of democratic politics. National control is undermined, as international movements of capital have greatly increased. Many people have become disillusioned, as a widened range of factors of vital importance to citizens and their well being, are no longer subject to democratic control.

Is democracy possible at all in this situation? If so, how can it be applied to decision-making bodies beyond the nation-state? It is in this regard that the establishment and widening of co-operation in Europe is of particular interest, both because it may be seen as an order particularly suited for handling globalization and also because it represents a form of voluntary but committing co-operation among *democratic* states.

Democracy, when considered from the vantage point of the deliberative perspective that is presented in this book, functions through the public discussion of important issues. Much of the literature on the EU portrays it as marked by technocracy, expert dominance and lack of transparency; bargaining and pork-barrelling between sectarian interests; and in general, as marked by lack of openness and political accountability. The European Union is also widely held to be a challenger, if not to the state, then at least to the nation. However, the EU is a dynamic entity and has increasingly taken on a set of supranational deliberative features. To a surprising degree it has shown itself capable of carrying out collective action. It has acquired competence to act in a wide range of policy fields and has established a set of institutions – however weak when compared to those of states – that are unprecedented and have revealed a remarkable ability to weather storms and handle crises.

The EU is a complex system of governance, and one that is hard to grasp in analytical terms. In particular we are faced with the question of how the process of integration in the EU can be explained. What are the integrative forces in the EU, and how can integration at a supranational level come about? Analytically speaking, integration may occur through *strategic bargaining* between the Member States or through *functional adaptation*, i.e. due to the performance and delivery of the system. These are the two conventional perspectives on integration in Europe and which have been developed by intergovernmentalists and neo-functionalists, respectively. Neither of these takes the question of democracy as an explanatory variable into consideration, however. These modes of thought are, then, not particularly well suited to address the question of democratic accountability and legitimacy which has become particularly pressing in the last decade. For instance, Pascal Lamy (Delors' *Chef de Cabinet*) said after the initial Danish no to the Maastricht Treaty, that: 'Europe was built in a St. Simonian way from the beginning, this was Monnet's approach. The people weren't ready to agree to integration, so you had to get on without telling them too much about what was happening. Now St. Simonianism is finished. It can't work when you have to face democratic opinion.' The important questions then, are: How can public opinion and will formation influence European politics? How can democracy at all be applied to the transnational system of governance?

This forms the backdrop for the assertion that this book is intended to clarify, namely that communicative processes in Europe must be taken properly into consideration if we are to account for post-national integration. Hence, our assertion is that integration also occurs through deliberation, or what is commonly referred to as *arguing*. This type of integration is very important, as stability depends on learning and alteration of preferences. Deliberation, when properly conducted, ensures communicative processes where the force of the better argument will sway people to harmonize their action plans and transfer agreements into binding contracts, with the aid of the legal structure in place. To understand integration beyond the nation-state, explanatory categories associated with deliberation are required, also because supranational entities possess far weaker and less well-developed means of coercion – bargaining resources – than do states. This is the main problem we are grappling with in this book, and which has encouraged the contributors to address topics such as constitution-making and democracy in the EU; deliberative supranationalism and the challenge of technocratic governance; the principle of subsidiarity; the role of interparliamentary discourse; the deliberative quality of the Council of the Union; the role of the public sphere; and the treatment of minority rights. These topics are the themes that inform the book. However, globalization forms the general background to the book and it was therefore necessary to devote an independent chapter to it.

To achieve the best possible exploration of these topics we arranged a conference on 'Democracy in Europe' in Bergen, Norway in February 1998. We invited people from different academic disciplines, different research milieus, and different countries. The contributors (with the exception of Jürgen Habermas whose contribution was originally delivered at the University of Oslo – as the Vilhelm Aubert lecture on 19 September 1997) presented papers and outlines, in response to a preliminary outline provided by the editors. Since then the chapters have gone through several major revisions in order to ensure the coherence we want readers to expect from a book, be it monograph or edited piece.

For comments on the various portions of the book that the editors have written together, as well as individually, we have incurred numerous debts. In addition to the comments from the contributors to this volume, and all those who have contributed to their chapters in various ways, we would in particular like to thank Svein S. Andersen, Jeffrey T. Checkel, Dag Harald Claes, Lars Fjell Hansson, Per Lægreid, Knut Midgaard, Johan P. Olsen, Stuart Robinson, Linda Sangolt, Anne Julie Semb, Helene Sjursen, Ulf Sverdrup, and Marianne Takle.

Special thanks are due to Maila Solheim for excellent technical assistance. We are also grateful for generous financial and administrative support from the Norwegian Research Centre in Organisation and Management, the Faculty of Social Science, and the Department of Administration and Organisation Theory, all at the University of Bergen, and from the ARENA programme at the University of Oslo.

Oslo/Bergen 1.6.1999
Erik Oddvar Eriksen and John Erik Fossum

1 Post-national integration[1]

Erik Oddvar Eriksen and John Erik Fossum

Introduction: post-national integration – a deliberative perspective

Reflecting on the revolutions in Eastern Europe in 1989, the late François Mitterand in his 1990 New Year's speech to the French people stated that 'Europe is returning home to its history and geography'. However, the revolutions in Eastern Europe should not be construed simply as an occasion to look back, to try to resurrect the past. They also represent a unique opportunity for Europe to try to recapture the aspects of the past that will produce a better future. Now that Europe is no longer divided, it can proceed with the *civilizational project* that was first initiated during the Enlightenment era, but which has since then faced a number of grave setbacks. European integration is rooted in the past, and ultimately draws its legitimating force from the humanistic developments that have been so important to the Western world. European integration has its foundations in the strongest institutional manifestations of this development, namely the successful establishment of national systems of democratic governance in all of Western Europe, but is also a response to their defects. European integration promises to expand the system of *democratic governance* to the international level, through the establishment of supranational institutions. Such institutions, it should be noted, are no doubt also efforts to remedy the particular contemporary challenges associated with globalization. Globalization alerts us to the fact that in important respects the state is too small to address some of the most pressing challenges we are faced with today. Globalization – proceeding along legal, cultural, economical and political dimensions – brings forth new and magnifies old challenges to legitimate governance. The state is not able to control international capital flows or technological developments. Nor can it stem the negative social and environmental effects of an increasingly global capitalism. It has become increasingly evident that many problems such as nuclear waste, carbon dioxide emissions, refugees, cross-border financial flows, criminal law problems, and technology transfer require solutions at the international level. In addition, in such a situation, it has become increasingly difficult for the state to uphold the socio-economic compromise, which has long sustained the welfare-state. This compromise consisted of measures to sustain economic growth, on the one hand, and measures to ensure social protection, on the other. In Chapter 2, Jürgen Habermas discusses the consequences of economic globalization and the need for a global welfare regime.

This particular project to develop democracy at the international level, from the vantage point of a system of democratic states, has no historical or contemporary precedents. In particular, the EU attaches citizens to a supranational entity in such a manner as to potentially undermine the nation-state. As such, Europe is facing a unique moment of institutional innovation which attests to what Robert A. Dahl (1994) has called the third transformation in the history of democracy. The first phase concerned the transformation of the undemocratic city-state and began in the fifth century B.C.; the second phase concerned the democratization of the nation-state and began in the wake of the French and American revolutions. There is a parallel between these two phases: as the city-state then became too small to cope with its problems, the nation-state today is too small to cope with its problems, as it has to grapple with the challenge of globalization. Decision-making authority is transferred to the international level, but here democratic structures are rather weak. International bodies of governance are, as a rule, not democratic. The EU, however, is not an ordinary international organization, neither is it a state. It is a unique type of entity. It is unique not only because it has developed a unique set of institutions, but also because there is such a great concern with democracy in the EU. This sets it apart from ordinary international organizations, which are rarely subject to democratic concern or public scrutiny. The democratic quality of the EU is assessed not only in terms of the outcomes that the EU produces, or in terms of its institutional and decisional make-up, but also in terms of its democratic accountability. Democratic accountability is directly linked to popular legitimacy. It is widely held that the EU suffers from a democratic 'deficit' and this is often attributed to weak popular legitimacy (Wallace 1993; Weiler 1996a). In Chapters 3 and 4, the notion of democratic 'deficit' will be critically scrutinized.

In this book, our point of departure is that innovations at such a scale require not simply attention to the empirical nature of the novel governance arrangements. They also require serious re-examination of the concepts available to depict these developments, and thereby theoretical frameworks and attendant standards that we can use to assess the democratic quality of this nascent system of governance. In this introductory chapter, our purpose is to clarify this assertion. We address the most common conceptual approaches that are used to analyse the EU and spell out how – and the extent to which – they assess the democratic quality of the EU. Conventional analyses of international integration are still informed by realist and neo-functional conceptions of political interaction. Realists are not really concerned with the prospects for democratic governance in contemporary Europe and neo-functionalists are prone to take the legitimacy of the EU-based institutions for granted. The *deliberative perspective*, which is only now gaining adherents among students of the EU, represents the most explicit departure from the dominant frameworks and standards that have thus far been employed. The deliberative perspective alerts us to achievements as well as shortcomings and enables us to assess critically the democratic quality of the EU without recourse to the often misleading standards associated with the nation-state.

The question is how the process of integration in the European Union (EU) can be explained. What are the integrative forces in the EU and how can integration at a supranational level come about? Integration may occur through strategic bargaining or through functional adaptation. However, it may also occur through deliberation or what is commonly referred to as arguing. This latter type of integration is very important, as stability depends on learning and alteration of preferences. Deliberation, when properly conducted, ensures communicative processes where the force of the better argument will sway people to harmonize their action plans. To understand post-national integration, or integration beyond the nation-state, explanatory categories associated with deliberation are required, as supranational entities possess far weaker and less well-developed means of coercion – bargaining resources – than do states.

We start with some observations on the limitations of the nation-state as ontological reality and on the limitations of the vocabulary of the nation-state as tool for the assessment of democratic governance in contemporary Europe.

Beyond the nation-state

The contemporary nation-state is facing many challenges, as manifest in increased interdependence and incorporation into an emerging global economy, and through the establishment of international, transnational and supranational organizations and structures of governance. The pressure on the state is heightened by important changes in the public sphere, such as the internationalization of social movements, transnational epistemic communities, and the emergence of some semblance of a 'global public opinion'. These developments have raised questions as to the continued relevance of core state attributes such as territorial boundaries and formal and *de facto* state sovereignty.

The state is 'Janus-faced'. One face of the state is oriented inwards, to the domestic arena, and the other is oriented outwards, to the international community or society of states. That the state has two 'faces' has had important implications for democratic accountability. The state has been seen as accountable to *its citizens*, whereas its obligations to non-citizens have been seen as weak, at best. This is the most widely held conception of democracy in both its liberal and republican trappings. It is from this notion of the state as a geographically confined and sovereign entity with a clearly defined *demos* that most standards of democratic governance have been derived. The doctrine of national sovereignty ensured that the interstate arena was seen as marked by anarchy, not in the sense of disorder, but in the sense of absence of an authoritative system of governance. This notion of accountability was wholly compatible with protection of borders and nationally based difference.

After the Second World War, in particular, the international arena has changed so as to heighten the salience of individual autonomy through universal human rights (Held 1993; Driscoll 1989).[2] The entrenchment in a body of treaty law of a set of individual and group-based rights at the UN and European levels has led to increased attention and heightened respect for individual and group-based rights other than those explicitly upheld by states. In the contemporary world the two faces of the state can not be kept separate, a development which might have profound consequences for established notions of accountability and democratic governance. The EU seems to reinforce this process of merging the state's two faces and the attendant sets of accountability.

In the EU, a set of institutions have been established over and above the Member States, which citizens of Member States, as well as aliens and denizens,[3] have recourse to, as additional outlets for settling their grievances. The EU is a complex entity without a clearly defined core and, compared to a state, with a far less hierarchical system of governance (Schmitter 1996a). It is a mixture of supranational, transnational, transgovernmental, and intergovernmental structures. Institutions such as the European Commission, the European Parliament and the European Court of Justice are 'supranational'. *Supranationality* refers to a system of law-making which exists and operates (partly) independently of the Member States and which supports and is supported by an accommodating process or style of decision-making.[4] The particular nature of supranationality in the EU (dynamic, non-hierarchical, and open to different kinds of co-operation and policy solutions) points us in the direction of the discourse theoretical perspective of deliberative democracy because those involved are compelled to sort out their disagreements and commonalities with reference to arguments. In order to reach an agreement and decisions that are binding, they can not simply rely on power or resort to procedures that terminate in voting or bargaining.

Institutions such as the European Council and the Council of the European Union (formerly known as Council of Ministers, and subsequently only referred to as the 'Council' here) are generally referred to as '*intergovernmental*' in the literature, since they are composed of the executive officials of the states. The former is composed of the heads of government, including foreign ministers, and their supportive staffs. The latter is composed of the ministers (including foreign ministers), organized along functional lines, so that one meeting will consist of the agricultural ministers and another of the energy ministers, and so forth. The Council, however, operates in close co-operation with organized interests which means that it operates within and promotes *transnational* relations, where transnational denotes 'transboundary relations that include at least one non-governmental actor' (Risse-Kappen 1996: 57). The EU is often referred to as a *multi-level structure of governance* (Marks *et al.* 1996; Jachtenfuchs and Kohler-Koch 1996a). The Committee of the Regions promotes transgovernmental relations, where transgovernmental refers to 'cross-boundary relations among sub-units of national governments in the absence of centralized decisions by state executives' (Risse-Kappen 1996: 58). The contemporary changes in the role of the state have led to renewed interest in democracy and democratic governance. This is discussed in several of the following chapters. In Chapter 2, Jürgen Habermas sheds further light on the limitations of the nation-state. In Chapter 3, Erik O. Eriksen discusses the democratic deficit in the EU, with particular emphasis on clarifying the nature of the underlying evaluative scheme. In Chapter 4, Richard Bellamy and Dario Castiglione address the problems of legitimacy in a mixed polity. In Chapter 5, Andreas Føllesdal discusses the status and role of subsidiarity in the EU. In Chapter 6, John Erik Fossum addresses the question of how constitution-making in the EU is legitimated, in order to see if or the extent to which the EU is accorded an independent normative status. In Chapter 11, Else Grete Broderstad examines the question of indigenous rights, with particular emphasis on the limitations inherent in the nation-state and the potential for the EU to address such.

Democratic governance

Analysts and policy-makers are greatly concerned with the challenges facing the nation-state. Mainstream analysts who have assessed the democratic implications of the challenges, have done so by means of terminology and standards which are direct transpositions of those conceptions of democratic governance that are generally associated with the nation-state. This is particularly evident in the debate on the quality of democracy in the EU. There is consensus among analysts and policy-makers that the EU suffers from a '*democratic deficit*'. Analysts have identified this as a multifaceted problem, which includes deficiencies in representation and representativeness, accountability, transparency, and legitimacy. The most widely held view is that the EU represents the establishment of an additional layer of governance, which has revealed an often surprising ability to take on added tasks. This process, it is often contended, has been largely unchecked.[5] The bounds between the EU and the Member States in terms of powers and competences are ill-defined and ambiguous.

That the standards of democratic governance used to assess the EU have been derived from the nation-state is perhaps not so surprising when it is recalled that the founders of the EU, such as Jean Monnet and Altieri Spinelli, agreed on the need to establish a new state-type structure on top of the established states (although they differed on how to proceed with integration) (Navari 1996; Holland 1996). Their view of the EU, as a 'United States of Europe in-the-making', is shared by many also today.[6] But whether the EU evolves into a state or not, the critics assert, the EU will magnify already existing problems of representativeness and accountability in the states and will also generate new problems. Decisions are further removed from the citizens, due to the greatly increased size of the entity, the added layer of governance, the lengthened chain of representation, and so on. In general terms, internationalization entails extending further the powers and prerogatives of the executive, that is the national officials who are the main actors in international co-operation (Moravcsik 1993, 1994, 1998). The intergovernmental bodies of the

EU, the European Council and the Council, are not properly checked by other institutions, such as the popularly elected European Parliament, nor are they properly checked by a system of constitutional controls. It is observed that whereas EU citizens can elect 626 MEPs directly, the EP is not able to hold the executives properly accountable. The Council is the one institution of the EU that comes closest to being the 'legislature' of the EU and consists of nationally elected representatives – government ministers (and their supportive staffs) – from each Member State. Increasingly, decisions are reached by qualified majority voting[7] and contribute to strengthening the supranational dimension of the EU. Also, the Commission, which is often considered to be the 'government' of the EU and 'the motor of integration', consists of twenty Commissioners and twenty-six Directorate Generals. The Commissioners are appointed by the Member States, but are required to act as EU officials and not as national spokespersons.[8] The Commission is required to place the interest of the EU first.[9] It operates on the majority principle, but when a decision is reached, all Commissioners are expected to give full support to all policies, which further reinforces the salience of the Commission as a supranational institution.

These institutions have a weaker popular basis than do ordinary states. There are no real European political parties that can act as vital intermediaries between the general populace and the central institutions at the EU level. Citizens of Member States are not able fully to control the actions taken by the executive officials that they have elected in national elections. The inter-institutional lines of accountability in the EU are hazy due to a byzantine legal structure – a legal structure made up of 'bits and pieces' (Curtin 1993) – and a multitude of complex voting procedures differentiated by policy content.[10] The EU has established an EU-based citizenship. EU citizens have obtained civil rights, but the legal enforcement of these rights at the EU level is weaker than in nationally based constitutional systems. EU citizens have also been granted political rights, but are not able to act as the ultimate authors of the laws that emanate from the EU.

This brief presentation of the EU serves to underline that the EU is quite different from a state. Further, there is no assurance that these differences will disappear. Therefore, the analogy with the nation-state is misleading[11] (whether we speak of the nation-state as model or whether we speak of an actual nation-state). In real terms, states differ considerably. But this observation does not alter the fact that the EU is qualitatively different. The question, however, is how the recognition of the EU as different from the nation-state will affect the standards that we must use to assess its democratic quality. Before proceeding with outlining an alternative set of standards, let us try to be a bit more explicit with regard to the shortcomings of the conceptual tools and the analytical perspectives that have dominated mainstream research on the EU.

The tyranny of concepts

In order to address the problem of democratic deficit in the EU, it is necessary to question the widely held conception of democracy and democratic legitimacy as intimately linked with and as dependent on the nation-state, and the vocabulary associated with the nation-state.[12] Hedley Bull has observed that 'one reason for the vitality of the states system is the tyranny of the concepts and normative principles associated with it' (Bull, cited in Linklater 1996: 78). This applies especially to the most fundamental and taken-for-granted concepts of political analysis, such as state and constitutionalism. Ulrich Preuss has observed that 'statehood has been the underlying premise of the concept of constitution-alism' (Preuss 1996a: 213), although 'constitutionalism as a doctrine and practice predated the development of the modern State and its scope is larger than the state' (Lane 1996: 16). The 'tyranny' of the concepts and principles associated with the nation-state, relate to how sovereignty, identity, community, citizenship and democracy have all been tied to the notion of nation-state and made subject to the territorial logic of the state. The state is sovereign which means that it controls a specific territory and those that inhabit that territory. The state as organization shapes conceptions of community and identity in such a manner as to highlight *national* communities. Such 'imagined communities' are sustained by sovereign states, which promote the development of a sense of national allegiance and an exclusive notion of citizenship (Anderson 1983). This sense of national allegiance is intended to crowd out competing forms of allegiance, and this has been done by various means, such as assimilation, integration, exclusion or even extermination. The world is made up of nation-states, or territorially based communities, which are able to exclude those that they deem to be non-nationals. In a world of territorially delineated nation-states, communities that are not states aspire to become nation-states in order to obtain recognition as sovereign entities and to ensure their continued survival.

The 'tyranny' of the state form is reflected also in the normative hegemony of the nation-state as the sole legitimate institutional source of democratic governance. The institutions of the state are intended to foster a sense of national allegiance – patriotism – and forms of participation that are compatible with the nation-state. Some conceptions of democracy and democratic governance are more compatible with these constraints than are other ones. The adequacy of institutionalized forms is assessed foremost in terms of the degree of coherence with a particular state form and national community, normally the unitary nation-state, rather than coherence with fundamental principles of democratic governance. The universally held embrace of nation-state-based conceptions of democratic governance has made this into a powerful tradition. There are no doubt merits in the state form of governance which are conducive to democracy, such as social justice, coherence and accountability. The problem is when each of these merits, as well as their interdependence, are taken for granted and assumed rather than assessed through examination and careful research. There is a certain propensity among students of the EU to derive institutional features or arrangements from democratic states and apply these to the EU without properly examining the normative status of these arrangements in the model of democracy from which they have been derived. Further, there is a certain tendency to fail to examine what the actual democratic quality of such a component is in current practice.[13] The 'tyranny', then, can manifest itself in a certain tendency to graft governance arrangements onto the EU from the actual arrangements of nation-states, without proper attention to democratic principles and whether the arrangements conform with such at a supranational level. Or it can manifest itself in the conflation of different conceptions and criteria of democratic governance which are based on quite different requirements. For instance, models of representative democracy are based on less stringent popular requirements than are participatory and deliberative ones.

That this taken-for-grantedness of the concepts and principles associated with the nation-state has become problematic is evident also in how these standards have been applied in actual research. Keohane and Hoffmann observe that:

> … (p)ortrayals of the state are often bedevilled by the image of an ideal-typical 'state' whose authority is unquestioned and whose institutions work smoothly. No such state has ever existed; viewed close-up, all modern states appear riddled with inefficiencies and contradictions.
>
> (Keohane and Hoffmann 1990: 279)

Therefore, when assessing the democratic deficit of the EU, we need to keep in mind that states often actually fail to adhere properly to the democratic standards associated with the nation-state model itself.

The taken-for-grantedness of the concepts and principles associated with the nation-state also manifests itself in a certain propensity to associate polity formation with state formation. Although the state form has become the dominant organizational form at present, there is no *a priori* assurance that this trend will continue.[14]

In recent years, some analysts have not only questioned the relevance of the nation-state, as the benchmark for the assessment of the democratic quality of the EU, but have also made efforts to think through which alternative standards can be applied. Clearly, the notion of democratic deficit (a term with a strong business–economic connotation: deficit/surplus) is more than a matter of definition, i.e. it entails something more than merely spelling out which aspects of the EU fail to adhere to conventional conceptions of democracy. The question of democratic deficit has direct bearings on what type of polity the EU is, what the EU aspires to be, and what we want the EU to be. It also means that we can not simply equate democracy at the national level with legitimacy. The precise relation between these two terms needs to be explored, because this set of questions relating to the democratic deficit has direct bearings on how the EU works. It also needs to be explored in terms of understanding the logic of integration, and in terms of the EU's normative status.

The EU is neither a market, nor is it a state. Therefore, to address the question of democratic deficit we are compelled to think carefully about what kind of entity the EU is and what can reasonably be expected from it. In counterfactual terms, one might ask what a 'democratic surplus' is,[15] or what a fully democratic order at the transnational level might look like. Once we start thinking about this counterfactual notion, it becomes quite clear that the question of democratic deficit revolves around both what type of polity the EU is and what standards of assessment can be applied to assess its democratic quality. It is therefore ultimately a matter of which analytical perspective informs our conceptions of democracy and democratic legitimacy.

The question of the democratic deficit reminds us that it is not enough to describe the EU and the integration process. We also need to understand and account for the fact that the EU prevails despite its many deficiencies and problems. It is quite easy to depict the many shortcomings and obstacles that beset the European integration process. It is more difficult and far more urgent to try to explain what makes the system keep on going. This difficulty stems partly from the intellectual hegemony of power-based and strategic action-based approaches that dominate so much of the theoretical and empirical analysis of the EU. What are the integrative forces in the EU? To shed light on this it is necessary not simply to look at stability as something that prevails by virtue of its already being in place. Something is in place not simply because it has existed for a while but also because it appeals to something that people can relate to and can support. Therefore, to understand the stability and longevity of the EU, it is necessary to clarify what are the 'virtues' of the EU system that contribute to its stability. The contention that informs this position is that in a democratic setting there is *no stability without validity*.[16] The normative visions, which have long been associated with the EU pertain to peace, freedom, democratic constitutionalism, and Europe as a common life world. Peace and prosperity were conceived of as common values that required co-ordinated and collective action in order to be brought about in the early post-war period.[17] These may be depleted today (cf. Offe 1998a), but are examples of the kinds of factors that help explain the attraction of the EU project.[18] Thus, it is necessary to let such values – which suggest that the EU has obvious merits – inform the discussion of the overarching question of what type of entity this is. What is the quality of the institutional make-up of the EU from the perspective of normative theory, and what are the prospects for its viability? There are, as mentioned, competing visions of the EU which emanate not only from uncertainty as to what kind of entity this is but which also relate to opposing views of the nature of politics.

Integration through what?

In order to understand the nature of the political system in the EU, in particular its democratic quality, it is necessary to supplement economic and realist perspectives in political science, because these perspectives consider democratic legitimacy as largely irrelevant. These perspectives consider the prospects for legitimate systems of democratic governance emerging at the international level as bleak indeed. State-centric, strategic perspectives – theories of international politics such as classical and structural realism – conceive of the international scene as marked by states seen metaphorically as 'billiard-balls' (Jønsson 1990: 128). State behaviour is driven by self-interest, and interstate relations are marked by 'balancing' behaviour (Morgenthau 1985; Waltz 1979). Standards of political behaviour do not exist independently of power. Even those theories that are concerned with the growth of interdependence and reject the billiard-ball conceptions of states such as (complex) interdependence and regime theory,[19] do not reject the core power-based assumptions of political realism, but rather seek to modify these so as better to reflect the changes on the international scene.[20] Regime theory, for instance, focuses on binding international co-operation in narrow functional areas ('low politics'), with little potential for spillover to vital state concerns ('high politics') and almost always as subject to utilitarian calculus (Krasner 1982; Fossum and Robinson 1998). These theories of international politics have certain basic assumptions about human behaviour that are surprisingly similar.[21]

In principle, there is a distinction between integration that occurs through *functional adaptation*, and integration that occurs through *interest-accommodation*, or strategic group activity. But integration can also occur through *deliberation*, i.e. through the process of arguing. Communication through reason giving is oriented at convincing opponents of the best or right course of action. There are other versions of integration, as well. These three modes are chosen because they adhere to distinctly different logics of explanation and can be seen as idealtypes (consistent with Max Weber's use of such). In the following pages, we will provide a brief presentation of these three modes of integration and link them to the relevant theoretical perspectives.

Neo-functionalism

Most of the theoretically informed work on the EU has drawn on two alternative but distinct theoretical approaches, neo-functionalism and intergovernmentalism. Neo-functionalism conceives of integration as essentially self-sustaining, albeit not at a constant rate. William Wallace defines integration as:

> the creation and maintenance of intense and diversified patterns of interaction among previously autonomous units. These patterns may be partly economic in character, partly social, partly political: definitions of *political* integration all imply accompanying high levels of economic and social interaction.
>
> (Wallace 1990: 9)

Wallace's definition is consistent with mainstream usage of the term.[22] Integration is effected through two kinds of 'spillover', functional and political. Spillover is seen to occur when 'imbalances created by the functional interdependence or inherent linkages of tasks can press political actors to redefine their common tasks' (Nye, cited in Keohane and Hoffmann 1991: 285). Functional spillover refers to the interconnection of various economic sectors or issue-areas, and how integration in one policy-area tends to spill over into others. Political spillover refers to how the existence of supranational organizations tends to generate a self-reinforcing process of institution-building. The institutions of the EU, in particular the Commission, would provide a modicum of leadership over, as well as an arena for, a burgeoning transnational society (Caporaso 1998: 9).

Supranational integration empties the state of policy content and normative salience, through an often mutually reinforcing process in which the actions by elites and interest groups reinforce the integrationist pull of a set of supranational institutional actors (Kirchner 1980; Caporaso 1998). The process is set in motion by some kind of imbalance and is carried forward by functional interdependence. The process of spillover-induced integration reinforces the salience of the supranational institutions at the EU level, to the detriment of the intergovernmental ones. The net effect is a set of institutions that are contingent on a wide network of substate actors but which themselves are relatively independent of the state actors for their operations and support. State power is therefore diffused onto a wide range of actors.

Neo-functionalism sees integration in process terms: polity-building is seen as the result of a wide range of converging processes. However, no conceptual link is established. Neo-functionalism has 'no theory to explain the transition from utility-maximizing self-interest to integration based on collective understandings about a common interest' (Risse-Kappen 1996: 56). Neo-functionalism conceives of integration as the effect of behaviour oriented towards fulfilling systemic requirements. Basically, the actors' behaviour appears to be driven by instrumental self-interest, largely conceived of in economic terms. The actors are more concerned with utility functions and expertise than with power (Caporaso 1998). The theory which neo-functionalism lacks, would have to account for at least two vital conversions. First, how instrumental self-interest can be converted into stable patterns of behaviour, and hence a sense of identity and allegiance. Second, how this conversion will enable a shift of allegiance from one level of governance to another, i.e. from the state level to the supranational level.

Neo-functionalism assumes that the process of integration will proceed from co-operation in the realm of 'low' politics (economic policies) to 'high' politics (foreign and defence policies) because the former is less contentious than the latter. But that is of little value to understand how identities and senses of allegiance are formed, sustained, and altered – common identities that are required to sustain co-operative patterns of behaviour. Without this vital information, neo-functionalism does not provide us with a good sense of how the two processes of spillover, functional and political, are related. Nor can it explain why each type of spillover is seen as acceptable by those affected by it. The EU is seen to survive because it is a functional answer to the problems of globalization. The question of its value basis and why those affected by integration accept it, i.e. the validity dimension, is left unanswered. The theory lacks microfoundations, and hence the problem of identifying feedback loops, which accompanies all kinds of functional analysis, prevails (cf. Elster 1984: 28ff.; Moravcsik 1998: 16).

Intergovernmentalism

Intergovernmentalism posits that integration proceeds as far as states permit it. This theory is founded on the basic realist premise that political action is based on power and that politics is a struggle among contending interests. In its more recent EU trappings, intergovernmentalism basically represents an attempt to apply the core assumptions of rationalist instrumentalism – rational choice – as reflected in realist, neo-liberal and neo-liberal institutionalist work on the EU. The recognition that the EU is something more than a mere intergovernmental arrangement has sparked considerable debate and important refinements and modifications. Perhaps the clearest and most recent example of this is Andrew Moravcsik's rational choice inspired approach which he terms 'liberal intergovernmentalism' (Moravcsik 1998). Moravcsik seeks to refute the neo-functional notion that integration weakens the state through diffusion of power and argues that integration strengthens the state.[23] The executive officials of the state control access to the international arena and have a strong incentive to 'cut themselves some slack' in relation to the domestic actors, i.e. to remove domestic constraints on their actions. European integration facilitates this because the executive officials who negotiate agreements have unique agenda setting powers and privileged access to information and policy-making fora. The process of integration, to Moravcsik, therefore 'internationalizes domestic politics' in the sense that executive officials bring domestic issues and concerns to the intergovernmental bargaining table and settle these issues with little domestic input. The executives seek to legitimate their actions with reference to 'the realization of common abstract values rather than self-regarding material interests …' (Moravcsik 1994: 14). This appeal to broader values, such as peace, prosperity, and cosmopolitanism provides executive officials with *added policy leverage*, since a wide range of policies can be justified with reference to such general values: 'The looser the links between broad ideals and concrete policies, the more flexibility the executive enjoys in framing domestic policy deliberations' (Moravcsik 1994: 25). The propensity for executives to seek to cut themselves domestic slack means that the democratic deficit of the EU is a characteristic feature of the integration process, rather than a recent phenomenon associated with the Single European Act (SEA), the Treaty on European Union (TEU) and the Amsterdam Treaty. The democratic deficit is a choice and a dilemma, between representativeness and effectiveness.

In empirical terms, intergovernmentalists – including Moravcsik – are hard put to account for the magnitude of integration that has occurred, in particular since the mid 1980s, when the ability of individual states to veto decisions has been greatly curtailed in a wide range of policy areas. What intergovernmentalism fails to properly acknowledge is that acts of integration are cumulative and foreclose states retaking their autonomy and sovereignty (Sandholtz 1996).

Intergovernmentalists conceive of states as actors who pursue their self-interests. This view of the state as unitary actor is incomplete. It attributes preferences and purposes to a collectivity – the state – without a proper explanation of where the preferences have been derived from and what their quality is.[24]

Intergovernmentalists also conflate the notion of state as actor with the notion of state as structure.[25] Therefore, they fail to examine how the complex institutional and structural make-up of the state affects the role conceptions and preferences of state officials. This is part of the wider problem of preference formation and justification facing both intergovernmentalists and neo-functionalists.

A new agenda

The perspectives briefly presented above, neo-functionalism and liberal intergovernmentalism are analytical perspectives, which differ profoundly in how they conceive of the nature and effects of the integration process, but which share two important features. First, they are both based on a common underlying conception of action motivation, and a means–end notion of rationality (*Zweckrationalität*, in Weber's terminology). Neo-functionalism is based foremost on the technical instrumental version, whose conception of action is derived from an observational perspective, whereas intergovernmentalism is based on the strategic version of means–end rationality. The latter is intentional and surpasses the former in the sense that actors' choices are seen not only as driven by expectations about the future, '[...] but also *on the basis of their expectations about the expectations of others*' (Elster 1984: 19). This basic similarity in behavioural assumptions places important constraints on the extent to which these can be seen as truly alternative conceptions. Second, both perspectives operate with a weakly developed and inadequate conception of democracy and democratic accountability. They therefore also understate the normative potential inherent in the European integration project. Neo-functionalism conceives of democracy in narrow terms and as ultimately contingent on a particular end product of the European integration process, i.e. a European federal state or a 'United States of Europe'. Neo-functionalism does not provide a convincing theory to explain how the EU might get to that end result.

The two perspectives listed above do not consider values and arguments to have any real or direct effect on behaviour. Moravcsik, for instance, sees appeals to values in instrumental terms, in particular as instruments for elites to augment their power and influence by 'cutting themselves slack' in relation to domestic interests. Moravcsik sees elites as able to appeal to general values, and the populace is only able to hold the elites accountable if the appeals refer to a specific set of policy measures which people can hold up against the values to see if they match. The executive officials are only accountable, it appears, when it is possible to match a specific policy with a specific value. The values and arguments are conceived of merely as aspects of a self-serving conception of justice. However, such an interpretation both underestimates the civilizing force of hypocrisy (Elster 1995),[26] and the potential force of the better argument. Another example of Moravcsik's narrow conception of accountability – typical of intergovernmentalism – relates to his view of domestic constraints. To him, each state's domestic arena is quite autonomous. State elites are only truly constrained by the domestic arena in their own country (cf. Marks *et al.* 1996:

345; Caporaso 1998: 12). Intergovernmentalism's shortcomings with regard to the notion of democracy are similar to those of the liberal, aggregative model, which we will return to.

Neither perspective places any emphasis on public discourse and the binding force of words in communicative practice, e.g. appeals to values can spark a public discourse on what the relationship between policy and value is and should be. Appeals to values raise normative expectations, a point which Moravcsik clearly fails to consider, and thereby also neglects how appeals to values have contributed to generate and sustain the supranational traits of the EU.[27] Preferences can not be taken as given, they are shaped, tested and reshaped in the many discursive and legal settings that the complex European integration process provides.

Recent research, in their efforts to conceptualize the EU, have gone beyond the simple supranationalism embedded in neo-functionalism and the state-centric view of intergovernmentalism, to conceive of the EU as *a system of multi-level governance* which consists of multi-tiered, geographically overlapping structures of governmental and non-governmental elites.[28] Some analysts term this the 'new governance agenda' (cf. Hix 1998). This term should not be construed as an expression of a uniform and coherent alternative theoretical position. The 'new governance agenda' is unified in its rejection of the nation-state bias and in its conception of the EU as a polity *sui generis*, but not in the conception of what the entity – the EU – really is. It draws on widely different theoretical perspectives in rejecting the nation-state analogy. However, striking findings are the EU's lack of accountability and the lack of popular influence on the EU. In the EU, it is the voice of the expert, rather than that of the people, that dominates. It is *steering without democracy* and governance without government (cf. Rosenau and Czempiel 1992).[29] These structures are then hard to validate in normative terms. The neo-liberal and postmodernist vision of post-national networks, as replacements for political government, can not make up for the lack of steering capacity and legitimacy that ensues at the national level. Functional efficiency and governance capacity do not justify outcomes, they are themselves in need of legitimation (cf. Habermas 1998a: 124).

These assessments by some of the adherents of the new governance agenda draw quite heavily on functional and instrumental outlooks: 'Proponents of multi-level governance, while adding a new and important institutional layer to neo-functionalist and intergovernmentalist arguments, do not challenge the rationalist microfoundations of either school' (Checkel 1998: 7). Multi-level governance, then, also presents us with an incomplete theoretical basis for addressing the fundamental questions: What keeps the Union together? What are the integrative forces? Why does the EU evoke popular support at all, and how can it undertake the following tasks:

> In addition to redistribution, through the regulation of social, environ-mental and health risk, EU citizenship, and competences over food safety, culture, tourism, immigration, combating racism and xenophobia, and

police and judicial co-operation, the EU is increasingly involved in the
allocation of social and political values throughout Europe.

(Hix 1998: 42)

These undertakings, in addition to enlargement to the East and the establishment of the EMU, require explanations that go beyond the ones provided by
functionalism and interest calculus – because they pertain to collective action
and norms of solidarity and fairness. These should not be reduced to the pursuit
of self-interest or to the requirements of functional adaptation.[30] This is so
because extra-material elements – norms or values – are required to motivate
collective action, because interests generate unstable outcomes. Interests make
parties friends one day and enemies the next (Durkheim 1893/1964: 204). Some
must contribute more than they receive, and some have to pay for the
misfortune of others, in order to realize collective goods, i.e. goods that can not
be reserved for the ones who produce them. In principle, compliance with
deontological norms, which tell what is a right and just course of action is
required to resolve collective action problems (cf. Olson 1965; Elster 1989). In
addition, articulations about identities, commitments and the common good are
often needed, however shifting they may be (cf. March and Olsen 1995: 35ff.,
1998; Olsen 1998). Generally speaking, established theoretical frames of
reference appear incomplete to explain integration because the force of shared
norms is left out. Functional interdependence and interest accommodation are
inherently unstable, as the moral point of view – or the normative procedural
element that is needed to bring about integration to override national interests –
is lacking.[31] This is, briefly stated, the general background which warrants the
quest for another theoretical frame of reference for research into European
integration. To highlight the particular features of this perspective, we will
briefly contrast it with the liberal and republican conceptions of democracy.

Deliberative democracy

The governmental structure of the EU contains processes that cannot be
captured or explained by realism and realism-derived perspectives. These
features are also based on something more and different from spillover-induced
integration. Basically, this contention stems from the fact that the EU, initially, is
based on *voluntary co-operation:* co-operation is not dependent on prevailing
patterns and distributions of power or on functional interdependence. The EU,
then, may be seen also as marked by actors who strive to solve problems and
realize common goals and whose behaviour is constrained by established
programmes and entrenched rules. The 'government' of the EU contains a legal
structure for collective decision-making – rules for the exercise of executive,
legislative and judicial powers. For quite a while now an *acquis communautaire* has
been in operation in the Community, i.e. a set of shared rules, norms and
procedures (Wiener 1998: 65ff.). According to this perspective, the EU already

possesses a constitution (Weiler 1991, 1995). This claim is substantiated by several judgments of the European Court of Justice and it is a claim that thus far has not been explicitly rebutted by national constitutional courts in their rulings. The founding treaties are based on the rule of law. The most recent Treaty of Amsterdam defines the common objectives of the Union more clearly and introduces the prospect of sanctions if the fundamental principles of the Union are breached or violated. In Chapter 6, John Erik Fossum discusses the question of the legitimacy of constitution-making in the EU by drawing explicitly on the deliberations during the Intergovernmental Conference, which produced the Amsterdam Treaty (IGC-96).

Basically, constitution means that the parties' common affairs are conducted within a set of norms and objectives, which are not up for grabs, as they constitute the very rules of the game. They provide a set of procedures that make problem solving and conflict resolution possible, i.e. 'rules that can be contested within the game, but only insofar as one first accepts to abide by them and play the game at all' (Benhabib 1994: 39, cf. Kratochwil 1991: 205ff.). Procedural arrangements bring people together to solve problems and conflicts, and encourage willing adherence to common rules. They are structures that constrain but which also enable action in so far as they create arenas for people to meet and to foster binding agreements. It is the legal medium that provides the binding force of words in a political context. This may explain the connection between the broad political ideas – of peace, freedom, and solidarity – to which politicians in the EU pay tribute and the rather prosaic and nitty-gritty manner in which – including bargaining and log-rolling – concrete decisions are made. Further, integration, in the true meaning of the term, depends on the alteration, not the aggregation of, preferences. *Integration is premised on learning and the alteration of preferences*: at least one of the contending parties must change his/her opinion in order to reach an agreement. Participation in co-operative processes is supposed to contribute to such a shift as actors have to frame arguments with reference to common standards in order to achieve agreement, a process that serves to override egoistic or national interests. This we may refer to as *normative learning* as it is not solely based on experience, but on arguments of a certain moral or ethical quality. It is this that forms the basis for the assumption that integration takes place through deliberation.

On the basis of this, there is a need for a conceptual framework which is not solely based on power and self-interest, but which complements such by acknowledging the role of deliberation and arguing in the establishment and validation of rules and by recognizing the potential for consensus formation among parties with conflicting interests and values. What are the prospects for reasonable action and rational argumentation within the EU structure? Does the EU embody institutional arrangements that can sway actors to adopt disinterested or third-party perspectives, or that, at least, enable working agreements and intermediate forms of consensus based on the force of the better argument? These questions are addressed in several chapters in this book. There are institutional dynamics that are based on egocentric behaviour as well as dynamics based on other-regarding behaviour. There are procedures that encourage strategic interaction – bargaining – and there are procedures that encourage participants to adopt a deliberative orientation, i.e. communicative action. In Chapter 7, Lars Chr. Blichner examines what the potential is of opinion formation in interparliamentary discourses, where deliberation is freed from the immediate requirements of action and decision-making. In Chapter 9, Roberto Gargarella explores whether or rather the extent to which the Council can be said to comply with the requirements inherent in the notion of deliberative democracy.

We need, however, to clarify what is meant by deliberative democracy and what the particular contribution of deliberative democracy is to international democracy. Political theory has long been concerned with *democracy as a method*, and as a means of aggregating preferences (cf. Schumpeter 1942; Downs 1957). One particularly important means of aggregating preferences has been through the establishment of voting procedures. In the liberal and pluralist tradition, democratic legitimacy is seen to emanate from the aggregation of votes cast by secret ballot. A voting procedure is seen to be just when the procedure treats people as equals by assigning their preferences equal weight in the collective decision-making process (Riker 1982). Voting procedures have generally been less relevant at the international level than at the domestic level. The establishment of institutions at the EU level that serve to aggregate preferences through voting procedures has therefore been conceived of as a major democratic improvement and much of the debate on the democratic quality of the EU has revolved around the nature and quality of these particular arrangements. The establishment of voting procedures at the international level is most likely a democratic improvement, but voting is not the only means to improve the democratic quality of the EU. The EU consists of approximately 350 million people and it is difficult by way of voting to secure that people are not subjected to laws they themselves have not consented to.

The problem with majority voting is that it permits the violation of freedom (Rawls 1971: 356). A majority vote is merely the reflection of the view of a particular majority at a particular point in time. It is, however, a general observation among analysts that a voting outcome, to stand over time, must be supported by substantive arguments – *reasons* (Dewey 1927: 207). A voting result can not claim to reflect the common will, but only the will of the winners. It therefore requires non-majoritarian sources or additional arguing in order to be held to be legitimate (Chambers 1997). The question which informs much of the present debate among political theorists is whether it is the act of voting or whether it is the antecedent debate that is the characteristic feature which lends legitimacy to outcomes. In an open debate decision-makers are forced to give reasons, and this enhances transparency and public accountability. Public debate is the single most important clue to the assessment of *democratic quality*, because the legitimacy of power holders can be tested in relation to affected interests.[32] In Chapter 8, Christian Joerges and Michelle Everson address the technocratic aspect of the EU. Here they ask whether comitology may be more of a remedy than a defect, i.e. more of a testimony to deliberative supranationalism than nascent bureaucratic governance. In Chapter 10, Philip Schlesinger and Deirdre Kevin address the question as to whether there is a European public sphere in the making.

Deliberative democracy does not preclude voting or bargaining, but it places the emphasis on obtaining a shared sense of meaning and a common will, both of which are the product of a communicative process. This is seen both as a normative requirement, and as an empirical fact. It takes a lot of arguing to get voting mechanisms to work, and a modicum of consensus is needed in order to establish alliances and voting alternatives. Without some kind of agreement and mutual understanding, a representative system such as a parliamentary one will be severely hampered in its ability to produce decisions, and those reached will be challenged on legitimacy grounds. In open societies political solutions have to be defended *vis-à-vis* the citizens in public debate. Outcomes will not be accepted unless they can be backed up by good reasons, as citizens require, and are expected to require, reasons of a certain quality. Constitutional democracy has, in fact, built in various types of safeguards that transform values and the perception of interests, so that citizens decide on 'who they are, what their values are, and what those values require. What "they" want must be supported by reasons' (Sunstein 1991: 13). The deliberative process of arguing and counter-arguing is a process 'that shapes *the identity and interests* of citizens in ways that contribute to the formation of a public conception of the common good' (Cohen 1991: 19). While aggregation may reflect only base preferences, and bargaining may only reflect actual resources and may yield suboptimal solutions, deliberation transforms preferences and compels actors to give reasons for why they seek a particular outcome, regardless of their resources. Deliberation is based on arguing which rests on reason giving and is considered superior to bargaining and voting. Among other things, deliberation improves decision-making while it pays attention to side effects, reveals private information, legitimizes the ultimate choice, contributes to Pareto-superior decisions, makes for a larger agreement, fosters mutual respect and is seen as good unto itself (Elster 1998b; Estlund 1997; Fearon 1998; Cohen 1991).

In such a perspective, *democratic legitimacy* does not stem from the aggregation of the preferences of all, but from 'the deliberation of all' (Manin 1987: 357). This perspective may be applied to international democracy at it does not base democratic accountability solely on the existence of formal aggregative procedures. The discourse theoretical variant of deliberative democracy associated with Jürgen Habermas also disconnects collective will formation in modern politics from the notion of a pre-existing system of common values and affiliations. In this perspective, there is a separation of politics and culture, of citizenship and nationality. Discourse theory departs from a substantive, or ethical conception of citizen autonomy, which emanates from the convergence of traditions and family-type bonds on the basis of which it is possible to reach an agreement. The republican or communitarian tradition of political theory presupposes an ascriptive membership in a common life form where it is possible to identify common goals, interests and affiliations. The people or citizens take the shape of a political subject – a nation:

> But this distinctive cultural identity does not designate it *as* a political com-munity of citizens. For the democratic process is governed by *universal* prin-ciples of justice that are equally constitutive for every body of citizens. In short, the ideal procedure of deliberation and decision making presupposes as its bearer an association that agrees to regulate the conditions of its common life impartially.
>
> (Habermas 1996a: 306)

Democracy is conceived of at a more abstract level: it is not seen only as an organization principle – e.g. representative or parliamentary democracy – but as a legitimation principle which ensures the conditions necessary for justification. In other words, it is not identical with a particular organizational form, but is rather a principle which sets down the conditions that are necessary for how to get things right in politics. Democracy is a way to find out what is fair or just. In a deliberative perspective, arguing is required for a norm to be seen as impartial.

From a conceptual point of view, then, supranationalism is a possible option, as co-operation in constitutional democracies is facilitated by procedures that do not require particular virtues or commonalities. They only require adherence to the rules of the game and a sense of fairness and justice, which can be seen essentially as a cognitive undertaking. People can reach agreement on what is fair or just when they proceed according to standards of communicative rationality (Habermas 1983, 1984).[33] It is possible to reach agreement on norms without presupposing common values and interests. The process itself is the guide to find out what is and what is not common, and how to treat equal and unequal cases.

Habermas understands democracy in political and not cultural terms, and shifts the focus on constitutions from seeing them as expressions of ethical substance (common life) to morality in the Kantian sense, i.e. as arrangements for respecting the integrity and freedom of the individual. Citizenship, then, requires membership and participation in the very structures that affect individual interests. State and world citizenship, then, form a continuum (Held 1993; Linklater 1996; Soysal 1994; Habermas 1996b). The EU can usefully be conceived of as an intermediate institution for grappling with transnational exigencies, and as such is an interesting experiment.

Deliberative supranationalism

In a complex world, people are affected both by decisions that have been made earlier and by present decisions that have not been subject to popular control. Modern societies increasingly have developed into *risk societies*, where there is a widening gap between what decision-makers decide and the possible dangers that the decisions pose to affected parties, and where this gap is difficult to bridge politically (Beck 1986, 1998; Luhmann 1991). At present, there are global structures of production, trade, and communication that permeate and transcend the boundaries of the state and which render these increasingly irrelevant. International legislative and policy-making bodies have emerged, and have added to the existing complex of local, regional and national centres of authority. The nation-state is challenged not only by internationalization, but also by regionalization and by changes in the dynamics of domestic decision-making brought about by global interdependencies. There are added layers of governance – and in Europe international as well as supranational and transnational levels of governance – which work to decouple citizens' participation and representation from concrete bodies. They serve to lengthen the chain of representation, control, and legitimacy. As this makes the process of aggregation more cumbersome, the liberal-aggregative model faces new shortcomings. The democratic deficit seems grave and insurmountable.

Likewise, the republican concept of deliberation becomes confining as it links democratic legitimacy to actual participation in the process of decision-making. Political decisions must reflect 'the will of all', something which is quite impossible in a large nation-state, let alone in an international polity. As a consequence, the liberal, aggregative and the republican, community perspective, each sees the development of international political institutions as incomprehensible, and an expression of obvious normative deficiencies, rather than a means to rectify persistent ills and normative challenges. Heteronomy prevails. The net effect is to conclude that there is no possible way to legitimize the growing process of internationalization. In what way may this development in any way be valid? At present, there is an obvious lack of proper assessment criteria by which the process of internationalization can be evaluated. Habermas' conception of discourse theory represents an innovation when compared to other conceptions of deliberative democracy because it is explicitly devised to overcome the traditional controversy between liberal (rights-based) and republican (community-based) theories of democracy. Human rights and popular sovereignty, constitution and democracy, presuppose each other reciprocally. It is only possible to form a common will in a qualified manner when individuals possess autonomy – negative freedom – to make up their minds independently. Even though liberties are among the topics of deliberation, they nevertheless constitute the framework that makes rational discussion possible.[34] In this manner discourse theory is a normative model of democracy that is not hampered by the shortcomings of liberalism, nor is it hampered by the shortcomings of republicanism. The latter does not properly emphasize the constitution and negative freedom. The shortcomings of liberalism relate to the failure to attend properly to collective will formation and to place an overly strong emphasis on individual (non-reflective) preferences. In the discourse theoretical reading of procedural democracy, both the atomistic individual and the supra-individual subject – the nation, the people – disappear. It is the flow of free communication in and between the associational network of civil society and the parliamentary complex that constitutes and ensures popular sovereignty, not the formal aggregative procedures that the liberals place their trust in or in the coming together in fora and 'halls' that republicans salute.

Legitimate governance

The discourse model of democracy, then, proposes to remedy some of the deficiencies of the existing models of democracy. The concept of sovereignty and the notion of autonomy are reframed in discursive terms, i.e. in terms of presuppositions for rational opinion and will formation. This makes the model of democracy not only more adequate in a normative sense, but also more suitable to face the challenges facing the territorially delineated and circum-scribed nation-state.

For a system of governance to be democratic, discourse theory claims that several requirements must be fulfilled. First, all people must be able to participate in the legislative process, which follows from the principle of popular sovereignty. Second, their rights to freedom must be respected, which follows from the principle of *human rights*. In a democracy, people are both the author(s) and the subject of the laws, and ultimately, a norm is only valid when it has been consented to in a free debate by all affected parties (Habermas 1996a: 107). In order for a governmental structure to be legitimate, it has to adhere to the principles of liberty, equality, security and participation. In more specific terms, the requirement is that it complies with the criteria of *congruence and accountability*. By congruence is meant the basic democratic principle which states that those affected by decisions should also be responsible for them (Zürn 1996: 39). This is an approximation: little congruence will lead to lack of legitimacy, while 'too much' is held to reduce efficiency in large polities. In real world democracies, there has to be 'a trade off' between legitimacy and efficiency. Accountability means the decision-makers can be held responsible by the citizenry and that it is possible to dismiss bad or incompetent rulers. What, then, is required is that basic liberties are guaranteed and that people also have participatory rights to initiate, influence and object to proposals in formal as well as in informal assemblies. A multifarious set of institutional arrangements may be needed to secure citizens' rights in complex and pluralist societies with several added layers of governance. Several checkpoints are relevant for assessing the democratic quality of a system of governance. In the discourse-theoretical perspective then, we do not solely focus on decision-making power, lack of parliamentary representation or separation of powers, but also on the possibility for wielding influence via institutions in civil society – press, media, non-governmental organizations – and the possibility of participation in opinion formation and the shaping and channelling of communicative power into the institutional complex of the EU. In addition to its focus on a wider range of fora, discourse theory is also concerned with whether the interaction processes within (and outside) elective bodies – assemblies, cabinets, committees, etc. – take on an arguing or a bargaining style, i.e. whether interaction is based on communicative or on strategic rationality. These criteria also informed the choice of the following themes, which have been addressed in the book.

First, there is a need to shed further light on the limitations of the nation-state. Jürgen Habermas does so in Chapter 2. The globalization of the economy serves to undermine a historical constellation, which made the compromise upon which the welfare-state is based possible. Thus, to find replacements there is a need to focus on the construction of supranational institutions and the prospects for post-national forms of solidarity. The potential of the European integration process, depends in social terms, on its ability to equalize living conditions across the whole territory. Individual states must be bound by co-operative supranational procedures that move the integration process beyond intergovernmentalism, if this process is going to succeed. Further, to succeed, the modernization process, of which the EU is part, must be taken a further step ahead and ensure that the citizens' national sense of solidarity is enlarged or turned outwards so as to include a sense of being citizens of the Union. It is important to note also that the survival of welfare-states at the national level may depend on some kind of global welfare regime in the future.

The discourse-theoretical perspective and the criteria for assessing demo-cratic quality are discussed in Erik Oddvar Eriksen's chapter of the book (Chapter 3). It is often claimed that the EU's democratic deficit is due to the lack of European political parties, representative accountability and a properly functioning public sphere. However, it may be argued that the underlying evaluative scheme which this diagnosis rests on, is based either on liberal aggregative or civic-republican assumptions about democracy. These perspec-tives offer a pessimistic assessment of the EU project and one that is premised on an overly confined notion of legitimacy. The author tries to show that discourse theory represents a promising theoretical alternative to atomist-liberal and civic-republican theories of democracy and the standards associated with these because the former conceives of the public sphere as a pluralistic institution for opinion formation and conceives of representative bodies, not only as bargaining 'markets', but also as deliberating 'fora', hence the notion of deliberative supranationalism.

Richard Bellamy and Dario Castiglione, in Chapter 4, explore the notion of the European democratic deficit. Is there a legitimation crisis in the European Union? They address this question by clarifying what is meant by democracy today and by examining some of the institutional limitations of contemporary democracy – in particular the notion of majority vote. Even if democracy is the only legitimate political regime possible in modern societies, democracy can not be confined to one particular institutional form. In regime terms, democracy is not clearly defined. Democracy can function only when embodied in certain institutions and decision-making procedures that cohere with the society to which they are meant to apply. As democracy is not to be acquainted with simple majoritarianism and thin procedural rules, the EU, to be democratic, requires a 'thick network of institutions'. The EU is a mixed polity and, thus, requires a mixed democratic regime.

The principle of subsidiarity was introduced in the Maastricht Treaty and there was a wide and lively discussion as to whether this was 'The Word that Saves Maastricht' (Cass 1992). Andreas Føllesdal, in Chapter 5, discusses the principle of subsidiarity, as presented in the Amsterdam Treaty, from the vantage point of deliberative democracy. His aim is twofold. First, he explores how subsidiarity may foster deliberation; and second, he discusses how compatible 'Amsterdam subsidiarity' is with deliberative democracy. There is no doubt that subsidiarity will foster deliberation. However, there are many different conceptions of subsidiarity, and the scope for deliberation varies considerably from one conception to another. Further, Amsterdam subsidiarity appears to grant unwarranted powers to Member States, which are not compelled in the same manner and degree to justify their actions as are the institutions of the EU.

Further, we need to understand the nature of the constitution-making process in the EU. John Erik Fossum, in Chapter 6, examines how comprehensive changes of a constitutional nature are legitimated in the EU, by focusing on how the question of the democratic legitimacy of the EU has been deliberated in the IGC-96 process. The emphasis is on whether or the extent to which the IGC-96 can be seen to bridge the gap that Joseph Weiler has identified between on the one hand the constitutional structure that the EU already has adopted, and on the other the reasons for why it is there. The gap stems from the fact that the EU has established a constitution, without an attendant constitutionalism to account for its normative justification. The chapter addresses two related questions: how can the gap be bridged, and in what sense or to what extent was the IGC-96, which led to the Amsterdam Treaty, an effort to bridge this gap? Three modes of legitimation are presented and discussed, namely legitimation through outcomes (indirect legitimation), through values, and through rights. It is found that although there is no overall uniform pattern, the arguments and reasons increasingly highlight legitimation through rights. Thus far, however, this is done without a sufficient attendant effort to clarify what type of entity the EU is or should be.

In Chapter 7, Lars Blichner looks at the prospects for interparliamentary discourses in the EU. Blichner assesses the democratic potential inherent in the Conference of European Affairs Committees (COSAC), a deliberative body that meets twice a year to discuss matters of common concern. Its purpose is to enhance the role of national parliaments in the EU. But it has no formal authority, so what value may it have, Blichner asks. Is this not just cheap talk? Blichner finds COSAC to be a sort of intermediate public sphere – inbetween a weak public sphere in civil society, and a strong public sphere within the governmental complex. This body can have positive democratizing effects on the EU partly because it makes up for the lack of a European-wide public sphere and partly because deliberation absent from decision-making may foster consensus and agreements of different kinds and qualities. A distinction is made between discursive and non-discursive agreement and between discursive disagreement and non-discursive disagreement. The latter is what is to be avoided, as it may lead to dissolution or repression. It undermines the legitimacy of every collective institution, and the integration process in Europe depends upon avoiding that possibility.

Can the way committees work contribute to deliberative supranationalism and remedy technocracy? This is the question that Christian Joerges and Michelle Everson pose in Chapter 8, when they address the system of comitology in the EU. This system refers to bodies that are engaged in the 'implementation' of secondary legislation. The authors' point is that comitology represents an institutional innovation that has contributed to the transformation of the economic community into a European polity. In hindsight, much of the dynamic of this process may be due to functional reasons and bureaucratic governance, with the result that the EU has become deeply involved in the regulation of social affairs. The location of 'non-unitary' regulatory bodies between the European and the national levels has contributed to deliberative supranationalism, which is different from both hierarchical, supranational law and international law, because legitimacy stems from democratic institutions. Accordingly, there is a need for constitutional reform and conceptual rethinking with reference to the legal constitution of comitology procedures.

What is the scope for deliberation in the Council, asks Roberto Gargarella, in Chapter 9. In this chapter Gargarella examines the deliberative potential of the Council of Ministers, by drawing on a set of normative propositions derived from the two main traditions of Anglo-American political thought, what he terms the conservative and radical tradition, respectively. The conservative tradition which defended the need for isolation of representatives *vis-à-vis* public discussion, is contrasted with the radical tradition which defended public accountability and open debate. He finds that the Council of Ministers is closer to the conservative position than to the radical one, also because of the critically important role of COREPER in the decision-making process. The Council, however, does contain certain restricted opportunities for public deliberation. All elected bodies have limits to public debate and limits are necessary for elected bodies to function properly as deliberative assemblies. Open discussion is time-consuming and prone to rhetorical deception. In recent years, there has been a certain trend in the Council towards '... more open debates on major issues of Community interest and major new legislative proposals' but the salience of this is tempered by obvious institutional shortcomings in the Council.

The last two substantive chapters provide an assessment of whether the EU meets the congruence and accountability criteria in the public sphere. In Chapter 10, Philip Schlesinger and Deirdre Kevin consider whether some forms of news media – press and television – contribute to produce something akin to a general debate at the European level. In short, is there a European public sphere for opinion formation conductive to a European identity? In order to examine this, they draw on a perspective that highlights the multifaceted character of the public sphere – there are many public spheres. They find that political communication about the EU is rooted in national contexts and the EU is more a disseminator of information than an initiator. Further, the debate is top-down and '... one of the most significant sectors in which a deliberative, media-sustained space is emerging is at the level of political and economic elites'. The rare examples of pan-European media are those set up to serve the market actors. However, it is also noted that there are elements of a European civil society organized around the political institutions of the EU. As of yet, this is at best a restricted public sphere.

The other contribution to offer an assessment of accountability, with specific attention to the status of minorities and regions, is offered by Else Grete Broderstad in Chapter 11. Broderstad focuses on how the European integration process affects indigenous peoples, with particular emphasis on the Saami people in Norway, Sweden and Finland. The article first sets out to clarify, in theoretical terms, the problems that indigenous peoples' role and status pose for established conceptions of citizenship and national belonging – which are based on conventional conceptions of democratic governance. Then, the article focuses – in empirical terms – on how these groups have been dealt with by the Member States in question. These states have adopted a wide range of different incorporation strategies, of which assimilation was the official one until after the Second World War. At present there are marked differences among the Nordic states in terms of how they respond to Saami demands. It is observed that homogeneous nation-states face important structural problems, which hamper their ability to handle claims for difference in a legitimate manner. The last part of the chapter, then, focuses on what possibilities the EU has to remedy this, i.e. to deal with difference and plurality in a legitimate manner. She discusses in what sense the establishment of a set of transnational institutions such as the EU represents a better way of treating the role and status of indigenous people. In Chapter 12 the editors conclude by addressing the many ways in which the EU – through its structures and procedures – is seeking legitimation through deliberation.

Notes

1 For comments on earlier drafts, we thank the researchers at ARENA.
2 Prior to the establishment of the UN, human rights were deemed a matter for domestic jurisdictions. Exceptions related to (a) certain minimum standards in the treatment of aliens; (b) slavery and the slave trade; (c) 'rights of certain persons in times of armed conflict'; and (d) rights of minorities (Driscoll 1989: 42).
3 A *denizen* can be defined as a long-term resident 'who possess[es] substantial rights and privileges ... The denizenship model [of citizenship] depicts changes in citizenship as an expansion of scope on a *territorial* basis: the principle of domicile augments the principle of nationality. Denizens acquire certain membership rights by virtue of living and working in host countries' (Soysal 1994: 138–139). Soysal critiques this model for being confined to the nation-state model.
4 To Ernst Haas, supranationality refers to 'a process or style of decision-making, "a cumulative pattern of accommodation in which the participants refrain from unconditionally vetoing proposals and instead seek to attain agreement by means of compromises upgrading common interests" ' (Haas cited in Keohane and Hoffmann 1991: 280).
5 Perhaps the clearest example is that of the Danish opponents to the Maastricht Treaty who sought and obtained a High Court ruling on the constitutionality of the

TEU. They claimed that article 235 of the TEU violated paragraph 20 of the Danish Constitution because it enabled the EU to take on issues that are not mentioned in the treaties (*Politiken*, April 7, 1998).

6 See e.g. Mancini and Weiler (1998), Pinder (1991, 1994). This view is also widely espoused by Euro-sceptics. See e.g. Holmes (1996).

7

> When a Commission proposal is involved, at least 62 votes must be cast in favour. In other cases, the qualified majority is also 62 votes, but these must be cast by at least 10 Member States. In practice, the Council tries to reach the widest possible consensus before taking a decision so that, for example, only about 14 percent of the legislation adopted by the Council in 1994 was the subject of negative votes and abstentions.
> (http://europa.eu.int/inst/en/cl.htm#methods, July 8, 1998)

8 Member States cannot remove Commissioners from office during their period of tenure. Further, Article 10(2) of the Merger Treaty states that a Commissioner who breaches the principle of autonomy can be compulsorily retired from office. The record thus far shows that Commissioners have been fully loyal to the EU.

9 Recent empirical findings reveal that the inclination to act as national representatives 'is highest among nationals with large personnel quotas in the Commission and nationals with strong supportive networks in Brussels' (Hooghe 1998).

10 The Amsterdam Treaty represents an important attempt to simplify the procedural arrangements of the EU by eliminating a large number of voting procedures.

11 The literature on this theme is vast, see e.g. Ruggie (1993); Caporaso (1996, 1998); Curtin (1997); Linklater (1996); Gowan and Anderson (1997); Moravcsik (1993, 1994, 1998); Schmitter (1992, 1998); Weiler (1995).

12 For an illuminating account of the vocabulary associated with the nation-state, consider M. Oakeshott (1975) and also Q. Skinner (1989).

13 For instance, consider the plea for European-wide political parties, which has been widely debated among analysts and which is even implied in Article 138a of the TEU (Lundberg 1995: 132). To address such a plea, we would need to specify which models of democratic governance are compatible with political parties; what role political parties are intended to play in each model; and what type of party and party system is required for the model to work. Then, once this is settled, it is necessary to examine how such parties and party systems fare today, i.e. are they well suited to address the particular democratic challenges that the EU is faced with now? Part of this answer can be found by examining their record at the national level. With regard to parties, many analysts contend that contemporary political parties are inadequate to address contemporary democratic challenges associated with more fluid allegiances and identities and more assertive citizens. It makes little sense to advocate the adoption of an institutional arrangement that is deemed to be crisis-ridden at the national level, straight to the European level, without first making sure that this arrangement does not simply replicate the problems at the European level.

14 Despite much effort to the contrary, there is still a tendency to engage in what Giovanni Sartori terms 'conceptual stretching' (Sartori 1970) when discussing the EU. For instance, if the EU is deemed a state-in-the-making, the denotation of the term 'state' has to refer not only to the characteristic features of an established state but also to those features that contribute to state-making. When there is no clear intent to establish a state, as is the case in the EU, it is easy to overstretch the connotation of the term state. A state is marked by fixed territory and a clear conception of sovereignty whereas the EU is marked by ambiguity on both counts. Since there are many possible end-states of the EU, to conceive of it merely as a state-in-the-making is akin to permit a desired result to determine the status of the present entity. This

type of teleological thinking would not only denigrate the independence of the institutional structure in place but also conceive of it in merely instrumental terms.

15 Consider for instance Gorm Harste, 'Demokratisk overskud' [Democratic Surplus], *Politiken*, May 26, 1998.

16 Tyrannies may be stable but lack validity, i.e. normative justification, and will therefore not be stable for very long. The EU is not only marked by a remarkable degree of stability, the high rate of change that it has undergone and continues to undergo is indicative of 'stability in motion'.

17 See for example Weiler (1999a: 240–255), and Bellamy and Castiglione in this volume.

18 They are also still widely drawn upon by EU officials in their efforts to legitimate the EU, as is amply demonstrated in the numerous submissions to the IGC-96. See also Fossum in this volume.

19 For a presentation of 'Interdependence', see Keohane and Nye (1977 and 1987). For regime theory, see Krasner (1982), Young (1986), Haas (1983), Rittberger (1993), and Breckinridge (1997).

20 In their classic work on 'Power and Interdependence', Keohane and Nye seek to *modify* the core assumptions of political realism rather than reject them. They note that complex interdependence is marked by a setting in which (a) there is a multitude of channels that connect societies; (b) interstate relations are characterized by an '*absence of hierarchy among issues*' which means that security does not dominate the agenda; and (c) governments do not use military force against other governments (Keohane and Nye 1977).

21 In more recent years a burgeoning literature that deals with value-based transnationalism, as conveyed through for instance issue networks and epistemic communities, has emerged (for a brief listing, see Keck and Sikkink 1998; Checkel 1997).

22 Consider for instance Phillippe Schmitter's definition of integration as 'the process of transferring exclusive expectations of benefits from the nation-state to some larger entity. It encompasses the process by virtue of which national actors of all sorts (government officials, interest group spokesmen, politicians, as well as ordinary people) cease to identify themselves and their future welfare entirely with their own national governments and its policies' (Schmitter, cited in Kirchner, 1980: 98). Similarly, Karl Deutsch has defined integration as 'the attainment, within a territory, of a "sense of community" and of institutions and practices strong enough and widespread enough to assure, for a "long" time, dependable expectations of "peaceful change" among its population' (Deutsch, in Wallace 1990: 9).

23 Caporaso argues that Moravcsik has modified intergovernmentalism by incorporating so much of neo-functionalism as to blur the distinction between classical realism and neo-functionalism: 'Realism can now embrace economic goals, can reject the hierarchy between security and economic issues, and can thoroughly disassociate itself from the systemic determination of preferences' (Caporaso 1998: 11).

24 Moravcsik does consider preferences that are formed through democratic processes at the national level but his normative framework does not enable him to assess their quality.

25 For this distinction, see Evans *et al.* (1985). See also Marks *et al.* (1996: 347–348).

26 The civilizing force of hypocrisy refers to the way public debate induces actors to replace the language of power by the language of reason, i.e. they have to appeal to common norms and values. This does not necessarily eliminate egocentric motives, but forces the actors to hide them, and in so doing they actually confirm the validity of norms and reproduce them (see Elster 1998c: 111; see also Eriksen and Weigård 1997a; Risse 1999).

27 John Hume, Nobel Peace Prize Laureate, recently noted that '(t)he Irish and British membership of the EU has really contributed to create the will to resolve the conflict in Northern Ireland. It has been almost embarrassing for the two countries to have a

nationalist civil war going on in their back yard, while they have participated in a grand scale anti nationalist project' (*Weekendavisen*, Denmark, 6–12 November, 1998: 2, authors' translation).

28 There is a large body of literature on this, see e.g. Marks (1993); Jachtenfuchs and Kohler-Koch (1996a); Hooghe (1998); Kohler-Koch (1996); Scharpf (1996a).

29 'One can distinguish between government based on representative democracy and governance based on a variety of different regulative, representative and authority processes' (Andersen and Burns 1996: 228). On this see also for example, Andersen and Eliassen (1996); Hix (1998); Majone (1996a); Marks *et al.* (1996).

30 This is to say that such forms of collective action could theoretically be modelled as rational choices from the actors' point of view by means of game theory. However, these are 'as if' explanations and seem highly speculative and unrealistic and quite often also cynical. On this see Eriksen and Weigård (1997a: 225). For instance, the tendency to explain integration and enlargement as necessary side-payments, does appear to be overly cynical.

31 Morality excludes egoism: 'By "the moral point of view" we mean a point of view which furnishes a court of arbitration for conflicts of interests. Hence it cannot (logically) be identical with the point of view of self-interest. Hence, egoism is not the point of view of morality' (Baier 1958: 189–190).

32 See e.g. Bohmann 1996; Gutmann and Thompson (1996); Bohman and Rehg (1997); Elster (1998a); Cohen and Sabel (1997); Rawls (1997).

33 Contractualists hold that this is obtained when parties proceed according to the principles of the original situation – behind a veil of ignorance (Rawls 1971, 1993).

34 The conditions for autonomy can only be accomplished through collective action as it is the political institutionalization and safeguarding of human rights through political activism that make them into real assets (Habermas 1996a: 14ff.).

2 Beyond the nation-state?

On some consequences of economic globalization[1]

Jürgen Habermas

Before the end of the welfare-state compromise

Ironically, developed societies at the end of the century are confronted with the return of a problem which, under the pressure of system rivalry, they just seemed to have solved. It is a problem as old as capitalism itself: How to exploit the allocative and discovering functions of self-regulating markets effectively without having to accept unequal distribution and social costs which are at variance with the preconditions for an integration of liberal societies? In the mixed economies of the West, the state, with a considerable share of the national product at its disposal, had gained a certain latitude for transfer and subsidy payments and, on the whole, for efficient policies in the fields of infrastructure, employment, and social security. It could exert a certain influence on the overall conditions of production and distribution, with the aim of achieving growth, price stability, and full employment. In other words, the regulatory state could at the same time, through growth-inducing action on the one hand, and social policy on the other, stimulate the dynamics of economy and guarantee social integration.

The key for solving the problem of guaranteeing both economic efficiency, on the one side, and political freedom and social security, on the other – i.e. of fitting capitalism to democracy – was the construction of a welfare-state which ensured, at a high level of employment, a relatively high average living standard and widespread prosperity. Different though they were, the social policy sectors of countries like the USA, Japan, and the Federal Republic had expanded till into the 1980s. But meanwhile, this trend is being reversed: benefits drop, while at the same time access to social security systems is toughened, and pressure on the unemployed is increased. The transformation and reduction of the welfare-state is the immediate consequence of a supply-side economic policy which is orientated to deregulation of markets, reduction of subsidies, and improving investment conditions. This policy-agenda has included anti-inflationary monetary and interest rate policies as well as reduction of direct taxes, transfer of state-owned enterprise into private ownership, and similar measures.

Revoking the welfare-state compromise, though, means new virulence for certain crisis tendencies which it had counterbalanced. Social costs arise which might well exceed the integration capacity of liberal societies. Indications of growing poverty and social insecurity as a corollary of growing disparities of income are unequivocal, and there are clearly recognizable trends towards social disintegration (Heitmeyer 1997). The gap between the living conditions of the employed, the under-employed, and the unemployed is widening. Moreover, the status of the employed is now much more differentiated – differentiated not only in terms of segments of the labour market, but according to the type of labour-contract (core *vs.* short-time staff), the degree of job stability (main companies *vs.* subcontracted suppliers), origin (nationals *vs.* immigrant labour), or legal *vs.* illegal status. The 'risk groups' of the labouring population – those who are considered 'hard to place in jobs' – can easily be classified in terms of gender, age, number of children, degree of education, ethnic origin, health handicaps, etc. These statistics reveal that the probability of the collective fate of becoming 'superfluous' may not be attributed to individual qualifications and dispositions. 'Underclasses' emerge where exclusions – from the employment system and from further education, from the benefits of transfer payments, from the housing market, from family resources, etc. – are bundled. These heterogeneous groups, largely segmentated from the rest of society and left to immiseration, are no longer able to change their social situation by their own efforts (Luhmann 1996). This kind of cumulative exclusion is what distinguishes an 'underclass' from traditional 'lower classes'.

In the long run, this de-solidarization will inevitably destroy a liberal political culture. For democratic societies are dependent precisely on those shared beliefs, attitudes and practices that articulate universalistic principles. Majority decisions which, while procedurally correct in coming about, merely reflect the reactions of self-defence of those who fear a loss of status and thus express just right-wing populist sentiments, would but erode the legitimacy of the very democratic procedures and institutions they apparently follow. Neo-liberals accept a higher degree of social injustice and believe that the manner in which world financial markets 'evaluate' the economies of competing countries is inherently 'fair'. They, of course, assess the present situation differently than those who still adhere to the 'socialdemocratic' era because they know that equal social rights are the stays of democratic citizenship. Both sides, though, start from a rather similar description of the dilemma. The gist of their diagnosis is that national governments are being forced into a zero-sum game in which the unescapable economic imperatives can be followed only at the expense of important social and political objectives.[2] In the context of a globalized economy, nation-states can achieve a higher degree of international competitiveness for their countries only by self-inflicted restrictions on their capacity to act; this, then, is a rationale for restrictive policies at home which erode social cohesion and are a severe test for democratic stability.

This dilemma is based on a plausible description, the detailed justification, or even illustration, of which I cannot go into here.[3] It boils down to two theses: (1) The economic problems of affluent societies can be explained by structural changes in the system of world economy – brought together under the heading of 'globalization'. (2) This transformation restricts the latitude of national governments, their remaining options no longer allowing them to 'cushion' undesirable social and political side effects of transnational economic transactions.

1 The by now fashionable talk of the 'globalization of markets' needs to be rendered more precise. Naturally, there is not such a thing like 'the' universal market. What the term 'globalization' in this context refers to is a *process* for which at least four indicators are presented (see Perraton *et al.* 1997):

- The expansion and growing density of interaction in international trade in various markets, above all in industrial goods, increasingly transform 'national' economies into dependencies of the world economy. At the same time, the composition of trade is changing in kind: as a consequence of the introduction of new communications technologies it is now possible to trade services which are produced as well as stored and then consumed at different locations far removed from one another (compare the outscoring of software tasks to developing countries).
- The global networking of financial markets encourages short-term investments and accelerates capital flows. One result is that capital, which has thus become more mobile, can more readily slip through the fingers of national fiscal authorities. Moreover, speculation in foreign exchange and derivates generates something like an independent 'symbolic economy'. On the other hand, governments come under pressure from the international stock exchanges, which swiftly react to interest rate policies and budgetary measures in general, thereby 'evaluating' national investment conditions.
- Increasing foreign direct investment results in the first place from the activities of multinational corporations, whose decisions become ever more independent of local concerns, since they have gained and can make use of (or efficiently threaten to make use of) new exit options. In this context, we are presently seeing a debate on the size of the 'exportation of jobs', for example from West Europe to low-wage countries in South East Asia, Latin America, and Central and Eastern Europe. In the developed countries it is the low-skilled blue-collar workers in industries with low-level technology and comparatively low productivity who are bearing the brunt of this.
- With the rapid increase in the export of industrial goods by the 'newly industrialized countries', the OECD countries are facing mounting competitive pressures that push their efforts to restructure their economies in favour of high-tech sectors.

2 If this is an appropriate description of prevailing trends, then the world economy can no longer be construed as an 'international' system of exchange in which nation-states take part as important actors, buttressed by their respective economies and competing with one another through the channels of foreign trade relations. The globalization of the economy, in the

sense just mentioned, rather appeals to the image of a 'transnational' system that blurs the boundaries between domestic and foreign trade and thus forces a changed perspective upon nation-states as actors on the world stage (Neyer 1995). To the extent that the power to design and structure interactions is now transferred to deregulated markets less and less confined by territorial borders, the political scope nation-states have is less and less curbed by the strategic decisions of other nation-states, but increasingly by *systemic* interdependencies. The aggregate impact of individual decisions taken world-wide by a huge and opaque number of market participants generates contextual constraints which can be calculated to a certain degree, but can certainly not be influenced in the sense that the behaviour of strategic opponents can be conditioned. The transnational model takes into account the fact that even the most powerful governments become dependent on globalized markets and are ever less able to politically frame economic processes.

The nation-state is being deprived of more and more options. Two of them can be discounted here: protectionism, and the return to a demand-side economic policy. As far as movements of capital can be controlled at all, the costs of a protectionist closure of domestic economy would soon, under the given conditions of world economy, soar to unacceptable heights. And state employment programmes today fail, not only because of the limits set to public debt, but because of their lack of effectiveness within a national frame. Under the conditions of globalized economy, 'Keynesianism in one country' no longer works.

Thus, a policy of anticipative, intelligent, and sustainable adaptation of national conditions to global competition is more promising – a strategy also pursued by 'New Labour'. It includes the well-known agenda of long-term industrial policy, promotion of research and development, that is, of *future* innovation, qualification of the workforce by better training and further education, and a reasonable degree of 'flexibility' for the labour market. In the medium term, these measures would bring about local advantages, but would not change the pattern of international competition between countries. Nor does it help the miners and dock workers who have been laid off. The unemployed in the lower strata would probably profit from a deregulation of the labour market, only if a low-wage sector were to be permitted on the condition that the cheap jobs thus created be subsidized, for example by means of a negative income tax – a programme that is now adopted by the campaigning Social Democrats in Germany (Scharpf 1997d).

If we give this idea a somewhat more radical twist, then we arrive at the notion of a general, state-guaranteed citizen-income, as originally proposed by André Gorz and now defended, among others, by Claus Offe. Severing the link between income and employment would place the current 'economic society', centred as it is on the traditional role of full-time wage labour, on a new footing and would create an equivalent for the disintegrating welfare system. The Basic

Income is expected to absorb the destructive impact the capitalist world market has on the personal life of those who slide into the growing segment of the 'superfluous' population. Such a radical redistribution programme calls, however, for a change in deep-rooted value orientations, which it is hard to bring about intentionally. Moreover, the question arises again how, under present conditions of global competition, the programme could be financed within the budgetary scope of individual nation-states if we assume that the target income is to be above the lowest level of welfare support.

So, the globalization of economy, no matter how we look at it, destroys a historical constellation in which, for a certain period and in a favoured region, the welfare-state compromise was possible. This compromise, to be sure, is by no means the ideal solution of a problem inherent to capitalism, but it has after all succeeded in keeping the social costs within accepted limits. In spite of the well-known features of bureaucratization and 'normalization', so convincingly critized by Foucault, the scale of social disparities were such that the actual state of society did not manifestly repudiate the normative promises of the democratic as well as liberal tradition as they are articulated in our constitutional principles.

Beyond the nation-state

The welfare-state is a rather recent achievement. In Europe, states characterized by their sovereign rule over a territory had emerged by the seventeenth century. Due to their larger capacities for control, they have proved to be superior to previous formations like the Ancient Empires or the city-states. Because of its functional specification as an administrative *state*, the modern state was differentiated from the private sphere of a legally institutionalized market economy; at the same time, as a *state based on taxes*, it became dependent on the capitalist economy. In the course of the 19th century it opened up to a democratic mode of legitimation. This kind of *nation-state* is by now a model all over the world. In certain privileged regions, benefiting from favourable post-war conditions, the nation-state could finally develop into the welfare-state by regulating national economies without, however, destroying the self-regulating mechanism of the market. This successful combination is now under threat as the globalized economy evades the grip of this *regulatory state*. Welfare-state functions, obviously, can only be maintained on the previous scale if they are transferred from the nation-state to larger political units growing to catch up, so to speak, with a transnationalized economy.

The focus, therefore, is now on the construction of supranational institutions and transnational forums of political co-operation (Held 1995). Such is the rationale of continent-wide economic alliances like NAFTA or APEC which allow governments to come to arrangements that are binding or, at least, provide for soft sanctions. Larger gains from co-operation are to be expected from more ambitious projects like the European Union. Continent-wide regimes like these not only allow for unified monetary blocs to emerge, thus diminishing the risks of fluctuating exchange rates, but for larger political units with a hierarchical organization of competencies.

In all probability the process of European unification will show how a currency union at first creates more problems than it solves – that is to say, if it does not go hand in hand with a unified social and economic policy for the states which relinquish their fiscal sovereignty but insist on retaining their sovereignty in most other policy fields (Streeck 1995). For not until independent collective actors have been transformed into members of a political community equipped with a democratic legislature would it be possible for equal social and environmental standards to be implemented. A union that emerges from various nation-states growing ever closer together – and which thereby itself assumes the qualities of a state – will first be able to make use of an extended regulatory capacity if, in line with the equalization of living conditions across the whole territory, there is progress in integration of another kind. *Citizens' solidarity*, hitherto limited to the nation-state, must be expanded to the citizens of the Union in such a way that, for example, Swedes and Portuguese, Germans and Greeks are willing to stand up for one another, as it is the case now with citizens from former West and East Germany. Only then would it be possible to expect them to accept the same minimum wages, let alone the same opportunities for their different collective forms of life and for their individual life-projects (Habermas 1996b: 128–191).

As it is, even such a regime would benefit from its larger geographical and economical basis, in the best of cases, by obtaining certain advantages in global competition and by strengthening their position *vis-à-vis* other global players. The creation of larger political units leads to defensive alliances opposed to the rest of the world, but does not change the *pattern* of competition between countries or continents as such. It does not *per se* bring about a change of mode, replacing adaptation to the transnational system of world economy by an effort to exert political influence on its overall frame. On the other hand, political alliances of this type are at least a necessary condition if politics should be put in the position to catch up with the pervasive forces of a globalized economy. With each new supranational regime, the number of political actors decreases, while the club of those few actors fills who are at all capable to act on a global scale, and are able to co-operate for reaching arrangements as to the project and the implementation of an economic world order.[4] The often discussed tax on speculative profits, the so-called 'Tobin-Tax', is a harmless example of such co-ordination in which all those involved get a better deal than in case of no decision and unco-ordinated action. Given that, despite supranational institutions and conferences, an economically stratified world society is politically still dominated mainly by international relations between a large number of strategic actors, even such an agreement, which could so easily be realized, does not arise, although it is evidently in the joint interest of all concerned.

If the making of the European Political Union is difficult, how much more so will it be to come to an arrangement on the project of an economic world order?

The task would be not only to implement, like the World Bank or the International Monetary Fund, transnational free market conditions, but to establish arrangements for the world-wide development of an informed political opinion and will formation and to guarantee binding political decisions. In view of the fact that coping with the demands of a globalized economy exceeds the competency of single nation-states, the obvious alternative, *in abstracto* and seen from the academic ivory tower, so to speak – is the very transfer of functions previously performed by the welfare-state to supranational agencies. However, at this level another mode of political co-ordination is lacking – something that would channel the undesirable social and ecological side effects of transnational economic flows and steer them in tolerable waters. There certainly is already a network of institutions interconnecting the 180 sovereign states even below the abstract level of the United Nations (Senghaas 1994). About 350 governmental organizations, more than half of them founded after 1960, are designed for economic, social, and peace-keeping functions. But they are too weak to take binding decisions and to assume any efficient regulatory function in the fields of economy, social security, and ecology.

From the viewpoint of mainstream social and political science, a *global welfare regime* seems a quite rapturous, if not bizarre idea. This is also true for those approaches which do not *a fortiori*, by the choice of the conceptual frame, rule out the possibility that complex societies can consciously exercise political influence upon themselves and self-reflexively cope with the failures of functional subsystems. Of course, nobody likes to keep heading for utopia, much less so today where all utopian energies *seem* to be exhausted.[5] Thus, in the absence of any noteworthy efforts on the part of established social sciences, the idea of supranational politics catching up with globalized markets has as yet not even reached the stage of a 'project'. It would first be possible to speak of such a project if, with regard to political opinion and will formation, we could present the outlines for new transnational procedures and institutions and, with regard to a global political order, we could at least provide some relevant examples for how compromises between obviously conflicting interests could be reasonably achieved. This abstinence of the social sciences were understandable if we had to assume that the justification of such a project would have to rely on the given interests of these states and their populations, and its realization on the action of *independent* political powers. In a stratified world society like ours, irreconcilable interests arise out of the asymmetrical interdependency between developed, newly industrialized and under-developed countries. But this perspective is valid only as long as there are no institutionalized procedures for a transnational political process inducing those few collective actors at all capable of global action to extend their range of preferences by including concerns of 'global governance'.

Through globalization processes, the nature of which is much broader than purely economic, we get more and more accustomed to a *different* perspective which sharpens our awareness of the growing interdependence of our social arenas, of shared risks, and of the inescapable impact of collective fates. While the acceleration and condensation of communication and traffic makes for shrinking distances in space and time, expanding markets come up against the limits of the planet, and exploiting resources against those of nature. Even at medium term, narrowing horizons by now all but prohibit the externalization of the consequences of many of our actions: it is increasingly rare that costs and risks can be shifted unto others – other sectors of society, remote regions, foreign cultures, or future generations – without fears of sanctions. This is as obvious for the risks of large-scale technologies, which can no longer be restricted to a local scope, as for the industrial production, by affluent societies, of harmful substances, which pollute all continents (Beck 1988). In such a setting, the question arises for how long we can still shift social costs of insecurity, poverty and misery unto those segments of the workforce that have become 'useless'? It is ridiculous that the increase of productivity should be paid for by the growth of underclasses which are excluded from the benefits of this very economic growth.

Governments certainly cannot be expected to enter international agreements, and to establish regulations counteracting such externalizations, as long as they are perceived as independent actors in those national arenas where they have to gain support from voters, i.e. re-election. The individual states must be tied into the binding procedures of co-operation within a transnational community of states in such a way that this commitment is in each case visible on the stage of domestic policy. The crucial question, therefore, is whether a consciousness of inevitable cosmopolitan solidarization is likely to emerge in the civil societies and the political public domains of large-scale regimes that are growing together. Only under the pressure of a change in the consciousness of citizens, one that has an impact on domestic affairs, those collective actors capable to act globally may come to perceive themselves differently, that is, increasingly, as members of a community that leaves them no choice but co-operation and taking one another's interests fairly into account. Still, ruling elites cannot be expected to accomplish this shift of perspective from 'international relations' to 'world domestic policy' unless this achievement is rewarded by the populations themselves.

A mild, but nevertheless encouraging example for this is the pacifist consciousness which, after the experiences of two barbaric World Wars, has been voiced in public and has spread originating from the nations immediately involved – to many countries. We know that this change of consciousness has been powerless to prevent countless local and civil wars in other regions of the world. Still, the change in mentalities has led to a change in the political and cultural parameters of international relations, thus succeeding in having the UN Declaration of Human Rights which proscribes wars of aggression and crimes against humanity gain the normative binding force, weak it is true, of conventions subscribed to in public. With regard to the institutionalization of procedures, practices and regulations, which would affect the world economy and allow global problems to be solved, this of course is insufficient. Here, we encounter a shortcoming, which we have already witnessed as a bottleneck in the process of European unification. What is lacking is the emergence of a cosmopolitan solidarity, less binding, of course, than the civic solidarity that has emerged within nation-states in the course of one or two hundred years. But a world population that is being welded together to form an involuntary risk-taking community is long since an objective fact. The hope for this pressure to bring about yet another stage of that far-reaching thrust for abstraction that has led from local and dynastic loyalty to national and democratic consciousness is, therefore, not completely without plausibility.

The institutionalization of procedures for the world-wide co-ordination and generalization of interests, as well as for the imaginative construction of shared interests, is unlikely to come about in the organizational form of a (not even desirable) world state. It will have to take into account the autonomy, particular mentality and even obstinacy of previously sovereign states. It is no coincidence that the UN General Assembly at best resembles an upper house. However, what is the path that leads there? The Hobbesian problem of how to create and to stabilize social order is too big a challenge, on the global scale as well, for the capacity of rational egoists to co-operate and to *bind* their own wills. Political elites are not capable of taking and carrying out such initiative, unless the institutional innovations are met by the response and support of previously reformed value orientations in their populations. Therefore, the first target groups of such a 'project' are not governments, but social movements and non-governmental organizations, e.g. the active members of a civil society which extends across the borders of a nation. At any rate, the idea of enhancing the capacity for political regulation in order to catch up with globalized markets highlights complex interrelations between the dispositions of larger political regimes to co-operate, and a new mode of integration, cosmopolitan solidarity, on the side of populations.

Ongoing modernity or taking modernity one step further forward?

A sociology that construes 'society' almost always as an object delimited by the nation-state, in other words as a national society, encounters conceptual difficulties when it comes to a politically underdetermined structure such as 'world society' (Giddens 1990a: 12ff.). Nevertheless, the question why social scientists hesitate to adopt such a perspective is not utterly trivial. Today, social scientists by no means close their eyes to the alarming facts and implications of economic globalization (Willke 1997: 83). However, only few sociologists are prepared to issue diagnoses of their times which serve to alarm a broader public.[6] It is not the diagnosis which is lacking, what needs explaining is the hesitation to adopt a perspective which would focus attention on the path, however rough it may be, toward a world domestic policy that is transnational in nature.

Why is it so strange to investigate the institutions and procedures necessary to construct common interests with a 'cosmopolitan intention' and to create a 'global welfare regime'? I suspect that social theories disarmed by a radicalized critique of reason can no longer make such a perspective their own, even if the diagnosis of 'reflexive modernization' suggests that a Modernity, the trends of which are continuing any way, needs to be taken one step further.

Heidegger is the key figure in the turn toward a post-Nietzschean critique of reason that sweeps the platform of Occidental rationalism clean only in order to ensure its re-enchantment. Whereas the dialectical self-critique of reason from Kant to Hegel and Marx endeavoured to strip Occidental rationalism of its limitations, Heidegger operates with a contextualizing critique of reason that confronts a subjective reason whose stubborn subjectivity is hidden from itself with its very own false pretensions. This critique is designed to expose, as it were from within, the local context from which a fathomless-abstract self-understanding emerges, to send the idol of reason crashing to the ground and therefore to pave the way for a new *Gelassenheit*. The intention: the sons and daughters of Modernity are meant to learn once again to genuflect in reverent expectation of the indeterminate fate of Being. However, this stance of 'apocalyptic attentism' looks suspiciously like the fatalistic mentality of traditional societies. The cultural critique which is fed by this source is therefore even less up to tackling the realities of the close of the 20th century than are those critical social theories in the tradition of Western Marxism to whose eroded credibility it is a response.

Like the modern critiques of the Enlightenment, the postmodern heirs to Heidegger take the side of the ruptured, the marginalized and the incomplete, for the excluded and the non-identical – that is, for the 'difference' and 'otherness'. They also renew the reservations against the abstract generalities and consuming totalities which ride roughshod over differences and steamroller the idiosyncratic particularity of the familiar and the local. To this extent, they bolster the distrust of any expansion of uncontrolled large-scale bureaucracies who threaten with the project of creating larger political units and with the agenda of some kind of world domestic policy. In addition, the postmodern critics of Enlightenment have taken a stand against the tradition of Enlightenment itself, including an Enlightenment of the Hegelian type which once endeavoured dialectically to grasp its own limits. These critics reject not only a wrong reading of the 'self' in acts of self-reflection, self-realization and self-determination – a reading in the misleading terms of possessive individualism – for they also reject Modernity's normative self-understanding *per se*. They not only celebrate the end of a philosophy of consciousness and a teleology of history, but bid farewell to the spirit of Modernity itself.

Postmodernism is aimed at bringing about a mental change which relieves society of the burden of collective responsibility for too much future, for too many future states of affairs, anticipated in too far a range. The intention is to shift the 'locus of control' away from over-strained subjects and over-taxed political communities and instead transfer it to the frenzy of contingencies, to the variance and over-complexity of environments, to the secondary nature of autonomous networks. And along with the normative self-understanding of

Modernity, the idea of the conscious, democratically organized exercise of influence by society on itself should and will also die out. However, this expectation is contradicted by persistent trends in social and cultural modernization fuelled from a pool of ideas that has remained the same. If we take our cue from descriptions that have been presented under the label of 'reflexive modernization' (Beck 1992; Beck *et al.* 1996), then what strikes the eye is that, for all the changes in the structures and prerequisites of Western societies, the cultural potential has remained the same. Those value orientations which jell around the notions of self-consciousness, self-realization and self-determination or self-government have been honed to an even finer edge. Moreover, our societies will have to draw on this pool of ideas if they wish to find answers to the global problems of the 21st century.

Anthony Giddens introduces the basic notion of 'reflexive modernization' in two sentences: 'Modernity, as it becomes globalized and turns back against itself, comes up against its own limits.' He concludes from this observation: 'Rather than entering a period of postmodernity, we are moving into one in which the consequences of modernity are becoming more radicalized and universalized than before' (Giddens 1990b). The one follows from the other, if we read the first sentence to mean that modern societies come up against their limits in two ways and perceive and cope with this state of affairs 'reflexively' or self-referentially. On the one hand, they are no longer able to externalize the side effects of social reproduction, which take the form of systemically generated risks; in other words, they cannot pass these risks on to other countries and societies, to future generations or to a self-regenerating nature. On the other, these societies are to an ever greater extent unable to resort to external resources such as nature or tradition, but instead increasingly have to reproduce the prerequisites necessary for their reproduction themselves. Modernity at the stage of industrialized society was able to feed off the stocks of its pre-modern heritage; for this reason, Ulrich Beck speaks now of the task of the modernization of 'semi-modern' societies.[7] This is only possible by 'reflexive' means, as handling the follow-up problems of social modernization has to rely on capacities generated by precisely that modernization.

'Reflexivity' can evidently be understood both in Niklas Luhmann's sense of the 'self-application' of systemic mechanisms, and in the sense of 'self-reflection', i.e. the collective actor's perception of, and operation upon themselves. An example of reflexivity of the first type would be the capitalist way the market economy copes with ecological problems generated by the market economy. An example of the second would be the political sector catching up with the globalization of markets by influencing the boundary conditions of the transnational economy. Assuming that the functional differentiation of highly specialized sub-systems 'continues', systems theory expects that reflexive mechanisms will cope with failures of *autopoiesis*. This expectation is implausible, for social sub-systems that only speak their own language remain blind to the external costs that they cause. It is with this in mind that Claus Offe takes up an idea of Adorno's when he writes:

It appears that the modernization of the parts comes at the cost of the modernity of the whole. Precisely because of the 'openness to the future' of the subsystems and of their innovation-intensifying sectoral rationalities, society as a whole seems to have become incapable of conceiving its own future as a project or even only of reining it in according to elementary goals and parameters.

(Offe 1996: 16)

The costs of opposed sectoral rationalities can clearly only be kept within limits that are socially tolerable by reflexivity of a different sort, namely self-reflection in the sense of a community's political influence upon itself.

Ongoing Modernity needs to be taken further forward. My intention is not to juxtapose some 'macro-planning model' to the model of the 'quasi-natural, incremental, and goalless adaptation' of systems and networks (Willke 1997: 83). The failed vision of state socialism shares an implicit assumption with the neo-liberal vision of the release of the individual from the liquidated community of solidarity among citizens into the arena of the free-for-all of the unregulated world market. Both approaches equally abandon the notion of democratic self-determination within complex societies. An abdication of politics goes hand in hand with the expectation that what will spread across the postmodern landscape will be a new form of that type of fatalism which was characteristic of the politically impotent, fellah-like populations of the Ancient Empires. But can we really expect that people who are supposed to master their private destinies as more or less rational egoists will adopt a quietistic stance with regard to the collective fates they have to suffer?

Empirically, such a fatalistic shift in attitude (be it inspired by systems theory or an ontologized notion of the history of being) is just not compatible with a continuation of the rationalization of lifeworlds. The classical social theories from Durkheim *via* Weber to Parsons have characterized the mentality of modern societies in terms of increasing reflexivity. Pluralist culture gets involved in hermeneutic conflicts on the constant revision of the traditions it can choose; existing institutions find themselves confronted with the need to provide rational justifications, so that legitimate orders increasingly become dependent on deliberate politics and democratic legislation; and the individual persons who are exposed to the pressure to decide between even more alternatives, are compelled to stabilize themselves by creating a highly abstract Ego identity (Habermas 1987: 140–148). Reflexive modernization will neither bring these prevailing trends toward de-traditionalization, universalization of values, and individualization to a halt, nor will it turn them around. Instead, all it will do is lend them a clearer shape and accelerate them. If this is a probable prospect, then a gap will open up between this increasingly pronounced normative self-understanding, on the one hand, and the experience, on the other, that politics fails to counteract the way our lifeworlds are mediated, that is colonized rather than supported by globalized systems.

Notes

1 Vilhelm Aubert Lecture given at the University of Oslo, September 19, 1997.
2 R. Dahrendorf terms this squaring the circle (in *Blätter für Deutsche und Internationale Politik*, no. 9, 1996), when writing: 'What is involved is the attempt to link three things that cannot be combined smoothly: first of all, to maintain and improve competitiveness in the harsh winds of the world economy; secondly, not to sacrifice social cohesion and solidarity in the process; thirdly, to do all this within the framework and by means of the institutions of a free society.'
3 My thanks are to the following authors who permitted me to consult their manuscripts: C. Offe (1997), J. Neyer and M. Seeleib-Kaiser (1995) and H. Wiesenthal (1995).
4 A. Gorz uses this argument to defend the necessity of a European Monetary Union in *Frankfurter Allgemeine Zeitung*, August 1, 1997, p. 35.
5 I do not, however, believe that my diagnosis of 1985 has been flawed by the unforeseen implosion of the Soviet Union. See J. Habermas (1985, 1990).
6 There is an evident turn away from classical social theory, which until Parsons coupled a social scientific analysis with a claim to providing a diagnosis of its age. In response to this shortfall, there have meanwhile been attempts to recover the ground for such diagnoses and not to abandon this field to the postmodern diagnoses in the humanities and among philosophers; see the foreword in Miller and Soeffner (1996: 9–27).
7 Beck (1996: 56ff.), see also the second section in Beck (1986).

3 Deliberative supranationalism in the EU

Erik Oddvar Eriksen

Introduction

The EU is a supranational construction that is demanding both in descriptive and normative terms.[1] It is a complex network of institutions for regulating common affairs, but it is not unitary and self-contained as a political unit. Even if its institutional structuring resembles a separation of powers, akin to the separation of power in a nation-state, there are profound differences. The Council of the Union consists of representatives from the Member States, and legislates on behalf of the Union. It decides some matters by qualified majority but most by unanimity. The European Parliament which is directly elected by the peoples of the Member States, have not until recently had much legislative power. Nor has it had much authority to hold the executive accountable. However, the Treaty of Amsterdam (1997) increased its role. The European Commission is the executor of Union policies and is endowed with the right of initiative, which includes the right to issue legislative proposals. In addition, hundreds of Committees, which were originally constructed to control delegation of powers from the Council to the Commission, are in operation. Such a system may blur the constitutional distinction between legislative and executive powers, between politics and administration. However, it may also represent a new emergent regime of governance contributing to *deliberative supranationalism*, as the authors of Chapter 8 in this volume contend.

What is the European Union, then? It is not a state based on a common identity, a fixed territory and an established *demos*, nor is it a loosely coupled system of allies who co-operate on the basis of mutual interest. The EU involves a lot more than international co-operation, meaning co-operation among states, but it is not a new state. The Community has no territory of its own, no taxing power no independent economic basis and it depends on Member States for implementation of its various legislative and other measures. It is not a body of organized citizens – the citizens' access to the system of government is mainly indirect, and 'there is no single polity which sets the standards of political behaviour' (Preuss 1996a: 215). There is a lot of discussion on the nature of the EU, such as what kind of organization it is, whether it is democratic or technocratic, whether it is moving towards a more firm supranational type of entity, and whether or not it should develop into a federal type of entity. The main problem that sparks frustration has to do with its presumed lack of democratic legitimacy.[2] People are expected to obey laws they themselves or their representatives have not authored. How is the popular will(s) reflected in the EU's political institutions and how can popular opinion be brought to bear upon the decision-makers? Without a uniform public sphere of opinion formation and without influence on decision- and law-making *via* elected representatives, the chain of democratic legitimation through citizens' consent is rather long and weak: Only indirectly through elected Member State representatives in the Council do the voters actually wield influence on political decision-making. In addition to an expert-dominated legislative process, the strong position of courts indicates a shifting balance of power in favour of law and administration. The prospects for popular governance seem rather bleak, indeed.

Many students of the EU, then, have suggested that we need to conceive of the Union as merely a functional arrangement which is to be assessed in accordance with efficiency standards. It is established and prevails because it guarantees market stability:

> After all, it was the presumed superiority of the Community's problem-solving capacity over those of the traditional nation-states which largely motivated the foundation of the Community in the fifties. In other words, reasons of efficiency and utility belong to the most significant founding rationales of the community.
>
> (Preuss 1997: 219)

Consequently, one way of assessing the EU is as a functional organization directed towards realizing collective goals as efficiently as possible. However, this should not be akin to saying that the EU is merely an economic association or a system of intergovernmental co-operation based on the self-interest of each Member State. The notion of utility calculus as the basis of legitimacy is problematic, for conceptual and empirical reasons. First, such an order will be unstable because actors opt out of co-operation whenever they face a better offer (cf. Olson 1965; Scharpf 1997c: 256). Second, it is not compatible with the fact that the EU takes decisions on a whole range of matters that are clearly beyond the immediate interests of the Member States. As was documented in Chapter 1, the EU makes binding decisions on social and cultural matters. It is also widely held that the EU is involved in a constitution-building process and this process has already produced a Union citizenship.[3] In no other international organization do we find such effective implementation of laws as in the European community where a recognized Court of Justice adjudicates disputes (Keohane and Hoffmann 1991: 11). This ability is due to the *doctrine of direct effect* which positions laws enacted in Brussels as if they were enacted by national parliaments and the *doctrine of supremacy* which albeit still a contentious issue – can be said to give the Court the 'Kompetenz-Kompetenz', i.e. the competence to increase its own competence. Lastly, the Treaty of Amsterdam is held to bring the EU one further step ahead as a polity, by enhancing the democratic quality of the EU, through somewhat strengthening its accountability and legitimacy:

> The opening section of the Treaty builds on the Treaty of Maastricht which strengthened the non-economic character of the Union's Constitution. The Treaty of Amsterdam underlines, in a number of different ways, the fact that the Union qua Union is a community of shared values. Article F(1) states that the Union is founded on 'the principles of liberty, democracy, respect for human rights and fundamental freedoms, rule of law, principles which are common to Member States'. This is followed by a provision for dealing with a 'serious and persistent breach by Member State of the principles' outlined in Article Fa(1) of the Treaty.
>
> (Laffan 1997: 14)

The EU is therefore a far-reaching polity, in territorial, functional and legal terms. Its depth and breadth, and its ability to act on several dimensions become quite incomprehensible from the reference point of a economic notion of democratic legitimacy. The EU's strive for openness, the strengthening of the Parliament, the status of the European Court of Justice, the forthcoming enlargement of the Union and its stand on social, environmental and political issues indicate that a broader sets of assessment criteria are required. These cases concern both questions of *identity* – who are we? – and questions of *justice* in a genuine moral sense, as both Member States' and citizens' interests are affected profoundly by decision-making activity of the EU. To understand and assess the EU, then, requires a conception of legitimation that extends well beyond that provided by economic calculus. Democracy, i.e. procedures based on deontological norms, is needed in order to make justifiable decisions when collective choices will interfere with or interrupt established interests and identity-based concerns. That is, to validate moral and ethical norms a popular-democratic concept of legitimation is needed, because only affected parties can decide what is fair treatment of equal and unequal cases, what is in the public interest, and what is the common good.

I would like to address the prospects for such a concept of legitimacy from a discourse-theoretical deliberative perspective on democracy, because the prevailing view of the democratic deficit of the EU is founded on a fixed set of – whether implicitly or explicitly stated – assessment standards. The prevailing judgement of democratic deficit (which is said to be due to lack of a public sphere, lack of European political parties and lack of voter influence through representative bodies), can be questioned by spelling out the evaluative standards that inform such a diagnosis. In particular, to conceptualize democratic legitimacy, the deliberative perspective emphasizes *arguing* and deliberative quality over and above interest representation, bargaining and voting procedures. Applied to the EU, it is necessary to have a closer look at the notion of the public sphere, the role of parliamentary discourse and negotiations in the committee system. I will start this endeavour by providing a short outline of the discourse-theoretical perspective.

From adversary to deliberative democracy

Problems of realism

The conventional criticism levelled against the EU is generally informed by a realist view of politics, i.e. politics as struggles over outcomes: what is in it for me? Resource allocation – the distributive aspects – is in focus: who gets what, how and when? In this perspective, democracy is understood as method of decision-making or a system for preference aggregation: A collective decision is just when it emanates from the aggregation of peoples' preferences through fair procedures. Realists or protagonists of the economic theory of democracy and of elitism and pluralism, rely on egoistic assumptions about human nature. They understand advanced industrial societies as conflict-ridden (Schumpeter 1942), and as 'inherently pluralistic and diverse' (Crick 1962). Decision-making refers to a mode of interaction in which private interests bargain with each other over how to maximize their own interest or given preferences. The only agreement needed in these kinds of co-operative undertakings is that on procedure, or the rules of the game. Consensus on the formal rules applied – in particular the principle of *majority vote* – is required to accomplish collective decision-making. Consensus on these rules is just presupposed, but not explained, even though it is this agreement that ensures political integration. Legitimacy is achieved in elections that are free, fair and secret. In the struggle and competition between contestants legitimacy stems from the aggregation of preferences in frameworks that are fair and neutral.

Likewise, realism in international politics conceives of international relations as interaction between states being in a 'state of nature'.[4] States are treated as 'rational' actors. Parties who are dependent on each other compete within a set of rules for the largest share (cf. Kaplan 1961). Game theory or rational choice is, then, the adequate tool for analysing interstate co-operation or intergovern-mentalism, not primarily because they are power-based relationships – 'a dog eat dog world'[5] – but because interaction is driven by mutual self-interest and strategic calculations.[6] The nature of co-operation is more about mutual advantage or utility than about reciprocity, impartiality or commonality (cf. Rawls 1993: 17; Barry 1989a). The formation of the preferences of the actors and '(T)the constitution of the interests of a nation are taken as established before negotiations among nations begin' (March and Olsen 1998: 951; cf. Moravcsik 1997).

Undoubtedly, this approach has improved the analytical precision in the hypotheses and the empirical foundation of the conclusions in political studies. But at the same time the selected scientific tools have surely favoured one particular way of understanding politics (Almond 1990). Ideals are a sham, an ideology or a mask to be exposed and debunked. The realist or economic approach to politics 'may explain adversarial politics, but it ignores other critical aspects, such as the unitary, the communitarian or the dialogue aspect of politics' (Scalia 1991: 205). It cannot explain the role of binding norms or the force of moral arguments in qualifying standpoints:

> Its medium is bargain, not argument. Its tools of persuasion are not claims and reasons but conditional offers of service and forbearance. Whether formally embodied in a vote or in a contract, or just informally carried out in social behaviours, a strategic outcome represents not a collective judgement of reason but a vector sum in a field of forces.
>
> (Michelman 1989: 293)

These models of politics and democracy, then, have been criticized on several accounts. Further problems arise with electoral authorization and majority vote within supranational institutions which serve to lengthen the actual chains of representation, control and legitimacy as the processes of aggregation become more cumbersome.

Majority rule may be seen as a response to the problem of finding one right answer. However, why does majority voting bind participants, when no voting procedure secures that the collective ranking of preferences reflects the preferences of the voters (cf. Arrow 1951; Riker 1982)? Why is the outcome of a formal, correct aggregation of non-reflective preferences respected when the outcome is insecure? Merely aggregative solutions '...can not live up to the ideals of democratic legitimacy because outcomes can only claim to represent winners and not a common will' (Chambers 1997: 1). Majority support is not sufficient to enact laws legitimately as many scholars have pointed out (Dahl 1989: 135ff.; Offe 1982). There has to be non-majoritarian sources of legitimacy, because:

> The majority principle itself depends on prior assumptions about the unit: that the unit within which it is to operate is itself legitimate and that the matters on which it is to operate is itself legitimate and that the matters on which it is employed properly fall within the jurisdiction of the unit. In other words, whether the scope and domain of majority rule are appropriate in a particular unit depends on assumptions that the majority principle itself can do nothing to justify.
>
> (Dahl 1989: 204)

Majority voting presupposes agreement on political boundaries and power assignments, as it affects the sovereignty of the nation-states. On one reading the majority principle is dependent upon a community of memory, of communication and of experience (Kielmannsegg 1996). Even though parliament does not necessarily represent the *demos* or the nation as such, it is only a legitimate and an effective mechanism for representation and majority voting when it rests on approved territorial bounds and authority structures that reflect approved power assignments. Only then will those who object to a majority decision actually comply with it out of volition. Majority voting, in fact, has increased in the EU and has been of vital importance for the creation of a single market. It has contributed to what amounts to a rather dramatic transforming of the norms that regulate decision-making in the EU (Weiler 1997: 107). This lends credence to the notion that the EU is something more than and different from an international organization. However, unanimity is the main decision rule and the search for consensus is a powerful norm.

Voting is not enough

In recent years the theory of deliberative democracy has received renewed attention in political analysis. This theory maintains that majority rule 'is never merely majority rule ...' because '...counting of heads compels prior recourse to methods of discussion, consultation and persuasion' (Dewey 1927: 207). Increasingly, political scientists have paid attention to the way discussion is required to facilitate collective decision-making. The voting mechanism can not stand alone, but presupposes discussion as an additional and supportive device, to foster decision-making. Empirically speaking, there is a whole lot of communication going on in a decision-making situation, as claims and proposals require justification. Logically speaking, there is no assurance that aggregation of exogenous preferences will produce robust results, as was shown by Arrow and Riker. Even though preferences may be rational and transitive the resulting social rankings are fundamentally arbitrary; majority decisions do not represent 'the will of the people' (Shapiro 1996: 34). Normatively speaking, aggregation of preferences is not enough to legitimate political decisions. However, the point about deliberative democracy is not only that discussion is needed in order to reach binding decisions – even though this is a vital concern. No model of democracy can do without discussion. It is an efficient means to represent preferences and to compensate for asymmetric information and contribute to better decisions (cf. Johnson 1993; Cohen 1998; Fearon 1998). Political decision-making is by its nature a choice under uncertainty and 'deliberation is in itself a procedure for becoming informed' (Manin 1987: 349). It is a way of reaching more security in an insecure world. Actors live lives that are limited in time and space. Consequently, they have bounded rationality: they do not possess all information and do not have all the competence and capability necessary to process it adequately (March and Simon 1958). Actors may be ill-informed; they may have badly or falsely grounded opinions, they therefore need the arguments of others in order to reach a more *enlightened understanding* (cf. Mill 1859/1984; Dahl 1989). In addition, there is the problem of complex or mixed motives that make coherent action difficult. Base preferences engender no respect, only laundered preferences that endure public scrutiny should prevail (cf. Goodin 1986, 1996a). In standard cases actors need communication to get a clear idea of what to do and to form a consistent opinion. Communication may also take the form of *bargaining*.

To bargain is to engage in communication for the purpose of *forcing* or *inducing* the opponent to accept one's claim. To achieve this end, bargainers rely on threats and promises that will have to be executed outside of the assembly itself.

(Elster 1992: 15)

In bargaining processes parties employ speech acts strategically in order to achieve results – to maximize preferences. They may even misrepresent their preferences and deceive one another by paying homage to virtue and social norms (Elster 1998c: 97ff.).

The claim on behalf of deliberative democracy is stronger than pointing to the way discussion is essential for pooling private information in order to make rational means–end calculations, or for making people more enlightened or self-confident. Many proponents of deliberative democracy contend that public communication is needed in order to legitimize outcomes *vis-à-vis* the citizenry. Thus, democracy is also an end in itself, not only a means. It is a (or the) way to secure right results – and is, thus, *a legitimation principle*. Only deliberation can get political results right as it entails the act of justifying the results to the people who are bound by them. This is the reason why contenders have to argue in relation to justifiable social norms in order to reach lasting agreements. To solve collective action problems there is a need for *normative argumentation*, i.e. shared notions of what ought to be done. Compliance with some deontological norms that in themselves command respect – e.g. democratic procedures or human rights – is often required. Even though appeals to norms in real discussions are liable to deception, the fact that parties at least are hypocrites – they have to 'pay homage' to norms in order to achieve agreement – does not only document to the importance of norms but also shows, I believe, that strategic communication is parasitic on authentic communication. Strategic rationality presupposes *communicative rationality*.

From a normative point of view legitimacy can only be achieved in a deliberative, public process between free and equal citizens. This is so because what is common will have to be decided in public and not prior to it (Cohen 1991: 29). The scope of politics is, thus, not confined to pragmatic dimensions of collective reason, i.e. as finding the best means to maximize given ends, but rather to the setting of goals and standards and the interpretation of values. Cognitive knowledge about voters' preferences and how to achieve ends efficiently does not suffice. In addition, normative articulations about what values and fulfilments are important to us and what norms or rules should be applied in dealing with common problems and conflicting interests are needed. In order to drum up support parties have to try to convince other parties with arguments that others understand and accept and which motivate them. In order to justify claims an actor has to compare his claims and beliefs to those of others and *enlarge his position* so that it becomes compatible with something that others say or hold to be true and correct. He has to speak from the position of *the generalized other* (cf. Mead 1962). This requires communicative rationality, i.e. parties try to talk themselves into consensus by applying standards of impartiality. Actors co-ordinate their aims by mutually respecting validity claims. By *arguing* in relation to inter-subjective standards of truth, rightness, and sincerity participants can reach an agreement and a base for judging what are reasonable choices (Habermas 1984: 392).

Arguing, then, not voting or bargaining, is the currency of democracy. Also, in politics, the social fabric is made up of parties that give and respond to reasons, even though prevailing disagreements – due to hostility and conflicts over outcomes – necessitate decision-making devices such as voting and bargaining. These non-deliberative procedures, however, in order to function adequately to a large degree also presuppose well-conducted arguing processes, not least because they must be justified – argued for – in order to be employed (cf. Johnson 1998; Gutmann and Thompson 1996).

Constitutional democracy

The challenge to civic-republicanism

It is, however, necessary to distinguish the discourse-theoretical concept of democratic legitimacy from the conventional civic-republican notion of legitimacy. The latter connotes the old Aristotelian model of deliberative democracy that conceives of politics as deliberation in relation to a common good. Here politics is the succession of ethics, and the constitution (Politea) is the institutional expression for the meaning of the good life. In modern pluralistic societies, however, there are conflicts over notions of the good life. The problem associated with the republican notion of deliberative democracy (and of communitarianism in general) is the priority of the good over the right. The shortcomings of civic-republicanism, which gives priority to collective will formation, represents a parallel to the one-sidedness of liberalism (in the tradition of Hobbes and Locke), which favours (pre-social and pre-political) rights. The defenders of civic-republicanism understand democracy as a *community* which deliberates upon what is equally good for the members. By implication, they do not recognize any commitment that is not in accord with the authentic understanding of the collectivity. It is only citizens that are the bearers of rights, not human beings in general (Arendt 1963). This theory pictures democracy as a process of collective self-discovery which only gives human rights a binding status as long as they correspond to the society's ethical self-understanding (Habermas 1996a: 100f).

It is this that enables Dieter Grimm to see the question of an EU constitution as a question of political self-determination. True self-determination is dependent on the existence of *demos*. And as there is no European *demos* – no European people – there can be no democracy.[7] To this tradition belongs the German Constitutional Court's Maastricht decision which supported the Maastricht Treaty with reference, not to supranationality, but to its being an association of states. Joseph Weiler has labelled this the *No-demos thesis*, saying that it 'is premised on an organic understanding of peoplehood deriving from the European nation-state tradition which conflates nationality and citizenship and can, as a result, conceive of Demos only in statal terms' (Weiler 1995: 219). It is also from this perspective that Jean-Marie Guéhenno can state that democracy is possible when the 'Gemeinschaft' from the outset is strong enough (1996: 398), and Fritz W. Scharpf can maintain that democratic self-government is dependent upon a high degree of cultural homogeneity (Scharpf 1996b).

If democracy is framed as deliberation on the good life, collective goals and communal ends, then the central point of modern politics, which pertains to the neutrality of the state regarding substantive conceptions of the good life, is left out. Modern constitutional democracies are united around a procedural commitment to treating people *equally and fairly* (Dworkin 1978; Rawls 1993). Constitutions have changed, and are no longer the embodiment of a concept of the good life as in premodern societies. It is now a device for limiting, controlling and civilizing statal power. It is supposed to secure societal autonomy, individual freedom and organize, legitimize and authorize political power (Preuss 1996a: 113, 1996b; Castiglione 1996; Bellamy 1996; Habermas 1993). Within modern societies there is a plurality of values and conflicting views about the good life among different groups, local communities and cultures. When a majority of the people share certain values, opponents and minorities may become threatened. Thus, a polity favouring certain values or virtues would be unfair to dissidents unless they are equipped with rights that protect their interests. Modern democracies are politically integrated on the basis of common notions of justice and fairness, rather than on the basis of substantive values (Kymlicka 1989: 21). A modern constitutional order is held to be neutral with regard to competing notions of the good life. Under pluralistic circumstances, a heroic deontologist or an authoritative interpreter of the good life will not do.[8] Therefore, a deliberative concept of politics has to reflect the way procedures and *the system of rights* institute and regulate the political process, how they intervene in the shaping of a collective will and in monitoring decision-making processes.

Theories of deliberative democracy that are modelled on deliberation within the city-state or a homogenous nation-state are challenged by pluralism and also by complexity due to societal differentiation. In opposition to conventional models of deliberative democracy that regard politics as deliberation in relation to the common good, Habermas reframes deliberation in Kantian terms, which means that he maintains a *liberal position*, giving priority to the right over the good. Citizenship is not conceptualized as based on a national or ethnic origin reflecting specific worldviews, but as based on a constitutionally entrenched notion of public and private autonomy.

Democratic legitimacy

The modern state is premised on the right of the individual – on the safeguarding of individual rights. Modern societies are pluralistic and conflict-ridden and the constitution makes it possible for different groups and subgroups to live together under a common law. They have to resolve their conflicts through the medium of law. Citizenship and nationality – *demos* and *ethnos* – are conceptually decoupled in the modern state and the state is, in principle, neutral regarding different conceptions of the good life. There are two points to be made:

First: The lessons to be learned from the political revolutions of Europe are instructive with regard to how we are to tackle the challenge of supranationalism:

> Indeed, in my understanding and construction of supranationalism its value system is, surprisingly actually wrapped up with the value system of European ethno-national liberalism of the 19th century and, as such, can offer great comfort for those concerned to preserve the values and virtues of the Nation-State.
>
> (Weiler 1995: 245)

Or as Habermas puts it 'Democracy and human rights form the universalist core of the constitutional state that emerged from the American and French Revolutions in different variants' (Habermas 1996a: 465).

Second: The discourse-theoretical concept of deliberative democracy sits very well with supranationalism as it decouples citizenship and nationhood and conceives the constitution as a system for *accommodating difference*. Modern states are premised on cultural diversity as there is a right to non-participation. The legislative structure of the modern constitutional state, and the modern idea of democratic citizenship makes solidarity between strangers possible. Actually, these states are not nation-states – Volksnationen – founded on an *ethical Sittlichkeit* or cultural substance, but rather nations of citizens integrated by common laws and legal procedures. The democratic constitutional state does not, in principle, need another basis than the recognition of and trust in the procedures that ensure participation in collective goal formation and that make peaceful conflict resolution possible (Habermas 1996b: 189). The democratic constitutional state (*Rechtsstaat*) institutionalizes the conditions necessary for integration through self-legislation. This practice is anchored in the medium of law as it simultaneously secures the *private autonomy* of the individual by certain protective rights, and secures the *public autonomy* of the individual by a right to participation. Both human rights and democracy are necessary for securing the private and the public autonomy of the citizens because individual rights cannot be formulated adequately unless those affected first have been engaged in public deliberation to discuss how to treat typical cases. The democratic process, which in itself is legally constituted, is the source of legitimation. 'The principle of democracy states that only those statutes may claim legitimacy that can meet with the assent (*Zustimmung*) of all citizens in a discursive process of legislation that in turn has been legally constituted' (Habermas 1996a: 110).

Discourse theory thus departs from both republican and liberal conceptions of popular sovereignty and democratic legitimacy. Whilst 'liberals' (or social choice theorists) conceive of the individual as bearer of rights and democratic legitimacy as a question of a fair aggregation of preferences, the republicans locate popular sovereignty in the public assembly of citizens. Discourse theory, in contrast, launches a de-substantialized and intersubjectivist concept of sovereignty and locates it in the anonymous and dispersed forms of communication in civil society – in the public spheres – combined with institutionalized discourses within the formal political complex. Democracy is conceived of as a set of argumentative or communicative presuppositions and procedural conditions. These bear the burden of legitimation: 'Only the principles of the *guaranteed autonomy of the public spheres* and *competition* between different political parties, together with the parliamentary principle, exhaust the content of the principle of popular sovereignty' (Habermas 1996a: 171).

The EU does not meet these conditions, it is contended, as there are no European political parties furthering the European interest, and since the Council of Ministers is the main legislative body. However, even though Parliament originally was given only a consultative role, subsequent Treaties – and consultation, co-operation, co-decision procedures – and the Amsterdam Treaty have extended Parliament's influence so that it now shares decision-making power with the Council in a larger number of areas. The Parliament emphasizes its own democratic quality and wishes for co-equal status with the Council in legislative and budgetary competence (Craig 1997: 110). Further, all major political currents are represented in the Parliament – (though the election turnout is low). Other claims are that there is no European public sphere and that the institutionalized deliberations within the politico-administrative complex adhere to the logic of power rather than to that of reason. Nevertheless, these findings are not uncontroversial as is shown in several recent publications. It has become obvious that what you see depends, to a large degree, on where you sit: The empirical findings are often the product of the conceptual lenses used. In this last part of the paper I will address the criteria for diagnosing the quality of the public sphere and the nature of the interaction within representative bodies that follow from the preceding outline.

Deliberative supranationalism

The public sphere revisited

The public sphere as such provides the sort of deliberative arrangement that fits the requirement of discourse theory. In principle, everybody is entitled to speak without any limitations, whether on themes, items, questions, time or resources. It is a common space for free communication secured by legal rights to freedom of expression and assembly. Among the generic set of conditions are *inclusion, freedom, equality, participation* and *open agenda*.

The pessimistic view of democracy in the EU maintains that as there is a lack of collective identity, the prospect for a viable European public sphere is rather bleak.

'In the absence of European media, European political parties, and genuinely

European processes of public-opinion formation, constitutional reforms could not, by themselves, overcome the present democratic deficit at the European level' (Scharpf 1994: 220). There is no agreement on common interests or values and different languages and disparate national cultures make opinion formation and coherent action unlikely. 'Plainly, "Europe" is not a simple politico-cultural space; nor is "Europeness" an unambiguous attribute' (Schlesinger 1995: 4). These moods have been fuelled by the notable upsurge in xenophobic and racist movements in Western Europe. While on the basis of simple empirical findings one may be disappointed, I think, that the pessimistic diagnosis reflects not only a rather constrained conception of the public sphere and of political opinion formation generally but also a national-constitutionalist view of supranational legitimacy. There has to be a common ground for deliberation; a common audio-visual space for interaction; and a shared identity to stimulate collective opinion formation, the moulding of common interests and the mobilizing of collective action.

There is a civic-republican, or rather a communitarian, string to this kind of critique, which conceptualizes politics as people reasoning together about the common good. This process of reasoning is seen as something quite different from discussion of private concerns, i.e. it appears as if a common will from the outset prevails. This view presupposes a homogeneous culture, a populace, a united people that comes together in public spaces to deliberate and decide about common concerns. It pictures the public sphere as something rather distinct and stable, as a place where enlightened and equal citizens can assemble to discuss public matters. This is the concept of *res publica* handed down from the Greeks where citizens meet in Agora as friends and brothers to deliberate before decisions are reached in Ekklesia, resurrected in the medieval republicanism and in seventeenth-century England, France and Germany. The Greek model of the public sphere which e.g. Hannah Arendt (1958) makes use of presupposes a homogenous political community (Benhabib 1992: 90ff.). A volonté genérale is possible because citizens are equal and share common values and notions of the public interest. In case of conflict, parties can reach an agreement on the basis of a hermeneutic interpretation of common values and affiliations about who they are and who they would like to be, and, then, develop into a collective subject – a nation – capable of action.

In this model there is no distinction between deliberation and decision-making, between opinion formation and will formation. Consequently, this conceptualization does not capture the way the modern public sphere is institutionalized in opposition to government, it is situated in *the civil society* and rendered possible by the fact that the citizens have rights that they are entitled to use against the state. However, also the bourgeois conception of the public sphere of the previous century is too narrow as it is conceived as *one* public arena and in this analysis:

> ... the emergence of additional publics (is interpreted) as a late development signalling fragmentation and decline. This narrative, then, ... is informed

by an underlying evaluative assumption, namely, that the institutional confinement of public life to a single, overarching public sphere is a positive and desirable state of affairs, whereas the proliferation of a multiplicity of publics represents a departure from, rather than an advance toward, democracy.

(Fraser 1992: 122)

There are many public spheres in modern states and they are not confined to national borders. There are subaltern, counterpublics and there are overarching publics transcending limitations of time and space made possible by new media technologies and audio-visual spaces. There are local publics, regional, national and international publics, and there are general publics, intermediate and semi- and quasi-publics, smaller ones nested into larger ones (Habermas 1996a: 374ff; cf. Cohen and Arato 1995; Taylor 1995). New forms of communication are evolving and citizens' involvement in public debate may be seen rather as voluntary and elective than obligatory and 'native'. The many publics may be seen as fostering democracy as they enhance the possibilities for popular participation in opinion formation. Even though the problem of fragmentation prevails it is fair to say that the more publics, the more debate, and consequently the more democracy. Fewer voices are excluded and more questions are asked: more publics provide more possibilities for testing the legitimacy of power.

Involved in the discourse-theoretical notion of the public sphere is a distinction between opinion formation, which is the domain for the public sphere, and will formation, which is the domain for decision-making units within the political system. Publics do not act, as they possess no decision-making agency. In public spheres it is only possible to deliberate and as such form opinions about what should be done. In pluralistic and complex societies public opinion is 'anonymous' – it is 'decentred' into the network of communication itself, it is dispersed, and has no power to govern:

In the proceduralist legal paradigm, the political public sphere is not conceived simply as the backroom of the parliamentary complex, but as the impulse generating periphery that surrounds the political centre: in cultivating normative reasons it has an effect on all parts of the political system without intending to conquer it.

(Habermas 1996a: 442)

These informal arenas for public discussion and opinion formation provide a *context of discovery*. In this context problems are identified, solutions articulated, thematized and dramatized in such a way that they potentially become relevant for parliamentary bodies (*ibid.*, 359). This is an open and inclusive network of public spheres with fluid boundaries that makes possible the formation of public opinion. The public sphere is a unique, European invention constituted by nothing outside the common action we carry out in it and where no authority can claim control but must seek approval. We may in fact be witnessing a transition from the speech of power, to *the power of speech*.[9] Habermas attacks the republican notion of popular sovereignty conditioned upon 'the will of all', as well as the notion of a centre of society, the legislature, as the locus of democratic legitimacy. In the discourse-theoretical reading of procedural democracy it is the public and informal opinion formation, freed from the necessities, compulsion and coercion involved in actual decision-making, that connects political action to the interests and needs of civil society. The constitutional protection of the public sphere makes possible free processing of opinions, information and formation of position taking and generation of communicative power.

In this view, the public sphere in Europe is not totally missing as there are new European audio-visual spaces – newspapers, television, Internet, and English maybe as a bound to be first language – and the new social movements, NGOs and identity politics cross borders (see Chapter 10 in this volume). In light of the new information technology, '(C)communication comes to be seen as *flows* among publics rather than as exchange among discrete commodities which can be owned and controlled privately as things' (Keane 1993: 243). Moreover, the point is that the public sphere is not an entity unto itself, as something, which may or may not exist. The public sphere is not prior to or independent of decision-making agencies but is created and formed in opposition to them – as a vehicle to test the legitimacy of legal provisions and as a counterweight to governmental power. This view of the emergence of the public sphere is based on the contention that the state originated, more or less, through war or brute force, and that state authority only subsequently was democraticized, i.e. subjected to the rule of law. First came the state, then came democracy. Collective identity has to be made rather than merely discovered. It is from this assertion that the contention 'no European demos without a European democracy' is derived.

However, it is not the public sphere alone that bears the burden of legitimation. Rather, it is the interplay between free and open debate in non-institutionalized (weak) publics and institutionalized debates – strong publics – in the political system that together secure the presumption of rational opinion and will formation. Popular sovereignty is to be secured by a 'two-track' model. The democratic procedures constitute, according to Habermas, a *context of justification*, as they provide the reference point for decision-making and negotiations that make clear which norms and goals are to be realized. Due to scarcity of resourses and because of political and constitutional constraints priorities always have to be set.

Deliberative bodies

Institutionalized discourses, in representative bodies, are necessary not only in order to narrow down alternatives for decision-making and voting, but also in order to reach more *enlightened opinions* about the public interest(s) or the common good(s). They improve decision-making. Representation contributes to refine and enlarge opinions by passing them through the deliberate concern of chosen members of the *demos*. As James Madison already made clear, representation contributes to political rationality by lifting elected members of the community out of parochial settings, potentially corrupted by local factions, to supra local settings where they have to ground their claims with regard to others' interests and needs. In national or federal settings the representatives have to take into consideration different interests and perspectives in order to justify particular claims and thereby can reach more reasonable and legitimate decisions. Representation may be seen as a precondition for political rationality as it secures institutional fora in which elected members of constituencies peacefully and co-operatively can seek alternatives and solve conflicts and problems on a broader basis: 'a central goal of constitutional democracy is to secure a realm for public discussion and collective selection of preferences while guarding against the dangers of factional tyranny and self-interested representation ...' and, further, principles of constitutional democracy 'include, above all, the effort to promote deliberation in government, to furnish surrogates for it when absent, to limit factionalism and self-interested representation, and help bring about political equality' (Sunstein 1988: 52, 1990: 171; cf. Weigård 1995).

However, if there is some credibility to the thesis of a non-existence of a European public sphere, there is no lack of representative bodies in the EU, as we have seen. There are bodies both for representing Member State citizens (the EU Parliament) and Member States (The Council, The Commission), and Regions (Committee of Regions). Regarding the notion of democratic deficit the argument now takes on a different turn. It is maintained that the deliberations adhere to the logic of power rather than to the logic of arguments; self-interests rather than common interests dominate. It is the large Member States that have the most votes, and it is the economic–functional interests of the society whose voices are most easily heard, due to lobbying and considerable bargaining resources. Decisions are reached by experts, and not by elected representatives, and laws are passed without due hearings and with little transparency and publicity – it is *an elite game* (Middlemas 1995a: 612). The representative system and the institutionalized discourses do not live up to democratic ideals (viz. equality of persons). The EU system on the whole is, on this reading, occupied by the special interests of big business and the ideology of free markets (Traxler and Schmitter 1995). The gap between power transferred to Community level and democratic control is 'filled by national civil servants operating as European experts or as members of regulation and management committees, and to some extent organized lobbies, mainly representing business' (Williams 1991: 162, cited from Føllesdal 1998c). 'The EU is characterized by principles of *national representation, interest representation*, and *representation of expertise*' (Andersen and Burns 1996: 227).

On another reading, however, the EU already does possess a constitution and laws that establish legal governance structures. The political process is legally constrained and the European Court of Justice, which has not formally adopted a European Bill of Rights, claims to be guided by constitutional rights, international conventions and in particular the European Convention on Human Rights (Bellamy and Castiglione 1998b: 171).[10] Small countries and rural interests are also systematically overcompensated in the voting formula of the Council of Ministers; and unanimity is required on a whole range of issues, which in fact gives Member States *veto power*, and thus puts them on an equal footing (akin to the principle of equality of states). Veto power is a main barrier to supranationalism, but on the other hand, it represents a constraint on discourse that induces communicative rationality: When parties can block outcomes actors have an incentive to convince all, not only the majority. In order to achieve consensus they have, in principle, to use arguments convincing to all of the participants. Moreover, veto or higher majority quorum may protect against professionals and lobbying. The emphasis placed on consensus in the Community is interesting also because representatives and delegates from Member State countries are brought together in many kinds of deliberating fora and arenas. They meet in committees, in boards and councils, in order to resolve conflicts and find solutions to common problems in a co-operative way. This interaction is governed by legal norms and procedures which means that parties have to raise *claims to correctness* even if they are subjectively following their own interests (cf. Alexy 1989: 219ff.). Regulatory acts establish missions and objectives for the bodies, and legal rules both enable and constrain action of their members in order to secure fair and reasonable results. There are different kinds of mandatory procedures and the objectives of the Commission are to identify the European interest, to consult as widely as is necessary and to respect the principle of subsidiarity.

The type of interstate interaction generally referred to as international co-operation – intergovernmentalism – may be described as strategic, and as conflict resolution through bargaining (Moravcsik 1994). The question of whether the EU is something more – representing a deeper form of integration[11] – then, can be addressed by examining the ability to act in concert, to achieve consensus on conflicting issues and to form a common will about how to solve common problems. If the EU is to be something more than an arrangement for interstate co-operation – the Union has to be able to act on a collective basis: The members have to have an open mandate from their constituencies in order to be able to identify common interests, that is interests that do not solely reflect nation-state interests, but which they can identify with. Forming a common will is conditioned on the ability to act communicative rationally. Actors that all have different interests or preferences must give priority to seeking agreement over self-interest maximization. The question of whether or not the EU is a supranational democratic polity can fruitfully be examined from the point of view of interaction modes. In short, is the interaction made up of Member States that compete for the biggest share or is it also constituted by some notions of common interests and shared identities? 'What supremacy requires is the identification of rules and principles ensuring the co-existence of different constituencies and the compatibility of these constituencies' objectives with the common concerns they share' (Joerges 1996a: 25). However, it is not enough to document interest incorporation and the formal structure of decision-making. We also have to study the actual deliberation and decision-making processes and examine the rationality, i.e. universality of the concrete decisions. Is there a European 'bonum commune'? In order to answer such questions we have to assess the quality of the agreements and not only the character of the procedure, because, even though we have *no procedure-independent criteria of what is a rational outcome* – a common interest – it is the 'arguments that provide the basis for rational judgements' (Peters 1994: 116).[12] In other words, the discussion itself must comply with certain standards of rationality – it must be of a certain quality – in order to satisfy requirements for legitimacy (Mauss 1996: 880f.). In a next step it is necessary to study if and how members voluntarily comply with decisions that may be detrimental to their self-interest, while furthering the common interests (Eriksen 1990: 348 ff.).

In order to examine the quality of the interaction process in representative and collegial bodies, the conceptual strategy of realism or the methodology of economics do not suffice, as they preclose the possibility for communicative action, and hence the alteration of preferences. Strategic interaction, on its part, merely mirrors prevailing preferences and actual resources. My contention is that the nature of co-operation may be of a different kind. Some institutions embody rules and procedures that facilitate communicative action while others favour strategic interaction. In a research programme there is need for criteria of demarcation, for how to decide when a process has been of a strategic nature and when it has been of an argumentative nature.

Compromise or consensus

If the critique of the public sphere is informed by the evaluative scheme of civic-republicanism, the critique of institutionalized negotiations is informed by the evaluative scheme of rational choice or the economic theory of democracy, seeing democracy primarily as a question of fair aggregation of preferences, and negotiations as strategic interaction.[13] In the process of *bargaining* between representatives of conflicting interests the object for each of the parties is to get a maximum outcome for their own interests, and for this end they have to be able to persuade their counterparts that, if necessary, they have the resources needed to force their interests through. An aspect of this is to persuade others that they also have *the will to employ* these resources. The hallmark of bargaining, then, is the latent presence of coercion. Use of hidden or open threats and warnings are central elements in bargaining situations (cf. Schelling 1960). Compromise procedures regulated by norms of fairness are called for when it comes to regulation of strategic behaviour.

The EU system is marked by consensual rather than by conflictual decision-making. Consequently, a simple distinction between unanimity and voting will not do. Agreements may, even when parties have veto power, be of a different kind. It may be a *compromise* which is the typical (positive) outcome of bargaining.

That usually means none of the parties gets exactly what he or she wants, but each regards the result as better than no outcome at all. How much the various actors have to deviate from their opening position depends on the strength of their bargaining power, i.e. the resources at their disposal, and on their ability to conduct the bargaining process in a (for each of them) favourable way. In that case parties will have different arguments for consenting. Another possibility is rational consensus which 'rests on reasons that convince all parties *in the same way* ...' (Habermas 1996a: 166). There has been a lot of controversy over the status of consensus, i.e. rational or qualified consensus, in Habermas' work. In the present use, however, communicative rationality only means trying to establish consensus by employing arguments, and as far as agreements are backed by mutually acceptable reasons one may say that there has been some sort of deliberative process going on. A transition to a higher level of abstraction – discourse or principled arguing – where participants examine what lies in the equal interest of all concerned, is not necessary, I believe, for reaching binding decisions in many cases involving political controversies.

The existence of formally correct procedures, and of rights and the knowledge of others' strong evaluations, is often involved in actual decision-making and sheds light on the fact that decisions come about which are neither compromises nor rational consensuses. In a deliberative process one sees the force of the good argument working to accommodate some points of view and values which make further co-operation possible. The participants do not agree on all matters, or on all premises of a conclusion, but the discussion makes the parties aware of the values at stake and of how the situation may be described from another angle. This means that there are a whole lot of situations where the force of the better argument influences decision-making without resulting in a qualified consensus. These agreements neither rest upon a pure convergence of interests nor are they negotiated compromises between contending parties. They are communicatively achieved *working agreements* (Eriksen 1999: 58f.).[14] Democratic legitimacy result from an open, public deliberative process, but the reasons that convince many need not convince all: the minority understands and respects the reasons provided by the majority and accepts the result because of a fair process. The problem of consensus and of majority vote has, among other things, led James Bohman to propose a less demanding principle of democracy stating that laws are legitimate if they stem from an open and fair process, the result allows for further deliberation, and 'the process makes the public deliberation of the majority the source of sovereign power' (Bohman 1996: 187).

Deliberative supranationality

Implementation of legislative acts by the Commission is assisted by hundreds of committees of experts from the Member States. *Comitology* is an EU expression designating this practice, which is analysed in more detail in Chapter 8 in this volume. The Council has been rather reluctant on conferring implementing powers to the Commission – they have, as Joerges and Neyer put it, not been:

willing to loosen their intergovernmental grip on the implementation process in favour of supranational institutions. In more constructive terms, the
Comitology decision rejects the idea of supranational central implementation machinery headed by the Commission, and thus indirectly forces
national governments into a co-operative venture.

(Joerges and Neyer 1997: 277)

Comitology, which is an EU invention, may be understood as an institutional
response to efficiency and legitimacy requirements. The Commission needs
unbiased information and expert knowledge as well as opinions of laymen
(and/or representatives of non-governmental bodies), in addition to loyalty and
support from representatives of national governments in order to be able to
implement measures effectively. Several hundreds committees are active in the
implementation of Council decision and enjoy extensive freedom of discretion.
It is a general point to be made that broad participation and fair decision-
making rules enhance legitimacy, but what is peculiar to comitology – contrary
to other international committees – is that these committees are involved in
decision-making that is binding on domestic governments. On the one hand this
contribution to Europeanization widens 'the gap between normal citizens and
policy matters' (Wessels 1998: 228). On the other hand, it has been proposed to
see comitology as a new political order that may help to repair democratic
deficit, and because Member-State and non-interest parties are included in the
decision-making process it also contributes to *deliberative supranationalism*. We then
have to ask: What conditions do the undertakings of the committees have to
comply with in order to contribute to deliberative supranationalism?

My proposal is that they have to take on a communicative style if they are to
mend the alleged democratic deficit or if they are to contribute to democratic
supranationalism. The problem of bargaining and voting procedures is that they
encourage a process of give-and-take, pork-barrelling, log-rolling etc. that does
not change opinions, necessitates learning or enlargements or refinements of
perspectives – there is no moulding of a common rational will.[15] In a way it
signals that the discussion has come to a standstill – a deadlock. It also indicates
that the parties have accepted an outcome, but not because it is an optimal
outcome. They accept it because of the resources and power relations involved.
Each participant would ideally like another and better outcome for themselves,
but can live with the agreement that has been obtained. It is a *suboptimal solution*
from the point of view of the actors.[16]

Arguing, in comparison, then is marked by a change of views, by the way the
discussion helps to mould preferences and to move standpoints. In case of
conflict at least one of the contenders has to change position in order to establish
agreement. And in case common problems are to be solved, agreement on
collective goals, about what should be done is needed, i.e. moulding of a
common will is required. When strategic rational actors change their views, it is
only to strike a better bargain: they are not moved by the force of the better
argument, but by the outlook for success. Which logic the deliberations in fact

adhere to is an empirical question. Whether they adhere to the logic of bargaining or to the logic of arguing can not be settled in advance. Christian Joerges and Jürgen Neyer (1997) conclude after having studied the working of food committees that different interests and affected parties are taken into account and thereby actually meet the congruence criteria.[17] They also contend that interaction takes on a communicative rather than the bargaining intergovernmental style.[18] Also reports from the deliberations of the working groups that the COREPER (Committee of Permanent Representatives) and the Council have to rely on in preparing the deliberations of the Council, point in this direction. 'Several authors argue that the national civil servants involved in these working group meetings are exposed to a spirit of co-operation and mutual understanding, to an *esprit de corps* ...' (Sasse *et al.* 1977; Pag 1987; Wessels 1991; Westlake 1995; Kerremans 1996) and, further: 'Obviously, informal communication is intense in the working groups manned by full-timers. These working groups also seem to enjoy a common leadership of core members. Among these core members the non-state institutional actors clearly are more than *primi inter pares*. They generally are the hub of the informal communication network. The principal fact emerging from the data is that our respondents appear to have adopted a common attitude to their different partners, ...' (Beyers and Dierickx 1998, 1: 21). There is a distinct supranationalist dimension to the way the interaction between experts is going on as they have to pay more attention to expertise and how to reach agreement and manage to 'get the work done' (Beyers and Dierickx 1997: 454). Even though the undertakings in committees may adhere to the logic of communicative action and as such possess normative quality, their democratic legitimacy hinges on whether the principles of representation and of the results withstand critical scrutiny in an open public debate.

Independent regulatory bodies, like courts of law and committees consisting of experts, national civil servants, and representatives of affected interest groups and NGOs seem to be more efficient in order to produce solutions. Recent empirical research indicates that they are 'more suitable for complex, plural societies than are mechanisms that concentrate power in the hands of political majority' (Majone 1996a: 286). However, the problem of democratic legitimacy prevails as they are linked to unequal chances of participation. They are based on expert knowledge and often power and contribute to the technocratization of politics. Institutional reforms for enhancing public accountability are called for.

Conclusion

When we address the EU system from a discourse-theoretical perspective we become aware of the rather complex set of institutions and procedures that is relevant for assessment of democratic quality. Democratic legitimacy does not solely rest on representative institutions for aggregating preferences, nor does it merely rest on citizens' participation in decision-making bodies. Both informal and formal institutions are needed, and both procedures for deliberation and for decision-making are required, because only full representation plus rational deliberation together ensure democratic legitimacy. The procedure itself guarantees, as mentioned, only the right to participation, not *the quality of discursive processes*. A more positive theoretical programme is possible as some institutional rules and institutional practices favour one type of behaviour while other favour others. Certain procedural norms and institutional settings are required to ensure that participants take on a communicative and not a strategic attitude.[19]

From this perspective we learn that in order to address the democratic deficit of the EU or its democratic quality we have to examine, first, the Member States and how well their democratic structure of governance is functioning. In fact national democracy already is in place, but are there really a free press, public spheres, party-competition and representative bodies, and is the way the Member States delegate power to the EU in accordance with democratic principles? Secondly, we have to address the network of intermediate organizations, NGOs, political parties, social movements and criss-crossing communicative channels of civil society. Do they contribute to opinion formation, maintain popular pressure on EU decision-makers and do they question the legitimacy of the EU's undertaking? Thirdly, we have to analyse the institutional complex of the EU itself. The EU Parliament is directly elected, but how much power does it really possess? The role of the Court and the Committee system are also to be addressed. Do they represent a broad spectrum of opinions and do they ensure a certain degree of popular influence on decision-making? And, lastly, how is the interaction conducted? From what sources do the decisive arguments extract their force and what is the quality of the debate? To what degree do decisions and laws stand up to a generalizing or universalizing test in a public debate?

Taken together, these checkpoints render it possible to address the problem of the democratic deficit of the EU in a more sophisticated way than the conventional theories of democracy make possible. In the end such an analysis may come to find that the EU embodies certain qualities that, from a democratic point of view, are important. The EU contains, after all, a rather complex 'constitution' comprising both voting and bargaining procedures, on the one hand, and procedures for ensuring both public and institutionalized deliberations. People are subjected to laws that they themselves have not authored, but the complex institutional set up of the Community contributes to the impression that citizens, at least partly, possess the possibility of being co-authors of the law. This may help us understand why the EU at all survives as a governmental structure capable of making binding decisions, despite all its obvious defects and all the criticism levelled at it. Its legitimacy is not solely derived from recognition by other states, because the EU itself contains procedures that lend some credibility to the presumption of democratic governance. This is supranationalism checked by Member States and without an established hierarchy that it can draw legitimation from, hence the term *deliberative supranationalism*.

Notes

1 Earlier versions of this chapter were read at the conference 'On Democracy in Europe – Integration and Deliberation', in Bergen, February 1998; at ARENA, May 1998, and at ECPR Joint Session Workshop 'Innovation in Democratic Theory', March 1999. I am grateful for comments made by the participants and to John Erik Fossum for also correcting language.

2 The literature on the 'Democratic Deficit' of the EU is enormous, see e.g. Castiglione 1996; Williams 1991; Middlemas 1995a; Scharpf 1996a, c; Schmitter 1992, 1996a, 1998; Weiler 1995; Gustavsson 1996; Andersen and Eliassen 1996; Pogge 1998; Lehning and Weale 1997.

3 'In the field of health and safety regulation, the Community has, "post-Maastricht", found itself unwittingly involved in a third phase of integration, being increasingly required to play a direct role in the implementation of European health and safety measures' (Vos 1997: 211).

4 There may be degrees of anarchy depending on whether only government is absent or whether there is lack of laws or norms altogether (cf. Østerud 1991: 294).

5 See Morgenthau [rev. by Thompson] 1993, Waltz 1959, see e.g. Müller 1994; Risse 1997 for the debate on international relations in Germany from the perspective of communicative action.

6 Strategic rational actors 'not only make choices on the basis of expectations about the future – *but also on the basis of their expectations about the expectations of others*' (Elster 1979: 19).

7 See Grimm 1995, and for a critical comment see also Habermas 1996b: 185ff.

8 This is one of great insights of B. Constant (1819/1980).

9 'Modern democracy invites us to replace the notion of a regime governed by laws of a legitimate power, by the notion of a regime founded upon *the legitimacy of a debate as to what is legitimate and what is illegitimate* – a debate which is necessarily without any guarantor and without any end' (Lefort 1988: 39). See also Taylor 1995: 266f.; Habermas 1962/1989, 1992a, 1997: 123ff.

10 A constitution for co-operation on the European level can not mirror nation-state constitutions, they cannot be a statal constitution writ large, because it is only through membership in a Member State that they have an EU membership. J. Weiler understands the European community as a new kind of integration and sees 'European demos and citizenship as part of a polity with multiple political demoi ... which may consist in what may be called the "concentric circles" approach' (Weiler 1997: 119): One is simultaneously a European and an Englishman. The EU is a union of peoples, not replacing the national with the European (p. 121).

11 Several proposals are launched to catch the post-national nature of EU, such as supranationalism (Weiler 1995), deliberative supranationalism (Joerges and Neyer 1997), a mixed polity (Bellamy and Castiglione 1997a), an imperfect state (Middlemas 1995a), Condomino or Consortio (Schmitter 1996a).

12 In this way legitimacy and democracy are conceptually linked: Democracy is a way to find out what justice consists in (Young 1990).

13 Bargaining is also a kind of speech acts as strategic action often involves communication among the parties. Giving and receiving orders between supervisors and subordinates is a typical example (Eriksen and Weigård 1997a; cf. Elster 1998a, b).

14 This resembles Habermas' recent notion of Konsens, but this kind of agreement is reserved for ethical political discourses: 'The consensus *(Konsens)* issuing from a successful search for collective self-understanding neither expresses a merely negotiated agreement *(Vereinbarung)*, as in compromises, nor is it a rationally motivated consensus *(Einverständnis)*, like the consensus on facts or questions of justice. It expresses two things at once: self-reflection and resolve on a form of life' (Habermas 1996a: 182).

15 The most that is to be expected is agreement on what the parties cannot subscribe to.

16 Nevertheless, they may even support it with rational arguments: considering the circumstances, a compromise is in fact 'a first best outcome' unless you waste some of the resources in the process of bargaining. Of course, you could achieve better results if you had more power, had more resources, and were more talented; but that is wishful thinking.

17 Congruence means that those who are affected should also be those responsible (cf. Zürn 1998: 8).

18 The following citation from an interview with an official from the German Bundesministerium für Gesundheit gives support to a hypothesis of arguing: 'During the course of working together, delegates approximate not only national legal provisions but also different problem definitions and problem-solving philosophies. They slowly move from representatives of the national interest to representatives of a Europeanized interadministrative discourse in which mutual learning and understanding of each other's difficulties surrounding the implementation of standards becomes of central importance. The emergence of shared feelings of interadministrative partnership is crucial to understanding the course of the negotiation because the control which national governments have on delegates is generally rather weak. Sometimes, governments have not defined their preferences and therefore leave delegates a wide margin of discretion. In other instances, delegates use their unique informational status to influence their governments' perception of their own preferences or even simply by-pass them.' (Interview conducted with official from the Bundesministerium für Gesundheit, Bonn, 28.02.96, by Joerges and Neyer 1997: 292.)

19 It may also be possible to establish the required communicative relationships in existing policy networks, triangulars, corporatist arrangements and the like to deal with conflict resolution and problem solving.

4 The uses of democracy

Reflections on the European
democratic deficit[1]

Richard Bellamy and Dario Castiglione

Like the child in the fairy tale, many European Union scholars protest the
'Emperor has no clothes'.[2] Though the EU dresses itself up in the rhetoric of
democracy – a fundamental requisite for Member States – it is covered at best
by only the scantiest democratic fig leaf. So far, however, the Union's failure to
acquire the trappings of democratic decency has been of little political
consequence. This fact should give commentators pause for thought. It suggests
either the European ruling elites are cynically testing how far they can get away
with their deception, or that current denunciations of a democratic deficit are
oversimplified.

A number of European analysts now take the latter view, and have become
more circumspect about just calling for more democracy. We agree with them.
Talk of a democratic deficit begs various questions that are rarely asked:
namely, why is democracy valuable, will Europe gain from using it as opposed
to other forms of decision-making, what form must it take to achieve these
results – deliberative, majoritarian, consociational, a mix of all three, or
something quite different from these – and how, if at all, can it be implemented
in the European context? This essay represents a modest attempt to address
them.

We begin, in the first section, by distinguishing two dimensions of the EU's
legitimation crisis, to which talk of a democratic deficit is intimately related.
The first concerns the genesis and character of the European polity, the second
the type of democratic regime most suited to it. Discussion of the latter
dimension often overlooks its connection to the former by regarding democracy *per se* as intrinsically good. However, as we argue in the second section,
the value of democracy is best measured by its benefits. These will only be
present if the forms and procedures of a democratic regime fit the complexion
of the polity and population to which they are applied. The next section
follows through this analysis by examining the weaknesses of what for many
defines contemporary democracy – namely, majority rule. The final section
concludes that if, by virtue of containing multiple *demoi*, the EU is a mixed
polity, it requires a mixed democratic regime involving a variety of decision
rules and the dispersal of sovereign power between different bodies and diverse
locations.

Legitimation crisis?

Maastricht focused the minds of supporters and opponents of the European project alike by raising fundamental questions about its methods and ultimate goal (cf. Weiler 1999a, Chapter 1). Up to then, question begging had been an intrinsic part of the principal integration strategy. According to the so-called Monnet or Community method, Europe was to be made 'in the details' through administrative means and elite bargaining. Legal rules and democratic decision-making merely offered ex-post endorsements of an already existing reality. This method had the advantage of allowing a federal structure to be formed by stealth, while keeping nation-states in control of the overall direction of the process. As a result, it pleased both federalists and intergovernmentalists, and has proved compatible with analyses from each of these perspectives. Political debate and directly consensual forms of legitimation were eschewed as either irrelevant to technical matters or inappropriate for interstate bargaining. Moreover, discussion of the ultimate shape and scope of the EU was carefully avoided.[3] The project possessed the social legitimacy offered by good economic performance and responsiveness to demands from infra-national groups and organizations (or European civil society at large), and the formal legitimacy provided by the international law framework (*pacta servanda sunt*) within which the various Treatises were agreed. But its political legitimacy was the indirect and weak result of the negotiations having been carried out by elected national politicians and their civil servants.

Recently, however, social and legal legitimacy have become more problematic, and the need for direct political legitimacy correspondingly greater (Beetham and Lord 1998b; Schmitter 1996a and 1998). In the immediate post-war period, peace and prosperity were seen as obvious public goods that needed co-ordinated European action to be achieved (Weiler 1999a, Chapter 7). The end of the Cold War and a slowing up of fifty years of steady growth have changed that perception. What is required to secure these basic goods is now more disputed. Many analysts contend peace depends on states simply being liberal democracies rather than on their joining together into a single unit. Likewise, global markets certainly necessitate interstate co-operation to establish free trade and regulate them, but how much beyond that is less clear. The old social democratic consensus on such matters has come increasingly under attack from the new right and the experiments with privatization adopted in almost all the Member States since the 1980s. The Common Agricultural Policy, for example, is likely to prove ever more contentious, as are the degree and character of regulations in areas such as health and safety and the environment which impose direct costs and produce only diffuse and indirect benefits. As friction over issues such as fishing rights reveals, nation-states are not averse to defecting from collective arrangements whenever it seems in their short-term interest to do so and free-riding on the efforts of others. The proliferation of opt outs over matters such as the Euro testifies to increasing disagreement over which economic and social policies are in the common interest. Meanwhile, expansion to the East and attempts to extend the public goods supplied by the EU are liable to heighten these tensions by raising the costs and decreasing the benefits available to existing members.

The formal legitimacy offered by law has been unable to make up for the lessening of the EU's social legitimacy. Indeed, in some respects the dramatic growth in legal integration may have exacerbated the situation. Even those scholars who believe the Member States still control the overall process accept that the gradual constitutionalization of the Treaties through successive judgements of the ECJ and Intergovernmental Conferences means some form of supranational constitution is in the making, requiring a reconsideration of the methods, aims and principal agents of integration (Moravcsik and Nicolaïdis 1998). However, this extension of legal integration has often appeared to overstep not only what seems socially and economically warranted, but also the substantive values and express wishes of the populations of the Member States. This conflict has been particularly evident in the clashes between the ECJ and national constitutional courts in cases such as Grogan, where the ECJ's defence of the EC's core principles, the four market freedoms, has been opposed to an even higher law emanating from the national Demos of the Member State involved (Coppel and O'Neill 1992; De Witte 1991). A similar concern lay behind the German Federal Constitutional Court's Brunner ruling (Grimm 1995) and the uneasy ratification of the Maastricht Treaty by the British parliament and in referenda in Denmark and France. In these situations, the formal legality of the ECJ's judgements proves no substitute for its lack of substantial legitimacy (MacCormick 1995 and 1996; Eleftheriadis 1998). The Court's increasing willingness to refer to notions of rights that strictly speaking lie outside the domain of European law indicates the dilemma it now finds itself in (Shaw 1996). However, since these rights can be subject to incommensurable interpretations by different national jurisdictions, this manoeuvre does not circumvent the possibility of conflict but merely moves it to a more fundamental level (Bellamy 1995). One prominent legal commentator has even likened the potential stand off between the ECJ and national constitutional courts to the Cold War policy of Mutual Armed Destruction (Weiler 1996a).

The retreat of the Community method and its associated political strategies and forms of legitimation has produced a shift to an 'intentionalist' paradigm that relies on more direct forms of consensual legitimacy (Streeck 1996; Offe 1998b). For the exhaustion of the EU's social and formal legitimacy can be remedied only through an explicit political commitment to a particular form of Union. As a result, academic attention has focused on the EU's democratic deficit with a renewed urgency and European studies have taken a correspond-ing 'normative turn'.[4]

A full diagnosis of the EU's current political legitimation crisis requires two interrelated tasks that EU scholars have too often kept distinct. The first involves analysing the nature of the emerging European polity, the second exploring what type of regime or system of governance best suits it so as to deliver the democratic goods on which political legitimacy rests. Integration theorists have tended to concentrate on the polity formation aspect of the question and democratic theorists on the regime aspect. However, theories of political integration that do not address its democratic character are normatively blind and lack a sense of where they ought to be headed, whilst democratic theories that are formulated in ignorance of the political shape of the EU prove empirically empty and so unable to make the democratic ideal a reality. Rendering the EU politically legitimate entails seeing how these two considerations might mutually influence each other, with the character of the EU polity shaping the form the democratic regime takes and being in its turn shaped by democratic decision-making.

The distinction between polity and regime (Schmitter 1996a) reveals two dimensions to political legitimacy. The polity dimension concerns the legitimacy of the political community as a bounded entity wishing to determine its affairs. Democratic theory *per se* cannot resolve this problem, since democracy presupposes a relatively autonomous group amongst whom its decisions are binding (Dahl 1989; Weale 1995, 1997 and 1998). In the modern world, nation-states have come to represent the 'natural' locus of political decision-making, sanctioned internally by their monopoly over the legitimate use of force and externally by a system of international law based on state sovereignty. Throughout the past two hundred years, claims to political autonomy and self-determination have been couched in terms of either nationhood or statehood, therefore, with the one very often meant to imply the other. Recent developments towards global governance, of which the European Union is considered one of the most developed instances, have been taken to prise open the internal connection between nation and state, as well as to undermine the logical structure of state governance. On the one hand, it is argued that nationhood no longer supplies the socio-cultural glue political integration requires to operate with the unconditional assent of the people living in a given territory (Curtin 1997; Habermas 1992b and 1996a; Ferry 1992). On the other hand, the congruence between territoriality and functional competence underlying (hierarchically ordered) state power is said to have broken down (Schmitter 1996a and 1996b). These developments supposedly point to the new European polity being post-national in character and post-state in form. At present, however, these are mere tendencies, defined in largely negative and ideal terms as 'non-state' and 'non-national'. They operate in a global environment of overlapping, and often depersonalized networks of governance, and have yet to emerge in their positive and concrete form. Nor is there any convincing teleology on which to argue that this is the shape of things to come.

Consequently, it seems more realistic to suggest we have a mixed system. Nation-states remain the dominant players, giving the EU many of the features of a confederation (Forsyth 1982; Warleigh 1998; Chryssochoou 1994). However, they sit alongside the supra- and to some extent post-national institutions of the Commission, Parliament, the European Court of Justice and now the European Central Bank. Meanwhile, the EU has encouraged the growth of political groups of a sub- and a transnational kind. For example, there are now over 3000 interest groups and 100 regional offices based in Brussels.

Many are directly involved in formulating policy via the process of comitology. Correspondingly new levels of decision-making have also emerged that vary according to the policy and groups involved. However, this is not a hierarchical system. There is growing disagreement over core policies, with only 10 of the 15 being members of the EU's putative defence arm, the Western European Union, 12 signing up to the Schengen accords on free movement of peoples, and 11 joining the single currency. Even at the centre there is a complicated mix between intergovernmental decision-making, as in the Council of Ministers; potentially transnational, as in the European Parliament; supranational, as in the Commission; and post-national, as with the ECJ. Moreover, all these institutions have to compete and incorporate the various levels of subnational – regional, local, workplace and community – decision-making. Yet there exist no clear lines of demarcated jurisdiction or overarching authority to decide disputes between them.

Even with nation-states, it would be wrong to assume that the legitimacy of the polity guarantees the legitimacy of its governing structure or regime. In a mixed polity, however, the legitimation offered by the regime plays an especially important role in determining the legitimacy of the polity itself. In the modern world, democracy has come to be seen as the only legitimate form of state. The resulting democratic imperative holds that the institutional organization of government (but not necessarily social governance) must reflect the main underlying principles of democracy. Denunciations of the European democratic deficit come into their own here. There is little doubt that the structure of European governance does not fully conform to any meaningful interpretation of the many standard definitions of democracy. There is no political equality in the present system of European representation. Small countries, for instance, are over-represented in both the Council, the Parliament and the Commission. The institutions of direct representation, namely the European Parliament, have no great power; the little they have is mainly as a brake upon other institutions, which are in full control of both the political agenda and legislative promotion. No clear majoritarian rule operates in European decision-making; or, when it does, it involves a majority of the Member States rather than their citizens. Finally, none of the main European institutions fully satisfies what are usually considered as the important democratic principles of popular responsiveness and accountability; nor is much of the business of government subject to the normative publicity associated with transparent decision-making and freedom of information.

If the European political regime must reflect the democratic imperative to pass the test of direct consensual legitimacy, there are a great many democratic deficits to be overcome. Yet why and how should the democratic imperative apply, given the new conditions in which the European polity and its component nation-states now operate? The very principles of democracy may need revision to meet post-national and global conditions, much as they did in taking on their modern representative form during this century as a result of democracy's extension to the masses and its application at a national scale. Addressing the

European democratic deficit is not as simple as it appears. It involves both an understanding of what democracy means today and what it can actually do for the legitimation of government.

The democratic imperative revisited

Democracy has three main meanings that appeals to the democratic imperative frequently conflate. First and most obviously, democracy is a form of government characterized by institutions, rights and practices designed to give people a say in how their community's political affairs are run. Second and more loosely, democracy refers to the underlying values, notably freedom and equality, that define it as a fair scheme of co-operation between formally equal people. Finally, democracy denotes a decision-making process, often identified with majority rule, that applies to groups irrespective of their scope and aims, and so extends beyond the political sphere narrowly conceived. The three meanings are intimately related, so their conflation comes as no surprise. Nonetheless, their analytical distinction reveals the need to disentangle the question of what makes arrangements democratic (and hence what is meant by a deficit of democracy) from what makes democracy a good thing.[5]

Democracy is often unquestioningly regarded as a self-evident and self-justifying good. The force of the democratic imperative clearly draws on this assumption. But if democracy just means a collection of political institutions of a certain sort, it is hard to see what is self-justifying about them. The worth of democracy must refer to other widely approved goods and values, therefore, that are supposedly given political currency by democratic institutions. A standard list consists of liberty, equality, independence and fairness, though different democratic theories combine them in various ways that often reflect divergent ontological assumptions (Held 1987; MacCormick 1997). Following the main contemporary democratic theorists (Habermas 1996a; Rawls 1993), we shall assume that modern democracy's main virtue lies in its tendency to underpin and promote value pluralism, at least in ideal conditions. This occurs through the formal incorporation and substantive balancing of different values within its very principles and procedures; through the promotion of consensual decision-making; and through the settlement of disputes arising from either the incommensurability of values or the non-composibility of rights and liberties, in ways that are recognized as fair and legitimate by the parties involved.

To unpack the value pluralism of democracy, we shall start with its inherent qualities. When considered as values intrinsic to democracy, then liberty, equality, independence and fairness help establish both the principle of democratic authorization and democracy's procedural character. Liberty entails the presumption that an agent should be free to choose a course of action and to shape the social context in which he or she operates in ways that maximize the conditions for autonomy. As a collective decision-making mechanism, democracy inevitably places limits on the liberty of individuals. But where collective decision-making is both inevitable, because of the social constraints within which agents operate, and necessary, because of the desirability of co-ordinated action in addressing common problems (Weale 1998), democracy offers a way of preserving the independence of individual members by allowing them to participate in shaping the rules that either limit or enable action.[6] Thus the equal right to liberty and self-determination[7] underlies the authoritative nature of democratic government and establishes the presumption of its legitimacy over other forms of collective decision-making. However, for authorization to be fully legitimate, some form of consent is needed, and so, inevitably, is some conception of autonomy. These two conditions ground the capacity of community members to make free and responsible choices, providing a formal legitimacy test for democratic authority and substantive criteria for the design of democratic institutions.[8]

Equality and fairness enter here to frame the procedures of democratic authorization itself. Such values are appealed to when arguing that we owe all individuals equal respect (Cohen and Sabel 1997), that they have equal claims over communal goods, and that their demands should be given equal considera-tion by the community itself (Dahl 1986, Chapter 8). The arguments for equal respect, claims and consideration are the basis for political equality, which is the guiding principle for establishing democracy's procedures in the aggregation of members' opinions and choices and the fair deliberation of reasons (Jones 1983; Sunstein 1991). These arguments also ground the assumptions about the superior legitimacy of democratic methods and arrangements over other forms of collective decision-making.

Both democratic authorization and its procedural framework rest on values that are considered paramount in modern, post-traditional societies. Herein lies much of the democratic imperative's plausibility. However, that liberty, equality, independence and fairness are intrinsically related to the idea of democracy does not, in itself, guarantee that the effects of democratic government will be consistent with those same values. Nor is there any *a prioristic* reason supporting the belief that democracy is conducive to social justice, however this is defined (Van Parijs 1996 and 1998). Strictly speaking, the asymmetry between intrinsic values and their promotion is neither a problem of the practical application of ideal requirements nor a question of the composibility of the demands arising from different values or their various interpretations. The asymmetry is the direct product of the absence of any logical connection between the conditions of choice and its results given the indeterminacy associated with *free* choice (besides various other problems usually associated with collective choice and unintended consequences). From this perspective, the relationship between democracy and either its own or other fundamental values becomes largely instrumental. At best, a virtuous circle may exist between democracy's intrinsic values and their reinforcement through the educative effect of democratic participation (Cohen and Sabel 1997).

Democracy's legitimacy cannot in any case rest on its intrinsic goodness alone, since this needs to be compared to and balanced against the substantial promotion of other values when taken independently (Shapiro 1996, Chapter 1).

This task involves looking at the beneficial effects of making decisions democratically, so far as these can be reasonably ascertained. Just as the value of democratic principles has been supposed to guarantee its intrinsic goodness, so the virtues of democratic governance are frequently considered self-evident. The literature often fails to indicate whether the benefits of democracy follow logically from its operations or are the empirically ascertainable results of them. To clarify this confusion, let's distinguish between three groups of benefits. A first group concerns the general effects of democratic governance. They consist in the goods of responsive government, adaptive governance and non-domination. The structure of democratic governance is meant to guarantee a two-way information flow that ensures government is controlled by the ruled and that the rulers are well informed about the needs and views of citizens. This process facilitates adaptive governance, by developing feedback mechanisms, the pooling of information for collective problem solving, and collective-learning mechanisms both in space and time (Cohen and Sabel 1997). Democracy's ability to adapt to the tasks in hand also means that, as a system of governance, it is apt to take different institutional forms according to the composition of its membership and its historical and cultural location. Democratic governance is also propitious terrain for securing liberty as non-domination (Pettit 1997). This condition consists not of an absence of interference either by the state or other private actors, but of guaranteeing an environment in which citizens can lead secure lives, plan ahead and feel generally in control, without a sense of their life choices being dictated by more powerful interests.

A second group of benefits concerns the quality of democratic decisions. These are harder to establish without precise empirical evidence. However, by checking arbitrary and self-interested uses of power, whilst encouraging the formulation of general laws that reflect the common good, democracy is generally conducive to the definition and protection of individual rights and liberties. Moreover, democratic mechanisms foster a degree of social equality by subsuming social and income differences under a commonality of concerns that calls for some redistribution of resources. Finally, democracy promotes domestic and international peace by establishing a framework within which people are expected to engage in discussion, exchange arguments and find reasonable agreements and compromises, rather than making use of their relative contractual position or physical force.

The third group of benefits follows more clearly from the manner in which democratic decisions are reached (Jones 1983). Democrats contend political participation educates citizens about each other's needs and ideals, thereby fostering toleration if not an equal regard, a concern for the common interest, and an awareness of the importance of co-operation to secure public goods. Some of these effects have already been mentioned in relation to the potential virtuous circle associated with the intrinsic values of democracy (Cohen and Sabel 1997), but they are probably better looked at from a more consequentialist perspective. Democracy encourages mutually beneficial types of bargain and forms of reciprocity in the construction of the general will; it formally requires frankness, mutual respect and taking the perspective of others when arguing for one's opinions. These processes facilitate interest and opinion filtering and transformation, so turning private individuals into citizens of the commonwealth (Offe and Preuss 1991; Mansbridge 1992). Involvement in public affairs may also foster solidarity and trust, contributing to the social capital needed to ease co-operation between different groups and particularly between long-standing majorities and minorities in both politics and society at large.

The catalogue of democracy's beneficial effects is certainly impressive. *Prima facie*, it reinforces the case for the democratic imperative in modern societies, particularly in view of their increasing pluralism and what Rawls (1993) calls the 'burdens of judgement' in ethical arguments (cf. also Habermas 1996a). However, like our earlier consequential refinement of arguments from democracy's inherent goodness, focusing on the good consequences of practising democracy also renders the endorsement of democratic arrangements more discriminating. In both cases, it turns democracy into a partly instrumental good. On the one hand, we value it for *realising* its intrinsic values, not just because they are inherent to democracy *per se*. On the other hand, our approval of democratic institutions is equally conditional to some degree on their delivering the beneficial effects associated with democratic decision-making. As we have seen, some of these effects are supported by empirical evidence, while others rest on the presumption that, given the right conditions and the appropriate institutional machinery, they are more likely to arise than not. The relatively instrumental and contingent nature of democracy, however, makes its legitimacy no longer self-standing, rendering the democratic imperative less compelling.

Of course, liberals and socialists have always qualified their approval of democracy in ways that appear superficially analogous to those proposed here. Whereas they make their support for democracy conditional on its fostering liberal or socialist values, however, our qualifications rest on the possibility that democratic institutions may either not further democratic principles or fail to produce the benefits that ideally follow from the democratic process. In each case, we evaluate democracy in terms of its instrumental ability to deliver democratic goods rather than those of some other kind. This is not to suggest that all good things are necessarily democratic. Many are only contingently so, and others may be undermined by democracy. As we saw, such reasoning led past European elites to conclude that we could do without democracy much of the time. Libertarians still hold this view, believing as much as possible should be left to the market (Hayek 1982; Buchanan 1975). Advocates of a rights-based constitution for Europe often take an analogous stance, seeing democracy as limited to and by its contribution to securing rights that might often be better promoted by other mechanisms (Mancini 1989). Much discussion of the democratic deficit involves such a purely instrumental view of democracy. However, these approaches cannot offer the EU the distinctively political legitimacy we have seen it now needs, given that the social and legal legitimacy it currently possesses have proven insufficient. To address this issue one has to consider the intrinsic merits of democracy. Although there are external limits to democracy in terms of economic performance and rights protection, which a comprehensive evaluation would have to consider, our concern has been with its own distinct contribution. Moreover, we have shown that many economic benefits and rights are intrinsic to democracy itself and only likely to be realized through it. By judging democracy by its own light, many of the limits that critics believe have to be imposed on democracy can be shown to be internal to it (Bellamy and Castiglione 1997b).

So even in the qualified form we have argued for, democratic values play a vital role in the direct and normative legitimation of regimes. European political integration is no exception. Nonetheless, opinions differ about why and how Europe fails the democratic legitimacy test. Having clarified what is good about democracy in general, we are now in a better position to answer these questions. We shall do so by briefly examining how Europe scores on the three kinds of goods provided by democracy: legitimate authorization, fair co-operation and the beneficial effects that stem from responsive governance.

The political authorization of European governance does not come directly from the people(s) of Europe. Direct and consensual authorization, through the election of the European Parliament, is still largely ineffective. Admittedly, the powers of the EP have recently been increased (see the Amsterdam Treaty), and the Parliament has become more of a partner in European decision-making through having certain powers of control or ratification. On the whole, however, the EP remains a secondary player in the business of European government.[9] Authorization of the main players, on the other hand, is only partial and indirect. The Commission is selected in ways that correspond more to bureaucratic and diplomatic criteria than to anything resembling democratic mechanisms. Similar notions inform the way it perceives itself and acts politically. The only effective branch of European government that can claim some form of democratic authorization is the Council. But such authorization is only indirect. Moreover, it is rare for national governments to be elected on a clear European agenda. Thus, referenda, like those on Maastricht, seem to be the only meaningful form of direct authorization so far used at the European level. Yet the electorate's message is far from clear on such occasions, given that the vote is often made with national issues in mind; a fact that also applies to elections for the European Parliament. In sum, the little democratic authorization that European governance can claim is partial, indirect, ineffective and unclear.

If we move to the question of political equality and fair co-operation, however, the bleak picture we have just painted of democratic authorization appears in a different and less gloomy light. There is no denying the failures on the authorization front, but the legitimacy that comes with authorization rests in turn on the legitimacy of the subject that transfers authority. Until some agreement is reached on who is the legitimate 'subject' of the European constitution: a European Demos of European citizens, the citizens of the Member States voting nationally, the governments of the Member States, or even, in a more cosmopolitan perspective, the values underlying the European constitution; the terms of both political equality and fair co-operation are uncertain. This problem is largely a question of political identity, to which we shall return in the next section when discussing democratic procedures in more detail. But it also partly depends on the issues raised in the first section concerning the legitimacy of the polity. As we pointed out, such matters cannot be solved democratically, since democracy itself rests on them. Political equality and fair co-operation presuppose we know who is equal with whom and who can be expected to co-operate or not. In Europe, these questions still remain unanswered.

A similar conundrum applies to the beneficial effects associated with democracy. Until European political institutions are explicitly designed according to democratic principles, arguments about the good consequences of European democracy can only be counterfactual, as can their supposed legitimating force. Supporters of the Community method often maintained that democratic methods and popular participation would bring about neither economic nor political integration. Whether this was true or not, the argument assumed that the benefits of democracy were outweighed by the goods associated with the integration process, mainly peace and prosperity. But now that a fair degree of economic and political integration has been achieved, a degree that most Europeans seem both to take for granted and approve of, the question has become how to sustain it – whether by deepening, widening or halting the process.[10] Hence the shift to a more intentionalist paradigm, which, for some of the reasons already outlined in this section, gives greater value to democracy.

The problem now confronting us is what kind of democratic institutions and what degree of popular participation are necessary to provide the democratic goods without jeopardizing the current level of integration. In this respect, critics of the democratic deficit take a sanguine view of the application of the democratic imperative to the European Union. They think political equality must surely apply to the citizens of Europe and that demands for the democratization of European institutions follow directly from the legitimacy of democratic authorization. They ask for a more thorough application of majoritarianism throughout the institutions of the Union, and propose we give more power to those involving direct representation. But is this a way out of the democratic deficit? We shall review the logic of these demands in the next two sections by discussing the other two meanings of democracy – as a decision-making procedure and as a form of government.

Political unity and democratic rules

Most democratic theories hold that majoritarianism – often defined as a majority 'principle' rather than a 'rule' – lies at the heart of democracy. This conviction is both trivial and unfounded. It is trivial because no one disputes that majoritarianism offers *an* application of the principle of political equality, which ensures the vote of each and every member of the community has equal weight. But it is unfounded as the guiding procedural principle of democracy.

The mistake arises from confusing people and majority. This error can best be illustrated by an example. If procedural democracy consisted in following the simple will of the majority of the members of a community, there would be nothing undemocratic in a society where a minority were excluded from the political process (but not necessarily from civil and social rights), as long as all decisions were taken by a majority of the whole community. Thus, for any single decision the majority of those having political rights (call them A) would need to be larger than the political minority (call them B) and the excluded minority (call them C) put together: A>B+C. On the face of it, this example seems consistent with majoritarianism, but is it consistent with democracy? In the past, many democracies sanctioned the permanent exclusion of minorities (and occasionally, majorities): women, slaves, unpropertied workers, blacks, indigenous populations. But with the universalization of fundamental human rights, this position is as untenable in practice as it is in theory. Moreover, none of these democracies were founded on the proviso we have specified in our hypothetical example. In the example itself, the minority is not excluded from the community (from the people, that is), but only silenced politically. Indeed, the proviso gives them a certain weight in the political process by allocating them a 'silent' veto power whenever the political and excluded minorities jointly represent the majority of the whole population. The political exclusion of a minority, therefore, does not contradict the majoritarian rule when this is applied to the entire community.[11] But such exclusion is evidently inconsistent with political equality. Indeed, it is the latter that should be regarded as the fundamental procedural principle of democracy, to which all decision-making rules ought ultimately to be subordinated.

To see how the principle of political equality renders democratic decision-making more complex, we shall briefly review some of the shortcomings of majority rule and contrast this procedure with the alternatives of super-majoritarianism, proportionality and deliberation. We will concentrate on three of the main features of majority decision: positive responsiveness, anonymity and issue neutrality (cf. Weale 1997). Each of them possesses certain virtues as part of a procedure that tends to respect the pluralism of preferences and opinions, if not necessarily of strongly held beliefs and values, in the community to which majority decision is applied.

Positive responsiveness implies that, *ceteris paribus*, changes in an individual's preferences should affect the function of social choice. Majority decision is extremely sensitive to such alterations, as is clearly illustrated in cases when a single vote alters the outcome. By contrast, super-majorities normally need preference shifts in more than a single voter to affect the collective choice. This lack of elasticity seems to give minorities a veto power, as is even more clearly illustrated by the unanimity rule (Saward 1998), so contradicting the principle of political equality. However, this conclusion may be too hasty if it involves the aforementioned confusion between the people and a majority. If, on a whole range of fundamental issues, a society were permanently divided along the same lines, persistent minorities might eventually lose interest in participating in the political process. In their view, such a system would fail to recognize their fundamental interests and contradict the principle of political equality. As Kelsen suggested some time ago (1929), in democracies it is more appropriate to speak of a majority–minority principle, since the one implies the other. The effectiveness of collective decision-making depends on keeping communities together, so that minorities can accept the legitimacy of majority decisions. Majoritarianism must be seen, therefore, as part of a wider process of democratic decision-making that tries to keep a balance between decisiveness in social choice (through competitive mechanisms, based on the equalizing function of democracy) and social integration (through co-operative mechanisms, based on the recognition function of democracy). From this perspective, the search for a wider consensus through consociational mechanisms such as the use of super- or concurrent majorities, or occasionally the unanimity rule, is not necessarily undemocratic. In certain circumstances, it may be considered as a way of adapting the principle of political equality to complex polities, where separate political identities coexist that reflect distinct and well-entrenched practices of co-operation and deep differences of interests (Weale 1998; Lijphart 1984; Schmitter 1996b).

Sensitivity to political identity is also central to a discussion of the anonymity feature of majority decision. This stipulates that only the number and not the identity or the status of the members determines the social choice function. As with positive responsiveness, the problem arises when there are persistent minorities. Political equality can be looked at either prospectively, by considering the equality of citizens to influence the making of collective decisions; or retrospectively, by considering whether the interests of citizens have been equally respected in the decision itself (Jones 1983; Saward 1998; Hyland 1995). Because of the anonymity feature, which precludes weighting an individual's voting power according to his or her interest in the matter, majority decision is insensitive to retrospective equality. So, a majority may take decisions on matters that mainly affect a minority, without due regard for the way the minority itself see things. Or, there may be cases in which a majority consistently outvotes a minority on related issues, so producing a winner-takes-all situation that reflects unfairly on the real divisions of interests and opinions within the society (Jones 1983). In all such instances, decision mechanisms that result in proportionate satisfaction would better reflect the principle of political equality.

The application of the proportionality rule is not always simple. The most obvious case involves systems of representation. Here majority rule is only undermined indirectly as a result of the consensus and coalition-building politics proportional representation seems to encourage. Moreover, the anonymity feature applies to PR. Things change when we move from second- to first-order decision-making; that is, from the selection of representatives to the making of decisions themselves. Here the only way of weighing the relative interest of the members of the electorate is to do away with anonymity. This can be done in various ways – such as giving stronger representation to certain groups, or by considering both horizontal (across society, through interest-based groups and associations) and vertical (across the territory, through federal and power devolving structures) decentralization of the decision process, depending on the issues at stake. Majority rule may still be applied in these decentralized structures, but the larger community *de facto* recognises that there are some (but clearly not all) collective issues for which a recognition of separate political identities may apply.

Finally, we turn to the neutrality of majority decisions. This feature implies the social choice function is determined solely by the number of votes favouring one or other option, rather than by the substantive merits of what is debated. Issue neutrality would raise no particular problem, besides those standardly treated in the public choice literature, if democratic politics just weighed individual subjective preferences. It is only when matters of intrinsic importance have to be discussed that difficulties arise. The application of a seemingly behaviouristic approach to politics (Weale 1992) fails to recognise the essential role played in a democracy by fair discussion and the appeal to arguments that are meant either to convince or to raise doubts in the minds of other voters. The idea of deliberative democracy emphasizes the importance of processes and institutions that foster the filtering and transformation of individual preferences by encouraging the educative engagement with others and reflective political judgements (Sunstein 1991). These practices change politics from a market of votes into a forum of principle. Majority decision is not overruled by such institutions, since in pluralist and complex societies there is still plenty of scope for reasonable disagreement and the clash of interests, but its place is hedged in by the forum institutions of politics and, more generally, by the critical function played by the modern public sphere (Habermas 1992a). Counting votes is normally the last stage of a process during which the issues have been discussed on their merits. The dialogic aspect of democracy is as important as the aggregation of views and preferences, and often more so. In simple majority decision, issues may not matter, but in democracy pushpin is not the same as poetry.

If democracy is not just simple majoritarianism, then democratic legitimacy depends on a thick network of institutions more than on thin procedural rules. This analysis also undermines calls for majority rule as the effective cure for Europe's democratic deficit (cf. also van Parijs 1998). If, as we have argued, majoritarianism is not the essence of democratic decision-making in the relatively homogenous conditions of the nation-state, there is even less reason to believe it can be placed at the core of a future European democracy. Indeed, a European democracy will probably have to wrestle with far more intractable problems of divided political identities than existing nation-states, since its component parts have a long history of common engagement, shared culture and feelings of mutual interest that cannot be brushed aside lightly. This sense of commonalty (meant dispositionally, rather than in a strong communitarian sense: cf. Barry 1989b; Weale 1997) is further reinforced by the national contexts in which civil networks, civic cultures, political structures and welfare insurance mechanisms mostly operate. The replacement of the sense of civic identity and of national institutions of co-operation, with equivalent structures of trust and reciprocity at a European level cannot be achieved overnight (Offe 1998b). Furthermore, the burden of proof must rest with those who attempt to either change or undo institutions that are reasonably efficient and socially legitimate, to show that the alternatives will do dramatically better.[12]

These are not arguments for the *status quo*. They suggest merely that calls for the diffusion of democratic procedures at a European level should give greater consideration to issues of political identity than has often been the case. For these are relevant to the fairness of the procedures themselves. More positively, the democratic recognition of different political identities can be incorporated within a Madisonian system of checking and balancing competing interests and powers. The retreat of the nation-state need not necessarily lead towards more centralization. Within the emerging system of European multi-level governance (Marks *et al.* 1996), there is scope for more decentralized and contextualized problem solving, for associative democratic governance and other schemes of dispersed and mixed sovereignty that offer an alternative to both top-down stateism and deregulated markets (Cohen and Sabel 1997; Schmitter in Marks *et al.* 1996; Hirst 1994; Bellamy and Castiglione 1997a, 1998a and 1998b). There are also opportunities for a less communitarian-based deliberative framework in which to embed democratic practices. These include the development of a pluralistic and interactive overlapping of national and European legal systems (MacCormick 1993 and 1995); the innovative use of European committees, where political interests are disciplined and made more deliberative by the contribution of expert knowledge (cf. Joerges' contribution to this volume); and the creation of a more strongly normative public sphere, applying the test of communicative rationality to the business of politics and administration (cf. Ferry 1992, and Eriksen's contribution to this volume).

Yet, however positive the chances for multi-governance, deliberation and self-reflection may appear, as Habermas reminds us in his contribution to this volume, there still remains an important demand for popular sovereignty and collective self-determination, with the community wanting to exercise 'political influence upon itself'. This is the role traditionally assigned to legislative power in democratic societies, and takes us back to the other reforms standardly invoked to address the democratic deficit in the European Union: more direct representation, more democratic control, more accountability. But can the traditional institutions of modern democracy be transferred to the Union?

Democracy, regimes and polities

As the main thrust of our argument implies, simple demands for more democratic European institutions make too easy a transition from the generic presumption in favour of the democratic imperative to its application to political regimes. There are *a prioristic* reasons for using democracy as the main strategy for direct regime legitimation, but these are not enough. Partly instrumental reasons need to be taken into consideration, but they in turn depend on the presence of mechanisms designed to bring about the various intrinsic goods and beneficial effects of democracy. As we have also seen, such mechanisms cannot be reduced to strictly procedural rules capable of universal application – the 'rules of the game', in Bobbio's phrase (1987) – but need more substantive specification to perform their tasks. So, what are the concrete institutions of a democratic society?

Talking, as we often do, of democratic societies is only shorthand for saying that some of their fundamental political institutions are run democratically. Neither markets nor families, which determine so much of our social life, are organized according to democratic criteria. Citizens spend most of their time in organizations (schools, firms, corporations) where democracy operates only at the margins, if at all. Even in the public sphere narrowly conceived neither the ordinary administration of justice, policing or the machinery of government are run democratically. There is a sense, of course, in which the passage from status to contract (Maine 1917 [1861]) has democratized social life through making it less hierarchical – a change in which modern political democracy is firmly rooted. But this is more a matter of social equality and independence than strict democracy. In ordinary language, we say that a society is democratic only by use of a synecdoche that treats a part as the whole. There are theories of democracy that argue for a diffusion of democratic practices beyond the confines of politics, maintaining that political democracy itself needs to be propped up by industrial, associational and other decentralized forms of democracy. But even these theorists rarely demand that most decision-making in society should be done democratically; for democratic criteria may not always be appropriate to either the scope or the locus of the kind of decisions to be taken. Furthermore, democracy may some times be too cumbersome and time-consuming to be put into operation, or in certain circumstances prove technically unworkable.

All this is fairly uncontroversial. But when we look at strict political democracy, we find precise limits imposed on its operations. These are embodied in some of the 'guardian' institutions of constitutional democracy (separations of powers, role and autonomy of the judiciary, super-parties roles, etc.), whose nature and function is open to interpretation, and whose justification as limits that democracy imposes on itself is questionable (Bellamy and Castiglione 1997b). So, in the relative sense already described, what is democratic about democratic regimes? The question can be answered from three different perspectives, reflecting issues already raised in discussing democracy's values, but which will now be treated at a more descriptive and institutional level. They are: political authorization, the systemic properties of the political regime, and the aims it pursues.

First, a democratic regime is one where the authorization of collectively binding political decisions is undertaken by the people. This is a very general pre-condition, whose fulfilment may require different institutions and rights, depending on how one understands the nature and extent of authorization. For instance, there are significant differences between direct authorization and authorization through representatives; there may be disputes over the criteria that are relevant to the assigning of participatory rights; and so on. But in essence, a regime can be defined as democratic if the people, as a collectivity, has the formal power, and a number of sufficiently effective means, through which to authorize the basic process of legislation.

Second, a regime is democratic if a number of its systemic features allow citizens, acting as free and equal members of the community, to participate in governance. So (partly following Schmitter 1996b), the regime must be organized in such a way that the forms and channels of access to governmental positions are in principle open to all and their holders significantly influenced by the people; the public realm where collective decision-making applies extends to all those issues that are relevant to ensuring the satisfaction of the members' common interests; and the rules followed in making publicly binding decisions ensure a balance between the competitive (voting, elections, individual interests, etc.) and co-operative (bounded nature of the democratic community, common interests, etc.) aspects of democracy.

Third, and from a more consequentialist perspective, a democratic regime is one that ensures that, on the one hand, ordinary citizens exercise both real influence (through selection and authorization) and control (through transparency and accountability) over their rulers; and, on the other, the political leaders gain sufficient information (through the electoral process and the public sphere) to be responsive in their decisions to the ideals and interests of the ruled.

In sum, democratic regimes are characterized by popular forms of authorization, governance and influence. However, institutional translation of these properties now clearly appears to be a matter of degree. Democratic regimes are not discrete entities. There are no institutions, rights and practices that in themselves can be regarded as sufficient for the establishment of democracy. Some institutional arrangements, such as universal suffrage, territorial representation, representative legislative assemblies, practices of parliamentary accountability, majority decision, etc., are well rooted in democratic theory and practice, but they have emerged historically, and often contingently, in order to fix ways in which to operationalize democratic authorization and governance. As a regime, democracy is underdefined, therefore: there is no necessary list of democratic institutions and procedures that are required for people to consent to, influence and control the decisions of their rulers. Nor has democracy even been fully realized in any given regime.

Herein lies the difficulty with talk of a democratic deficit. As Neil MacCormick (1997) and Philippe van Parijs (1998) have recently commented, the issue of the legitimacy of political regimes is not whether there is enough (or a maximum) of democracy, but whether there is an adequate (or an optimum) amount. The implications for Europe are that an injection of democratic institutions is not sufficient to give political legitimacy to its system of governance; and, conversely, that addressing the question of the legitimacy of the

European regime does necessarily require more democracy. So, what is to be done?

The first task is to make a realistic assessment of how the European system of governance currently works. Of course, there is a vast empirical literature, but from a normative perspective the crucial fact to recognize is that most regimes are of a mixed nature. This point has recently and convincingly been made by Neil MacCormick (1997) with particular reference to Europe. The three main branches of European governance form, in his view, a mix of bureaucratic-oligarchic elements, mainly embodied in the Commission (but one could also add the ECJ), with forms of direct (Parliament) and indirect (Council) democratic control. This clearly makes for a mixed constitution, but, as he says, one not 'wholly lacking in democratic elements or democratic spirit' (p. 344). From this perspective, reform of the European mixed regime[13] with regard both to its efficacy (in sustaining integration) and an increase in direct forms of legitimation (which are required by the new intentionalist paradigm) is more a matter of prudence, in designing and adapting institutions, than of acting on democratic imperatives (cf. also Schmitter 1996b, and Craig 1997). As we have argued elsewhere, the constitution of Europe should be seen as reflexive bricolage rather than grand architecture (Bellamy and Castiglione 1997a, 1998a, cf. also MacCormick 1997, and Curtin 1997).

The second task is to take seriously the new demands that globalization and multiculturalism pose to democracy in the twenty-first century. As we have argued, a European democracy needs to confront the issue of political identity by finding institutional means through which to parcel out democratic power in ways that are consistent with the principle of subsidiarity (cf. MacCormick 1997). This is a particularly complex task, not only because of the confusion that still surrounds this principle, but also because regime legitimacy meshes with the legitimacy of the polity at this point. As we saw, the mixing and overlapping of sovereignties (multiple *Demoi* and multi-level governance) make Europe a 'mixed polity'. Yet it is also a 'mixed regime' (or commonwealth), in that there is a mixing of different elements of rule (in the classical sense of the three forms of government). As things stand, these cannot be considered transient features of the European Union. For its political legitimacy depends on the mixture of elements making up the EU being given democratic recognition and expression through a careful and sensitive allocation of powers and the design of inclusive institutions. A mixed polity requires a mixed regime.

Conclusion

The underlying values of democracy favour its status as the only legitimate political regime for modern non-hierarchical societies. On the one hand, it ensures that people (both individually and collectively) are in charge of their own affairs. On the other, its general procedures possess a certain fairness appropriate to egalitarian societies. But though the effects of democratic government are generally positive, they cannot be assumed to be so *a priori*. Democracy only works if its embodied in a mix of institutions and decision-making procedures that suit the society to which they apply. The democratic deficit can only be addressed in ways that will resolve the EU's current crisis of political legitimacy, therefore, if the proposed democratic regime matches the mixed character of the European polity.

Notes

1 Research for this paper was supported by an ESRC Research Grant on 'Sovereignty and Citizenship in a Mixed Polity' (R000222446). For helpful comments, we thank the editors of this volume and participants at the Bergen Conference on 'Democracy in Europe – Integration and Deliberation', February 1998.
2 Weiler (1999a, Chapter 7).
3 On the process of integration so far and on its ethics, cf. Bellamy and Warleigh (1998).
4 The list of works taking such a turn is growing rapidly. These are some of them, in no particular order: de Burca (1996), Mancini (1989), Curtin (1997), Weiler (1995, 1996a and 1999a), MacCormick (1993, 1995 and 1997), Habermas (1992b), Joerges (1997a), Lehning and Weale (1997), Weale (1994), Weale and Nentwich (1998), Shaw (1996, Chapter 6), Preuss (1996a), Føllesdal and Koslowski (1998), Bellamy and Castiglione (1996, 1997a and 1998b).
5 All three meanings cut across the descriptive/evaluative distinction. We can describe the institutional arrangements of a democratic regime, but we can also prescribe the minimum (or maximum) level of popular involvement required for a regime to be considered a democracy. Similarly, we can identify the values that are supported by actual democratic arrangements; but also reverse the perspective and argue that political arrangements are only truly democratic if they support certain values. Finally, the identification of democratic procedures is not just an empirical question, as it will be shown in the next section of this essay.
6 cf. Kelsen, 1929, who expounds on arguments advanced by classical authors such as Rousseau, Kant and Mill.
7 The democratic ideals of liberty and self-determination can be interpreted from either an individualistic or a holistic perspective. For different views, cf. Weale (1997 and 1998), Føllesdal (1998d) and Offe (1998b).
8 The criteria of consent can take various forms: explicit, tacit or hypothetical; original, recurrent, or sustained. Different theories of democracy may require some or all of these forms. Autonomy can also be given different contents in its specification. From the particular interpretations given to consent and autonomy depends the kind of tests to which democratic institutions can be put in order to satisfy the criteria of democratic authorization. For instance, with regard to consent, the form of representation and consultation needed in different moments of democratic politics; or, with regard to autonomy, the extension of the franchise and the extent of participation.
9 For an extended discussion of the normative role of the EP, cf. McCormick (forthcoming).
10 We are assuming that, from a very general perspective, supporters of the various strategies are in favour of the kind and level of integration so far achieved (let us call it the '*acquis communautaire*' in a non-technical sense), and that their different suggestions are aimed at sustaining it. We are therefore excluding those who may simply wish to undo the Union, who we take to be a very small minority at this stage. As things move on, of course, supporters of the 'halting' strategy may become less satisfied with the integration process. For some of these, who genuinely proclaim to be in favour of Europe, monetary union may represent a critical threshold.

11 This is true at least for all those instances where a 'positive' decision is taken; the political exclusion of a minority may instead make a difference for all those cases in which the *status quo* is upheld.

12 cf. Føllesdal (1998a) and Weale (1998). Pogge (1998: 184) suggests that, because there is no 'pressing emergency' in Europe, this favours the democratic reshaping of European institutions. This is only partly true, for the reason we have just stated in the main test. The lack of emergency may favour a more considered change, but poses a greater normative burden on the arguments for change.

13 MacCormick calls it a 'mixed commonwealth'. We also used 'mixed commonwealth' in Bellamy and Castiglione (1997a), partly borrowing from MacCormick; but, in fact, we there meant what we now call 'mixed polity' as opposed to 'mixed regime'.

5 Subsidiarity and democratic deliberation[1]

Andreas Føllesdal

The Amsterdam Treaty seeks to bring the European Union closer to the people of Europe by aligning the institutions closer to conceptions of *subsidiarity* and *democracy*. Subsidiarity is made operational in a Protocol to the Amsterdam Treaty. This 'Amsterdam Subsidiarity' regards Community action as appropriate if 'the objectives of the proposed action cannot be sufficiently achieved by Member States' action in the framework of their national constitutional system and can therefore be better achieved by action on the part of the Community' (art. 5). Thus the *determination of relative efficiency* of Community and Member State action is crucial for this conception of subsidiarity. Democracy is furthered by reforms which increase the European Parliament's powers *vis-à-vis* both the Commission and the Council of Ministers. These reforms move the Union towards a bicameral model of parliamentary democracy (Nentwich and Falkner 1997).

Subsidiarity may seem attractive for deliberative democrats concerned with the opportunities for preference formation in 'decentralized processes of decision making ... within constitutional political structures' (Bohman 1999: 25; Miller 1992: 54, 67). While there are such reasons for supporting subsidiarity, the Amsterdam conception of subsidiarity also conflicts with the concern for democratic deliberation when it comes to institutional arrangements. The paper identifies three main areas of tension between Amsterdam Subsidiarity and deliberative democracy. Firstly, an urgent but unanswered task is how to secure accountable applications of Amsterdam Subsidiarity. Secondly, this conception of subsidiarity seems to grant unwarranted powers to Member States. Other entities, such as sub-state regions, might also appeal to considerations of subsidiarity, yet such applications and arguments are not recognized. Finally, Amsterdam Subsidiarity may hinder the development of trans-European values and commitments necessary for a stable European political order.

The first section provides a brief historical backdrop about the role of subsidiarity in the European Union. To understand and assess the Amsterdam conception of subsidiarity it is then helpful to consider aspects of deliberative democratic theory, as well as alternative theories of subsidiarity. The second section sketches some relevant aspects of deliberative democratic theory. The third section surveys some competing theories of subsidiarity. The aim is twofold: to see how subsidiarity may foster deliberation, and to identify some peculiar features of the conception of Amsterdam Subsidiarity. The last section considers conflicts and tensions between Amsterdam Subsidiarity and deliberative democracy.

Subsidiarity in the European Union

The Principle of Subsidiarity regulates the *allocation* or the *use* of authority within a political order where there is no unitary sovereign. The principle holds that powers or tasks are to rest with the sub-units of that order unless a central unit is more effective in achieving certain specified goals. Appeals to subsidiarity take on particular salience in periods of institutional transformation, often as part of the bargain among sovereign communities agreeing to a common authority in federal fashion. A Principle of Subsidiarity reduces the risks for members of being overruled in common decisions, by limiting the common agenda.

How are we to assess the Principle of Subsidiarity? The principle seems to reflect the same normative ideals as democracy: policies must be controlled by those affected, to ensure that institutions and laws reflect the interests of the individuals under conditions where all count as equals. Only when these considerations counsel joint action, is central authority warranted.

In the context of the European Union, the Principle of Subsidiarity has served to quell fears of centralization. The Union was established to enhance and complement domestic sovereignty in areas where there was a recognized disparity between state borders, electorates, and affected parties. The European level of governance ensured beneficial co-operation, regulation of externalities, and options for collective action.

Talk of subsidiarity was introduced in the late 1980s through the initiative of the European Parliament, Britain and Germany. Britain feared European federalism, and the German Länder sought to maintain their exclusive powers enjoyed in the German Federal Republic. To constrain centralizing tendencies, they sought to place the burden of argument with integrationists. A Principle of Subsidiarity was included in the 1992 Maastricht Treaty on European Union (TEU), and further elaborated in a Protocol of the Amsterdam draft Treaty of 1997.

In the European setting, state governments' fears of excessive centralization are understandable, for the safeguards against centralization found in many federations are absent in Europe. There is no doctrine of enumerated powers, and rather than enjoying competencies for specific fields of legislation, Community institutions enjoy whatever competencies they need for specified ends. Member States enjoy little exclusive legislative authority, due to doctrines of 'Direct Effect', 'Supremacy' and 'Absorption of Community Law', and due to the use of qualified majority voting.

One reason why subsidiarity serves to constrain European integration is that the Member States presently disagree about common ends, shared standards, and the likely results of separate and common action. These disagreements hinder applications of the principle, and thus prevent joint action. To illustrate, some Member States already address ecological problems better than can be hoped for at the level of the EU, while other states support EU action.

However, the Principle of Subsidiarity may also foster agreement by indicating the issues which must be resolved, including such topics as the aims of the Union, the feasible strategies and their expected effects. This is because subsidiarity requires that certain arguments must be made when joint action is contemplated. Thereby subsidiarity stimulates common deliberation, which in turn may lead to further integration – contrary to the constraining role Member States envisioned.

There are further reasons why subsidiarity is unlikely to alleviate worries about undue integration. The Principle of Subsidiarity can be interpreted in several different ways, so as to protect against intervention – or to the contrary, require intervention by the central unit. These and other issues are addressed in the third section. Moreover, the Principle of Subsidiarity does not prohibit centralization, but only places the burden of proof on integrationists. Thus it can be disadvantageous to those sceptical of integration, by providing warrant for new forms of centralization. Finally, Subsidiarity may be invoked against Member States by their regions, draining national state powers from within. Regions may argue that the Principle of Subsidiarity must apply all the way down to ensure that 'decisions are taken as closely as possible to the citizen'.

Some of these aspects have been addressed in the Treaty formulations of the Principle of Subsidiarity. In the Maastricht Treaty the principle is explicitly linked to the uncontested objectives of the Treaty, and stated thus:

> In areas which do not fall within its exclusive competence, the Community shall take action, in accordance with the principle of subsidiarity, only if and in so far as the objectives of the proposed action cannot be sufficiently achieved by the Member States and can, therefore, by reason of the scale or effects of the proposed action, be better achieved by the Community.
>
> Any action by the Community shall not go beyond what is necessary to achieve the objectives of this Treaty.

As a result of the inclusion of the Principle of Subsidiarity, the Commission has apparently changed its mode of operation: 'The Commission has undertaken to justify each of its new proposals in the light of the subsidiarity principle. It makes more regular use of Green Papers and White Papers, prompting broad public debate, before new proposals are submitted' (European Council 1996: 4).

The 1997 Amsterdam Treaty goes further, and includes a Protocol on the application of the Principle of Subsidiarity which offers a more precise interpretation of subsidiarity.[2] This 'Amsterdam Subsidiarity' applies to issues where competencies are shared between the Union institutions and Member States. Subsidiarity provides some safeguards against centralization by laying down certain requirements for central action, and by increasing transparency about these arguments. *Comparative effectiveness* of Community action must be determined, by showing that the objectives of the proposed action cannot be sufficiently achieved by Member States, and can be better achieved by the Community. Community action is required if

- the issue under consideration has transnational aspects beyond control by Member States;
- actions by Member States alone or lack of Community action would violate the Treaty;
- action by the Community produces benefits of scale or effects, as compared with action at the level of the Member States.

The Community is also required to legislate in the weakest form necessary, leaving discretion to Member States. Thus directives are preferred over regulations, and framework directives over detailed measures.

At present, the EU institutions are still in flux: the allocation of competencies and modes of operation are adjusted at the frequent intergovernmental conferences. In this phase deliberation about the purposes and functioning of the Union is particularly important. For this reason Amsterdam Subsidiarity serves a valuable function. It facilitates public discussion and deliberation about the ends and means of the European Union in at least three ways. It requires openness and arguments among Member States and the Union institutions about comparative effectiveness.

Secondly, these arguments must draw on arguments within the Member States themselves about the ends and means of common action. And finally, the common directives identify certain outcomes, which must be reached through domestic legislation, but leave the states free in their choice of how to secure these outcomes. Directives thus require each Member State to choose policies on the basis of their comparative advantage. Such domestic discussions may consider expected results, local circumstances, and domestic history and customs, thus facilitating deliberation.

Deliberative democracy

We may use 'democracy' as a term for certain procedures for deliberation and decision. After public deliberation, the electorate votes and runs for office in elections, decided by majority rule, to bodies which legislate after public deliberation, and execute rules by majority rule. Thus rulers are held responsible to electoral majorities (Dahl 1989: Chapters 10, 11; Arneson 1993). Theories of democracy in this broad sense have also endorsed other features such as constitutionally specified procedures and constraints.

A broad range of liberal theories hold that institutions are legitimate only if they can be justified by arguments in the form of a social contract of some specific kind. The aim of such theories is not to justify morality from an assumption of self-centred individuals. Rather, they assume that individuals generally have an interest in acting justly, in being 'able to justify one's actions to others on grounds they could not reasonably reject' (Scanlon 1982: 116). They 'desire to act in accordance with principles that could not reasonably be rejected by people seeking an agreement with others under conditions free from morally irrelevant bargaining advantages and disadvantages' (Barry 1989a: 8). The implications are in accordance with the principle that 'only those norms may claim validity that could find acceptance by all those concerned as participants in a practical discourse' (Habermas 1991a: 235). This commitment to give reasons 'manifests our respect for the reasonableness of others' (Macedo 1990).

The aim of these liberal theories is to bring the commitment to justice to bear on our rules, institutions and practices. The principles of legitimacy we should hold institutions to, are those that the affected persons would unanimously consent to under conditions, which secure and recognize their status as appropriately free and equal. The specific conditions, and the significance of consent, vary among theories in ways which need not concern us here. The set of social institutions as a whole should secure the interests of all affected parties to an acceptable degree, including our interests in peace, stability, basic needs, and shares of goods and powers. Among the important interests we must take each other to have, are interests in joint activity as well as an interest in developing our preferences under acceptable conditions.

An important challenge to any normative theory is the plurality of life plans and conceptions of the good which flourish today and the range of views which will flourish in the future. While much is shared among citizens, there are also conflicting views about what the good life and polity consists in. Respect for all entails that a broad range of such views must be respected by the social institutions. All the same, social institutions affect our lives profoundly: they determine our prospects and life plans. Moreover, they are important for character formation, as they affect our preferences and values deeply. So an important good to be distributed is the power to influence the institutions that shape one's lives. Hence the importance of allocating political rights, the subject of theories of democracy.

The justification of deliberative democratic political arrangements over other arrangements is not, on this view, ultimately that they best carry out the will of the majority, but rather that they best secure the interests of all affected parties. The case for majority rule, for instance, must draw on empirical evidence that, when properly regulated and circumscribed, such mechanisms best secure substantive justice, i.e. that all affected parties' interests are expressed and taken care of acceptably well – as compared to other arrangements. A general statement of such justifications of democratic institutions runs as follows:

> The central virtue of democratic forms is that, in the presence of a suitable social background, they provide the most reliable means of reaching sub-stantively just political outcomes consistently with the public recognition of the equal worth or status of each citizen. Democratic forms succeed in achieving this aim, when they succeed at all, less because they aggregate existing preferences efficiently than because they foster a process of public

reflection in which citizens can form political views in full awareness of the grounds as well as the content of the (possibly competing) concerns of others.

(Charles Beitz 1989: 113)

Note that there are two sets of reasons for democratic arrangements, when combined with public deliberation. Deliberation followed by majority rule provides both acceptable interest *formation* and acceptable interest *aggregation*. The discussion of subsidiarity that follows focuses on the former, and following the conventions of this book, 'deliberative democracy' is used about the former features. The discussion leaves aside important issues pertaining to the aggregation of votes through majority rule and mechanisms of representation.

Let us consider some reasons why deliberation is important.

Deliberation about ends

Deliberation about ends as well as means is not a new concern in democratic theory, unique to recent liberal theories. David Hume (1752/1882), influenced by James Harrington (1656) and in turn influencing James Madison, was concerned with institutional mechanisms conducive to deliberation and criticism. He considered such arrangements as bicameralism and submission of arguments for new pieces of legislation, with the aim of 'refining' the opinion of voters (Beer 1993: 265–270). J.S. Mill supported the creation of deliberative bodies to identify and pursue common interests among those sharing national sentiments.

Deliberation about common ends and means affects preference and option formation, and are crucial input for defining the problems. Will formation is fostered by public deliberation, which allows for the development of a necessary sense of solidarity, a shared political culture and possibly a sense of community. Thus John Stuart Mill (1859/1962) insisted on the role of deliberation for making individuals understand themselves as responsible citizens who consider the views of others. A focus on the constitutional allocation of powers easily ignores these effects on preferences. An important question concerns the opportunities for arguments and the use of public reason under various institutional arrangements, which also must serve as a backdrop for bargains and co-ordination (cf. Dahl 1956; Dewey 1927). The formal powers of putting issues on the political agenda, and the allocation of bargaining power within the political process, shape the form, content and results of informal norms and arrangements (Føllesdal 1998a; Joerges and Everson in this volume).

Deliberation which uncovers arguments for positions may shift the participants towards mutual accommodation. Presenting arguments to one another, based on premises one assumes all can share, fosters willingness and ability to take an interest in the interests of others (Miller 1992). That is:

the need to reach an agreement forces each participant to put forward proposals under the rubric of general principles or policy considerations that others could accept ... By giving these reasons, however, I am committing myself to a general principle, which by implication applies to any other similarly placed group.

(Miller 1992: 55)

Nino argues that democratic procedures are 'regimented surrogates of moral discussion' (1996: 117) that allow us to determine one another's interests, and turn bargaining procedures in the direction of arguments (cf. Bohman 1999: 18). This is an element also found in certain 'integrative' bargaining approaches, which first seek agreement on principles for settling disagreements, before applying such principles to the conflict at hand (Fisher and Ury 1987; Raiffa 1982).

Preference adjustment can occur even when arguments are presented with the intention of own gain, for hypocrisy has a civilizing impact on character formation (Elster 1998a). Hypocrisy can remove blatant violations of shared norms, it fosters some adherence to these norms, and may make people prune their own preferences, since they feel obliged to 'report only those reasons that others might plausibly be expected to share' (Elster 1998a: 238, cf. Goodin 1996b: 86–89).

One contested issue concerns to what extent such public political deliberation affects preferences, as compared to other inputs on character formation. (cf. Femia 1996). Thus Miller holds that deliberative democratic theory:

relies upon a person's capacity to be swayed by rational arguments and to lay aside particular interests and opinions in deference to overall fairness and the common interest of the collectivity. It supposes people to be to some degree communally orientated in their outlook.

(Miller 1992: 45)

It is important to be clear about both the efficacy and objectives of preference formation by public deliberation. This is because each individual faces a dual threat under partial compliance possibly wrought by unilateral preference adjustment.

On the one hand, there is a risk of exploitation. My willingness to abide by principles required by the common interest as I see it, may be abused by others who claim to be guided likewise, but who actually pursue their own self-interest under the guise of common interests. When the stakes are high, such partial compliance is a risk which institutions should try to protect individuals against (Elster 1983a: 37–38). To allay this risk it is important to consider evidence of the claim that 'base prejudices will be transformed, and worthy intuitions like hatred of racism vindicated, through rational criticism and dialogue' (Ackerman 1980: 353, discussed by Sanders 1997: 351). One mechanism for preference adjustment is the civilizing impact of hypocrisy mentioned above. It is unclear, however, whether this and other mechanisms reduce the harms of partial compliance sufficient to protect against exploitation.

The second challenge is to lay out publicly observable limits to appropriate self-interest. There is a legitimate place for self-interest where issues of just distribution of benefits and burdens arise, since the complete subjection of self-interest for the sake of 'common interests' of others seems illegitimate. Yet there are few standards available to determine the reasonable limits to subjection to altruistic goals (cf. Sanders 1997: 361). While deliberation should not be thought to extinguish self-interest, the appropriate level and content of self-interest must be clarified, to allow limited self-interest without provoking suspicion of partial compliance.

Deliberation about means

To be legitimate, decisions must be made by voters with the appropriate preferences, who are informed about the available policy alternatives, and the candidates' performance and promises. Deliberation in this sense, scrutinizing such claims, improves the chance that voters identify the best policy choices, and the best candidates, among those available. There are at least four reasons for this.[3]

- *Option creation.* Deliberation may help identify better alternatives, for instance by discovering trade-offs and side payments for mutual gain. This is consistent with recent bargaining theory, which suggests that public discussion – or the use of trusted mediators – is helpful for discovering areas of mutual gain and opportunities for linked bargains (cf. Raiffa 1982; Lax and Sebenius 1986).
- *Option assessment.* Deliberative procedures can improve voters' assessments of existing policy choices. Miller holds that 'deliberative democracy has the resources to attenuate the social choice problems faced by the political community' (1992: 60). The reason is that many rankings are eliminated through three reasons: fact checks which remove preferences based on false beliefs; through the condition of publicity which removes morally repugnant preferences; and through requirements of universalizability: 'To be seen to be engaged in political debate we must argue in terms that any other participant would potentially accept, and "It's good for me" is not such an argument' (61). The main point seems sound, though important social choice problems may well remain, as noted by Nino (1996).
- *Option choice.* Voters of good will are more likely to cast their votes according to their conception of the common interest when they are convinced, through public debate, that they know what choice it requires. David Miller underscores this role of deliberation even after deliberation has changed the preferences expressed in votes:

  > finally when a decision has to be reached there may still need to be a vote taken between two or more options, what participants are doing at that point is something like rendering a judgement or a verdict on the basis of what they have heard. They are expressing an opinion about

which policy best meets the various claims that have been advanced, or represents the fairest compromise between the competing points of view that have been expressed.

(Miller 1992: 55–56)

It is unclear why Miller's conjecture will always be the case. There is no guarantee that voters who through deliberation are more likely to *understand* the common good, *always* will vote accordingly. The more cautious claim seems more plausible.

• *Constraints on the majority*. Deliberation can also indicate the limits to majority rule. Public deliberation can identify weaknesses of majoritarian decisions. Consider Brian Barry's argument for majority rule (Barry 1991). He claims that majority rule is wise under four conditions: when there is only one decision, only two alternatives, when the constituency is not open to doubt, and when the outcome is not of vital importance. The majority principle itself offers no guidance for identifying which issues should be on the agenda, the set of alternatives, the constituency, or the set of vital interests which should be kept off the agenda. Public deliberation may provide answers to these important questions, and remind people that under majority rule no one should be permanently in the minority. This may also be Miller's point, when he claims that:

> The emphasis in the deliberative conception is on the way in which a process of open discussion in which all points of view can be heard may legitimate the outcome when this is seen to reflect the discussion that has preceded it, not on deliberation as a discovery procedure in search of a correct answer.

(Miller 1992: 57)

The challenge for Miller is to show how the outcome 'reflects' the discussion, beyond for instance identifying the alternatives.

Democratic deliberation at the European level?

The reasons in favour of deliberation for interest formation rests on assumptions that are presently less plausible at the European level than at the national level (see Schlesinger and Kevin, this volume, for a careful consideration of these arguments). The opacity of European institutions, the present lack of a well-developed European public space, and the relative absence of European political parties reduce the opportunities for character formation, and limit the informational bases and range of political choice. Additional problems arise in the scenario of multiple Europes – that is, extensionally different sets of Member States forming a 'Defence Europe', 'Common Currency Europe', 'Human Rights Europe'. Different arenas for public deliberation may arise clustered around each functional regime, without arenas for addressing the issues arising across functions. Segments of citizens, including those in small states, harbour reasonable fears of becoming permanent minorities in the absence of trans-sectoral arenas for public deliberation.

One might hope that the Principle of Subsidiarity as found in the Amsterdam Treaty alleviates some of these hindrances to democratic deliberation, and brings the European Union closer to the citizens. However, the Amsterdam conception of subsidiarity has characteristics which suggest that high hopes are premature.

Traditions of subsidiarity

To get a better grasp of the features of the Amsterdam conception of Subsidiarity it can be contrasted to five alternative theories of subsidiarity, each of which has different implications both for institutional arrangements and for the role of political deliberation. The five accounts draw on insights from Althusius, the American Confederalists, Economic Federalism, Catholic Personalism, and Liberal Contractualism, respectively (Føllesdal 1998b). These accounts may regard subsidiarity as *proscribing* or prescribing central intervention, apply subsidiarity to the *allocation* of political powers or to their *exercise*, and *add* or *remove* issues from the sphere of political decision-making altogether. Some of these features reduce the room for democratic deliberation, while some may foster deliberation.

Liberty: Althusius

Althusius, 'the father of federalism', developed an embryonic theory of subsidiarity drawing on Orthodox Calvinism. Communities and associations are instrumentally and intrinsically important for supporting ('subsidia') the needs of the holy lives of individuals. Political authority arises on the basis of covenants among associations. The role of the state is to co-ordinate and secure symbiosis among associations on a consensual basis. The notion of symbiosis may be interpreted as requiring deliberation about common ends among sub-units, since it involves 'explicit or tacit agreement, to mutual communication of whatever is useful and necessary for the harmonious exercise of social life' (Althusius 1614: Chapter 28). At the same time, Althusius recognized that deliberation will not always yield agreement, particularly not in matters of faith. In such cases, he counselled religious toleration:

> the magistrate who is not able, without peril to the commonwealth, to change or overcome the discrepancy in religion and creed ought to tolerate the dissenters for the sake of public peace and tranquillity, blinking his eyes and permitting them to exercise unapproved religion.
>
> (Althusius 1614: Chapter 28)

This interpretation of subsidiarity would appear to take the existing sub-units for granted – a feature it shares with Amsterdam Subsidiarity. While this account allows for negotiation among sub-unit representatives based on existing preferences, agreement on ends is not expected – which is why subsidiarity is required in the first place. Althusian subsidiarity thus seems based on a fundamental pessimism regarding the complete obliteration of disagreement by means of preference formation through deliberation.

Liberty: American Confederalists

Similar conclusions emerge from confederal arguments for subsidiarity based on the fear of tyranny. On this view, individuals should be free to choose in matters where no others are harmed. This is thought to be best secured by decentralized government enjoying veto powers. Thus sub-units may veto decisions, or super-majoritarian mechanisms must be established. An added reason for local politics often found in this tradition is that participation – and possibly subsidiarity – might be thought to facilitate learning and to secure political virtue, clearly embracing preference formation.

Two drawbacks of this view should be mentioned. Firstly, the exclusive focus on tyranny as the sole ill to be avoided is questionable. In the context of the European Union, similarly, abuse of centralized powers is not the only risk: inability to secure necessary common action is also a threat.

Secondly, as Madison pointed out, the plight of minorities is uncertain, since it is unlikely that smaller units are completely homogeneous. Indeed, tyranny may emerge more easily in small groups. It might also be easier for minorities to muster courage in larger settings (Sanders 1997).

Regarding deliberation, let us note that there is room for deliberation regarding ends within sub-units, but not between them. Thus subsidiarity and veto powers may reduce opportunities and need for agreement, rendering such solutions unattractive for discourse democrats. If we agree that it is easier to reach agreement about ends in local polities, i.e. that individuals are likely to come to agreement on ultimate values, this may be an argument for subsidiarity. Montesquieu (1748) held that common interest is easier to see in a smaller setting. We may note that Scharpf (1988) makes similar arguments for subsidiarity in the European Union.

Agreement may be easier to reach in small democracies with homogeneity of socio-economic circumstances and closed borders, where politicians are less likely to pursue own advantage, and where demands are stable over time. However, these conditions are unlikely – as the American Federalist debate made clear. Perfect homogeneity is never achieved and:

> the fewer the distinct parties and interests, the more frequently will a majority be found of the same party; and the smaller the number of individuals composing a majority, and the smaller the compass within which they are placed, the more easily will they concert and execute their plans of oppression.
>
> (Madison 1787)

These risks should be kept in mind when considering the deliberative implications of Amsterdam Subsidiarity.

A final implication for deliberation of this kind of subsidiarity might be illustrated by Montesquieu's suggestion, that once agreement was secured by homogeneity in sub-units, this should be combined with a limited central agenda. For instance, an agreement on the common end of defence should move on to a discussion of the best means of defence, rather than a more expansive discussion of other common ends (Beer 1993: 230). In effect this argument supports a proscriptive version of subsidiarity, and limits deliberation of ends from the outset. It is similar to the Amsterdam conception of subsidiarity in that the objectives of co-operation are laid down in advance.

Efficiency: Economic Federalism

This theory of subsidiarity holds that powers and burdens of public goods should be placed with the populations that benefit from them. Decentralized government is to be preferred insofar as a) local decisions prevent overload, or b) targeted provision of public goods is more efficient in economic terms. This conception of subsidiarity seems to match the Euro-sceptics' wariness of European co-operation – though they might object to the label 'federalism'.

This theory is concerned with competence allocation, and provides standards for sub-unit identification and tasks. Sub-units do not enjoy veto powers, since free-riding individual sub-units may be overruled to ensure efficient co-ordination and production of public goods, namely non-excludable and inexhaustible goods. Weaknesses of this view include the following: it is limited in scope to such public goods. Moreover, it suffers from the standard weaknesses of economic theory regarded as a theory of normative legitimacy. Standard economic theory does not address the important issue of preference formation, and relies on Pareto improvements from given utility levels, ignoring the pervasive impact of unfair starting positions.

Deliberation about means and strategic co-operation is important on this view, partly in order to determine win–win situations. The focus on expressed preferences without regard for how the preferences develop sets this approach apart from deliberative democracy. Also note that arguments of economic federalism may recommend that issues are removed from democratic and political control, and left to market mechanisms or other non-political arrangements within sub-units. Finally, of relevance for Amsterdam Subsidiarity, we may note that this argument questions the presumption in favour of Member States as the appropriate sub-units, and instead supports placing powers with sub-state regions. Subsidiarity, on this view, may go 'all the way down'.

Justice: Catholic Personalism

The Catholic tradition of subsidiarity is expressed clearly in the 1891 Encyclica *Rerum Novarum*, and further developed in the 1931 Encyclica *Quadragesimo Anno* against fascism. The Catholic Church sought protection against socialism, yet protested capitalist exploitation of the poor. As developed in Personalism, a tradition which influenced Delors, the human good is to develop and realize one's potential as made in the image of God. Voluntary interaction is required to find one's role and promote one's good. A hierarchy of associations allow persons to develop skills and talents, and assist those in need. The state must serve the common interest, and intervene to further individuals' autonomy.

Subsidiarity should regulate both competence allocation and exercise. It allows both territorial and functional applications of the principle, possibly placing issues outside of the scope of democratic politics. Sub-units do not enjoy veto rights, and interpretation of subsidiarity may be entrusted to the centre unit.

Christian Democratic governments and the European People's Party hold views on subsidiarity close to this, for instance supporting just wage constraints on market economies.

This view rests on contested conceptions of the social order as willed by God, and of the human good as a particular mode of human flourishing. Thus it cannot settle beyond reasonable disagreement which sub-units and cleavages should be embedded – e.g. families, or labour unions – and what their responsibilities should be regarding care for infirm, wages, or unemployment. Deliberation might reduce these disagreements for purposes of reaching public consensus.

This theory recognizes an important role for deliberation, both so that individuals and social groups may discover their proper function, and in the exercise of powers regulated by considerations of subsidiarity. This aspect is shared by Amsterdam Subsidiarity, which holds in paragraph (1) that subsidiarity primarily regulates how institutions exercise their powers, and not how these powers should be allocated. However, the Catholic view would deny that standards and functions are determined by deliberation, paralleling Amsterdam Subsidiarity in that the objectives of the social order are to be taken as given. Aspects of the natural social order are at most discovered, and not constituted, by deliberation.

A Liberal Contractualist case for subsidiarity

Liberal Contractualism of the kind associated with Rawls, Scanlon or Barry might acknowledge a limited role for subsidiarity. Socialization into a sense of justice is important. However, this does not amount to full-fledged support for a Principle of Subsidiarity. Even though political virtue must be fostered, possibly through political participation, local democracy need not be given priority in the form of subsidiarity as long as some learning takes place locally.

Two other arguments within this tradition provide better support for subsidiarity. Firstly, individuals must be acknowledged to have an interest in controlling the social institutions that in turn shape their values, goals, options and expectations. Such political influence secures and promotes two important interests. Agreeing with the republican claim of Confederalists, it protects our interest in avoiding domination by others. In modern polities this risk is reduced by a broad dispersion of procedural control. And control over institutional change serves to maintain our legitimate expectations. We have an interest in regulating the speed and direction of institutional change. This interest is secured by ensuring our informed participation, to reduce the risk of false expectations. When individuals share circumstances, beliefs or values, they have a *prima facie* claim to share control over institutional change to prevent subjection and breaking of legitimate expectations. Those similarly affected are more likely to comprehend the need and room for change. Insofar as this holds true of members of sub-units, there is a case for subsidiarity. However, this account does not single out Member States as the only relevant sub-units, contrary to Amsterdam Subsidiarity.

The second argument for subsidiarity concerns its role in character formation. The Principle of Subsidiarity can foster and structure political argument and bargaining in ways beneficial to public deliberation, and to the character formation required to sustain a just political order. By requiring impact statements and arguments of comparative efficiency, Amsterdam Subsidiarity facilitates the socialization of individuals into the requisite sense of justice and concern for the common good. For this purpose the Principle of Subsidiarity need not provide standards for the resolution of issues, as long as it requires public arguments about the legitimate status of sub-units, the proper common goal, and the likely effects of sub-unit and centre-unit action.

This argument underdetermines subsidiarity. That is: other rules for the exercise of political power could serve the same purpose, which is to ensure public argument about shared ends and suitable means, leading to preference adjustment. Furthermore, this argument must be supplemented by theories of institutional design in order to suggest suitable institutional reforms. Whether sub-units should enjoy veto, votes or only voice is a matter of the likely institutional effects on character formation, and on the likely distributive effects.

Summary: subsidiarity improving deliberation

In light of these brief sketches, we may conclude that Amsterdam Subsidiarity may improve the deliberative aspects of democratic decision-making. This is in accordance with some deliberative theorists, who prefer decentralization and direct democracy (Bohman 1999: 20). Thus Miller seeks a 'reshaping of those [liberal democratic] institutions in the light of a different regulative ideal', including subsidiarity to allocate decisions downwards to the sub-constituencies according to who are affected (Miller 1992: 54, 67). The five accounts of subsidiarity sketched above suggest several reasons to support these claims that subsidiarity and deliberative democracy are compatible and indeed mutually supportive.

- Sub-units are better able to secure shared interests, particularly if shared geography, resources, culture or other features make for similar interests and policy choices among members of the sub-units. *Option assessment* and *option choice* are facilitated.

- A reduction of issues on the agenda and parties to agreements serve to reduce the risk of information overload, and foster joint gains. *Preference formation, option assessment* and *option choice* are made easier.
- The deliberation fostered by subsidiarity can help build community, partly by *preference formation* towards the common good. The deliberation about ends also supports an important sense of community for a minority, that these decisions are 'ours', and can foster a sense among the majority about *majority constraints*. Deliberation may thus enforce the boundary within which majoritarianism is accepted as a legitimate decision procedure (cf. Miller 1995: 257; Manin 1987: 352).
- Subsidiarity helps protect against subjection and domination by others, by proscribing intervention into local affairs. *Option choice* is fostered.
- Deliberation outside direct political control may be warranted by considerations of subsidiarity, since it allows for *preference formation* without the risks associated with political domination. Thus Habermas stresses the importance of deliberation in the public sphere, rather than deliberation in state institutions. This can be said to express a non-territorial application of subsidiarity, where some important aspects of preference formation are placed outside political control.

Subsidiarity versus deliberation?

This final section considers some unresolved dilemmas between Amsterdam Subsidiarity and deliberative democracy. Classical features of democratic rule – free agenda setting and accountability – appear to conflict with political orders as regulated by Amsterdam Subsidiarity. Some of these objections are presented only to be rebutted. Other criticisms survive scrutiny. In particular, the Amsterdam conception of subsidiarity embeds states in ways incompatible with deliberative democracy, and it remains an open question whether the present institutions can foster the requisite trans-European values and commitments.

Agenda setting

Subsidiarity constrains political agenda in ways which might appear incompatible with fundamental norms of democratic theory, by moving some issues away from democratic control in the same way as federal arrangements split the agenda (Dahl 1983: 95–105). Constraints on the political agenda are of course particularly worrisome if some affected parties are not part of the sub-unit which deliberates and decides. However, when subsidiarity regulates the allocation of competencies, the agenda of political discourse is reduced correspondingly. This immunity from majority control is indeed central to several arguments for subsidiarity, and is crucial for the protection of minorities and other protections of individuals through legal powers and immunities (Lijphart 1991).

In response, we must first note that the alternatives to splitting competencies are also problematic. Allocation of competencies according to who is affected makes for an opaque distribution of authority. The problem is that it easily leads to overlapping and competing jurisdictions of 'communication flows' (Habermas 1992b: 11, and Schlesinger and Kevin, this volume).

From the point of view of liberal political theory, the removal of some issues from day-to-day political debate is not necessarily to be regretted. Surely, allegiance to the political system may be threatened if everything can be put on the agenda. If the elected representatives are able to redefine the basic rights of all, or revoke minority protections, trust may not be forthcoming. More importantly, constitutional protections and competence allocations by such means as subsidiarity do not remove issues from public debate, even though the issues are taken off the day-to-day political agenda. Thus some objections to constitutional constraints should be reconsidered. Dryzek, for one, argues against constitutional guarantees which violate a claim to 'unconstrained political debate' which should allow discussion of 'the authority of prior norms or requirements' (Dryzek 1990: 170). But constitutional constraints on the political agenda, for instance by a constitutional court, remove issues from ordinary legislative debate, but do not remove issues from political debate *tout court*. Instead, such measures may serve to give notice to the public that the political process now yields extraordinary effects; or that the unintended systemic effects of political decisions now cross certain limits defined as trigger issues by a constitution. Such warnings do not stifle political debate. To the contrary, they may indicate that further public deliberation is in order, for there are ways of revising the constitution or the Union treaties. Such procedures typically involve further political debate and deliberation, and further opportunities for reconsideration, than the deliberations required for ordinary legislation (Ackerman 1988: 192, and cf. Sunstein 1994: 13–14). Requisite arenas for public constitutional deliberation must be present – a requirement which is not satisfied as yet in the European Union (cf. Schlesinger and Kevin, this volume).

These considerations aside, there are clear risks in limiting local or central agendas, e.g. through rights. The current allocation of authority between the EU and Member States is biased in favour of some conception of the proper relations between Member States and the Community, which may not be legitimate (Femia 1996: 370). Other divisions than those based on citizenship – class, gender, profession or age – might be more appropriate for certain issues, but states are identified in the treaties as the main sub-units. We consider these issues further below.

Moreover, institutional arrangements for reassigning competencies must be available. Miller suggests that this task might be handled better by deliberation than by other means. Apparently, only deliberative democracy reveals what sort of issue is at hand – whether it is indeed a topic where:

> personal preferences should reasonably play a large role in deciding them. This will be true of many ordinary public goods, for instance. If we have to

make a budget allocation as between football pitches and the swimming pool in the local park, the main consideration is likely to be the general direction and strength of preference between these options. ... this is a case where the role of deliberation is to identify a procedure for making a decision rather than to arrive at a substantive agreed judgement.

... deliberative democracy, precisely because the content of people's preferences emerges in the course of deliberation, can in theory select the decision procedure most appropriate to the case in hand.

(Miller 1992: 66)

On Miller's argument, observe that it is unclear whether such deliberations avoid the problems of partial compliance and strategic arguments shared by deliberative democracy and integrative bargaining. Individuals may reasonably fear that others will promote principles which favour them, in the guise of allegedly reasonable principles. A second concern arises if we grant that deliberative democracy might in theory be better equipped to select procedures, and allocate authorities. Still, empirically informed arguments are needed to support Miller's view about the likely effects of deliberative procedures for institutional redesign and competence reallocation.

Accountability

A further challenge to some applications of subsidiarity stems from the requirement of accountability. Subsidiarity can prevent the public from placing responsibility for actions on particular officials, who may appeal to vague and complex notions of comparative effectiveness and limited room for independent action. Such responses hinder accountable government. This opacity may occur when competencies are shared between sub-units and central units, as in the European Union, or when the principle of subsidiarity guides discretion without making the deliberations public. These features also hinder the desired effects of subsidiarity on preference formation.

In response, we may note that Amsterdam Subsidiarity partly alleviates these fears by requiring public, substantiated arguments for comparative effectiveness of central action (paragraph 4). However, the objection points to general challenges to institutionalizing deliberative democracy. The information required for making and assessing claims for centralization is exceedingly complex, and relies in part on counterfactual hypotheses. Recall that Amsterdam Subsidiarity requires a comparison of the likely effects of decentralized action with the effects of central action, assessed by some standard of efficiency. Information overload threatens. On the other hand, withholding information also violates precepts of democratic deliberation. Robert Dahl warns against institutionalizing deliberative democracy on such grounds: as long as governments fail to inform the public about the problems of health care services, well-grounded political choices are impossible (Dahl 1997). A major challenge of liberal, deliberative institutional design is thus to enhance the public's ability to hold officials accountable.

Equality vs democratic sovereignty

We may also note a problem which arises for subsidiarity from the perspective of egalitarian political theories, such as John Rawls' theory of Justice as Fairness (Rawls 1971). For such theories it would appear that few distributive decisions should be left to sub-units and domestic democratic institutions. Instead such theories support centralization and uniformity of several policies. These egalitarian distributive implications are consistent with the EU objective to 'promote ... economic and social cohesion and solidarity among Member States' (Art 2 ECT). But this egalitarianism appears to conflict both with our judgements regarding the priority of compatriots (Beitz 1983) and with the traditional scope of domestic sovereignty, since egalitarianism puts drastic constraints on the legitimate outcomes of democratic decision-making.

An unresolved challenge to the egalitarian objective concerns whether and how to reduce differences in living conditions across Member States when some differences may be due to costly local policy choices made according to the principle of subsidiarity. Given that some egalitarian objectives are found in the treaties, Amsterdam Subsidiarity might support Community action which overrides such local variations. However, Member States then risk a complete erosion of such kinds of autonomy that matter.

As a preliminary response, the egalitarian commitment requires careful delineation of which goods and burdens must be secured on an equal basis across sub-units. Furthermore, this commitment to equal respect may allow some democratically generated distributive variations among sub-units. It remains, however, an open question whether the best justification for equal political control among Europeans also supports equal shares of other goods and benefits – and how this egalitarianism is to be squared with subsidiarity.

The tension between equality and sub-unit autonomy points to a central problem of Amsterdam Subsidiarity: the status of states.

Political equality: among persons or states?

Subsidiarity arrangements often grant small states powers beyond what the number of inhabitants should suggest, so too in the European Union. Historically, in the EU and in other systems of pooled sovereignty, the prominent role of states is no doubt due to the historical bargain that took place among the formally equal sovereign joining members. This feature ensured the concerns of smaller states within the community. Such arrangements seem illegitimate, as they violate the ideal of one person, one vote. Note, however, that such discrepancies between voting powers of individuals are not a necessary feature of subsidiarity or of federal arrangements. David Hume, in defending a federal design, suggested electorates of equal size. However, the apparent anti-egalitarian feature occurs when sub-units are of different sizes – as is the case in Europe.

The future institutional design of the EU is at stake. In order to increase the equal influence of citizens, institutional reform could increase the powers of the

European Parliament, a 'federal' institution. Furthermore, the electoral bases of the seats should be reallocated to equalize representation, roughly reflecting the influence of the population of Spain. The populations of Germany, the United Kingdom, Italy and France should then receive seats from the rest. This conception of political equality also suggests that state votes in the Council of the European Union should reflect population size. Thus the influence of large states should be increased so that individuals of those states gain more equal control over the conditions shaping their lives.

Alternatively, 'peoples', that is states, should be represented as equals in federal arrangements. From this perspective, small states should continue to wield power irrespective of population size. The question might then be whether Germany, with 10 votes in the Council, are too influential in comparison to Luxembourg's two and Ireland's three – even though Germany has a population more than 200 times that of Luxembourg and 22 times that of Ireland.

One might argue that such federal features can be endorsed by considerations of subsidiarity, in that they allow states to protect their vital 'national interests' through co-operation restricted by veto powers and blocking abilities. A defence of this kind must indicate how a system of checks and balances serves these ends, and how it constrains the day-to-day political bargaining between tiers, possibly giving the bargaining more of a deliberative bent. The grounds for veto or blocking must be specified, perhaps through a list of individual and state rights. A definite list of the objectives of the federation, coupled with a Principle of Subsidiarity, must provide further guidance. Such an account must draw on a theory indicating which interests and values are at stake, and what are the legitimate ends of state and federal institutions. However, these 'national' interests must be specified in terms of the interests of individuals. Why should states otherwise enjoy political powers? After all, democratic deliberation is fundamentally concerned not with the interests of states but the interests of persons.

In response, skewed representation can be justified on one of two grounds compatible with deliberative democracy. Such arrangements can ensure that representatives of all affected parties are able to participate as equals in the deliberations. States' representatives present the views and interests of citizens, and it is not obvious that proportional representation is required. Instead, skewed voting weights, veto, double majorities or qualified majority mechanisms, typical of federal arrangements, may be appropriate to give citizens of small states both voice and clout.

Alternatively, one might argue that states are appropriate units for controlling cultural and institutional change. Small states may properly be over-represented in federal decision-making bodies, since equal concern for the similar interests of all is sometimes appropriately secured by allowing citizens of small states to enjoy influence in deliberative settings beyond what their population size should entail. Citizens of small states are threatened in other ways than citizens of populous states. For instance, if decisions were made by majority vote, small states will tend to be permanent policy-takers rather than policy-makers, risking massive and systematic changes to the expectations of their citizens. It therefore seems acceptable to allow small states extra opportunities for voicing concerns and receiving a fair hearing for their arguments, for instance through disproportionate votes, or by veto rights.

To illustrate how subsidiarity might be defended along this line, recall that subsidiarity insulates sub-units from majority rule in the larger polity, by offering sub-units a veto or by separating competencies. This effect is similar to that of consociational arrangements (Lijphart 1979); and federal arrangements (Dahl 1983). True, majority rule is constrained. But for deliberative democrats, this is not an objection, since it is not clear that the preferences of the majority should always win out. What matters is that the interests of all should be secured to an acceptable degree, after preference formation through public deliberation has run its course. Majoritarianism is plausible when everybody benefits acceptably in the long run (Barry 1991). One problem arises for minorities in polities with deep structural cleavages. Two assumptions in favour of majority rule are broken for permanent minorities in small Member States: their chances of being in the majority are not equal to the chances for citizens of larger states, and the compounded outcome of several decisions against their votes can amount to major disadvantages for them. Subsidiarity would secure these minorities control over such issues among others.

Liberal theories of the kind explored here recognize that majoritarianism poses risks, even when we grant an important role for democratic deliberation. If possible, institutions should protect against miscarriages of deliberation wrought by partial compliance with the norm of voting one's conception of the common interest. Institutional safeguards should protect against these risks.

Why are states the appropriate sub-units?

This strategy in defence of subsidiarity against majoritarianism highlights a problem for Amsterdam Subsidiarity. The case for states as sub-units remains to be made. Given pluralism of values and shared circumstances both within and across state borders, claims that states should be privileged parties regulated by Amsterdam Subsidiarity must be substantiated better than as yet. Why allocate powers precisely at the level of nation-states, rather than insisting that decisions must be local? It would seem that subsidiarity sometimes should go 'all the way down', at least to the various regions of states, as argued by the Committee of the Regions. Individuals' concern for political control suggests precisely that jurisdiction should be local except insofar as larger scale arrangements are required for co-ordination or externalities.

State governments have traditionally enjoyed control over institutional design, so citizens' expectations have to a large extent reflected the domestic institutions and cultures. As primary implementors of policies, these governments are also the most plausible agents of Union directives. Yet this does not mean that state governments are the primary locus for shared purposes and goals. Pluralism of cultures and values within states suggest that they are too large and heterogeneous for inhabitants to agree to common ends. Indeed, regional unrest and regionally based political parties indicate that the unit of the state is too large. Moreover, permanent minorities within states, such as migrant workers, cultural minorities or the unemployed, have needs that are not secured by Amsterdam Subsidiarity. It regulates co-decisions by states and the Community, and does not recognize other units. Arguments for subsidiarity as explored in the third section can support non-territorial representation in some functional areas, since non-state units may be better equipped to ensure efficacious responses.

A central problem with Amsterdam Subsidiarity is thus that it embeds states even further, together with any injustice that exists between them, for instance unfair shares of resources. Amsterdam Subsidiarity perpetrates the original status of groups clustered by state borders, freezing patterns, rather than accommodating groups under common institutions as counselled by some deliberative democrats (cf. de Beus 1997, and Eriksen this volume). The embedded partitioning may limit mutual respect, and reduce the interest in political participation beyond sub-units, as witnessed in consociational arrangements (Lijphart 1979, cf. de Beus 1997). The problem from the point of view of deliberative democracy is not that some groups have counter-majoritarian power, but that the *wrong* groups may have it. Those likely to benefit unfairly from unjust advantages may enjoy disproportionate control over political decisions, and they may be insulated from the processes of public preference formation. Insofar as the present system of nation-states in Europe is taken for granted, Amsterdam Subsidiarity does nothing to alleviate such injustices.

How secure support for polity-wide values and solidarity?

A second problem with the status of states in Amsterdam Subsidiarity has to do not with the lack of justification, but with problematic and unintended effects. It is unclear that stability and support for basic democratic values is likely across Europe, if local cultures and political culture flourish within Member States, but not between them.

This is indeed one reason why one may object to subsidiarity, consociational democracy and other quasi-federal arrangements which embed, rather than remove, entrenched divides among inhabitants. Borders between sub-units may limit mutual respect, and limited political participation beyond the sub-unit. Appeals to a historically shared European identity is unhelpful for these purposes. Indeed, several writers note that the essence of Europe in fact is diversity and complexity of localized societies (Kundera 1984; Enzenberger 1987), with competing attempts at redefining the concept of Europe (Wæver 1990). Thus the quest for shared values, identities and loyalties through deliberation may be arduous and yield few suggestions about the ends of Europe.

The significance of this worry depends on the extent that shared values and commitments are needed in a polity. If 'thicker' sentiments are needed, as e.g.

indicated by David Miller (1995), this may challenge subsidiarity. On the other hand, Habermas' 'Constitutional Patriotism' may make modest demands on empathy and compassion. Empathy generated on the basis of shared history or deliberation plays a small role. On this point, we might agree with Habermas' recommendation, that 'our task is less to reassure ourselves of our common origins in the European Middle Ages than to develop a new political self-confidence commensurate with the role of Europe in the world of the twenty-first century' (Habermas 1992b:12).

Of course, it also remains to be seen what sort of institutional arrangements can foster Europe-wide deliberation. Interaction in a shared public sphere might be necessary to foster and maintain mutual respect and solidarity. Considerations of subsidiarity might support local deliberation and action, either to foster the required shared sense of justice (Blichner and Sangolt 1994), or because Amsterdam Subsidiarity requires a comparison of the effects of Member States acting on their own, with the effects of common action. The comparisons required by Amsterdam Subsidiarity may *require* domestic deliberation about common ends and proper means. We should also be aware that this practice of justification may become a model for domestic political decision-making.

Insofar as popular support for institutions is required, considerations of subsidiarity might also require local measures to ensure support for whatever common endeavours are needed. Thus, if a common political culture must be developed among all members of the polity, including a commitment to justice or the European common-weal (Habermas 1992b: 9), this is no objection to subsidiarity in general. However, it may be a problem for Amsterdam Subsidiarity insofar as that conception of subsidiarity limits the interaction between citizens of different Member States.

One lesson to be drawn is that important dilemmas may occur where system capacity suggests centralization, while deliberative preference formation requires local decision-making. In the European Union, cumulative impact of policies and responses to international market competition suggests central responses. At the same time, there is still reason to doubt whether individuals across the EU are able to achieve deliberative agreement in the relative absence of European public spheres. The Principle of Subsidiarity as expressed in the Amsterdam Treaty offers little hope for resolving these issues.

Deliberation and subsidiarity may both be crucial components of a legitimate European order securing the equal dignity of all Europeans. The tensions and risks suggest that there is a long way to go. Three main challenges have been identified. Amsterdam Subsidiarity must be applied transparently and accountably. Member States are institutionally entrenched in ways difficult to justify by any theory of subsidiarity. This is particularly problematic in the absence of procedures for institutional redesign and competence reallocation. The task of generating and maintaining the requisite trans-European values and commitments is a daunting challenge, given the current flaws of a European public sphere. European institutions may one day embody the ideals of deliberative democracy and subsidiarity, and secure and express respect for all Europeans as equals. Careful and public deliberation is needed to get us there.

Appendix

Protocol on the application of the principles of subsidiarity and proportionality, in Amsterdam Treaty 1997

The high contracting parties

Determined to establish the conditions for the application of the principles of subsidiarity and proportionality enshrined in Article 3b of the Treaty establishing the European Community with a view to defining more precisely the criteria for applying them and to ensure their strict observance and consistent implementation by all institutions;

Wishing to ensure that decisions are taken as closely as possible to the citizens of the Union;

Taking account of the Interinstitutional Agreement of 25 October 1993 between the European Parliament, the Council and the Commission on procedures for implementing the principle of subsidiarity;

Have confirmed that the conclusions of the Birmingham European Council on 16 October 1992 and the overall approach to the application of the subsidiarity principle agreed by the European Council meeting in Edinburgh on 11–12 December 1992 will continue to guide the action of the Union's institutions as well as the development of the application of the principle of subsidiarity, and, for this purpose,

Have agreed upon the following provisions which shall be annexed to the Treaty establishing the European Community:

(1) In exercising the powers conferred on it, each institution shall ensure that the principle of subsidiarity is complied with. It shall also ensure compliance with the principle of proportionality, according to which any action by the Community shall not go beyond what is necessary to achieve the objectives of the Treaty.

(2) The application of the principles of subsidiarity and proportionality shall respect the general provisions and the objectives of the Treaty, particularly as regards the maintaining in full of the acquis communautaire and the institutional balance; it shall not affect the principles developed by the Court of Justice regarding the relationship between national and Community law, and it should take into account Article F (4) of the Treaty on European Union, according to which 'the Union shall provide itself

with the means necessary to attain its objectives and carry through its policies'.

(3) The principle of subsidiarity does not call into question the powers conferred on the European Community by the Treaty, as interpreted by the Court of Justice. The criteria referred to in the second paragraph of Article 3b of the Treaty shall relate to areas for which the Community does not have exclusive competence. The principle of subsidiarity provides a guide as to how those powers are to be exercised at the Community level. Subsidiarity is a dynamic concept and should be applied in the light of the objectives set out in the Treaty. It allows Community action within the limits of its powers to be expanded where circumstances so require, and conversely, to be restricted or discontinued where it is no longer justified.

(4) For any proposed Community legislation, the reasons on which it is based shall be stated with a view to justifying its compliance with the principles of subsidiarity and proportionality; the reasons for concluding that a Community objective can be better achieved by the Community must be substantiated by qualitative or, wherever possible, quantitative indicators.

(5) For Community action to be justified, both aspects of the subsidiarity principle shall be met: the objectives of the proposed action cannot be sufficiently achieved by Member States' action in the framework of their national constitutional system and can therefore be better achieved by action on the part of the Community.

The following guidelines should be used in examining whether the abovementioned condition is fulfilled:

- the issue under consideration has transnational aspects which cannot be satisfactorily regulated by action by Member States;
- actions by Member States alone or lack of Community action would conflict with the requirements of the Treaty (such as the need to correct distortion of competition or avoid disguised restrictions on trade or strengthen economic and social cohesion) or would otherwise significantly damage Member States' interests;
- action at Community level would produce clear benefits by reason of its scale or effects compared with action at the level of the Member States.

(6) The form of Community action shall be as simple as possible, consistent with satisfactory achievement of the objective of the measure and the need for effective enforcement. The Community shall legislate only to the extent necessary. Other things being equal, directives should be preferred to regulations and framework directives to detailed measures. Directives as provided for in Article 189 of the Treaty, while binding upon each Member State to which they are addressed as to the result to be achieved, shall leave to the national authorities the choice of form and methods.

(7) Regarding the nature and the extent of Community action, Community measures should leave as much scope for national decision as possible, consistent with securing the aim of the measure and observing the require-

ments of the Treaty. While respecting Community law, care should be taken to respect well established national arrangements and the organization and working of Member States' legal systems. Where appropriate and subject to the need for proper enforcement, Community measures should provide Member States with alternative ways to achieve the objectives of the measures.

(8) Where the application of the principle of subsidiarity leads to no action being taken by the Community, Member States are required in their action to comply with the general rules laid down in Article 5 of the Treaty, by taking all appropriate measures to ensure fulfilment of their obligations under the Treaty and by abstaining from any measure which could jeopardize the attainment of the objectives of the Treaty.

(9) Without prejudice to its right of initiative, the Commission should:

- except in cases of particular urgency or confidentiality, consult widely before proposing legislation and, wherever appropriate, publish consultation documents;
- justify the relevance of its proposals with regard to the principle of subsidiarity; whenever necessary, the explanatory memorandum accompanying a proposal will give details in this respect. The financing of Community action in whole or in part from the Community budget shall require an explanation;
- take duly into account the need for any burden, whether financial or administrative, falling upon the Community, national governments, local authorities, economic operators and citizens, to be minimized and proportionate to the objective to be achieved;
- submit an annual report to the European Council, the European Parliament and the Council on the application of Article 3b of the Treaty. This annual report shall also be sent to the Committee of the Regions and to the Economic and Social Committee.

(10) The European Council shall take account of the Commission report referred to in the fourth indent of point 9 within the report on the progress achieved by the Union which it is required to submit to the European Parliament in accordance with Article D of the Treaty on European Union.

(11) While fully observing the procedures applicable, the European Parliament and the Council shall, as an integral part of the overall examination of Commission proposals, consider their consistency with Article 3b of the Treaty. This concerns the original Commission proposal as well as amendments which the European Parliament and the Council envisage making to the proposal.

(12) In the course of the procedures referred to in Articles 189b and 189c of the Treaty, the European Parliament shall be informed of the Council's position on the application of Article 3b of the Treaty, by way of a statement of the reasons which led the Council to adopt its common position. The Council shall inform the European Parliament of the reasons on the basis of

which all or part of a Commission proposal is deemed to be inconsistent with Article 3b of the Treaty.

(13) Compliance with the principle of subsidiarity shall be reviewed in accordance with the rules laid down by the Treaty.

Notes

1   I am grateful for comments at a conference in Bergen on Deliberative Democracy, and constructive suggestions from the editors and from Knut Midgaard. This paper is part of a project on Democracy and Citizenship under the auspices of ARENA, a research programme on the Europeanization of the nation-state.

2   Included as an appendix, above.

3   A distinct additional role of political deliberation associated with 'ideal pure procedural deliberation' should be noted. Sunstein holds that answers to political problems 'are understood to be correct through the only possible criterion, that is, agreement among equal citizens' (Sunstein 1993: 137). One reading of this claim is compatible with the arguments laid out above, that deliberation plays roles in preference formation, in discovering correct or good policy outcomes, and in enhancing majority mechanisms of preference aggregation. Such deliberation is the most reliable method for attaining correct answers. However, an additional claim may also be ascribed this position, regarded as 'ideal pure procedural deliberation' (Estlund 1989, 1997). On this interpretation, the standard for moral truth is constituted as the result of actual deliberation under certain conditions. These issues go beyond the arguments of concern in this paper. There are particular challenges to this view concerning why majority rule should be included as a democratic feature, and how to identify intentional and unintentional political abuse. These issues are not pursued here.

6 Constitution-making in the European Union

John Erik Fossum

Introduction

The purpose of this chapter is to discuss how comprehensive changes of a constitutional nature are legitimated in the European Union. The EU has gone through three such comprehensive changes since the mid 1980s, the Single European Act (SEA), the Treaty of European Union (TEU), and the Amsterdam Treaty. Many analysts claim that this almost continuous process of treaty-making or treaty change can best be conceived of as a process of constitution-making.[1] The EU has developed a system of law-making which is based on the principles of supremacy of EU law (within the EC's sphere of competence) and direct effect. This development presents the EU with a pressing problem of legitimacy. Joseph Weiler asserts that the 'condition of Europe ... is not, as is often implied, that of constitutionalism without a constitution, but of a constitution without constitutionalism. What Europe needs, thus, is not a constitution but an ethos and telos to justify, if they can, the constitutionalism it has already embraced' (Weiler 1995: 220, cf. Weiler 1999a). The basic challenge confronting the EU, then, is not that of its legality, but rather that of its weak legitimacy. Political legitimacy refers to popular approval and to how authority and approval can be justified, i.e. which normative principles that can be brought to bear on it.[2]

Following Weiler, there is a European constitutional structure but not a corresponding constitutional discourse. The EU has developed a set of binding norms and rules, but their principled and practical status is unclear and incomplete. They have not been properly debated. It is therefore reasonable to assume that there is a gap between the structure of rules and the arguments that are used to justify the rules. It is quite unlikely that such a gap or inconsistency can exist for very long. The main reason for this is that the EU has developed in such a manner as to seriously weaken or even undermine the manner in which it has been legitimated in the past. The legitimacy of the EU has generally been related to its outcomes and seen as 'indirect' or 'derivative', i.e. conditioned on the legitimacy of the democratic nation-states of which it is composed. Its own legitimacy has been foremost seen as based on its performance. This mode of legitimation has become problematic. First, the EU has emerged into a polity in its own right, however defined, and is no longer a mere derivative of the

Member States. The indirect or derivative mode of legitimation is thus inadequate. This is not only because the EU has become a polity, but also because this process has affected or even transformed the Member States so much that the question of the legitimacy of the democratic Member State can no longer be seen as separate from or independent of the EU. Second, legitimation through outcomes is based on performance, and as such is highly conditional. It can not draw on anything but actual performance and as such is highly unstable (Held 1987: 238). These two elements of change no doubt interact and make the problem of legitimacy one of the most important challenges presently facing the EU and its Member States.

In this chapter, I will examine how the question of the democratic legitimacy of the EU has been deliberated in the IGC-96 process, with particular emphasis on whether this can be seen to bridge the gap that Weiler identified between on the one hand the structure in place and on the other the reasons for why it is there and what its normative basis is. The chapter will address two related questions. First, how can this gap be bridged? Second, in what sense or to what extent can the IGC-96, which led to the Amsterdam Treaty, be deemed as an effort to bridge this gap?

With regard to the first question, it is necessary to clarify how constitution-making can be legitimated and specify criteria that permit us to identify the relevant arguments and reasons that can be given in support of these. Three approaches to legitimation can be identified, namely legitimation through outcomes, through values, and through rights. The relevant criteria refer to (a) utility; (b) values; or (c) rights. 'Utility' refers to ability to produce substantive results, in particular economic ones ('weak evaluations'). This approach to legitimacy is incomplete, at best. The two latter criteria, values and rights, explicitly refer to normative justifiability ('strong evaluations' (Taylor 1985, 1986)). As such, they can be used to bridge the gap. 'Value' refers to something which is seen to be valuable, or ethically salient, and which is important to a group's or community's sense of identity and conception of the good life 'Right' is a legal entity which presupposes mutual recognition and respect, which every rights holder is compelled to offer and essentially entitled to receive from other rights holders. In a modern democracy, rights ensure individual protection and participation and foster community-based allegiance and consent. In the next section these approaches to legitimation will be presented in further detail and applied to the EU, in order to clarify which arguments and reasons are associated with each. The two differ considerably, with regard to the sense of allegiance, the nature of arguments and reasons appealed to, and in terms of the nature of the polity that they envision.

With regard to the second question, I will examine arguments and reasons presented during the IGC-96 in order to clarify which of the three approaches to legitimation predominated. For the IGC-96 to constitute an effort to bridge the gap, we have to find evidence of a change from legitimation through outcomes to one or both of the other forms, namely legitimation through values or through rights.

How to study this? First, I will specify the three approaches to democratic legitimation which inform the three criteria and clarify their relevance to the EU. Second, the three approaches will be used to clarify the arguments and reasons presented during the IGC-96. The focus will be on arguments presented by EU officials – in the European Council, Commission and European Parliament – as well as in two member countries, the UK and Denmark. These countries were selected because they have consistently opposed an independent normative basis for the EU and because they have had the strongest and most vocal popular opposition. There is little doubt that if a change from utility to values and rights is afoot, it would be detected here. Such a change could manifest itself in opposition based on defence of national identities, values, rights and nationally based democracy. Or it could manifest itself in more inclusive conceptions of identity and embrace of European rights.

Legitimacy and constitution-making in the EU

In the following section, I will briefly present the three approaches to legitimation that the criteria listed above are derived from. The relevance of these to the EU will also be clarified.

Legitimation through outcomes

Legitimation through outcomes is premised on a means–end type of rationality that highlights those outcomes or results that best reflect the relevant actors' preferences. The onus is on finding ways to ensure that a set of given interests or preferences is converted into those types of outcomes that best represent initial preferences. This can be done by assessing and weighing the costs and benefits of various possible solutions as well as through devising and assessing various interest accommodation schemes.

This approach to legitimation, modified to suit particular European requirements, has marked the EU since its inception. Helen Wallace has observed that 'much of the justification by politicians of the case for the EC has been couched in terms of its utility in providing substantive results for the participating countries and therefore for their populations' (Wallace 1993: 100). Proponents and opponents of European integration could agree to this notion, because it did not presume that the EU become an independent governance structure, which would require its own normative justification. Legitimation through outcomes is, at least in principle, consistent with the notion of indirect or derivative legitimacy for the EU. Indirect legitimacy entails that the EU is based on the democratic character of the Member States. It is this combination of legitimation through outcomes and indirect legitimacy that has marked the EU (Beetham and Lord 1998b: 11–16).

This approach which is based on outcomes and indirect legitimation is problematic. Indirect legitimacy is premised on each Member State retaining its right to veto. The right to veto, if used frequently, can easily undercut effective performance (Beetham and Lord 1998a: 26–27). Efficiency considerations will also discourage the use of veto. These problems are compounded the further the integration process proceeds. The indirect mode of legitimacy is being undermined by several important developments. The EU is a source of authoritative rules and allocations which impinge on citizens directly and 'which require *their* acknowledgement of them as authoritative and binding, as well as the acknowledgement on the part of state officials' (Beetham and Lord 1998b: 13). Further, the EU has strong supranational elements. It is also a dynamic system, which has taken on a wide range of activities that have been seen as the preserve of states. The EU, as a result, is 'increasingly involved in the allocation of social and political values throughout Europe' (Hix 1998: 42).

If this process continues to be legitimated with reference to outcomes, then it becomes increasingly difficult to specify performance standards by which the outcomes can be assessed, which means that the outcomes will be more contentious and less stable. Further, when faced with this problem, to avoid conflict, there is a strong temptation to try to convert issues that have deep implications for people's values, identities and sense of belonging and which require open discourse, into matters that can be bargained over by elites in closed quarters. The legitimacy of such outcomes – if they ensue – will be unstable. The risk, then, is that this is couched as pragmatic co-operation (where pragmatic revolves around technical, practical and economic issues and concerns and is premised on 'acceptable' and identifiable interests, where means–end relations can be specified, and where efficient or 'technically best' solutions can be found), but where precisely those ingredients that ensure pragmatic agreement will be missing. Continued reliance on legitimation through outcomes, will exacerbate the problems associated with the gap that Weiler identified.

What arguments and reasons will be used by those that continue to see the EU as founded on legitimation through outcomes? They will argue that binding European co-operation is tenable as long as it (a) leads to favourable results, and (b) does not undermine the democratic character of the Member States. The discourse will reflect this dual character of legitimation through outcomes. On the one hand, it will revolve around the costs and benefits of co-operation to differently situated self-interested actors. On the other hand, it will revolve around the question of how to ensure that the EU does not challenge the democratic legitimacy of the Member States.

Efforts to initiate treaty change such as the IGC-96 will be presented as means to rectify performance shortcomings or means to improve outcomes, and generally measured in economic terms. Treaty changes will be assessed and discussed in terms of the anticipated costs and benefits that will be conferred on the interests involved, as well as whether or how they affect the legitimacy of the Member States. This approach to legitimation is about self-interest and utility and not about the rights or values of the peoples of Europe. If such terms are used, the assumption is that they are merely intended to sustain the common market. For instance, rights will be considered not as entitlements but as instruments to ensure the proper functioning of the EU, and in particular the common market. This approach to legitimation is therefore incompatible with polity-building or constitution-making in the EU.

In sum, legitimation through outcomes is revealed by arguments and reasons that highlight (a) costs and benefits of co-operation, (b) 'indirect legitimation', and (c) concepts such as rights and values are merely instrumental and functional.

Constitution-making and legitimacy

Precisely how we conceive of constitution-making is important to how the gap may be bridged.

Constitution-making refers to a 'process of change in which the norms, principles, decision-procedures, and modes of justification that underpin and inform a written body of rules are presented, deliberated, and eventually encoded in a constitution or in binding constitutional interpretations' (Blichner and Fossum 1997: 3). The notion of process is important and relevant to the EU which has gone through several major bouts of treaty change. It is possible to conceive of constitution-making, either foremost in 'contractual' or in 'conversational' terms. If constitution is conceived of primarily in contractual terms, then constitution-making is the search for a privileged moment 'where constitutional essentials are unambiguously settled and made binding into the future' (Chambers 1998: 149). The absence of such a moment thus far in Europe would seem to lend the structure in place little credibility. As an alternative, it is possible to conceive of:

> a model of agreement based on maintaining a conversation over time rather than concluding a contract [and which is] a more realistic approach to constitution making, especially in multicultural societies as well as a better articulation of the conditions of democratic legitimacy in the late twentieth century.
>
> (Chambers 1998: 143–144, cf. Chambers 1996)

It is this latter approach to constitution-making that informs this analysis.

In the EU, constitution-making is complicated by the particular problems surrounding the nature of *demos* and *telos*. Democracy is premised on a *demos*. That there is no clearly delimited European demos, in the traditional sense, is by many seen as one of the main defects of the EU.[3] Such a consideration is 'only conclusive, however, if we think of political identities and loyalties in ethnic, or backward referring terms, based on a common past, rather than upon an agreed political project for a common future' (Beetham and Lord 1998b: 29; Habermas 1992b). In the EU this is best seen as a question of *who*, and in what sense individuals, groups and collectives should be included or excluded, as well as *which* sense of identity and attachment such inclusion requires. The question of a European *demos* does require some sense of a European identity, and changes in national identities, but there is no reason to assume or require that this has to be backward-looking.

The question of identity is steeped in what Charles Taylor has termed 'strong evaluation'. Therefore, constitution-making requires an approach to legitimation that is founded on strong evaluations. Both weak and strong evaluations are reflective of 'the power to *evaluate* our desires, to regard some as desirable and others as undesirable' (Taylor 1985: 15–16). But whereas weak evaluations are simply related to outcomes, strong evaluations also refer to the *quality* of the motivation. Strong evaluations are characteristically and distinctively human in the sense that they reflect the particular human ability not only to assess the quality of the motivation, but also to attach worth to our desires. Taylor observes that:

> to define my identity is to define what I must be in contact with in order to function fully as a human agent, and specifically to be able to judge and discriminate and recognize what is really of worth or importance, both in general and for me.
>
> (Taylor 1986: 258)

Strong evaluation refers to what is valuable in life, it is 'not simply a condition of articulacy about preferences, but also about the quality of life, the kind of beings we are or want to be. It is in this sense deeper' (Taylor 1985: 26). Strong evaluations offer standards through which our preferences can be assessed. Strong evaluation will shed light on the question of legitimacy, as it refers to those elements of our sense of being and belonging that are most likely to generate the type of allegiance and consent that are intrinsic to legitimacy.

Identity is created and sustained in interpersonal contexts. Such interpersonal contexts are shaped by the values that are embedded in the social context in which individuals operate as well as by the structure of rights that individuals hold (Honneth 1995; Habermas 1996a; March and Olsen 1989, 1995). As such, a person's identity is shaped in the 'networks of solidarity and shared values within which the particular worth of individual members of a community can be acknowledged' (Honneth 1995; Taylor 1989, 1994, 1995). Communitarians emphasize shared values, whereas Liberals stress rights (Honneth 1995). Both the language of values and of rights is reflective of strong evaluations. In the following, the two different approaches to legitimation through strong evaluations will be briefly presented and applied to the EU.

Legitimation through values

Legitimation through values is based on a value-oriented notion of rationality (*Wertrationalität*, in Weber's terminology). It asserts that human motivation is deeply shaped by certain norms and values and that these values, once embraced, actually inform and drive human conduct.

The value-based approach to legitimation presented here is derived from the republican conception of democracy, in its communitarian trappings. The republican view of democracy conceives of politics as a process of deliberation that is particularly oriented to the common good and the constitution of society as an ethical community (Eriksen 1994a: 10).[4] The basic communitarian premise is that the individual is shaped by the community:

> (t)he community is not simply an aggregation of individuals; nor is there a causal interaction between the two. The community is also constitutive of the individual, in the sense that the self-definitions which define him are drawn from the interchange which the community carries on.
>
> (Taylor 1985: 8, cf. Thompson 1998: 185–186)

The community is made up of people whose histories, experiences and identities are important to me because they are part of an intersubjectively shared form of life (Habermas 1995a). A person's identity is steeped in and shaped by a set of collective identities that are founded on a shared set of traditions and a common sense of history.[5] The communitarian approach is premised on the notion that 'there is a necessary connection between the deliberative concept of democracy and the reference to a concrete, substantively integrated ethical community' (Habermas 1996c: 24). This common sense of identity permeates the institutional structures, which are promotive of the common values of the collectivity and protective of the uniqueness of the community in relation to the external world. Such communities are seen as infused with ethical values, which shape identities and lend credence to that particular community's sense of uniqueness. The criteria of evaluation are therefore also largely internally derived, i.e. they are derived from and based on the norms and values and self-conceptions of a particular community.

Communitarians are particularly concerned with the question of what makes a political society possible (Thompson 1998). In answering this central question, they privilege the good over the right; i.e. they emphasize the role of a particular sense of identity, belonging and set of values over more universalist conceptions of justice which are not bound to specific communities or traditions. This deeply affects their view of political legitimacy. Janna Thompson notes that 'Communitarianism ... is best understood as a theory of political legitimacy which holds that the authority of principles of justice and political institutions, including democratic institutions, depends on an identity of individuals with their political society' (Thompson 1998: 190). Political leaders express, reflect, and enact the self-conception of a particular community, and the political leadership is expected to be in congruence with the cultural life-form which is constitutive of the community (Habermas 1998b).

Communitarians see identity as communally based. There are several problems with this position, which presents identity in terms as 'oneness'; as a 'one-dimensional' relationship; conceives community identity as a value consensus; and sees identity as 'fate' (Thompson 1998). First, total identification with a particular community can easily become oppressive and can be abused by those in power. Second, this type of identification fails to appreciate that people are able to belong to a wide range of associations and also that they are capable of different types and intensities of allegiance, depending on level and type of association. Third, this position downplays the problems of obtaining a value consensus, in particular in multicultural settings. It is not even clear that value consensus is a desirable trait in a democracy. Finally, it is premised on the assumption that those relations that were constitutive of a person's identity are those that the person necessarily will value. This, however, is something that can not simply be assumed.

The value-based approach to legitimation, then, explicitly addresses the question of identity and belonging and *demos*. But it also presents a particular view of identity, which highlights an ethically salient sense of community. It seems much better equipped to explain how established identities can be sustained than how new ones may be created. It also appears better equipped to deal with the question of exclusion than inclusion, in the sense that it can provide a set of clear-cut criteria for who should belong and who should be excluded. In multi-level and culturally and linguistically heterogeneous entities such as the EU, the question of inclusion and exclusion is more complex and may require a more nuanced approach to who should be included and excluded, because it is necessary to consider not only whether to exclude or include but also in what sense they should be included or excluded. The EU presents the communitarian approach with a particularly vexing challenge and which also promises to tell us much about how far the communitarian approach to identity, community and belonging can be extended.

The arguments that inform the discourse on legitimation through values will highlight the ethical salience of European traditions and values and how these traditions and values can contribute to create and/or sustain a particular and unique sense of European identity. The EU, in this view, is a community that is in the process of being (re)constructed which means that there will be considerable emphasis on establishing precisely *who* is a European and who *is not*, as well as to identify the particular values that are associated with a European community and a European way of life. The ultimate objective is to clarify a particular European sense or conception of the good life and embed this in a constitutional shape. Therefore, it must be assumed that the interlocutors are able to identify a set of European traditions and values and that they also consider these to form the basis of a distinct European identity and sense of belonging.

This means that the value-based discourse will not only focus on which values but also on how the process of treaty change can be brought into greater conformity with people's conceptions of community. Treaty changes will therefore be conceived of and discussed as efforts to ensure that the EU comes to reflect or is brought as closely as possible to the most central European traditions and values. This means that it will be important both to those conducting the process and to those affected by it that there is a shared understanding of what the process is about. Insofar as this is not the case at the outset, if the process is truly and self-consciously constitutional, there will be much attention to how such heightened congruence can be obtained. This means that the deliberative process will be marked by efforts to clarify which values and traditions are the most important, that these are shared by all, and that the process is conducted in a manner that is consistent with this.

In sum, legitimation through values is revealed by arguments and reasons that highlight (a) a set of European values and traditions that are constitutive of European identity, (b) a set of criteria that clarify who are Europeans and who are not, and (c) people are addressed as and encouraged to see themselves, not as market actors, but as fellow compatriots. Legitimation through values, as noted, is inadequate to address integration in a multicultural and multinational setting.

Legitimation through rights

Legitimation through rights is based on a communicative notion of rationality. It asserts that human beings are social beings, compelled to justify their actions by means of reasons, in order to reach agreements that are legitimate. Rights offer a framework for discourse and are also established through discourse. Habermas observes that 'the principle of democracy derives from the interpenetration of the discourse principle and the legal form. I understand this interpenetration as a *logical genesis of rights* ...' (Habermas 1996a: 121–122).

The rights-based approach to legitimation is concerned with entitlements and obligations. It also asserts that in modern societies, rights are vital to foster the allegiance and consent that a modern constitutional democracy can draw upon.[6] Rights are 'legally institutionalized relations of universal respect for the autonomy and dignity of persons ...' (Anderson, in Honneth 1995: xi–xii). Legal rights are founded on the notion of reciprocal recognition and as such foster a sense of community allegiance because:

> we can only come to understand ourselves as the bearers of rights when we know, in turn, what various normative obligations we must keep vis-à-vis others: only once we have taken the perspective of the 'generalized other', which teaches us to recognize the other members of the community as the bearers of rights, can we also understand ourselves to be legal persons, in the sense that we can be sure that certain of our claims can be met.
>
> (Honneth 1995: 108, cf. Habermas 1996a: 88–89)

Legal relations highlight the general and universalizable aspect of the recognition relationship because what is recognized is the person as a holder of rights, not the particular personality traits or attributes of the person.

But individual rights do not only pertain to individuals, they also have implications for people's sense of community. Although it is the general aspect of the recognition relationship that is highlighted in the notion of 'right', this does not mean that the nature and composition of rights will be uniform or independent of the specific setting in which the rights were granted. The modern view of law, as positive law, is bounded law in the sense that it applies to specific settings. Therefore, 'one can count as the bearer of rights of some kind only if one is socially recognized as a member of a community' (Honneth 1995: 109). The particular values of a given community will therefore also be reflected in the system of law that this community adopts (Habermas 1994a: 124).

What also matters, then, is *precisely how* a person is socially recognized, i.e. what the precise composition of civil, political, social, and economic rights is in a given community. But this is not simply a matter of the range of rights, what is also important is what *function* the rights have. Rights are not single, isolated entitlements but vital ingredients in the *system of law*, and which is based upon a number of normative presuppositions.[7] Rights are important to democracy, in the sense that they offer individuals protections and entitlements. When used to the full, they are vital in a deeper sense, because they enable a given community of rights holders the ability in substantive and symbolic terms to conceive of itself as a democracy. The point is that a modern democratic community can not act as a source of legal norms independently of individuals. To clarify this, it is important to recall that modern law, in normative terms, is founded on the dual notions of private and public rights, and the vital link between these two sets of rights. Together, they constitute the *Rechtsstaat* and popular sovereignty (Habermas 1994a, 1996a).

The *Rechtsstaat* is constrained from acting upon the citizens according to its own devices because all citizens have a set of rights that protect them from random state actions. These rights are required for citizens to operate as autonomous legal persons. They enable each person the protection necessary to deliberate disputed norms. The *Rechtsstaat* is constrained by democracy, as reflected in the notion of popular sovereignty and expressed through public participatory rights. These rights provide people with access and enable them to question whether the principles of justification that are applied are sufficiently inclusive to protect their basic interests. Personal autonomy, then, is the sum of both the private protective and the public participatory rights. This combination of rights enables citizens to be both subject to the legal requirements whilst they also retain the possibility to act as the ultimate authors of the law (Habermas 1994a, 1996a). Once this set of rights is established, the citizens deliberate over how extensive their social and economic rights will be.

In the extension of this, the rights-based model of legitimation presupposes that there are a set of rights that 'define' the EU as polity and political community. In other words, it must be assumed that there are a specific set of rights that are seen as constitutive of the European Union and that these form the basis of a distinct European entity. Of particular importance in this regard are those rights that ensure the autonomy of the person, i.e. private protective and public participatory rights.

The arguments that this approach to legitimation will highlight will necessarily focus on rights. Actors who support this view of the EU will conceive of the

EU as a constitutional structure which is an independent granter of rights and which therefore provides persons with real entitlements as rights bearers. Rights will be conceived of as vital to foster a sense of community allegiance and to ensure that all rights holders are properly recognized as such depending on the type and composition of rights that they hold. Rights will not only be seen as important in fostering a sense of allegiance but also in establishing a rights-based system of democratic governance. The question of rights therefore ultimately revolves around the constitutional status of the EU.

Since rights are founded on the notion of reciprocal recognition, it is not only those in charge of the process that are able to decide the salience of the entitlements and obligations involved. All those identified as rights bearers are in principle involved in the process and it is intrinsic to the nature of the modern institution of 'right' that all rights holders need to be consulted for there to be a proper sense of reciprocal recognition. Therefore, to understand the salience of a rights-based approach to legitimation, it is necessary to examine if this commitment to rights is readily expressed and that not only those directly involved in granting rights but also that all those affected by the rights are properly included in the process. If this approach to legitimation predominates, those formally in charge of the process would consider and address those affected by the process as rights-bearing individuals and/or as the ultimate authors of the law, rather than consider and address them as utility-seeking market actors or as fellow compatriots.

In sum, legitimation through rights is revealed by arguments and reasons that highlight (a) the EU as a granter of rights, (b) rights ensure citizens' private *and* public autonomy, and (c) citizens as rights holders.

The IGC-96 and democratic legitimation

The IGC-96 was the first Intergovernmental Conference to place governance issues at the very centre stage of treaty-making in the EU.[8] The IGC-96, at least formally, was explicitly focused on the political aspects of the EU, whereas the IGC that produced the Maastricht Treaty had been concerned with both Economic and Political Union. Was this concern of such a nature as to bridge the gap listed above; i.e. between the structure in place and the arguments used to support it? The strongest and most conclusive evidence of such a change would be a widely announced self-conscious assertion on the part of the process-based insiders that the EU was involved in constitution-making; that the IGC-96 was a means to further this process; and that special steps were taken to foster constitution-making, such as for instance setting up a constitutional convention. That was not the case. None of the documents presented by the EU-based institutions directly involved in the IGC-96 process spoke of 'constitution', referred to the IGC-96 process as one of constitution-making, or set out to clarify the status of the constitutional structure that had already been embraced. There was also a virtual ban on talking about 'constitution' in Brussels.[9]

The European Parliament, which was not directly involved in the process of treaty change, was more attuned to the constitutional dimension. This was most evident in the report on the Amsterdam Treaty issued by the EP Committee on Institutional Affairs in November 1997, which stated that 'the Union Treaty is an organic process of political and constitutional development' (CONF 4007/97: 13). Thus, whilst the executive officials or process-based insiders did not portray the IGC-96 as 'the moment of constitutional choice for Europe', the IGC-96 could still qualify as a 'constitutional conversation'.

There was a great concern with the need for legitimation in the IGC-96, as revealed both in the wording and in the sheer volume of discussion. No doubt, the concern with legitimation was more pronounced during the IGC-96 than it had been during the Maastricht Treaty process. For instance, in 1995, a reflection group was established to discuss the issues and to report on the items on the agenda for the IGC-96. Further, the various EU-based institutions and the Member States all submitted numerous discussion papers and proposals to the IGC-96, both to provide feedback on their experiences with the Maastricht Treaty, and to present more concrete proposals for the IGC-96. The European Parliament held open hearings and received over 100 submissions. All the institutional proposals and the submissions are rife with statements on the need to address the democratic challenges facing the EU.

The many documents presented during the IGC-96 reveal a widely recognized need to replace the prevailing sense of the EU as a remote technocracy, based on elite rule, and an unaccountable bureaucracy. Further, in many of the submissions, the populations of the Member States are referred to as citizens, as opposed to aliens and denizens, and there are frequent references to European citizenship. Further, it is not only recognized that the EU suffers from a democratic deficit, but the vocabulary has been expanded with several new terms and many of the old terms have been given added emphasis. Relevant terms are the need for *proximity* to citizens (to counteract the sense of remoteness to citizens and people); the need for *transparency* (with regard to procedures and which is required to combat complexity and lack of procedural clarity); *openness* (which is needed to replace closedness and 'cosy inwardness' and which refers both to procedures and to new entrants, and which was included in Article 1.4 of the Amsterdam Treaty); *subsidiarity* which was seen as a remedy against remote and centralized rule; *flexibility and solidarity*. These terms indicate that the evaluative standards, as expressed in official submissions to the process, have become more explicitly linked to democratic legitimacy. The Report on the Amsterdam Treaty by the Institutional Committee of the EP also concluded that the Amsterdam Treaty is a significant step forward for the European Union, compared to the Maastricht Treaty, in terms of democracy, freedom, the rule of law, social policy, solidarity and cohesion (CONF 4007/97: 15).

Legitimation through outcomes

Does the heightened recognition of the need to address the problem of democratic legitimacy involve a change from legitimation through outcomes to legitimation through values or rights? As noted, legitimation through outcomes is revealed by arguments and reasons that highlight the costs and benefits of co-operation; 'indirect legitimation'; and rights and values are considered in instrumental and functional terms only.

The increased concern with democracy, as reflected in the reports, suggests that the officials in charge of the process no longer would embrace the notion of indirect legitimation and instead explain what type of political project the EU was and what type of political community was being built. The Reflection Group reiterated the European Council's position (as expressed in the Presidency Conclusions from the December 1995 Madrid European Council Meeting) and stated that 'The Union is not and does not want to be a super-state. Yet it is more than a market. It is a unique design based on common values. We should strengthen these values ...' (SN 520/95 and 5082/95 in EP White Paper I: 154, 29). The failure to state precisely what type of entity the EU is may be due to the fact that the Reflection Group was deeply divided on these questions. But the problem runs deeper. The Commission, in its report, referred to the EU as an 'organization of states' (White Paper I: 238), a description which is hardly much more enlightening. The executive officials in the European Council, in the Council and in the Commission had no doubt abandoned the notion of indirect or derivative legitimation but they did not specify precisely what kind of entity would command their allegiance in Europe.

The principles most frequently referred to were democracy and effectiveness. The Commission, in its report on the Maastricht Treaty, noted that 'Democracy comprises the very essence of the Union, while effectiveness is the precondition for its future' (White Paper, I: 239). The reports issued by the process-based insiders in the Council were ambiguous on the relation between these terms. The arguments and reasons presented here suggest that the emphasis was more on effectiveness than on democracy, which helps account for the ambiguous way in which the EU was depicted. For instance, when the European Council spoke of the need for proximity to the 'citizens', there was great emphasis on the need to bring the institutions closer to the 'citizens' so that they could better see that the Union was doing things that people deem useful and valuable. Insofar as this was the case, the challenge would not be to include the citizens into the structure in such a manner as to engage their hearts and passions, or even to grant them rights that enable them to see themselves as the authors of the laws and hold the structure accountable, but rather to do such things that the citizens would find valuable. The European Council at the Turin Council 'asks the IGC to base its work on the fact that the citizens are at the core of the European construction: the Union has the imperative duty to respond concretely to their needs and concerns' (Presidency Conclusions, Turin European Council, 69). The Union had to ascertain what were the needs of the citizens and to respond to their needs. The statement does refer to the Union as being obligated to do so and as such is clearly reflective of the Union as based on some sort of popular sanction and as deriving its legitimacy from the peoples of Europe. Much of this legitimacy, then, does appear to derive from what the EU actually does, and is therefore reflective of legitimation through outcomes. The EU is said to have a *duty* to respond, an element of popular constraint which suggests a certain ambiguity with regard to the appropriate status of the EU.

The case of Britain

No such ambiguity was apparent in the statements and reports by the UK Conservative government. It saw the EU in explicit derivative terms and whose legitimacy was entirely founded on the democratic Member State. The UK position paper to the IGC-96 stated that 'The bedrock of the European Union is the independent, democratic nation state … The EU is not a state, and should take care not to develop ideas which feed people's fear that it has a vocation to become one' (UK: A Partnership of Nations 1996, 1: 24). This statement is telling also of the government's view of the process, in that it seeks assurances that there is no *intent* on the part of the Union to develop into a state. Obviously, to the UK Conservatives, there was only one direction in which the EU could develop, provided its political role was further enhanced, and that would be into a full-fledged state. This position was further underlined by the unwillingness to accept the EU as a guarantor of fundamental human rights: 'The Government does not consider that the EU is the right context for the protection of fundamental human rights, or for a general clause … prohibiting discrimination for example on grounds of gender, sexual orientation, race, religion, age or disability' (ibid. 24). Similarly, with regard to European Union citizenship, it was stated that 'The Treaty provided that citizens of the Union "shall be subject to the duties" imposed by the Treaty, but these have not been developed and the Government believes it is right that they should not be' (ibid.). The reason was that the duties could include military service and taxation which would lead to statehood. It is hard to find a more explicit statement of the *No-demos thesis* and the binary logic associated with it than the UK government's stance on European Union citizenship.

That the UK government wholly endorsed the primacy of the nation-state is also evident in its view on enlargement. In the position paper to the IGC-96, the government noted that '(t)he European Union must never become a cosy inward-looking club. We have an obligation to consolidate the new unity of the continent, and actively to help our central European neighbours as they prepare for membership.' This view coincided with acceptance of the notion of 'variable geometry', but it was underlined that geometry had to stay flexible, i.e. it should not permit the establishment of a cemented two-tier Europe or a Europe with a firmly established inner core. The overriding concern of the British government, therefore, was to prevent the establishment of either a strong supranational entity of which it was part, as well as to prevent the establishment of a strong inner EU core of which it was not part. The commitment to the nation-state was systemic and referred to a defence also of the state system in Europe. The EU should therefore remain explicitly based on the continued primacy of the nation-state and the nation-state system. The UK government's position is clearly reflective of Hedley Bull's statement to the effect that 'one reason for the vitality of the states system is the tyranny of the concepts and normative principles associated with it' (Bull, in Linklater 1996: 78).

The British government supported binding interstate co-operation but noted that:

> (a)bove all, we shall be guided by a cool assessment of the British interest. Common European decision-making, as opposed to cooperation, can only be justified where it brings benefits for British security, prosperity and quality of life which are so significant that they justify some loss of unfettered national control over decision-making in the area concerned, or where common action enables nation states to exercise joint control which is not open to them individually.
>
> (UK: A Partnership of Nations 1996: 5)

A part of this was the need to defend national parliaments and to reject any new powers to the EP, as the government was not willing to accept the EP as a real parliament. The UK Conservative government also refused to sign the Social Charter. In sum, the UK Conservative government was motivated by a value-laden defence of the particular British nation-state and the concepts and normative principles associated with the nation-state system in general. The EU was acceptable insofar as it did not threaten either and could be assessed in terms of its performance with regard to a range of activities that would be narrower than those the EU presently undertook.

The Conservatives failed to obtain popular support for their strong European stance, which was labelled as 'phobic' by one commentator (Hugo Young, *the Guardian*, 2 May 1997) and the Conservative government was ousted from office in the landslide national election in May 1997. The election debate was influenced by the impending Amsterdam European Summit Meeting and although there were many different issues on the agenda, the Conservatives' attempt to highlight the salience of a relatively exclusive sense of national (English) identity and belonging, failed to obtain the support of the voters to renew their term in office. The Blair Labour government adopted a more conciliatory, pragmatic and inclusive approach to Europe and European integration which has somehow defused the emphasis on national identity. Once in power, the new British Labour government stated that:

> We must avoid the mistakes made at the time of Maastricht when the people came close to rejecting a Treaty they saw as largely irrelevant to their needs. We will only be able to restore popular legitimacy in the European Union if we get away from the politicians agenda and onto the peoples agenda.[10]

The people's agenda, Cook believed, could be met by improving the policy-making and instrumental aspects of the EU, in particular in the field of employment. This instrumental stance was foremost directed at the existing EU. With regard to the prospect for enlargement, the language changed:

> if we are going to recapture some of the idealism that marked the early years of the European Community, perhaps we need something which we pragmatic Britons are sometimes accused of lacking – a vision. I believe that vision lies in the unprecedented opportunity to unite our continent through the enlargement of the European Union. We have the chance to right the wrongs of the last half century.

The Foreign Minister did not say how the EU was to entrench democracy in the East, but it is obvious that action was required beyond strengthening the instrumental aspects of the EU. Labour signed the Social Charter and supported proposals to strengthen some aspects of individual rights, notably protections against discrimination. Labour therefore adopted a more conciliatory stance to European co-operation. Its far more inclusive stance than its predecessor included acceptance of a more independent role of the EU in employment, social and environmental policy and human rights.

The Blair government also initiated a constitutional reform process which includes a commitment to address regionally based claims for difference, through establishing regional parliaments in Scotland and Wales. The Blair British government has therefore adopted a more inclusive view of cultural and identity-based difference, and this applies to other parts of Europe and to the UK, as well.

The British case reveals that the Conservative government embraced the notion of legitimation through outcomes. The EU was to be seen as entirely derived from and dependent on the Member State and the range of issue-areas available for the EU to produce outcomes was to be quite narrow and circumscribed. The election which was held during the IGC-96 process revealed that the Conservative government did not have much popular support for its vehement stance. The newly elected Labour government adopted a more conciliatory position on the EU, a position which still reflects an element of legitimation through outcomes but which was more ambiguous with regard to the independent salience of the EU, also as rights granter.

The case of Denmark[11]

The Danish government, in light of the initial Danish rejection of the Maastricht Treaty in 1992, was widely believed to present – if not itself embrace – a deeply sceptical view of the EU. The official Danish position on the EU, as expressed by the PM and supported by the majority of Danes, has long been one of the EU as founded on binding interstate co-operation.[12] It is important to recognize, when examining the statements of Danish executive officials, that they are subject to uniquely strong popular constraints, both through parliamentary controls and through the requirement to hold a popular referendum on every major treaty proposal.

The Danish officials have consistently rejected the notion that the EU is involved in a constitution-making process. But their efforts have not prevented the issue from being raised. Opponents of further European integration in Denmark succeeded in activating the courts in their effort to strike down the Maastricht Treaty. In 1993, twelve persons charged the PM with having violated the constitution because he signed the Maastricht Treaty. The High Court decided to hear the case and handed down its verdict on April 6, 1998. The High Court found for the PM and asserted that (a) Danish membership in the EU is consistent with the Danish Constitution; (b) the 1953 Danish Constitution permits quite a comprehensive relinquishment of national sovereignty to an 'interpopular' authority; (c) the question of relinquishment of sovereignty is to be based on political considerations; and (d) the particular manner in which the EU has expanded its powers and competences, through article 235, is consistent with the Danish Constitution. But the High Court also noted that if a legal act by the EU Court of Justice conflicts with the Danish Constitution, the latter shall prevail. The Danish High Court therefore did not acknowledge that the European Court of Justice had *Kompetenz-Kompetenz*. The Danish High Court also opened up the possibility for further court rulings on EU-related matters (Information, 07.04.1998). The opposition to the Maastricht Treaty thus served to activate a legal and constitutional discourse in Denmark. This discourse was conducted among experts but nevertheless revealed that the constitutional dimension of the European integration process extended into the internal legal deliberations of a Member State.

At the Amsterdam Summit meeting, the Danish PM placed strong emphasis on the EU as a 'rational' pragmatic type of co-operation, but he also observed that this type of co-operation is founded on a set of values that Europeans share. One obvious such value is the emphasis on peace. The EU is important to ensure continued peaceful relations in Europe. The PM also underlined that there is a common cultural heritage that the European interstate construction is based on. This common cultural heritage has contributed to the uniqueness of the European experience, an experience which has enabled this type of close co-operation. Neither the cultural heritage nor the common experience, he asserted, offers a solid basis on which to found a European polity, however. The statement is suggestive of the binary logic associated with the *No-demos thesis*, but the official Danish position and the Danish debate on the EU are more complex than that.

The official Danish negotiating position on the IGC-96 was far more open and inclusive than the position adopted by the UK Conservative government, when viewed in terms of legitimation. The Danish government did not simply refer to the virtue of the nation-state as the legitimate foundation of the EU. Rather, the government professed a strong commitment to binding interstate co-operation. For instance, at Amsterdam, the Danish government was prepared to consider the inclusion of a statement on fundamental human rights, which refers both to human rights and to democratic rights (Det Åbne Europa, 11/12, 1995: 5 INTERNET version). This did not include European citizenship, and the government did not clarify *which* 'democratic rights' could be included in the treaty.

The Danish position departs from conventional conceptions of interstate co-operation because there was so much emphasis on the need for this type of co-operation to be *open, democratic and accountable*. The Danish government was clearly concerned with democratizing the diplomatic interstate relations in Europe and to ensure that binding interstate co-operation was openly accountable. The Danish commitment to openness and transparency and to democratize interstate relations was stronger than that of any other state. Perhaps the Danish position could be seen as transnational, rather than either international or supranational. There was a strong commitment to bring the EU closer to the citizens, simplify the procedures, and generate more openness and transparency in the workings of the EU. The Danish position was transnational rather than international because it was explicitly oriented to the EU (including the expanded EU) and emphasized the need for strong and binding European co-operation. Further, it was transnational rather than supranational because it was not intended to violate or undercut the national traditions, cultures and histories in Europe (Det Åbne Europa, 11/12, 1995: 2) and because it opposed the measures that would greatly strengthen the supranational components of the EU. The Danish exemption from Union citizenship would prevent Denmark from pushing participatory rights. There was no real Danish commitment to strengthen the EP which was conceived of mainly as a controlling agent (Det Åbne Europa, 4), and the government was more concerned with strengthening the national parliaments in the process.

From the above it is quite apparent that the notion of legitimation through outcomes has continued to play a major role in the discourse on European integration during the IGC-96. But there is also a willingness, even among those deeply sceptical of the EU, to attribute a more independent role to the EU in areas that are clearly important to people's values and conceptions of rights. That such an ambiguity exists is not so surprising when we consider how the process of integration has been conceived.

Legitimation through values

Legitimation through values can be revealed through arguments and reasons that highlight European values and traditions constitutive of European identity; through efforts to specify explicit criteria that clarify who are Europeans and who are not; and through efforts to address people as fellow compatriots.

The need to focus on a set of values that can legitimate the European construction has been recognized throughout its existence: '(t)he search for new principles of European legitimacy is inextricably bound up with the attempt to create a space in which collective identities can be formed' (Delanty 1995: viii).

The EU has made numerous efforts, in substantive and symbolic terms, to foster a European identity and sense of belonging. There is a European Parliament, a European Court, a European flag, a European anthem, Europe Day, European Citizenship, and a common European Currency. There are also numerous efforts to preserve the European heritage. The EU is often said to have a cultural foundation rooted in Latin Christendom, humanist values and liberal democracy, all of which have been drawn upon to support the European construction.

Much of the symbolism that is used to depict the EU has normally been associated with the nation-state. An important question is whether the EU has merely copied this onto the EU level, in an effort to foster a conventional European state, or whether the EU represents something new and different. The nature and composition of values that were appealed to will shed light on this.

During the IGC-96 there was much concern with 'European' values. The values most frequently referred to were peace, peaceful co-existence with other peoples, democracy, freedom, human rights, the rule of law, social justice, solidarity, equality, non-discrimination, cohesion, security, efficiency, cultural diversity, and national identity (respect for the national identity of the Member States).

All the EU institutions referred to these values, albeit to varying degrees and intensities. For instance, the Commission, in its initial report on the Maastricht Treaty, spoke of the need to balance democracy and effectiveness (White Paper I: 239). The European Parliament placed particular emphasis on democracy and democratic legitimacy. The EP Committee on Institutional Affairs noted that '(d)emocracy is not only one of the goals of integration but at *the same time a prerequisite*' (CONF 4007/97: 14). The Committee was concerned with another means of balancing effectiveness:

> (t)he European Parliament sees the European Union not only in the narrow sense of a common market but also as *a system of values*. One of the characteristics of this system of values is that it aims to create real competitiveness which is essential for the common market within the framework of a system of social justice without which the common market would not be viable.
>
> (CONF 4007/97: 15)

The EU institutions listed a wide range of values that could generate a sense of attachment to the structure, because they reflect many of the most important concerns of modern people throughout the world. But this is also what Communitarians would consider problematic in terms of polity formation. Whilst the values are obviously important, in what sense can these values be appealed to in order to generate a distinct and exclusive European identity and sense of belonging? Most of the values do not refer to a specific or exclusive European history or a set of traditions that mark the European experience. Insofar as explicit European values are referred to, the reference is either to values associated with the Member States (national identity), or to the cultural diversity of Europe. Communitarians would not consider this adequate to produce a sense of belonging strong enough to support a state. But is the EU an attempt to establish a conventional state? This suggests that the assessment of the role of values in legitimating the construction can not be undertaken in complete isolation from the question of what type of entity the EU is.

As noted, very few of the documents had much to say on this. The most explicit statement is found in the report on the Amsterdam Treaty by the EP Committee on Institutional Affairs, which stated that:

> the goal of integration inherent in the European Treaties, including the Treaty of Amsterdam, does not require a federal State in the conventional sense, which is inspired by the traditional concept of the State. The Union should rather be understood as a legal order sui generis in a state of change, the characteristics of which will ultimately be determined by its own history, in other words by developments in the desire of the peoples of the Union for integration.
>
> (CONF 4007/97: 15)

The report highlights the importance of European integration as *process*. It is implied that the process has proceeded so far as to place the important governance issues squarely on the popular agenda but the issues are complex and may require novel solutions.

Did the reports seek to specify a precise cultural identity of Europe that could be identified independently of the national identities of the Member States, and which could be fostered by the institutions of the EU, in order to derive criteria to establish who were European and who were not? None of the documents submitted to the IGC-96 referred to a set of European values that could be unambiguously used to determine who were Europeans and who were not. Insofar as such criteria have been developed, this is done through rights, and not values. The EP underlined the need for the EU to be inclusive and respectful of diversity:

> There should be no restrictions on the number of official or working languages of the European Union. In view of the multicultural nature of European society, explicit reference should be made to the need to promote intercultural dialogue aimed at improving mutual understanding and tolerance.
>
> (EP Resolution, 17 May 1995)

This is also underlined by the stated need for protection of minority languages. The EP sought to reconcile and find common ground amidst a complex set of allegiances and refrained from appealing to or even seeking to identify a set of pre-political European values that could highlight its own role.

Were people addressed and encouraged to see themselves as 'fellow compatriots?' The documents did not refer to 'We, the people.' In the explanatory portions of the Dublin II and the Amsterdam Treaty proposals, the executive officials referred to people, persons and citizens as 'they'. The impression one gets from reading these statements is that the authors speak *of* the people rather than directly to them. The statements appear almost as reminders. It is apparent that the executive officials are aware of popular constraints, but precisely how these constraints are to be addressed is a contentious issue because it brings forth the question of what entity the EU is, and what entity they would want it to be, questions that were and still are, deeply controversial.

Finally, was there a change from utility to values afoot among the strongest opponents, in the UK and Denmark? In the UK, as noted above, the change in government marked a change from value-based opposition to a more pragmatic and ambiguous embrace of the EU. What kind of change took place in Denmark, given that the Danish position may be termed 'transnational'? Transnational implies a more inclusive approach – was that also reflected in the popular debate that led up to the referendum on the ratification of the Amsterdam Treaty?

In Denmark, the Amsterdam Treaty had to be ratified by popular referendum. The parties to the comprehensive debate – which covered a broad spectre of political parties and popular movements – included a wide range of positions, along three main dimensions, which may be labelled European federalists, intergovernmentalists (committed to more or less binding transnational co-operation), and nationalists. The debate was political and with hardly any emphasis on economic benefits. It revolved around basic human rights, the need for enlargement, environmental protection, the fight against international crime, the need to protect borders, and the need to protect the Danish national identity. It was marked by a wide range of views as to what type of entity the EU was and ought to be. In general, however, the proponents were at a greater loss to clarify precisely what type of entity they wanted than were the opponents. Few of the opponents wanted Denmark to leave the EU, however, and most recognized the need for binding interstate co-operation in at least some areas.

The debate was inclusive, in several ways. It was inclusive in a geographic sense, in that almost all the interlocutors agreed on the need for enlargement to the East and to strengthen the protection of basic human rights. Enlargement was considered an expression of international solidarity. This recognition was so strong as to largely defuse the onus on national exclusion and protection of what the strongest opponents (Dansk Folkeparti) referred to as the unique Danish identity. The no side included committed ethno-nationalists (Dansk Folkeparti) and cosmopolitans (Enhedslisten and parts of SF) and was deeply divided on precisely what it was opposed to.

The debate was inclusive also in the sense that so many of the interlocutors were aware of and willing to consider the arguments set forth by the opponents. In fact, opinion research has revealed that many individual Danes have divided allegiances.[13] The general sense of the referendum debate was that it was focused on political issues; it revolved around identity but not an exclusive sense of identity. Rather, the debate was on 'which Denmark in which Europe'. These two questions were entangled so as to make the debate complex and inclusive.

The debate also revolved around the question of national sovereignty, but it was inclusive in the sense that there was no uniform conception of sovereignty which could serve to exclude outsiders. Instead, there were different views on which components of sovereignty mattered most, such as for instance the need to retain territorial borders, as opposed to the need to protect national culture and identity. The two did not necessarily correspond so as to reinforce each other. The debate revealed that what constitutes national identity and sovereignty has become less certain and it is recognized that these are multi-dimensional phenomena, where the merits of each dimension has to be considered. The concerns of non-nationals were also actively considered, which made it more difficult to appeal to and defend an exclusive and coherent sense of Danish national identity and sovereignty. The various components that used to add up to form a coherent and comprehensive national identity that could be largely taken for granted now increasingly are becoming disassociated and the value of each must be considered more independently, since each has to be defended in a more open and other-including discourse than before. The result is a more comprehensive and nuanced discourse on precisely which identities, values, and rights are essential in today's and tomorrow's Europe. Therefore, in Denmark, although the executive officials did not view this as a 'constitutional' discourse, the opponents succeeded in raising the question of *Kompetenz-Kompetenz* and the referendum debate revolved around relatively open and inclusive conceptions of identity, values and rights.

In sum, insofar as values have informed the European discourse up to and during the IGC-96, it is precisely those values that are sufficiently general and 'inclusive' that have been referred to. The EU has not been able to, nor has it wanted, to draw on a set of prepolitical values and traditions that could (re)create a sense of community, as Taylor conceives of such. Thus, although the EU has embraced much of the symbolism and the vocabulary of the nation-state, the values it appeals to are more inclusive and less reliable to support the type of identity and allegiance associated with the nation-state. This is not akin to say that values need be less important to sustain the European project. Rather, it is apparent that for the EU to be able to foster a sense of legitimation through values, it can not draw very much on a set of prepolitical values in the manner that many nation-states have done. The European project, this suggests, must rely less on past experiences and common traditions and, as will become evident, more on the role of rights and the deliberative quality of the ongoing process of integration, in order to foster identity and sense of allegiance.

Legitimation through rights

As noted, legitimation through rights is revealed by arguments and reasons that see the EU as a granter of rights; rights ensure citizens private *and* public autonomy; and citizens are addressed as rights holders.

The EU is an independent granter of rights. The Maastricht Treaty also greatly increased the concern with rights, a concern that harks back to the Treaty of Rome. Since then the notion of 'right' has expanded. The Treaty of Rome referred to freedom of movement for 'workers', whereas the Single European Act referred to 'people'. As one analyst has noted:

> The metamorphosis of workers into persons was no semantic accident: it reflected the transformation of the Community from being a merely economic organisation into one that affected, and benefited, all its inhabitants irrespective of their economic function and, indeed, irrespective of whether they had any economic function.
>
> (Moxon-Browne 1996: 89)

This transformation prepared the ground for the considerably widened conception of rights that was introduced in the Maastricht Treaty. Article F (2) stated that:

> The Union shall respect fundamental rights, as guaranteed by the European Convention for the Protection of Human Rights and Fundamental Freedoms signed in Rome on 4 November 1950 and as they result from the constitutional traditions common to the Member States, as general principles of Community law.

The Maastricht Treaty also introduced Union citizenship. This notion of citizenship is significantly weaker than that of nation-states because it falls well short of ensuring the public autonomy of persons and does not enable them to act as the ultimate 'authors of the law'. Still, the rights already granted are of such a kind as to have obvious community-building implications. It is noteworthy, however, that the expanded role of rights occurred through the legal interpretative actions of courts. Politicians have generally incorporated rights into the treaties as a response to the actions of courts on rights.

How did the process-based insiders, the executive officials, appeal to persons – as customers, as clients, as fellow compatriots, as rights-bearing individuals, or as the ultimate law-makers? When consulting the explanatory portions of the draft treaties (Dublin II and Amsterdam), it appears that none of the terms listed above fully captures the nature of the relation, as the executive officials themselves appeared to conceive of it: 'People wish to live in a Union in which their fundamental rights are fully respected. They also want to be able to live and to move freely within the Union, without fear of threats to their personal safety' (Draft Treaty of Amsterdam, CONF/4000/97: 4). Given the democratic character of the Member States of the EU, it seems somewhat odd that they would refer to fundamental rights protection as a mere *wish*? Is it not something that most people take for granted? One reason for the careful language could be, as Finn Laursen (1997) has observed, that the EU officials used carefully worded language to avoid committing themselves to more than really necessary, in order to get on with their important business, which was economic. Another reason for the careful wording could be that a strong commitment to civil rights to ensure the citizens' private autonomy would not be supported by those who saw the Union as no more than an economic arrangement (notably the Conservative British government).

The actual suggestions in the draft treaty support the second interpretation. The Conservative British government had opposed an EU-based commitment to civil rights but once they were out of office, in May 1997, the road was open for the EU to include such. The Amsterdam Treaty, which was concluded in June 1997, included provisions that for the first time would enable the EU to initiate sanctions against persistent breaches of fundamental human rights. The salience of national opposition was reflected in the provisions on citizenship, however. The Amsterdam Treaty included an important constraint on how European Union citizenship was to be conceived. It stated that 'Every person holding the nationality of a Member State shall be a citizen of the Union. Citizenship of the Union shall complement and not replace national citizenship.' The European Council was concerned with reconciling the need to promote European citizenship with the need to protect essential features of the nation-state: 'The Council has taken the necessary decisions to implement the Treaty provisions on "citizenship of the Union" which give Member States' nationals additional rights and protection without in any way supplanting national citizenship' (White Paper, 1996, I: 51). European Union citizenship is also far from uniform because it is based on the particular rules of incorporation that each nation-state has adopted. The status of non-EU nationals can vary considerably from one member country to another.

The statements on the role of persons may therefore best be seen as part of an ongoing process of deliberation on precisely what should be the status of the EU on civil and political rights. The statements and provisions in the Amsterdam Treaty revealed, however, that there was no firm commitment to citizens as the ultimate authors of the law in the EU. There is also no mention of the notion of popular sovereignty in any of the publications produced by the European Council.

The explanatory portion of the draft treaty contained stronger wording when addressing those rights that were more explicitly – in legal and substantive terms – associated with the Common Market. It stated that:

> The people of the Union rightly insist that they should be allowed to benefit fully from the freedom of movement which the development of the European Union makes possible, and at the same time be protected from threats to their personal safety.
>
> (Draft Treaty of Amsterdam CONF/4000/97: 4)

This statement was more strongly worded than the one listed above, and is most likely reflective of the agreement that has emerged on those rights that are associated with the operation of the Common Market. The statements extended beyond the mere functional aspects of the market, to cover the effects of the market; notably the effects on the labour market, the unemployment rate, the environment and the social conditions. Despite the fact that most of the officials involved were representatives of the Member States, the nature of the arguments and the reasoning behind do seem to move in the direction of universalism, i.e. an increased focus on those issues and concerns that pertain directly to citizens as holders of rights. Rights were portrayed as entitlements and not as instrumentalities, but the strong onus on economic and social as compared to political rights supports the notion that the executive officials no longer see the EU as founded on outcomes, but do not have a very clear conception of precisely what they seek.

The EP adopted the most explicit stance on legitimation through rights. The EP also appears to have developed a clearer view of the legitimacy of the EU 'as a Union of the states and a union of the peoples of Europe ...' (EP Committee on Institutional Affairs, 1997: 5). It was concerned with strengthening both the substantive content of rights and made numerous proposals to that effect, as well as the symbolic aspect of rights as a legitimating device: 'The existing preamble of the Treaty should be rewritten in more inspiring language, and the provisions concerning citizens' rights should be placed at the beginning of the Treaty' (EP Resolution, May 17, 1995).

Precisely which rights were involved and how far would the rights go in polity-terms? In its May 17, 1995 resolution, the EP stated that:

> European integration which, since its very beginnings, has been synonymous with peace, political stability and harmonious economic development for the benefit of all citizens, now faces new challenges ... [which] call for initiatives by the European Union enabling it ... fully to assume its responsibilities in promoting peace, respect for human rights and the democratic stability of the European continent and neighbouring regions ...
>
> (White Paper, I: 214)

The EP thus underlined the need not only to recognize the direct link between preservation of peace, respect for human rights and democratic governance, but also to take action to strengthen this link further. Action on rights was an obvious requirement. The EU, it was noted, should 'ensure that its citizens can exercise their rights and freedoms, and contribute to maintaining the security of the individual, while safeguarding national and regional cultural identities ...' (White Paper, I: 215). The EP thus sought both to expand the number of rights of European citizens, as well as to strengthen the rights that they had already been granted in the TEU. The EP was also concerned with the present nature of rights protection in the Member States and stated that 'European citizens must under no circumstances be treated as foreigners within the European Union.'[14]

Several means were proposed to strengthen the rights already granted citizens. One important proposal was that the treaty should be unified in structure in order to make it more simple and comprehensible and the pillar structure should be abolished. The latter provision is important in terms of rights protection, as the pillar structure of the TEU placed obvious constraints on the jurisdiction of the Court of Justice and served to fragment and weaken rights exercise. Another such means was for the EU to accede to the Council of Europe's Convention on Human Rights and Fundamental Freedoms. The main reasons stated for the EU to accede to the Convention was both to entrench human rights as strongly as possible but also to enable an outside legal body specifically concerned with human rights to examine how human rights were addressed within the EU (EP Resolution, March 13, 1996: 3). The EP was concerned with the need to spell out a specific procedure in the treaty for how human rights were to be addressed (EP Note, Strasbourg, 12 December 1996). Whilst not explicitly stated, such a move could serve to reinforce the impression of the European Union as an independent legal body. It could also give the European Union added credibility at the international level, thus strengthening the case for a distinct European identity on the international level.

In addition to accession to the ECHR, the substance of European citizenship was to be strengthened through a wide range of concrete measures.[15] The measures proposed reveal that the EP attached particular importance to strengthening the private autonomy of citizens. The EP underlined the individual as a rights-bearing individual and argued for the need to take measures that highlighted the universal aspects of personhood, irregardless of religion, race, nationality and gender. The appeal to the need for the EU to ensure the private autonomy of persons was therefore a vital part of the EP's approach to legitimacy. The EP also argued for the need for further institutional changes to reinforce this. One important such change was to alter the institutional balance in the EU by the EP obtaining equal status with the Council. That would make the EP a co-legislator with the Council, in line with the dual notion of legitimation, cited above.

The emphasis on economic and social rights should be seen as compatible with the general concern with fundamental human rights because the latter are also linked to the individual and there is no concern voiced as to possible incompatibilities as to the overall scope of rights. In fact, it would appear from the manner in which the EP presents some of the arguments, that rights that have been hitherto associated with the open market must be made more universal and include not only workers but all persons. There is therefore a strong universalist thrust in the arguments presented by the EP.

But despite the emphasis on the private autonomy of persons, none of the resolutions (May 17, 1995; December 14, 1995 and March 13, 1996) mentioned 'popular sovereignty'. The EP highlighted the salience of the EU in ensuring the private autonomy of persons over and above that of the public autonomy of persons. It was explicitly stated that EU citizenship should not replace national citizenship but supplement it. The manner in which it was to be supplemented, more precisely, was for most of the political rights to reside with the respective populations of each Member State.

In sum, the EU is an independent granter of rights and rights played a central role in the effort to legitimate the EU. The concern with rights was more pronounced in the EP than among the process-based insiders in the European Council. With regard to the nature and range of rights, there was particular emphasis on ensuring the *private* autonomy of persons, whereas the commitment to public autonomy was notably weaker. Rights were also more important than values to all the institutions. But despite the concern with rights protection and promotion, it was not entirely clear what would be the salience of rights to legitimate the European constitution, because the institutions did not specify precisely what type of entity they wanted. There is no doubt that the great emphasis on rights can help bridge the gap but that is premised on an ongoing constitutional conversation which helps sort out precisely what role and status rights would have in the overall constitutional structure.

Conclusion

The purpose of this chapter was to discuss how comprehensive changes of a constitutional nature were legitimated during the IGC-96, which had to respond to the politicization of the process during Maastricht. Two questions were posed. First, how can the gap be bridged that Weiler identified between the structure in place and the arguments that were used to justify the rules? Second, in what sense was the IGC-96 an effort to bridge the gap?

Three approaches to legitimation were identified, namely outcomes, values, and rights. These three were considered individually. It was found that the notion of legitimation through outcomes is clearly inadequate to bridge the gap. If anything, it may widen it. Legitimation through values is also problematic. 'Communitarian' values are too exclusive to accommodate the diversity of multicultural and multinational entities such as the EU. 'Cosmopolitan' values offer no reliable basis on which to build a sense of community allegiance. Legitimation through rights is probably the most promising avenue, but it does depend on the nature and range of rights, as well as how rights are entrenched in the constitutional structure. No effort was made in this chapter to combine these modes of legitimation, which is necessary to get an overall sense of how entities are legitimated. Lack of space prevented this.

The core objective of this chapter was to assess whether the IGC-96 was an effort to bridge the gap. This chapter has revealed that there has been a change from legitimation through outcomes, as understood in a European context, to the other two approaches on legitimation presented above. Particularly important was the emphasis on legitimation through rights. This is the overall trend or tendency. It is a development that is underway, and not yet a fixed outcome. There are also important variations here. First, at the EU level, there is evidence to suggest that the change was more salient among the process-based outsiders, in the EP, than among the process-based insiders, in the European

Council. The former appeared more willing to abandon the notion of legitimation through outcomes, and instead promote rights and values, than were the latter. Second, the brief presentation of the debates in the two member countries suggests that there were important changes in the nature of opposition to the EU. In the UK the discourse revolves around legitimation through outcomes. The reasons have changed from a value-laden defence of an exclusive and perhaps even 'ethnic' English notion of identity to a more pragmatic and open discourse on the role of Britain in a wider Europe. This far more pragmatic approach also includes a certain commitment to EU-based rights. In Denmark, the discourse during the Amsterdam referendum was more focused than before on political issues, related to rights, values and identities. The two cases, the UK and Denmark reveal that increased integration during Amsterdam has not heightened the level of opposition-based conflict. If anything, the national positions have become more open and inclusive. Both Maastricht and Amsterdam portray the EU as a rights-granting entity. The question of identity is therefore hardly a zero-sum game.

There is no single European constitutional discourse, although there appears to be a movement afoot in many countries to test precisely what is the role of the national constitutional structure in relation to the one erected in Europe. The limited evidence presented here also suggests that much of the discourse at the elite level as well as at the popular level is focused on fundamental principles that are relevant to constitutionalism. The constitutional salience of this discourse may be less apparent than what the nature of the discussion would appear to warrant. Two possible reasons may account for this. First, many still think of constitution in state-based terms and simply extract the standards of reference directly from the nation-state model. In other words, constitution and how it is assessed, is directly associated with nation-state. Second, there may be a propensity to think of constitution too much as a type of contractual arrangement and understate the importance of 'constitutional conversation'. This may help account for the present situation in Europe. There is now much discussion of rights and values, but this discussion is not well tied in with or even related to any clear attempt on the part of the interlocutors to specify what they want the EU to be. There is an obvious need to clarify the constitutional implications of the discourses that are already taking place. This is one way to bridge the gap that Weiler identified. The other is to continue to re-examine central concepts such as identity, citizenship, democracy and not least constitution. This process of reconsideration, which is still largely confined to academic circles, must become part of the wider popular discourse, if the normative potential that is inherent in the European integration process is to be brought to fruition.

Notes

1 cf. EP, Institutional Committee: Report on the Amsterdam Treaty, CONF 4007/97; Curtin 1993; Weiler 1993, 1995, 1997, 1999a; Laffan 1996; Preuss 1996a; Blichner and Fossum 1997.
2 cf. Held 1987; Habermas 1996a.

3 Weiler notes that 'the No Demos thesis is premised on an organic understanding of peoplehood deriving from the European Nation-State tradition which conflates nationality and citizenship and can, as a result, conceive of Demos only in statal terms' (Weiler 1995: 219).

4 There is a general tendency among contemporary republicans to 'give this public communication a communitarian reading' (Habermas 1996c: 23).

5 According to Anthony Smith, national identity consists of the following fundamental features: '1. an historic territory, or homeland; 2. common myths and historical memories; 3. a common, mass public culture; 4. common legal rights and duties for all members; [and] 5. a common economy with territorial mobility for members' (Smith 1991: 14).

6 Rights are central to Habermas' notion of constitutional patriotism. cf. Habermas 1994a, 1996a.

7 Modern law is *formal, individualistic, coercive, positive, and procedurally enacted* (Habermas 1994a: 121).

8 The mandate for the IGC-96 was threefold: (a) to ensure a Union closer to its citizens; (b) institutional reforms so as to obtain a more democratic and effective Union; and (c) to increase the Union's ability and capacity to operate abroad (Udenriksministeriet 1996).

9 Interview with Commission official, Brussels, January 1998.

10 Foreign Secretary, Mr Robin Cook, 'Planning the Future of the European Union', The European Press, 15–16 June, 1997.

11 The information gathered here is derived from personal attendance at Danish press briefings at the Dublin and Amsterdam Summit meetings; referendum debates (live and televised) during my stay in Copenhagen in May 1998; and Danish newspaper coverage of the referendum debate during May 1998.

12 The Danish PM summarized his view of the Amsterdam Treaty in the following manner: 'a model which is more strongly entrenched than before; with more human and, in my opinion, more explicit Northern European features in its structure than before: employment, environment, and ideas are more strongly entrenched than before, fundamental human rights, and non-differentiation and non-discrimination are more explicitly stated in this than in the former treaty. It is not the great, new breakthrough which signals an entirely novel structure – that was also not the intention, but a treaty that will make it possible to continue the process of enlargement ... I would conclude that sensible, practical work is conducted ...' (PM Poul Nyrup Rasmussen, at Press Briefing, Amsterdam, June 18, my translation).

13 Public opinion research commissioned by Grindsted Public has revealed that many individual Danes were divided as to what to vote. A very large portion of the voters offered both arguments in favour of as well as against the Amsterdam Treaty which reveals that they were willing to consider both positions. See Grindsted Public, April 20, 1998, presented by Folketingets EU-Opplysning.

14 cf. Opinion of Parliament on the Convening of the IGC, in Collected Texts of the Italian Presidency, prepared by the General Secretariat of the Council of the European Union, 46.

15 The proposals were: (a) 'a new right of all EU citizens to information on EU matters'; (b) 'an explicit reference in the Treaty to the principle of equal treatment irrespective of race, sex, age, handicap or religion ... also incorporation of an article specifically referring to a ban on capital punishment' ...; (c) 'the development of political citizenship, inter alia through measures that facilitate participation in political life in the Member State of Union citizens residing in that State'; such measures related for instance to the need to establish a common electoral system to the EP and the development of political parties at the European level; (d) 'the strengthening of provisions needed to achieve fully the free movement of persons'; (e) 'the preservation of Europe's diversity through special safeguards for traditional minorities in terms of

human rights, democracy and the rule of law'; and (f) 'the application of the provisions in the Treaty on equal rights not only to economic rights but to all aspects of equality for women' (EP Resolution, 17 May, 1995). In the March 13, 1996 EP resolution it was noted that gender-based equality should be considered a fundamental right.

7 The anonymous hand of public reason

Interparliamentary discourse and the quest for legitimacy

Lars Chr. Blichner

Introduction

Over the last few years the importance of continuous contacts between parliaments throughout Europe has been stated on more than one occasion both at the national and the European level. The European Council meeting in Rome (1990) concluded that national parliaments should be more active in the process of European integration. Declaration 13 in the Maastricht Treaty emphasizes the importance of contacts between the European Parliament and national parliaments. The Committee on Institutional Affairs in the European Parliament stresses the need for reinforcing co-operation between the parliaments of the Union and the European Parliament. With the possible exception of the British House of Commons, national parliaments and elected representatives stress the importance of these contacts (M.P. Smith 1996: 290).

At the national level efforts have been made in order to secure a greater say in European affairs for the national parliaments. Although the solutions differ from one country to another and give the national parliaments different degrees of influence over national decisions directed at Community affairs, by now all national parliaments within the European Union have at least established special European Affairs Committees. Co-operation between these committees at the European level (including representatives from the European Parliament) has been institutionalized through the Conference of European Affairs Committees (COSAC),[1] which has met twice a year since 1989 when it was first established in Paris.

Most recently concern about the limited role played by national parliaments has been expressed in the Amsterdam Treaty by the adoption of the Protocol on the role of the national parliaments and for the first time interparliamentary co-operation has been given treaty status. The first part of the Protocol covers the need to improve the flow of information, in particular the need for national parliaments to get necessary information in time. In the second part the role of COSAC is commented on. It is recommended that COSAC in the future formally will be asked to comment on proposals with bearing on the rights and freedoms of individuals, fundamental rights and on the application of the principle of subsidiarity. Still, according to the Protocol COSAC may 'make any contribution it deems appropriate for the attention of the EU institutions'.

So there seems to be almost full agreement on the importance of increased contact between national parliaments. The question is why? Why should parliamentarians throughout Europe speak to each other, in institutional settings such as for example COSAC when these institutions have no formal power to act? In what way can this be seen to strengthen democracy at the European level? I will try to answer these questions from the perspective of deliberative democracy.

My aim with this chapter is limited. I will make three points about the role that interparliamentary discussions in Europe may fulfil in order to, at least partly, meet the democratic challenge. First, however, in order to provide some general background to interparliamentary co-operation I will briefly go through some of the developments towards what has been interpreted as a more active role for the national parliaments. The emphasis will be on the European Affairs Committees. Second, I will discuss how the network of interparliamentary co-operation can serve as a kind of intermediary public sphere, a public sphere which is more institutionalized than public spheres in civil society, but less institutionalized than parliamentary institutions both at the national and the European level. Third, I argue that talk is not only directed at consensus, but is as important in creating respect and understanding for the arguments presented even in situations where any sort of agreement seems out of reach. In a pluralist and multicultural setting as the EU talk is as much directed at avoiding the pitfalls of non-discursive disagreement as reaching a discursive agreement. Fourth, I argue that democratic legitimacy at the EU level is dependent on arenas where it is possible to talk relatively unrestrained by strategic considerations pertaining to national or party interests, interests which may be activated as soon as a concrete decision has to be taken. I argue that institutions such as the COSAC, which only talks and has limited capacity to act, may be especially well suited for this task.

Reparliamentarization of European politics?

The claim that European integration, by weakening parliamentary power at the national level, tends to weaken the democratic political element in Member States is not new. Almost thirty years ago Niblock (1971: 7) stated that as 'the involvement of governments in each other's domestic policy making' increases, they 'escape to some extent the controlling influences which have been exerted upon them by their respective Parliaments'. Since then the EU agenda has continued to expand into policy areas previously excluded from the EU's competence. The resulting tendency of increased Europeanization of domestic issues, which earlier had been the domain of national parliaments, has made elected representatives all over Europe question the traditional primacy of the executive in external relations. The justification for the traditionally weak position of national parliaments in foreign affairs is called into question.[2]

Still, the national parliaments have been slow to respond to the challenge of Europeanization, as compared to other institutional or political actors. The question of whether the national parliaments have left too much power in the hands of national governments in their relation with the EU has only recently become an issue that transcends national borders. The process has been called a reparliamentarization of European politics and may be seen as part of a larger debate over the democratic deficit in the EU.

It may also be seen as a more direct result of the changing status of the European Parliament (EP). Before 1979 when direct elections to the EP were introduced, most of the EP representatives were also representatives of the national parliaments. With direct elections this link between the national and the European level disappeared. In addition the EP has grown in importance over the last years. Both developments may have triggered fears at the national level over a possible development towards a federal system. In a federal system the relationship between the federal parliament and the 'national' parliaments is established constitutionally. A clear division of tasks would mean that the federal parliament would be accountable for decisions taken at the federal level and the 'national' parliaments accountable to decisions at the national level. Clearly this is not the case in the EU where the European Parliament has limited, although increasing powers and where decisions at the European level, in the Council of Europe, are democratically accountable through each national government's duty to answer to the national parliaments (Lord 1991). Still, the increased use of majority voting in the Council of Ministers and the European Parliament's increasing powers, demonstrated by the recent unprecedented resignation of the European Commission, tends to undermine national parliamentary control.

The national parliaments' discretion has also been limited by decisions taken at the European level. The national parliaments have, in the process of integration, voluntarily transferred substantial decision-making power to EU institutions. The evolving role of the European Court of Justice is a case in point. The court has gradually expanded its supranational powers, not only through its right to a simple form of judicial review, but also by its implied powers to rule in cases where it has no formal powers, where the ruling is deemed necessary in order to achieve the treaty's purposes (Weiler 1991: 2413–2417). Within the EU, the supremacy of Community law over national law has been established since the early 1960s (van Gend en Loos 1963 and Costa *v.* Enel 1964). It was in the Simmenthal case (1978) that the principle got its classical formulation; national courts must 'set aside any provision of national law which may conflict with it, whether prior or subsequent to the Community rule'. What has been referred to as the 'aggressive activism' of the European Court of Justice throughout the history of the EU has challenged the supremacy of national laws. At the same time national courts have increased their powers domestically through the authority to invalidate national legislation on the basis of Union law (Caldeira and Gibson 1995: 358). Thus, national parliaments, in their legislative role, especially in those countries where judicial review has played a less important part, are challenged both by developments at the national and the European levels.[3]

Institutional expressions of the increased concern with the role of national parliaments in relation to the Europeanization process can be seen both at the European and the national level. At the European level, in addition to the establishment of COSAC, annual meetings between the presidents of national parliaments have been institutionalized to deal with matters concerning practical administrative co-operation between the parliaments, and there has also been a growing number of joint meetings between committees with the same field of responsibility (Corbett 1998: 79).

At the national level an indicator of the increased concern is the establishment of European Affairs Committees. Many of these have only been established during the last ten years. Table 7.1 provides a general overview and indicates the relative power of the different national European Affairs Committees in relation to their respective governments.[4]

Denmark is the country where the European Affairs Committee is the most powerful in relation to the national government. The minister responsible needs a mandate from the committee to adopt a position in the Council of Ministers. Rules secure that the committee gets the information it needs in order to give this mandate. The government transmits about 1000 proposals a year to the committee and the government's position is presented to the committee before all Council meetings. The extended powers of the European Affairs Committee in Denmark has been critiqued on the grounds that it is the 17 members that represent the Danish people and the rest of the parliament is not much involved. Denmark, in this sense, they assert, has in fact established a kind of two-tier system. This has led to a restructuring of the Parliament's working methods. The specialized committees now co-operate more closely with the European Affairs Committee and they have the right to examine any Community issue they may wish and to submit their proposals to the European Affairs Committee.

If one compares the powers of the Danish European Affairs Committee to that of its Greek counterpart the vast difference between EU member countries, when it comes to parliamentary scrutiny powers, becomes apparent. No constitutional provision obliges the Greek government to inform or consult the Greek parliament before agreeing to a proposal in the Council. The Greek government has only to inform the parliament about European issues through a report issued to the parliament before the end of each parliamentary session. Portugal, Luxembourg, Ireland, Belgium and the Netherlands are countries which resemble Greece in that each parliament has no or limited scrutiny reserve power. In France, Italy and Spain the parliament may suspend or postpone a decision in the Council of Ministers, while in Germany[5] and Austria the government is bound by a mandate, if the parliament chooses to issue one. In the UK the government is obliged to consult parliament before adopting a position, and in the House of Commons every 'depositable document' has to be examined by the European Legislation Select Committee which decides on the proper parliamentary procedure before the responsible minister can adopt a position in the Council (Miller and Ware 1996).

Table 7.1 European Affairs Committees in the national parliaments

Country	Chamber in parliament	Established	Number of members	Weeks between meetings	Scrutiny power
Denmark	Folketinget	11.10.72	17	1	Requires mandate from committee for all decisions
UK	Commons	7.5.74	16	1	Obliged to consult parliament
	Lords	10.4.74	20	2	Obliged to consult parliament
Germany	Bundestag	14.12.94 (91)	50 (11 EP)	1	Government is bound by a position if it is adopted by the Bundestag
	Bundesrat	20.12.57	23	3	Obliged to respect the views of the Bundesrat
Austria	Nationalrat	15.12.94	27	2	Minister bound by mandate if given
	Bundesrat	14.12.94	21	On request	Minister bound by mandate if given
Sweden	Riksdagen	16.12.94	17	1	Not formally binding, but parliamentarily binding*
Finland	Riksdagen	1.1.95	25	1	Not formally binding, but parliamentarily binding
France	Assemblée National	6.7.79	36	1–2	Government may request suspension in Council with reference to parliament
	Senat	6.7.79	36	2–3	Government may request suspension in Council with reference to parliament

* meaning that the cabinet or single ministers may be held accountable to the parliament for any decision made in matters concerning the EU

Table 7.1 European Affairs Committees in the national parliaments (continued)

Country	Chamber in parliament	Established	Number of members	Weeks between meetings	Scrutiny power
Spain	Congresso/ Senado (joint)	27.12.85	39	4	Congress can postpone the adoption of a position in Council
Netherlands	Tweede Kam.	18.5.94	26	2	No general scrutiny power
	Eerste Kam.	June 1970	13	4	No general scrutiny power
Italy	Camera dei deputati	10.10.90	50	1–2	May ask government to postpone adoption of Council's position; no formal parliamentary scrutiny power
	Senato	17.7.68	24		No formal parliamentary scrutiny power
Belgium	Rep.	25.4.85	20 (10 EMP)	4	No scrutiny power
	Senat	29.3.90	22	3	No scrutiny power
Greece	Vouli ton ellinon	13.6.90	31 (10 EMP)		Government does not have to consult or inform parliament
Ireland	Dil/Seanad (joint)	14.3.95	17	2	Government does not have to consult or inform parliament
Luxembourg		6.12.89	11		No scrutiny power
Portugal	Assemblée de la république	29.10.87	27	1	No scrutiny power

Even if the national parliaments exert quite different influence on their respective governments on European issues, the overall tendency seems to be that the national parliaments through the European Affairs Committees gradually have taken on a more important role. Since the COSAC was established in 1989, most notably during the process of ratification of the Treaty on European Union, the national parliaments have made efforts to increase their powers (Judge 1995). This may be seen as a process towards a more active role for the national parliaments in European politics. With this in mind I now turn to the question of whether, and if so, in what sense interparliamentary co-operation can be seen as part of the ongoing effort to make the European Union more democratic?

The anonymous hand of public reason

Any democratic theory in some way has to explain how the will of the people is transformed into authoritative decision-making. Economic theories of democracy (Elster 1983b) answer this question with reference to a process of preference aggregation. Much of the criticism directed at the EU for lack of democracy is based on such a model. In different ways it is shown that the process of aggregation from individually held preferences to decisions at the EU level is incomplete, distorted or both. The critics claim that elections to the European Parliament are not based on one member one vote,[6] that the discussions tend to turn around national rather than genuinely European issues, that turnouts for elections are too low and that the European Parliament lacks sufficient power. The European Council is only indirectly accountable to the people in whose name decisions are made, and because of the lack of openness, the public has no way of knowing if the compromises reached are comprehensive or if they only represent special interests. This critique is no doubt highly relevant, but still it falls short of grasping the process of popular opinion and will formation, which according to democratic theory represented by for example John Rawls and Jürgen Habermas, is essential to any stable democracy. As the tragic developments in the former Yugoslavia make clear, words written on a paper and signed by the contending parties, give no guarantee of stability no matter how much physical force that is put behind it, if the solutions reached are not based on genuine deliberation anchored in the hearts and minds of those involved (Chambers 1998).

The question is what alternative deliberative democracy can come up with? Through what kind of process is the will of the people transformed into binding decisions, and how does the EU live up to standards emanating from such a model of democracy? I will try to answer only a part of this question by focusing on the interparliamentary discourse that is going on between different parliaments throughout Europe. My point of departure is the following: if the democratic institutions of the EU are to live up to the standards of deliberative democratic theory, they have to reflect, not only the preferences and priorities of the electorate, but more importantly, they must also reflect the process of justification that is going on in the civil sphere. This is in line with what Kerstin Jacobsson (1997: 84–86) argues in a recent article 'that the challenge is to develop the porous relationship between civil society and the decision making system in open, non-exclusive ways', that the EU's legitimacy problem is linked to the non-communicative nature of the legislative process. This would mean that formal power given to for example the European Parliament, would have little democratic significance in itself if the link to the civil sphere was lacking (Habermas 1995b).

While economic democratic theory focuses on the aggregation process and the formal power to decide, deliberative democracy focuses on the communicative power emanating from free and open discussions that eventually are turned into collective preferences. The problem at the European level is that the public spheres have been poorly developed. And even if there are some signs that European public spheres are now emerging, it does not seem very likely in any foreseeable future that these can live up to the requirements which a deliberative model of democracy normally would demand.[7]

This is one reason why many Euro-sceptics would trust the national parliaments to be better guardians of democracy than the European Parliament. Still, as long as decisions continuously are made at the European level, decisions which affect people across Europe equally; there will still be a need for deliberation across borders, if European democracy can hope to come anywhere near the deliberative democratic ideal. When decisions made in one country increasingly affect people in other countries, realization of deliberative democracy entails that discussions have to be expanded to include even those non-citizens that are affected. If we accept deliberative democracy as a normative ideal, international democracy is not something we can choose, but rather something that follows by necessity from the normative theory justifying deliberative democracy. When decisions are taken at the supranational level, the need for deliberation across national borders becomes all the more apparent.

The EU has since its beginning tried to legitimize itself in instrumental terms. If only citizens throughout Europe could experience the benefits from economic co-operation they would also accept the EU. This strategy is bound to fail partly because it depends on stable economic growth, but more importantly because genuine political questions cannot be answered by hypothetical imperatives, but are linked to questions of ethics and morality. These are questions that cannot or should not be solved by reference to empirical evidence or by retreating to power politics. What is at stake is 'the relationship between morality and ethical life or the internal connection between meaning and validity' which refers to the question as to 'whether we can transcend the context of our respective language and culture at all or whether all standards of rationality remain bound to specific world-views and traditions' (Habermas 1993: 136).

According to Ghita Ionescu (1993) parliamentary sovereignty is defined as 'the network of communication and consultation between the sovereign people and its representatives in parliament'. This definition emphasizes the idea of government by discussion. The original idea was that the representatives should consult the electorate to inform them and give reasons for their actions. In line with this the frequently expressed ambition at the EU level to improve information to the public is important, but in itself it is not enough. A deliberative version of democracy takes the principle of accountability even further. It claims that in a democracy each should in principle be accountable to all.

Ideally this is only possible if everyone affected takes part in the same discussion. In a modern, complex, large-scale society this is impossible in practice. The result is that deliberation has to be institutionalized. The parliament has to deliberate for all and on the basis of such deliberations take action (Gutmann and Thompson 1996). This is also true at the supranational level. In the words of Cohen and Arato 'frameworks of representative democracy provide the only access for large numbers of people to global processes of democratic will formation', still, 'in representative democracies, political society both presupposes and must be open to the influence of civil society' (Cohen and Arato 1995: 412–413).

A deliberative perspective on democracy will focus on talking and the ways in which talking eventually affects voting, as well as how it affects the level of mutual understanding in a society. Its basic tenet is that the highest authority in a democratic society, when a practical decision is to be taken, is the free and open discussion among all affected parties. People are able to rationally co-ordinate their actions through open-minded discussion aimed at genuine agreement and not only with reference to some pre-political societal norms, or with reference to their own self-interest. This means that deliberative democracy breaks with the assumption made in much of scholarly debate on international relations, that preferences are formed exogenously to interaction.[8] It is rather premised on the idea that collective identities and interests may be formed at the supranational level through a process of democratic opinion and will formation that surpasses domestic politics. Preferences are not given prior to discussions. As Seyla Benhabib (1996: 71) puts it, 'the formation of coherent preferences cannot precede deliberation; it can only succeed it.' Rationality is understood inter-subjectively and is established through a process of reason giving. Only what can be explained to others is considered rational (Chambers 1996: 90).

Deliberative democracy makes the link between the civil sphere and parliamentary decision-making with reference to the development of communicative power emanating from partly autonomous public spheres. In a public sphere problems are ideally detected, identified, thematized and dramatized, and possible solutions are presented (Habermas 1996a: 359). Ideally, discussions in civil society should not be restricted in any way by the state. There should be no restrictions on participation and no restrictions on deliberation. The state's role is to make sure that free and open discussion in the civil sphere is made possible, and as far as possible protected from any kind of manipulation. This is done by establishing and actively protecting civil, political, and social rights. The state also has a responsibility to keep the public informed about public matters, in accordance with the publicity principle (Luban 1996), and in order to ensure accountability. The role of the civil sphere is crucial if state legitimacy is to mean something more than simply adherence to the formal process of decision-making, i.e. that the law-makers abide by the law when making laws. Ideally, what is needed is a process of democratic legitimization that precedes any use of force by the state or any other party. Legitimacy is derived from the process, which explains the need for state power, a process, which logically should not be restrained by the state.[9] As Habermas observes:

> If binding decisions are legitimate, that is if they can be made independently of concrete exercise of force and of the manifest threat of sanctions, and can be regularly implemented even against the interests of those affected, they must be considered as the fulfillment of recognized norms.
>
> (Habermas 1972/1992: 101)

Still, we cannot expect a public sphere in a modern large-scale democracy to reach a conclusion on the actual policies to be carried out. A public sphere cannot and should not make binding decisions. To make binding decisions representative institutions like parliaments are needed. Parliaments transform the influence of the public sphere into communicative power, which in turn legitimates political decisions in parliament (Habermas 1996a: 371).

This does not mean that the civil sphere is not institutionalized in any way. Both the private spheres and the public spheres are sometimes highly institutionalized. The main point from a liberal point of view is that the state should not play a part in this in any direct way. Nancy Fraser (1992: 134) has challenged this conception of public spheres by making a distinction between weak publics 'whose deliberative practice consists exclusively in opinion formation and does not also encompass decisions making' and strong publics 'whose discourse encompasses both opinion formation and decision making'. She argues that a sovereign parliament functions as a public sphere within the state and this is what she has labelled strong publics. In this way parliamentary democracy entails a blurring of borders between state and civil society. My argument in this chapter is that interparliamentary co-operation, as it has been institutionalized in the EU, represents a 'hybrid form' situated between weak and strong publics. It entails a further blurring of the border between state and civil society, one that may serve to enhance the democratic transformation of opinions in a process of collective will formation at the European level. Inspired by Nancy Fraser I have tried to sum up the argument so far in Table 7.2.

One way to envision the process of opinion and will formation that is going on in the public spheres and between public spheres, is as a sifting process where the same arguments are tried over and over again in different situations and in relation to different problems, and where some arguments survive the process, because they tend to convince others. Thus, there is not one debate, but many criss-crossing semi-autonomous debates, within different public spheres, which are different in many ways but which still remain porous to one another (Habermas 1996a: 374). One may speak of this as the anonymous hand of inter-subjective reason. People accept worthy arguments and reject those that do not make sense and this happens without any centralized co-ordination. It is more like a decentralized learning process. By engaging in discussion with others, you get a reaction, a reaction that is not only negative or positive, but that also provides you with a reason for why it is negative or positive. If these reasons are

Table 7.2 Weak and strong publics

	Institutions			
	Weak public spheres (e.g. media; NGOs)	*Intermediary public spheres (e.g. inter-parliamentary debates)*	*Strong public spheres (e.g. parliaments)*	*Government organizations*
State-controlled restrictions on participation	Weak			Strong
State-controlled restrictions on deliberation	Weak			Strong
Effectiveness of collective decision-making	Low			High
Power		Public influence	Communicative power; legislative power	Administrative power

convincing you may change your mind or your mind is reassured depending on the response you get. As John Stuart Mill states, the human mind is 'capable of rectifying his mistakes by discussion and experience', experience alone is not enough (Mill 1931: 81–82). The expectation is that in free and open discussion the more universally acceptable arguments will survive more easily than arguments based purely on self-interest or tradition.

In order for this learning process to be effective, at least three preconditions have to be met. First, people have to be able, willing and permitted to speak their mind on any subject matter (Eriksen 1995: 58). The learning process feeds on variation and any restriction on deliberation will reduce the effectiveness of the learning process. In real life no democratic system will ever be able to fully realize this ideal. Across Europe the practical problems with free and open deliberation probably vary. The media, for example, play different roles and set different standards in their capacity as fora for discussion and broadcasters of viewpoints. This may pose a problem to the establishment of a forum for a common European learning process.

Second, people have to have enough information in order to pass judgement on government policies and administrative practices. This poses a more serious problem in a European context where the language problem, the amount of information processed and the complexities of the many compromises made, make it almost impossible for the ordinary citizen to grasp clearly the rationale behind and the content of the many decisions made.

Third, there has to be some kind of contact between the different discourses that are going on in different public spheres. Nancy Fraser (1992) has pointed to the importance of what she calls subaltern counter-publics, public spheres where interests that are excluded by the dominant publics, or not currently considered relevant for discussion, can be developed and refined through a language that is at least potentially understandable to others. Still, the arguments and world-views represented by such a group, at some point in time have to be tested against standards shared by the dominant publics, if the group's claims are to be recognized by society at large. This becomes increasingly difficult when arguments have to travel across state borders and across different political cultures where what is seen as relevant for discussions in the dominant public spheres may vary from one country to another.

As a result European democracy is in need of public spheres which cut across national borders. My argument is that the interparliamentary discussions may serve as such an intermediary public sphere. Although this intermediary public sphere does not emerge spontaneously out of civil society, but is organized by the parliaments involved, it shares some traits with other public spheres. It has limited power to act, and its institutional structure is not ordered according to any pre-established organizational principles. The prevailing norm seems to be the more contact the better, and this results in a network of criss-crossing contacts between parliamentary representatives interchangeably acting on behalf of the parliament, a parliamentary committee, a political party, or a particular region (Corbett 1998). It has its institutional expressions in multilateral arrangements such as the Conference of the Parliaments of the Union (Assizes), recommended by the Maastricht Treaty (Declaration 14), the assembly of the WEU (West European Union which deals predominantly with security matters), and COSAC. There are also an increasing number of bilateral arrangements between parliaments in Europe (Nentwich and Falkner 1997: 24). Contacts between the European Parliament and parliaments in other parts of the world have also been institutionalized and more firmly established during the last few years. The ACP–EU Joint Assembly, for example, made up of 71 members of the European Parliament and an equal number from African, Caribbean and Pacific (ACP) states, meets twice a year to discuss matters concerning the interdependence of the North and the South.

Still, does all this have any real significance? Is it not just an effort to try to justify a system that is plagued by damaging criticisms, and without giving away any real power – is it merely justification without any real content? It depends on what is meant by content. If content means the power to decide, the sceptics are right. Interparliamentary co-operation, in the way it has been institutionalized in the EU, will not take us much forward. If, on the other hand, we take the idea that talk matters seriously, that in some way arguments that are presented in one setting – a setting in which discussions are not aimed at reaching compromise, but rather consensus – make their way to the deciding fora of the EU, we will at least have to investigate further, both theoretically and empirically, in what way this may be the case.

By design, at least, the COSAC is what may be termed a purely deliberative body. The conference is deliberative in the positive sense in that it is designed for the articulation and exchange of information and ideas between national delegates and also serves as a forum where it should be possible to identify the climate of opinion in relation to more specific issues. It is deliberative in the sense that its sole purpose is to deliberate and not to make any binding decisions. The closest the assembly comes to making decisions is on matters concerning its own organization and even these have to be approved by the other EU institutions. Even though the conference does not make binding decisions, it may issue communiqués on any issue that is found appropriate. It is also difficult to see that the conference is trying to establish itself as something other than a purely deliberative assembly. To the degree that COSAC can be said to represent a particular interest, it reflects the interests of the national parliaments acting in the capacity of sovereign national legislative bodies. The conclusion of the Dublin Summit in 1996 that one should strive 'to enforce the role of the national parliaments in the legislative procedures of the Union', shows that COSAC does express the need to strengthen the national parliaments. But it has not done so by trying to increase its own powers as a representative of the national parliaments in the same way as the EP for example has worked to increase its formal powers.

On the contrary, the conference has decided that any communiqué that is issued requires consensus, and even if consensus is reached, this should not be seen as binding upon the national parliaments. An example of such a consensus is the decision at the Paris meeting in 1995 not to endorse a proposal to establish a second chamber at the Union level which would be made up of delegates from the national parliaments. This was not a self-evident result, but one that emerged out of the discussions following a proposal set forth by the French delegation. Even if this decision does not have any binding force it is difficult to imagine a process in the EU where the COSAC in fact would be turned into a second chamber without seriously damaging the legitimacy of the EU. From the point of view of deliberative democracy, once a clear consensus emerges out of the discussions in COSAC it will be difficult for other EU institutions to act against it without first engaging the national parliaments in further discussions.

Still, consensus is rare in a modern complex society and when it is achieved it is often general enough to allow for a broad range of interpretations by those responsible to make the actual decisions. The consensus rule is nevertheless important because it is this rule that constitutes COSAC as a purely deliberative assembly. The question is if deliberation has anything to offer in situations where consensus is not possible, at least in the short run. Why is it important to keep on talking even in case of deep diversity and when no viable agreement seems in sight? Why not just take a vote and move on?

Deliberation and disagreement

One of the problems facing the European Union is how to reach agreement on issues which not only relate to questions of efficiency and distribution, but which also extend beyond economic considerations. Such issues cannot be settled by reference to empirical evidence, and qualified majority voting will not be deemed an acceptable procedure. At some point in time economic integration creates a need for solutions that involve genuinely political issues, i.e. issues where moral or ethical questions are involved, and where agreement based on compromise alone is not possible. These are issues where agreement cannot be reached without some kind of change in the goals involved or at least a change in the ordering of these goals.

For example, people in the European Union are now free to work in any member country they wish. Still the many different national pension laws make it difficult for them to plan their retirement. This has obvious political implications because the choice of a national policy based on private pensions as compared to state pensions involves ethical and moral questions and is not simply a matter of finding the most effective way to reach established goals. This means that discussions that cut across national borders will have to include normative-political questions. Agreement cannot be reached by reference to efficiency considerations alone. Another example may be the different national policies on drugs and alcohol – policies based on different national traditions and conceptions about the relationship between state and civil society in Europe. The Dutch liberal policy on drugs, for example, is not only based on pragmatic concerns where efficiency criteria apply, but also has a more basic foundation. It boils down to a question as to whether individuals should have the right to choose their preferred way of life by themselves, or whether the state is obliged to regulate society in such a way as to make it difficult for 'weak souls' to lead what is considered a destructive life. When the border controls between European countries are relaxed, this, to a certain extent at least, implies that the liberal Dutch policy, becomes the 'European policy'. This creates the need for discussions where agreement will be difficult to reach with reference to efficiency criteria alone.

Still, is it realistic to presume that interparliamentary discourse can establish an absolute agreement on such issues? Not necessarily full agreement, but then deliberation cannot only be seen as directed at consensus. Gutmann and Thompson (1996) make a distinction between agreement concerning the validity of single arguments and agreement concerning what should be done. In fact they argue that a position on an issue may be worthy of moral respect even if one finds the position morally wrong. For example, through a process of reason-giving marked by reciprocity, even a pacifist may be able to understand the morally relevant reasons for intervening in the conflict in Yugoslavia by use of force. Gutmann and Thompson also make a distinction between discursive and non-discursive procedures. From these distinctions it is possible to identify four types of agreements or disagreements (see also Table 7.3):

1   Discursive agreement is an agreement reached through discussions, which lead to a change of preferences and where in the end everyone agrees for the same reasons. The result is consensus.
2   Non-discursive agreement is an agreement reached through some sort of preference aggregation, but where everyone in principle may have different reasons for accepting the agreement. The result is a compromise solution.

3   Discursive disagreement describes a situation where no agreement has been reached as to what to do, but where the validity claims of the arguments put forth are respected by all. This means that everyone accepts the arguments as valid from the point of view of those who bring them forth, resulting in a degree of mutual understanding.

4   Non-discursive disagreement describes a situation where the validity claims set forth are not respected and where no agreement is reached on what to do, which results in isolation, and possibly hostility or violence.

Gutmann and Thompson argue that in complex modern societies it is difficult to achieve discursive agreement on most moral (or ethical) issues. There are many reasons for this, but maybe the two most important ones are, first, the practical difficulties involved in actually carrying out a conversation where every person is heard in an equal manner and where no force or coercion is applied. In most cases it is simply too time-consuming and inefficient. Second, there are moral and ethical disagreements that run so deep that they will not be solved, no matter how long one is able to talk (Elster 1986: 115).

With this in mind, rather than focusing on how it is possible to achieve discursive agreement, much of their effort will focus on how to avoid the pitfalls of non-discursive disagreement. This is a situation where what people say has no effect on what others say and do, and where there is no way of establishing inter-subjective standards by which to evaluate the different arguments put forth by conflicting interests. The likely outcome in case of severe conflict would be repression or more direct violence. The distinction between this radical version of deliberative democracy and other versions that make less room for deliberation may be understood better by comparing it with John Rawls' idea of overlapping consensus[10] (Rawls 1993).

The concept of overlapping consensus does not fit easily into any of the four categories presented in Table 7.3. For Rawls talking is important, but he starts from the presumption that in order to reach agreement it is necessary to leave out some issues from the public agenda. Thus he argues for the need to limit what can be said in public. This breaks with the idea of deliberative democracy presented here. Rawls holds that in making justifications in matters

Table 7.3 Four different types of agreement and disagreement

	Discursive	*Non-discursive*
Agreement	Agreement for the same reasons	Agreement for different reasons
	Result: consensus	Result: compromise
Disagreement	Disagreement as to what to do, but mutual respect for each other's reasons	No discussion, and voting is not respected
	Result: a degree of mutual understanding	Result: hostility/isolation

of constitutional essentials and basic justice 'we are to appeal only to presently accepted general beliefs and forms of reasoning found in common sense, and the methods and conclusions of science when these are not controversial' (Rawls 1993: 224). Rawls is trying to avoid arguments based on comprehensive 'religious and philosophical doctrines'. For Gutmann and Thompson such limitations on public discourse would be problematic, since it would make it difficult or impossible to identify and understand the reasons people have for accepting or rejecting specific proposals to changes in the political order. If we abandon the idea of consensus as the ideal and rather focus on the importance of continuous discussion in order to establish a degree of mutual respect, we also have to leave the idea that some issues are better left out of discussion. Agreement on some issues, according to such a view, is easier to reach if we respect each other's reasons for not agreeing on other issues. Thus, what we may realistically aim for most of the time is discursive disagreement, which implies willingness and ability to talk, even when disagreement runs deep.

My basic point in the last two sections has been that the interparliamentary discussions may serve as an intermediary public sphere that has little actual power to act, but that still, simply by keeping a discourse alive across national borders in Europe may have an influence on other EU institutions. These suggestions depend heavily on the belief that talk in some way matters and that interparliamentary fora are well suited for talking.

Why talk?

As argued one reason why discourse is important even if it does not lead to consensus is that it creates at least a degree of mutual respect and understanding for each other's arguments. With the absence of talk different positions on a particular issue will tend to be interpreted in terms of self-interest. The language of efficiency and self-interest travels well across national borders in Europe because it is this language that has thus far been most developed in the EU. The arguments for a single currency in Europe, for example, tend to focus on questions of efficiency and on who should be in control of economic decision-making. The single currency issue may, however, also be presented as a question of cultural integrity, where the currency you use symbolizes who you are in a more fundamental way, and defines what kind of society you are part of. Thus, the currency issue may not only be a pragmatic question, but may also involve a deeper question of meaning. The only way to decide if this normative attachment to the currency should have any influence on the decision that is reached is through talking.[11]

Through such an effort one may at least start to understand why, for some, the cultural meaning attached to the currency issue is more important than efficiency considerations. No empirical evidence, however well presented, will convince a cultural sceptic that a common European currency will not represent a threat to national self-understanding. If a decision on introducing a common currency is made without discussions on the meaning attached to the currency, and especially if such considerations are ridiculed as irrational by the proponents of a common currency, the EU may lose legitimacy.

If the proponents of a common currency are able and willing to listen to arguments that are not based on economics, a majority decision, based on efficiency considerations, may be more acceptable to those who prefer to keep the national currencies for other reasons. The broader interparliamentary discussions where there is little prestige and strategic positioning attached to particular outcomes, because no real decisions are made, may contribute to enhance the democratic quality of decision-making, on such issues, in the European Union.

A second reason why deliberation is important is to decide when majority voting can be legitimately used. When is an aggregative procedure acceptable? As a general rule one may argue that non-discursive agreement may be accepted when pragmatic issues are involved, but not when moral or ethical questions are involved. Still, voting as a legitimate decision procedure presupposes a more basic normative agreement, and for this reason it is a question that ideally should be decided by discursive agreement. Majority voting, for example, cannot on principle be legitimized by majority voting, and the same goes for deciding which issues can be legitimately dealt with by majority voting. An institution like COSAC, where majority voting is not an accepted procedure, may be especially well suited to discuss such issues.

A third reason why deliberation is important is because it prepares the ground for a more acceptable compromise in situations where consensus is impossible, but where a collective decision has to be taken. Sometimes collective decisions have to be made, and for this reason democratic collective decision-making in the end has to depend heavily on non-discursive agreement, that is compromise, majority voting or any other democratic aggregative decision-making procedure. Deliberative democracy claims that a majority decision will be easier to justify to all involved if it is preceded by a process of deliberation which not only seeks to establish a solution that may obtain a majority, but also seeks as far as possible to take into account the reasonable objections of a minority. A practical example of such a compromise, which may at least serve to illustrate this point, is the decision to print national symbols on one side of the new European ECU coins. This solution may not satisfy the sceptics who build their argument on non-economic reasons, but it may at least show a willingness to take such considerations into account.

The reason why interparliamentary fora may serve an important role in preparing for a more legitimate compromise or to discuss when majority voting is acceptable, is the fact that it has limited power to act in the sense of having the power to make binding decisions. Voting, once a particular procedure is accepted by all, solves the problem of arriving at an authoritative decision, but the fact that voting is a possibility and the last retreat in case of disagreement, may negatively affect how people talk (Chambers 1997). From this point of view, the suggested alternative to the development of a federal order in Europe, which

Erik Jurgens (1994) refers to as 'an embryonic pre-federal parliament' based on co-operation between national parliaments through the Interparliamentary European Assembly (IEA), and which Christopher Lord (1991) refers to as an interparliamentary union, may reduce the quality of the deliberations among the parliaments. The reason for this is that the voting element will play a greater role and this may tend to focus attention on strategic motives rather than on mutual understanding.

In deliberative versions of democracy it is presumed that mutual respect develops through talking to each other as equals, which means that any argument has to be taken seriously before it is criticized. Convictions, which emanate from history, tradition or religion cannot be refuted by refuting the relevance of these deep-seated beliefs. Only by finding a solution, which makes them irrelevant from the point of view of those who hold them, may agreement be reached.

As a consequence, a fourth reason why deliberation is important is because it may lead to the questioning of the limits of formal decision-making power at the collective level. One of the most important questions to be settled by deliberation is to establish the limits that ought to be set on state intrusion into the public and the private spheres. According to Habermas (1996a: 313) 'every affair in need of public deliberation should be publicly discussed, though not every legitimate object of public discussion will in fact be politically regulated'. This implies that when parliaments are discussing the possibility of regulating a certain activity they also have to discuss if this activity ought to be regulated by the state. At the EU level this problem becomes even more complicated as the question is not only if an activity should be open to regulation, but also at what level, national or European, the decision to regulate should be made.

The introduction of the subsidiarity principle has focused attention on these issues within the EU.[12] The principle states that decisions should be taken at the lowest possible level of government in order to reach EU goals. The preamble to the Maastricht Treaty potentially gives the concept an even wider application when it states that decisions should be taken 'as close as possible to the citizen in accordance with the principle of subsidiarity'. Within the EU, one may argue that the experience of deep diversity in the Maastricht Treaty process increased the relevance of the subsidiarity principle. This principle urges one to question the decision-making powers at any level of government.

Thus disagreement where deep diversity is involved may be solved by non-decision, or as implied by the subsidiarity principle by moving a decision to a lower level of government. The question is why interparliamentary fora may be especially well suited to discuss these matters.

After the subsidiarity principle was written into the Maastricht Treaty and established as a guiding principle for the EU, much discussion has focused on who should in practice decide on what level a decision should be taken. The European Court of Justice (ECJ) has been mentioned as one possibility. From the point of view of deliberative democracy, this solution is clearly unacceptable. The decisions which should be taken with as broad a public participation as possible, and where deliberation is more important than anywhere else, are those concerning who should decide a particular issue, and in what way the issue should be decided (e.g. majority vote). If anything, this is what the popular resentment directed at the Maastricht process has shown.

The most radical suggestion made is, as mentioned earlier, the proposal to establish a second chamber to the European Parliament, constituted by the national parliaments, and which would have as one of its primary responsibilities, the monitoring of the subsidiarity principle. A second, less radical suggestion, has been to establish an interparliamentary committee made up of national representatives from each Member State. And a third suggestion has been to leave decisions concerning subsidiarity to the national parliaments which are seen as the prime source of democratic legitimacy (M.P. Smith 1996: 288).

All these suggestions seem to break with the main content of the subsidiarity principle which, as noted, explicitly gives a higher level 'the burden of proof', which emphasizes the central importance of open deliberation in any such relationships (Blichner and Sangolt 1994). Thus, the principle of subsidiarity seems to necessitate interparliamentary deliberation, rather than a division of labour between different parliamentary bodies.

The introduction of the subsidiarity principle in the Maastricht Treaty, and which was further developed in the Amsterdam Treaty, is an example of how a concept is used in an effort to make a political order more democratic, without directly changing the institutional set-up. Since the concept was first introduced, there has been an ongoing discussion on what the concept entails and how it is best applied. It reminds us that constitution-making is not only about changing rules and procedures, but also about conceptualizing a political order in terms common to all. Thus, a fifth and final point in this section is that deliberation institutionalized in the form of interparliamentary co-operation may be important in the process towards a common conceptualization of the European polity.

In contrast to the debates on economic issues, which refer to general economic principles, the debates on democracy are more often linked to the democratic institutions in each of the Member States, or as David Judge (1995: 96) puts it: 'European institutions still seem remote to many citizens of the EU and European issues still tend to be seen through national lenses.' Common idealized democratic principles that everybody agrees on have not developed very far. Words like federalism, judicial review or democratic legitimacy have different meanings in different countries. Solutions that are all considered democratic, differ substantially. Each country has its own interpretation of democratic principles and their own institutional ethics. Thus, there is no common standard by which the political institutions of the European Union can be judged. Thus far, each country tends to evaluate the European Union as a political entity on the basis of concepts and ideas that are used in each country to discuss, describe and legitimize the democratic institutions of that country.[13]

Conceptual clarification opens up for new ways of thinking as well as acting. It makes a particular worldview possible, a worldview which may be difficult to understand for an outsider. More importantly it makes certain choices possible. Without a concept of honesty, one cannot choose to be either honest or dishonest (Connolly 1983).

To be more specific, the way Europe as a political unit is interpreted in ethical terms, combined with interpretations of more universally valid political principles, will have an impact on concrete decisions concerning the organization of EU institutions and on the relationship between them. Consider the European Council as a case in point. There is a discussion going on about what kind of political institution the Council really is. The reason for this is that the Council, with its mixture of executive and legislative functions, does not easily compare with the political institutions at the national level in member countries. Even so discussions on what the European Council is tend to make use of national analogies. Sometimes it is compared to the Cabinet in parliamentary systems and sometimes it is compared to the legislature and sometimes it is seen as a mixture between the two (Miller and Ware 1996: 185). It has, for example, been suggested that the European Council should serve the role of a second chamber much in line with the American Senate or the German Bundesrat, where representatives are elected with reference to territory, and not with reference to the size of the constituency. Such and other interpretations may have a direct impact when deciding how the general principle of transparency and openness is interpreted in relation to the Council. The tradition throughout Europe is that cabinets deliberate and decide behind closed doors while most decisions in parliaments are presided by open debate. The interpretation of what the Council is may then have a direct impact on how the principle of transparency is implemented in the context of the Council.

Common conceptualization will depend on a rather complicated process of translation, where the content of a concept and its relation to other concepts will be discussed continuously, at different levels and in different types of communities, both nationally and internationally, and where the discussions at one level help inform discussions at another level. Thus, if a concept such as transparency is presented for example in the COSAC, as something wanting within the EU, the national delegates may go home and try to make sense of this concept in a national context, for example by introducing this concept in private discussions, in public debates or in the national parliaments. They may then go back to the COSAC for new discussions, better prepared to explain to other delegates what the concept means in a national context and how it sits with the meaning it is given at the European level. Each time the concept is evoked in practical politics the content of the concept may be reaffirmed, changed or further refined.

In order to do this there has to be continuous communication in the form of reasoned deliberation between representatives that speak different languages, and where the meaning of a concept in one context continuously is compared to the meaning in another context. In the process, a common understanding may be reached on what the concept entails. My point is that the interparliamentary discussions have an important part to play in this process. First, because they bring a democratic element into the process of conceptualization; second, because they are transnational; and third, because they have little formal power to decide and the discussions may be less open to the influence of strategic manoeuvring.

Conclusion

Deliberative democracy claims that it is possible to reach understanding across different cultures even in situations where deep diversity threatens to destroy any hope of future co-operation. For deliberative democracy to function the link between society and the political system has to be secured in a way that reflects the process of justification that is going on in the civil sphere. In order to secure this link will formation has to be institutionalized. It may be institutionalized in different ways. Deliberative democracy does not prescribe certain institutional solutions; rather it develops standards by which existing and proposed solutions may be evaluated and possibly changed. In light of such an evolving democratic project, the focus in this chapter has been the possible positive democratizing effects on the EU from the efforts to institutionalize interparliamentary co-operation in Europe.

To sum up, a democracy needs public spheres which are able to stand up to state institutions, put issues on the public agenda, define the lines of conflict, and transform issues into distinguishable alternatives. My main argument has been that interparliamentary discourse is important in democratic terms because it may partly make up for the lack of European-wide public spheres. Even though the level of co-operation between parliaments in Europe is still fairly low, this activity is on the increase, and there are also a wide variety of different forms of co-operation already in place.

A main argument in this chapter has been that deliberation is not only directed at consensus, deliberation is as important in promoting understanding and respect for each other's arguments. Through interparliamentary co-operation at the EU level deliberation is institutionalized in a way that at least in principle gives priority to free and open discussion. As an intermediary public sphere situated at the border between civil society and parliamentary democracy it may prove to be an important link in the chain of democratic opinion and will formation. According to a deliberative version of democracy this chain should start by unrestrained discussions in the civil sphere, discussions which ideally should end up influencing concrete decisions at the EU level.

Further I have argued that there are some kinds of issues for which this intermediary public sphere is especially suitable. When it comes to discussing questions that cannot be solved simply by reference to efficiency criteria and where power politics is not accepted, interparliamentary discourse has a special role to play. My last point has been that the parliaments (including the EP), acting in concert, may serve as the only truly democratic body to discuss and come to an understanding on how to conceptualize the European polity, and doing so while actively engaging the public at the national level in the process.

The interparliamentary discussions may be seen as a way of institutionalizing self-reflectivity on the parliament's own decisions. Some would ridicule this whole idea as utterly naive. How can interparliamentary discussion influence decision-making if it in the end has no power to decide? This objection is of course right if we presume that there is no such thing as the power of the better argument and it is not possible to achieve a higher level of understanding and respect for each other's arguments through discussion. Formalized and extensive interparliamentary co-operation is in its very beginning. From the point of view of economic democratic theory it can easily be written off as a futile effort to lend some justification to a political system in need of popular support. From the vantage point of deliberative democracy it gives the promise of developing into one important link between the national civil spheres and EU decision-making. If interparliamentary co-operation actually will live up to such a task remains to be seen. I have argued in theoretical terms that it is a possibility and indicated that developments thus far within the EU at least move in the right direction.

Notes

1　Conférence des organes spécialisés dans les affaires communautaires.
2　The perhaps most remarkable example of this turn is the French parliament's effort, during the last few years, to increase its powers in Community affairs which previously has been considered foreign policy under the control of the executive (Judge 1995: 91).
3　See Weiler (1994) for a discussion of how and why the European Court of Justice has been so successful in limiting national autonomy.
4　Based on national and EU internet sources (http://www.europarl.eu.int/natparl/cosac). For a review see David Judge (1995).
5　Of the six founder Member States Germany is the country where procedures were first established to enable the legislative bodies control over the executive (Judge 1995: 82).
6　Based on the fact that smaller states are over-represented in the EP.
7　See for example Schlesinger and Kevin (1999).
8　For a discussion see, for example, Alexander Wendt (1993).
9　Theoretically at least this opens up for a democratic dilemma if democracy in the form of free and open discussions independently of the state is dependent on democratic institutions. In a democracy citizen communication has to be institutionalized legally. Still, democratic institutions in order to be considered democratic have to be established through free and open discussion. This interdependency means that democracy and democratic institutions will have to develop hand in hand. See Habermas (1995b) for a brief account of the relevance of this for the development of a democratic Europe.
10　Overlapping consensus broadly covers the idea that it is possible to agree on moral matters even if the reasons for agreeing are not the same.
11　This does not mean that deliberation may also be important in order to raise the level of competence on factual matters concerning European issues among national parliamentarians. Scholars have shown relatively little interest in parliamentary debates, but at least one study of debates in the British House of Commons indicates a deterioration in factual accuracy of contributions by MPs on European issues up until 1993 (Garnett and Sherrington 1996). A main premise in this chapter, however, is that deliberation may also have an impact on the contending parties' position on normative issues.

12 Miller and Ware (1996), for example, suggest that the introduction of the principle of subsidiarity is one reason why the flow of legislative proposals in the EU has slowed down.
13 Martyn A. Bond (1997), for example, notes that 'Member States have been more mindful of their national traditions, which vary widely, than of the need to lend greater legitimacy to the European Parliament'.

8 Challenging the bureaucratic challenge[1]

Christian Joerges and Michelle Everson
(translated by Iain L. Fraser)

I Introduction

This contribution takes its assigned task seriously. It deals with the most Kafkaesque among the very many European institutional developments, namely the committee system. This system, or comitology[2], would readily seem to represent – and indeed was early qualified as such[2] – the bureaucratic challenge *par excellence*: the administrative incubus, which is steadily superseding more conventional structures of democratic governance (cf. Weiler 1999b). However, this widely held view, may still, and will be contrasted as against a far more optimistic view.

'The challenge to the bureaucratic challenge', or the 'redemption' of the committee system, rests primarily upon a more closely considered examination of the place and role of committees within the overall institutional and contextual structure of the European Communities (*infra* II). A presentation of the full range of arguments which led to the institutional preference for committees, together with a detailed examination of the forms of social regulatory action in which they engage, sets the scene for a questioning of widely held perceptions and allows for a different interpretation (*infra* III and IV). European committees cannot simply be classified as the agents of a bureaucratic revolution. Rather, with all its sensitivity for the modern complex of risk regulation and for the intricacies of internationalized governance within non-hierarchical and multi-level structures, the committee system may be argued to possess a normative, if underformed, character of its own; or, more precisely, to operate within a novel constitutional framework informed by the notion of 'deliberative supranationalism' (*infra* V).

Such rosy optimism apart, however, this contribution similarly seeks to avoid the dangers of misplaced generalization. The point is not to claim that a Panglossian European Community has successfully circumnavigated the iron cage of Max Weber's tragic scheme of bureaucratic governance. Rather, the assertion is that the process of European integration has of itself led to institutional innovations, which challenge the European Community's own bureaucratic image and heritage. Where once doyens of *Europawissenschaft*, such as Hans-Peter Ipsen (cf. Ipsen 1972), characterized the European Communities as a 'Zweckverband funktioneller Integration', whose legitimacy derived exactly from its political limitations – or bureaucratic nature – the process of European integration has seen European institutions evermore deeply implicated in social and thus politically relevant regulation. From technocratic regime to 'political administration': the novel institutional evolution of the European Communities has questioned conventional paradigms of bureaucratic governance. Furthermore, to the extent that new European institutions of governance may be argued to be founded upon a legally structured and deliberative balancing of national and supranational claims to protect and promote social and ethical interests against the demands of rational economic integration, they may likewise be claimed to represent 'good governance' in the making: or, an experimental process of multi-level integration through deliberation.

II   Contextualizing the bureaucratic challenge

The EC's committee structure, following its long history of steady, seemingly irresistible rise in practice, now seems well on the road to a second, this time academic career. Understandably, given the multiplicity and variety of European committees in almost all areas of European policy,[3] studies which seek to go beyond mere description, but which likewise eschew only very abstract theoretical statements, must strictly delimit their focus and clearly specify their objects of investigation. The starting point and focus of this contribution is, accordingly, the committee system as an *institutional form of regulatory policy* in the European internal market. The committee system is therefore of interest, not because of its alleged peculiarities or its Kafkaesque features, but since it represents an innovative institutional response to the unforeseen challenge of regulatory policy-making at the European level. Accordingly, the committee system will be studied in this, its specific context of action. This context is still notably ambitious. The institutional preference for committees represents nothing less than a systematic and empirically based contribution to the development and formation of a core area of European policy; and with this, the transformation of the European Economic Community into a European polity with its own peculiar governance structures, policy objectives, regulatory techniques and problems of legitimacy. Inherent to the choice of this framework of reference, is an assertion that the specific objects of investigation within this contribution are of exemplary importance for the study of the European Communities as a whole. This is true, first, of the concentration on questions of risk regulation as a feature of internal market policy, and, second, of the focus on the 'implementation' problems that came to the fore after the supposed 'completion' of the internal market in 1992: the term 'comitology', it should be noted, stands not for the European committee system as a whole, but merely denotes those bodies involved with the 'implementation' of secondary legislation.[4]

This introductory section seeks to present these complex reference problems in a systematic manner and to develop from them the specific approaches which guide and structure the study as it unfolds. Accordingly, this introduction will deal with the three underlying themes: regulatory policy; institutionalization; and constitutionalization. These are kept separate for analytical reasons, though their interdependence will also be underlined: the manner in which the committee system is rooted in internal market policy (1); the institutional attraction of comitology (2); and, the demand for a legal constitution in line with the quasi governmental tasks of comitology (3).

1   Regulatory policy

This contribution responds to the intensification of the Community's 'new' regulatory policy as launched by the Commission's 1985 Internal Market Initiative (EC Commission 1985a) and the Single European Act that entered into force in 1987.[5] Accordingly, it forms a part of a body of integration research that by now comprises a barely graspable volume of theoretical and empirical studies,[6] but which, nonetheless, also raises controversial issues of fundamental importance. More specifically, why did a policy that aimed to open frontiers and which was based on market economy principles itself generate new regulatory programmes? Economists, political scientists and lawyers all have well equipped theoretical arsenals for answering this question. 'Market failure – policy failure – failure of law' are the landmarks in this debate which are familiar from national contexts. These are landmarks that have also had an impact upon debates on European internal market policy; though, in this case, they must be approached with new analytical tools and patterns of argument.

In our area of study, however, wide-ranging theoretical debates are now probably less helpful than are interpretative specifications of exemplary importance. This contribution seeks to specify its interpretation in two ways. First, by shifting the focus of study from the production to the 'implementation'[7] of legislatively prescribed regulatory policies; that is, the question of what remains to be done in the Community irrespective of the supposed 'completion' of the internal market in 1992. Secondly, by concentrating upon the markets for 'technical goods' and 'foodstuffs'; and further, by placing special emphasis upon safety or risk control product regulations within these markets. Note, however, that the relevance of these specifications is by no means a given. Undoubtedly, 'product regulations' are an indispensable prerequisite for the realization of the internal market. The specific circumstances that give rise to these regulatory activities, however, appear to be fairly specific and do not operate in the same way in all policy areas,[8] while even the conceptualization of product regulation as *risk* regulation is in need of an explanation and justification of its own.[9]

2   Institutionalization

If and because the European internal market is an integration policy project requiring not simply the adoption of the sparse 280 legal acts mentioned in the Commission's 1985 White Paper, but also – as the Commission soon realized – constant management to keep it going,[10] the number of regulations and directives adopted by the Commission now many times exceeds the number of legal acts adopted by Council and Parliament.[11] It is therefore essential, when analysing the manner in which this undertaking works, to also address its institutional dimensions.

Its practical significance in this regard notwithstanding, the committee system has received little theoretical attention in relation to its role in fostering the functioning of the internal market. Instead, two institutional alternatives – of themselves far more transparent and better in line with the internal market policy programme – were to be highlighted: (1) the legal obligation of 'mutual recognition' of binding regulations, making authoritative harmonization superfluous and seeking to replace it with regulatory competition;[12] (2) the handing over of regulatory tasks to 'non-majoritarian institutions', particularly independent agencies in line with the American pattern.[13] Yet, in Community policy areas regulated in the 'old European' manner, particularly in agricultural policy (Bertram 1967; Schmitt von Sydow 1980: 131–185; Falke 1996: 138ff.), though by no means only there (cf. Falke 1996: 152ff.), the committee system already had a long, albeit somewhat obscure,[14] history behind it. In the two areas selected for study here – technical standards and foodstuffs law – which both had their own institutional traditions and were now required to revise them under the influence of internal market policy, the analogous adoption of the committee system seemed immediately appropriate, even though, in the area of food safety, the institutionalized concentration of expert knowledge in a European agency was to be considered long before the BSE scandal.[15] Similarly, those studying the new policy of mutual recognition, for instance in the insurance sector or in relation to Commission documents on the setting up of a European pharmaceuticals agency, noted that committee structures were created or maintained even though the Community announced alternative regulatory programmes.[16] *Summa summarum*: the successful institutionalization of the internal market seemed to be fully dependent upon this particular institutional oddity. This is reason enough to seek explanations for the vitality of the committee system with regard to the comparatively high problem-solving capacity of these hybrid institutions.

3   *Constitutionalization*

'Regulative competition' – 'independent regulatory agencies' – 'committee system' – this threefold constellation does not simply designate regulatory techniques or alternatives from amongst which European policy-makers could chose as they saw technocratically fit. Rather, each of the three represents a regulatory alternative that, when chosen, has 'constitutional' significance, since it apportions responsibility for governmental or administrative action and likewise structures this responsibility. 'Regulatory competition' between jurisdictions which must demonstrate locational advantages is certainly an unavoidable consequence of opening frontiers (Scharpf 1997c: Chapter III; *idem* 1997a); yet, guaranteeing mutual recognition of regulatory policies and the transition from checks by the state of destination to checks in the state of origin are creative steps that go far to replace the usual competition for electoral votes in constitutional states. 'Non-majoritarian institutions' that remain outside the cycle of general elections and are confined to handling defined specific tasks are not, by definition, anti-democratic; yet, if they are constructed as an exclusive form of government, their democratic credentials may be questioned. Finally, committees, in which an objectively interdependent problem-solving task is nonetheless distributed among separate bodies according to competence, are familiar from federative multi-level systems.[17] However, as regular forms of action within a system that has strictly formalized its legislative processes, yet in principle has no central administrative competences, the committee system is evidently, if not 'extra-legal', at least something consequent – a forum developed as an answer to a practical need for formal and informal co-operation between various bearers of distinct functions. This statement applies both to the forms of action in internal market management used in practice and those recommended in theory.[18] Even if the options mentioned are fundamentally different in their underlying regulatory philosophies, taken together, they nonetheless represent developments which, while not 'unlawful', are irregular to the extent that the EC's founding fathers or 'masters of the treaty,' had not envisaged their appearance or that they would systematically be deployed to supplement legal provisions or, indeed, replace legal harmonization procedures.

While it may be superfluous to define and to compare the degree to which legal innovations are irregular, the committee system nonetheless deserves prior attention, if only because, in the practice of Community policy-making, a greater importance attaches to it, and it has similarly proved to have extraordinary vitality even after the 'completion' of the internal market. Accordingly, in the light of regulatory policy, and institutional and constitutional considerations, the following may be observed:

1   The committee system is a form of action by which the Community handles long-term policy tasks. To the extent that such 'comitology' is marked by more recent internal market policy, it must be analysed in the context of the creation and 'management' of this market; that is, seen against the background of the specific rationalities and contents which characterize this policy (*infra* II).

2   The committee system is a facet of the institutionalization of the European internal market which is specific to the Community, and the practical shape of which depends on the tasks from time to time associated with market integration. Accordingly, one may anticipate a flexible internal structure, and also that the demands made upon its performance capacity will vary (*infra* III).

3   Last but not least, because the committee system presents itself as a specific Community form of governance, or of market management, its institutional pattern is a question of constitutional significance (*infra* IV).

III   Social regulation and internal market policy

What were the policy objectives that guided the European internal market policy and that continue to accompany it? Some minimal theoretical reconstruction of this development seems an indispensable prerequisite to the explanation and assessment of the particular institutional patterns which have been chosen or rejected.

1   Negative integration, positive integration and re-regulation

Since its conception (see Tinbergen 1965) the concept of negative integration, with all its ambivalent connotations, has accompanied European policy for the creation of a single market. At the analytical level, the term is acceptable if used to distinguish between integration oriented 'merely' to removing non-tariff barriers, on the one hand, and integration oriented to developing European policies ('positive integration'), on the other.[19] Yet, the positive/negative dichotomy tends to lead to two forms of misperception. It seems to suggest that the creation of uniform market conditions is merely a matter of paying tribute to pre-legal 'freedoms' and thereby neglects the politically creative element in removing barriers to trade. Just as importantly, the distinction between, first, a 'negative' policy aimed at removing legal differences, and, second, a 'positive' policy determining what will take the place of the 'removed' regulations, is analytical rather than 'real'; in practice, all legal harmonization measures were always also 'positive' legislative policy decisions – any implementation of economic freedoms was always associated with a testing and assessment of the regulatory interests of Member States.[20]

The negative/positive dichotomy has had effects well beyond the original context it emerged from. In particular, the now legendary internal market initiatives of the 1980s were seen at the time by many commentators – and, indeed, equally so by sceptics and partisans – as a project to overcome stagnatory Member State regulation, as an implementation of freedoms guaranteed in the EC Treaty and as a limitation – which was supported by the legal precept of 'mutual recognition'[21] – upon the regulatory discretion of Member States. This perception was, as very quickly emerged, rather short of the mark. The internal market initiative did not, say, remove national regulations acting as non-tariff barriers to trade, leaving no residue, but instead replaced them by European regulatory arrangements: it did not bring about 'de-regulation', but revealed itself to be a 're-regulatory' programme.[22]

2   Re-regulation as the modernization of regulatory approaches and a restriction of regulatory objectives

To be sure, the assertion that internal market policy was aimed at re-regulating the European economy is as such neither theoretically surprising, nor exciting in terms of practical politics or even illuminating. Instead, substantial evaluation was to depend upon the substantive regulatory concepts which were to find room within the new regulatory provisions. Two observations typified the debate on the implications of internal market policy, not only in respect of the particular fields of product regulation highlighted here, but also with regard to the full range of internal market regulation.

The first concerns the 'level' or 'stringency' of regulatory policy. That the harmonization measures needed to 'complete the internal market' should aim at a 'high level of protection' is a legal requirement pursuant to Article 100a (3) ECT. It was at first thought to be surprising that this provision did not remain a mere and general programme; but, its detailed application is no longer controversial.[23] Certainly, the identification of a particular level of protection and therefore also the distinction between 'stricter' and 'looser' rules is often troublesome. Although lawyers have learned to attribute important practical implications to the wording of various general clauses referred to in regulating risks,[24] they have problems with 'grading' regulatory approaches where such grading presumes the existence of an overreaching reference framework, or alternative concepts built upon incompatible preconditions.[25] It is, in any case, more appropriate to term the 'high level of protection' an internal market policy 'modernization' of regulatory policy. This at the same time fits its conditions of action: the Commission must, per Article 100a (3) ECT, present regulatory proposals that bring a 'high level of protection', which at least – but also only! – meet with the approval of a qualified majority of Member States and are at the same time suitable for circumnavigating the individual national approaches that may seem to threaten internal market policy. In the 'positive integration' of regulatory policies which is, as a consequence, unavoidable, the Community is confronted by differing national regulatory traditions and interest groupings. Even in terms of the constraints of finding consensus, the Commission cannot without further ado take on some particular national regulatory model. Obviously the prospect of consensus is the greater the better a regulatory proposal may be presented as an 'objective' and 'neutral' measure of mediation between the objective goal of market integration and the guaranteeing of protective interests (such as, health, safety, environment protection or consumer protection).[26]

Is all this just too idealistic an assessment? Can the conditions that promote decisions where the agents involved are guided by 'objective' criteria be more precisely defined in theoretical terms, if not for the planning, then at least for the implementation of Community policies? These key questions are not new. The first to 'discover' them and treat them systematically was, without doubt, Giandomenico Majone. In its regulatory activities, runs his central thesis, the Community should and must pursue economic efficiency criteria, confine itself to the correction of market failure, and refrain from all redistributive activities.[27] This is not to deny that decisions for this or that regulatory standard have different effects in the regions or Member States. Nor is there any dispute that the agents involved will assert their interests through their governments or other national agents. Majone is, instead, concerned with the conditions for the success of Community policies. Among these are, in his view, deliberate neglect of controversial distributive objectives and a correspondingly narrow treatment of 'social regulation' (Majone 1993c).

We shall very shortly return to the institutional and normative dimensions of this approach. Here, however, we would first like to draw attention to two types of (*inter alia*) empirical difficulties. First, Majone's assertion that Community regulatory policy tends to avoid distributive questions certainly finds backing in the rejection, or rather redefinition, of 'industrial policy' interests. Such interests have long, in the area of product standards (EC Commission 1990a and 1990b) and now explicitly in foodstuffs law (Commission 1997b), been simply redefined as being commensurate with an increase in the performance of the European economy, and have thereby been freed both from interventionist practices and from protectionist or national economic interests. Yet, this assertion is also incompatible with the practical importance of the committee system and the major part still played by national bureaucracies and experts close to government. It only then becomes plausible if one assumes that the distributive effects of regulatory policies spread so wide that it is no longer possible to allocate particular economic interests to individual governments, and/or assumes that the anti-protectionist legal provisions of Community law are actually observed in the decision-making processes (cf. Joerges and Neyer 1997: 295ff.). Second, Majone's thesis that it is possible to portray the objects of decision and regulatory policy as 'technocratic' questions, the answering of which is a function that can be delegated to experts, is, at the very least, counter-intuitive. Judgements on the social acceptability of risks associated with the consumption of food require a balancing of benefits and costs which cannot meaningfully be performed without the help of experts but which, at the same time, must also pay due regard to normative, political and occasionally even ethical considerations. For present purposes, it may be sufficient to note that, to date,[28] no constitutional state has delegated risk assessment entirely and exclusively to expert bodies.[29] The normative, ethical, cultural and political dimensions of risk calculations will make themselves felt at Community level: not only do they militate against the delegation of risk assessments to bodies of experts; but they also render it highly unlikely that one single body will be able to provide uniform decisions which are socially acceptable within the entire internal market. The institutional implications of these considerations are far-reaching. If and because risk assessments must also include normative-political considerations, the committee system needs equally to mediate between 'universal' (Europe-wide agreed upon) criteria and 'national concerns'. Thus, it must not be replaced by a central authority which would be politically unaccountable for its risk assessments (Joerges and Neyer 1997: 278).

3   Re-politicizing social regulation

Even were Majone's rejection of distributive considerations empirically justified or normatively sustainable, his reduction of politics to distributive questions would nonetheless remain untenable. The ethical and normative dimensions of risk management described above are just one justification for this objection. Of equal importance is the circumstance that the objectives of regulatory policy are constantly being expanded and that regulatory complexity renders illusory the notion of delegation to non-political bodies of experts. Foodstuffs law and areas connected with it offer very rich illustrative material here. Suffice it to point to the example of genetic engineering, or the debate on taking nutritional policy aims into account in foodstuffs law (Commission 1997b). In the area of standardization, one may refer to the debate on the consequences of technologies in safety at work law (Bücker 1997: 58ff.) and the efforts to include environmental policy objectives within product standardization (Falke and Joerges 1995).

In the same manner as the developmental phases sketched out above, so the trends here designated 're-politicization' suggest further institutional and normative considerations. Thus, notwithstanding European regulatory policy-making's bedrock eschewal of socially redistributive issues, the impact upon it of the ethical and normative dimensions of risk assessments and of the growing complexity of social regulatory measures, seems nonetheless to preclude any interpretation of it as nascent technocratic governance. Further, it is equally inadequate to justify the delegation of implementations to bodies of experts on the basis of this form of characterization. From this very 're-politicization' of social regulation a consequential problem emerges, namely the question whether present institutional framework conditions are appropriate to their decisional contents. The European Community system has become established as an intergovernmental 'administrative' counterpart to the supranational European legislature. If it would function merely as an institutional counterweight, it would not by any means be a promising candidate in the search for a legitimate form of regulatory European policy.[30]

4 Product and process regulation

The impact of product regulations on the free circulation of goods in the EU is immediately evident. To focus on product regulation and to neglect the so-called process regulations, which deal with production processes and tend to impose differing costs on producers in different Member States,[31] may at first sight seem a very questionable, if not misleading device. However, the famous negative/positive integration dichotomy, or the analytical differentiation between product and process regulations often seems not to provide a distinction sharp enough for the practical process of decision-making with regard to internal market policies. This is true, first, for the decisional procedures on product regulations – often also with environmental relevance! – pursuant to Article 100a ECT and on process regulations pursuant to Article 130s (1) ECT, the earlier differences between which have been rendered less stark by the Maastricht Treaty, and will be still further levelled out by Articles 95, 175, 176 of the Amsterdam Treaty. But it is also true since product regulations increasingly include environmental policy requirements (cf. Falke and Joerges 1995) – construction products are an exemplary case.[32] Further, our analysis aims at showing the institutional preconditions for 'legitimate' problem solving by the European committee system. This approach may overlap with the study of process regulations.[33]

IV The legal and institutional options for internal market policy

The foregoing sketch of the development of internal market policy should have made it clear that the deepening of market integration was always associated with the expansion of institutional frameworks to achieve regulatory objectives; in view of the different problems and interest configurations to which these regulatory frameworks must respond, it comes as no surprise that their design is highly variable. The possible reactions are limited, but not determined, by the institutional peculiarities of the Community. Three basic patterns have already been mentioned. They will now be presented once again, but this time in such a way as clearly to bring out interdependencies between the institutional alternatives and the definitions of regulatory problems.

1 Mutual recognition and regulatory competition

The first alternative, namely abandoning 'positive' Community policy in favour of the 'mutual recognition' of national provisions – underpinned by information policy measures and a consistent product liability law[34] – will not be pursued in any more detail given this study's focus on risk issues.[35] To be sure, market competition for goods also encompasses risk information and risk communication. Yet, for clear practical and normative reasons, no legal system might dispense with regulatory policies for risk control. This fact alone determines that the choice of risk regulation as an exemplary specification within this study is not an arbitrary one. This form of regulatory activity has survived the trend to eschew interventionist policies. It is inconceivable that the 'completion' of the European internal market could be based upon a deregulation of risk controls – and always was so, even before the BSE crisis made it clear to all parties that a market without frontiers is not just simply economically advantageous, but may also dangerously intensify risk-based problems.

2 Agencies

The US inspired alternative of independent regulatory agencies, has also been recommended, particularly by Giandomenico Majone, as an institutional priority for the EC.[36] His plea is to be understood in theoretical and constitutional-normative terms.[37] The delegation of regulatory powers to non-majoritarian institutions is said 'internally' to stabilize political commitments against short-term, tactical policy priorities, and 'externally' to enhance the credibility of programmatic commitments.[38] On the other hand, this form of political 'renunciation of power' can be tolerable only if a sort of technocratic self-restraint is imposed on those agencies; their tasks must be clearly defined by legislative requirements, and their regulatory practice must meet procedural standards that are substantiated and monitored by the courts.[39]

The European agencies established to date[40] fall far short of this ideal. Even the London Pharmaceuticals Agency, set up in 1995,[41] ultimately remains tied to the committee structure which it was allegedly supposed to replace.[42] The practical political and formal legal reasons for reserve on the part of Member States and the Commission need not be detailed here. All we wish to note is that the new 'agencies' are auxiliary institutions for the Commission and are chiefly assigned tasks of preparing information, but lack the legally specific feature of their American namesakes, namely a genuine regulatory competence – which need not, though, mean that these supposedly weak institutions will be spared the experiences of the sorcerer's apprentice.[43]

3   Committees

The apparently irresistible rise of the committee system as a forum for and form of regulatory policy in the internal market seems, at least in hindsight, to be a simple result of functionalist reason. It is no coincidence that the committee system was first developed in the most intensively regulated area of the European economy, namely the agricultural sector (cf. Bertram 1967; Falke 1996: 138ff.). It is equally clear that the Community continually gave precedence to that institutional option when it became apparent that policy sectors needed continuous 'accompaniment', to guarantee that new legislative acts met with the necessary assent in Member States and that strictly circumscribed implementation programmes would compensate for the lack of genuine European administrative powers. The specific shape of the committee structure is, however, not adequately explained by such general considerations. Particularly in the area of internal market policy, such a structure also owes to various specific regulatory problems and traditions.

a   Examples

A first look at the fields investigated here may illuminate this point, while, at the same time, may also give a key to their exemplary significance:

(1) MACHINE SAFETY AND CONSTRUCTION PRODUCTS

The whole area of technical safety law, and not just in Germany, is traditionally a domain for co-operation between administrative bodies and non-governmental and by no means only 'economic' organizations. The EC was able to deploy this tradition as a springboard when it thoroughly reshaped its traditional legal harmonization policy in the framework of the new internal market policy.[44] In the entire area of technical harmonization, Community directives content themselves with setting binding safety requirements.[45] Achieving these objectives is formally a task of the Commission. It is supported here by the Advisory Committee on Technical Standards and Regulations set up by Directive 83/189/EEC (OJ L 108/1983, 8) and works together with the European Standardisation Organisations, CEN and CENELEC. The Committee is, in particular, involved in allocating standardization mandates (cf. Article 6 [4e] of Directive 88/1182/EEC [amendment of Directive 83/189/EEC]) and is competent to hear objections to the appropriateness of standards in safeguard clause procedures.[46] The directives adopted in the course of applying the New Approach regularly refer to that committee in their safeguard clause procedures.[47] Directive 89/392/EEC harmonizing the legal provisions of Member States for machines (OJ L 183/1989, 9; amended by Directive 93/44; OJ L 175/1993, 12) admittedly distinguishes, in Article 6, between the Committee on Standards and Technical Requirements, which reviews the appropriateness of standards (Article 6 [1]), and a Standing Committee that deals with questions arising from the implementation and practical application of the Machine Directive (Article 6 [2]). However, such standing committees with advisory functions specific to groups of products – which back up the 'umbrella committee' pursuant to Directive 83/189/EEC – are also provided for by other directives under the New Approach, such as the directives for medicinal products (Directive 93/84, OJ L 169/199).

Yet, similarly in the area of technical safety law, the delegation of regulatory tasks to non-governmental bodies and the retreat by Member States to a merely consultative status is not 'perfect'. In the framework Directive 89/391/EEC (OJ L 183/1989, 1), based on Article 118a ECT, on safety and health protection at work, which uses a similar distinction to the one made in foodstuffs law, a distinction is made between its realization through individual Council directives (Article 16) and through technical adaptations by the Commission (Article 17). The committee that collaborates on such adjustment measures is a regulatory committee; for the area of labour protection there also exists, by Council decision of 27 June 1974 (OJ L 185/1974, 15), a 'triple parity' advisory committee for safety, labour hygiene and health protection at the workplace.

(2) FOODSTUFFS

Following the 1985 White Paper on the completion of the internal market (EC Commission 1985a), the Commission explained in an additional communication (EC Commission 1985b) that the new harmonization policy should ideally also be applied in the foodstuffs sector; though here other forms of application would need to be found. Legislative acts ought accordingly to focus on the 'traditional' foodstuffs law objectives, namely the safety of food, the protection of consumers against deception and fraud, the support of fair trading practices. This, in particular, included a move away from 'compositional regulations' for specific product categories.[48]

The new approach in foodstuffs law was achieved with the aid of the already established committees; though, at the same time, their tasks were redefined. The committee structure reflects the dimensions of regulatory problems in foodstuffs law and their development: (1) the 'Standing Committee for Foodstuffs' set up by the Council resolution of 13 November 1969 (OJ L 291/1969, 9) is, as emerges from the Council resolution on procedures for consultation of the Standing Committee for Foodstuffs of the same date (OJ C 148/1969, 1), a so-called regulatory committee consisting of Member State representatives. This status was never called in question even after the reorientation of harmonization policy in foodstuffs law, or after the amendment of Article 145 by the Single European Act. Through the Standing Committee for Foodstuffs, Member States or their administrations take part in exercising the implementing powers conveyed to the Commission. (2) The Scientific Committee for Foodstuffs set up by Commission decision of 16 April 1974 (OJ L 136/1974, 1) has a merely advisory function. The fact that its members are appointed not according to national proportions but ought simply to be 'highly scientifically qualified persons' reflects the form of authority allotted to this committee. The growing dependency of the Community's regulatory policy on scientific advice is, moreover, evident from Directive 93/5/EEC 'on support to the Commission and Member State collaboration in the scientific testing of foodstuffs' of 25 February 1993 (OJ L 52/1993, 18). (3) The Advisory Committee on Foodstuffs, finally, set up in 1975 (OJ L 182/1975, 35 and L 251/1978, 18; cf. the amending Resolution of 24 October 1980, OJ L 318/1980, 28), consists of permanent members and experts intended to represent agriculture, commerce, consumers, industry and workers (Article 2 [1] and [2]); as the mode of appointment shows, these groups are intended to articulate private and cross-European interests.

b   The state of the debate in legal and political science

The rise and vitality of the European committee system is clearly an expression of its functional superiority over the alternatives sketched out above. It may also be asserted, however, that such superiority has important normative dimensions. This thesis is, however, in need of further substantiation. Even the very cursory references to the examples of standardization and the foodstuffs sector have, after all, made it clear that the structures and regulatory functions of the committee system are not constant. They have, like regulatory policy itself, changed – and only recently, further major changes were made.[49] Our thesis must accordingly be related back to the internal market policy development detailed above. It may then be more ambitiously formulated, though not without risk: the committee system is an element in the transformation of the economic community into a European polity which is not informed by 'nation building', but which nonetheless requires a 'constitution'. So extended, our thesis requires various delimitations (and normative underpinnings).

(1) LEGAL SCIENCE

The debate upon the legal questions to which the committee system gives rise, has not been systematically related to the regulatory functions of the committees in the context of European 'social regulation'. It has, above all, dealt with and responded to conflicts among institutional actors.[50] This is true especially of the theorem of the so-called 'anti-delegation' doctrine and the principle of the 'institutional balance of powers',[51] the debate on the new version of Article 145 inserted into the SEA in 1987,[52] as well as the EP's constant, and relatively successful efforts to enhance its legal position within comitology procedures.[53]

There exists, however, a second series of judicial decisions, less spectacular but important to our approach, which deals with the 'procedural modalities' of the committee system.[54] The number of decisions that directly tackle committee procedure is admittedly still astonishingly small; but the statements in the relevant judgements are of fundamental importance.[55] They contain procedural requirements on the finding and justification of decisions that could and should be further developed through transparency requirements and the recognition of participation rights.

(2) POLITICAL SCIENCE

How, asks a standard political science analysis, does comitology fit within paradigms of integration research? Do the defence of the committee system by the Council and the transposition of the 1987 Comitology Decision (Weiler 1999b), confirm the practical relevance of intergovernmentalism?[56] Or, has the degree of co-operation between national administrations and the Commission instead intensified to the degree that one might now speak of a merged, denationalized and, to that extent, supranational administration (Wessels 1990, 1992, 1996)? Alternatively, is it more appropriate to designate such forms of co-operation as a network (cf. e.g. Héritier 1993; Ladeur 1993 and 1999)? What is common to all these approaches, however, is that their conceptualizations aim to provide *explanations* of comitology and its decision-making practices, and that institutional and legal requirements are treated as external data, but not taken into account through an 'internalization' of the principles and commitments that can lead to a normative structuring of practice in comitology.

It is this internalization of normative principles that this contribution will underline.[57] It assumes that conceptualizations of the committee system – not just in political science but in legal science, too – must match general developments in the integration process. It therefore assumes that these conceptualizations must go beyond intergovernmental, functionalist and neo-functionalist theoretical approaches (and their parallels in legal science). It adapts analyses of the EU as a multi-level system in integration research[58] and will seek to show the relevance of this analytical approach to the debate in legal science on the interaction of European, national, governmental and non-governmental actors. We see the intrinsic advantage of the multi-level approach as lying in the fact that it does not assign governance functions in the EU to a central body, and that it further assumes the co-existence of formally independent but factually interdependent political actors. Equally, with regard to the problem-solving capacities of governments, the multi-level approach is advantaged since it frees itself from the territorial demarcation of political entities and no longer equates governance structures with the form of the nation-state. In legal science conceptualizations of the EU, similar realignments are unavoidable. To point again to the exemplary importance of the field under scrutiny: those possibilities for action in social regulation areas, which arise from the EC's competences, always only concern certain subsets of functionally cohesive sets of problems, or are merely 'selective', leaving many problem-solving tasks in the hands of the Member States; in addition to this, the Community is dependent for the administrative implementation of its programmes on the Member States. The location of functionally connected powers at differing levels, determines that the supremacy of European law is not sufficient for the consistent development of centralist, hierarchical forms of government. Solutions to problems are dependent on the development of lasting forms of co-operation – and it seems equally inevitable that networks of governmental and non-governmental actors will become established for this.

4   *Innovations*

Yet, just how imprudent it would be to declare forms of problem solving developed in the integration process to be definitive has been confirmed anew by the BSE crisis and its institutional consequences: the committee system in its present shape does not follow some preconceived model, but has instead evolved with a constant eye to its necessary readjustment in the light of unforeseen sets of problems; equally, comitology will retain its practical importance only if it continues to meet the Community's needs in a constant process of self-transformation.

Three responses to the 'institutional failure' prompted by the BSE crisis should be stressed.[59] The European Parliament was to adjust its hitherto abolitionary stance upon the committee system and was instead to seek a (presumed!) strengthening of its institutional role in implementing Community law.[60] Using the investigation committee procedure based on Article 138c ECT, it found an effective avenue publicly to warn the actors involved at both European and national level of their political responsibility.[61] Among the various measures secured is a reorganization of the committee system inside the European Commission: all (currently six) scientific committees involved with risk recognition and assessment are assigned to a scientific steering committee (SSC) (to be 'evaluated and monitored' by it), operating under the umbrella of DG XXIV, competent for consumer protection.[62] It is noteworthy that the decision establishing the steering committee puts into practice principles that were only partially existent in positive secondary law, or the general validity of which could be derived from the case law solely through extensive interpretation. Thus, the SSC is assigned rights of initiative (Article 2 [3] e), thereby implicitly recognizing that the Commission cannot autonomously determine whether a technical question needs to be scientifically assessed or not.[63] Further important provisions guarantee the independence and technical competence of the SSC and the transparency of its activities in Articles 4, 6 and 7, which are more precisely formulated than in the principles developed in the case law.[64] Last but not least, now that the importance and complexity of the committee system has entered the public awareness, the shaping of criteria for allocating tasks and forms of committees, something neglected in the 1987 Comitology Decision (cf. Weiler 1999b), can no longer be avoided.[65] All these are questions that belong in the broader context of the constitutionalization of the committee system.

V The constitutional framework of risk politics in the internal market

Summarizing the argument so far in thesis form: the newly integrated European product markets present the Community with a two-dimensional task. (1) Product regulations should, on the one hand, take account of the functional requirements of market integration, and thus, in particular, guarantee free movement of goods – which admittedly speaks not for the abolition of regulatory requirements but for their unification or else mutual recognition. (2) On the other hand, the Community cannot deny the normative political dimensions of dealing with risks. In this, the second dimension of its regulatory policy the Community ought not to aim at blanket or unitary responses simply since it has not been transformed into a unitary polity and would thus not appear to possess sufficient legitimation for the hierarchical imposition of European solutions. On the other hand, however, a decentralization of risk policy and its location at the level of the nation-state would amount to no less than the negation of the market integration project.

The desire to locate a 'non-unitary' European regulatory policy somewhere between the European and national level is compatible with the institutional dominance of comitology as such. This is, though, true only if the interpretation of the tasks and modes of operation of comitology is liberated from traditional patterns of integration research. Thus, on the one hand it is inappropriate to regard European regulatory policy as intergovernmental action, proceeding from and controlled by autonomous political entities – the Member States. It is equally misplaced to interpret the committee system as a supranational body, as if it were merely a preliminary stage on the road to politically autonomous European agencies (cf. Wessels 1996: 183f).

The attempt to coin a term which most adequately expresses the underlying approach which informs this study is bedevilled by the fact that most available terms repeatedly arouse associations with nation-state or with federal models.

The notion 'fusioned administration' introduced by Wessels[66] fits our view to the extent that it departs both from the concept of a supranational, hierarchically structured bureaucracy on the one hand, and from intergovernmental steering machinery on the other, and is further intended to designate a co-operative relationship. Yet, Wessels' term is intended to cover a much wider field of action than is studied here. In particular, it is not related to the question that seems to us to be central within risk regulation, namely the tensions between the functional requirements of the internal market and the normative political dimensions of risk regulation. In order to give expression to this tension, we therefore resort to a conceptual oxymoron, namely the term 'political administration'.[67] Product regulation through the committee system seems to be more an administrative and less of a governmental activity since all actors involved – at Community level and in the Member States – must adhere to legally defined requirements; it is nonetheless a 'political' activity because the implementation of the legal framework is conceivable neither as a mere application of law, nor as purely technocratic activity. The term remains a makeshift one.[68] National administration, too – and the administration of risks is only one example of this – has long ceased to see itself as a mere executor of given programmes or a neutral agent in the solving of clearly defined problems. Yet, the specific feature of European action, namely its intergovernmental residues and the constraint to solve problems in a non-integrated, plurally composed polity, is not adequately expressed by the term 'political' – 'good governance' might be an alternative which may capture the normative commitments of risk regulation, but carries with it connotations which at present do not seem to correspond to the daily work and routines of committee actors.

1   Deliberative supranationalism as constitutional basis

The term 'political administration' implies that 'law' is intended to 'guide' the involved actors, but does not yet explicate which constraints this brings with it and how these are or ought to be patterned in the specific circumstances of the European internal market policy. Any discussion of these questions requires considerations at three levels. First, a pinpointing of the 'constitutional' bases of European risk management – an area for which the term 'deliberative supranationalism' will here be used. Second, political science theorems will be used to clarify the question whether, and if so under what conditions, one might expect the practical realization of the normative perspectives of deliberative supranationalism (*infra* 2). Thirdly, a question has to be asked as to which additional infra-constitutional legal rules are necessary for a juridification of these perspectives (*infra* 3).

The term 'deliberative supranationalism' denotes a constitutional perspective for European law different, on the one hand, from orthodox interpretations of the Community as a system integrated through supranational law, and, on the other, from the quasi international law downgrading of the Union to a mere alliance of states.[69] In terms of legal or constitutional theory, the notion of deliberative supranationalism is borrowed from theories of 'deliberative' democracy,[70] according to which the legitimacy of modern law is constituted by the democratic institutions of the constitutional state. Accordingly, if seen from this theoretical perspective, Europe's much vaunted 'democratic deficit' is in fact an objection against the claims of European law to immediate validity and primacy – and this objection only gains in strength where one assumes that the European Union will not transform itself into a statal entity in the foreseeable future.

As deployed here, the term 'deliberation' designates a mode of legal structuring of political processes, which can be seen in isolation from the model of the national constitutional state, but which also tackles comprehensive tasks and involves real powers, and so offers a viable normative perspective, first, for the maintenance of supranational legal links among the EU's constitutional states and, secondly, for the legal constitution of the Community's political projects. The specific characteristic of this approach is that it conceives of 'supranational' law not as given rules, which pre-empt and have supremacy over national legal systems, but as law that derives its validity from the 'deliberative' quality of its production. Two sets of questions must therefore be distinguished here:

1   First, it need be recalled, and this is a familiar notion in all disciplines of international law, that the validity claims of national constitutional law are extremely 'one-sided'. National constitutions are normatively sealed organisms which nonetheless have universal implications. Thus, a statute created within the logic of the constitution will ordinarily also have an impact upon people outside the normative reach of the given constitutional system without their once having had a chance to take part in internal decision-making or to guarantee that their interests have been taken into account. European law contains, in a number of its core provisions – such as the ban on discrimination in Article 6 ECT or the anti-protectionist precepts of Article 30 ECT – correctives to this 'failure of the constitutional state'. The supranational constitutionalization of such correctives is not only compatible with the democratic principle that rule should be based on the consent of the governed, but is indeed a requirement of this principle.

2   For numerous practical reasons – especially in view of the external effects of individual state policies, but also simply as a consequence of the opening up of frontiers to goods, services and to ideas – interdependencies arise that undeniably require supranational problem solving.[71] Risk management in the internal market is a paradigmatic case. Is an institutionalization of 'deliberative' problem solving conceivable outside integrated constitutional states? An analogous approach suggests itself. At the domestic level, institutional deficits also arise. Can proposed domestic correctives be transferred to supranational level? Analytical conceptualization of regulatory policy accordingly furnish us with various starting points for the debate.

Primary amongst such correctives is Giandomenico Majone's advocacy for the establishment of 'independent' (non-majoritarian) institutions capable of, and having their tasks limited to, the credible implementation of non-distributive regulatory objectives.[72] A second approach, though to date barely tackled at supranational level,[73] is based on analyses by Cohen and Rogers (Cohen and Rogers 1992), recently renewed and modified by Cohen and Sabel.[74] The failings within traditional constitutional institutions are to be compensated for by new forms of directly deliberative problem solving to be organized by those involved for themselves.

The transposition of theories of directly deliberative problem solving to the sphere of European regulatory policy-making involves complex issues which cannot be exhaustively dealt with within this contribution. Nonetheless, it is possible to make mention of those existent rules and principles within European law, which do not pre-empt the outcome of the decision-making process, but which instead structure such processes so as to promote 'deliberative' problem solving. Among these are the rules of primary law and secondary law – such as the market freedoms' commitment to rational economic development and a corresponding structuring of that development to take, say, health and safety requirements into account – which narrow down the range of arguments that are admissible within debate so that only generally reproducible and justifiable grounds or concerns, and not mere protectionist interests, can be used to justify restrictions on manufacture and trade. Equally important amongst these rules and principles, however, are those which promote pluralist discourse and the presentation of all relevant viewpoints within debate, so shaping the committee system into a forum for rational problem solving. Vitally, such pluralism is guaranteed not simply through the secured independence of expert discourse, but also arises since *all* of the varied national, supranational and private actors involved within the comitology system are forced to generalize their arguments, thus not merely pursuing their own interests but also tackling problems with an eye to the legitimate (under EC principles of discourse) concerns and interests of those who do not directly participate within the committee system.[75]

2   *Political science theorems and empirical investigations*

What are the requirements for the practical transposition of these forms of normative postulate? This question must be dealt with on two levels:

a   *Theoretical analyses*

The considerations underlying the thesis advocated here do not simply arise from normative notions of what *may* be desirable. A multiplicity of studies on international regimes in general, and with reference to the EC in particular, already exist, which diagnose in international negotiating and decisional processes a turn from interest-led to problem-oriented decision-making, from negotiative to argumentative, from strategic to discursive communication.[76] None of these terms, with their positive connotations, is identical with the category of 'deliberative' politics. Nonetheless, the various theoretical approaches do demonstrate that the structuring of decisional processes by means of principles and rules is not merely a *de jure* expectation but can also be observed *de facto*.

b Empirical findings

'Deliberation' is a theoretical category. It cannot be operationalized in such a way as to allow for the corresponding qualities of political processes of discussion and decision to be 'proven'. Nor can the assumption that the national representatives within comitology do more than merely formulate and assert national positions be made directly demonstrable. Yet, a whole range of indicators can be mentioned and tested that do make such assumptions, at the very least, plausible. To what degree are Member State representatives at all capable of indicating the economic and distributive effects of a product regulation in their Member State? Where are their nationally specific concerns and standpoints on product risks? How do the committees deal with such differences?

Without pre-empting the presentation of a detailed study on these points, or indeed denying the inevitable indeterminacies in its findings, two points may nonetheless be stated:[77]

1 The process of negotiation and opinion-forming within comitology certainly takes national positions into account but does not fit within current conceptualizations of intergovernmental action; the discussions and debates in the committees document involve such an intensive interweaving of interests and arguments that it would be hopeless and artificial to attribute them to individual states or companies; putting that positively, they document the emergence of a, however rudimentary, European polity.

2 The debates on questions of risk policy are real discussions of problems; all the actors, including the Commission as agenda setter, are aware that they are not operating in a hierarchically structured system but that solutions must be found through co-operative approaches.

3 Constitutionalizing comitology

These findings, which fit our initial theoretical considerations, are a challenge to political science and legal science. They are a challenge to political science at least to the extent that even the approaches just mentioned, which diagnose discursive, argumentative, problem-oriented behaviour and thus enter into the normative dimensions of social action, neglect the social functions of European law, and, in particular, do not seem to reckon with the possibility that by reflectively deploying law it might by possible to structure political processes normatively; or, that, conversely, such links are only achievable through the use of legal institutions. They are equally a challenge to legal science since in their controversial conceptualization of a European law as a deliberative steering mechanism, the question of the exact character of the European polity is side-stepped, so that the problem of its substantive constitutional structuring (notions of supremacy, etc.) does not arise.

The exact working out of a legal constitution for comitology procedures would, without doubt, require more detailed theoretical considerations and broader empirical studies than those offered by this contribution.[78] It seems nevertheless safe to summarize and repeat:

1   The adequate analytical reference point for the conceptualization of risk policy in comitology is the treatment of the EU as a non-hierarchical multi-level system of governance.[79]

2   To this analytical reference frame corresponds, in normative terms, the turn towards a 'deliberative' vision of supranationalism as opposed to both 'orthodox' perceptions of supranationalism, on the one hand, and the revitalization of the nation-state, on the other.[80]

3   The task of committees in the internal market policy can be termed 'political administration'. This is intended to express the fact that the risk regulation tasks arising in the implementation of internal market policy can neither be handled purely legalistically (as mere application of law) nor tackled purely functionally (by delegating them to expert bodies).[81]

4   The constitutionalization of the committee system must take account of both the objective-technocratic and the normative (political) problem content of its decisional tasks. It is exactly this multinational, multicultural, social and academic plurality within the committees and exactly this lack of a hierarchical structure that promotes and requires recognition of norms that give the committee system's decisional processes a 'deliberative' quality. In particular, the manner in which primary law binds the committees, as well as the collaborative duties of Member States and their administrations, can be understood in this way.

5   Below the level of primary law, however, there still remains a considerable need for rules. This need concerns the composition of the committees, the guarantees of the independence and plurality of expert bodies, the pattern of delegation of decisional powers, the transparency of procedures and the publication of findings. These rules may be treated as a 'European administrative law', which however has constitutional functions, namely those of guaranteeing the generation of legitimate decisions.[82]

6   In activating the justification requirements of Article 190 ECT and activating individual possibilities of legal protection at European level, it should be borne in mind that the comitology procedure is, as a rule, aimed not at individual decisions but at 'executive' law-making.[83] As a corollary, any extension in the participatory rights of private and non-governmental social actors, is not a matter of simply securing individual accountability, but instead entails a reshaping of the institutional conditions for deliberative policy.[84]

7   The reshaping of the committee system as a forum for deliberative politics should be planned to supplement existing institutions and correct their

deficits. That such reshapings can, as it were, arise spontaneously – even if in connection with crises – has been documented by the BSE scandal. It is not the participatory rights won by the European Parliament in the context of the institutional conflict over comitology procedures, but the subsequent, targeted analysis of errors, which proved to be the most constructive contribution to overcoming the efficiency and legitimacy problems of European social regulation. Here a promising solution to the problem of 'political accountability' of regulatory market management can be seen to be emerging (cf. Joerges 1993, 1997b: 323).

Notes

1 This essay originates from a project on 'Die Beurteilung der Sicherheit technischer Konsumgüter und der Gesundheitsrisiken von Lebensmitteln in der Praxis des europäischen Ausschußwesens ("Komitologie")', funded by the Volkswagen-Stiftung (cf. for the design of this research Joerges 1995; the final report was completed in 1998 and will be published in 1999). It thus owes much to many, especially Josef Falke, Jürgen Neyer, Andreas Bücker and Sabine Schlacke, all from the Centre for European Law and Politics (ZERP), Bremen. It profits equally from parallel research activities at the European University Institute, Florence, especially the collaboration with Michelle Everson and Ellen Vos.
2 cf. Ipsen (1972), esp. at 176ff.
3 See the pioneering works by IEP (1989), Schaefer (1996) and Falke (1996).
4 Council Decision 87/373/EEC of 13 July 1987 laying down the procedures for the exercise of implementing powers conferred on the Commission, OJ L 197/1987, 33.
5 See the new version of Article 145 (3), 3rd indent, the basis of the Comitology Decision.
6 For topical analyses see Eichener (1997), Majone (1996a), Voelzkow (1996).
7 The legal concept of 'implementation' (Article 145) is just as embarrassing a concept as any other would be: it includes tasks of 'executive law-making', of discretionary problem solving over and above legislative programmes, routine decisions, and intergovernmental co-operative action – paraphrasing, one might say, that not just Europe's legislative policy needs a 'constitution'.
8 For more detail see III.4 below.
9 Implicit in *infra*, for explicit treatment, cf. Joerges and Neyer (1997: 296f): though briefly, the shift in emphasis to risk regulation has specific analytical consequences – 'risk' entails a notion of ethical or social disturbance, and so, its regulation takes on political connotations.
10 cf. the analysis in Dehousse *et al.* (1992).
11 For figures see Dehousse (1999) .
12 These viewpoints, represented particularly by economists, are documented in Gerken (1995).
13 For the current development cf. the documentation in Kreher (1998 and 1997); based on Majone's seminal articles (1993a, b, c, 1994).
14 But see Schmitt von Sydow (1980), IEP (1989).
15 See the documentation in Snyder (1994).
16 cf. Joerges (1991); for an analysis of the new 'agencies' cf. Dehousse (1997: 254ff.), and especially on the pharmaceuticals agency Gardener (1996), Vos (1999: 203ff.).
17 cf. only Scharpf (1985, 1992a and 1992b).
18 cf. III.4 below.
19 In this sense, e.g. Scharpf (1997c: Chapter II).
20 cf. Joerges (1988: 178ff.), with references.

21 cf. the notorious (over-)interpretation of the legendary 1979 Cassis de Dijon judgement in Commission (1980).
22 cf. the debate documented in Majone (1990).
23 For product safety law cf. in detail Joerges *et al.* (1988) and Joerges (1990); on protection at work cf. Eichener (1993) and Bücker (1997); on foodstuffs law cf. e.g. Hufen (1993) and now in more detail Schlacke (1998). For a markedly sceptical view of environment policy with regard to the example of the UVP directive see now Albert (1998), who admittedly neglects the – now outdated – institutional context; cf. also III.4 below.
24 Among many, see Joerges *et al.* (1988: 144ff.).
25 The best know example is from the ECJ's case law: German woodworking machines can be declared unsafe in France if based on a different safety concept: Case 188/84 [1986] ECR 419.
26 For more detail see Joerges (1994).
27 The term 'social regulation' denotes not the whole of social policy, but 'merely' so-called 'quality-of-life issues such as risk, consumer safety, the environment or the protection of diffuse interests and non-commodity values'; so runs Majone's (1996b) definition; cf. earlier Majone (1993a).
28 For summaries in sociology and political science on which our argument is based cf. Bechmann (1994), Shrader-Frechette (1991).
29 For a summary of underlying considerations cf. Köck (1996), Pildes and Sunstein (1995).
30 cf. III.4 and IV below.
31 cf. Scharpf (1997b: 522ff.), and earlier Rehbinder and Stewart (1985: 9ff.), on the use of this pair in the American federalism debate cf. Mashaw and Rose-Ackerman (1984: 129ff.), and the references in Scharpf, *op.cit.*
32 cf. IV 3 a (1) below.
33 cf. only Gehring (1999) .
34 As in fact at the time said by the Scientific Advisory Council (1986); on the later debate, see Gerken (1995).
35 On what follows see Joerges *et al.* (1988: 437ff.).
36 See references in note 13 above.
37 See the analysis by Everson (1995a).
38 Most recently, see again Majone (1999).
39 cf. Majone (1993c) and the analysis by Everson (1995a and 1997).
40 For a complete current survey see Kreher (1997 and 1998).
41 'European Agency for the Evaluation of Medicinal Products', OJ L 214/1993, 1; details in Gardener (1996), Vos (1999: 203ff.).
42 cf. e.g. Dehousse (1997: 254ff.), and earlier Joerges (1991).
43 cf. the disputes between Majone (1997) and Shapiro (1997), and also Kreher (1997 and 1998).
44 See below; in detail, Joerges *et al.* (1988: 341ff.), specifically on the law of machine safety Bücker (1997: 179ff.).
45 As per Council Decision of 7 May 1985, OJ C 136/1985, 1.
46 See the position paper from DG III, 'Compatibility of harmonised standards with directives in accordance with the New Approach', 22 June 1990, DIN-Mitteilungen 70 (1991: 106f).
47 cf. e.g. Article 7 (2) of the Toys Directive, OJ L 187/1988,1; Article 9 (2) of the Directive on Electromagnetic Compatibility, OJ L 139/1989, 19. Special features apply e.g. to construction products (see Directive 89/106; OJ L 40/1989: 12). In the light of the 'underdeveloped' state of standardization here, regulatory committee procedures are provided for the production of basic documents. Similarly, Directive 93/42/EEC on medical products (OJ L 169/1) provides for a regulatory committee procedure (variant IIIa) for particular classifications (see Article 7 taken together with

Article 9 [3]; otherwise, for general standardization questions competence remains with the Committee for Standards and Technical Requirements, Article 6).

48 For details see Vos (1999: 131ff.).

49 See IV.4 below.

50 For details on this see Bradley (1997 and 1999), Vos (1999: 83ff.).

51 Case 25/70, *Einfuhr- und Vorratsstelle v Köster* [1970] ECR 1161; Case 23/75, *Rey Soda v Cassa Conguagli Zucchero* [1970] ECR 1279; Case 5/77, *Tedeschi v Denkavit* [1977] ECR 1555.

52 The complaint brought by the European Parliament against the Council's comitology resolution was rejected by the ECJ as inadmissible, without going into the legal questions of comitology (Case 302/87, *Parliament v Council* (Comitology) [1988] ECR 5615; Case 70/88, *Parliament v Council* [1990] ECR I-2041.

53 cf. esp. the '*modus vivendi*' agreed between EP; Council and Commission on 20 December 1994, OJ C 102/1996, 1.

54 On this see Joerges (1997b), Joerges and Neyer (1997: 284ff.).

55 cf. esp. case C-269/90, *Hauptzollamt München-Mitte v TU München* [1991] ECR I-5469, 5499; case 12/91, *Angelopharm*, [1993] ECR I-171.

56 As most recently in Pollack's principal/agent model (1997).

57 For the following see Joerges and Neyer (1997) and on the general theoretical and methodological premises, Joerges (1996b).

58 cf. only Jachtenfuchs and Kohler-Koch (1996b).

59 On this see for more detail Chambers (1999) .

60 For a description and a criticism see Bradley (1997).

61 See the Committee Report of 17.7.1996; OJ C 239/1996, 1; and Europäisches Parliament (1997): cf. Commission (1997a).

62 Commission Resolution 97/404/EC setting up a scientific steering committee of 10.6.1997; OJ L 169/1997, 85.

63 On this cf. V below and the debate on the importance of the Angelopharm judgement, case C-212/91 [1994] ECR I-171 (Bradley 1999).

64 See, e.g. ECJ, case C-269/90 *Hauptzollamt München-Mitte v TU München* [1991] ECR I-5469, 5499 (14).

65 cf. case C-417/93, ECR I-1185, Para 24 (I-1217) and the remarks of AG Ph. Léger Para 88 (I-1204).

66 Wessels (1992), cf. the diagram in Wessels (1996: 167).

67 cf. Everson (1997) for the slightly more nuanced notion of market administration within an evolving climate of political regulation: a notion reflecting both the empirical presence (even at national level) of politics within administration, as well as allowing for the capture of the possible transformation of an administration into a nascent polity.

68 The term 'political administration' was probably first coined by Wiethölter (1972: 532) in order to express the discrepancy between the implementation of purposive provisions, as, e.g. the Act on Restraints of Competition (Gesetz gegen Wettbewerbsbeschränkungen) and the application of 'classic' private law legislation.

69 On all this see in more detail Joerges (1996b) and Joerges and Neyer (1997: 292ff.).

70 We would refer here merely to the systematic portrayal in Gerstenberg (1997a).

71 See III.3 b above, and the survey and analysis in Scharpf (1997b).

72 See the references in note 13; a German predecessor that should be recalled is H.-P. Ipsen (1972: 176ff.), Majone (1993c) has explicitly recognized this intellectual connection.

73 But see V. Eichener (1997: Chapters 5 and 6), cf. also earlier Voelzkow (1996: 261ff.).

74 Cohen and Sabel (1997), on which see Gerstenberg (1997b).

75 This is vital: comitology is currently a matter of representation rather than participation. Note powerful critiques, cf. Weiler (1999b), which bemoan the limited numbers of actors, however, who actively participate within comitology start with the

assumption that legitimation is furnished by participation. By contrast, given the current evolution of a European polity with uncertain characteristics, cf. Everson (1999), rule-based representative legitimacy – or a duty placed upon actors within comitology to take only generalizable and thus universal interests/concerns into account during decision-making – might better compensate for the Sisyphus-like task of securing participatory legitimation through the incremental inclusion within the comitology system of a series of interests which are still in the process of formation.

76 cf. Gehring (1995, 1996, 1997), Risse-Kappen (1995, 1996), Müller (1994), Prittwitz (1996), from the chorus of sceptical voices, see Zürn and Zangl (1996).

77 cf. earlier Joerges and Neyer (1997: 277ff).

78 See note 50 above.

79 cf. III 3 above.

80 cf. 1 above.

81 cf. 1 above.

82 cf. Everson (1997: 3): European administrative law is less concerned 'with the formal investigation of whether an existing will has been faithfully executed, and more with the "fair structuring" of ongoing political processes'.

83 On this concept cf. Falke and Winter (1996).

84 cf. note 75.

9 Demanding public deliberation

The Council of Ministers: some lessons from the Anglo-American history

Roberto Gargarella

In this paper, I will critically examine the role and functioning of the European Council of Ministers. Given the growing importance of the Council, and its quite recent creation, it seems particularly important to discern which are the main virtues and the main weaknesses of this institution. In order to have a 'standpoint' from where to examine the Council, I will resort to the institutional discussions held both in England and in the United States, at the end of the eighteenth century. The reason for this choice is the following: the political debates held at that time constitute an enormously rich source of arguments about how to design institutions, and why to choose a particular institutional model. Those arguments are particularly helpful given the questions that I want to examine in my analysis of the Council: Could we reasonably expect to obtain impartial decisions from this institution? How could we evaluate the relationship that this institution establishes between its members and the European citizenry? Could we expect the Ministers to properly represent their countrymen? Could we expect them to be properly accountable to the European people?

In my critical approach to the Council of Ministers I will suggest that this institution has its philosophical roots in one of the two main traditions that distinguished the Anglo-American debates: the conservative tradition. As I will present it, the conservative Anglo-American tradition distinguished itself by defending centralized institutions; a low level of 'mass' political participation; restricted opportunities for public discussion; and many 'counter-majoritarian' devices (typically, indirect elections; or a system of judicial review). This conservative tradition was opposed to another, more radical position, which defended, by contrast, a more decentralized institutional project; an active political role for the citizens; ample opportunities for public discussion; and a more clearly 'majoritarian' political system.

In order to expose the conservative foundations of the Council, and some of the weaknesses of this conception, I will examine this institution in the light of some of the most significant values defended by the opposite Anglo-American radical tradition. The values to which I will refer are, mainly, a properly representative and accountable government (what we could call an 'accountability conception of representation');[1] and a 'simple' and transparent political system. In particular, and regarding this latter issue, I will consider the value of having 'open debates'. Before directly addressing this analysis I will briefly describe the Council of Ministers and the way it works.

What is the Council of Ministers and how does it work: a few basic notes

Originally, the Council of Ministers was conceived as a means to help the different state members in co-ordinating their work. However, and since its creation, the Council consolidated its position as a legislative body with the capacity to take final decisions in many, although still not clearly defined, areas. At present, the Council not only constitutes the main decision-making body of the Union (a mission that it shares with the European Parliament and the European Commission), but it also exercises some executive tasks under the treaties. It represents the European Union before other countries, and constitutes an important and more or less permanent negotiating forum within the Union (Binseil and Hantke 1997; Hayes-Renshaw and Wallace 1997).

The Council is composed (according to the EEC article 146) of 'representatives of the Member States, at ministerial level, authorized to commit the government of that Member State'. Although the Foreign Affairs Ministers have a *de facto* supremacy within the Council, the other Member States' ministers also take part of this body, through other more specific committees. In fact, it does not exist of only 'one' but of 'multiple Councils', specialized in different areas. The most important among them are the Agriculture Council; the Economic and Financial Council (Ecofin); the Internal Market Council; as well as the Councils of Budget; Development; Environment; Transport; Labour and Social Affairs; Education; Industry; Culture; Health; Civil Protection; Telecommunications; and Energy. Some of the Councils celebrate a meeting every month, but some others do it only every six months.

The Council's decision-making process is quite complex and includes, very schematically, the following steps. In the first place, the President of the Council hands a legislative proposal – which he or she normally receives from the European Commission – to the Council's General Secretariat.[2] At that moment, it comes into play to the COREPER (Committee of Permanent Representatives) that begins to study the technical aspects of the project through one of the different Working Parties that work under its supervision. The chosen Working Party tries to reach an agreement on the proposal from a technical standpoint. When the agreement is reached, the proposal is again submitted to the COREPER, for its approval. Then, the COREPER tries to secure the political agreement of the different Member States. When the proposal achieves a sufficient consensus, the COREPER submits it to the Council. The Council may consider the proposal as an 'A' or 'B' item. 'A' items are normally approved without discussion, while 'B' items are discussed. In those rare cases where the proposal does not achieve the necessary consensus, it is sent back to the COREPER.[3]

The Council takes its decisions by simple majority, qualified majority, or unanimity. The votes are weighted according to the size of Member States (until recently, France, Germany, Italy, and the UK had 10 votes each; Spain 8 votes; the Netherlands, Portugal, Greece and Belgium 5 votes; Sweden and Austria 4 votes; Denmark, Finland and Ireland 3 votes; and Luxembourg 2 votes). Most of the decisions of the Council are taken by qualified majority; only in some cases is unanimity required (unanimity is mainly reserved for constitutional decisions). Where the Council acts as a result of a Commission proposal (the most common situation), the qualified majority required amounts to 62 votes which would require, at least, the agreement of eight Member States. Where the Council acts in the absence of a Commission proposal, the qualified majority again amounts to 62 votes, but composed of at least ten of the Member States.[4] With this voting concludes the first and fundamental round of the Council's decision-making process. Then, and under the so-called Co-decision Procedure, the European Parliament approves, amends, or rejects the Council's decision. It is worth noting, in this respect, that after the Amsterdam Treaty the European Parliament was put, basically, on an equal footing with the Council. Thus, presently, the Parliament acts as a co-legislator at least in thirty-seven different types of issues although – we must recognize it – certain imbalances between the two institutions remain. In effect, as we will see, the Parliament still plays a secondary role in some central legislative issues.[5]

In what follows I will examine the described decision-making process of the Council in the light of the radical values that I mentioned above.

Composition of the representative branches of the government/Accountability

The Anglo-American discussion on representation

Both in Europe and in the United States the conservative and radical traditions opposed each other, among other things, in their evaluation of the representative system. Typically, the conservatives tended to favour representative institutions composed of few and well-prepared individuals, isolated in their deliberations from the pressures of 'the many'. The radicals, by contrast, defended larger institutions, strictly controlled by the people at large.

Within the British conservative tradition, Edmund Burke represented one of the most influential opinions. As Hanna Pitkin stated, according to Burke's view 'representation mean[t] government by a true elite and elections [represented] a means for finding that elite'.[6] In his opinion, political deliberation had to be a practice monopolized by the 'enlightened few'. He characterized the deliberations of the people, instead, as 'hasty, passionate, prejudiced, [and] subject to violent ... fluctuations' (Pitkin 1967: 181).

In North America, the so-called Federalists (the defenders of the American Constitution of 1787) advanced a similar view, rejecting the role of (what they called) local factions and emphasizing the importance of deliberation as the main feature of an adequate political system. The reasons given for this 'total exclusion of the people' were clear. Above all, they assumed that the people were not able to engage in adequate political discussions. In fact, the Federalists used to affirm that large groups of people, in public assemblies, were unavoidably driven by passions and not by reason. They were certain that 'only those who r[o]se above the ambition, bias, prejudice, partial interest, and immediate interest of ordinary men will be in a position to see ... the true interests of the community' (M. White 1987: 216). These features defined what was called the Federalists' political elitism.

Morton White explained this political elitism affirming that:

[The Federalists] thought the people were subject to momentary passions which could lead them to make grave political mistakes; that rational, wise, and virtuous leaders could refine the people's passions and speak more effectively for them than they could for themselves; that could flatter the people while leading them into subjugation; that the people tend to focus on the immediate, short-term advantages of certain courses of action; that the people tend to be influenced by local, partial interests while disregarding the interests of the community as a whole; that discerning leaders would be better able than the people themselves to see what the people's true interests were; and last, but not least, that the people might not see the truth, much less the self-evidence or possibility to demonstrate the truths which served as the major moral premises of arguments advanced for the adoption of the Constitution.[7]

There are still some obvious reasons to support the rather elitist conception of representation defended by the Federalists. First, as Madison put it, direct ('pure') democracy appears to be possible only within very small communities. In addition, the conservative model might be defended through (what we could call) a 'division of labour' argument, according to which 'it is reasonable to leave to the politicians the discussion and the resolution of most political issues, as a way of facilitating other people's life'. In connection with this argument, someone could also resort to a motivational argument, according to which, normally, people are not willing to spend so much time discussing political issues.

The radicals strongly opposed the conservative model of representation. In England, this opposition became particularly intense after the so-called 'Wilkes affair' which made it apparent that the political system was not properly sensitive to the will of the people.[8] In the U.S., the issue of representation became the main point of the dispute between the radical and the conservative traditions. The radicals, mostly through the voice of the so-called anti-federalist writers, affirmed that the institutional system that their opponents – the Federalists – were creating, was elitist. Most of them described the proposed system as 'aristocratic', and considered that its adoption would imply the end of federalism – no more political powers to the decentralized States.

In addition, the radicals argued that the proposed conservative model was unable to 'process' all the information required in order to reach impartial decisions. According to their claim, one should not assume that the representatives – whoever they might be – could recognize and understand the claims of the majority just by making an effort at assuming the majoritarian viewpoint. Therefore, and in addition to a more decentralized system, the radicals defended what we could call a 'mirror-model of representation': the main representative institution of society had to mirror, in its composition, the composition of society. This was a claim both for a *more numerous* body, and for a *more diverse* composition, within this body.

The radicals had good arguments in favour of including, in the political discussions, the viewpoints of 'all those potentially affected'.[9] Among them, we could mention the need to reduce the risks of misunderstanding the others' preferences (i.e. considering important something that the others do not really value, or disregarding as unimportant what is actually significant to them). Also, in the defence of the same ideas the radicals could resort to a motivational argument. They could affirm that, without the actual presence of all those possibly affected, they would not be able to defend the viewpoints of these people with the required intensity and the required commitments.[10]

In addition, the radicals practice of 'town meetings' – popular assemblies through which the community discussed the most significant political issues that they confronted – disproved some of the conservatives' main concerns: public discussion neither implied discussion of 'all' types of issues, nor the resort to 'gigantic' meetings.

Finally, both the British and the American radicals defended institutional mechanisms oriented to 'reduce the distance' between the representatives and their constituency. This emphasis on *accountability* went hand in hand with their distrust of representation. The radicals knew that, even an ideally large representative body, composed of a diverse group of people that 'mirrored' society would not adequately secure the people's self-government. Even good representatives – they believed – would be tempted to rule by and for themselves, unless the people had appropriate devices for punishing or threatening them. Regular elections were not sufficient for this purpose if – as it was proposed by the conservatives – elections were not so frequent. Therefore, the radicals proposed additional mechanisms like *the right to write instructions to the representatives*;[11] which was normally supplemented by a *right to recall* the elected;[12] and the establishment of *mandatory rotation* (that prevented the possibility of immediate re-election).[13] There are obvious problems that, presently, would make some of these devices for accountability inadequate.[14] However, we may still have good reasons for keeping in mind some of the radicals' institutional concerns: periodical elections are not necessarily sufficient for the objective of securing a good representative system. We may discuss and disagree about which mechanisms to adopt, for achieving that end, but we should not neglect that discussion.

The Council of Ministers and the problems of representation

At this point, we should go back to the Council of Ministers and try to find out whether the Council – as a 'key' political and representative institution, within the European Union – is adequately organized with regard to both goals mentioned above: i) securing that the different State-members are properly represented, and ii) guaranteeing that the constituency has adequate chances for controlling their representatives.

In my opinion, it is not difficult to conclude that the Council is not adequately designed for achieving any of those ends. In the first place, recall that the Council consists of 'representatives of the Member States, at ministerial level, authorised to commit the government of that Member State'. This means that the members of the Council are not directly elected by the people at large. In addition, the former are not subject to direct popular controls: they keep their power as long as their respective States decide it.[15] Moreover, we should remember that still 'there is no single clear view shared by all Member States of what the Council does or should do' (Hayes-Renshaw and Wallace 1997: 17).

Clearly, the mere fact that the delegates are only indirectly elected (or removed) by the citizenry does not imply that the latter has no control at all of the representatives. However, when we combine these mere indirect powers with the secrecy and opacity that – as we will see – distinguish the Council's procedures, and the indeterminacy of its functions, we can recognize the significant problems that this institution has, as a representative body.

Given the mentioned facts, what actually happens, in most cases, is that the people know very little about their representatives and their particular work and, accordingly, they have few incentives (as well as rather poor institutional mechanisms) for rewarding or punishing them. The mentioned problems appear to be much more serious when we think in terms of the 'European citizens'. In effect, the powers of the 'European citizens' with regard to their representatives, taken as a whole, seem very diluted. What could they do, for example, if they wanted to reproach some of the Council members' labour? How could they react against those who appear to represent them?

Things have been improved – although not that substantially – after the adoption of the Amsterdam Treaty. On the one hand it is true that, after the Treaty (and, in particular, with the reform of the Co-decision Procedure), the European Parliament increased its capacity to control the Council's decisions. On the other hand, however, it is also true that there are still a number of important policy areas outside the scope of the Co-decision Procedure. Among these areas, for example, we find most decisions on asylum and immigration (decisions that – it was said – 'touch the essence of citizenship'); decisions on agricultural policy; or decisions on the harmonization of legislation concerning indirect taxes. In addition, as A. Weale affirms, one has to consider that 'many of the other formal powers of the EP are either weak or so apocalyptic in their consequences that rational actors are precluded from using them'.[16]

The fact that the Council's participation in the European decision-making process is undergoing continuous change makes it very difficult to evaluate it. However, and just taking into account the manner in which is organized at this point in time, I would affirm that, even assuming a very relaxed position on the accountability of the representatives, we would have good reasons to complain about the degree of political freedom enjoyed by the representatives. If, as the radicals assumed, impartial decisions are best guaranteed by ample discussion among a properly representative group of people, we should see the significant political freedom and independence (independence with regard to its constituency) enjoyed by the Council's members as a threat to the goal of impartiality.[17]

To adequately understand the seriousness of these observations, we should also consider the following additional facts. First, we have to acknowledge that the procedures and decision rules of the Council have changed significantly in the last few years, and become increasingly difficult for outsiders to understand (Hayes-Renshaw and Wallace 1997: 25). Also, we must take into account that the COREPER – one of the (thus considered) 'most obscure' organisms within the European Union's institutional structure – is, many times, the real responsible of the Council's final decisions.[18] This fact, of course, affects the people's chances to control the legislative process.

In addition and closely related to the previous point, we should take note of some particularities that normally distinguish the Council's decisions. For example, most of the agreements that the Council's signs are (according to the used language) agreements 'in principle' that the Members are 'invited to confirm'. This indication, as some commentators exposed, actually implies that '90 per cent of the final text of legislation is decided at sub-Council levels' (Wessels and Rometsch 1994: 213). Finally, we must also acknowledge that the representative's significant degree of independence has encouraged an increased activism of lobbyists and pressure groups behind the Council.

In summary, as a representative institution in charge of adopting fundamental political decisions, the Council of Ministers exhibits significant flaws: its members are not directly elected; and it concentrates too much authority through vaguely defined powers. It is then very difficult for the European citizens to reward or punish its members (although, presently, there are better chances to control the Council than before); and (given the way in which its members are elected) the Council is not institutionally well prepared to register the internal political and social differences that exist within each country.[19]

Accessibility/simplicity

The radical's defence of 'political transparency'

In addition to the mentioned demand for a properly representative and accountable system, many radical thinkers – both in the British and the American context – argued in favour of other values, equally important in the task of securing the protection of the people's will. I am referring to values like those of 'accessibility' and 'simplicity', which all belonged to the same principle of 'political transparency'. It seemed obvious, for these radical authors, that if the people had to have a chance to control their representatives, they needed to be informed about the content of their discussions (about the reasons to which they resorted) and they also needed to understand the actual meaning of these discussions. I believe that, presently, we still have good reasons to accept the radicals' claims. Clearly, the representatives cannot assume that their political responsibility is fulfilled, say, simply by 'facilitating' to the people the documents that they demand. The representatives need to speak in a clear and comprehensible language; have to avoid the use of jargon; and avoid the use of overly technical words. In sum, they have to force themselves to make their decisions easily understandable to the citizens. This obligation is particularly important when the representatives are discussing problems that may imply the use of the coercive powers that they control. In these cases, we need to see that the representatives use reasons that are publicly acceptable among free and equal citizens with different and conflicting interests: we need them to resort to reasons that are accessible to citizens and interpretable by them.[20]

These claims of transparency and simplicity, I believe, have characterized the best radical traditions both in England and the U.S., since the eighteenth century. For example, the British radical activist, Thomas Paine, adopted the ideal of simplicity as the 'core' value of one of his main books, 'Common Sense'. The defence of 'simple' constitutional or basic documents had a clear explanation, in this case: Paine was opposing the conservative constitutional model (the so-called 'mixed Constitution') that – he thought – was distinctively complex. Notably, Paine's influence became significant in the State of Pennsylvania, in the U.S., where he finally produced most of his intellectual work. In particular, Paine contributed to the creation of (what would become) the most radical Constitution in U.S. constitutional history.

Paine's multiple suggestions for the Pennsylvanian Constitution were basically oriented to secure these ideals of simplicity and transparency. In this respect, for example, he stated:

> to the end that laws before they are enacted may be more maturely considered, and the inconvenience of hasty determinations as much as possible prevented, all bills of public nature shall be printed for the consideration of the people, before they are read in general assembly the last time for debate and amendment; and, except on occasions of sudden necessity, shall not be passed into laws until the next session of assembly; and for the more perfect satisfaction of the public, the reasons and motives for making such laws shall be fully and clearly expressed in the preambles.
>
> (Blaunstein and Sigler 1988: 29–30)

Paine understood that, in a proper political system, the people had to be able both to know and understand the legislative initiatives of their representatives.

The claim for a more transparent and simple political system was also popular among many American anti-federalists. In particular, the anti-federalists made this demand clear through their opposition to the system of 'checks and balances' (the system of 'internal' controls that the Federalists defended at the Federal Convention). According to the radicals, a system of 'checks and balances' would be, on the one hand, too complex to be properly understood by the people and, on the other hand, too obscure to secure a proper relationship between the different branches of governments. The anti-federalists, thus, tended to accept the idea of a division of powers but not (what Madison called) the 'partial intermixture' between the different branches of power (that is, the radicals defended a 'strict separation of powers').[21] Beyond our agreements or disagreements regarding the radicals' institutional proposals, what is important, at this point, is to acknowledge the emphasis that they usually put on the idea of 'political transparency'.

The Council of Ministers on transparency and simplicity

Since its creation, the Council of Ministers has been widely criticized for the opaqueness and complexity of its procedures. These objections seemed not only descriptively adequate, but also reasonable, if we recognize the extent and significance of the Council's tasks, and the validity of a 'principle of legitimacy' similar to the one we referred to above (a principle according to which the exercise of coercive powers is justifiable only if they are exercised according to reasons that may be endorsed by all those potentially affected).

Acknowledging these types of criticisms, the same Council tried to secure a higher level of transparency in its decision-making process. In this sense, the Council decided that 'When a formal vote is taken in the Council, the record of the vote (including explanations of vote where delegations request them) shall be published.' This initiative came together with some recommendations concerning the provision of more adequate information about the Council's decisions. In addition, the 1992 Edinburgh Council made reference to the need for *simplifying the language* of the Council's decisions, normally too technical, detailed, and obscure, and distinguished by the use of abbreviations, jargon, and cross-references to other legislation. Also, the Edinburgh Council called for greater consistency between texts.

In coherence with the mentioned suggestions, declaration N. 17 of the Maastricht Treaty affirmed that:

> The Conference considers that transparency of the decision-making process strengthens the democratic nature of the institution and the public's confidence in the administration. The Conference accordingly recommends that the Commission submit to the Council no later than 1993 a report on measures designed to improve public access to the information available to the institutions.

These commitments were later reaffirmed by the Copenhagen European Council, in 1993 and, later on, the Council adopted some implementing decisions on public access.

All the measures that I mentioned represent, I believe, initiatives oriented to reorganize the Council in the right direction. However, there are multiple considerations that drastically reduce the attraction of these initiatives. As a general problem, we have to consider that the Council does not always move to a formal vote.[22] This mere fact deprives the citizenry of very basic information. In effect, if we take the principle of political transparency seriously, it follows that the people need to know which representative voted for which resolution and as a result of what reasons. Also, we have to take into account the fact that the Council's rights and responsibilities are still not clearly established: the Council has – as we mentioned – executive and legislative duties that it normally shares with other EU institutions. This very situation – that the radical anti-federalists would describe as a complex and confusing distribution of power – makes it even more difficult for the outsider to properly understand and evaluate the Council's work.

Other difficulties in this quest for transparency are the following. First, the Council's rules of procedure still recognize the Council's right to deny the publication of its legislative acts. In addition, the Council still has the right to refuse the petition of certain documents, in order to protect the confidentiality of its proceedings. Also, we have to take into account that, according to the Council's recent dispositions the request for documents has to be made 'in a sufficiently precise manner', something that seems to imply that the petitioner more or less precisely knows what, in fact, she wants to know.

At different institutional levels, the continuous importance of this problem is widely recognized. In the opinion of the European Commission, for example, the public's expectations for increased political transparency within the European institutions are far from satisfied and the Council is the more problematic institution, in this respect (see Wessels and Rometsch 1994). Also, and according to the Council's Legal Service:

> statements in the Council minutes, which have been a handy negotiating tool, have developed in such a way that they now threaten to undermine legal certainty and that in any event they form an absolute impediment to the making of Council minutes. That development runs counter to the efforts being made by the Council to improve the openness of its proceedings and the quality of Community legislation.
>
> (Helm 1995)

The same Council admits that:

> [the] practical arrangements for applying the principle of transparency are still the subject of differences of assessment among Member States as to the best way of ensuring a balance between the confidentiality required for any

negotiation to be effective and the need for the proceeding to be transparent, especially in the legislative field ... Some progress is possible in this area.

(Quoted in Westlake 1995: 192)

In sum, it is true that the Council has taken significant steps in its quest for transparency and that, in this respect, the situation is much better than it was a few years ago. However, it also seems clear that much needs to be done.

Open debates: its virtues and defects

The Anglo-American debate

The fight for open political debates has always characterized the radical political and philosophical tradition. In the British context the claim for open debates was typically used as a political weapon against the conservatives' defence of 'secrecy' (see Gargarella 1995 and 1996). In the American context, the debate about open or secret meetings, and about the importance of 'openness' in favouring deliberation, occupied a significant place during the initial constitutional discussions. As it is known, the American constitutional convention deliberated behind 'closed doors', something which provoked sharp criticisms among the members of the more radical groups. Radical politicians like Thomas Jefferson, for example, opposed the conservatives' position, according to which it was not necessary to allow the citizenry to somehow participate in the debates of the Constitutional Convention. A significant example of his position appears in a letter that he wrote to John Adams, in 1787, where he presented his criticisms, and referred to the importance of 'openness' for the sake of achieving better discussions. He stated:

> I am sorry [that the Federal Convention] began their deliberations by so abominable a precedent as that of tying up the tongues of their members. *Nothing can justify this example but the innocence of their intentions, and ignorance of the value of public discussions.*[23]

The conservative approach always tended to object to the ideal of having open debates. In order to defend this position, for example, the conservatives affirmed that the influence of the public tended to 'contaminate' and deteriorate the value of the representatives' discussions. In addition, they resorted to various related beliefs: the belief according to which, by opening the doors of the Convention, they would allow 'the spirit of faction' to hinder the debates; the idea that the Convention was already formed by 'virtuous people'; and the idea that a 'chosen body' of delegates could define adequate political solutions for the whole community, better than the community itself. More than anything, this latter belief moved them to reject a disclosure of the notes of the debates, even when the sessions were over.[24] Probably Jared Sparks presented the best summary of this conception. After a visit to James Madison, with whom he discussed this issue, Sparks justified the secrecy of the debates in these terms:

> Had the members committed themselves publicly at first, they would have afterwards supposed consistency required them to maintain their ground, whereas by secret discussion no man felt himself obliged to retain his opinions any longer than he was satisfied of their propriety and truth, and was open to the force of argument. Mr. Madison thinks no Constitution would be ever adopted by the convention if the debates had been public.[25]

Clearly, some of the opinions of the 'Founding Fathers' and their allies were simply an expression of their elitism (the belief according to which only the 'enlightened few' were able to adopt impartial decisions). However, part of their argument is suggestive of other reasons (against open debates) that could be reasonably used in more contemporary discussions. For example, someone could say that open discussions could move the representatives to adopt certain positions 'simply' in order to 'please' the audience. Or, it could be said that publicity hinders the possibility of a more frank exchange of ideas: the representatives feel too much constrained under the scrutiny of the 'public eye'. In addition, someone could affirm that having public debates work against the possibility of self-correction. These are not simply 'elitist' arguments.

Although it is true that publicity has significant effects on political discussions, it is far from clear that all of them are necessarily 'bad' effects. In effect, frequently we should celebrate the fact that the representatives had to avoid certain arguments (i.e. racist arguments) and had to resort to different ones. The existence of 'public constraints on public statements' may be seen as something positive for democratic politics.[26] In this sense, too, we have to recognize that the celebration of open debates makes it somehow more difficult, for the representatives, to engage in merely self-interested negotiations.[27] Obviously, if the representatives want to engage in self-interested negotiations they can actually do it, even against our best efforts to the contrary. But we should not facilitate this type of behaviour through the institutions we design. Open political debates, in this respect, make it more difficult for them to deceive us. I will return to this point below.

The Council of Ministers and open debates

Considering the previously exposed ideas, we would have reasons to object to the organization of the Council of Ministers. In effect, since its origins, the Council had as a regulative principle that of private meetings: the Council could meet in public – it was established – only if all the Member States unanimously decided to do so. The idea behind this decision was that 'no government meets in public'. Thus, since the 1950s and during forty years, the principle of secrecy has reigned supreme.

In the late 1970s the principle of secrecy was challenged, not as a result of new moral convictions, but simply as a result of pragmatic needs. Some members of the Council of Ministers began to defend more open debates, under the assumption that a few reluctant Member States blocked the integration. Thus, they demanded public debates only for strategic reasons.

In the latter years, and in particular since 1993 and the Maastricht Treaty, the situation – very slowly – began to change: it was so obvious that the Council's decision-making process was objectionable that the principle of confidentiality enshrined in the 1958 rules of procedure began to be seriously challenged from within. These pressures became stronger than ever before at the time that Denmark decided to hold a referendum on its integration into the Community, and had to convince its citizenry that things had changed in the organization of the Community.

However, although it is true that, in recent times, the Council of Ministers decided to have more open debates on major issues of Community interest and major new legislative proposals, it is also true that negotiations on legislation within the Council remained confidential, and decisions to hold debates on major issues had to be taken by unanimity. According to the Council's own opinion, 'open debates have tended to be about subjects on which consensus existed. Request for open debates on other subjects have failed to secure the required unanimity.'

In addition, one has to consider to what extent the participation of the COREPER (and its dependent groups) in this decision-making process affects the general goal of having more open legislative debates. As we examined above, the COREPER has a pre-eminent role in the decisions on almost all issues (only the Special Committee for Agriculture and the Monetary Committee escape from its control).[28] It analyses each of the topics that the Council of Ministers has to resolve and decides most issues in advance. In fact, it is possible to assert that the COREPER and its Working Parties on many occasions actually replace the Council as a decision-making institution. Then, and given the lack of openness that marks the discussions within these advisory bodies, we have reasons to insist on our previous worries.

Some officers and academics tried to justify the described decision-making process and its lack of openness. Thus, for example, one author suggested that:

> By its nature a negotiation cannot be open to the public view. The negotiator needs to be able to take positions and change them in a way which would upset particular interest groups and weaken his bargaining stance. Open sessions are for the delivery of set piece speeches. The negotiation goes on out of view, and if pushed out of the conference room by the cameras, in the back rooms.[29]

In addition, some other commentators considered these open discussions as merely 'time-consuming' – a loss of time.

In spite of these arguments, however, I believe that we have very good reasons to still fight for the adoption of more open legislative debates. In general terms, the demand for open debates seems a just claim within any just society: free and equal citizens may reasonably demand to clearly know what their representatives are discussing – to know, in the end, how the decision-making process is working. In addition, by having open political debates, we make the representatives more accountable to the people (in fact, we cannot punish or reward our representatives if we do not know what they are doing) and (more important for the purposes of this paper) we may also secure the adoption of more impartial decisions. In effect, as I suggested above, within an open deliberative framework the representatives are forced to filter out mere self-interested arguments: proposals that have their foundation in proper names or particular interests or in non-universal reasons are not likely to prevail in any genuinely deliberative assembly (see Gargarella 1998). Also, by having open political deliberations we contribute to the legitimacy and, finally, to the stability of the political system. In this respect, it seems reasonable to assume that i) when the people know the reasons that moved their representatives to adopt a certain decision, and ii) the latter are properly checked, iii) the institutional system increases its chances of obtaining the public confidence – something that would not tend to happen if the mentioned conditions were absent.[30]

I must say that one does not need to subscribe to a radical political position in order to point out the problems that I examined in the previous pages. I think that, in spite of their differences, both radical and conservative thinkers (say, Thomas Jefferson and James Wilson; Thomas Paine and James Madison) would recognize that the Council of Ministers, as an institutional project, still requires substantial readjustments. Examining the Council, the radicals would mainly criticize its lack of 'external' – popular – controls (how can the people check their representatives? how can they force the representatives to take their will seriously?), and the conservatives would criticize, at least, its lack of proper 'internal' – institutional – controls (are the Council's decisions properly balanced? how is it possible that some of the most important legislative decisions adopted by the Council still suffer from the lack of proper institutional checks?).

A few final words

In this paper, I tried to demonstrate that, since its creation, the Council has been built under the influence of a conservative philosophical conception. I also insisted that we have good reasons to object to the general orientation of this conception. Although I looked for support for my objections in the Anglo-American radical philosophical tradition, my intuition is that the best contemporary theories of democracy would ratify the line of criticisms that I followed. At the moment, it is sufficient for me to affirm that we *still* have good reasons to critically reflect upon the worth of the philosophical conception on which the Council's organization is based.

Notes

1 I take this term from Przeworski (1997).
2 The presidency of the Council (which, among other tasks, sets the agenda of the Council meetings) rotates among its members: the idea is that each of the Member States presides the Council during a six month period.
3 See, in this respect, Raworth (1993), Hoscheit and Wessels (1991).
4 The increasing importance of majority voting in the Council substantially changed the negotiating behaviour of the Member States: previously, unanimity granted all members a veto power. Presently, in order to 'block' a certain proposal, a coalition of members is necessary. See Hosli (1996).
5 See some important discussions over this issue in Weale and Nentwich (1998).
6 In what came to be the most famous exposition of the conservative position on deliberation, Edmund Burke stated that: 'Parliament is not a congress of ambassadors from different and hostile interests, which interests each must maintain, as an agent and advocate, against other agents and advocates; but Parliament is a deliberative assembly of one nation, with one interest, that of the whole – where not local purposes, not local prejudices, ought to guide, but the general good, resulting from the general reason of the whole. You choose a member, indeed; but when you have chosen him he is not a member of Bristol, but he is a member of Parliament' (Ross *et al.* 1949: 116).
7 M. White (1987: 213). 'This is only part of the political elitism which is blatantly present in The Federalist' – White added – 'in spite of the many genuflections that are made in the direction of the people' (*ibid.*). As J. Fishkin stated, from this (Madisonian) model 'we get some deliberation among political elites in representative institutions'. See Fishkin (1991: 44).
8 John Wilkes was a British journalist who was refused a place in the Parliament even in spite of his repeated victories in the polls (in Middlesex 1770). See Gargarella (1995).
9 See, for example, Habermas (1992a), Nino (1996).
10 The idea of evaluating the opinion of all those potentially affected seems to match some of our most basic intuitions about justice. Our common sense opinions about justice, in fact, say that even the most heartless criminals have a right to present their opinions in the judicial process. Their opinions have to be taken into account because they may have something important to say, in order to justify – or at least to make less disputable – their acts.
11 For example, in his famous 'Political Disquisitions', written in 1774, the radical English James Burgh defended this right, given that the representatives – in his opinion – were simply the people's advocates. At the same time, and following Burgh's ideas, Joseph Priestly and Richard Price, radical religious figures in eighteenth-century England, defended similar ideas and recommendations: 'civil governments – they affirmed – are only public servants and their power, by being delegated, [should be] by its very nature limited'. See, for example, Peach (1979: 48 and 138). In addition, we should not be concerned about the possibility of transforming the representatives into mere 'mouthpieces' of the people. The decision to closely follow the representatives' actions, and even the decision to force them to take certain particular choices does not preclude deliberation: a strong control over the representatives is not incompatible with the possibility of having open discussions, or representatives who change their initial thoughts, in Storing (1985, vol. 2: 445).
12 This right, for example, was formally demanded by the States of Rhode Island and New York, when consulted about the proposed Federal Constitution, but it was actually a common demand among the critics of the Constitution. The idea behind this proposal was a reasonable principle according to which, when a person authorizes someone else to do a certain job, the former has to retain the right to replace the

latter, whenever she sees the need to do it. In this respect, for example, 'Brutus', quoted in Storing (1985, vol. 2: 445).

13 The idea of rotation seemed to offer at least two important benefits: first, it opened the deliberative body to a greater number of people; and second, it helped to stop one of the worst evils perceived in many representative institutions, like the creation of a quasi-independent, autonomous, and self-interested elite. More recently, some authors suggested the adoption of *reserved seats for particular minorities*, as a way of improving the defence of minority rights. This suggestion (which does not necessarily imply that only the members of the 'affected' group can defend their rights) simply tries to improve our chances to secure the informational and motivational needs (that all representative bodies have and) to which I referred above. See, for example, Kymlicka (1995).

14 I discuss some of these problems in Gargarella (1995).

15 The only partial exception to this general rule seems to be the case of Denmark, whose parliament can bind its representatives.

16 See, for example, Weale (1998). In particular pp. 55 and 56.

17 In addition, consider that 'Convinced federalists had always seen the Council as an alien, intergovernmental body in the Community's supranational institutional structure. They took solace from the conviction that the foreign ministers and their traditional diplomatic methods would, sooner or later, be ousted by sectional minister and technical specialists. Vertical division would weaken the Council's grip and strengthen the Commission's hand; international diplomacy (as the federalists perceived it) would give way to specialized negotiations'. See Westlake (1995).

18 A good analysis, concerning this point, in Westlake (1995).

19 An interesting analysis of the Council, also, in Føllesdal (1998a).

20 See, for example, Freeman (1992: 25). This idea summarizes what John Rawls named 'the principle of political legitimacy'. According to this principle, 'our exercise of political power is proper and hence justifiable only when it is exercised in accordance with a constitution the essentials of which all citizens may reasonably be expected to endorse in the light of principles and ideals acceptable to them as reasonable and rational' Rawls (1993: 217).

21 See, for example, Vile (1967), and Storing (1985).

22 Among the reasons that explain this fact would be the following: on the one hand, many times, its members simply give their acquiescence to the decisions already adopted by the Council, instead of voting on them; and, on the other hand, these members are sometimes reluctant to promote a formal vote, because they see this measure as a way to slow down the decision-making process.

23 Italics are mine. I discuss this position in Gargarella (1995).

24 For example, Hamilton affirmed that '[had] the deliberation been open going on, the clamours of faction would have prevented any satisfactory result. Had they been afterwards disclosed, much food would have been afforded to inflammatory declamation. Propositions, made without due reflection, and perhaps abandoned by the proponents themselves on more mature reflection, would have been handles for a profusion of ill-natured accusation', Hamilton in Farrand (1937/1966, vol. 3: 368).

25 Farrand (1937/1966, vol. 3: 479). Madison's opinion on this issue was also clear. He emphasized, as most Federalists did, the importance of secret deliberation, and deemed that the majoritarian will could only 'vitiate' the discussions by transmitting to them the passions and prejudices characteristic of local politics. He explicitly defended the secrecy of the debates on these terms, in *The Federalist* no. 37. There, he affirmed that the debates 'had enjoyed in a very singular degree, an exemption from the pestilent influence of party animosities; the diseases most incident to deliberative bodies, and most apt to contaminate their proceedings'. Even stronger, Rufus King suggested destroying the Journals of the Convention (*ibid.*, vol. 2: 648).

26 See, in this respect, for example, Sunstein (1996). See, also, Goodin (1986), and Elster (1995).
27 As some contemporary political theorists affirm, in effect, secret procedures tend to foster bargaining, while open procedures tend to favour deliberation. See, for example, Elster (1991).
28 The COREPER is divided into two branches: COREPER I, that studies most technical matters; and COREPER II – the one which is important for us, in this context – that is in charge of the study of political and institutional issues (foreign affairs; regional policies; among others).
29 See Nicoll (1994: 192). For a similar argument, see Hayes-Renshaw and Wallace (1997: 7).
30 See, in general, Habermas (1996a).

10 Can the European Union become a sphere of publics?[1]

Philip Schlesinger and Deirdre Kevin

Introduction

In late modern democracies, the role of mediated communication is becoming ever more central to public life. Popular deliberation about matters of public interest is for the most part heavily dependent upon information and perspectives provided by the news media. Since the key framework for democratic politics and the formation of a public sphere remains that of the nation-state, the emergence of a supranational polity changes the relations between media, publics and state power.

This chapter will consider whether European Union (EU) integration is bringing changes in the organization of public spaces for debate and discussion. To what extent are developments in some news media and the communicative efforts of political institutions at the European level likely to produce generalized public deliberation inside the EU?

We shall argue first, that there are conceptual problems inherent in thinking about the prospect of a *single* European public sphere: we need to replace that notion with one of an increasingly articulated sphere of European publics with the potential to develop deliberative processes broadly in line with the evolution of a European civil society.

Secondly, we shall draw attention to two crucial features that structure the flow of news and information about the EU and have a direct impact on the nature of wider European deliberation. One is the overwhelming 'nationalization' of political communication about the EU: it is generally produced, distributed and received from within standpoints rooted in the nation-state. Moreover, in some fields, the EU operates more as a disseminator of pronouncements than as an initiator of broadly based dialogue.

Our analysis will reveal a twofold impediment to the present-day articulation of a single European public sphere: on the one hand, there is the fracturing of politico-communicative space along nation-state lines; on the other, there is the EU's tendency to 'pronunciamentism', to top-down communication rather than dialogue.

Finally, we wish to suggest that one of the most significant sectors in which a deliberative, media-sustained space is emerging is at the level of political and economic elites. But this is not a public sphere. Rather, the evidence indicates that the transnational market for news tends to sustain a restricted communicative space. While this does not match up to normative ideals of generalized access to the public domain, and is very far from offering universal participation in debate about key public matters, it is nonetheless an important indicator of the incipient 'Europeanization' of politico-economic discourse. The dominant focus on the role of public intervention in creating a new European public may well have obscured the workings of the media market in sustaining and perhaps developing transnational elite audiences and readerships in Europe.

The 'national' public sphere

Jürgen Habermas and his followers see the public sphere as a realm in which a range of views and opinions can be developed in relation to matters of public concern. It is a space that exists outside the institutions of the state but in which all who are concerned with questions of public interest and the conduct of civil society may engage in debate. This perspective emphasizes the possibility of achieving rational agreement between publicly competing opinions (Habermas 1962/1989). A key underlying condition for the development of public opinion, according to this view, is guaranteed universal access to the public sphere for all citizens. The liberal, constitutional public sphere is presented as permitting a rational, well-informed conversation between equals capable of resolving their differences by non-coercive means. The existence of such a public domain is central to the freedom of expression commonly associated with democracy.

Of course, Habermas' conception of the historic emergence of the public sphere imagines a set of ideal conditions. These are not met anywhere. As Habermas himself recognizes, the contemporary political public sphere is peopled by groups organized in the pursuit of sectional interests rather than individual citizens intent upon discussing the common good. Moreover, he has also acknowledged the importance of public relations and political marketing in shaping processes of mass communication and therefore in influencing public opinion. For Habermas, the original rational ideal has become corrupted, being turned into a public display or spectacle, with major interests, political parties, and the state all pursuing their communicative goals through techniques of information management.

However, as numerous critics have pointed out, even the historical, bourgeois public sphere was incompletely open, excluding various groups – such as the labour movement, women suffragists, people of colour – who needed to fight their way into the framework of public debate and attention (Calhoun 1994). The generalized pursuit of communicative strategies in the public domain has become part of our contemporary understanding of political action. There is, however, highly differentiated access to public debate by players of various kinds in the political field. In addition, the media of communication do not invariably operate as equal voices that express a range of rational arguments.

Habermas' normative argument provides us with a useful starting point for discussion of a possible European public sphere. His earliest account is simultaneously utopian and dystopian. It is a tale of the descent from a state of grace, that which he elsewhere formulates as undistorted communication, into the messy realities of the world of distorted communication – of spin doctors, political consultants, and media feeding frenzies. These are today's idioms rather than those of Habermas' classic treatment. But they reflect his well-articulated concern with the 'refeudalization' and spectacularization of the public domain.

This line of argument has recently been given a distinctive twist by Leon Mayhew. Synthesizing the work of Talcott Parsons and that of Habermas, Mayhew (1997: 51) has postulated the creation of a 'New Public ... constituted by the rise of professional experts in persuasion. These experts aspire to more than particular acts of persuasion; they aim to build, and to help others to build, the general capacity to persuade that we call *influence*.' According to this analysis, it is the rationalization of persuasion through the building of forms of irredeemable influence exercised by professional politicians and communicators that short-circuits the deliberative capacities of the public. Like Habermas, therefore, Mayhew considers contemporary trends in political communication to be inimical to democracy.

It is insufficiently recognized that Habermas' early theory took as its framework the European *nation-state* addressed as a political community. Mayhew, likewise, takes the USA as his unquestioned political space. In fact, the historical formation of the public sphere has been closely connected to the process of creating nation-states (Eley 1994: 296). Thus, Craig Calhoun (1995: 233) has emphasized the intimate relations that exist between conceptions of the political community, its public sphere, and the boundaries of the nation. However, it is crucially important to recognize the contingency of these relationships.

The view that communicative processes are crucial in delineating the boundaries of the political community, and at the heart of the public sphere, is closely aligned with a consistently articulated strand in the theory of nationalism (cf. Schlesinger 2000). Karl Deutsch (1966) first gave a name to the 'social communications' approach, whose axial premise is that nations are set apart from other collectivities because of the special nature of their internal communications, their 'communicative complementarity'. Communication processes, broadly understood, are argued to have played a crucial role in the historical formation of nation-states. This line has been followed by other influential writers. Ernest Gellner (1983) identified the crucial importance of national systems of education in developing a common cultural literacy and also in sustaining 'high cultures' that could be claimed as expressions of the nation. Benedict Anderson (1983), for his part, has singled out the historical development of a print culture as a key influence which, he suggests, ensured the entrenchment of a national language of state out of competing vernaculars. Through the medium of a reading public, it brought about the participation of diverse localities in the creation of an 'imagined community' of the nation.

Consequently, one way of looking at the nation-state, as Stuart Hall (1992: 292) has suggested, is as a 'system of cultural representation'. The public sphere, from this point of view, may be seen as a space in which the national political community talks to itself, as a 'discursively constituted subject' that provides itself routinely with images of its very constitution as a body politic (Calhoun 1995: 251). Crucial to their existence is the production of public discourse about themselves, which in conditions of late modernity, is a pre-eminently *mass-mediated* discourse. But discourses on the nation are not *just* ideal processes: rather, the symbolizing and marking out of the national cultural terrain, in a public domain, are materially underpinned by a range of institutions, political, economic and communicative.

A serious shortcoming of the early Habermas was to depict the national polity as a *single* public sphere. This is a limiting case that suggests a degree of cultural homogeneity to be found in few societies, if any. Nancy Fraser (1992) has suggested that the Habermas' model is unduly restrictive when it proposes a sole authoritative centre to the public sphere. Rather, she has argued that the ideal of equal participation in public debate is better served by imagining a *plurality* of competing publics. This lays stress on a diversity of interests and backgrounds in any given society while at the same time presuming the possibility of 'interpublic discursive interaction' (Fraser 1992: 126). Calhoun has glossed this idea by suggesting that we therefore think in terms of a 'sphere of publics', of 'multiple intersections among heterogeneous publics, not only as the privileging of a single overarching public' (Calhoun 1995: 242). Arguably, therefore, a plausible image for the expression of public life in late capitalist democracies is that of a plurality of discourses in contest for a dominant position in national public space. This presupposes that there is a democratic order permitting diverse groups to organize themselves to wage the battle for public opinion, although it does not necessarily mean that they do so on equal terms.

However, even this revised approach needs further amendment because it still treats public space too unproblematically: it thinks of it as prototypically bounded by a nation-state. But consider political discourse in the space of the European Union, which is certainly not a nation, nor is it a polity easily characterized in conventional terms. In Europe, the national, state-bounded, context can no longer be taken for granted as a viable framework for defining the scope of communicative communities. Whereas nation-states are enormously important focuses of collective identity, to analyse the emergent European communicative spaces, the focus needs to shift to the new, *supranational* arenas and their constituent publics. To complicate things further, it is also necessary to address another level as well: that of the political spaces *below* the level of the nation-state that are being redefined by the EU's regionalist dynamic (cf. e.g. Schlesinger 1998).

The European Union as communicative space?

Is a sphere of publics that is distinct from those of the Member States actually emerging at the European level? One of the clearest recent efforts to address this question has come from Habermas in an obvious outgrowth of his concern with the constitution of the national public sphere. The argument about how a

European public sphere might be formed – and along with this, the kind of collective identity that it might have – is closely linked to his proposal of a 'post-national' identity for Germany after reunification. In a nutshell, what he has argued is that the ideal identity for the Germans is one that detaches itself from the antecedent, ethnic, *Kulturnation* and embodies itself in the civic *Staatsnation*. The stress is upon universalistic principles of state citizenship. The commitment to the collectivity, on this model, derives from a 'constitutional patriotism' that offers a 'non-nationalist understanding' (Habermas 1991b: 94, 97).

This perspective has been transposed wholesale to the European level by Habermas, writing in the context of post-unification Germany, ethnic conflicts in the former Soviet Union and ex-Yugoslavia, and the continuing process of economic and political integration in the EU. He observes that the 'classic form of the nation-state is at present disintegrating'. A 'republican' approach to the nation, argues Habermas, would therefore shift the emphasis from any ethnic or cultural properties of nationality to stress a citizenship based upon communal self-determination (1994b: 21–23). A democratic state does not require a common ethnicity or language. Instead, Habermas (1994b: 27) proposes, 'the political culture must serve as the common denominator for a constitutional patriotism which simultaneously sharpens an awareness of the multiplicity and integrity of the different forms of life which exist in a multicultural society'.

The term 'political culture' here refers to a set of legal principles, institutions, and political norms and practices commonly diffused throughout a given polity. A political culture, then, is a kind of frame and medium for political activity. It tends more towards a notion of principles and rules of the game than to the broader, anthropological notion of culture as a way of life. Thus, two senses of 'culture' are relevant to the overall argument: the 'common political culture' quite narrowly understood (in this sense, widespread knowledge of, and adherence to, the rules of the game); and national culture as the 'branching national traditions of art, historiography, philosophy' which importantly involve cultural elites and mass media (Habermas 1994b: 33). For Habermas, national culture remains relevant because the persisting basis of collective difference is the medium through which common legal principles are to be variously interpreted in the coming European federation.

What is needed to develop this political culture is a liberal and egalitarian European order in which decision-making bodies are open to scrutiny. Habermas assumes that there will be intensified networking across existing national boundaries and argues for an ideal interplay between 'institutionalized processes of opinion and will formation' and 'informal networks of public communication' (1994b: 31). Habermas (1996a: 171) postulates a radical form of popular involvement in public affairs as the essential corrective to profession-alized politics. Parliamentary democracy, therefore, 'demands a discursive structuring of public networks and arenas in which anonymous circuits of communication are detached from the concrete level of single interactions' – in other words, a communicative space.

In his later work, Habermas has accepted, to some extent, the argument of his critics by partially dethroning the *single* public sphere: the discursive diversity in 'arenas' of public life is now expressly recognized. Based on civil society, the public sphere is described as 'a highly complex network that branches out into a multitude of overlapping international, national, regional, local and subcultural arenas' (Habermas 1996a: 373–374). Yet, inconsistently, there does remain an underlying conception of 'the' public sphere, for it is within this logically presupposed integrative frame that so-called 'hermeneutic bridge-building' between different discourses occurs.

Habermas also now portrays the public sphere as potentially *unbounded*, as having shifted from specific locales (such as the nation) to the virtual presence of citizens and consumers linked by public media. A European public sphere would therefore be open-textured, since its communicative connections would extend beyond the continent. Of course, this makes a certain sense: contemporary communication flows and networks ensure that no – or hardly any – political community can remain an island. But how does the suggestion that we all really belong to a global village sit alongside the postulate of a European identity? We are compelled to ask *which* communicative boundaries are significant for the development of a distinctive political identity and political culture in the EU. In other words, how might communicative processes contribute to the Union's social cohesion?

Habermas' latter-day conception of the unbounded public sphere also sits somewhat uneasily with his thinking about the supersession of the nation-state and its reconstitution at a federal level with a political culture to match. Habermas wants to argue that any eventual European political community would be linked not by means of thickly textured common symbols, and the deep layers of affect that go with these, but rather through the rule-governed matrix of a constitutional patriotism. This deliberative conception tends to overemphasize the role of rationality. It is hard to see how a discursively linked community could develop a collective political loyalty and identity if completely unbounded. A European political community without some distinctive communicative boundary-markers simply cannot be imagined as a sociological possibility.

This relates to the general problem of an emergent European collective identity. Habermas offers a federalist model of political involvement by Europeans in which the content of their collective identities is different at each level. At the level of the nation-state it is 'thick' and articulates with a national political culture elaborated within a highly institutionalized public sphere. At the level of Europe, it is 'thin' and legalistic, and overwhelmingly refracted through the medium of nation-state politics. Behind this characterization of two levels of collective identification lies the unresolved broader issue of what makes collectivities cohere, and whether any conceivable constitutional patriotism ultimately presupposes a hinterland of *non-rationalistic* assumptions and sentiments in order to make its civic appeal work (Schlesinger 1997: 385–388).

While the EU's future trajectory is uncertain, it is already reframing political life within its boundaries. We might invoke as an instance the rather uncertain redefinition of citizenship presently under way in the EU. The Maastricht Treaty of 1991 took an important step when, under Article 8, it formally established citizenship of the European Union for everyone holding the nationality of a Member State. It is true that the real content of such citizenship still needs to be defined and the relationship between the Union and the individual is mediated by the Member States. Some have taken an optimistic view of this developing relationship, which Elizabeth Meehan (1993: 185) has characterized as follows:

> a new kind of citizenship is emerging that is neither national nor cosmo-politan but which is multiple in enabling the various identities that we all possess to be expressed, and our rights and duties exercised, through an increasingly complex configuration of common institutions, states, national and transnational interest groups and voluntary associations, local or provincial authorities, regions and alliances of regions.

Whether this formulation resolves matters is open to question. It makes a virtue of present ambiguities as EU citizenship still stands in potential contradiction to national citizenship. Conventionally, modern citizenship is a relationship in which individuals assume duties to the commonality in exchange for the exercise of rights within the boundaries of a state. An essential aspect of the exercise of citizenship is the availability of a diverse range of information on matters of public interest on the basis of which political judgements can be made. The workings of the public sphere therefore directly intersect with the exercise of citizens' rational capacities to choose and decide.

Apart from involving membership of the political community of a state, the concept of citizenship is also closely tied to that of belonging. The growing complexity of the relationships between citizenship, nationality and statehood opens up the question of *who* is permitted to belong to a given community and *why*. In other words, we are directed to the criteria for inclusion or exclusion that might be applied in drawing the boundaries of a collectivity. For Habermas, in the choice between two divergent, ideal typical, conceptions of the nation – the 'civic' and the 'ethnic' – it is the 'civic' identity that offers the only possible answer for what it is to be a 'European'.

Indeed, Joseph Weiler (1996b: 22) has reinforced this view, pointing out that the European (federal) project has necessitated a decoupling of citizenship from nationality:

> The substance of membership (and thus of the demos) is in commitment to the shared values of the Union as expressed in its constituent documents, a commitment to the duties and rights of a civic society covering discrete areas of public life, a commitment to membership in a polity which privileges exactly the opposites of classic ethno-nationalism – those human features which transcend the differences of organic ethno-culturalism.

In a nutshell, the Habermasians' argument is that a European identity (and its citizenry, its demos) has to become denationalized, leaving behind that prior conception of national identity which is rooted in the existing state system. This leaves open a couple of key questions. First, how will the new identity articulate with the old (which are not going to disappear, as for the conceivable future nation-states will remain the foundation stones of the EU)? Second, will the new *demos* in due course become, in some widely recognized and felt sense, a new nation, albeit a highly complex one?

The Euro-polity and its publics

Habermas' argument broadly places him among those who think that a distinctive Euro-polity is emerging, even though they might not characterize themselves as federalists. Some, such as Philippe Schmitter (1996a, 1996c) would contend that the EU's economic integration process and the incremental growth of political power have now run their course. Schmitter accepts the widely aired claim that the EU is facing a crisis of legitimacy due to the lack of citizen involvement in its decision-making process. There is no alternative, he thinks, but to democratize further, and this entails re-imagining European institutions. It means setting aside the conventional view that the choice lies either between the formation of a new supranational state or staying with the existing state system. He envisages the formation of a non-state, non-national polity, which he describes as a condominium. In this political formation the functions of government and the territorial dimension do not coincide. There will be a 'plurality of polities at different levels of aggregation' (Schmitter 1996c: 18). Our commonly held conception of the polity as a sovereign state, or state with a centre of sovereignty, will have to be set aside, argues Schmitter. By contrast, 'the Euro-polity will have to invent and implement new forms of ruler accountability, new rights and obligations for citizens and new channels for territorial and functional representation' (Schmitter 1996c: 21). This means that there will have to be new experiments in citizenship, representation and decision-making. And that would mean rethinking the articulation of the public sphere: indeed, thinking in terms of overlapping spheres of publics would make much more sense than imagining a single centre of authority.

Others, however, would disagree that reform can actually democratize the EU. Michael Mann (1993: 127) argues that the post-Maastricht EU gives the misleading impression of being a superstate. It is true, he acknowledges, that sovereignty has been undercut by Community law, the Single Market, and the European Monetary System, together with the extension of qualified majority voting. But at root, the EU 'regulates only the capitalist activity of a region'. Common actions are limited, there is no common sense of identity or citizenship, national politics prevails, and there is no common defence policy. In his view, then, there is some divided sovereignty but no serious evidence of a shift towards a 'single state or even a federal state'. Mann believes that to overcome any shortcomings in democratic representation would entail a far-reaching restructuring of Europe in the direction of fully-fledged federalism, an outcome he considers hardly feasible. This view is not too distant from that of Alan Millward *et al.* (1993), who in an influential thesis, have argued that European integration has actually strengthened the nation-state, which remains the key brokerage point in the EU. Any shift towards supranationalism, Millward contends, would depend upon Member States giving up their present powers, which would cut across the intergovernmentalist logic of the EU.

Certainly, an argument such as Mann's or Millward's rests on conceptually safe ground in that it deploys existing categories of political analysis. These tend to interpret European developments in terms of what is already known rather than what might be. On this basis, we could not expect that, in due course, a European public sphere might emerge as a locus of accountability for the exercise of power. Moreover, it follows that questions about the role of communication at a supranational level are of little relevance. However, to keep an open mind about the potential emergence of a communicative space at the EU level does not require one to endorse a post-nationalist position and to write off the continuing importance of the nation-state. There is already an emergent supranational civil society in the shape of organized policy communities. And there is also a linguistically- and class-restricted media space opening up. Neither of these implies that the nation-state is a dead letter, but they may be taken as indices of an emergent supranational politico-communicative space.

Arguably, the long-term impact of collaborative practices inside the EU is bringing about a gradual modification of the ways in which political life is conducted. Looked at comparatively, the EU's drive towards the creation of common political institutions is quite distinctive and far-reaching when compared to other trading blocs around the world (Katzenstein 1996). Hirst and Thompson (1996: 153–154) consider the EU to be 'the most ambitious project of multinational economic governance in the modern world'. Since the sharing of economic decision-making has eroded national sovereignty, the Union may be seen as 'a complex polity made up of common institutions, Member States, and peoples' that combine their efforts in governance.

Complementary to the conventional political science focus on the formal systems of the EU – its legal instruments and its intergovernmentalism – is a consideration of its informal workings as a 'unique political market-place', in the words of Keith Middlemas (1995b: 684). From this point of view, the question of the EU's potential statehood, while properly addressed as a problem, is subordinated to a view of the Union as a long-term game, without a clear-cut outcome, but in which the continuous involvement of the players modifies both the Community and themselves. As Middlemas (1995b: 685) puts it:

> The game also induces a process of socialisation, habituating players to each other, forcing them to think through other points of view and subsequently live with them. Indeed, this Euro-civilising aspect may come to be seen, looking back from early in the next century, as informal politics' largest contribution to the European Union.

While Middlemas (1995b: 687) recognizes that there are many obstacles to any 'necessary linkage between economic and political union' he draws attention to the impact of the continuous practice of co-operation, likening this to other historical processes of state formation in Europe: 'If a game which is common to all twentieth-century industrial nations exists in the EU, then the Community's informal statehood must develop further …' This historical perspective directs attention to the gradual shaping of a political community and a common culture. While it is framed in terms of statehood, it points to something different from what we now take as conventional.

The EU's institutional heartland

The impact of the EU's institutional framework on political and media discourse is not surprising. From its earliest origins in 1950, its political space has evolved and a policy community has grown around it. Moreover that space is the object of routine attention. Thus, while the EU is a political space, we may also see it as the junction of a range of communications activities. The European Commission's information efforts regarding EU policy processes are aimed at European publics and are filtered through national or regional information structures. At the same time, the elites – especially those in business and in Euro-politics – are increasingly being served and addressed as a single entity by a developing, specialized, European media structure.

The way in which communication is shaped by national political and cultural frameworks is most obvious during European Parliament (EP) election campaigns and when referenda are held. Elections for the Parliament do not take place among a single European electorate. Rather, they focus on national political issues, are still fought by national political parties (one exception, for instance, being the development of European parties in Denmark), and are reported through national media using the same reporting conventions used for national elections (Blumler 1983; Wober 1987; Leroy and Siune 1994). Analogously, the information campaigns of the European Union have addressed national political, media and PR structures, but they are now increasingly focused on regional media and regional representative bodies. This both reflects an EU commitment to a 'Europe of the Regions' and is a response to regional political and economic self-assertion.

Considered as a quasi-polity, the EU consists of four main institutions: the European Commission; the European Council; the European Parliament; and the European Court of Justice. Together, these constitute a unique institutional arrangement. The Commission is the 'motor of the integration process' (Christiansen 1996: 78). A supranational institution led by twenty Commissioners, it is a bureaucratic body that formulates policy and implements European Union legislation. The Commission is the EU's main focus of lobbying activities. Commission employees involved in formulating policy often suffer an information deficit and departments are usually understaffed. Commission officials are 'increasingly reliant upon groups and firms to supply them with good information and expertise and to suggest policy solutions which can be made to work in each of the twelve [now 15] Member States' (Mazey and Richardson 1992). Lobby groups with an interest in the policy area will 'befriend' such people, gain their trust and supply them with expertise.

While the Commission pushes the political and legislative agenda, it is the Council of Ministers that is the key focus for interstate bargaining and the representation of national interests. Consultation on policy occurs quite early and working groups are set up to assess proposals. The Council's procedures are, however, more secretive than those of the Commission due to the intergovernmental nature of negotiations and there has been serious resistance to offering wider public access to information (Edwards 1996: 143). This makes the Council less amenable to lobbying groups than the Commission and more dependent on national civil servants (Mazey and Richardson 1992).

What we learn of these rather opaque decision-making processes comes primarily through *national* news media, a process of framing that allows national governments to emphasize their victories and to play down compromises reached with other Member States. Morgan's analysis of the Brussels news beat (from a UK perspective) shows that the Commission is most open to news reporting and the Council most closed. It is also apparent that national editorial values influence coverage whereas national governmental sources are still of key importance for journalists covering European Union issues. Morgan argues that most journalists were 'conscious of having to report with a highly developed sense of the domestically acceptable so far as EU news is concerned' (Morgan 1995: 327). Current reporting styles mean that we are more likely to learn about legislation that has been decided on rather than the policy process itself. What reporting patterns tend to obscure is where, and by whom, influence has been exerted, as well as leaving shrouded the compromises that have been entered into by national representatives.

The European Parliament is the only directly elected body in the EU. Since the Single European Act 1987, and even more so since the Treaty on European Union 1991, its powers have expanded and latterly it has had an increased role in 'co-deciding' legislation with the Council of Ministers (Earnshaw and Judge 1996). Its increased power has made it more of a focus for lobbying activities. The Parliament often transmits the causes of interest groups and lobbyists by pressuring the Commission, the Council and even national MPs.

The European Court of Justice (ECJ) is perceived by many as having done most to further the process of European integration by its judicial activities, decisions on the interpretation of EU legislation, challenges to Member States over the non-implementation of regulations and also the resolution of arguments between the institutions over the legal basis of regulations. Citizens and interest groups from the Member States have also taken cases to the ECJ challenging Member States' implementation of legislation. Many cases are referred by national courts to the ECJ for clarification of EU legislation which, according to some commentators, allows the European Court considerable scope in interpreting the intentions of the original treaty. The Court's interaction with other institutions and interests in developing both Community law and policy has been crucial for European integration (Wincott 1996).

An indication of the impact of EU legislation on the national political space – to take the British case – and the extent to which power has moved beyond national boundaries, can be seen from the following figures. In a recent report by the think-tank Demos, it is claimed that 80 per cent of economic and social legislation and 50 per cent of all legislation is decided at EU level; that 20–30 per cent of civil service time is taken up with EU matters; and that 90 per cent of EU decisions are taken by national civil servants behind closed doors. As with other Member States, EU law has precedence over UK law, impinging on all areas except housing, civil liberties and domestic crime (Leonard 1997).

This extensive 'Europeanization' of governmental processes is reflected in the development of a truly transnational European political community. It is apparent that a supranational public space has indeed evolved around the policy-making actors in the various institutions, but even here much of this activity ultimately relates back to national or regional interests. There are certain organizations which play an active role in policy-making and thus take a more pan-European approach. These include the Union of Industries in the European Community (UNICE) and the European Trade Union Confederation (ETUC) both of which are regularly consulted by the EU.

The officially recognized regions of Member States tend to have representative offices in Brussels. Despite criticism of this development by some national governments the Commission established a Consultative Council of Regional and Local Authorities which is consulted on policies regarding regional development (Mazey and Richardson 1992). However, because there is such a variety of regional bodies in the EU, they do not constitute a common tier of government and Member States continue to be the key players (Keating and Hooghe 1996: 226–227). It is estimated that there are some sixty territorial offices in Brussels (Mitchell 1995: 289). These actors often co-operate with particular industries important for their region. According to Gardner (1991) the involvement of regional representatives in a lobbying campaign 'can impart a thoroughly European "spin" to an issue'. Canel's (1994) analysis of the activities of EU regional agencies shows that the majority of the work involves 'information mediation' through provision of details of EU policies and plans to other national and regional bodies. The regional agencies' main promotional activity involves developing a 'regional corporate identity', namely providing information about the region and attending trade fairs and promotional events. Their contact points are concentrated in the Commission (Canel 1994: 16). In general, regional bodies, like other sectoral and industrial groups have to liaise with central government representatives in the EU on common lobbying strategies (Mazey and Mitchell 1993: 101).

The above sketch outlines the political space of the EU. The political communication processes, which take place in terms of policy consultation, lobbying, public affairs, and interest representation reflect the 'multi-level governance' of the European polity. Consequently the processes are at times national, supranational and sub-national, and often combine all three levels. This greater complexity of view about the nature of political society in Europe means that we can no longer think of political space as just contained within the nation-state nor of the role of information as adequate if all it is intended to do is to assist the conduct of the citizen within the national democratic polity. As the European Union's policy-making and political direction impinge increasingly on Member States, it is evident that the European dimension increasingly shapes the content and sets the agenda of the mediated political discourse of national polities (Fundesco 1997; Morgan 1995: 323; Schlesinger 1998: 58–60).

Campaigning for the EU

In 1991, at Maastricht, the European Union stated its intention to improve access to information regarding the decision-making process (EC 1991). The difficulties in ratifying the Maastricht Treaty and the subsequent debate on the EU accelerated the momentum of reform. EU information policies could also be seen as a response to negative media coverage and part of an overall attempt to 'market' Maastricht (Tumber 1995). The process culminated in codes of conduct concerning public access to information, excluding material classified as 'secret', 'confidential' or 'restricted' (and later, a further classification of 'top secret') while certain Council meetings were to be made public.

The EU has accepted in principle that informing and involving the public about the process of integration is necessary. Since Maastricht it has been recognized that levels of public hostility towards the EU project are considerable. A recent think-tank report has argued that the EU is suffering from a lack of popular legitimacy, with only 46 per cent of citizens supporting their countries' membership. Scant public knowledge and a widespread perception of the EU's irrelevance are also noted. However, it is suggested, the Union might be able to redeem the situation by tackling 'problems without frontiers' (such as a common defence and foreign policy, the environment, international crime and terrorism, and job creation). It is widely believed that such issues cannot be dealt with by individual Member States. Additionally, it is held, there may be a stronger basis for a European identity rooted in everyday transnational cultural consumption and tourism rather than in official attempts at cultural promotion such as the EU passport and a common anthem, flag and day (Leonard 1998: 5–9).

Following the report of a 'reflection group' set up to assess the information and communication policies of the EU, the Commission decided that its lack of public support was largely due to inadequate information and understanding and so endeavoured to increase the transparency of its policy-making. Further integration was to be 'based on information, which means giving the facts and explaining, communications which means listening and dialogue, and transparency, which means priority to total openness in pursuing the first two objectives' (EC 1994).

The extent to which these aspirations have succeeded is highly questionable. EU efforts to date have included the Public Information Relay initiative, designed to give access to the people through the use of the public library network and documentation and information centres throughout Europe. The scheme emphasizes the 'need for easily accessible, neutral and accurate information on European matters' (EC 1995). The regional approach to this initiative was intended to:

> bring facts concerning established policies and programmes of the EU closer to the users in the localities where they have the greatest impact and to draw public attention to the fact that EU policies form an integral part of the national and local system of law government and administration.
>
> (EC 1994)

The more recent information drives have included the 'Citizens First' campaign which outlined the 'four freedoms' of EU citizenship, the 'Building Europe Together' campaign which set out to explain the purpose and aims of the 1996 Intergovernmental Conference, and the 'Euro' campaign which was aimed at promoting a positive attitude towards the single currency before decisions were made at the national and EU levels. The objectives of the 'Euro' campaign were to:

> inspire confidence and win the support of the general public and the different categories of players; to stimulate and help economic and financial operators and other players in the public and private sectors to prepare and implement the necessary mechanisms for the transition to the Euro; to prepare all the citizens of the countries of the European Union for the change-over to the single currency.
>
> (EC 1996: 2)

According to EU documentation 'a currency is the expression of identity. There cannot be a real acceptance of a European currency without an awareness of a certain European identity' (EC 1996: 3). The majority of EU Member States moved into the 'Euroland' of the single currency in January 1999. It remains to be seen what impact trading in the new currency will have in the longer term on conceptions of collective identity. At present, instrumental concerns rather than symbolic ones seem to be prevalent amongst Europeans.

The EU has set up internet sites, information offices, phone lines and resource centres which serve those seeking information, particularly in the areas of education and research. In the business community the EU Commission's 'Groupeuro' project has involved the recruitment of economists and specialists to promote the positive aspects of EMU. The EU has also hired PR agencies across Europe to run campaigns and make contacts at a national level. These efforts include TV advertising and the distribution of leaflets to households. It has also been claimed that the Commission has tried 'product placement' in encouraging soap operas to include positive references to the EU in their dialogue (Conradi 1997: 8).

Such initiatives are, strictly speaking, intended to be carried out in the spirit of 'subsidiarity' wherein the individual Member States control the manner in which the campaign is organized. The 'Citizens First' campaign was given a low profile in the UK as its launch coincided with the general election campaign of 1997. As regards the 'Euro' campaign, EU documentation states that 'the priority information action will need to be adaptable in view of different economic and political situations of the Member States, particularly with regard to the state of public opinion and the results of democratic consultation' (EC 1996: 3).

The EU's approach reflects the recognition that to reach the mass of citizens it is necessary to have 'information materials adapted to the needs of the media at the national and regional level' (EC 1996: 3). Certainly, whereas involvement in the EU policy process by pressure groups and lobbies conforms at least to some deliberative ideals, it may be doubted that the Commission's pronunciamentism fits that frame at all. It is hardly surprising that the Commission's various initiatives have been criticized by both pro- and anti-European voices in the UK. One critic described the initiatives as 'black propaganda' and claimed that as there was already 'a vigorous and well-informed debate over the merits of the Euro [that] the use of European funds to advertise the single currency is a perversion of the democratic process' (Heathcoat-Amory 1998). The EU's top-down approach to fostering a European identity has also been attacked by arguing that the focus should instead be on the 'surreptitious identity ... carefully stored away in holiday snapshots and memories of art, literature, music and buildings and landscape' (Leonard 1998: 27).

The mediation of the EU

Thus far, the argument has suggested that elements of a European civil society have begun to emerge, organized through the mobilization of diverse and often competing interests, and oriented towards the political institutions of the EU. As we have seen, political communication – broadly understood – while focused on those institutions is at the same time complexly mediated by national and regional political actors. To the extent that information about, and the interpretation of, EU activities is disseminated outwards from the Union's administrative heartlands, this characteristically flows along the grooves of established national and regional networks of communication.

This means that to think of the EU as constituting a *single* public sphere, as something fully centred – based on the model of a nation-state – is to produce a misleading image. Multi-level governance, and the continuing tensions and divergences between the supranational level and those of the Member States and regions, rather require us to think in terms of overlapping spheres of publics. There is little evidence of a single, *official* mode of address to the publics of Europe.

It is this very lack that has made the search for evidence of a *common* public sphere capable of transcending Europe's diversity a matter of some theoretical and practical interest. To the extent that the issue has been a public policy concern, over the past two decades this has taken various forms. There has been an attempt first to develop a so-called 'European audio-visual space' through the promotion of cross-border film and television production. This has been followed more recently by a drive to create a 'European information area' based on the convergence of telecommunications, computing and media. Each of these policy initiatives has presupposed a common communicative space, but in the first instance it has been cultural value and heritage that have been emphasized, whereas in the latter it has been the image of a wired society and informational exchange that has predominated.

Neither of these approaches has really been driven by a direct concern with *political* communication as such. However, to the extent that they each embody conceptions of either cultural, or alternatively, informational aspects of citizenship, they do clearly have a bearing on the construction of a political space in which communication is afforded some centrality. The idea of an 'audio-visual space' was attuned to the role of entertainment in building a public by way of fictional film and television distribution. By tempering the usual concern with news and information, it corrected the rationalism and cognitivism of most theorizing about the public sphere. It also recognized the likely importance of the affective dimensions of collective belonging and social cohesion, as I have pointed out elsewhere (Schlesinger 1997: 387, cf. McGuigan 1998).

An explicit relationship between media and political citizenship has been much more evident at the heart of efforts to devise a common framework for assuring media pluralism in the EU. However, thus far this has foundered on the opposing interests of those who want a single EU market place for large media conglomerates to operate with a minimum of constraint and those who argue for the protection of consumer interests at the level of the Member State. Significantly, the space in which pluralism is to be secured is one of the moot points: should it be the Member State or should it be the Union itself? This dilemma neatly encapsulates the ambiguous politico-communicative status of the EU.

As public communication inside the EU is largely produced for national markets bounded by the political confines of states, there is little scope for pan-European modes of address. The short history of attempts to fashion Europe-wide public service satellite television channels has been above all a tale of casualties (Collins 1993). Nor, with some signal exceptions with which we deal below, have there been good grounds for thinking that a European market exists for print media. Without European media consumers organized transnationally as common audiences or readerships there is no basis for talking about a single European public for political communications.

On this reading, then, public policy on media and communication at the EU level has been rather fragmented and inconsistent in its attempts to create a common communicative space. From the standpoint of political communication, rather more interesting than official interventions have been the contemporary dynamics of the transnational market for news.

For analytical clarity, it is essential to distinguish between information made available to elites engaged in the policy process or economic decision-making and that produced for mass publics. The press is preferred by elites whereas television is the most-used mass medium. That said, however, television is now increasingly capable of finding niche markets prepared to pay for specific services, as the growth of digital technology is ensuring that this medium, too, will be capable of targeting elites. Top professionals are increasingly also gravitating to the Internet for certain kinds of specialist information-seeking, and their use of the World Wide Web and of e-mail is increasingly taken as an index of elite status in business surveys.

Selling news is not, in general, primarily motivated by the idea of creating and serving a new public. Its marketability is not especially susceptible to political engineering. In exceptional circumstances, such as the era – now largely past – of public service or state broadcasting monopolies, it has been possible to use news along with other programming to produce an audience, addressed as a national public. But those are no longer the prevalent conditions.

Thus, what is of particular interest about the European space today is how some news media are in effect creating specialized audiences and readerships by way of seeking markets. An incipient change is taking place in the collectivities to be addressed, one ultimately due to the development of the European Union as a novel political form. It has started to make sense to think of such emergent media audiences as occupying a *transnational* space. Although driven by profit-seeking, some Europe-wide media are creating a distinct space or spaces for a form of collective debate, albeit a highly restricted one. This contrasts strongly with the policy-makers' failure to create a new European public in the face of the deep-rooted barriers of language, culture, ethnicity, nation and state that make Europe into such a mosaic (Schlesinger 1993, 1994).

Supranational mediation

Although at the present stage of development of European media markets it is evident that the press remains an almost exclusively national medium, there are, nevertheless, newspapers and magazines that do self-consciously address a European (as well as a global) *elite* audience conceived as composed of political and economic decision-makers, the preferred language being English. In television, too, there are indications of related developments which will be illustrated by the case of Euronews.

A press for the politico-business elite

Economic elites are a key battleground for the printed press. How media enterprises and their journalists regard the European arena plainly depends greatly upon their vantage point. We need to distinguish an 'internal' perspective from an 'external' one. From inside the EU, the key concerns of elites are with the ramifications of creating a common economic order supported by law and regulation and how this is translated into the practice of politics. Viewed from without, the nature of the European space changes dramatically. From the standpoint of external capitalist interests, Europe is a *region* about which it is prudent to gather intelligence. What happens in the interior is ultimately interesting because it bears on the political stability of the continent, the sharpness of economic competition between blocs and states, and the attractiveness of investment conditions. The difference between internal and external points of view, then, is akin to that between having a stakeholding and maintaining a more general prudential interest in the performance of an investment. We may assume that these underlying attitudes are conveyed in journalistic practices.

Europe is a distinct regional market whose specificity is underlined when we consider its attractions for a daily newspaper with world-wide distribution such as the *Financial Times* (FT). The FT sells itself as the 'world business newspaper', as 'the best source of world-wide business', claiming its authoritativeness against 'a background of increasing globalization of markets' and using a reporting perspective that is represented as 'international'. Its circulation is over 300,000, the readership more than one million, and distribution occurs in 140 countries (http://www.FT.com, 27 January 1999). According to one authoritative trade survey, the FT – with a 9 per cent share of the elite's 'important business reading' – is the most widely-read daily in the 15 EU countries, Norway and Switzerland. For these purposes, Europe's elite is defined as 'the top 4 per cent in terms of income and executive activity' (RSL 1996: 17).

The FT is owned by Pearson plc and headquartered in London. But the paper *has* globalized its market place. Like Britain itself, Europe is undoubtedly a crucial regional market for the FT, which publishes in the UK, France, Germany, Sweden and Spain. Within Europe, among senior people in the continent's largest businesses in 17 countries the newspaper outstrips key daily competitors that include *Die Frankfurter Allgemeine Zeitung* (FAZ), *Das Handelsblatt*, *Der Spiegel*, the *International Herald Tribune* and the *Wall Street Journal*. It is noteworthy that in the key EU Member States, especially France and Germany, the economic elites are willing to read a newspaper written *in English* because of its international standing.

According to Morgan's study of news reporting from Brussels (1995: 333) the FT is 'usually cited as being favoured by official sources' because of its 'European-wide readership'. Arguably, therefore, despite its global reach and ambitions, the FT's European edition contributes to a common agenda for a fraction of Europe's elite. Illuminatingly, in this regard, on 9 February 1998, when 155 German economists wrote to the press calling for a delay in the implementation of European Monetary Union, they sent their letter both to the FT and the FAZ.

Along with the Benelux countries, France and Germany are also the continental states of greatest interest to *The Economist*, owned by the London-headquartered Economist Newspaper Ltd. Like the FT, but in the weekly market, *The Economist* is the most widely read paper of its category across Europe, taking 3 per cent of the possible readership. Inside the company it is held that there is 'a pan-European business-government elite, which (sic) are speaking English in a daily basis, using it in business and personal life'. Certainly, survey figures bear this out: of the top 4 per cent of employees across 14 of the richest European countries examined (a mere 5.7 million people), 68 per cent speak or read English (with French at 42 per cent and German at 23 per cent way behind), and of these more than 38 per cent use some English at work, albeit with major variations between countries (RSL 1995: 11). For *The Economist*, the EU's development offers 'transnational cultural opportunities' for selling its product (Interview, Simon Philips, Marketing Executive, *The Economist*, 21 April 1998).

The company has also recognized the potential of the political microculture in Brussels described above, launching *European Voice* in October 1995 on the model of Washington DC's *Roll Call*. *European Voice* is a weekly newspaper with a 'village feel' to it aimed at all the top people in the Brussels micro-polity. This publication has 'the exclusive co-operation of the European Commission, the Council of Ministers and the European Parliament, who circulate 7,000 individually addressed copies of the newspaper to Commissioners, their Cabinets, MEPs [Members of the European Parliament] and A grade civil servants'. Other targets are registered lobbyists, the business community and the press, with total circulation reaching 16,000. (URL: http://www.european-voice.com/advertise/2.p15, 27 January 1999; Interview, Hugh McCahey, Marketing Executive, *The Economist*, 21 April 1998).

Doubtless the FT's regional acceptance in Europe is ultimately connected to its British provenance. This may be underlined by considering the position occupied by the *International Herald Tribune*, whose major market is Europe although it proclaims itself to be thoroughly international. Edited in Paris and printed around the world, this is *par excellence* 'the daily international newspaper' of the mainly corporate *American* citizen abroad, and above all, by its own report, of seriously wealthy decision-makers who travel both often and rather expensively. Circulation is over 210,000, distribution takes in 181 countries, and there are half a million readers. More than two-thirds of copies are sold in Europe, the rest in the Asia/Pacific region ('Who Reads the IHT?'; 'Circulation, January–December 1997', URL: http://www.iht.com/IHT/HELP/27 January 1999). Politics, business, sport and culture are the keystones of a paper that draws on the *New York Times* and the *Washington Post* for its copy. In short, US east coast elite perspectives are published daily in seven European countries to address an audience principally resident in Europe. But the IHT is differently positioned from the FT and *The Economist*. The reason is important: it resides in the dual attributes of readers' citizenship and interests rather than the place of publication or even the geographical location of the readership. Since readers of the IHT do *not* mostly enjoy relevant European national citizenship rights they do not participate in political activities that are formally constitutive of the Euro-polity – notably national and European elections. Yet, on a different reading, they could still be said to constitute a part of European civil society as denizens who doubtless do play an important role in key areas of economic decision-making that substantially affect Europeans' well-being.

Thus far, we have discussed printed media that reach a specific kind of European market but are by no means entirely dependent upon it for their revenues, and certainly do not make it their *raison d'être*. The short, eight-year life of *The European* (launched in May 1990, closed down in December 1998) may well be instructive about the risks involved in relying largely (if not exclusively) upon building up a European market, as well as of letting a political agenda strongly critical of the EU predominate.

The European began first as a weekly broadsheet intended to contribute to European unity under the aegis of the UK-based Mirror Group Newspapers, then run by the late Robert Maxwell. It ended its life as a weekly tabloid-style news magazine with a 'Euro-sceptical' vocation, owned by the Barclay Brothers' European Press Holdings. In its last, anti-EU incarnation, the editor-in-chief, Andrew Neil, aspired to reach the status of *The Economist*, namely to offer an 'essential read for the people ruling Europe' (*Media Guardian*, 2 June 1997: 6). The paper's executives believed that 'The true Europeans now are the businessmen ... people who might be operating in one, two, or three different countries at one time ...' and that US decision-makers needed a 'one-stop shop' when reading about Europe (Interview, Sue Douglas, editorial consultant, European Press Holdings, 4 February 1998).

While *The European*'s latter-day sense of its potential business elite audience was well founded, it had to fight against established titles and there can be little doubt that its editorial policy under Neil was disastrous, leading to a major downturn in its sales from some 155,000 to around 133,000 in 1997. The paper's eventual collapse, amidst accusations of cronyism, misdirection, and sheer lack of management, is of less interest here than the fact that it did, for some years, manage to hold a modest share of a cross-national readership. While one-third of sales were in the UK, its home base, it did achieve a more than negligible presence in the big EU states and in Belgium, principal home of the EU institutions. Some insiders expressed the private view that in political terms it was 'before its time', that Europe had yet to become a political entity. Should this eventually occur, the implication is that as the EU's politico-communicative space develops, a more successful successor venture of this kind will not be out of the question.

Television news for the upmarket consumer

Euronews was launched in January 1993 in an attempt to produce a distinctive news agenda for a broader, European, public. It came in the wake of a number of failed experiments in pan-European television. The Euronews project, supported by a consortium of eighteen European public service broadcasters and the European Parliament, arose in the context of global competition to dominate the international news agenda. It reflected the desire in some quarters (notably the French government) to produce a 'European' perspective on world news (Hjarvard 1993). Television programme sales (which include news and journalism) are part of a global struggle for commercial and political hegemony that is perceived as having an impact on national sovereignty and cultural identities.

The pressure to enter the market place became especially marked after the Gulf War in 1991, when CNN's success both in reporting from the front line and in acting as a vehicle for television diplomacy marked out new territory subsequently entered by the BBC's World Television News. Although global in reach, both the Anglo-American companies are firmly rooted in their national journalistic cultures, with distinctive corporate identities and brand recognition.

By comparison with Euronews, which has always broadcast in five major European languages (English, French, German, Italian and Spanish) and also since 1997 in Arabic, both CNN and BBC World are monolingual channels, transmitting solely in English. As a transnational broadcaster, Euronews presently embraces some of the major features of the linguistic and national diversity of the European cultural space.

Despite major financial losses, Euronews has twice proved attractive to firms rethinking their strategies in the European communications market. Its operating company was purchased in 1995 by a subsidiary of the French telecommunications giant, Alcatel-Alsthom, because of the weakness of public sector finance provided by the European broadcasters and the EU. Alcatel sought to combine its communications distribution capacity and the information services offered by Euronews (Machill 1998).

The French telecommunications enterprise entered into a rather short-lived acquisition of news-producing capacity. Alcatel's shares were purchased by ITN, the British television news provider, in November 1997. ITN took operational control because of the conditions of national and international competition for broadcast news producers. By finding a new 'niche product' – Europe-wide broadcasting in the public service tradition – the company diversified, breaking into broadcasting after forty years as a news supplier. Multi-language broadcasting was seen as giving ITN a competitive edge in the European market place, with added potential for international sales. The strategy is premised on the longer-term view that over time, and especially with a single European currency, the EU's national publics will gradually develop a sense of a common news agenda (Interview, Stuart Purvis, Chief Executive ITN, 20 April 1998).

Euronews is the only pan-European broadcaster to transmit in more than two languages. Audience research indicates that Euronews reaches 90 million households via cable, satellite, or terrestrial broadcasting, three times the reach of BBC World, and that the channel is the number two pan-European news broadcaster after CNN. To CNN's 28.1 per cent share of pan-European viewing in one month, Euronews has 21.3 per cent ('Euronews', ITN Information Pack, 1998; http://www.euronews.net/en/about/about.htm, 21 January 1999). Widespread distribution, however, does not equate to actual viewing and as has justly been pointed out, transnational news of this kind actually reaches very small audiences indeed by comparison with those of news broadcasters aiming at specific national audiences (Sparks 1998: 117) .

Moreover, although such crude figures do not tell us what audiences make of the news programmes that they view, it is worth noting that Euronews has its highest distribution by far in the largest media markets of the EU Member States: France (20.9 million viewers), Italy (20.2 million), Germany (12.9 million), Spain (11.7 million). These are the main non-Anglophone states in whose languages Euronews broadcasts. In the UK, in sharp contrast, the potential viewership is a mere 1.2 million, far exceeded by both Belgium and Finland, with much smaller populations.

Euronews is attempting to harness linguistic diversity to commercial advantage. Digital distribution offers the means to meet specific audience tastes in a fragmenting market place where viewer choices can be more directly expressed.[2] ITN's Chief Executive, Stuart Purvis, has observed that '[p]art of our plan is to create two separate products: a core pan-European service and national versions of it in partnership with our local partners' (Plunkett 1998: 19). ITN believes that there is a growing market for news about Europe amongst those dissatisfied with increasingly parochial national news programmes. Purvis says that he is aiming for such upmarket viewers who prefer to have the news in their own languages (Plunkett 1998: 19; *The Economist* 22 November 1997: 50; Interview, 20 April 1998). The company has sought the financial support of the European Commission and the European Parliament as a way of bolstering itself, recognizing the need for political support to sustain this kind of venture over the longer term, and anticipating that digital technology will eventually make of a European Union public affairs channel possible.

It remains to be seen whether this niche audience for news can offer a route to creating a transnational public. The original French government policy of pushing back Anglo-Saxon dominance in the international news market has apparently failed on two counts. First, effective control has shifted to London, although production is still located in Lyon in France. Secondly, ITN is reshaping the company along the lines of what its British managers see as good journalism. Will British-influenced practice therefore increasingly provide the common idiom for growing segments of the continental European viewing public, competing with national stations?

If Euronews were ever able to be a major news agenda-setter on the continent, sufficiently enterprising in journalistic terms to grab the interest of the political class and able to create stories for other media to follow, the station's reach and potential penetration could indeed become significant in the formation of a sphere of European publics – albeit one addressed multilingually.

The above discussion revisits some earlier speculations (cf. Schlesinger 1994: 40–42) and suggests how we might think about the EU's changing communicative space. First, the core of the emergent European political class and the business elite *do* have a number of print media that they use intensively and variously. Secondly, despite the well-known complexities of language politics in the European Union, English already functions to a considerable extent as a *lingua franca* amongst elites. Thirdly, a transnational market for information about the European space does exist – and not just in Europe. Arguably, that is because global business and political elites across the Atlantic (and elsewhere) do see the EU, and Europe more generally, as a distinct *region* within a global economy.

Concluding remarks

There is a case for taking seriously the emergence of a distinct, complex, Euro-polity which is generating multi-level forms of political communication that encompass lobbying, official information campaigns, and news reporting. Such communicative activity takes place *not* in a single coherent European public arena but rather in an often contradictory field of political forces. Consequently, rather than imagine a *single* European public sphere as the likely outcome of economic and political integration, we should think about the growth of interrelated spheres of European publics. How these will evolve is open to conjecture. However, we may speculate that ultimately what Keith Middlemas (1995b) has called the 'Euro-civilizing' process will continue to knit these discursive spaces together, and that the drift towards a more coherent articulation might in the *longue durée* contribute to the conditions for a distinctive Euro-political culture that offers a potential focus for a new layer of political identity. A necessary precondition for this, however, would be broad public engagement in European public affairs. Presently, at best, some European elites have begun to constitute a restricted communicative space.

If we think beyond elites to a putative network that knits together a range of European publics, ideal-typically these would be composed of *transnational citizens* who have: (1) an equal and widespread level of communicative competence; (2) relatively easy access to the full range of the means of communication; and (3) a generalized communicative competence which embodies sufficient background knowledge, interest, and interpretative skills to make sense of the EU and its policy options and debates.

A hypothetical *European sphere of publics* would, amongst other things: (1) involve the dissemination of a European news agenda; (2) need to become a significant part of the everyday news-consuming habits of European audiences; and (3) entail that those living within the EU have begun to think of their citizenship, in part at least, as transcending the level of the member nation-states. Moreover, these rational attributes would need to be accompanied by an affective dimension. Without such conditions obtaining, we could not meaning-fully talk of the development of a genuine sphere of publics at this level.

In reality, any common European public agenda is likely, in the process of media reception, to be diversely 'domesticated' within each distinctive national or language context (Gurevitch *et al.* 1991). This does not foreclose the question of how national audiences might – in some significant respects – still be oriented towards a common 'European' frame of reference. As noted above, we already have some nascent forms of 'European' journalism. For this to evolve, it needs to find a mass, transnational audience that recognizes it to offer something distinct from national forms of reporting, with a different institutional focus and agenda from that of the individual Member States. This will have both to interest and be significant for large numbers of Europe's citizens. Public engagement with the centrality of EU decision-making and the effectiveness of its workings would not eclipse public interest in the politics of nation-states, regions or other meaningful territorial entities.

The record of public policy intervention to create a common European media space, or to engage the public via official information, has not been a notable success. If there are some signs that the news market is taking a 'European' shape, and thereby helping to build a restricted communicative space for some, it is important to recognize that his could not have occurred without the prior institutional framework of the European Union. It is the very existence of the emergent Euro-polity that has created the conditions for a transnational, elite media to develop. To the extent that pan-European media have begun to emerge in the press and in television – and these are still rare birds indeed – their market-seeking behaviour has been the driving force rather than the search for the new public imagined in normative theory. The result is that an elite conversation is now under way in the European space – and much of it is taking place in English.

Notes

1   Research for this chapter has been conducted as part of a study of 'Political Communication and Democracy' (Reference No.: L126251022) funded under the UK Economic and Social Research Council's 'Media Economics and Media Culture' Programme. The constructive comments of Jay Blumler, John Corner, Daniel Dayan, Simon Frith, Erik Oddvar Eriksen, Tore Slaatta, Peter Larsen, Graham Murdock and Richard Paterson are all gratefully acknowledged. This work was first presented at the conference on 'Democracy in Europe – Integration and Deliberation', University of Bergen, Norway, 20–22 February 1998 and subsequently at the ARENA Seminar, University of Oslo and at the Institute for Media Studies, University of Bergen on 5 and 6 October 1998 respectively. The present chapter expands substantially on Philip Schlesinger (1999).
2   This turns on its head the view that Europe's cultural mosaic is a *blockage* to building a pan-European market. In 1994, be it noted, this kind of approach had already been aired by EU Industry Commissioner, Martin Bangemann's report (1994) on the construction of a European information society.

11 Indigenous rights and the limitations of the nation-state[1]

Else Grete Broderstad

Introduction

It is by now commonplace to assert that the nation-state is undergoing profound transformations. The idea of the homogeneous nation-state, which is associated with a uniform conception of citizenship, and a common sense of national community and identity, is challenged by ethnic and cultural revival within and among states. This revival is associated with more complex conceptions of citizenship and notions of community and identity – which may be more or less inclusive and exclusive – than those associated with the nation-state. A particularly important set of challenges emanates from indigenous people, due both to their particular history of incorporation, as well as their present status.[2] These developments affect the state both from 'above' and from 'below', in the sense that indigenous groups have obtained special status and group rights in international law, as well as special legal protections and representative bodies within certain nation-states.

The focus of this chapter is on how the European integration process affects the role of indigenous groups and peoples, as illustrated by the Saami people in three of the Nordic countries, namely Norway, Sweden, and Finland.[3] The Saami are an indigenous people in each of the countries, a fact which has been acknowledged by granting the Saami special status. In each of these states, to varying degrees, legal and political arrangements have been established which are intended to promote a greater measure of Saami self-government. In institutional terms, an important result of these legal and political reforms has been the establishment of Saami Parliaments in each of these countries.[4] The establishment of Saami Parliaments in Norway, Sweden and Finland, combined with the entrenchment of certain Saami rights, has affected the constitutional status of the Saami. There are now specific rights, rules and procedures for decision-making and handling of Saami issues and concerns, both in a Saami context and on a common Saami/majority arena. The institutionalization of the management of Saami issues also includes cross-border co-operation. The increasingly formalized and extensive co-operation between the Saami Parliaments has resulted in the establishment of the Saami Parliamentary Council. This contemporary Saami form of political co-operation has emerged in addition to the voluntary work of Saami organizations through the Saami

Council.[5] These developments can be viewed as a means of further institutionalization of regional cross-border Saami co-operation.

At the same time, the development of Saami rights and other political
arrangements could still be said to be in a constituting phase. It is frequently
noted that there is a need for a new period of legislation, to further develop
Saami rights and to strengthen the Saami community (cf. plan 1998–2001 of the
Saami Parliament in Norway, C. Smith 1996).[6] This applies to all the three
countries discussed here, namely Norway, Sweden and Finland. However,
despite these obvious similarities, the developments in the respective Nordic
states since the 1970s, reveal less of a convergence in the Nordic states' policy
towards the Saami than might have been expected, given the obvious similarity
in objectives (cf. Sillanpää 1994, 1997; Lewis 1998).

Thus, from the above it is quite clear that the Saami challenge is not a matter
that can be confined to or discussed merely as a matter between an individual
state and 'its' Saami minority. A more transnational perspective is required if we
are to improve our understanding of the Saami as an indigenous people, and as
a people whose traditional settlement areas were divided up by the states.

The focus of this chapter is on how the role and status of the Saami are
affected by the process of European integration. This process affects both
national policy towards indigenous peoples and the Saami directly in several
areas. It is only in very recent years that these effects have started to show up
which means that the current assessment must be based on trends and
developments rather than very tangible effects. Sweden and Finland, as EU
members since 1995, are adapting their societies and systems of government to
the EU, and this process of adaptation also influences Saami policy and politics.
For instance, the European regionalization process, which is clearly evident in
Sweden and Finland, is also important in the Saami context. Norway, albeit not
a member of the EU, is affiliated through the EEA, and is 'an adaptive non-
member' (Sverdrup 1998).

The EU's regional policy, as manifest for instance in its programmes of
regional development, could over time constrain national governments in
qualitatively new ways with regard to their policy towards the Saami. Several
factors must here be considered. On the one hand, the success of international
policy and law, as instruments for increased indigenous self-determination, does
of course depend on how these instruments are adopted and implemented
within the larger framework of each Member State. On the other hand,
Member States and/or Saami political activism, could contribute to the
development of indigenous policy on the international arena, so as for instance
to foster a future EU policy towards indigenous peoples and national minorities.
The question to be addressed in this chapter is: *Given the structural constraints
inherent in the notion of a homogeneous nation-state and a uniform conception of citizenship,
what are the prospects for the EU to remedy such defects with regard to indigenous groups?*

In order to address this question, we have to clarify first what is the nature of
the challenge that indigenous people pose, i.e. in what sense are their claims a
problem for conceptions of citizenship and belonging based on national systems

of democratic governance. This is not merely an empirical issue but also relates to the conceptual lenses we apply: the problems inherent in the liberal and communitarian conceptions of nationally based democracy are particularly relevant. Second, we need to clarify how these groups have been dealt with by the Member States in question; i.e. describe and compare how these groups have been incorporated into their states historically, as well as how their concerns are addressed and possibly limited in these states today. Third, it is necessary to clarify how the European integration process could affect them. The EU is often conceived of as a post-national entity, which promotes a more inclusive sense of identity and belonging. This may be addressed by means of the following question: In what sense does and should the EU affect the manner in which Member States address the role and status of indigenous people? This question will be addressed by looking at some aspects of the debates conducted in the EU. Deliberation at the EU level may contribute to generate and cement a sense of obligation.

In the following pages, these questions will be addressed. In the next section, the liberal and communitarian conceptions of citizenship will be briefly outlined and assessed with explicit attention to how amenable they are to address Saami claims for citizenship and status. In the following section, a brief presentation of the different national incorporation strategies will be provided in order to shed light on how the states dealt with their Saami minorities and also to clarify the nature and range of challenges that these minorities posed to the states. In the next section, the onus is on clarifying how the Europeanization process might affect the Saami in the three Nordic countries. The final section holds the conclusion.

Concepts of citizenship and models of democracy

Indigenous claims for political autonomy – self-determination in internal affairs and joint decision in common affairs – represent an important challenge to the manner in which citizenship is understood in both the traditional liberal and in the communitarian model of democracy.

Within a traditional liberal conception I understand political rights as individual rights, which 'give citizens the opportunity to activate their private interests in such a way that through voting, the composition of elective bodies and formation of cabinet, they can aggregate their interests into a political will which in turn can influence the administration' (Habermas 1995c: 31).

The most widely held understanding is that the liberal tradition does not include cultural membership. The model claims that equal rights are independent of the existence of indigenous and minority cultures (Kymlicka 1989). According to this orthodox liberal view, the maintenance and reproduction of ethno-cultural groups should be left to the free choices of individuals in the private sphere (Kymlicka 1997: 72). The liberal tradition is primarily concerned with the relationship between the individual and the state, and does not take the individual's membership in a community and a culture into account. Nation-states that comply with this view, are able to and have, ignored the distinctness of indigenous or minority cultures. The result has been assimilation of distinct minority cultures into the dominant majority society.

The liberal interpretation of democracy is at pains to explain how a common will is formed (cf. Eriksen 1995: 13). This perspective, which highlights interests, cannot explain the role of the Saami Parliament as an important vehicle for Saami identity and opinion formation (Broderstad 1994/1995). The traditional liberal view sees cultural identity as a private concern. This is a question of individual choice, not of public policy. But questions about cultural identity and indigenous rights have a public dimension, and are dependent on collective public actions. The reason for considering these questions as public is not that they are unable to exist without state regulations (cf. Miller 1997: 89). Rather this is a question about political rights not merely as means of protecting individuals from state incursions, but also as action-generating vehicles, as means to give citizens access to political participation. 'Only such rights may be used to increase autonomy in that they equip the citizen with the "self-referential competence" that enables him/her to affect matters which will influence his/her role in society' (Eriksen and Weigård 1997b: 4).

The communitarian tradition embraces a collective understanding of citizenship, and a shared conception of the good, based on common traditions and practice. Common values and practices are viewed as authoritative horizons, which set goals for us (Kymlicka 1989: 50). The focus is on ethical-political questions, collective processes and self-interpretation. However, 'as most communitarians admit, this "politics of the common good" cannot apply at the national level. ... A common national identity, therefore, is not a useful basis for communitarian politics, which can only exist at a more local level' (Kymlicka 1995: 92). A more nationalist claim is that the society is held together by a culturally defined nation and a shared conception of community. The nationalist response to cultural diversity is assimilation of indigenous and minority cultures, due to the state's active efforts to make the citizens as culturally alike as possible. This is of course highly disconcerting to those culturally distinct minorities that face the threat of being assimilated. But also communitarians, who seek ethical community, can run into problems in their response to cultural diversity because of conflicting views about the good within different groups, local communities and cultures (cf. Eriksen 1994b: 15).

The communitarian interpretation of democracy does not provide compelling reasons for the need for human rights (cf. Eriksen 1995: 13). The onus on the common good within a community lends itself to paternalism, an attitude which is incompatible with the individual's right independently to consider and to dismiss any given tradition. The pluralistic society of today requires that traditions have to be merited, i.e. their value must be demonstrated and can not be taken for granted. The members of a cultural community can, through the public, consider what is worthy of recognition in their cultural traditions. However:

in order to be able to consider which traditions are valid, one must know the actual traditions. The traditions must be given an opportunity to assert

themselves as valid or invalid. This is an internal connection between cultural dissemination, cultural criticism and cultural innovation in the sense
that conditions for cultural survival can be guaranteed only to the extent
that conditions for cultural criticism can be guaranteed.

(Oskal 1995: 73, 74)

From this the need emerges for an institutionalization of frameworks for
'explicit distribution of traditions and criticism of traditions' (Oskal 1995).

A basic requirement for a just indigenous policy is the need for a dialogue
within the democratic constitution. The challenges that indigenous issues pose to
existing arrangements necessitate a dialogue also about the common democratic
constitution. It could be necessary to lift this dialogue above the context of the
nation-state in order to become properly aware of the particularities of the given
nation-state, and the taken-for-grantedness of the concepts and principles
associated with the nation-state (cf. Chapter 1).

This problem does not only pertain to the state but also, as James Tully has
observed, to the 'language of modern constitutionalism which has come to be
authoritative [and which] was designed to exclude or assimilate cultural diversity
and justify uniformity' (Tully 1995: 58). This not only underlines the difficulties
associated with recognizing and affirming cultural diversity, it also further
demonstrates the need for such a debate – which presupposes equal conditions
for indigenous minorities and majorities to enter into and participate in the
debate. Indigenous cultures must publicly be acknowledged and affirmed in the
basic institutions of their society (cf. Tully 1995: 198).

In practice, there is evidence to suggest that the need for explicit acknowledgement of indigenous cultures has, at least to a large extent, been recognized
in Norway. The political rights that the Saami as a people have obtained – as
revealed for instance in the establishment of the Saami Parliament and in the
amendment of the Norwegian Constitution to include a Saami clause – indicate
that the Saami as Saami are more strongly and explicitly related to the national
constitution than before (cf. the plan for the Norwegian Saami Parliament 1991–
1993: 13). This is the result of increased Saami political rights, and is not merely
a policy objective. A Saami political system of participation has been established
at the same time as these political rights are anchored in a common constitution.
Political rights give access to political participation, and according to Habermas
(1992b), political rights have priority as the core in the notion of citizenship. A
precondition for political rights exercise is that the individuals can make use of
their private autonomy (Habermas 1994a). This in turn is conditioned on the
notion that cultural belonging is viewed as a primary good, which creates a
necessary context for execution and realization of our potentialities as
autonomous individuals (Kymlicka 1989). Saami rights are meant to guarantee
cultural belonging as a basic good for the individual. The democratic process has
to safeguard cultural identity as a precondition for individual autonomy and
freedom. Thus cultural identity must be connected to the notion of citizenship.

This also includes deliberation about the recognition of political rights of indigenous peoples. Focusing on this deliberation attention must be directed at three core principles: Cultural and political rights claimed by indigenous peoples might be related to the principle (1) that everybody should be recognized as a member of an ethnic or cultural group with a cultural identity. Everyone should be recognized for his or her unique identity. We should not just recognize differences, but also foster cultural particularity (Taylor 1994: 43; Oskal 1998a: 143). This principle seems to be at odds with a principle (2) that acknowledges that everybody should be recognized as an irreplaceable individual and treated equally, irrespective of ethnic and cultural belonging. A third principle (3) is the demand to be recognized as a citizen, with full citizenship in the political community, which entails the right to participate in the execution of political power and political representation (Oskal 1995. cf. Habermas 1992b). According to the most widely held view, there might seem to be little consistency between these principles. However, as Kymlicka (1989) argues, one should recognize the importance of culture (first principle) as a precondition for individual autonomy and freedom (second principle). And individual autonomy is intrinsically connected to the citizen's public autonomy. The private and public autonomies are equiprimordial (third principle) (Habermas 1994a). With reference to these three ideal principles, to what degree are they reflected in the national constitutions which are addressed here? In the next section, the different national incorporation strategies in the three Nordic countries will be presented in order to shed light on this question.

The alternatives of state minority politics

The idea of the homogeneous nation-state

The minority political status of indigenous peoples emerged as a result of the dual process of state formation and nation-building. The historical relationship between the Saami and the nation-state has taken several distinct forms, which can be identified as distinct historical periods. The central aspect of the first period, which lasted from the Middle Ages to the middle of the nineteenth century, is state formation. This period is marked by state penetration and attempts to establish hegemony in the Northern areas, but the attitude towards the Saami people was accommodating (Niemi 1997a). Historically, Saami rights were acknowledged by both the Swedish–Finnish and the Danish–Norwegian state. In the second period, which runs roughly from 1850 to 1950, a different relationship emerged. Several efforts at colonization were carried out. Local rights were removed and a new management system was established, which sought to encourage as many Norwegians as possible to settle in the Saami areas (Pedersen 1999). Assimilation became official state policy.[7] In Sweden, segregation was even encouraged. Segregation implies that minority groups are excluded from the mainstream society and live their own way of life. Aspects of the Swedish 'let the Lapp remain a Lapp' policy just after the turn of the century could be understood in light of this concept. According to this notion, a 'real

Saami' was one committed solely to herding and to living a 'natural/traditional' nomadic way of life (Lewis 1998: 27). The Saami outside the reindeer society should assimilate because they lived an artificial Saami life. The result of this has been that Swedish Saami policy up until today has been marked by reindeer-herd management policy, with obvious political consequences (Jernsletten 1994), such as a split between the reindeer-herders and the Saami outside the reindeer-herding industry (Erikson 1998).[8]

Assimilation has for over two hundred years been part of European nation-building. Norwegian and Nordic minority policy towards the Saami in the period from 1850 and until 1950–60 can be understood in these terms. Many Saami consequently suppressed their claim to belong to the Saami culture. Many old trades and occupations disappeared as a result of adaptation to economic and social changes. Conversely, Swedish nationalism did not need to establish and motivate the struggle for an independent nation and could take its historical identity for granted (Østerud 1994: 42). This could be one explanation for the Swedish 'let the Lapp remain a Lapp' policy. In overall terms, assimilation to ensure cultural homogeneity among the citizens of the nation has been the dominant policy and practice. In line with both the ethnic nationalist and the orthodox communitarian conception of citizenship, people who do not belong to the majority culture, must assimilate in order to be regarded as citizens.

However, the third period, which covers the post-war period ushered in an attitudinal change, in terms of how the nation-state conceived of the Saami. In Norway the Norwegian parliament agreed that the previous assimilation policy belonged to the past.[9] At the same time, such a change was not obvious in Sweden. According to Roung (1982) the Swedish state policy towards the Saami was still characterized by a paternalistic attitude. Not until the beginning of the 1970s did some readjustments in the state's policy appear (N.J. Nystø 1993: 30, 31). With regard to the Finnish situation, Finland was the first to inquire into aspects of Saami affairs and devise some institutional channels for managing Saami demands (Lewis 1998: 55).[10]

The previous policy of assimilation was gradually abandoned[11] and the new policy stance was marked by the need to recognize Saami as equal members of the state. But their equality was that of individual members, not members of a separate ethnic group or nation (cf. Stordahl 1994). Such a standardized policy of equality does not acknowledge the existence of permanent minorities, only the principle of 'one person, one vote'. This policy could be viewed as a result of both liberal principles of equal rights and communitarian principles based on a shared conception of common traditions and practice, independent of the existence of indigenous and minority cultures.

The indigenous challenge

In 1963 the Norwegian parliament admitted that this policy failed (Stordahl 1994) and this admission resulted in policy change. The beginning of the 1980s represents a clear turning point in the three Nordic states' policy towards the

Saami. In Norway, the Alta conflict[12] was the event that instigated a lengthy process of legal and political reform. The Norwegian Saami Rights Commission started its work in 1980. It conducted its work during the same period as did similar inquiries in Finland and in Sweden (1983–1990). In Finland, a series of four separate official inquiries were undertaken in the early 1970s, and in the period 1987–1990 an inquiry was undertaken to enhance the status of the Saami. During this period, new legislation and legal reforms were introduced in Norway, Sweden and Finland to accommodate Saami demands and recommendations, albeit at different lengths. Unlike Norway[13] and Finland,[14] Sweden does not have Saami language legislation. But although Finland has a Saami language law, the ability to execute and implement its objectives is hampered by budgetary cut backs (M. Aikio 1994). An investigation done by the Finnish Saami Parliament shows that the law does not assure Saami-speaking people a basic service in Saami language.[15] In Sweden, a report on the status of minority languages, including the Saami language, was published in December 1997.[16] The report is said to form the basis for a Swedish minority policy, and recommends measures to strengthen the role of minority languages. But the report has been criticized for not having adopted a broader indigenous perspective as its point of departure.[17]

One explanation for these national differences relates to the fact that the new policy, at least in principle, does not differentiate between different types of group rights, such as for instance minority rights as opposed to indigenous rights, and therefore does not take into account the Saami claim for aboriginality. In actual fact, Norway[18] and Finland[19] with their respective constitutional amendments of 1988 and 1995, have gone to the greatest length in this respect, as they amended their Constitutions so as to recognize the Saami people as a distinct cultural community and people. In contrast to Norway and Finland, the Swedish parliament did not want to change the Constitution. According to the Swedish government, the Saami already are afforded general protection by the amendment on ethnic minorities.

Let me thus make one distinction, which is relevant to my empirical focus: Indigenous peoples have historic home areas, which often cut across the borders of the nation-state in which they live.[20] Although subjected to state rule through the process of state formation, indigenous people have never chosen citizenship. And when the state borders were drawn through the traditional areas of the Saami people, some were forced to choose where to belong. Further, and which distinguishes Saami from both historic as well as more recent patterns of immigration, the Saami occupied their traditional home areas long before the state borders were settled.[21] Thus, members of indigenous peoples did not become citizens on an individual level, or as families, their areas were collectively incorporated into the state. Although collectively incorporated, their collective interests as Saami were ignored by the states. Their position as minority, in numerical terms, was further underlined when their traditional geographical and cultural regions were divided by municipal, regional and state borders (cf. Danley 1991; Oskal 1998a; Kymlicka 1996).

There is a Nordic agreement on the states' responsibility to safeguard and develop the industrial base, language and culture of the Saami (Nordic Saami Convention, report, June 1998). However, there are differences concerning implementation. This can be illustrated by reference to the Finnish situation. Even if the formal framework for larger political and cultural autonomy is apparent in Finland, the real situation is characterized by difficult conditions concerning resources and influence. Legal rights are not necessarily of great value, if there is no political agreement on how these rights should be codified in the actual context. There are even more diverse opinions concerning the Saami claims for self-government, i.e. political and territorial rights.[22] This could be illustrated both by debates within each state and by the fact that the three states have gone to different lengths in strengthening the legal status of their respective Saami communities.

Based on the coherence between the principles of cultural recognition, individual autonomy and citizen's public autonomy, I would prefer to talk about political participation. A central question would for instance be how to include Saami considerations into regional and local politics and administration on Saami premises. With reference to the Canadian context, Borrows (1999: 110) puts it like this: 'Aboriginal control of Canadian affairs has the potential to facilitate the acquisition of political control, the continued development of culture, and respect for difference because it could change the contemporary notions of Canadian citizenship.' The focus will be on the rights of citizenship – that is the rights to political participation and communication. These rights are understood as positive rights, which guarantee participation in a common praxis and where citizens are understood to be politically responsible subjects (Habermas 1995c: 32). With reference to the Australian context, Ross Poole (1999) notes that 'As most Aboriginal leaders recognise, the claim on the material and moral resources which Aboriginal people need is best made, not merely in terms of right, but in the discourse of citizenship.' The model of the Saami Parliament within a common democratic constitution, could be viewed as an answer to indigenous claims for political and cultural self-determination, and at the same time a contribution to political co-operation supporting collective problem solving between the indigenous minority and the majority in a common political system. This could be illustrated by the Norwegian Saami Parliament which has developed into a central and influential political actor in the Norwegian political system as a whole.[23] The development of the Saami Parliament is not only a result of conflicts. It is also a result of a learning process with increased and new insight into the historic and contemporary relationship between the Saami people on the one side and the state and majority society on the other side, i.e. a result of a communicative process.

Fundamental questions concerning the status of the Saami people can not be isolated to just an internal Saami debate. All Saami participate in some important aspects of the daily life of the majority society and some are indistinguishable from it. In addition to the Saami perspective on self-government, there is a need to talk about incorporation of Saami perspectives into significant decision-making structures of the majority society.

Thus, the Saami political movements in all the four Northern states (including Russia),[24] have presented claims for political arrangements to their respective nation-states in order to secure the right to difference and the right to equal participation in matters of common interest.

This understanding of political rights must be applied to concrete contexts where relevant circumstances for indigenous peoples legitimate various self-government powers. 'The fact that indigenous communities continue to be referred to as nations – or as "first nations" or "national minorities" – is an implicit recognition that a certain political status has not been lost completely' (Poole 1999). The acknowledgement that the Norwegian state is founded on the territory of two peoples – the Saami people and the Norwegian people – (St. meld. no. 52 (1992–93)), supports the Saami's position as an indigenous people with inherent rights.[25] This position forms the basis for the Saami strive for political institutions.

Territorial rights – rights to land and water – are grounded on these considerations, and acknowledged by international law, such as International Labour Conference (ILO) convention no. 169 concerning indigenous and tribal peoples in independent countries, adopted by the ILO in June 1989. In contrast to Norway,[26] neither Finland nor Sweden has ratified ILO convention no. 169, which is the main international instrument directly affecting indigenous peoples. The Convention states that indigenous peoples have the right to decide their own priorities for development and to exercise control over and participate in the process of development.

According to this Convention, indigenous peoples are secured 'the right to own and possess' the areas of land they have traditionally lived in, and they have the right to actively participate in decisions on how natural resources should be exploited.

The greatest obstacle to its ratification by Sweden was previously considered to be the fact that Sweden does not fulfil the conditions set down by the Convention with regard to land rights[27] (SOU 1999: 25). There is an ongoing process in which Finland and Sweden consider what is required to enable them to accede to the Convention. In Finland this is done in co-operation with the Saami Parliament. The obstacle to ratification is viewed to be insufficient land rights in the Finnish legislation.[28] In Sweden the measures required to enable Sweden to comply with the provisions in the Convention, are discussed in SOU (1999: 25) (SOU is a public report issued by the Swedish government).

The basic considerations that inform the Saami debate about territorial rights, are that such rights must be regarded as inherent and of a permanent nature. In a joint statement from August 1997 in connection with the UN International Decade of Indigenous People, the Saami Parliaments point out that large parts of the states of Finland, Sweden, Norway and Russia are established on Saami land.

As a consequence, the Saami, as a people that has used the land since time immemorial, are recognized as having the right to make decisions concerning their own culture, social life and own areas. It therefore follows that the basic principle in the relationship between the Saami and the Finns, Swedes and Norwegians must be one of negotiations to reach understandings and mutual agreements between the representative organs of our peoples. It must be accepted that in the same way it is impossible that Saami should have total domination in the areas inhabited by them, it is equally impossible that the non-Saami should be allowed such domination. One should evaluate the possibility of delimiting fields of responsibility and influence between Saami and other state authorities through genuine negotiations and agreements.[29]

Similar principles appear in the Canadian debate on indigenous rights. Principles of mutual respect, recognition, responsibility and sharing were identified in the Report of the Royal Commission on Aboriginal Peoples, and negotiations[30] between the Canadian governments and the First Nations are referred to as 'nation to nation'. If transferred to the Saami context, this would imply the right for the Saami, as well as the obligation on the part of the sovereign state authorities, to negotiate over the distribution of authority and influence between the Saami and the state.

This brief overview of how the Saami were incorporated into the three Nordic states has made it evident that there are important limitations in the state's dealing with indigenous issues. First, there are clear differences between the Nordic states' responses to Saami demands. Each state's policy contains a set of premises for Saami political development, not only at the national level, but also at the pan-Saami level. These constraints are exacerbated by the fact that the states' policies diverge. Second, although each state has developed a more well-meaning attitude to the Saami, the Saami's claim for aboriginality is not satisfactorily taken into account by the state, i.e. ideal cultural expressions are accepted, but the claims for political and territorial rights are complied with differently by the respective states. Third, democratic processes have been limited to the borders of the nation-state, and the public has been fragmented into national units (cf. Habermas 1992b). In the Saami context this can be illustrated by the manner in which each nation-state pursues and interprets international instruments such as the ILO convention, which is of vital importance to the Saami people as a whole.

Let me thus focus on the possibility of viewing the EU as a means to accommodate difference and plurality. Is it conceivable that the EU and the Saami share similar views, 'while the state actors are in a category of their own'? (cf. Joenniemi 1994: 217).

The effects of Europeanization on the status of the Saami as an indigenous people: a brief overview

The EU represents an important political and institutional framework that affects state policy towards the Saami people. Policy framed at the EU level may promote Saami institution-building through policy expansion, and the Saami case is becoming a policy-area also within the EU. Based on the indigenous peoples' experience with the establishment of modern nation-states, a specified notion of rights is addressed. This notion relates to the fact that indigenous peoples and the development of their culture are greatly dependent on the resources in their traditional settlement areas.

In order to understand Saami questions as indigenous issues, it is important to clarify whether, or the extent to which, the EU system can be seen as a type of norm-context that will somehow affect the Member States in such a manner as to strengthen Saami rights and conceive of Saami questions as indigenous issues. Further, it is conceivable that the process of regionalization, as a significant feature of contemporary Europe and European integration, could lead to the adoption of a new framework in which to consider Saami political development.

Analysts often assess the EU as a functional type of organization directed towards realizing collective goals in as efficient a manner as possible. The EU is then viewed merely as an economic association or a system of intergovernmental co-operation based on the self-interest of each Member State (cf. Chapter 3). But the EU takes decisions on a whole range of matters that are clearly beyond the functional interests of the Member States, and makes binding decisions on social and cultural matters (*ibid.*). Political statements and programmes such as the First European Community Framework Programme in Support of Culture (2000–2004), illustrate this nicely.

As regards rural development, the policy of diversification of activities in rural areas must endeavour to take into full consideration the possibilities offered by cultural activities. This would cover the fact that projects presented must aim to promote rural diversification, notably through the use of cultural activities. This would, in turn, cover the following fields: promotion of territorial identity; exploitation (in line with the principles of sustainable development) of the vernacular cultural heritage (material, heritage, folklore, linguistic heritage, etc.); creation of permanent cultural infrastructures (eco-museums, arts centres, etc.); and the organization of specific cultural activities.[31]

If the implementation of programme objectives such as these should appear as instruments for future possibilities in Saami areas, the concept of culture and rights must be based on the understanding of the Saami's dependence on the material resource base for Saami culture.

The notion of rights

With regard to international law, the Saami people may seek support in two main groups of legal norms. The first group can be linked to general sources of law, which apply to minorities (article 27 of the International Covenant on Civil and Political Rights from 1966). The second group refers to special sources of law with exclusive application to indigenous peoples (ILO convention no. 169) (cf. Smith 1995).

Article 27 is regarded as a strong source of law for Saami rights, including the rights to the natural resources in areas which the Saami use and have settled

(Smith 1990). The securing of the material foundation for cultural enjoyment is seen as a central prerequisite for Saami society. This 'material base' argument stresses that cultural survival is dependent upon a material resource base. The Saami Rights Commission (1984) in Norway came to the conclusion that cultural survival is dependent upon a material resource base. This conclusion was later approved by the Norwegian parliament when adopting the constitutional entrenchment of its obligations towards the Saami people, and it is further corroborated by the ratification of ILO convention no. 169 (Thuen 1995: 246, 247).

The importance of this 'material base' argument became obvious in the context of the Norwegian and Saami debate on EU membership in 1994. The opponents of Norwegian membership in the EU argued that if Norway were to become a member of the EU, the special Saami material interests like reindeer nomadism, fjordal fisheries and small-scale agriculture would be even more negatively affected than today by an expanding and integrated European market economy (*ibid.*). It would be more difficult for the Saami to claim the right to control their land and resources in the EU, if large enterprises wanted to exploit them. Saami politicians also expressed this uncertainty:

> The major uncertain issue today is perhaps the ongoing European integration process, which carries many promises for the future but can also be detrimental to a small culture if the Saami are left without any special rights and just exposed to free economic expansion of the European state.
>
> (P. Aikio 1994: 43)

In this perspective, from a Saami point of view, it would be of vital importance to stress the second group of rights, territorial rights, which had the ILO convention as their main legal source. In 1994 the European Parliament focused on action required to provide effective protection for indigenous peoples, and adopted the definition of indigenous peoples that the ILO convention had embraced. The EP calls on the Member States of the European Union to show their determination to provide tangible protection for indigenous peoples by acceding to ILO convention no. 169 and by calling on other states to do the same (A3-0059/94: Official Journal of the European Communities).

Even though the ILO convention has not yet been ratified by Sweden and Finland another obligation concerning Saami rights is now in force. As a result of the EU negotiations, a Saami Protocol (Protocol three – regarding the Saami) gives the Saami special rights to reindeer herding in the Saami traditional areas[32] despite the basic EU principle about non-discrimination between EU-citizens. Until the Saami entered the EU, there were no ethnically based rights that had been incorporated into EU legislation. In the Norwegian negotiations with the EU this aspect was viewed as a problem. However, the Norwegian delegation emphasized the indigenous status of the Saami and obtained understanding for this argument (St. meld. nr. 40 (1993–94)). The Protocol can also be extended to include a further development of Saami rights connected to the traditional industrial base of the Saami. It is worthwhile to note that the EU has accepted protectionist legislation that will benefit the Saami.

The Commission has pointed out the possibility to expand the Protocol to include a broader understanding of Saami rights in primary industries and society in general.[33] The Protocol on Saami issues is signed by Norway,[34] Sweden, Finland and the European Union, and is now in force concerning the Saami in Sweden and Finland. All parties acknowledge that the three countries have 'obligations to the Saami according to national and international law'. It is this obligation that the Saami Council refers to when it criticizes Finland's preparations regarding the take over of the presidency of the EU. In a letter[35] to the government of Finland, the Council questions the Finnish government's commitment to the EU's Northern dimension. Finland is criticized for ignoring the obligations of the Protocol and the fact that the Saami is an indigenous people divided between four states.[36]

Despite acknowledged obligations and formal legislation in place, the Member States appear to constrain or stall the implementation of Saami rights, understood as indigenous rights. But these limitations are not necessarily given, and can be challenged in public discourse at the national level, as well as at the international level.

Does the EU promote a more inclusive sense of identity and belonging for the Saami of Northern Europe?

Composing norms

One point of departure for addressing this question will be the assumption that the EU can be seen to represent a normative context with implications for the nation-states. Applied to the EP, one could look at the role of parliamentary discourse, as illustrated by the Parliament's resolutions concerning indigenous peoples. The Parliament has on several occasions demanded actions and focus on indigenous situations around the world. During the period 1988–94, the Parliament made 28 decisions concerning indigenous peoples.[37] The EP[38] called on the Australian government to respect the status of the park and the land rights of the Aborigines, because of the Australian government's decision to consider the development of the Uranium project in a world heritage park on legally recognized Aboriginal territory. The EP therefore wanted the project halted and for the Member States to ban all imports of uranium from mines where land rights of minority peoples are threatened. The Australian government, in response to this resolution, referred to the lack of state efforts concerning Saami affairs, and challenged the Member States to tidy up their own policy towards indigenous peoples.[39] Is there then any likelihood for the EU to admit political and territorial rights to the Saami people? The EU's policy on indigenous issues in developing countries, could be seen to lend support to such an assertion.

The EU's concern with the rights of indigenous peoples has for the main part been concentrated on developing countries. Here it is worthwhile to note that the Saami Council with its NGO-status, is playing an influential role in this process, and is trying to establish a network within the EU. They also participate in the EU Parliament's indigenous delegation (cf. activity plan 1999 of the Saami Council). By virtue of suggestions and recommendations from the Saami Council, a 'Working Document of the Commission on Support for Indigenous Peoples in the Development Co-operation of the Community and the Member-States,'[40] will be used for development projects in Africa, Asia and South and Central America. Two such projects in developing countries are carried out by the Swedish section of the Saami Council.[41] It might also be adopted for projects aimed to support indigenous peoples in Russia. Based on the working document the Council of Ministers has adopted a resolution.[42] According to the chairman of the Swedish Saami Association – SSR, the work done by the Saami can now be put to use on the global scene. However, he observes that

> The weakness is that it is limited to developing countries, we would have preferred a general policy on indigenous matters, yet now the foundation is made indirectly and it will guide how the EU will handle matters for other native peoples.[43]

There is a parallel to this development in the Norwegian government's positive attitude at the end of the 1960s and beginning of the 1970s concerning the relationship between indigenous issues and human rights internationally, but which was not yet a policy for the home field related to the Saami case. By establishing standards concerning indigenous political and territorial rights in other parts of the world, the EP and the rest of the EU also obligate themselves to implement these standards towards the Saami people. For instance, the European Commission co-operates with and supports indigenous peoples through programmes and projects, and has taken several initiatives in order to prepare a more comprehensive approach towards indigenous peoples. The Commission's work with the External Global Environment Policy[44] and Human Rights Policy has identified the protection of indigenous peoples, their rights and cultures as one main area of focus.

> The European Community plays its part in international action to promote respect for the human rights and fundamental freedoms of indigenous peoples, lending its support to innovative practical projects carried out in partnership with the local authorities with the aim of improving the organizational abilities of indigenous communities and, if necessary, consolidating the demarcation of their territories. These kinds of project emphasize the link between the promotion of human rights and respect for the environment, in line with the conclusions of the Rio conference of 1992, in which the concept of environmental rights was developed.[45]

Concerning land rights, the Working Document of the Commission for Indigenous Peoples states that: 'A basic recognition of indigenous peoples and their territorial rights form the essential preconditions for indigenous peoples to participate in development processes in a meaningful way'. With the Saami indigenous status[46] as a point of departure, we have to ask if these political statements also have relevance for the Saami as an indigenous people.

Illustrated by the Finnish prospects developing forest industries in the EU (cf. Lipponen 1997), the question about an indigenous influence and 'say' appears as a challenge. This approach became evident in 1995 when Finland entered the EU. Mining companies got over 100 prospecting licences in Saami areas. But Saami from the reindeer-herding industry complained and argued that this permission was inconsistent with article 27 of the International Covenant on Civil and Political Rights from 1966. The Supreme Administrative Court of Finland (Högsta Forvaltningsdomstolen) abolished each and all of the licences, and returned the case to the Ministry of Trade and Industry. The decision influenced the practice so that possible damaging effects must be considered in co-operation with the Saami Parliament (SOU 1999: 25).

In formal terms, such influence has a legal basis in Finland. The Finnish governments, at all levels, are obligated to negotiate with the Saami Parliament on matters concerning interference and exploitation of resources, such as mining and forestry on so-called state-owned land in Saami areas. A major concern is whether this obligation to negotiate implies that the Saami Parliament will become part in the discussions at an early stage in the process and will obtain influence beyond that of mere consultation. This does seem realizable after two new decisions where the Supreme Administrative Court in March 1999 tightened up its earlier decisions claiming that the Ministry must consult with Saami interests prior to any new encroachments.[47] Such a right of consultation may be reinforced within the EU. On inquiry from the Finnish Ministry of Justice, a report from Lapland University suggests that the president of the Saami Parliament should have the right to be consulted in the Council of Ministers when Saami issues are at stake.[48]

Another area where the EP could contribute to develop a new set of transnational norms, is in the field of language policy which is of vital importance to the Saami. In 1981 the EP adopted the Arfé Resolution as a result of a series of motions on regional or minority languages and cultures. A second Resolution was adopted two years later in which the Commission was asked to continue to intensify its activities to promote these languages. In 1987 the EP pointed out that EU Member State governments and the European Commission should propose some concrete directives for the conservation and promotion of regional or minority languages and cultures of the EU. In 1994 the EP – almost unanimously – adopted the Killilea Resolution on linguistic and cultural minorities. This text endorses the previous Resolutions and urges the Member States to support the European Charter for Regional or Minority Languages of the Council of Europe. It also calls on the European Council and the European Commission to continue their support and encouragement for European organizations representing linguistic communities, particularly the European Bureau for Lesser-Used Languages (EBLUL).[49]

Since Sweden and Finland are members of the EU, they are also members of the EBLUL which co-ordinates the efforts of national committees in the EU Member States. Saami representatives participate in the national committee of this Bureau in Sweden and Finland. Each Member State has to report on the situation of the minority languages. The Bureau could, however, be viewed to have minimal impact, and this picture is reinforced by the lack of financial resources available for regional and minority languages.[50] But still, together with resolutions of the EP on minority languages, these discourses could over time provide new possibilities for Saami language development.

The concept of regionalization

Another point of departure with regard to the possible effects of European integration on the role and status of the Saami as an indigenous people, is to focus on the concept of regionalization. The traditional Saami areas can be viewed both as a historical region based on a common culture and a more recent creation based on networks of public and private actors. There is also an increasing political mobilization and institutionalization of European regions (Erikson 1997). The regionalization process in Europe becomes more and more important for political and cultural identity, and may be seen as a claim for cultural survival and self-determination, but does not manifest itself in a claim for separate statehood (Hylland Eriksen 1994). As a parallel to these perspectives, emerges the ambition for a Saami region.

The question of regionalization was for the first time raised in 1991 in a joint Nordic Saami meeting. In 1992 the Saami Conference presented several claims ahead of the EU negotiations, such as protection of the resource base of Saami, their lands and waters, the harmonizing of national laws concerning the Saami situation through a Nordic Saami Convention, and the establishment of a Saami region.

In connection with the Norwegian application for EU membership, the Council of the Norwegian Saami Parliament, in 1992, raised the possibility of establishing a Saami region within the EU. This idea was elaborated in a report from 1993: 'The Saami region – a tool for Saami self-government' (S.R. Nystø 1993). Here a scheme for the development of Saami self-government on an interstate regional basis is formulated, which for the first time brings to the fore a number of perspectives on the future rearrangement of political authority concerning the Saami's status as a people within the Nordic countries (Thuen 1995: 241). The realism of these suggestions may today be questioned, especially since a major part of the Saami people are outside the EU. The concept of a Saami region has so far not been further developed and accomplished.

Other processes of regionalization have contributed to more concrete forms of collaboration. The Barents Euro-Arctic co-operation consists of the Northern parts of Norway, Sweden, and Finland, and of Murmansk and Arkhangelsk

Oblast including the Nenest area in Russia and the Republic of Karelia. The establishment of the region must be seen as a part of the process of developing European co-operation and integration. The region was formally established in 1993, and came also to include the co-operation between the indigenous peoples of the region.

The indigenous peoples that are represented in different boards in the Barents Region, are the Saami, the Nenets and the Vepsians. There is established a Committee of Indigenous Peoples, with representatives from the Saami Parliaments in the Nordic countries and Kola Saami Associations, in addition to Nenets and Vepsians representatives. Both regional and international questions can be put on the agenda of the Barents Council and the Barents Regional Committee via the Committee of the Indigenous Peoples.[51] Thus, the Saami, Nenets and Vepsians already have a more established position in the Barents co-operation than the Saami have in the Nordic Council.[52] The fact that the Saami were granted a more influential role in the system of Barents co-operation than in the Nordic Council, could be due to the fact that the Nordic Council is a forum for parliamentarians from the five Nordic countries with the states as the main actors, whereas the main focus of the Barents system of co-operation is regional, and as such compatible with the process of institutionalization of European regions.

However, the indigenous people of the region have claimed that indigenous co-operation must be granted a higher degree of status, legitimacy and representation, than is the case today. Indigenous co-operation must be regarded as a third dimension of the co-operation, in addition to the central and regional one, and not be regarded as a part of today's regional co-operation. But this request has not been complied with.

Another framework connected to the processes of regionalization with significant impact on Saami politics and co-operation, is the EU's regional policy, as concretized through programmes for regional development. Through the Saami sub-programmes connected to the EU Interreg II-programme[53] and another regional development fund – the so-called Objective 6 area,[54] the EU's regional policy influences Saami political co-operation. The responsibility for all these programmes is given to the Saami Parliament in Sweden. Both Interreg Sápmi, Interreg for the South Saami areas, and the Saami sub-programme within the Objective 6 area, are divided into two main development areas – Saami industry and culture. The Saami Parliaments are now co-operating in order to establish and promote to the Commission, a frame programme of the Saami people for the period 2000–2006.[55] On the basis of this development, it seems likely that EU programmes bring new possibilities for creating organizational frameworks for political influence and further development of Saami culture.

This point is emphasized by the Saami in Sweden. The chair of the Swedish Saami Association (Svenska Samers Landsforbund)[56] points out that EU membership and the EU's regional programmes have given the Saami community new political tools for developing industries through the regional funds. These possibilities have not been present before. The Saami Rights Commission[57] in

Sweden indicated the need to formulate regional policy in a way that might create better employment opportunities and enhance activity in Saami settlement areas. But the Swedish government did not comply with this request. Saami expectations to new political tools such as the EU's regional funds, must thus be understood in light of absence of state efforts, and one could ask if Sweden's entry into the EU could compensate for the lack of state efforts towards the Saami.

Regionalization also implies 'cross-boundary relations among sub-units of national governments in the absence of centralized decisions by state executives' (Risse-Kappen 1996: 58). The Committee of the Regions represents such transgovernmental relations. In this committee regional authorities can participate directly in the EU system, and express concerns on relevant regional matters.[58] Swedish central authorities appoint twelve, whereas Finnish authorities appoint nine members to the Committee.[59] The Swedish Saami Parliament's claim for Saami representation in the EU Committee of the Regions was denied by the Swedish government.[60] According to the former chair of the Swedish Saami Parliament, Ingwar Åhrén, this has been denied by the Swedish government with reference to the practice that only political parties represented in the Swedish parliament can be represented in the Committee. The denial of Saami representatives in the Committee ignores the Saami people's status as an indigenous people and the consideration related to the need to include Saami perspectives into significant political arrangements. This example illustrates that political responses by national authorities to Saami claims, are often made in the context of established arrangements, and according to a given 'pattern of response' in the actual cases (Rakoff and Schaefer 1970: 70, 71).

Within a rapidly changing European context, the Saami are facing new challenges concerning influence and participation. One of these challenges is connected to the nation-state as the main actor in international co-operation. However, the Saami case is becoming a policy area within the EU. And if the states more or less ignore the Saami part because of established arrangements and given structures, the EU could represent a type of norm context that might induce or compel the Member States to deal with Saami issues, in accordance with Saami claims. In addition, regionalization processes affect the possibilities for Saami political influence. As the EU ambassador[61] to Norway observed, at an information seminar in Karasjok, the future of Europe lies in the regional variations and the flourishing of cultural heterogeneity, not in the hegemony of nation-states. Their borders will crumble, and the Saami should be all the more pleased with this prospect, since they have a long historical experience of state borders dividing their settlement area (Thuen 1995: 246).

Conclusion

A central idea throughout this chapter has been that political rights are the core of any notion of citizenship and are needed to ensure respect for cultural identity and individual freedom. This was especially stressed in the second and third sections. There is thus a need to highlight the indigenous people's experience with the modern nation-state. The relationship between the state and the Saami people was marked by several alternative sets of state policy, of which assimilation was the official one until the post-war period. But the formal departure from this policy did not end the assimilation process. Awarding collective rights to indigenous peoples or minority groups was seen as incompatible with the orthodox liberal and communitarian notion of equality. However, the work of the Saami political movement resulted in a break with this policy and the beginning of a new development of legal and institutional reforms, including the establishment of political rights to participate in national decision-making.

So is it possible to presume that there should be some kind of an 'EU–Saami alliance against recalcitrant nation-states', as I have indicated? In assessing this question, I have decided to focus on the following aspects:

- The states' different responses to Saami political claims. The challenge concerning these considerations becomes especially evident, illustrated by the handling and interpretation of ILO convention no. 169. Further, the authorities of Finland, Norway and Sweden have recognized the Saami people as an indigenous people, but only Finland and Norway have expressed this acknowledgement in their respective constitutions.
- The states' dealing with Saami claims for aboriginality. The development of Saami rights has taken place mainly within the different nation-states. The arrangements are on an intra-state level (cf. S.R. Nystø 1993), and such a perspective could be viewed as restrictive in terms of understanding the notion of aboriginality.
- The Saami's own ability to adapt to shifting contexts. 'The Saami culture has survived so far due to its ability to adapt to the surrounding nations shifting policies and ideologies and to incorporate and control new technology and ideas' (Stordahl 1994: 62).

The Saami Council can serve as an illustration of this ability. As an NGO in an international context, the Council seems to be quite efficient at playing an influential role in the work with the indigenous policy of the EU. The Council is part of a network of indigenous organizations that provides indigenous peoples with presence and voices at both national and international levels, and serves to provide partnership in negotiations and actions.[62]

Also, Saami participation in different processes of regionalization seems to bring new possibilities for cultural and political influence. 'Political arrangements must secure the Saami people the right to self-determination where self-determination also means the capacity to participate in the process of change, not isolation from it' (Poole 1999).

So, even if the Saami thus far have no political rights or representation at the EU level, compared to representation at the level of the nation-state, the prospect of the EU as a post-national unit with more inclusive conceptions of indigenous and minority identities, could become an important integrative force.

This assertion is supported by the fact that the EU, in structural terms, is more flexible and has a greater degree of flexibility regarding the handling of difference and plurality, than does the nation-state. But if this is to come into fruition, it is clear that the EU's obligations to the Saami as an indigenous people – dependent upon a material resource base – must be reflected in increased political influence for the Saami, especially with regard to rights to land and resources. The parliamentary discourses in the EP concerning indigenous issues could be seen as part of such a process. At the same time such a development requires an active involvement from the Saami part.

The Swedish and Finnish accession to the EU means that a large portion of the Saami people are also EU citizens, and Saami claims for increased self-government cannot be isolated from questions concerning political globalization, economic internationalization, increased EU integration and regionalization, such as Barents co-operation. The system of Barents co-operation and the EU's regional programmes imply new instruments for cross-border co-operation among the Saami people. The establishment of regions can also be regarded as the development of new arenas where different actors can meet. These developments can stimulate the 'discourse involving several voices – something rather pluralistic, reflecting forms of culture and values long suppressed by the uniformity required by the statist logic and strict conceptualizations of the essence of international relations' (Joenniemi 1994: 216).

Furthermore, questions about the relationship between citizenship and identity are general aspects in the European debate about integration. In a complex society the activating of different identities is going to be a more central aspect of political processes (Olsen 1993). The Treaty on European Union expresses the intentions of the Member States, to 'mark a new stage in the process of European integration', to 'deepen the solidarity between their peoples while respecting their history, their culture and their traditions', and to 'establish a citizenship common to nationals of their countries'.[63]

Such ambitions and intentions concerning the relationship between nation-states and peoples in the EU, could contribute to a better understanding of indigenous peoples' claims for recognition and self-government, where the aim is to strengthen and develop language, culture, and social life.

Notes

1 I would like to thank Erik Oddvar Eriksen, John Erik Fossum and Will Kymlicka for comments. I also want to thank Nils Oskal for discussions, through which many of the ideas in this chapter have developed.
2 Will Kymlicka (1996) distinguishes between two main forms of ethnic diversity. The first category, that of 'multinational' refers to a state in which more than one nation coexist, and where nation means a historical community, more or less institutionally complete, occupying a given territory or homeland, and sharing a distinct language and culture. Many of these nations have become national minorities. The second concept 'polyethnic' refers to a state marked by a large influx of immigration, and where groups constitute subcultures within the state, but do not demand their own forms of political autonomy within the state in the same way as for instance indige-

nous peoples do. National minorities in the former category can be divided in two: so-called stateless nations or ethno-national groups, and indigenous peoples. Stateless nations were contenders but losers in the process of European state formation, whereas indigenous peoples were entirely isolated from that process until very recently, and so retained a pre-modern way of life until well into this century (Kymlicka 1999). My concern here is with indigenous people.

3 The traditional territory of the Saami people is divided between Norway, Sweden, Finland and Russia. The parallels between the Saami political development in the Nordic countries are obvious, compared to the situation on the Russian side. Each of these three countries represents a developed industrial democracy with a capitalist market economy, an advanced institutional welfare-state and a similar political culture (Lewis 1998: 18). However, the present pan-Saami movement is character-ized by increased participation by Saami from the Kola peninsula (cf. endnote 5).

4 In 1995, a new Saami Act was adopted in Finland, and a new Saami Parliament entered into force on 1 January 1996. The Finnish governmental bodies are now obliged to negotiate with the Saami Parliament on any matter which may have a special influence on the Saami's position as an indigenous people. The Norwegian (1987) and Swedish (1992) Saami Acts do not contain a corresponding obligation. These Saami Acts form the basis for the establishment of the respective Saami Parliaments. The Norwegian Saami Parliament was established in 1989, and the Swedish Saami Parliament in 1993.

5 The Council was established in 1956 as a co-operative body to support voluntary Saami organizational work in Finland, Norway and Sweden. The Kola Saami Association, established in 1989, has been an ordinary member of the Saami Council since 1992.

6 Within a Canadian context a similar view is expressed: 'At a time when non-aboriginal government are streamlining and restructuring government organizations, aboriginal governments are just in the beginning of their institution building process' (Doerr 1997).

7 The geographical position in the border areas in the North has been seen as one explanation for the harsh assimilation policy. This is due to the concern with national security which was present during this period of assimilation (Eriksen and Niemi 1981). This did not only affect the Saami as an indigenous people, but also affected a minority group called Kvens. They are descendants of Finnish immigrants.

8 This split could explain the conflict lines in today's Swedish Saami Parliament (Erikson 1998).

9 In May 1963 the Norwegian Parliament discussed the report from the Saami Com-mission which had been formed in 1956. The report from 1959 stressed the impor-tance of mutual respect between the Saami and the Norwegians (Stordahl 1994).

10 During 1949–1952, by the Committee on Lapp Affairs. In 1960, an Advisory Council on Saami Affairs was established by the Finnish government.

11 Still, during the 1950s and 1960s, the effects of the determined Norwegian assimilation policy became apparent (cf. Broderstad 1997).

12 The building of a hydro-electric power station on the river Alta, gave rise to huge protest actions. These conflicts stimulated Saami activism and self-defence, and where the awareness of being Saami was considerably increased (Stordahl 1994).

13 The Norwegian Saami law was amended in 1990 so as to recognize Saami language as a second official language in five municipalities in Finnmark county (where the total number of municipalities is twenty) and one municipality in Troms county (where the total number of municipalities is twenty-five). This means that the Saami in these areas now have a right to receive public services in Saami language.

14 In Finland, a law on the authorities' use of the Saami language was established in 1992, and some changes were made when the law was revised in 1995.

15 cf. *Min Aigi*, a Saami language newspaper, 5 February 1999.

16 The Committee of Minority Languages suggests that Saami, Finnish and Romani will be officially recognized as minority languages in Sweden. In addition, the country must recognize the following minorities as domestic: Saami, Tornedal Finns, Romanies ('Gypsies') and Jews.

17 cf. *Samefolket*, no. 3, March 1998.

18 According to Article 110a of the Norwegian Constitution Act: 'It is the responsibility of the authorities of the State to create conditions enabling the Saami people to preserve and develop its language, culture and way of life'.

19 Finland has made an enactment regarding Saami cultural self-government, concerning a more precisely defined area in which the Saami can exercise cultural autonomy. This Saami home area is limited to the municipalities of Enotekio, Enare, Utsjok and parts of Sodankylä. It is the Saami Parliament which, on behalf of the Saami, is going to clarify Saami self-determination (Henriksen 1996).

20 Einar Niemi (1997b), has shown how governments since 1700 have used concepts like 'the oldest, the original, the native', when speaking about the Saami.

21 Historically, the Saami found themselves victims of competing tax claims and exercise of jurisdiction from the surrounding states. From 1300 onwards, the rivalry between the Russians/Karelians, Swedish/Finnish and the Norwegians resulted in multiple tax claims and exploitation (cf. the report concerning a Nordic Saami Convention 1998; Pedersen 1999).

22 The Saami Rights Commission (SRC) in Norway has clarified territorial rights in Finnmark (the largest Saami county in Norway) since its first report was issued in 1984. The Commission's final report was published in 1997 (The Norwegian Official Report – NOU 1997: 4 Naturgrunnlaget for Saamisk kultur). The report's objective was to ensure real equality between Saami culture and other cultures in Norway. According to the mandate, natural resources are the basis for Saami culture and must therefore be protected so that the Saami can secure and develop their own culture. The Commission recommends, amongst other things, the establishment of a Land and Territorial rights management agency in Finnmark, with responsibility for the management of land and territory and non-renewable resources in the county. The Finnmark county council and the Saami Parliament should each appoint four representatives to the board of the Land and Territorial Rights Committee. A minority in the Commission recommends the appointment of a separate Saami board of Land and Territorial Rights. The Commission recommends that the majority of members of the board of the Saami Land and Territorial Rights agency should be appointed by the Saami Parliament. It would be left up to each individual municipality to decide whether it would come under the Saami Land and Territorial Rights Committee instead of the Finnmark Land and Territorial Rights Committee. The administration of natural resources in the remaining municipalities will come under the Finnmark board for Land and Territorial Rights (cf. Oskal 1998b). A majority of the SRC also suggests that the Saami Parliament should be equipped with a suspensive veto to refuse interference in Saami areas in the whole of Norway. Its suspensive power should be limited to six years.

23 In Norway, the Saami Parliament's almost unanimous acceptance by the Norwegian political system may be put to a harder test when questions of territorial control, veto powers and decisive authority within specific fields of public affairs are raised (cf. Thuen 1995: 175).

24 Also, the Saami in Russia have presented claims for political and cultural self-determination and claimed the right to establish and elect their own Saami Parliament (Vatonena 1993).

25 In a report (White Paper) from the Norwegian government to the Norwegian parliament (St. meld. nr. 41 (1996–97)), regarding Norwegian Saami policy, the government specifies that the Saami constitute one of the two state-constituting peoples in Norway.

26 By March 1998, ILO convention no. 169 had been ratified by Norway, Mexico, Bolivia, Peru, Columbia, Costa Rica, Paraguay, Honduras, Denmark, Guatemala and the Netherlands. The Norwegian government has admitted that it is important how the regulations in the ILO convention are interpreted by Norway, and that this interpretation could influence international interpretations of the regulations in the convention (St. meld. nr. 18 (1997–98)). The Norwegian discussion on land and water rights has revealed that although the ILO convention has been ratified, precisely how the obligations are interpreted varies considerably.

27 This article deals with two different categories of indigenous land rights. First are property rights (so-called category 1 territories). Then there are territories with co-existing indigenous and non-indigenous land-use (so-called category 2 territories).

28 Report to the Finnish parliament, from the Finnish government, April 1996.

29 http://www.suri.ee/uc/4/samiobj.html

30 The federal government confirms that both historical and modern treaties constitute the basis for the relationship between the indigenous peoples and Canada as a nation-state ('Gathering Strength' – Canada's Aboriginal Action Plan, presented in January 1998). Negotiations are taking place all over Canada. For instance, in British Columbia, the governments of Canada and the province of BC anticipate fifty negotiations with First Nations in the province.

31 cf. Chapter 3 – Integrating cultural aspects explicitly into the Community's actions and policies, in the First European Community Framework Programme in Support of Culture (2000–2004).

32 The area of reindeer herding in Sweden covers the whole of the counties of Norrbotten, Wästerbotten and Jämtland, and parts of the counties of Kopparberg and Västernorrland. In Finland this area includes most parts of Lapland county and the Northernmost part of the county of Uleåborg (cf. NOU 1997: 5, pp 95, 105). In Norway the area of reindeer herding covers the whole of Northern Norway in addition to the counties of North and South Trøndelag and Hedmark.

33 cf. Report from a meeting on November 4, 1998 in Brussels between the Saami Parliaments and the EU Commission.

34 Norway played a leading role in the EU negotiations concerning Saami issues. From a Swedish Saami point of view, the situation was described as follows: 'The result of the negotiations revealed that Norwegian leaders were instrumental in defending Saami issues while Sweden and Finland blocked them. The Norwegian negotiators' platform had been created in co-operation with Norway's Saami Parliament.' (Web page of the Saami Parliament in Sweden: http://www.sametinget.se/).

35 Letter from the Saami Council of February 15, 1999 to the government of Finland, Prime Minister Paavo Lipponen.

36 Lars Anders Bær, Saami Council: Saami Radio interview, 8 February 1999.

37 These are collected by Lydia van de Fliert in 'Indigenous Peoples and International Organizations' (1994).

38 Resolution on Protection of the Aboriginal people in Australia of January 15, 1998. In the debate, Allan Macartney (North East Scotland, ERA) stressed that it was a broader issue covering the land rights of indigenous peoples across the world. He mentioned with approval the resolution of the Australian Senate calling on its government to proceed no further with the Uranium project (cf. Web page of the European Parliament: http://www.europarl.eu.int/dg3/sdp/pointses/en/p980112. htm#39).

39 According to *Nordlys*, a Norwegian newspaper, 24 and 28 January 1998.

40 A new policy on Indigenous Peoples by the European Commission, SEC (1998)773 final, Brussels, 11.05.1998.

41 cf. Activity plan 1999 of the Saami Council: Project on Indigenous Peoples: 'International Human Rights Standards and the Policy Process' and 'Regional Studies in Indigenous Areas'.

42 'Indigenous peoples within the framework of the development co-operation of the Community and the Member States', 30.11.1998.

43 cf. *Samefolket*, August 1998.

44 http://europa.eu.int/search97cgi/s97_cgi: Budget line B7-8110: External Environment Policy: Global Environment.

45 http://europa.eu.int/search97cgi/s97_cgi: Activities – The External Dimension of Human Rights Policy From Rome to Maastricht and Beyond – European Commission: DG 1A.

46 With the accession of Finland and Sweden into the EU, the Saami is the only people within the EU that is granted indigenous status (cf. St. meld. nr. 40 (1993–94) Om medlemsskap i Den europeiske union). The authorities of Finland, Norway and Sweden have recognized the Saami as an indigenous people, but only in Finland and Norway is this expressed in the respective constitutions.

47 Information from Heikki J. Hyvärinen, secretary of legal affairs, Saami Parliament, Finland.

48 Kristian Myntti: Suomen saamelaisten yhteiskunnallinen osallistuminen ja kulttuuri-itsehallinto. Raportti oikeusministeriölle, osa I, Pohjoisen ympäristö- ja vähemmistöoikeuden instituuttii/Lapin yliopisto, 1997 (Report from the Northern Institute for Environmental and Minority Law, University of Lapland).

49 The European Bureau for Lesser Used Languages (EBLUL) is an independent organization. Its members are volunteer associations and institutions active in the promotion of minority languages throughout the European Union. The Bureau's purpose is to promote and defend the autochthonous regional or minority languages of the countries of the European Union and the linguistic rights of those who speak these languages (cf. http://www.eblul.org/what-gb.htm).

50 cf. European Dialogue. The magazine is a forum for discussion, and therefore its contents do not necessarily reflect the policies or views of the EU institutions or Member States.

51 The Committee of the Indigenous Peoples has initiated a wide range of projects to support language preservation and legal and economic development for the people in question. These projects have been important for the indigenous people on the Russian side. Examples of such projects are: regional medical health centres in Lovozero and Najan Mar, handicraft projects and a pre-project for establishing a slaughterhouse in the Autonomous region of Nenets and in Lovozero (S.R. Nystø 1996).

52 The Faeroe Islands, Greenland and Åland have been given a special form of representation on the Nordic Council together with the five states. But the Saami people, who were settled here before the formation of the Nordic states, are the only Nordic people without such a representation. One of the arguments for not giving the Saami an ordinary membership has been that the Saami didn't have any representative bodies. But today Finland, Norway and Sweden have their own Saami Parliaments and a common Saami Parliamentary Council. The Saami have got status as observers, but have not been granted an ordinary membership like the other small nations. The granting of full Nordic Council membership to the Saami, is one of the main objectives of the Saami Parliaments.

53 Interreg Sapmi as a sub-programme under Interreg Nordkalotten, includes co-operation with the Saami on the Norwegian side of the borders.

54 The Objective 6 area programme covers Norrbotten and Lapland county in Sweden and Finland. The programme is financed by a 50 per cent EU contribution. The rest has to be covered by national financial sources. The overall aim of this programme is to promote the creation of new jobs to enable people to continue to work and live in the region. This involves diversifying the economy while safeguarding the viability of local communities and exploiting natural resources. Special emphasis is placed on the preservation of the Saami people's culture, language and way of life. In the reform of

the Structural Funds 2000–2006, the current Objective 6-regions will be considered equivalent to Objective 1-regions.

55 Report from a working group appointed by the presidents of the Saami Parliaments, February 1999.
56 Lars Anders Bær: Riikkasearvvi bargguid ja ulbmiliid birra go Sápmi lea jagi 2000:a uksagaskkas – RSS work and aims for Sápmis entering year 2000, speech to the national meeting of the Swedish Saami Association 1997.
57 SOU 1990: 84 Språkbyte och språkbevarande.
58 For instance, the work with the First European Community Framework Programme in Support of Culture (2000–2004), a response to concerns expressed by the Community institutions and the Committee of the Regions (cf. Web page Communication from the European Commission to the European Parliament, the Council and the Committee of the Regions).
59 The then Minister of Foreign Affairs, Thorvald Stoltenberg, said in a speech to the Norwegian Saami Parliament in 1993, that on the assumption that Norway, Sweden and Finland became EU members, it was reasonable that the Saami people be represented in the Committee of the Regions.
60 cf. § 8 'Samerna och EU', Sammanträdesprotokoll, 25–27.10.1994.
61 Aneurin Hughes, the EU ambassador to Norway, Karasjok, November 1991.
62 The Saami Council participate in the UN system as a NGO, is a member in the World Council of Indigenous Peoples (WCIP) and has a permanent participant status in the Arctic Council together with the Inuit Circumpolar Conference, the Association of Indigenous Minorities of the Russian Federation and the Aleut International Association.
63 From the preamble of the Treaty on European Union, cf. Web page: Communication from the European Commission to the European Parliament, the Council and the Committee of the Regions – First European Community Framework Programme in Support of Culture (2000–2004: http://europa.eu.int/en/comm/dg10/culture/program-2000-part1_en.html).

12 Conclusion

Legitimation through deliberation

Erik Oddvar Eriksen and John Erik Fossum

European integration derives much of its momentum from the process of globalization, and in particular economic globalization. The process of globalization challenges the conventional model of governance based on the nation-state, as was discussed in Chapter 2. *Political integration* in Europe – in both depth and breadth terms – exerts a strong independent pressure on the nation-state, beyond that of globalization. Since its inception, we have witnessed a considerable increase in the EU's ability to carry out collective action. This is reflected in its institutional make-up. It has acquired competence to act in a wide range of policy fields and has established a set of institutions – however weak when compared to those of states – with no real precedents and a remarkable ability to weather storms and handle crises.

In order to account for these developments, this book has sought to demonstrate that we need to supplement the repertoire of intellectual tools already in place and which have been applied to the European integration process. This addition to prevailing realist and functionalist perspectives (and their derivatives) must draw on a theory of human action that is based on an alternative set of micro-foundations. The realm of international politics is not marked solely by power struggles between entrenched parties, which pursue their national interests defined in power terms and are free to harbour deep hostilities towards each other. Nor is it marked solely by the functional imperatives of a burgeoning capitalist economy.

How can integration come about in a system, which lacks an independent decision-making structure, based on:

- central authority and the rule of law (in a hierarchical sense);
- a collective identity derived from a common history, tradition or fate;
- sovereign immunity based on fixed, contiguous and clearly delimited territory; and
- a set of explicit principles established and sanctioned by international law?

Recent treaty changes have underlined that the integration process proceeds also along non-economic tracks, and involves issues of a more explicit political, social and cultural nature, where the nature of co-operation involved cannot be explained with mere reference to cost–benefit calculations or fixed interests. Why this occurs is a puzzle to conventional theories of co-operation in general and international politics in particular. A modicum of *non-egoistic commitment* is necessary for community co-operation to come about. Intergovernmentalists are prone to presuppose the puzzle, because they take preferences as givens (cf. Scharpf 1988). In this book we suggest another way of looking at integration and of addressing the puzzle of why the EU holds together. A deliberative perspective posits that co-operation comes about when the process of reason giving generates a capacity for change of viewpoints. In that respect, *arguing* is the glue of the integration process. Consequently, it asserts that it is possible to explain the puzzle, without either presupposing the answers or ignoring the questions.

In analytical terms, integration is about the transferral of perceptions of benefits and burdens to a larger political community. In Chapter 1, we outlined the key features of a deliberative perspective. Our assertion is that integration can be brought about by adherence to legal and argumentative procedures. These procedures unleash the force of normative reason that is required to override national interests. This forms the backdrop for the thesis of *integration through deliberation*. Needless to say, integration can take place through strategic bargaining and through functional adaptation, but insofar as these processes are not stabilized by normative arguments that refer to what is good or right, they are insecure. From this derives our point of departure for the book: there is no stability without validity. For a democratic political order to become integrated and remain stable, it has to comply with certain normative requirements. In actual terms, power holders also, in one way or the other, claim legitimacy; they claim that the support they obtain is somehow deserved. In a modern post-metaphysical context, only the democratic procedure, and the way it incorporates and deals with interests and values, can test this claim to legitimacy. It is the procedure itself, and how it fosters democratic processes, that bears the burden of legitimation in a modern state, and this also applies to the EU.

The merit of a deliberative perspective, as a vital supplement and also corrective to conventional theories of politics, is the emphasis it places on how procedures ensure communicative processes. We present this perspective as a supplement rather than a substitute to mainstream theorizing. We suggest that it will account for 1) the 'anomalies' left unexplained by mainstream theories, and 2) the conditions that are necessary for bargaining and other power-induced forms of integration to take place at all. The first refers to integration in issue-specific areas and within particular time-sequences that are hard to account for in power and interest terms. Obvious examples are citizenship, enlargement to the East, environmental policies and human rights protection and promotion. The second refers to the need to clarify precisely which conditions of fairness that bargaining and power relations presuppose and have to comply with, in order to claim legitimacy. Similarly, it helps clarify which kinds of agreements and common understandings on issues, goals and procedures that are necessary for log-rolling, bargaining, voting, and so forth to come about. As such, this perspective compels the analyst to pose 'deeper questions'. Questions pertaining to justice and identity require deliberation to be properly dealt with (see Chapter 3).

In this concluding chapter, we will first elaborate on these points, and then highlight the role of *procedures* and *processes* in the EU that may bring about integration through deliberation. Next we will try to support the contention that the EU requires a measure of *direct legitimation*, beyond whatever indirect legitimacy it may derive from the Member States. Finally, democratic legitimacy, however, does hinge on the prospects of a *public sphere*, which may be hard, but not impossible to emerge in a post-national European context.

Integration through deliberation

In a sense the EU is remarkable precisely because it is less of a given fact than any state. As political entity compared to the by now well-established and almost taken-for-granted notion of political entity labelled nation-state, it can not simply draw on a set of fixed reasons to justify its existence. Nor is it equipped with a set of goals and objectives, or a sense of identity, that can be readily drawn upon. Rather, it must be seen as something that is undergoing *constant change* and evolution, and as something that in a more fundamental sense is still 'in the making'. It is a system, which to a large extent is premised on preferences and interests, not as exogenously set, but rather as endogenously shaped through complex patterns of interaction. Preferences are moulded – reinforced and transformed – in the political process, they are rarely to be acted upon as given properties. Hence, the EU is conceived of as the embodiment of a set of structural and procedural arrangements that induce actors to override national self-interests, a process which is supportive of and which also requires *communicative rationality*. Ulrich Preuss observes that:

> The EU is a dynamic polity. In contrast to the modern state's objective to maintain and reproduce the given order, the Community is directed at change, namely an ever further integration of the Member States. This is an open-ended process of the Community's continual self-transformation which requires institutional devices of permanent learning, self-observation and self-adaptation.
>
> (Preuss 1996c: 138)

As such, present-day EU is less the manifestation of a particular conception of governance and more of a meeting ground in which different conceptions of democracy and justice are discussed and assessed. The EU is therefore also marked by the search for a set of principles that can help ensure that the normative potential inherent in this meeting place of ideas and standards is properly harnessed. We argue that the best option here is the discourse-theoretical conception of democracy. It asserts that democracy, as a concept, has to be detached from substantive assumptions of popular governance that restrict it to certain organizational forms, such as representative (parliamentary or presidential) systems of governance. Central to this perspective are the notion of rights and the discourse principle – the latter asserts that a norm is valid only when agreed to by all in a free public debate.

The idea of modern democracy basically entails two types of rights: *human rights* and rights ensuring *popular sovereignty*. These rights are necessary for compatriots to sort out their affairs through the medium of law. In discourse-theoretical terms this requires an institutional make-up that is able to protect the interests of individuals, both as private and public persons. In other words, citizens must be equipped with participatory rights on an equal basis, so that they can conceive of themselves as the authors of the very laws of which they are the addressees. It is through a procedure based on non-exclusion and fair debate, and in a process not predetermined by substantive values and commitments, identities and pre-fixed loyalties, that people can come to terms with their commonalities in a valid manner. In principle, this applies regardless of the particular conditions in which they exist. Deliberations do not presuppose broad agreements, except on the terms of interaction, which must be fair. Lasting agreements can be formed, because actors are involved in a process of justification and *reason giving* that compel contestants to change established preferences and outlooks, due to the authority of good arguments and that the outcomes are written into binding law. Incoherent adjudication and inconsistent argument bring parties into painful performative contradictions that are unbearable to those who claim to be involved in a serious discussion.

The critical questions to ensure rational outcomes, public accountability, and popular authorization of a mode of governance, then, revolve around the central tenets of public freedom; the nature, scope and composition of representative bodies; and the quality of debate.

Integration through procedure

The traditional view holds that there is less deliberation in the EU than in conventional states. The EU was established as a type of interstate co-operation in a world marked by anarchy (at least in the minimum sense of absence of compelling rule or hierarchical authority) in which diplomacy played a very important role. Diplomacy is marked by secrecy, hierarchy, and fixed mandates (officials represent their states) – hardly features that are overly conducive to deliberation. But the EU has changed, and so has the international context, and both have changed in the same direction, namely one that is far more conducive to deliberation.

It is widely recognized that modern societies are marked by the decline of hierarchies and an attendant questioning of traditions and value-based consensus in critical public discourse. Actors are compelled to justify their actions with reference to rational arguments, to a greater extent than before. We believe that there are aspects of the EU that further promote this onus on reason giving. First, in order to ensure that peaceful international co-operation will take place at all, actors need to establish bodies in which affected parties can come together to find out how much co-operation is tenable. As such, they need to establish bodies, which can ensure some form of deliberation, however constrained that may be. A purely voluntary association of states, however, does not give rise to collective binding agreements: it is a fragile and unstable order. It is likely to run into problems such as those faced by the *League of Nations*, which failed to authorize anyone to defend the shared principles. This example actually reveals a tension in Immanuel Kant's proposal for perpetual peace, which is so central to cosmopolitan thought. Kant envisioned a federation of sovereign states, without a superior authority – only a 'permanent congress of states' (Kant 1795/1985). 'Just how the permanence of this union, on which "civilized" resolution of international conflict depends, can be guaranteed without the legally binding character of an institution analogous to a state constitution Kant never explains' (Habermas 1998b: 161). The process of reaching collectively binding decisions is, ultimately, institutionally dependent: post-national law must be made binding on Member States. For this the coercive power of a constitutional order is required.

The EU has clearly progressed beyond this initial stage of a purely voluntary association of states. In its present, incomplete form, there are structural aspects of the EU that lend themselves to a democratic constitution, as is touched upon in several of the chapters. The EU is an entity with strong supranational elements. Of particular importance is the supranational character of the legal structure, which is supported and enhanced in particular by the European Court of Justice. In its rulings, the Court has long asserted the principles of supremacy and direct effect, principles, which have informed the actual operations of the EU, albeit their precise status in relation to national constitutional orders remains ambiguous. Although the Member States respect the basic principles of EC law, they have been reluctant to recognize a legal hierarchy with EC law on top. This is evidenced for instance in the rulings by the German Constitutional Court and by the Danish High Court, on the constitutionality of the Maastricht Treaty, where both national courts refused to grant the European Court *Kompetenz-Kompetenz*. But the fact that the national Constitutional Courts did not reject outright the principles established by the Court of Justice also demonstrates their willingness to continue the search for valid principles. Given the status and role of in particular the German Constitutional Court, such willingness is important unto itself. This is suggestive of how the EU is based on deliberation and itself serves to foster deliberation. With regard to the German Constitutional Court's ruling on the constitutionality of the Maastricht Treaty, Joseph Weiler observes that 'the German move is an insistence on a more polycentred view of constitutional adjudication and will eventually force a more even conversation between the European Court and its national constitutional counterparts' (Weiler 1996a: 119). This means that both levels will be forced to offer compelling reasons for why one set of principles associated with one level of governance should have preponderance over the other.

This non-hierarchical aspect of the EU's legal structure is also reflected in the other institutions at the EU level. The European Parliament which is directly elected by the peoples of the Member States, is supranational, and has recently increased its powers *vis-à-vis* the European Commission. The EP has constantly sought to improve the political status of the EU, by demanding heightened accountability, and more openness and transparency in the EU. The Commission is the executor of Union policies and is endowed with the right of initiative, which includes the right to issue legislative proposals. The particular non-hierarchical nature of supranationality that marks the EU is, among other things, a result of its peculiar and rather fuzzy 'separation of powers', which ensures the Member States a strong and consistent say in the decision-making processes of the EU. The Council of the Union consists of representatives from the Member States, and legislates on behalf of the Union. It decides some matters by qualified majority and other by unanimity, and where the tendency is more frequent use of qualified majority voting. The European Council consists of the heads of governments and their supportive staffs and is in charge of treaty changes and other particularly important matters. Its decisions are made by unanimity. In principle, when all have to agree, comprehensive deliberation is required before decisions can be made (cf. Chapter 3). However, considerable secrecy surrounds the activities of the Council of the Union and of the European Council, as their decision-making – through deliberation and bargaining – takes place behind closed doors. Preparations are undertaken by the COREPER (Committee of Permanent Representatives) which 'works most effectively out of the limelight' (Hayes-Renshaw and Wallace 1997: 83). However, it is watched by 'a network of well-informed lobbies' (Wessels 1991: 150). The role of the Council of the Union is further discussed in Chapter 9 by Roberto Gargarella, who, despite portraying it as a closed body, does detect certain signs of heightened openness. In addition to these central institutions, at the EU level, hundreds of Committees are in operation. These were originally constructed to control the delegation of powers from the Council to the Commission. Such a system may further contribute to blur an already unclear constitutional distinction between legislative and executive powers, but does contribute to deliberative supranationality.[1]

These examples serve to illustrate that the structure in place is incomplete, in principled and substantive terms, due to its particular character *qua polity*, which is marked by dynamism, openness, and polycentricity. Its incompleteness in principled terms is reflected in the widely recognized need for legitimacy. It is for instance recognized that despite three comprehensive treaty changes since the mid 1980s, there is a gap between the system in place and the arguments and reasons that are used to legitimate it, as was fleshed out in Chapter 6. It is noteworthy that there have been numerous efforts to address this gap. But the role of the gap and how it is discussed changes with every turn of the integration process. In other words, as the integration process expands, more ambitious efforts to expand the gap are also initiated. For instance, at the outset European integration was legitimated with reference to values, in particular to establish a stable system of co-operation in order to protect peace and democracy in Western Europe. The legitimacy of this structure was entirely indirect, i.e. derived from the democratic nature and status of the Member States. As the integration process expanded, the EU became increasingly legitimated with reference to its outcomes and its procedures. The SEA and Maastricht Treaties represented a significant widening and deepening of integration and underlined the need to think of the EU as an entity in its own right, which required a direct mode of legitimation. Present-day EU is involved in clarifying precisely what type of legitimation this will be and how independent of the Member States it can be.

That this problem was not resolved during the Maastricht Treaty process was quite evident. For instance, the Maastricht Treaty contained a provision to hold another intergovernmental conference in 1996. This decision prompted a comprehensive review of the Maastricht Treaty at a point in time when few of the effects had yet been properly felt. This evaluation therefore had to focus more on principles than actual effects of institutional arrangements. This has also been noted: '(f)ar from laying down a comprehensive and final identity for Europe, the Maastricht Treaty has instead ushered in a dynamic process of development which may or may not lead to European statehood' (Everson 1995b: 78).

One particularly important development we have seen in the EU since its inception is the strengthened commitment to rights. This development has enabled the EU to reach more deeply and directly into the Member States, and appeal to people as rights holders rather than mere market actors. Concomitantly, it has dramatically increased the range of normative claims people can make on the EU. As such, it is a development that is bound to foster more deliberation in and on the EU.

Integration through process

The EU is labelled *post-national*, as it is an entity *sui generis* with sufficient independence to require a more direct mode of legitimacy, beyond that conferred upon it by the Member States. However, the EU is 'not just a state of affairs', rather it is 'a process of integration … that requires normative justifications' (Beetham and Lord 1998a: 32). This process is not unidirectional, nor is it clear exactly what its end point will be. This uncertainty is due to the fact that the process is also based on consent. This need for consent has affected the structure in place and also made it more important to explain what type of process it is. *Consent-based integration* implies resistance against hierarchical authority or institutional preponderance, unless such is founded on a coherent set of principles. The absence of such has not only produced a set of non-hierarchical structures that are conducive to deliberation, the same applies to the process of decision-making in the EU.

There is great onus on process-oriented legitimation built into the very nature of EU decision-making, in that basically all the various decision-making procedures require extensive inter-institutional interaction and deliberation. The Amsterdam Treaty reduced the number of decision-making procedures to three: consultation, co-operation, and co-decision, but strengthened the role of that procedure which requires the greatest amount of deliberation and reason giving, namely co-decision. However, in the second and third pillars – i.e. in the Common Foreign and Security Policy and Justice and Police Affairs Co-operation – it is still only the less arduous consultation procedure that is employed. The role of process-oriented legitimation has also been enhanced as a result of the heightened role of the European Parliament in the EU's decision-making structure. Its decision-making powers have increased and its scope of action is widened, as it will increasingly be a co-legislator with the Council.[2]

The incomplete nature of the EU constitution is reflected also in the emergence of deliberative bodies that are merely oriented at discussion and habituation. One example is the establishment of bodies of interparliamentary co-operation, such as COSAC, which is foremost oriented at deliberation, and not formal decision-making, as was shown by Lars Blichner in Chapter 7. There is an urgent need for exchange of views among Member-State parliaments, and this need may even exceed that of formal decision-making power. Interparliamentary discourse may somewhat compensate for the lack of European-wide public spheres, and deliberation not directly oriented at achieving consensus is important to promote learning, self-reflexivity, and understanding which are all necessary for consent-based integration to come about.

Consent-based integration is evident in the onus on deliberation apparent at every stage of the decision-making process in the EU. There is extensive consultation of affected interests, through lobbying and sounding out. In addition to committees of advisory and expert groups, the Commission, on an *ad hoc* basis is 'committed to the equal treatment of all special interest groups, to ensure that every interested party, irrespective of size or financial backing, should not be denied the opportunity of being heard by the Commission' (Commission 1993b, cited in Nentwich 1998: 131). The legitimacy of the EU partly derives from the deliberation that emanates from the non-hierarchical networks and webs of communication among actors who address substantive concerns, and who are involved in the process of decision-making. This mode of interaction is very much the result of the process of integration itself. Although the initial setting up of a network can be seen as a result of conscious design, subsequent efforts are more the result of copying and adaptation, due to favourable results. Integration to come about, however, is less a matter of an initial plan or motives, and more a reflection of the process of *reason giving* that is required when actors from different contexts – national, organizational and professional – come together to solve various types of issues. Comitology is one such obvious example, as revealed by Joerges and Everson in Chapter 8. The composition, interaction and outcomes of committees in themselves bear the burden of legitimation, not established hierarchies of one sort or the other. They do possess normative quality but whether or not they contribute to democratic legitimacy in overall terms, remains to de demonstrated.

Further, the principle of subsidiarity may contribute to legitimation through deliberation, as the burden of proof is placed on the higher-level units, which must provide reasons for why a task should be undertaken at that level.[3] Subsidiarity prompts justification and polycentric views on adjudication, something witnessed in the weak form of legislation. As Andreas Føllesdal observes, in Chapter 5: 'The Community is also required to legislate in the weakest form necessary, leaving discretion to Member States. Thus, directives are preferred over regulations, and framework directives over detailed measures.' Consequently, extensive extra-legal communication is needed for adjudication and decision-making in concrete cases.

Direct legitimacy

The EU is not a conventional international organization. Recent treaty changes and developments have produced an entity that requires direct rather than merely indirect legitimacy (legitimacy based on the democratic authority of Member States). After Maastricht this has become far more obvious, both to analysts and decision-makers. The EU has a far-reaching direct impact on citizens and their affairs (Beetham and Lord 1998b; Graeger 1994: 69ff.), as it affects them in their capacity as consumers, producers, employees, and rights holders. The 'direct effect' principle of EC law not only affects the Member States profoundly. What is also important is how the Court seeks to justify its intervention. 'Increasingly the Court has justified its claims to judicial competence-competence as the authority interpreter of a "higher" European law by reference to the protection of basic human rights' (Bellamy and Castiglione 1998b: 165). The universal nature of these rights makes them into one of the most potent sets of reasons that any political entity can employ to support its claim for legal sovereignty.

The question of direct legitimacy is not merely a matter of clarifying the status of the EU in principled terms. It is also an empirical matter, as the EU profoundly transforms the Member States, through relinquishment and 'pooling' of sovereignty. However, the relationship is complex. For instance, the EU can be seen to contribute positively to Member State authority, insofar as the Union can serve as a means to handle externalities in an effective manner. On the other hand, it can also be seen to weaken the authority of the Member States, when mismanagement and the democratic deficit in the EU institutions generate legitimation problems for Member States. There is strengthened emphasis on measures to heighten the direct legitimacy of the EU. Some of these result from the peculiar dynamics of decision-making in the EU. For instance, Member States may use the EU to relieve the national agenda of difficult issues. This highlights the autonomy and visibility of the EU and makes it more exposed to public questioning.[4]

The EU itself also claims popular approval, and claims to be a source of legitimacy in its own right. Both the rhetoric of 'bringing the Union ever closer to the people' – the Community as 'a political union' – a polity – and the many referenda on treaty changes to increase the depth of European integration, are reminders that the power resides directly with the people. In value terms, the European tradition supports a wide range of values, all of which are currently drawn upon to support the new European construction. For instance, during the IGC-96, which produced the Amsterdam Treaty, the values most frequently referred to were peace, peaceful co-existence with other peoples, democracy, freedom, human rights, the rule of law, social justice, solidarity, equality, non-discrimination, cohesion, security, efficiency, cultural diversity, and national identity (respect for the national identity of the Member States).

It is possible to see these value notions as mere pretence and window dressing, as many analysts do. But whether they are really intended as window dressing or not, if the EU is at all to respond to the many calls for a more direct mode of legitimacy, it has to specify the principles on which it is to be based. The values listed above are not only unavoidable as means of interpreting the history of the Union and as means of defining what it is about – its identity – but they also constitute the very language codes for dealing with common affairs, such as the question of enlargement to the East. With regard to the latter, democracy and human rights are employed directly as admission criteria, which applicants must adhere to, in order to obtain membership. The basic norms and values that are appealed to, in order to justify the EU, are powerful weapons in the hands of democrats.[5]

The efforts to reform the EU to heighten its democratic legitimacy demonstrate the force of direct legitimacy, albeit the sheer complexity of the EU and the fact that these efforts must be consensually based, suggest that this will be a lengthy and difficult process. The conflict-ridden relationship between the Commission and the EP, due to the absence of a clear-cut division of powers, is producing efforts to hammer out a more coherent and democratically based system of accountability. Consider the 1999 crisis. The Committee of Independent Experts was set up to report on various allegations and produced the report entitled *Allegations regarding Fraud, Mismanagement, and Nepotism in the European Commission*, which led to its dissolution and the reappointment of members. This was due to vociferous criticisms by the Parliament. The dissolution of the Commission in 1999 may signal a watershed change in the development of the EU. The crisis promises to further increase the power of the EP and further enhance the supranational features of the EU, and base these on strengthened and more coherent conceptions of accountability, transparency, and honesty.[6] However, this struggle for public recognition is hard to understand, unless the terminology and criteria associated with popular sovereignty are employed.

One thing is that the EU requires direct legitimacy, quite another is whether this claim can be warranted by the structure in place. In Chapter 4, Richard Bellamy and Dario Castiglione, drawing on a normative model associated with republicanism, assert that the structure in place has limited prospects of obtaining an acceptable measure of democratic legitimacy. In Chapter 3, a broader set of assessment criteria of democratic legitimacy was presented. For these to be realized, massive improvements are required. But we should not ignore the progress already made. A rather complex 'opportunity structure' of accessibility is already in place in the EU. There are voting-rights and the right to petition the legislature at the EU level, there are hearings and conferences organized by the Parliament and the Commission, there is a European Ombudsperson, and there are possibilities for direct contact, letter writing, etc. (Nentwich 1998: 126ff.). Nevertheless, the main requirement in order to assess democratic quality is a public sphere, in which all, on a free and equal basis, can participate. This is necessary for the public authorization of political power and for the testing of power-holders' claims to legitimacy. Without a public sphere, no democracy!

Prospects for a pan-European identity?

In Chapter 10, Philip Schlesinger and Deirdre Kevin address the vital problem of whether or not there is a European public sphere – or spheres – for opinion formation. When seen from a discourse-theoretical perspective, a person's identity *as citizen* is not to be found in his/her pre-political cultural or ethnic heritage, tradition or other historical sense of belonging, but is established through legal entitlements and political discourse. It is conceivable, then, that the political institutions at the European level, whose historical foundation and anchoring in a particular cultural and ethnic tradition is weak indeed, may actually be quite well placed to contribute to the formation of a European citizen or political identity. A constitution with a clearly specified system of rights will probably have a 'catalytic effect' on identity formation (Habermas 1998a: 156).

There are certain developments that offer some hope in terms of developing a viable public sphere. Schlesinger and Kevin find that the EU has a potential space for the creation of collective identity through pan-European press and media based on English as *lingua franca*. The poly-lingual TV-channel 'Euronews' operates on a large scale. In addition *The Financial Times, The Economist*, BBC World, Deutsche Welle, and also CNN – and certainly not least the Internet – create audio-visual spaces in Europe that are conductive to a European identity. Most of these are, needless to say, market driven initiatives. The authors caution us that this is still an elite conversation and one propelled by market-seeking behaviour.

The public sphere is, however, complex and multifaceted. It is composed of smaller webs of communication which are nested on to larger ones, and communication takes place in criss-crossing channels and networks, which greatly heighten the prospects for protest by social movements and NGOs in a European-wide context (cf. Tarrow 1995) and which foster heightened inclusiveness and self-reflection. The sheer complexity of the public sphere also requires a far greater research effort than was possible here, if we are to understand its overall salience to democracy in the EU. It is also important to recall that, as noted in Chapter 3, the public sphere at the national level was not developed prior to the establishment of government, but arose in opposition to state-based authority. It was a consequence of constitutionally actionable entitlements, i.e. citizens were endowed with rights that could be used against absolute power. The public sphere developed around and in opposition to decision-making centres. It is not something prior to such centres, reflective of some kind of natural identity – 'a people', 'a nation' – or other 'natural' or 'intrinsic' and contextually based senses of loyalty. The public sphere has to be created.

Popular sovereignty hinges not on the existence, or the presence of 'a people', but rather on the possibilities of the different groups with a distinct identity within a territory under common legislation to come together to form opinions and hold power holders accountable. In this sense a public sphere in which identities can be shaped is a necessary prerequisite for democracy. The public sphere in Europe that emerged in English coffee houses from 1680 until 1730, and correspondingly in clubs and lounges in France, was first of a literary nature and later developed into political publics (Habermas 1962/1989). Rather than posing an overt challenge to political authority, they established the ideal of conflict resolution through debate, and sought to subject political authorities to the force of reason. 'Indeed, this society was wider than any one state; it extended for some purposes to all of civilized Europe' (Taylor 1995: 266). Theoretically speaking, the public sphere is a common *meta-topical space* of discourse outside of state power, and is based solely upon communicative rationality, i.e. on secular, universalistic and impartial argumentation. The public sphere is no hierarchy and as such offers scant prospects for the establishment of a novel hierarchical sense of attachment in Europe. But this is precisely one of its most important merits – it fosters inclusiveness and the potential for multiple identities to co-exist, features very much conductive to European constitution-making.

It should also be recalled that the public sphere rooted in *civil society* outside the realm of the state is a unique European invention with a rather long history. As Charles Taylor (1995: 204ff.) points out, the resilience of the notion of civil society is derived from 'the medieval constitution', which was based on disjuncture between political organization and society, division and even fragmentation of authority, the legal development of individual rights, the dependent nature of political rule and the later notion of popular legitimation of any given system of rule. The state system appropriated several of these principles but never succeeded in rooting them out entirely. Instead, many of these principles have returned in revised form and with both old as well as new institutional moorings, from churches in the East to social movements in the West, to the support of a realm outside of political control. Thus, there is a favourable common background for the Member States in the history of ideas and as also reflected in political practices that the Member States can draw upon in creating a European identity based on civic principles.

Post-national integration

There are threads of common history in Europe that the process of integration can draw on.[7] The emergence of public spheres is also a reminder of what the

'European civilizational project' is about, in spite of grave disasters and setbacks, such as the two world wars that initiated the integration process in the first place. Europe can be seen to have a normative political culture whose self-understanding is based on *recognition of difference* and a constitutional order that is compatible with pluralism and which does not require homogenization in nations for democracy to thrive. In Chapter 11, Broderstad draws attention to the growing recognition of the rights of indigenous peoples. In Northern Europe the traditional Saami settlement area has been divided up into several nation-states. Even though the nation-states, in the last two decades increasingly have come to recognize minority rights, there are obvious limits to their ability. European integration fosters a process of Europeanization, which 'affects both national policy towards indigenous peoples and the Saami directly in several areas. Sweden and Finland, as EU members, are adapting their societies and systems of government to the EU, and this process also influences Saami policy and politics'. As a post-national entity, the EU may promote a more inclusive sense of belonging with potential, at least, to enable people to learn to cope with deep diversity in a more respectful manner than the nation-state has thus far been able to. At this level minorities such as the Saami, are just one minority among many other. In the EU every people is a minority.

In this respect the EU pursues the modern idea of statehood, as divorced from nationhood: the polity is not bound by pre-political bounds. It is not necessary for citizens to be each other's brother or sister, or neighbour, or native inhabitant, for political integration to come about. In modern societies, citizenship has taken *a cognitive turn*, which reflects the onus on basic equal rights: If compatriots are to regulate their common affairs by law, they must concede equal rights to each other. Modern states are, according to Kant, based on entitlements entrenched in constitutions as individual rights which turn human beings into a unified body of citizens capable of making the very laws they are to obey (cf. Habermas 1998a: 165; Apel 1997: 79ff.). Increasingly, nationality and citizenship have been disconnected in modern, Western societies. After the French Revolution, nation-states have not 'existed in isolation as bounded geographical totalities, and they are better thought of as multiple overlapping networks of interaction' (Held 1995: 225). This is a process very much speeded up by the EU, which has 'established the bold idea to disconnect nationality from citizenship, and this idea may well evolve to a general principle which ultimately transforms the ideal of cosmopolitan citizenship into a reality' (Preuss 1998: 149).

Though the European integration process suffers from many defects and shortcomings, it provides us with an attractive ideal. On the threshold of a new millennium, the prospect of a renewed 'balkanization of the world' in a horrifying manner yet again serves to remind us of the crisis-ridden history of Europe. When faced with the possibility of such a past to re-emerge as the future, we are compelled constantly to remind ourselves of the normative foundations of the European integration process. Czech President Vaclav Havel presented the following scenario when he spoke on enlargement to the EP in 1994:[8]

Anything else would be a return to the times when European order was not a work of consensus but of violence. And the evil demons are lying in wait. A vacuum, the decay of values, the fear of freedom, suffering and poverty, chaos – those are the environments in which they flourish. ... For if the future European order does not emerge from a broadening European Union, based on the best European values and willing to defend and transmit them, the organization of the future could well fall into the hands of a cast of fools, fanatics, populists and demagogues waiting for their chance and determined to promote the worst European traditions.

(cited from Schimmelfenning 1999: 35)

Notes

1 'European committees cannot simply be classified as the agents of a bureaucratic revolution. Rather, with all its sensitivity for the modern complex of risk regulation and for the intricacies of internationalized governance within non-hierarchical and multi-level structures, the committee system may be argued to possess a normative, if underformed, character of its own; or, more precisely, to operate within a novel constitutional framework informed by the notion of "deliberative supranationalism" ' (Joerges and Everson, Chapter 8 in this volume).
2 As a result of Amsterdam, the EP will be a co-legislator with the Council in thirty-seven different types of issues: '... codecision will henceforth be perceived as the standard procedure in legislative matters, while consultation or cooperation will increasingly be considered as exceptions to the rule' (Nentwich and Weale 1998: 8).
3 For instance, in its report on the TEU, the European Council and Council of the Union stated that: 'The Commission has undertaken to justify each of its new proposals in the light of the subsidiarity principle. It makes more regular use of "Green Papers" and "White Papers", prompting broad public debate, before new proposals are submitted.' The European Council and Council of the Union: Report of 6 April on the Operation of the Treaty on European Union (5082/95, p.4).
4 '[T]he tendency of national governments to offload the odium for unpopular decisions onto the EU level only further exposes the character of its decision making and the nature of its authority to public questioning' (Beetham and Lord 1998b: 14).
5 cf. 'If the European Union was a state, it would not qualify for membership in the Union because of the inadequate democratic content of its constitution' (Offe 1996: 145, our translation).
6 The EMU appears to be a step in the same direction: 'The introduction of a single currency in 1999 under the authority of a Central bank is an irreversible step in the same direction towards a real federation' (Anderson 1997: 126).
7 See for instance Rokkan (1975) and Fossum and Robinson (1999).
8 Europe Documents 1874 (16 March 1994), 3.

Bibliography

Ackerman, B. (1980) *Social Justice in the Liberal State*, New Haven: Yale University Press.

—— (1988) 'Neo-federalism?', in J. Elster and R. Slagstad (eds) *Constitutionalism and Democracy*, Cambridge: Cambridge University Press and Norwegian University Press, pp. 153–194.

Aikio, M. (1994) 'The Saami language – a living language', in *Majority–Minority Relations. The Case of the Saami in Scandinavia*, Report, The World Commission on Culture and Development, Diedut, no. 1, Kautokeino, Norway: Nordic Saami Institute.

Aikio, P. (1994) 'Development of the political status of the Saami people in Finland', in *Majority–minority relations. The case of the Saami in Scandinavia*, Report, The World Commission on Culture and Development, Diedut, no. 1, Kautokeino, Norway: Nordic Saami Institute.

Albert, D. (1998) 'Supranationale Problemlösung oder nationale Interessenwahrung? Die umweltpolitische Handlungsfähigkeit der E', *Integration* 21: 32–42.

Alexy, R. (1989) *A Theory of Legal Argumentation*, Oxford: Clarendon Press.

Almond, G.A. (1990) *A Discipline Divided: Schools and Sects in Political Science*, Beverly Hills, Calif.: Sage.

Althusius, J. (1614/1995) *Politica Methodice Digesta* (trans. Frederick Carney), Indianapolis: Liberty Press.

Andersen, S.S and Burns, T. (1996) 'The European Union and the erosion of parliamentary democracy: a study of post-parliamentary governance', in S.S. Andersen and K.A. Eliassen (eds) *The European Union: How Democratic Is It?*, London: Sage.

Andersen, S.S. and Eliassen, K.A. (eds) (1996) *The European Union: How Democratic Is It?*, London: Sage.

Anderson, B. (1983) *Imagined Communities*, London: Verso.

Anderson, P. (1997) 'The Europe to come', in P. Gowan and P. Anderson *The Question of Europe*, pp. 126–145, London: Verso.

Apel, K.O. (1997) 'Kant's idea of peace and the philosophical conception of a world republic', in J. Bohman and M. Lutz-Bachmann (eds) *Perpetual Peace. Essays on Kant's Cosmopolitan Ideal*, Cambridge: The MIT Press.

Arendt, H. (1958) *The Human Condition*, Chicago: University of Chicago Press.

—— (1963) *On Revolution*, New York: Viking.

Arneson, R.J. (1993) 'Democratic rights at national and workplace levels', in D. Copp, J. Hampton, and J.E. Roemer (eds) *The Idea of Democracy*, Cambridge: Cambridge University Press, pp. 118–148.

Arrow, K. (1951) *Social Choice And Individual Values*, New Haven: Yale University Press.

Baier, K. (1958) *The Moral Point of View: A Rational Basis for Ethics*, Ithaca, NY: Cornell University Press.

Bangemann, M. (Chairman) (1994) *Europe and the Global Information Society*, Brussels, 26th May.

Barry, B. (1989a) *Theories Of Justice. A Treatise on Social Justice*, vol. 1, Berkeley: University of California Press.

—— (1989b) *Democracy Power and Justice*, Oxford: Clarendon Press.

—— (1991) 'Is democracy special?', in *Democracy and Power. Essays in Political Theory*, Oxford: Oxford University Press, 1: 24–60.

Bechmann, G. (1994) 'Risiko und gesellschaftlicher Umgang mit Unsicherheit', *Österreichische Zeitschrift für Soziologie* 19: 8–33.

Beck, U. (1986) *Risikogesellschaft. Auf dem Weg in eine andere Moderne*, Frankfurt: Suhrkamp.

—— (1988) *Gegengifte, Die organisierte Unverantwortlichkeit*, Frankfurt: Suhrkamp.

—— (1992) *The Risk Society*, London: Polity Press.

—— (1996) 'Wissen oder Nicht-wissen? Zwei Perspektiven "reflexiver Modernisierung" ', in U. Beck, A. Giddens and S. Lash, *Reflexive Modernisierung. Eine Kontroverse*, Frankfurt: Suhrkamp.

—— (1998) *Politik der Globalisierung*, Frankfurt: Suhrkamp.

Beck, U., Giddens, A., and Lash, S. (1996) *Reflexive Modernisierung*, Frankfurt: Suhrkamp.

Beer, S.H. (1993) *To Make a Nation: The Rediscovery of American Federalism*, Cambridge, Mass.: Harvard University Press.

Beetham, D. and Lord, C. (1998a) 'Legitimacy and the European Union', in A. Weale and M. Nentwich *Political Theory and the European Union*, London: Longman.

—— (1998b) *Legitimacy and the European Union*, London: Longman.

Beitz, C.R. (1983) 'Cosmopolitan ideals and national sentiment', *Journal of Philosophy* 80: 591–600.

—— (1989) *Political Equality*, Princeton, NJ: Princeton University Press.

Bellamy, R. (1995) 'The constitution of Europe: rights or democracy?', in R. Bellamy *et al.* (eds) *Democracy and Constitutional Culture*, London: Lothian Foundation Press, pp. 153–175.

—— (1996) 'The political form of the constitution: the separation of powers, rights and representative democracy', *Political Studies* 4, 3 (Special Issue): 436–456.

Bellamy R. and Castiglione, D. (eds) (1996) *Constitutionalism in Transformation. Theoretical and European Perspectives*, Oxford: Blackwell.

—— (1997a) 'Building the union: the nature of sovereignty in the political architecture of Europe', *Law and Philosophy* 16: 421–445.

—— (1997b) 'Review article: constitutionalism and democracy – political theory and the American constitution', *British Journal of Political Science* 27: 595–618.

—— (1998a) 'The normative challenge of a European polity: cosmopolitan and communitarian models compared, criticised and combined', in A. Føllesdal and P. Koslowski (eds) *Democracy and the European Union*, Berlin: Springer Verlag, pp. 254–284.

—— (1998b) 'Between cosmopolis and community: three models of rights and democracy within the European Union', in D. Archibugi, *et al. Re-imagining political community. Studies in cosmopolitan democracy*, Cambridge: Polity, pp. 152–178.

Bellamy, R. and Warleigh, A. (1998) 'From an ethics of integration to an ethics of participation: citizenship and the future of the European Union', *Millennium: Journal of International Studies* 27: 447–470.

Bellamy, R., Bufacchi, V. and Castiglione, D. (eds) (1995) *Democracy and Constitutional Culture in the Union of Europe*, London: Lothian Foundation Press.

Benhabib, S. (1992) *Situating the Self. Gender, Community and Postmodernism in Contemporary Ethics*, New York: Routledge.

—— (ed.) (1994) *Democracy and Difference: Contesting the Boundaries of the Political*, Princeton: Princeton University Press.

—— (1996) 'Towards a deliberative model of democratic legitimacy', in S. Benhabib (ed.) *Democracy and Difference*, Princeton, NJ: Princeton University Press.

Bertram, C. (1967) 'Decision-making in the E.E.C.: the management committee procedure' *Common Market Law Review* 5: 246–264.

Beus, J. de (1997) 'The place of national identity in a well-ordered consociational democracy', *Acta Philosophica Groningana* 24, December.

Beyers, J. and Dierickx, G. (1997) 'Nationality and European negotiations: the working groups of the Council of Ministers', *European Journal of International Relations* 3, 4: 35–471.

—— (1998) 'The working groups of the Council of the European Union: supranational or intergovernmental negotiations?', *The Journal of Common Market Studies* 36, 3: 289–317.

Binseil, U. and Hantke, C. (1997) 'The power distribution in decision making among EU members states', *European Journal of Political Economy* 13: 171–185.

Blaunstein, A. and Sigler, J. (1988) *Constitutions that Made History*, New York: Paragon House.

Blichner, L. and Fossum, J.E. (1997) 'Modern constitution making', paper published in 'The Proceedings of the Annual General Meeting of the Canadian Political Science Association', St. John's, Newfoundland.

Blichner, L. and Sangolt, L. (1994) 'The concept of subsidiarity and the debate on European cooperation: pitfalls and possibilities', *Governance* 7, 3: 284–306.

Blumler, J. (1983) *Communicating to Voters: Television in the First European Parliamentary Elections*, London: Sage.

Bobbio, N. (1987) *The Future of Democracy*, ed. Richard Bellamy, Cambridge: Polity Press.

Bohman, J. (1996) *Public Deliberation. Pluralism, Complexity, and Democracy*, Cambridge, Mass.: The MIT Press.

—— (1999) 'The coming of age of deliberative democracy', *Journal of Political Philosophy* 1 (March)

Bohman, J. and Rehg, W. (1997) *Deliberative Democracy*, Cambridge, MA: MIT Press.

Bond, M.A. (1997) 'The European Parliament in the 1990s', *The Journal of Legislative Studies* 3, 2: 1–9.

Borrows, J. (1999) ' "Landed" citizenship: Narratives of Aboriginal political participation', to be printed in A. Cairns *et al.* (ed.) *Citizenship, Diversity and Pluralism*, Montreal: McGill-Queen's University Press.

Bradley, K.St.C. (1997) 'The European parliament and comitology: on the road to nowhere?', *European Law Journal* 3, 3: 230–254.

—— (1999) 'Institutional aspects of comitology', in C. Joerges and E. Vos (eds) *EU Committees: Social Regulation, Law and Politics*, Oxford: Hart, pp. 71–93.

Breckinridge, R. (1997) 'Reassessing regimes: the international regime aspects of the European Union', *Journal of Common Markets Studies* 35, 2: 173–187.

Broderstad, E.G. (1994/1995) 'Samepolitikk – interessemaksimering eller identitetsskaping?', Hovedfagsoppgave, Institutt for samfunnsvitenskap, Tromsø: Universitetet i Tromsø, 1994, also issues as LOS Nord-Norge: Notat, 1995.

—— (1997) 'Saami identity in cultural and political communities', Oslo: ARENA, Working Paper no. 97/9.

Buchanan, J. (1975) *The Limits of Liberty: Between Anarchy and Leviathan*, Chicago: University of Chicago Press.

Bücker, A. (1997) *Von der Gefahrenabwehr zu Risikovorsorge und Risikomanagement im Arbeitsschutzrecht*, Berlin: Duncker & Humblot.

Caldeira, G. and Gibson, J.L. (1995) 'The legitimacy of the court of justice in the European Union. Models of institutional support', *American Political Science Review* 89, 2: 356–376.

Calhoun, C. (ed.) (1994) *Habermas and the Public Sphere*, Cambridge: The MIT Press.

—— (1995) *Critical Social Theory*, Oxford: Blackwell.

Canel, M. J. (1994) 'Lobbying and communication: regional bodies in the European Union', Working Paper, Pamplona: University of Navarra.

Caporaso, J. (1996) 'The European Union and forms of state: Westphalian, regulatory or post-modern?', *Journal of Common Market Studies* 34, 1: 29–52.

—— (1998) 'Regional integration theory: understanding our past and anticipating our future', *Journal of European Public Policy* 5, 1: 1–16.

Cass, D.Z. (1992) 'The word that saves Maastricht...', *Common Market Law Review*, 29.

Castiglione, D. (1996) 'The political theory of the constitution', *Political Studies* 44, 3 (Special Issue): 417–435.

Chambers, G.R. (1999) 'The BSE crisis and the European parliament', in C. Joerges and E. Vos (eds) *European Committees: Social Regulation, Law and Politics*, Oxford: Hart, pp. 95–106.

Chambers, S. (1996) *Reasonable Democracy*, Ithaca: Cornell University Press.

—— (1997) 'Talking versus voting, democratic trade-offs and tensions', University of Colorado, mimeo.

—— (1998) 'Contract or conversation? Theoretical lessons from the Canadian constitutional crisis', *Politics and Society* 26, 1: 143–172.

Checkel, J. (1997) 'International norms and domestic politics: bridging the rationalist–constructivist divide', *European Journal of International Relations* 3 (December).

—— (1998) 'Social construction and integration', Oslo: ARENA, Working Paper no. 14.

Christiansen, T. (1996) 'A maturing bureaucracy? The role of the commission in the policy process', in J. Richardson (ed.) *European Union: Power and Policy-Making*, London and New York: Routledge, pp. 77–95.

Chryssochoou, D.N. (1994) 'Democracy and symbiosis in the European Union: towards a confederal consociation?', *West European Politics* 17: 95–128.

Cohen, J. (1991) 'Deliberation and democratic legitimacy', in A. Hamlin and P. Pettit (eds) *The Good Polity*, Oxford: Basil Blackwell.

—— (1998) 'Procedure and substance in deliberative democracy', in J. Bohman and W. Rehg (eds) *Deliberative Democracy*, Cambridge, Mass.: The MIT Press.

Cohen, J. and Arato, A. (1995) *Civil Society and Political Theory*, Cambridge: MIT Press.

Cohen, J. and Rogers, J. (1992) 'Secondary associations and democratic governance', *Politics and Society* 20: 393–472.

Cohen, J. and Sabel, C. (1997) 'Directly-deliberative polyarchy', *European Law Journal* 3, 4: 313–343.

Collins, R. (1993) 'Public service broadcasting by satellite in Europe: Eurikon and Europa', *Screen* 34, 2: 162–175.

Connolly, W.E. (1983) *The Terms of Political Discourse*, Oxford: Martin Robertson.

Conradi, P. (1997) 'EU bankrolls sitcoms to sell its message', *The Times*, 1 June, p. 8.

Constant, B. (1819/1980) 'De la liberté des anciens comparée à celle des modernes', in M. Gauchet (ed.) *De la liberté chez les Modernes*, Paris: Le Livre de poche.

Coppel, J. and O'Neill, A. (1992) 'The European Court of Justice: taking rights seriously?', *Common Market Law Review* 29: 669–692.

Corbett, R. (1998) *The European Parliament's Role in Closer EU Integration*, London: Macmillan Press.

Craig, P.P. (1997) 'Democracy and rule-making within the EC: an empirical and normative assessment', *European Law Journal* 3, 2: 105–131.

Crick, B. (1962) *In Defence of Politics*, London: Weidenfeld & Nicolson.

Curtin, D. (1993) 'The constitutional structure of the Union: a Europe of bits and pieces', *Common Market Law Review* 30: 17–69.

—— (1997) *Postnational democracy: The European Union in Search of a Political Philosophy*, The Hague: Kluwer Law.

Dahl, R.A. (1956) *A Preface to Democratic Theory*, Chicago: University of Chicago Press.

—— (1983) 'Federalism and the democratic process', in J.R. Pennock and J.W. Chapman (eds) *Liberal Democracy, Nomos 25*, New York: New York University Press, pp. 95–108.

—— (1986) *Democracy, Liberty and Equality*, Oslo: Norwegian University Press.

—— (1989) *Democracy and its Critics*, New Haven and London: Yale University Press.

—— (1994) 'A democratic dilemma: system effectiveness versus citizen participation', *Political Science Quarterly* 109, 1 (Spring): 23–34.

—— (1997) 'On deliberative democracy: citizen panels and medicare reform', *Dissent* (Summer).

Danley, J.R. (1991) 'Liberalism, Aboriginal rights, and cultural minorities', *Philosophy and Public Affairs* 20, 2 (Spring): 168–185.

de Burca, G. (1996) 'The quest for legitimacy in the European Union', *The Modern Law Review* 59: 349–376.

Dehousse, R. (1997) 'Regulation by networks in the European community: the role of European agencies', *Journal of European Public Policy* 4: 246–261.

—— (1999) 'Law implementation in a polycentric community: towards a regulation of transnational governance', in C. Joerges and E. Vos (eds) *EU Committees: Social Regulation, Law and Politics*, Oxford: Hart, pp. 109–127.

Dehousse, R., Everson, M., Joerges, C., Majone, G. and Snyder, F. (1992) 'Europe after 1992. New regulatory strategies', EUI Working Paper Law 92/31, San Domenico di Fiesole/FI.

Delanty, G. (1995) *Inventing Europe – Idea, Identity, Reality*, London: Macmillan.

Deutsch, K.W. (1966) *Nationalism and Social Communication*, Cambridge, MA: MIT Press.

Dewey, J. (1927) *The Public and its Problems*, London: George Allen & Unwin.

De Witte, B. (1991) 'Droit communitaire et valeurs constitutionelles nationales', *Droits* 14: 87–96.

Doerr, A.D. (1997) 'Building new orders of government – the future of Aboriginal self-government', *Canadian Public Administration*, 40, 2: 274–289.

Downs, A. (1957) *An Economic Theory of Democracy*, New York: Harper & Row.

Driscoll, D.J. (1989) 'The development of human rights in international law', in W. Laqueur and B. Rubin *The Human Rights Reader*, New York: Meridian, pp. 41–56.

Dryzek, J.S. (1990) *Discursive Democracy: Politics, Policy, and Political Science*, Cambridge: Cambridge University Press.

Durkheim, E. (1893/1964) *The Division of Labour in Society*, New York: Macmillan.

Dworkin, R (1978) 'Liberalism', in S. Hampshire (ed.) *Public and Private Morality*, Cambridge: Cambridge University Press.

Earnshaw, D. and Judge, D. (1996) 'From co-operation to co-decision: the European parliament's path to legislative power', in J. Richardson (ed.) *European Union: Power and Policy-Making*, London and New York: Routledge, pp. 96–126.

Edwards, G. (1996) 'National sovereignty vs integration? The Council of Ministers', in J. Richardson (ed.) *European Union: Power and Policy-Making*, London and New York: Routledge, pp. 127–147.

Eichener, V. (1993) 'Social dumping or innovative regulation? Processes and outcomes of European decision-making in the sector of health and safety at work harmonization', EUI Working Papers SPS 92/28, San Domenico di Fiesole/FI.

—— (1997) 'Entscheidungsprozesse in der regulativen Politik der Europäischen Union', Habilitationsschrift Bochum.

Eleftheriadis, P. (1998) 'Begging the constitutional question', *Journal of Common Market Studies* 36: 255–272.

Eley, G. (1994) 'Nations, publics and political cultures: placing Habermas in the nineteenth century', in C. Calhoun (ed.) *Habermas and the Public Sphere*, Cambridge: The MIT Press, pp. 289–293.

Elster, J. (1979) *Ulysses and the Sirens: Studies in Rationality and Irrationality*, Cambridge: Cambridge University Press.

—— (1983a) *Sour Grapes: Studies in the Subversion of Rationality*, Maison des Sciences de l'Homme, Cambridge: Cambridge University Press.

—— (1983b) 'Offentlighet og deltakelse. To teorier om deltakerdemokratiet', in T. Bergh (ed.) *Deltakerdemokratiet*, Oslo: Universitetsforlaget.

—— (1984) *Ulysses and the Sirens. Studies in Rationality and Irrationality*, Cambridge: Cambridge University Press.

—— (1986) 'The market and the forum: three varieties of political theory', in J. Elster and A. Hylland (eds) *Foundations of Social Choice Theory*, Cambridge: Cambridge University Press.

—— (1989) *The Cement of Society*, Cambridge: Cambridge University Press.

—— (1991) 'Arguing and bargaining in two constituent assemblies', *The Storrs Lectures*, New Haven: Yale Law School.

—— (1992) 'Arguing and bargaining in the federal convention and the Assemblée Constituante', in R. Malnes and A. Underdal (eds) *Rationality and Institutions*, Oslo: Universitetsforlaget.

—— (1995) 'Strategic uses of argument', in K. Arrow *et al.* (eds) *Barriers to the Negotiated Resolution of Conflict*, New York: Norton, pp. 236–57.

—— (ed.) (1998a) *Deliberative Democracy*, Cambridge: Cambridge University Press.

—— (1998b) 'Introduction', in J. Elster (ed.) *Deliberative Democracy*, Cambridge: Cambridge University Press.

—— (1998c) 'Deliberation and Constitution Making', in J. Elster (ed.) *Deliberative Democracy*, Cambridge: Cambridge University Press.

Enzenberger, H.M. (1987) *Ach Europa*, (English translation: *Europe, Europe: Forays into a Continent*, 1989), Frankfurt: Suhrkamp.

Eriksen, E.O. (1990) 'Towards the post-corporate state?', *Scandinavian Political Studies* 13, 4: 345–364.

—— (ed.) (1994a) *Den politiske orden*, Oslo: Tano.

—— (1994b) 'Europeanisation and democratic theory', in Eriksen, Malnes and Føllesdal *Europeanisation and Normative Political Theory*, Oslo: ARENA, June.

—— (1995) 'Statsvitenskapen og konstitusjonstenkningen. Bidrag til en konstruktiv politisk teori', in E.O. Eriksen (ed.) *Deliberativ politikk*, Oslo: Tano.

—— (1999) *Kommunikativ Ledelse. Om Styring av Offentlige Institusjoner*, Bergen: Fagbokforlaget.

Eriksen, E.O. and Weigård, J. (1997a) 'Conceptualizing politics: strategic or communicative action', *Scandinavian Political Studies* 20, 3: 219–241.

—— (1997b) 'The end of citizenship? New roles challenging the political order', Exeter: University of Exeter, Department of Politics, Rusel Working Paper no. 30.

Eriksen, K.E. and Niemi, E. (1981) *Den Finske Fare. Sikkerhetsproblemer og Minoritetspolitikk i Nord 1860–1940*, Oslo: Universitetsforlaget.

Erikson, J. (1997) 'Partition and redemption: a Machiavellian analysis of sami and Basque patriotism', Ph.D. dissertation, Umeå: Umeå Universitet, Statsvetenskapliga institutionen.

—— (1998) 'Samepolitikens kända problem och okända framgångar', in *Samefolket*, (Östersund, Sweden), no. 8 (September).

Estlund, D. (1989) 'Reply to Grofman and Feld', *American Political Science Review* December.

—— (1997) 'Beyond fairness and deliberation: the epistemic dimension of democratic authority', in J. Bohman and W. Rehg (eds) *Deliberative Democracy*, Cambridge, MA: MIT Press.

Evans, P.B., Rueschemeyer, D. and Skocpol, T. (1985) *Bringing the State Back in*, Cambridge: Cambridge University Press.

Everson, M. (1995a) 'Independent agencies: hierarchy beaters', *European Law Journal* 2, 1: 180–204.

—— (1995b) 'The legacy of the market citizen', in J. Shaw and G. More *New Legal Dynamics of the European Union*, Oxford: Clarendon Press.

—— (1997) 'Administering Europe?', *Journal of Common Market Studies* 36, 2: 195–216.

—— (1999) 'The constitutionalisation of European administrative law', in C. Joerges and E. Vos (eds) *EU Committees: Social Regulation, Law and Politics*, Oxford: Hart, pp. 281–309.

Falke, J. (1996) 'Comitology and other committees: a preliminary empirical assessment', in R.H. Pedler and G.F. Schaefer (eds) *Shaping European Law and Policy. The Role of Committees and Comitology in the Political Process*, Maastricht: European Centre for Public Affairs, pp. 117–165.

Falke, J. and Joerges, Ch. (1995) 'Rechtliche Möglichkeiten und Probleme bei der Verfolgung und Sicherung nationaler und EG-weiter Umweltschutzziele im Rahmen der europäischen Normung. Gutachten erstellt im Auftrag des Büros für Technikfolgen-Abschätzung des Deutschen Bundestages', typescript Bremen.

Falke, J. and Winter, G. (1996) 'Management and regulatory committees in executive rule-making', in G. Winter (ed.) *Sources and Categories of European Union Law. A Comparative and Reform Perspective*, pp. 541–558, Baden-Baden: Nomos.

Farrand, M. (1937/1966) *The Records of the Federal Convention*, New Haven, Conn.: Yale University Press.

Fearon, J.D. (1998) 'Deliberation as discussion', in J. Elster (ed.) *Deliberative Democracy*, Cambridge: Cambridge University Press.

Femia, J. (1996) 'Complexity and deliberative democracy', *Inquiry* 39, 3–4: 359–397.

Ferry, J.-H. (1992) 'Une "philosophie" de la communauté', in J.-H. Ferry and P. Thibaud *Discussion sur l'Europe*, Paris: Calmann-Levy.

Fisher, R. and Ury, W. (1987) *Getting to Yes*, Boston: Penguin.

Fishkin, J. (1991) *Democracy and Deliberation: New Directions for Democratic Reform*, New Haven: Yale University Press.

Føllesdal, A. (1998a) 'Democracy, legitimacy and majority rule in the European Union', in A. Weale and M. Nentwich *Political Theory and the European Union*, London and New York: Routledge, pp. 34–48.

—— (1998b) 'Subsidiarity', *Journal of Political Philosophy* 6, 2: 231–259.

—— (1998c) 'Democracy and the European Union: challenges', in A. Føllesdal and P. Koslowski (eds) *Democracy and the European Union*, Heidelberg: Springer Verlag.

—— (1998d) 'Democracy and federalism in the European Union', in A. Føllesdal and P. Koslowski (eds) *Democracy and the European Union*, Berlin: Springer Verlag, pp. 231–253.

Føllesdal, A. and Koslowski, P. (eds) (1998) *Democracy and the European Union*, Berlin: Springer Verlag.

Forsyth, M. (1982) *Union of States – The Theory and Practice of Confederation*, Leicester: Leicester University Press.

Fossum, J.E. and Robinson, P.S. (1998) 'Regimes or institutions? The search for meaning in the study of international society', mimeo, Bergen and Tromsø.

—— (1999) 'A Phoenix arises: the social reconstruction of Europe', *Policy, Society and Organisation* (Australia) 18.

Fraser, N. (1992) 'Rethinking the public sphere. A contribution to the critique of actually existing democracy', in C. Calhoun (ed.) *Habermas and the Public Sphere*, Cambridge, Mass.: The MIT Press.

Freeman, S. (1992) 'Original meaning, democratic interpretation, and the constitution', *Philosophy and Public Affairs* 1, 1: 3–42.

Fundesco/AEJ (1997) *The European Union in the Media 1996*, Madrid: Fundesco.

Gardener, J.S. (1996) 'The European agency for the evaluation of medicines and European regulation of pharmaceuticals', *European Law Journal* 2: 48–82.

Gardner, J.N. (1991) *Effective Lobbying in the European Community*, The Netherlands: Kluwer Law and Taxation Publ.

Garnett, M. and Sherrington, P. (1996) 'UK parliamentary perspectives on Europe 1971–93', *The Journal of Legislative Studies* 2, 4: 383–402.

Gargarella R. (1995) *Nos los representantes*, Buenos Aires: Miño y Dávila.

—— (1996) *La justicia frente al gobierno*, Barcelona: Ariel.

—— (1998) 'Full representation, deliberation, and impartiality', in J. Elster (ed.) *Deliberative Democracy*, Cambridge: Cambridge University Press, pp. 260–280.

Gehring, Th. (1995) 'Regieren im internationalen System. Verhandlungen, Normen und Internationale Regime', *Politische Vierteljahresschrift* 36: 197–219.

—— (1996) 'Arguing and bargaining in internationalen Verhandlungen zum Schutz der Umwelt. Überlegungen am Beispiel des Ozonschutzregimes', in V. von Prittwitz (ed.) *Verhandeln und Argumentieren in der Umweltpolitik*, Opladen: Leske & Budrich, pp. 207–238.

—— (1997) 'Governing in nested institutions: environmental policy in the European Union and the case of packaging waste', *Journal of European Public Policy* 4: 337–354.

—— (1999) 'Bargaining, arguing and functional differentiation of decision-making: the role of committees in European environmental process regulation', in C. Joerges and E. Vos (eds) *European Committees: Social Regulation; Law and Politics*, Oxford: Hart, pp. 195–217.

Gellner, E. (1983) *Nations and Nationalism*, Oxford: Blackwell.

Gerken, L. (ed.) (1995) *Competition Among Institutions*, New York: Macmillan.

Gerstenberg, O. (1997a) *Bürgerrechte und Deliberative Demokratie*, Frankfurt: Suhrkamp.

—— (1997b) 'Law's polyarchy: a comment on Cohen and Sabel', *European Law Journal* 3, 4: 343–358.

Giddens, A. (1990a) *The Consequences of Modernity*, Cambridge: Polity Press.

—— (1990b) 'Introduction', in A. Giddens *The Consequences of Modernity*, Cambridge: Polity Press.

Goodin, R.E. (1986) 'Laundering preferences', in J. Elster and Å. Hylland (eds) *Foundations of Social Choice Theory*, Cambridge/Oslo: Cambridge University Press/ Universitetsforlaget.

—— (ed.) (1996a) *The Theory of Institutional Design*, Cambridge: Cambridge University Press.

—— (1996b) 'Institutionalizing the public interest: the defense of deadlock and beyond', *American Political Science Review* 90 (June): 331–343.

Gowan, R. and Anderson, P. (1997) *The Question of Europe*, London: Verso.

Graeger, N. (1994) 'European integration and the legitimation of supranational power', Oslo: Institutt for statsvitenskap.

Grimm, D. (1995) 'Does Europe need a constitution?', *European Law Journal* 1, 3: 282– 302.

Guéhenno, J.M. (1996) 'Europas Demokratie erneuern – Stärkung der gemeinschafts- bildende Kraft der Politik', in W. Weidenfeld (ed.) *Demokratie am Wendepunkt*, Berlin: Siedler Verlag.

Gurevitch, M., Levy, M.R., and Roeh, I. (1991) 'The global newsroom: convergence and diversities in the globalization of television news', in P. Dahlgren and C. Sparks (eds) *Communication and Citizenship*, London: Routledge, pp. 195–216.

Gustavsson, S. (1996) 'Double asymmetry as normative challenge', in A. Føllesdal and P. Koslowski (eds) *Democracy and the European Union*, Heidelberg: Springer.

Gutmann, A. and Thompson, D. (1996) *Democracy and Disagreement*, Cambridge, Mass.: The Belknap Press of Harvard University.

Haas, E.B. (1983) 'Words can hurt you; or who said what to whom about regimes', in S.D. Kraser (ed.) *International Regimes*, London: Cornell University Press, pp. 23–60.

Habermas, J. (1962/1989) *The Structural Transformation of the Public Sphere*, (trans. T. Burger and F. Lawrence), Cambridge, Mass.: Cambridge University Press.

—— (1972/1992) *Legitimation Crisis*, London: Polity Press.

—— (1981/1984/1987) *The Theory of Communicative Action*, vol. 1–2, Boston: Beacon Press.

—— (1983) *Moralbewusstsein und kommunikativen Handeln*, Frankfurt: Suhrkamp.

—— (1985) 'Die Krise des Wohlfahrtsstaats und die Erschöpfung utopischer Energien', in J. Habermas *Die Neue Unübersichtlichkeit*, Frankfurt: Suhrkamp, pp. 141–163.

—— (1990) 'Nachholende Revolution und linker Revisionsbedarf', in J. Habermas *Die nachholende Revolution*, pp. 179–204, Frankfurt: Suhrkamp.

—— (1991a) 'Justice and solidarity: on the discussion concerning stage 6', in Thomas E. Wren (ed.) *The Moral Domain*, Cambridge, Mass.: MIT Press, pp. 224–252.

—— (1991b) 'Yet again: German identity – a unified nation of angry DM Burghers?', *New German Critique* 52: 84–101.

—— (1992a) 'Further reflections on the public sphere', in C. Calhoun (ed.) *Habermas and the Public Sphere*, Cambridge, Mass.: The MIT Press.

—— (1992b) 'Citizenship and national identity: some reflections on the future of Europe', *Praxis International* 12, 1: 1–19.

—— (1993) 'Struggles for recognition in constitutional states', *European Journal of Philosophy* 1, 2: 128–155.

—— (1994a) 'Struggles for recognition in the democratic constitutional state', in A. Gutmann and C. Taylor (eds) *Multiculturalism: Examining the Politics of Recognition*, Princeton: Princeton University Press.

—— (1994b) 'Citizenship and national identity', in B. van Steenbergen (ed.) *The Condition of Citizenship*, London: Sage, pp. 20–35.

—— (1995a) *Diskurs, Rätt och Demokrati – Politisk-filosofiska Texter i Urval av Erik Oddvar Eriksen och Anders Molander*, Gøteborg: Daidalos.

—— (1995b) 'Remarks on Dieter Grimm's "Does Europe need a constitution?" ', *European Law Journal* 1, 3: 303–307.

—— (1995c) 'Tre normative demokratimodeller: om begrepet deliberativ politikk', in E.O. Eriksen (red.) *Deliberativ Politikk. Demokrati i Teori og Praksis*, Oslo: Tano.

—— (1996a) *Between Facts and Norms. Contributions to a Discourse Theory of Law and Democracy*, Cambridge, Mass.: The MIT Press.

—— (1996b) *Die Einbeziehung des Anderen. Studien zur politischen Theorie*, Frankfurt: Suhrkamp.

—— (1996c) 'Three normative models of democracy', in S. Benhabib (ed.) *Democracy and Difference – Contesting the Boundaries of the Political*, Princeton, NJ: Princeton University Press, pp. 21–30.

—— (1997) 'Kant's idea of perpetual peace, with the benefit of two hundred years' hindsight', in J. Bohman and M. Lutz-Bachmann (eds) *Perpetual Peace. Essays on Kant's Cosmopolitan Ideal*, Cambridge, Mass.: The MIT Press.

—— (1998a) *Die Postnationale Konstellation. Politische Essays*, Frankfurt: Suhrkamp.

—— (1998b) *The Inclusion of the Other*, London: Polity Press.

Hall, S. (1992) 'The question of cultural identity', in S. Hall, D. Held and T. McGrew (eds) *Modernity and its Future*, Cambridge: Polity Press, pp. 274–316.

Harrington, J. (1656/1883) *The Commonwealth of Oceania*, London: Henry Morley.

Hayek, F.A. (1982) *Law, Legislation and Liberty*, London: Routledge.

Hayes-Renshaw, F. and Wallace, H. (1997) *The Council of Ministers*, London: Macmillan.

Heathcoat-Amory, E. (1998) 'Selling citizenship', *The Spectator*, 7 February, p. 15.

Heitmeyer, W. (1997) *Was treibt die Gesellschaft auseinander?*, Frankfurt: Suhrkamp.

Held, D. (1987) *Models of Democracy*, London: Polity Press.

—— (1993) 'Democracy: From city-states to a cosmopolitan order?', in D. Held (ed.) *Prospects for Democracy: North, South, East, West*, Cambridge: Polity Press, pp. 13–52.

—— (1995) *Democracy and the Global Order*, Cambridge: Polity Press.

Helm, S. (1995) 'Report challenges EU's hidden deals', *The Independent*, June 23.

Henriksen, J.B. (1996) 'Betenkning om Samisk parlamentarisk samarbeid', Utredning fra Nordisk Samisk Institutt, Kautokeino, Norway.

Héritier, A. (1993) 'Policy-Netzwerkanalyse als Untersuchungsinstrument im europäischen Kontext: Folgerungen aus einer empirischen Studie regulativer Politik', in A. Héritier (ed.) *Policy-Analyse. Kritik und Neuorientierung*, Politische Vierteljahresschrift SH 24, Westdeutscher Verlag, pp. 432–448.

Hirst, P. (1994) *Associative Democracy*, Cambridge: Polity.

Hirst, P. and Thompson, G. (1996) *Globalization in Question*, Cambridge: Polity Press.

Hix, S. (1998) 'The study of the European Union II: The "new governance" agenda and its rival', *Journal of European Public Policy* 5, 1: 38–65.

Hjarvard, S. (1993) 'Pan-European television news: towards a European public sphere?', in P. Drummond, R. Paterson and J. Willis (eds) *National Identity and Europe: The Television Revolution*, London: British Film Institute, pp. 71–94.

Holland, M. (1996) 'Jean Monnet and the federal functionalist approach to European unity', in P. Murray and P. Rich *Visions of European Unity*, Boulder, Colorado: Westview Press, pp. 63–91.

Holmes, M. (ed.) (1996) *The Eurosceptical Reader*, London: Macmillan.

Honneth, A. (1995) *The Struggle for Recognition: The Moral Grammar of Social Conflicts*, Cambridge: Polity Press.

Hooghe, L. (1998) 'Consociationalists or Weberians? Top commission officials on nationality', Oslo: ARENA, Working Paper no. 20.

Hoscheit, J. and Wessels, W. (1991) *The European Council*, Maastricht: European Institute of Public Administration.

Hosli, M. (1996) 'Coalitions and power: effects of qualified majority voting in the Council of the European Union', *Journal of Common Market Studies* 34, 2: 255–273.

Hufen, F. (1993) 'Kooperation von Behörden und Unternehmen im Lebensmittelrecht. Neue Instrumente des Verwaltungsrechts, insbesondere: Akkreditierung, Zertifizierung, Betriebsbeauftragte und kooperative Qualitätssicherung', *Zeitschrift für das gesamte Lebensmittelrecht*, 3: 233–249.

Hume, D. (1752/1882) 'Idea of a perfect Commonwealth' (first publ. in *Political Discourses*), *Philosophical Works*, vol. 3 (eds. T.H. Green and T.H. Grose), Darmstadt, Germany.

Hyland, J.L. (1995) *Democratic Theory*, Manchester: Manchester University Press.

Hylland Eriksen, T. (1994) 'Nye former for politisk identitet i Europa og Norge?', in T.H. Eriksen, N. Græger, J.H. Matlary and T. Myhre *Kan EU være Demokratisk. Politisk Identitet og Legitimering i en ny Tid*, Oslo: Ad Notam Gyldendal.

IEP, Institut für Europäische Politik (1989) 'Comitology' – characteristics, performances and options. Research project under contract by the EC-Commission', Preliminary Final Report, Bonn.

Ionescu, G. (1993) 'The impact of the information revolution on parliamentary sovereignties', *Government and Opposition* 28, 2: 221–241.

Ipsen, H.-P. (1972) *Europäisches Gemeinschaftsrecht*, Tübingen: Mohr/Siebeck.

Jachtenfuchs M. and Kohler-Koch, B. (eds) (1996a) *Europäische Integration*, Opladen: Leske & Budrich.

—— (1996b) 'Regieren im dynamischen Mehrebenensystem', in M. Jachtenfuchs and B. Kohler-Koch (eds) *Europäische Integration*, Opladen: Leske & Budrich, pp. 15–44.

Jacobsson, K. (1997) 'Discursive will formation and the question of legitimacy in European politics', *Scandinavian Political Studies* 20, 1: 69–90.

Jernsletten, R. (1994) 'Samisk etnopolitisk mobilisering i et komparativt perspektiv', University of Tromsø, Centre for Saami Studies, November, mimeo, http://www.uit.no/ssweb/dok/j/r/94ksdg.htm

Joenniemi, P. (1994) 'Region-building as Europe-building', in O.S. Stokke and O. Tunander (eds) *The Barents Region, Co-operation in the Arctic Europe*, Oslo: PRIO/ London: Sage Publ.

Joerges, C. (1988) 'The new approach to technical harmonization and the interests of consumers: reflections on the necessities and difficulties of a Europeanization of product safety policy', in R. Bieber, R. Dehousse, J. Pinder and J.H.H. Weiler (eds) *1992 One European Market? A Critical Analysis of the Commission's Internal Market Strategy*, Baden-Baden: Nomos, pp. 157–225.

—— (1990) 'Paradoxes of deregulatory strategies at community level: the example of product safety policy', in G. Majone (ed.) *Deregulation or Re-regulation? Regulatory Reform in Europe and in the United States*, London: Pinter and New York: St. Martin's Press, pp. 176–197.

—— (1991) 'Die Europäisierung des Rechts und die rechtliche Kontrolle von Risiken', *Kritische Vierteljahresschrift für Gesetzgebung und Rechtswissenschaft* 3–4: 16–434 ('Product Safety in the European Community: Market Integration, Social Regulation and Legal Structures', in F. Snyder (ed.) (1993) *European Community Law*, vol. II: 297–320, Dartmouth: Aldershot.)

—— (1993) 'Soziale Rechte und regulative Politik in der Europäischen Gemeinschaft' in

SPD-Bundestagsfraktion (ed.) *Besser leben mit Europa? Chancen einer Europäischen Verfassung'. Texte der Anhörung am 27. Mai 1993 in Bonn,* Anhang 4: 1–17, Bonn, pp. 24–28.

—— (1994) 'Rationalisierungsprozesse im Recht der Produktsicherheit: Öffentliches Recht und Haftungsrecht unter dem Einfluß der Europäischen Integration', *Jahrbuch für Umwelt- und Technikrecht* 27: 141–178.

—— (1995) 'Die Beurteilung der Sicherheit technischer Konsumgüter und der Gesundheitsrisiken von Lebensmitteln der Praxis des europäischen Ausschußwesens ("Komitologie")', ZERP-Diskussionspapier 1/95.

—— (1996a) 'The emergence of denationalized governance structures and the European Court of Justice', Oslo: ARENA Working Paper no. 16.

—— (1996b) 'Die Rolle des Rechts im Prozess der Europäischen Integration – Ein Plädoyer für die Beachtung des Rechts durch die Politikwissenschaft', in M. Jachtenfuchs and B. Kohler-Koch (eds) *Europäische Integration,* UTB, Leske & Budrich, pp. 73–108; 'Taking the law seriously: on political science and the role of law in the process of European integration', *European Law Journal* 2, 3: 105–135.

—— (1997a) 'The impact of European integration on private law: reductionist perceptions, true conflicts and a new constitutional perspective', *European Law Journal* 3: 378–406.

—— (1997b) 'Scientific expertise in social regulation and the European Court of Justice: legal frameworks for denationalised governance structures', in C. Joerges, K.–H. Ladeur and E. Vos (eds) *Integrating Scientific Expertise into Regulatory Decision-Making,* Baden-Baden, pp. 295–323.

—— (ed.) (1999) 'Die Beurteilung der Sicherheit technischer Konsumgüter und Gesundheitsrisiken von Lebensmitteln in der Praxis des europäischen Ausschusswesens ("Komitologie"). Ein Projekt zu den Rechtsgrundlagen, zur Funktionsweise und zur Legitimationsproblematik der Sozialregulierung in der Europäischen Gemeinschaft' , Baden-Baden (forthcoming).

Joerges, C. and Neyer, J. (1997) 'From intergovernmental bargaining to deliberative political processes: the constitutionalisation of comitology', *European Law Journal* 3, 3: 274–300.

Joerges, C., Falke, J., Micklitz, H.–W., and Brüggemeier, G. (1988) *Die Sicherheit von Konsumgütern und die Entwicklung der Europäischen Gemeinschaft,* Baden-Baden.

Johnson, J. (1993) 'Is talk really cheap? Prompting conversation between critical theory and rational choice', *American Political Science Review* 87: 74–86.

—— (1998) 'Arguing for deliberation: some skeptical considerations', in J. Elster (ed.) *Deliberative Democracy,* Cambridge: Cambridge University Press.

Jones, P. (1983) 'Political equality and majority rule', in D. Miller and L. Seidentop (eds) *The Nature of Political Theory,* Oxford: Clarendon Press, pp. 155–182.

Judge, D. (1995) 'The failure of national parliaments?', *West European Politics* 18, 3: 79–100.

Jurgens, E. (1994) 'A federal option for the European community or a permanent democracy deficit?', in Flinterman *et al.* (eds) *The Evolving Role of Parliaments in Europe,* Antwerp: Nomos Verlag.

Jønsson, C. (1990) 'Den transnationella maktens metaforer: Biljard, schack, teater eller spindelnæt', in G. Hansson and L.G. Stenelo (eds) *Makt och Internationalisering,* Stockholm: Carlsson.

Kant, I. (1795/1985) 'Perpetual peace', in H. Reiss (ed.) *Kant's Political Writings,* Cambridge: Cambridge University Press.

Kaplan, M.A. (1961) 'Problems of theory building and theory confirmation in international relations', in K. Knorr and S. Verba (eds) *The International System: Theoretical Essays,* Princeton, NJ: Princeton University Press.

Katzenstein, P.J. (1996) 'Regionalisation in comparative perspective', Working Paper 95/1, Oslo: ARENA.

Keane, J. (1993) 'Democracy and the media – without foundations', in J. Forester (ed.) *Critical Theory and Public Life*, Cambridge, Mass.: The MIT Press.

Keating, M. and Hooghe, L. (1996) 'By-passing the nation state? Regions and the EU policy process', in J. Richardson (ed.) *European Union: Power and Policy-making*, London and New York: Routledge, pp. 216–229.

Keck, M.E. and Sikkink, K. (1998) *Activists beyond Borders. Advocacy Networks in International Politics*, Ithaca, NY: Cornell University Press.

Kelsen, H. (2nd ed., 1929) *Vom Wesen der Demokratie*, Tübingen: J.C.B. Mohr.

Keohane, R.O. and Hoffmann, S. (1990) 'Conclusions: Community politics and institutional change', in W. Wallace (ed.) *The Dynamics of European Integration*, London: Pinter Publishers.

—— (1991) *The new European community: Decision-making and Institutional Change*, Boulder, Colorado: Westview Press.

Keohane, R.O. and Nye, J. (1977) *Power and Interdependence – World Politics in Transition*, Boston: Little, Brown and Company.

—— (1987) 'Power and interdependence revisited', *International Organization* 41, 4: 725–753.

Kerremans, B. (1996) 'Do institutions make a difference? Non-institutionalism, neo-institutionalism and the logic of common decision-making in the European Union', *Governance* 2: 217–240.

Kielmansegg, P.G (1996) 'Integration und Demokratie', in M. Jachtenfuchs and B. Kohler-Koch (eds) *Europäische Integration*, Opladen: Leske & Budrich.

Kirchner, E.J. (1980) 'Interest group behavior at the community level', in L. Hurwitz (ed.) *Contemporary Perspectives on European Integration*, London: Aldwych Press.

Kohler-Koch, B. (1996) 'Die Gestaltungsmacht organisierter Interessen', in M. Jachtenfuchs and B. Kohler-Koch (eds) *Europäische Integration*, Opladen: Leske & Budrich.

Krasner, S.D. (1982) *International Regimes*, Ithaca, New York: Cornell University Press.

Kratochwil, F.V. (1991) *Rules, Norms, and Decisions*, Cambridge: Cambridge University Press.

Kreher, A. (1997) 'Agencies in the European community – a step towards administrative integration in Europe', *Journal of European Public Policy* 4: 225–245.

—— (ed.) (1998) *The EC Agencies Between Community Institutions and Constituents: Autonomy, Control and Accountability*, San Domenico di Fiesole, EUI Florence.

Kundera, M. (1984) 'The Tragedy of Central Europe', *New York Review of Books* 26 (April).

Kymlicka, W. (1989) *Liberalism, Community and Culture*, Oxford: Clarendon Press.

—— (1995) *Multicultural Citizenship. A Liberal Theory of Minority Rights*, Oxford: Clarendon Press.

—— (1996) 'Social unity in a liberal state', *Social Philosophy and Policy: Community, Individual and the State* 13, 1: 105–136.

—— (1997) 'Do we need a liberal theory of minority rights? Reply to Carens, Young, Parekh and Forst', *Constellations* 4, 1: 72–87.

—— (1999) 'Theorizing indigenous rights', *University of Toronto Law Journal* 49, 2.

Köck, W. (1996) 'Risikovorsorge als Staatsaufgabe', *Archiv für öffentliches Recht* 121: 1–23.

Ladeur, K.–H. (1993) Von der Verwaltungshierarchie zum administrativen Netzwerk? *Die Verwaltung* 10: 137–165.

—— (1999) 'Towards a legal concept of the network in European standard-setting', in C. Joerges and E. Vos (eds) *European Committees: Social Regulation, Law and Politics*, Oxford: Hart, pp. 151–170.

Laffan, B. (1996) *Constitution-building in the European Union*, Dublin: Institute for European Affairs.
—— (1997) 'The IGC as constitution-building – what's new at Amsterdam?,' Paper prepared for ARENA Annual Conference 'The Amsterdam treaty-implications for Nordic countries: Analytical approach and empirical results', Oslo 6–7 November.
Lane, J.E. (1996) *Constitutions and Political Theory*, Manchester: Manchester University Press.
Laursen, F. (1997) 'The lessons of Maastricht', in G. Edwards and A. Pijpers (eds) *The Politics of European Treaty Reform*, London: Pinter.
Lax, D.A. and Sebenius, J.K. (1986) *The Manager as Negotiator: Bargaining for Cooperation and Competitive Gain*, New York: The Free Press, Macmillan.
Lefort, C. (1988) *Democracy and Political Theory*, Cambridge: Cambridge University Press.
Lehning, P.B. and Weale, A. (eds) (1997) *Citizenship, Democracy and Justice in the New Europe*, London and New York: Routledge, pp. 125–141.
Leonard, M. (1997) *Politics without Frontiers: The Role of Political Parties in Europe's Future*, London: Demos.
—— (1998) *Making Europe Popular: The Search for European Identity*, London: Demos.
Leroy, P. and Siune, K. (1994) 'The role of television in European elections: the cases of Belgium and Denmark', *European Journal of Communication* 9, 1: 47–69.
Lewis, D. (1998) *Indigenous Rights Claims in Welfare Capitalist Society: Recognition and Implementation. The case of the Saami people in Norway, Sweden and Finland*, Rovaniemi, Finland: University of Lapland, Arctic Centre Report.
Lijphart, A. (1979) 'Consociation and federation: conceptual and empirical links', *Canadian Journal of Political Science* 22, 3: 499–515.
—— (1984) *Democracies. Patterns of Majoritarian and Consensus Government in Twenty-one Countries*, New Haven and London: Yale University Press.
—— (1991) 'Self-determination versus pre-determination of ethnic minorities in power-sharing systems', in D. Schneiderman (ed.) *Language and the State: The Law and Politics of Identity*, Montreal: Les Editions Yvon Blais, pp. 153–165.
Linklater, A. (1996) 'Citizenship and sovereignty in the post-Westphalian state', *European Journal of International Relations* 2, 1: 77–103.
Lipponen, P. (1997) 'The European Union needs a policy for the northern dimension', in L. Heininen and R. Langlais (eds) *Europe's Northern Dimension: The BEAR Meets the South*, Rovaniemi, Finland: University of Lapland Press.
Lord, C. (1991) 'From intergovernmental to interparliamentary union', *Contemporary European Affairs* 4, 2/3.
Luban, D (1996): 'The publicity principle', in R.E. Goodin *The Theory of Institutional Design*, Cambridge: Cambridge University Press.
Luhmann, N. (1991) *Soziologie des Risikos*, Berlin: de Gruyter.
—— (1996) 'Jenseits von Barbarei', in M. Miller and H.G. Soeffner (eds) *Modernität und Barbarei*, Frankfurt: Suhrkamp, pp. 219–230.
Lundberg, E. (1995) 'Political freedoms in the European Union', in A. Rosas and E. Antola (eds) *A Citizens' Europe – In Search of a New Order*, London: Sage.
McCormick, J.P. (forthcoming) 'Parliament and the Court in the European Union: an evaluation of their potential as supranational democratic institutions', in J. Donnelly (ed.) *Democracy, Community and Social Justice in an Era of Globalization*, mimeo.
MacCormick, N. (1993) 'Beyond the sovereign state', *Modern Law Review* 56: 1–19.
—— (1995) 'The Maastricht-Urteil: sovereignty now', *European Law Journal* 1: 255–262.
—— (1996) 'Liberalism, nationalism and the post-sovereign state', in R. Bellamy and D. Castiglione *Constitutionalism in Transformation*, Oxford: Blackwell, pp. 141–156.

—— (1997) 'Democracy, subsidiarity, and citizenship in the "European Common-wealth" ', *Law and Philosophy* 16: 331–356.

Macedo, S. (1990) *Liberal Virtues: Citizenship, Virtue, and Community in Liberal Constitutionalism*, Oxford: Clarendon Press.

McGuigan, J. (1998) 'What price the public sphere?', in D.K. Thussu (ed.) *Electronic Empires: Global Media and Local Resistance*, London and New York: Arnold, pp. 91–107.

Machill, M. (1998) 'Euronews: the first European news channel as a case study for media industry development in Europe and for spectra of transnational journalism research', *Media, Culture and Society* 20, 3: 427–450.

Madison, J. (1787) 'Federalist Paper no. 10', in A. Hamilton, J. Madison, and J. Jay (1787–88 (1961)) *The Federalist* (ed. J.E. Cooke), Middletown, Conn.: Wesleyan Univ. Press.

Maine, H. (1917 [1861]) *Ancient Laws*, New York: Dutton and Co.

Majone, G. (ed.) (1990) *Deregulation or Re-regulation? Regulatory Reform in Europe and in the United States*, London: Pinter and New York: St. Martin's Press.

—— (1993a) 'The European community between social policy and social regulation', *Journal of Common Market Studies* 31: 153–150.

—— (1993b) 'The European community. An "independent fourth branch of govern-ment?" ', in G. Brüggemeier (ed.) *Verfassungen für ein ziviles Europa*, Baden-Baden: Nomos, pp. 23–44.

—— (1993c) 'Wann ist Policy-Deliberation wichtig?' in A. Héritier (ed.) *Policy-Analyse. Kritik und Neuorientierung*, *PVS* Sonderheft 24: 97–115.

—— (1994) 'Independence and accountability: non-majoritarian institutions and democratic government in Europe', in J. Weiler, R. Dehousse and S. Cassese (eds) *Collected Courses of the Academy of European Law*, London: Kluwer.

—— (1996a) *Regulating Europe*, London/New York: Routledge.

—— (1996b) 'Which social policy for Europe?', in Y. Mény, P. Muller and J. Quer-monne (eds) *Adjusting to Europe: The Impact of the European Union on National Institutions and Policies*, London: Routledge, pp. 123–136.

—— (1997) 'The new European agencies: regulation by information', *Journal of European Public Policy* 4: 262–275.

—— (1999) 'Europe's "Democratic Deficit": the question of standards', *European Law Journal* 4, 1: 5–28.

Mancini, G.F. (1989) 'The making of a constitution for Europe', *Common Market Law Review* 26: 595–614.

Mancini, G.F. and Weiler, J.H.H. (1998) 'Europe – The case for statehood … and the case against an exchange', Harvard Jean Monnet Chair, Working Paper Series, 6/98.

Manin, B. (1987) 'On legitimacy and political deliberation', *Political Theory* 15, 3: 338–368.

Mann, M. (1993) 'Nation-states in Europe and other continents: diversifying, developing, not dying', *Daedalus* 122, 3: 115–140.

Mansbridge, J. (1992) 'A deliberative theory of interest representation', in M.P. Petracca (ed.) *The Politics of Interests. Interest Groups Transformed*, Boulder, Colo.: Westview Press, pp. 32–57.

March J.G. and Olsen, J.P. (1989) *Rediscovering Institutions: The Organizational Basis of Politics*, New York: The Free Press.

—— (1995) *Democratic Governance*, New York: The Free Press.

—— (1998) 'The institutional dynamics of international political orders', *International Organization* 52, 4: 943–969.

March, J.G. and Simon, H. (1958) *Organizations*, New York: John Wiley & Sons.

Marks, G. (1993) 'Structural policy and multilevel governance in the EC', in A.W.

Cafrany and G.G. Rosenthal (eds) *The State of the European Community, vol. 2: The Maastricht Debates and Beyond*, London: Longman.

Marks, G., Hooghe, L. and Blank, K. (1996) 'European integration from the 1980s: State-centric *vs.* multi-level governance', *Journal of Common Market Studies* 34, 3: 341–378.

Marks, G., Scharpf, F.W., Schmitter, P. and Streek, W. (1996) *Governance in the European Union*, London: Sage.

Mashaw, J.L. and Rose-Ackerman, S. (1984) *Federalism and Regulation, in The Urban Institute, The Reagan Regulatory Strategy*, pp. 111ff. Washington D.C.

Mauss, I. (1996) 'Liberties and popular sovereignty: on Jürgen Habermas' reconstruction of the system of rights', *Cardozo Law Review* Part I 17, 4–5: 825–882.

Mayhew, L.H. (1997) *The New Public: Professional Communication and the Means of Social Influence*, Cambridge: Cambridge University Press.

Mazey, S and Mitchell, J. (1993) 'Europe of the regions: territorial interests and European integration: the Scottish experience', in S. Mazey (ed.) *Lobbying in the European Community*, Oxford: Oxford University Press, pp. 95–121.

Mazey, S. and Richardson, J. (1992) 'British pressure groups in the European Union', *Parliamentary affairs* 45, 1: 92–107.

Mead, G.H. (1962) *Mind, Self and Society from the Standpoint of a Social Behaviorist*, Chicago: University of Chicago Press.

Meehan, E. (1993) 'Citizenship and the European community', *The Political Quarterly* 64, 2: 172–186.

Michelman, F.I. (1989) 'Conceptions of democracy in American constitutional argument: the case of pornography regulations', *Tenn. Law. Rev.* 291.

Middlemas, K. (1995a) *Orchestrating Europe. The Informal Politics of European Union, 1973–1995*, London: Harper Collins.

—— (1995b) *Orchestrating Europe: The Informal Politics of European Union, 1973–1995*, London: Fontana Press.

Mill, J.S. (1859/1962) *On Liberty* (ed. M. Warnock), Glasgow: Collins.

—— (1859/1984) 'On Liberty', in *Utilitarianism, on Liberty and Considerations on Representative Government*, London: Everyman's Library.

—— (1931) 'On Liberty', in *Utalitarianism, Liberty and Representative Government*, London: Dent and Son Ltd.

Miller, D. (1992) 'Deliberative democracy and social choice', *Political Studies* 40 (Special Issue: Prospects for Democracy): 54–68.

—— (1995, 1997 pbk) *On Nationality*, Oxford: Oxford University Press.

Miller, M. and Soeffner, H.G. (eds) (1996) *Modernität und Barbarei*, Frankfurt: Suhrkamp.

Miller, V. and Ware, R. (1996) 'Keeping national parliaments informed: the problem of European legislation', *The Journal of Legislative Studies* 2, 3: 184–197.

Millward, A., Lynch, F.M.B., Romano, R., Ranieri, R. and Sørensen, V. (1993) *The Frontier of National Sovereignty: History and Theory, 1945–1992*, London: Routledge.

Mitchell, J. (1995) 'Lobbying Brussels: the case of Scotland Europa', *European Urban and Regional Studies* 2, 4: 287–298.

Montesquieu, C. (1748/1991) *The Spirit of Laws* (trans. by T. Nugent; revised by J.V. Prichard), Littleton, Colo.: F.B. Rothman.

Moravcsik, A. (1993) 'A liberal intergovernmental approach to the EC', *Journal of Common Market Studies* 31, 4: 473–524.

—— (1994) 'Why the European community strengthens the state: domestic politics and international cooperation', Paper presented at 'the Annual Meeting of the American Political Science Association', New York.

——— (1997) 'Taking preferences seriously: a liberal theory of international politics', *International Organization* 51, 4: 513–553.

——— (1998) *The Choice for Europe*, London: UCL Press.

Moravcsik, A. and Nicolaïdis, K. (1998) 'Keynote article: federal ideas and constitutional realities in the treaty of Amsterdam', *Journal of Common Market Studies* 36 (Annual Review): 13–38.

Morgan, D. (1995) 'British media and European news', *European Journal of Communication* 10, 3: 321–343.

Morgenthau, H.J. (1985) *Politics Among Nations: The Struggle for Power and Peace*, Sixth Edition, New York: Alfred A. Knopf.

——— (1993) *Politics Among Nations. The Struggle for Power and Peace*. New York: McGraw Hill (rev. K.W. Thompson).

Moxon-Browne, E. (1996) 'Citizens and parliaments', in B. Laffan *Constitution-Building in the European Union*, Dublin: Institute for European Affairs, pp. 71–92.

Müller, H. (1994) 'Internationale Beziehungen als kommunikatives Handeln. Zur Kritik der utilitaristischen Handlungstheorien', *Zeitschrift für Internationale Beziehungen* 1, 1: 15–44.

Navari, C. (1996) 'Functionalism versus federalism: alternative visions of European unity', in P. Murray and P. Rich *Visions of European Unity*, Boulder, Colorado: Westview Press.

Nentwich, M. (1998) 'Opportunity structures for citizens' participation: the case of the European Union', in A. Weale and M. Nentwich (eds) *Political Theory and the European Union*, London: Routledge.

Nentwich, M. and Falkner, G. (1997) 'The treaty of Amsterdam: towards a new institutional balance', *European Integration Online Papers (EIoP)* 1, 15, (http://eiop.or.at/eiop/texte/1997–015a.htm).

Nentwich, M. and Weale, A. (1998) 'Introduction', in A. Weale and M. Nentwich (eds) *Political Theory and the European Union*, London: Routledge.

Neyer, J. (1995) 'Globaler Markt und territorialer Staat', *Zeitschrift für Internationale Beziehungen* 2: 287–315.

Neyer, J. and Seeleib-Kaiser, M. (1995) 'Bringing Economy Back in', Zentrum für Sozialpolitik, University of Bremen, Working Paper 16/95.

Niblock, M. (1971) *The EEC: National Parliaments in the Community Decision-making*, London: Chatham House: PEP.

Nicoll, W. (1994) 'Representing the states', in A. Duff *et al. Maastricht and Beyond*, London: Routledge, pp. 190–206.

Niemi, E. (1997a) 'Kulturmøte, etnisitet og statlig intervensjon på Nordkalotten. Et historisk perspektiv', in *Den nordiska mosaiken*, Uppsala: Uppsala universitet, Humanist-dagarna 15–16 mars, rapport, pp. 261–272.

——— (1997b) 'Politikken: Staten og minoritetene', Foredrag ved symposiet 'Tre stammers møte', 13.–15.11.97, Tromsø: Universitetet i Tromsø.

Nino, C. (1996) *The Constitution of Deliberative Democracy*, New Haven, Conn.: Yale University Press.

Nystø, N.J. (1993) 'Najonalstat og minoritet. En komparativ studie av norsk og svensk samepolitikk', M.Phil. thesis, Tromsø: Institutt for samfunnsfag, Universitetet i Tromsø, hovedfagsoppgave.

Nystø, S.R. (1993) 'Sameregionen – et redskap for samisk selvstyre', Oslo: NSR-utredning.

——— (1996) 'Framtidige utfordringer for urfolkssamarbeidet i Barentsregionen', foredrag på 'Barents urfolkskonferanse', Murmansk, Russland, konferanse 16.10.96.

Oakeshott, M. (1975) 'The vocabulary of the modern European state', *Political Studies* 2–3: 319–341, and 4: 409–415.

Offe, C. (1982) 'Politische Legitimation durch Mehrheitsentscheidung', *Journal für Socialforschung* 22, 3: 294–318.

—— (1996) 'The utopia of the zero option', in C. Offe *Modernity and the State*, Cambridge: Polity.

—— (1997) 'Precariousness and the labor market', Berlin: manuscript.

—— (1998a) 'Demokratie und Wohlfahrtsstaat: eine europeische Regimeform unter dem Stress der europeischen Integration', Berlin, mimeo.

—— (1998b) 'The democratic welfare state: a European regime under the strain of European integration', mimeo.

Offe, C. and Preuss, U.K. (1991) 'Democratic institutions and moral resources', in D. Held (ed.) *Political Theory Today*, Cambridge: Polity.

Olsen, J.P. (1993) 'Utfordringer for den offentlige sektor og for statsvitenskapen. Noen sentrale spørsmål og problemstillinger', *Norsk Statsvitenskapelig Tidsskrift*, 1: 3–28.

—— (1998) 'Skiftende politiske fellesskap', in J.P. Olsen and B.O. Sverdrup (eds) *Europa i Norden. Europeisering av Nordisk Samarbeid*, Oslo: Tano-Aschehoug.

Olson, M. (1965) *The Logic of Collective Action*, Cambridge, Mass.: Harvard University Press.

Oskal, N. (1995): 'Liberalisme og urbefolkningsrettigheter', *Norsk Filosofisk tidsskrift* 30, 2–3: 59–76.

—— (1998a) 'Urfolksvern og demokrati: Om det moralske grunnlaget for Samiske rettigheter. Noen betraktninger om Samerettsutvalgets innstilling (NOU 1997:4) med vekt på grunnsynet', in E.G. Broderstad (ed.) *Samiske rettigheter – utfordringer lokalt, regionalt, nasjonalt og internasjonalt*, Tromsø: Senter for Samiske studier, Universitetet i Tromsø, Skriftserie nr. 5.

—— (1998b) 'Saami situation in Norway – Normative foundations of claims on securing a voice and place for Aboriginality in a context of a nationstate', International Arctic Social Sciences Association (forthcoming).

Østerud, Ø. (1991) *Statsvitenskap: Innføring i Politisk Analyse*, Oslo: Universitetsforlaget.

—— (1994) *Hva er Nasjonalisme?*, Oslo: Universitetsforlaget.

Pag, S. (1987) 'The relation between the commission and national bureaucracies', in S. Cassesse (ed.) *The European Administration*, IISA.

Peach, B. (1979) *Richard Price and the Ethical Foundations of the American Revolution*, Durham, NC: Duke University Press.

Pedersen, S. (1999) 'Statens eiendomsrett til grunnen i Finnmark – en del av den interne "kolonihistorie" ', in H. Eidheim (ed.) *Samer og Nordmennn*, Oslo: Cappelen Akademisk Forlag.

Perraton, J., Goldblatt, D., Held, D. and McGrew, A. (1997) 'The globalization of economic activity', *New Political Economy* 2, 2 (July).

Peters, B. (1994) 'On reconstructive legal and political theory', *Philosophy and Social Criticism* 20, 4: 101–134.

Pettit, P. (1997) *Republicanism: A Theory of Freedom and Government*, Oxford: Clarendon Press.

Pildes, R.H. and Sunstein, C.R. (1995) 'Reinventing the regulatory state', *Chicago Law Review* 62, 1–129.

Pinder, J. (1991) *European Community – the Building of a Union*, Oxford: Oxford University Press.

—— (1994) 'Building the union: policy, reform, constitution', in A. Duff, J. Pinder, and R. Pryce (eds) *Maastricht and Beyond: Building the European Union*, London: Routledge.

Pitkin, H. (1967) *The Concept of Representation*, California: University of California Press.

Plunkett, J. (1998) 'What's the story with euronews?', *Broadcast* 3 April, pp. 18–19.

Pogge, T.W. (1998) 'How to create supra-national institutions democratically. Some reflections on the European Union's "democratic deficit" ', in A. Føllesdal and P. Koslowski (eds) *Democracy and the European Union*, Berlin: Springer Verlag, pp. 160–185.

Pollack, M.A. (1997): 'Delegation, agency and agenda setting in the European community', *International Organization* 51: 99–134.

Poole, R. (1999) 'Autonomie gouvernmentale et peuples autochthones: libération nationale ou citoyenneté? ('Self-determination and indigenous people: National liberation or citizenship?'), in Michel Seymour (ed), *Nationalité, Citoyenneté et Solidarité*, Montréal: Éditions Liber.

Preuss, U.K. (1996a) 'Prospects of a constitution for Europe', *Constellations* 3, 2: 209–224.

—— (1996b) 'Two challenges to European citizenship', *Political Studies* 44, 3 (Special Issue): 534–552.

—— (1996c) 'Two challenges to European citizenship', in R. Bellamy and D. Castiglione (eds) *Constitutionalism in Transformation: European and Theoretical Perspectives*, Oxford: Blackwell, pp. 122–140.

—— (1997) 'Migration – A challenge to modern citizenship', *Constellations* 4, 3: 307–319.

—— (1998) 'Citizenship in the European Union: a paradigm for transnational democracy', in D. Archibugi, D. Held and M. Köhler (eds) *Re-imagining Political Community*, Cambridge: Polity Press.

Prittwitz, V. von (1996) 'Verständigung über die Verständigung. Anmerkungen und Ergänzungen zur Debatte über Rationalität und Kommunikation in den Internationalen Beziehungen', *Zeitschrift für Internationale Beziehungen* 3: 133–147.

Przeworski, A. (1997) 'Democracy and representation', paper presented for 'the II Inter-American Congress of CLAD', Venezuela.

Raiffa, H. (1982) *The Art and Science of Negotiation*, Cambridge, Mass.: Harvard University Press.

Rakoff, S.H. and Schaefer, G.F. (1970) 'Politics, Policy and Political Science: Theoretical Alternatives', *Politics and Society* 1: 51–77.

Rawls, J. (1971) *A Theory of Justice*, Cambridge, MA: Cambridge University Press.

—— (1993) *Political Liberalism*, New York: Columbia University Press.

—— (1997) 'The idea of public reason', in J. Bohman and W. Rehg (eds) *Deliberative Democracy*, Cambridge, MA: The MIT Press.

Raworth, P. (1993) *The Legislative Process in the European Community*, Deventer, Boston: Kluwer Law and Taxation Publ.

Rehbinder, E. and Stewart, R. (1985) *Environmental Protection Policy. Integration Through Law*, vol. 2, Berlin/New York.

Riker, W.H. (1982) *Liberalism Against Populism*, San Francisco: Freeman.

Risse, T. (1997) ' "Let's talk!" Insights from the German debate on communicative behavior and international relations', Paper presented to the 'Annual Convention of The American Political Science Association', Washington DC, Aug. 27–31, 1997.

—— (1999) 'International norms and domestic change: arguing and strategic adaptation in the human rights area', in K. McNamara and S. Berman (eds) *Europeanization and Domestic Change*, Cambridge: Cambridge University Press.

Risse-Kappen, T. (1995) 'Reden ist nicht billig. Zur Debatte um Kommunikation und Rationalität', *Zeitschrift für Internationale Beziehungen* 2: 171–184.

—— (1996) 'Exploring the nature of the beast: international relations theory and comparative policy analysis meet the European Union', *Journal of Common Market Studies* 34, 1: 53–80.

Rittberger, V. (ed.) (1993) *Regime Theory and International Relations*, Oxford: Clarendon Press.

Rokkan, S. (1975) 'Dimensions of state formation and nation building: a possible paradigm for research on variations within Europe', in C. Tilly (ed.) *The Formation of National States in Western Europe*, Princeton: Princeton University Press, pp. 562–600.

Rosenau, J.N. and Czempiel, E.O. (eds) (1992) *Governance Without Government: Order and Change in World Politics*, Cambridge: Cambridge University Press.

Ross, J., Hoffman, S. and Levack, P. (eds) (1949) *Burke's Politics*, New York: A. Knopf.

Roung, I. (1982) *Samerna*, Stockholm: Bonniers.

RSL (1995) *The Pan European Survey 6: The Results of the 1995 Fourteen Country Survey*, Harrow: Research Services Ltd.

—— (1996) *The European Business Readership Survey 1996*, Harrow: Research Services Ltd.

Ruggie, J.G. (1993) 'Territoriality and beyond: problematizing modernity in international relations', *International Organization* 47, 1: 139–174.

Sanders, L.M. (1997) 'Against Deliberation', *Political Theory* 25 (June): 347–377.

Sandholtz, W. (1996) 'Membership matters: limits of the functional approach to European institutions', *Journal of Common Market Studies* 34, 3: 403–429.

Sartori, G. (1970) 'Concept misformation in comparative politics', *The American Political Science Review* LXIV, 4: 1033–1053.

Sasse, C.E., *et al.* (1977) *Decision Making in the European Community*, London: Praeger.

Saward, M. (1998) *The Terms of Democracy*, Cambridge: Polity Press.

Scalia, L.J. (1991) 'Self-interest and democratic theory', in K.R. Monroe (ed.) *The Economic Approach to Politics*, New York: Harper Collins.

Scanlon, T.M. (1982) 'Contractualism and utilitarianism', in A.K. Sen and B. Williams (eds) *Utilitarianism and Beyond*, Cambridge: Cambridge University Press, pp. 103–128.

Schaefer, G.F. (1996) 'Committees in the EC policy process: a first step towards developing a conceptual framework', in R.H. Pedler and G.F. Schaefer (eds) *Shaping European Law and Policy. The Role of Committees and Comitology in the Political Process*, Maastricht: European Centre for Public Affairs, pp. 3–23.

Scharpf, F.W. (1985) 'Die Politikverflechtungs-Falle. Europäische Integration und deutscher Föderalismus im Vergleich', *Politische Vierteljahresschrift* 26: 323–356.

—— (1988) 'The joint decision trap: Lessons from German federalism and European integration', *Public Administration* 66: 239–278.

—— (1992a) 'Einführung: Zur Theorie von Verhandlungssystemen', in A. Benz, F.W. Scharpf and R. Zintl (eds) *Horizontale Politikverflechtung. Zur Theorie von Verhandlungssystemen*, Frankfurt, pp. 11–27.

—— (1992b) 'Koordination durch Verhandlungssysteme: Analytische Konzepte und institutionelle Lösungen', in A. Benz, F.W. Scharpf and R. Zintl (eds) *Horizontale Politikverflechtung. Zur Theorie von Verhandlungssystemen*, Frankfurt: Campus, pp. 51–96.

—— (1994) 'Community and autonomy: multi-level policy-making in the European Union', *Journal of European Public Policy* 1: 219–242.

—— (1996a) 'Democratic policy in Europe', *European Law Journal* 2: 136–155.

—— (1996b) 'Föderalismus und Demokratie in der transnationalen Ökonomie', in K. von Beyme and C. Offe (eds) *Politische Theorien in der Ära der Transformation*, Oplanden: Westdeutscher Verlag.

—— (1996c) 'Negative and positive integration in the political economy of European welfare states', in G. Marks, F.W. Scharpf, P. Schmitter and W. Streeck *Governance in the European Union*, London: Sage.

—— (1997a) 'Economic integration, democracy and the welfare state', *Journal of European Public Policy* 4: 18–36.

—— (1997b) 'The problem-solving capacity of multi-level governance', *Journal of European Public Policy* 4: 520–538.

—— (1997c) *Games Real Actors Play. Actor-centered Institutionalism in Policy Research*, Boulder: Westview.

—— (1997d) 'Die Malaise der deutschen Politik', *Frankfurter Allgemeine Zeitung* June 5, p. 35.

Schelling, T.C. (1960) *The Strategy of Conflict*, Cambridge, Mass.: Harvard University Press.

Schimmelfennig, F. (1999) 'The double puzzle of enlargement', Oslo: ARENA, Working Paper.

Schlacke, S. (1998) *Risikoentscheidungen im europäischen Lebensmittelrecht: Eine Untersuchung am Beispiel des europäischen Zusatzstoffrechts unter besonderer Berücksichtigung des europäischen Ausschußwesens ('Komitologie')*, Baden-Baden.

Schlesinger, P. (1993) 'Wishful thinking: cultural politics, media and collective identities in Europe', *Journal of Communication* 43, 2: 6–17.

—— (1994) 'Europe's contradictory communicative space', *Daedalus* 123, 2: 25–52.

—— (1995) 'Europeanisation and the media: National identity and the public sphere', Oslo: ARENA Working Paper no. 7.

—— (1997) 'From cultural defence to political culture: the European Union, the media and collective identity', *Media, Culture and Society* 19, 3: 369–391.

—— (1998) 'Scottish devolution and the media', in J. Seaton (ed.) *Politics and the Media Prerogatives and Harlots at the Turn of the Millennium*, Oxford: Blackwell, pp. 56–75.

—— (1999) 'Changing spaces of political communication: the case of the European Union', *Political Communication* 16, 3: 263–279.

—— (2000) 'The nation and communicative space', in H. Tumber (ed.) *Media, Power, Professionals and Policies*, London and New York: Routledge (forthcoming).

Schmitt von Sydow, H. (1980) *Organe der erweiterten Europäischen Gemeinschaften – die Kommission*, Baden-Baden.

Schmitter, P. (1992) 'Representation and the future Euro-polity', *Staatswissenschaft und Staatspraxis* III, 3: 379–405.

—— (1996a) 'If the nation state were to wither away in Europe, what might replace it?', in S. Gustavsson and L. Lewin (eds) *The Future of the Nation-state: Essays on Cultural Pluralism and Political Integration*, Stockholm: Nerenius and Santérus.

—— (1996b) *How to Democratize the Emerging Euro-polity: Citizenship, Representation, Decision-making*, mimeo.

—— (1998) 'Is it really possible to democratize the Euro-polity?', in A. Føllesdal and P. Koslowski (eds) *Democracy and the European Union*, Heidelberg: Springer Verlag, pp. 13–36.

Schumpeter, J.A. (1942/1976) *Capitalism, Socialism, and Democracy*, London: George Allen and Unwin.

Senghaas, D. (1994) 'Interdependenzen im internationalen System', in G. Krell and H. Müller (eds) *Frieden und Konflikt in den Internationalen Beziehungen*, pp. 190–222. Frankfurt: Suhrkamp.

Shapiro, I. (1996) *Democracy's Place*, New York: Cornell University Press.

Shapiro, M. (1997) 'The problem of independent agencies in the United States and the European Union', *Journal of European Public Policy* 4: 276–291.

Shaw, J. (1996) *Law of the European Union*, 2nd ed., London: Macmillan.

Shrader-Frechette, K.S. (1991) *Risk and Rationality*, Berkeley: University of California Press.

Sillanpää, L. (1994) *Political and Administrative Responses to Saami Self-determination. A Comparative Study of Public Administration in Fennoscandia on the Issue of Saami Land Title as an Aboriginal Right*, Helsinki, Finland: The Finnish Society of Sciences and Letters, Commentationes Scientiarum Socialium, 48.

—— (1997) 'A comparative analysis of indigenous rights in Fennoscandia', *Scandinavian Political Studies* 20, 3: 197–217.

Skinner, Q. (1989) 'The state', in T. Ball, J. Farrand and R.L. Hanson *Political Innovation and Conceptual Change*, Cambridge: Cambridge University Press.

Smith, A.D. (1991) *National Identity*, London: Penguin.

Smith, C. (1990) 'Samiske interesser i fiskerireguleringssammenheng. Sakkyndig vurdering av hvilke rettslige forpliktelser myndighetene er bundet av overfor den samiske befolkningen ved reguleringer i fisket'. Avgitt til Det kgl. fiskeridepartement, Oslo, 9 July.

—— (1995) 'The development of Saami rights since 1980', in T. Brantenberg, J. Hansen and H. Minde (eds) *Becoming Visible. Indigenous Politics and Self-government*, Tromsø: University of Tromsø, Centre for Saami Studies.

—— (1996) 'Fra Samerettsutvalget til Sametinget' (From the Saami Rights Commission to the Saami Parliament), speech to the Norwegian Saami Parliament 27.02.96, Karasjok, Norge.

Smith, M.P. (1996) 'Democratic legitimacy in the European Union: fulfilling the institutional logic', *The Journal of Legislative Studies* 2, 4: 283–302.

Snyder, F. (ed.) (1994) 'A regulatory framework for foodstuffs in the internal market', EUI Working Paper Law 94/4, San Domenico di Fiesole.

Soysal, Y. (1994) *Limits of Citizenship – Migrants and Postnational Membership in Europe*, Chicago: University of Chicago Press.

Sparks, C. (1998) 'Is there a global public sphere?', in D.K. Thussu (ed.) *Electronic Empires: Global Media and Local Resistance*, London and New York: Arnold, pp. 108–124.

Stordahl, V. (1994) 'Identity and Saaminess: Expressing world view and nation', in *Majority–minority Relations. The Case of the Saami in Scandinavia*, report, The World Commission on Culture and Development, Diedut, no. 1, Kautokeino, Norge: Nordic Saami Institute.

Storing, H. (1985) *The Anti-federalist*, 2 vols., Chicago: University of Chicago Press.

Streeck, W. (1995) 'Neo-voluntarism: A new European social policy regime?', *European Law Journal* 1, 1: 1–59.

—— (1996) 'Neo-voluntarism: A new European social policy regime?', in G. Marks *et al. Governance in the European Union*, London: Sage, pp. 64–94.

Sunstein, C. (1988) 'Constitutions and democracies: An epilogue', in J. Elster and R. Slagstad (eds) *Constitutionalism and Democracy*, Cambridge/Oslo: Cambridge University Press/Universitetsforlaget.

—— (1990) 'Political self-interest in constitutional law', in J.J. Mansbridge (ed.) *Beyond Self-interest*, Chicago: The University of Chicago Press.

—— (1991) 'Preferences and politics', *Philosophy and Public Affairs* 20, 1: 3–38.

—— (1993) *The Partial Constitution*, Cambridge, Mass.: Harvard University Press.

—— (1994) 'Approaching democracy: a new legal order for Eastern Europe – Constitutionalism and secession', in C. Brown (ed.) *Political Restructuring in Europe: Ethical Perspectives*, London: Routledge, pp. 11–49.

—— (1996) 'Public deliberation, affirmative action, and the Supreme Court', *California Law Review* 84, 4: 1179–1200.

Sverdrup, U. (1998) 'Norway: an adaptive non-member', in K. Hanf and B. Soetendorp (eds) *Adapting to European Integration. Small States and the European Union*, Harlow, Essex: Addison Wesley Longman, pp. 149–166.

Tarrow, S. (1995) 'The Europeanisation of conflict: Reflections from social movements research', *West European Politics* 18, 2: 223–251.

Taylor, C. (1985) *Human Agency and Language*, Cambridge: Cambridge University Press.

—— (1986) *Philosophy and the Human Sciences*, Cambridge: Cambridge University Press.

—— (1989) *Sources of the Self: The Making of the Modern Identity*, Cambridge, MA: Harvard University Press.

—— (1994) 'The politics of recognition', in A. Gutmann and C. Taylor (eds) *Multiculturalism*, Princeton, NJ: Princeton University Press.

—— (1995) *Philosophical Arguments*, Cambridge: Harvard University Press.

Thompson, J. (1998) 'Community identity and world citizenship', in D. Archibugi, D. Held and M. Kohler *Re-imagining Political Community: Studies in Cosmopolitan Democracy*, London: Polity, pp.179–197.

Thuen, T. (1995) *Quest for equity. Norway and the Saami Challenge*, Newfoundland: Institute of Social and Economic Research (ISER), Memorial University of Newfoundland, Canada.

Tinbergen, J. (1965) *International Economic Integration*, 2nd edition, Amsterdam: Elsevier.

Traxler, F. and Schmitter, P. (1995) 'The emerging Euro-polity and organized interests', *European Journal of International Relations* 1, 2: 191–218.

Tully, J. (1995) *Strange Multiplicity. Constitutionalism in an Age of Diversity*, Cambridge: Cambridge University Press.

Tumber, H. (1995) 'Marketing Maastricht: the EU and news management', *Media, Culture and Society* 17, 3: 511–519.

van Parijs, P. (1996) 'Justice and democracy: are they incompatible?', *The Journal of Political Philosophy* 4: 101–117.

—— (1998) 'Should the European Union become more democratic?', in A. Føllesdal and P. Koslowski (eds) *Democracy and the European Union*, Berlin: Springer Verlag, pp. 287–301.

Vatonena, L. (1995) 'The Saami in Russia today', in T. Brantenberg, J. Hansen and H. Minde (eds) *Becoming Visible. Indigenous Politics and Self-government*, Tromsø: University of Tromsø, Centre for Saami Studies.

Vile, M. (1967) *Constitutionalism and the Separation of Powers*, Oxford: Oxford University Press.

Voelzkow, H. (1996) *Private Regierungen in der Techniksteuerung. Eine Sozialwissenschaftliche Analyse der technischen Normung*, Frankfurt/New York: Campus.

Vos, E. (1997) 'The rise of committees', *European Law Journal* 3, 3: 210–229.

—— (1999) *Institutional Frameworks of Community Health and Safety Regulation – Committees, Agencies and Private Bodies*, Oxford: Hart.

Wæver, O. (1990) 'Three competing Europes: German, French, Russian', *International Affairs* 66, 3: 477–494.

Wallace, H. (1993) 'Deepening and widening: problems of legitimacy for the EC', in S. Garcia (ed.) *European Identity and the Search for Legitimacy*, London: Pinter, pp. 95–105.

Wallace, W. (ed.) (1990) *The Dynamics of European Integration*, London: Pinter Publishers.

Waltz, K.N. (1959) *Man, the State and War: A Theoretical Analysis*, New York: Columbia University Press.

—— (1979) *Theory of International Politics*, New York: McGraw-Hill.

Warleigh, A. (1998) 'Better the devil you know? Synthetic and confederal understandings of European unification', *West European Politics* 21: 1–18.

Weale, A. (1992) 'Social choice', in S. Hargreaves Heap *et al. The Theory of Choice. A Critical Guide*, Oxford: Blackwell, pp. 199–215.

—— (1994) 'Single market, European integration and political legitimacy', Paper presented at the 'Evolution of rules for a single European market', ESRC Conference, University of Exeter, 8–11 September.

—— (1995) 'Democratic legitimacy and the constitution of Europe', in R. Bellamy *et al.* (eds) *Democracy and Constitutional Culture in the Union of Europe*, London: Lothian Foundation Press, pp. 81–94.

—— (1997) 'Majority rule, political identity and European Union', in P.B. Lehning and A. Weale (eds) *Citizenship, Democracy and Justice in the New Europe*, London and New York: Routledge, pp. 125–141.

—— (1998) 'Between representation and constitutionalism in the European Union', in A. Weale and M. Nentwich (eds) *Political Theory and the European Union*, London and New York: Routledge, pp. 49–62.

Weale, A. and Nentwich, M. (eds) (1998) *Political Theory and the European Union. Legitimacy, Constitutional Choice and Citizenship*, London and New York: Routledge.

Weigård, J. (1995) 'Representasjon og rasjonalitet', in E.O. Eriksen (ed.) *Deliberativ politikk. Demokrati i teori og praksis*, Oslo: Tano, pp. 70–104.

Weiler, J. (1991) 'The transformation of Europe', *Yale Law Journal* 100: 2403–2483.

—— (1993) 'Journey to an unknown destination: a retrospective and prospective of the European Court of Justice in the arena of political integration', *Journal of Common Market Studies* 31, 4: 417–446.

—— (1994) 'A quiet revolution. The European Court of Justice and its interlocutors', *Comparative Political Studies* 26, 4: 510–534.

—— (1995) 'Does Europe need a constitution? Demos, Telos and the German Maastricht decision', *European Law Journal* 1, 3: 219–258.

—— (1996a) 'European neo-constitutionalism: in search of foundations for the European constitutional order', in R. Bellamy and D. Castiglione (eds) *Constitutionalism in Transformation*, Oxford: Blackwell, pp. 105–121.

—— (1996b) 'Legitimacy and democracy of union governance: the 1996 intergovernmental agenda and beyond', Working Paper 96/22, Oslo: ARENA.

—— (1997) 'The reformation of European constitutionalism', *Journal of Common Market Studies* 35, 1: 97–131.

—— (1999a) *The Constitution of Europe, 'Do the New Clothes have an Emperor?' and Other Essays on European Integration*, London: Cambridge University Press.

—— (1999b) 'Comitology' as revolution: infranationalism, constitutionalism and democracy', in C. Joerges and E. Vos (eds) *EU Committees: Social Regulation, Law and Politics*, Oxford: Hart, pp. 339–350.

Wendt, A. (1993) 'Collective identity formation and the international state', *American Political Science Review* 88, 2: 384–396.

Wessels, W. (1990) 'Administrative interaction', in W. Wallace (ed.) *The Dynamics of European Integration*, London/New York, pp. 229–241.

—— (1991) 'The EC Council: The community's decision-making center', in R.O. Keohane and S. Hoffmann (eds) *The New European Community*, Boulder: Westview Press.

—— (1992) 'Staat und (westeuropäische) Integration. Die Fusionsthese', in M. Kreile (ed.) *Die Integration Europas, Politische Vierteljahresschrift*, Sonderheft 23: 36–61, Opladen, Westdeutscher Verlag.

—— (1996) 'Verwaltung im EG-Mehrebenensystem: Auf dem Weg zur Megabürokratie?', in M. Jachtenfuchs and B. Kohler-Koch (eds) *Europäische Integration*, Opladen, pp. 165–192.

—— (1998) 'Comitology: fusion in action. Politico-administrative trends in the EU system', *Journal of European Public Policy* 5, 2: 209–234.

Wessels, W. and Rometsch, D. (1994) 'The commission and the council of the union', in G. Edwards and D. Spence (eds) *The European Commission*, London: Cartermill, pp. 213–239.

Westlake, M. (1995) *The Council of the European Union*, London: Cartermill.

White, M. (1987) *Philosophy, the Federalist, and the Constitution*, Oxford: Oxford University Press.

Wiener, A. (1998) *'European' Citizenship*, Boulder: Westview Press.

Wiesenthal, H. (1995) 'Globalisierung. Soziologische und politikwissenschaftliche Koordinaten eines unbekannten Territoriums', Bremen, manuscript.

Wiethölter, R. (1972) 'Wirtschaftsrecht', in A. Görlitz (ed.) *Handlexikon zur Rechtswissenschaft*, München: Ehrenwirth, pp. 531–539.

Williams, S. (1991) 'Sovereignty and accountability in the European community', in R.O. Keohane and S. Hoffmann (eds) *The New European Community*, Boulder: Westview Press.

Willke, H. (1997) *Supervision des Staates*, Frankfurt: Suhrkamp.

Wincott, D. (1996) 'The Court of Justice and the European policy process', in J. Richardson (ed.) *European Union: Power and Policy-making*, London and New York: Routledge, pp. 170–199.

Wober, J.M. (1987) 'Voting in Europe: television and viewers' involvement in the 1984 European parliamentary election', *European Journal of Communication* 2, 4: 473–489.

Young, I.M. (1990) *Justice and the Politics of Difference*, Princeton, NJ: Princeton University Press.

Young, O.R. (1986) 'International regimes: toward a new theory of institutions', *World Politics* 39: 104–122.

Zürn, M. (1996) 'Über den Staat und die Demokratie im Europäischen Mehrebenensystem', *Politische Vierteljahresschrift* 37: 27–55.

—— (1998) 'Democratic governance beyond the nation state', Bremen, mimeo.

Zürn, M. and Zangl, B. (1996) 'Argumentatives Verhandeln bei internationalen Verhandlungen. Moderate Anmerkungen zur post-realistischen Debatte', *Zeitschrift für Internationale Beziehungen* 3: 341–366.

Official documents

Commission of the European Communities: 'First European community framework programme in support of culture (2000–2004)'.

Commission of the European Communities (1998) 'A new policy on indigenous peoples by the European commission', SEC (1998) 773 final, May, Brussels, 11.05.98.

Council of the European Communities (1992) 'Treaty on European Union', Brussels.

Council of Ministers (1998) 'Indigenous peoples within the framework of the development co-operation of the Community and the Member States', 30.11.1998.

Council of the Union (1996) Report of 6 April 1995 on the operation of the treaty on European Union, in European Parliament, intergovernmental conference task force: 'White Paper on the 1996 Intergovernmental Conference', vol. I, Luxembourg.

Denmark, Grindsted Public, April 20, 1998, presented by Folketingets EU-Opplysning.

Denmark, Udenriksministeriet (1995) 'Det Åbne Europa', 11/12, 1995 INTERNET version.

Denmark, Udenriksministeriet (1996) 'På vej mod det åbne Europa'.

Denmark, Udenriksministeriet (1997) 'Tæt på det åbne Europa'.

EC (1963) Van Gend en Loos, Case 26/62 ECR1.

EC (1964) Costa v. Enel, Case 120/24 ECR593.

EC Commission (1980) 'Commission Report on the effects of the ECJ judgment of 20 February 1979 on Case 120/79 ("Cassis de Dijon").'

EC Commission (1985a) 'Commission White Paper to the European Council on the completion of the internal market', COM (85) 310 final of 14.6.1985.

EC Commission (1985b) 'New concepts in the field of technical harmonisation and standardisation', COM (85) 19 final of 31.1.1985.

EC Commission (1990a) 'Green Paper – standardisation –' COM (90), 456 final (OJ C 20/1991, 1).

EC Commission (1990b) 'Industrial policy in an open and competitive environment: guidelines for a community approach', COM (90), 556 final of 16. 11.1990.

EC Commission (1991), 'Declaration No. 17 annexed to the final act of the treaty on European Union, on the right of access to information', Maastricht Conference, 7 February.

EC Commission (1994), 'Information, communication, openness', ISEC/B25/1994 Luxembourg.

EC Commission (1995), 'Background report on information and relay networks', BR/14/95, Luxembourg, November.

EC Commission (1996), 'Information programme for the European citizen', CC-99-96-803-EN-C, Luxembourg.

EC Commission (1997a) 'Final consolidated report to the temporary committee of the European Parliament on the follow-up of recommendations on BSE', COM (97) 509 final of 20/10/1997.

EC Commission (1997b) 'General principles of food law in the European Union – Commission Green Paper on Food Law', COM (97) 176 final.

European Council (1995) '1996 Intergovernmental conference: Reflection group report', Brussels.

European Council (1995) 'Report of the council on the functioning of the treaty on European Union', Luxembourg, 1995:15.

European Council, conference of the representatives of the governments of the member states (1996) 'The European Union today and tomorrow – adapting the European Union for the benefit of its peoples and preparing it for the future', Dublin II, CONF 2500/96.

European Council, conference of the representatives of the governments of the member states (1997) 'Draft treaty of Amsterdam', CONF/4000/97.

European Council (1997) Turin European Council (29 March 1996): 'Presidency conclusions on the intergovernmental conference', in Italian Presidency, collected texts, Brussels.

European Council 'Presidency conclusions', Dublin and Amsterdam summit meetings.

European Council and Council of the Union (1996) 'A report of 6 April 1995 on the operation of the treaty on European Union', in European Parliament, Intergovernmental Conference Task Force: 'White Paper on the 1996 intergovernmental conference', vol. I, (5082/95), Luxembourg.

European Council and Council of the Union (1996) Reflection group report of 5 December 1995, in European Parliament Intergovernmental Conference Task Force: 'White Paper on the 1996 intergovernmental conference', vol. I, Luxembourg. Also available as SN 520/95 (REFLEX 21).

European Parliament (1994) 'Official Journal of the European Communities', A3–0059/94.

European Parliament, 'Resolution of 17 May (1995) on the operation of the treaty on European Union with a view to the 1996 intergovernmental conference', in European Parliament, Intergovernmental Conference Task Force: 'White Paper on the 1996 intergovernmental conference', vol. I, Luxembourg.

European Parliament, 'Resolution of 14 December (1995) on the agenda for the 1996 intergovernmental conference with a view to the Madrid European Council'.

European Parliament, Secretariat Working Party (1996) 'Note to Mr. Hansch, President, and Mr. Vinci, Secretary-General, on parliament's views regarding the IGC and current progress of the negotiations', Strasbourg, 12 December 1996.

European Parliament (1996) 'Resolution om Europaparlamentets yttrande om sammankallande till regeringskonferensen och utvardering av reflektionsgruppens arbete och precisering av Europaparlamentets politiska prioriteringar infor regeringskonferensen', Bulletin EU 3–1996.

European Parliament (1996) 'Opinion of parliament on the convening of the IGC', in 'Collected texts of the Italian presidency', prepared by the General Secretariat of the Council of the European Union.

European Parliament, Intergovernmental Conference Task Force: 'White Paper on the 1996 Intergovernmental Conference', vol. I–III, Luxembourg.

European Parliament (1997) 'Bericht über behauptete Verstöße gegen das Gemeinschaftsrecht bzw. Mißstände bei der Anwendung desselben im Zusammenhang mit BSE unbeschadet der Zuständigkeiten der nationalen und gemeinschaftlichen Gerichte', session documents, PE 220.544/end/Teil A (A4–0020/97).

European Parliament (1997) 'Report of the Commission for Environmental Issues, Public Health and Consumer Protection on the proposal of the commission for a council directive on commission support and member states cooperation in the scientific examination of food issues' (PE Doc. A 3–97/92).

European Parliament (1997) Committee on Institutional Affairs, Rapporteur: Ms Annemie Neyts-Uyttebroeck, 22 May, 'On the relations between the European Parliament and national parliaments', Report A7 4–0179/9.

European Parliament's General Secretariat Working Party Task Force on the Intergovernmental Conference (1997) 'Note for the attention of Mr. Jose Maria Gil-Robles Gil-Delgado, President of the European Parliament and Mr Julian Priestley, Secretary General, on the European Parliament's priorities for the IGC and the new Amsterdam Treaty: Report and initial evaluation of the results', DOC_EN\DV\332\332457, 15 July 1997.

European Parliament, Committee on Institutional Affairs (1997) 'Report on the Amsterdam Treaty', (CONF 4007/97–C4–0538/97) Strasbourg, 5 November 1997.

Germany, Scientific Advisory Council (1986) 'Stellungnahme zum Weißbuch der EG-Kommission über den Binnenmarkt', Schriften-Reihe 51, Bonn.

Government of Canada, 'Canada's Aboriginal action plan (1998) "Gathering strength" ', Ottawa, Ontario: Department of Indian Affairs and Northern Development, January.

ILO convention no. 169 concerning indigenous and tribal peoples in independent countries, Oslo, Norway: Kommunaldepartementet.

Nordic Saami Convention (1998) 'Behov og grunnlag for en Nordisk Samekonvensjon', (Report about the need and foundation for a Nordic Saami Convention), June, Oslo, Norway: Kommunal- og regionaldepartementet, rapport fra den nordiske arbeidsgruppen for nordisk samekonvensjon, desember 1996 – juni 1998.

Norway, Utenriksdepartementet (1994), 'Protocol three – about the Saami, Traktat om Kongeriket Norges, Republikken Østerrikes, Republikken Finlands og Kongeriket Sveriges tiltredelse til Den europeiske union', June, Oslo.

NOU 1997:4 (Public report issued by the Norwegian government) 'Naturgrunnlaget for Samisk kultur'.

NOU 1997:5 'Urfolks landsrettigheter etter folkerett og utenlandsk rett. Bakgrunnsmateriale for Samerettsutvalget'.

Saami Council (1999): 'Activity Plan 1999', Utsjok, Finland: Document from the Saami Council.

Saami Parliament, 'The Norwegian Saami Parliament: Sametingsplanen 1991–1993, 1998–2001', Karasjok, Norway.

Saami Parliament, 'The Swedish Saami Parliament: Sammanträdesprotokoll', 25–27.10.1994, § 8 'Samerna och EU', Kiruna, Sweden.

SOU 1990:84 (Public report issued by the Swedish government) 'Språkbyte och språkbevarande'.

SOU 1999:25 'Samerna – ett ursprungsfolk i Sverige. Frågan om Sveriges anslutning till ILO:s konvention nr. 169'.

St. meld. (Norway White Paper) nr. 52 (1992–93) 'Om norsk samepolitikk'.

St. meld. nr. 40 (1993–94) 'Om medlemsskap i Den europeiske union'.

St. meld. nr. 41 (1996–97) 'Om norsk samepolitikk'.

St. meld. nr. 18 (1997–98) Tillegg til St. meld. nr. 1 (1996–97) 'Om norsk samepolitikk'.

UK (1996) 'A partnership of nations: The British approach to the European Union Intergovernmental Conference 1996', March 1996.

UK (1997) Foreign Secretary, Mr Robin Cook, 'Planning the future of the European Union', The European Press, 15–16 June, 1997.

Newspapers/magazines

Aktuelt, various issues (Denmark).

Berlingske Tidende, various issues (Denmark).

Information, various issues (Denmark).

Jyllandsposten, various issues (Denmark).

Min Aigi, 5 February, 1999 (Saami language newspaper).

Nordlys, 24 and 28 January, 1998 (Norway).

Politiken, various issues (Denmark).

Samefolket, March and August editions, 1998 (a monthly magazine about Saami and indigenous events and issues).

Name index

Subject index

More Praise for *Making Millions in Direct Sales*:

"Mike Malaghan's book will help you overcome the number-one reason salespeople quit their jobs or their profession: rejection. He shows you how to accept it, he shows you how to deal with it mentally, and he shows you how to overcome it in a way that you will win for your customer and win for yourself."

Jeffrey Gitomer, author of *The Sales Bible* and *Jeffrey Gitomer's Little Red Book of Selling*

"Use the tools in *Making Millions in Direct Sales* and the doors in *face-to-face* selling are sure to open. Mike's outline of the 8 essential things sales managers must do every day will keep you on track. With a book like this, anybody can sell anything to anybody, I LOVE IT!"

—Joe Girard, Worlds #1 Retail Salesperson, attested by the Guinness Book of World Records, speaker/author, *How To Sell Anything To Anybody; How To Sell Yourself; How To Close Every Sale*, and *Mastering Your Way To The Top* www.joegirard.com

"With vision and heart, Mike Malaghan lays out a sure course that will take you step-by-step to successful sales management. Building and leading sales teams requires more than just goal setting and teaching how to overcome objections. Managing teams to sell products and services requires personal discipline, compassion, cultivating relationships, and more. It's all in *Making Millions in Direct Sales*."

—Jack D. Wilner, speaker, trainer, and author of *7 Secrets To Successful Sales*

"This is the practical everyday 'how do do it' manual for the sales management who is paid on an incentive income basis. It's a paradigm to instant success."

—Joe Adams, former CEO for Encyclopedia Britannica, United Kingdom.

"The book is the blueprint for success in the face-to-face industry."

—Michael Batten, president of Learning Technologies, licensee, and distributor of Disney World of English.

"Would you like to double, maybe even triple, your income? If so, this book is the definitive manual for helping you improve your recruiting process, generate more leads, and motivate your sales force to perform to their potential. Malaghan doesn't waste time on theories that don't relate to the real world. He provides proven, step-by-step techniques you can use immediately to catapult your effectiveness. Read it and reap."

—Sam Horn, author of *Tongue Fu!* and *What's Holding You Back?*

"In direct sales, cold calling is essential; getting over that fear of rejection is a priority. In *Making Millions in Direct Sales*, Malaghan shares openly, with a genuine desire to teach others the methods that have led him and so many others to success. This book will help you GET SALES AND CLOSE THE DEAL!"

—Stephan Schiffman, America's "Cold-Call King" and author of many books, including *Cold Calling Techniques That Really Work* and *25 Most Dangerous Sales Myths and How To Avoid Them*

"Mike Malaghan's book shows how to transfer your dream of building a sales empire into reality with the eight proven steps steps-to-success formula."

Nicki Keohohou, CEO of the Direct Selling Women's Alliance—www.mydswa.org

"When I managed direct salespeople many years ago, I wish I'd had all the tools and techniques revealed in *Making Millions in Direct Sales*. The eight essential activities successful sales managers must do every day is worth several times the price of the book for sales managers who want to get the most out of their sales teams. Read it and reap—BIG sales dividends!"

—Dr. Tony Alessandra, author of *Collaborative Selling* and *The Platinum Rule* www.alessandra.com

"*Making Millions in Direct Sales* is destined to be the dog-eared reference book for any sales empire builder. Hundreds of ideas on conducting sales meetings and training, workable suggestions on prospecting, and a blueprint on building a leadership personality."

—Lisa Jimenez, M.Ed., www.Rx-Success.com

DEDICATION

This book is dedicated to the remarkable pioneer men and women of Taiwan who trusted me with their future in 1992 as we started to build a $75 million a year business from scratch. Thank you Sophia, Max, Tom, William, Dan, Rhett, and Richard. You took a chance that first week. You were soon joined by Bernie, Amos, Caesar, Monica, Hsiao Hui, Elizabeth, Violet, Jimbo, Judy, Christina, Henry, Marian, Jessy, and Frieda. And Chung Tu, thank you for allowing me to concentrate on what I did best. The watch you all gave me is still on Taiwan time. Finally to my wife, Tomoko, who took care of me so that I could take care of business.

MAKING MILLIONS IN DIRECT SALES

The 8 Essential Activities
Direct Sales Managers
Must Do Every Day
to Build a Successful Team
and Earn More Money

Michael G. Malaghan

McGraw-Hill
New York • Chicago • San Francisco • Lisbon • London • Madrid • Mexico City •
Milan • New Delhi • San Juan • Seoul • Singapore • Sydney • Toronto

The *McGraw·Hill* Companies

1 2 3 4 5 6 7 8 9 0   FGR/FGR   098765

ISBN 0-07-145150-1

This publication is designed to provide accurate and authoritative information in regard
to the subject matter covered. It is sold with the understanding that the publisher is not
engaged in rendering legal, accounting, or other professional service. If legal advice or
other expert assistance is required, the services of a competent professional person should
be sought.

> —*From a declaration of principles jointly adopted by a committee of the
> American Bar Association and a committee of publishers.*

McGraw-Hill books are available at special quantity discounts to use as premiums and
sales promotions, or for use in corporate training programs. For more information,
please write to the Director of Special Sales, Professional Publishing, McGraw-Hill, Two
Penn Plaza, New York, NY 10121-2298. Or contact your local bookstore.

 This book is printed on recycled, acid-free paper containing a minimum of 50%
recycled, de-inked fiber.

Library of Congress Cataloging-in-Publication Data

Malaghan, Michael G.
    Making millions in direct sales : the 8 essential activities direct sales managers must
do every day to build a successful team and earn more money / Michael G. Malaghan.
        p. cm.
    ISBN 0-07-145150-1 (alk. paper)
    1. Direct selling. 2. Sales management. I. Title.
    HF5438.25.M3255 2005
    658.8'72—dc22
                                                                            2005000204

CONTENTS

EIGHTH ESSENTIAL ACTIVITY

LEAD

INTRODUCTION

If you are not going all the way, why go at all?

—Joe Namath, Football Player

WHY DO YOU NEED THIS BOOK?

Making Millions in Direct Sales is a practical and valuable "how to" book for sales managers in the direct-to-the-consumer sales industry, written by a veteran sales manager with international experience. If you work in this ever-growing industry, this book is for you!

This simple distinction separates *Making Millions in Direct Sales* from the rest of the pack. Most other books on sales management are usually written by academics and are primarily directed toward traditional business-to-business selling or are written by a former sales manager for one Fortune 500 company selling to another Fortune 500 company—again, the business-to-business sales industry.

The "tell it like it is, show me the money" voice and style of this book should appeal to your practical nature. And the useful, bite-sized instructions on how to build a powerful sales force with any product in any location will ring true regardless of your time and experience in the industry.

WHY ME?

In September 1994, I addressed a group of *my* top sales managers and made this pledge: "I will not leave my post until at least 10 of you are millionaires." I kept that pledge, in fact fulfilling it twice over. I was able to do so because, over my four-decade-plus career in sales, I had cultivated an effective system for developing great sales managers.

I'll admit, when I began my sales career, I had no idea that it would take me and my sales partners to such heights. Like many people who make a career in sales, my first position was humble and, I thought, temporary until I found a "real job." I started as a door-to-door encyclopedia salesperson when I was a college student in the 1960s. After a stint in the Peace

Corps, I began a direct-sales "conglomerate" in the Caribbean, setting up direct-marketing groups throughout the islands selling educational programs and waterless cookware. After leaving the Caribbean in 1978 I led face-to-face sales divisions in Japan, American, and England. My big break came in 1991, when I was offered the opportunity to build a full-commission sales force from scratch in Taiwan. I would be able to do it "my way," using all the skills I had learned over three decades.

I arrived in Taiwan with an empty office in 1991. Eight years later, 1,100 full-commission sales consultants, spread among four separate companies in Taiwan and Hong Kong, were selling $75 million annually. Based on that track record, the company added Japan to my territory and promoted me to president. Annual sales in Japan jumped from $40 million to $125 million in the next three years.

For 11 consecutive years, my group of sales companies collectively sold more products and services than the previous year. The company's profits grew in a similar fashion. Even during those times when a country's economy plummeted, our sales still increased. I believe that the continued success of our sales force resulted from my system for developing and honing world-class sales managers. I had hit on the right formula.

You can use that very same formula. It's waiting for you to discover within the pages of this book.

WHY NOW?

For 42 years I have looked for a very specific sales management book—one that would tell me how to improve my ability to recruit, train, and motivate a sales team that sold directly to the end consumer on a "results count" compensation system. I never found that book. So I wrote it.

Don't get me wrong. I found many worthwhile and respected books with long shelf lives that focus on motivation and salesmanship. A couple of my favorites include Zig Ziglar's *See You at the Top* and Joe Girard's *How to Sell Anything to Anybody*. They are still best-selling classics in both print and audio. Zigler and Girard learned their stuff in the trenches, both of them having sold on commission and directly to the consumer. Tom Hopkins's and Jeffrey Gitomer's excellent books teach the practices of face-to-face selling. Up until now however, there has been no similarly compelling book on *managing* a direct-sales force. *Making Millions in Direct Sales* addresses that need.

It is my fondest hope that the more than 2.3 million direct-sales managers in action today, along with the countless people who want to be sales managers, will recognize this book as the manual that they have been searching for, now and for many years to come.

WHY YOU?

No matter how capable you already are, you can always be a more effective leader and a more successful sales manager.

I was well into my forties before I had all the tools I needed to build and manage 2,000 direct-to-the-consumer sales representatives. You shouldn't have to wait that long.

Every week or month, you receive a double report card—one on your sales results, and the other on your personal income. You make an immediate connection between effort and results. You want to be better. I can help you.

When I was 35 years old, I had been in sales management for 15 years. I was a cocky young buck who knew it all. Yet 90 percent of what I know today I learned *after* I knew it all. Much of what you will learn in this book is what I learned after I knew "everything."

WHY THIS WAY?

Most sales managers do not have time for long treatises on management theory; they just want to know what works and how to do it. They need direct language for direct sales. This book not only shares its advice concisely, but presents more than a hundred human-interest stories to make those recommendations come alive.

Making Millions in Direct Sales can be read cover to cover or used as a guidebook to apply to daily problems and specific situations. Each chapter targets a key function of sales management, allowing the reader to access needed information immediately without having to read through the entire book. It is designed to be the dog-eared reference book that is always within easy reach.

Making Millions in Direct Sales revolves around the *eight essential activ-*

ities that successful sales managers must perform every day. These activities are sequenced to follow a particular logic. However, each chapter stands on its own, as well as being a slice of the greater sum of the parts. You are invited to read the chapters out of order. Pick the area where you need help at the moment; come back to another at a different time.

Here's a quick preview of what you'll find in the following pages:

■ *The first Essential Activity: sell.* Our industry is a "show and tell" industry, so the first Essential Activity is to set the example. "Do as I say, not as I do" may work for parenting occasionally, but it's a failed strategy for sales management. These first two chapters emphasize why it is important for a sales manager to stay in the field and explains how a sales manager's field time is quite different from that of a salesperson. Coaching techniques are clearly laid out.

■ *The second Essential Activity: prospect.* Facts and belief must collide at the prospecting opportunity to give you the confidence to keep your manpower growing. The number of prospects *always* exceeds the ability of your current salespeople to contact them all. Few sales managers use all the prospecting tools available. So, at the beginning of this section, you will review how to determine the extent of your immense prospecting base. Once you recognize the greater opportunity, a host of proven prospecting techniques is presented in a "how to" fashion, so that you can embrace *all the market, all the time.* In turn, this potent marketing combination gives you the swagger and confidence to recruit an ever-growing sales empire.

■ *The third Essential Activity: hire.* Always, always, always recruit. Today may be the day that an eagle needs a new perch. The first of two chapters on recruiting review 17 proven recruiting methods. The companion chapter provides a clear 10-step interview process that will fill your training room with more and better sales recruits than ever before.

■ *The fourth Essential Activity: train.* Sales training is a mix of showmanship, planning, and skills transference. You control the training. If your sales partners can't find customers or close orders, it is your fault. Six distinct chapters address the complete range of training opportunities: the how and why of field training; getting new recruits to their first order; retaining new salespeople one more week, every week; the challenge of training veterans; scores of classroom training techniques; the power of off-site training; and 60 sure-fire ways to keep your sales meetings interesting. You might be tempted to jump to one of these chapters right away if you're due to conduct a training class soon. Go ahead.

■ *The fifth Essential Activity: replicate yourself.* Get ready for your next promotion. Increasing sales is the first step; developing new sales managers to replace you is the second. The first of these management development chapters concentrates on how to find, define, and train the group leader, field manager, or whatever you choose to call that first level of sales management. A chapter on delegation follows, which not only makes the case for delegating, but illustrates precisely how to do it. The trilogy of chapters on replicating yourself concludes by proposing a five-day key-person training course that you conduct to fast-track your managers to excellence.

■ *The sixth Essential Activity: motivate.* Four robust chapters tackle this ever-important, ever-illusive, always asked-about sales management skill. Since motivation starts with the leader, the first chapter helps you set the type of goals you need in order to maintain self-motivation so that you will have the credibility to motivate others. The second chapter explains how you can *use* the 14 greatest motivators to inspire your team members to be the best they can be follows. The third motivation chapter walks you through the goal-setting steps to use with your sales representatives. The final chapter covers how to weave sales contests into your total motivation matrix.

■ *The seventh Essential Activity: manage.* Peter Drucker's famous assertion, "Management is doing things right; leadership is choosing the right thing," explains why these two responsibilities are separated in this book. The four management chapters advance focused time-management practices, promote customer service as a referral opportunity, suggest prospecting and selling tools for your troops, and advise you how to take advantage of the Internet age without its taking over your life.

■ *The eighth Essential Activity: lead.* The first chapter in this section is the most unusual in the book. It lists the 12 personality or character demons that can destroy all that a sales manager has built. The following chapter helps you recognize the characteristics of leadership that you already possess, encourages you to determine what leadership attributes you would like to develop further, and gives you specific suggestions on how to upgrade those targeted leadership abilities. This chapter closes with 50 ideas on how to build a leadership persona. Charisma need not be limited to a chosen few. You can cultivate magnetism and assure your recognition as a leader by practicing these techniques.

There it is, all laid out for you so that you can pick and choose your path to the sales management success you crave and deserve.

The following is a sample of how we will go about building up the leadership skills you already have.

WHY ASK FOR THE GOOD NEWS?

Most great men and women are not perfectly rounded in their personality, but are instead people whose one driving enthusiasm is so great it makes their faults seem insignificant.

—Charles A. Cerami, Author

For more than 30 years, I routinely asked my salespeople how they were doing with phrases like "How many orders did you get?" or "How did it go yesterday?" I didn't realize that what the salesperson heard was, "How much money did you make for me?"

My fiftieth birthday had passed before I started greeting my sales associates by asking, "What's the good news?" Let's face it: More often than not, a salesperson will not get an order on any particular day. Sales managers have more "off" days than "on" days. However, there is *always* good news. If the person got an order or hired a new salesperson, she will tell you immediately. However, the respondent can also let you know about the new referral program that produced three leads, the new newspaper ad that added more sales recruits, the big selling event scheduled at the mall this coming weekend—you get the drift.

When I converted most of my conversations to start with, "What's the good news?" the effect was immediate. Most people were eager to tell me something positive.

Making Millions in Direct Sales advocates successful sales management practices to build on the success you have already achieved. You have already proved that you have the personality and the work ethic to be successful in the direct-sales industry. As your career progressed, you received training to enhance the skills and potential that you already had when you entered this industry. You have already faced and conquered obstacles. You have overcome the fear of failure and rejection. In short, you have what it takes to be a successful sales manager.

You have the raw material to become a millionaire. What you may not have are all the skills it takes to be successful. However, the skills and competencies of successful sales managers can be learned by anyone who has already come as far as you have. That is very good news indeed. You can become a millionaire by managing commission salespeople and/or sales personnel whose salary and bonuses are directly tied to performance, because you can acquire all the practices and habits of successful sales management. There is no skill or habit that is beyond your competence.

Making Millions in Direct Sales covers all those tools and shows how to use them to build your sales empire.

ACKNOWLEDGMENTS

The writing of a book is a lonely exercise; getting it done right is a community project. Never again will I gloss over an acknowledgments page in a book. Now I understand how important so many others are to a completed project.

First, volunteer readers reviewed my early drafts. Jimbo Clark, who had helped me train for a decade, asked, "Where are the stories?" to bring my recommendations alive. Former president of Encyclopedia Britannica, England, Joe Adams, sharpened my attention on my direct-sales audience. Housewife Martha Cooper provided hints on tightening my sentence structure.

My first draft of the book proposal was appraised by Bob Scott of *Writer's Digest*. My next stop was the Maui Writer's Conference, where Sam Horn took me under her wing and sharpened my proposal so that an agent would see the promise in it.

David Trunzo, an accountant by profession, was an early reader who sent back memos that resulted in an easier read. Patrick Antonio, a young sales manager in the telecommunications industry, helped broaden the book's scope.

Fletch Shipp helped organize the book in a more logical order. My final personal editor, Vicki McCown, spent four months of her life sending drafts back and forth to hone a shorter, punchier manuscript.

My agent, Roger Jellinek, and my editor, Donya Dickerson, gave this project an enthusiastic boost. Their belief in this book gave me the motivation to spend the extra hours making the final manuscript a much better read than those earlier versions.

Finally, I want to acknowledge all the sales managers I have been privileged to work for and learn from over four decades. This book represents the successful ideas we used to build sales empires. It's your book too.

FIRST ESSENTIAL ACTIVITY

SELL

Successful selling. That's what earned you the opportunity to see if you have what it takes to be a good sales manager. To make the most of that management opportunity, you must *continue* to sell. Sales managers double their selling effectiveness when members of their team can watch them in action.

In an early scene in the movie *Troy*, Achilles destroys a Goliath-sized soldier in personal combat to settle a war. As a general in the army, Achilles did not have to participate in the actual fighting. That the soldiers in his regiment gained renown as Greece's fiercest warriors is a testament to the power of his leading by example.

Shakespeare brings Henry V to life with his St. Crispin's Day speech. However, Henry V doesn't just tell his men what to do; he personally leads the charge in the assault on the French castle at Agincourt.

Alexander the Great has gone down in history as one of the most successful conquerors of all time. Reports of his scarred and battered body, earned by his fighting in the trenches with his men, were legendary. His Greek legions fought with unparalleled loyalty and passion to protect their fighting king.

These are all dramatic examples of leaders using their own dynamic acts to motivate their followers. Sales managers who employ this style of leadership will enjoy enduring success through the achievements of the people they lead.

CHAPTER 1

SET THE EXAMPLE

Industry is a better horse to ride than genius.

—Walter Lippman, Journalist

Selling sales managers lead by example. If Missouri is the "show me" state, then the face-to-face sales industry is the "show me" business. Leading by example sets the tone in any business. But in sales, the boss's attitude and action reign supreme in managing salespeople. Salespeople start every pay period essentially unemployed until they sell their first order. They have the freedom to quit at any time. In my early days, I kept a plaque on my desk for all my salespeople to see: "The speed of the boss is the speed of the team." It reminded me—and let my team know—that what I *did* mattered more than what I preached. How well I remember the following epiphany moment when I was attempting to make clear the advantages of leading by example:

My training clinic for our new sales managers on the importance of their continuing to sell had covered all the necessary points. The nods and note taking suggested that I had once again persuaded everyone to embrace this concept. I couldn't help but admire the fine job I'd done, silently stroking my inner vanity. Then Jane broke my smug reverie by asking the dreaded question: "At what point can we stop personal selling and just manage the other salespeople?"

I felt my prickly temper rise, popping my balloon of self-importance. At one time I might have shouted at her exasperatedly, "Where have you been for the last hour? Don't you get it?"

But I had learned to cool down, to smile, to be patient, because I'd come to understand that Jane—and many other new sales managers—truly didn't "get it." Jane had recently been promoted. She was typical of most new sales managers I have encountered. Throughout my presentation, she had been focusing on the one answer she wanted to hear: When could she "just manage and leave the selling to the salespeople"?

I tried to make my point a different way. "Jane, at some point, when you are managing a sales force of between 50 and 100, you may be too busy to have the time for personal selling. You will have managers under you to fill that role. The problem is, most sales managers never get to that point, because they stop personal selling too soon."

You set the pace by your example. You do not have to be the best salesperson on your team (although that helps), but you must continue to engage in personal selling until you have sufficient managers under you to fulfill this mission. To be successful, you must endeavor to impersonate those heroes we so admire in action movies: You must lead from the front lines.

By continuing to sell, not only do you maintain a high income, but you create a positive and powerful model for the team. As a sales manager, you send the message that selling *is* the job. Some sales managers talk about good selling; other sales managers sell. Which type do you think leads more effectively?

My best selling years took place *after* I became a sales manager. I felt a personal and professional pressure to maintain a high sales level. Why? I might have doubted my leadership abilities, but I felt confident that I could, and should, set a good example. This approach worked.

People in direct sales work alone; sales managers working in the field are watching or being watched. Sales managers who sell infrequently, and/or who do not sell with their sales force, impose an enormous handicap on both manpower growth and sales force retention.

Personal selling can even be used as the exclusive method for training new sales recruits. Several times in my career, I entered a new territory by myself. I had to recruit and train a sales team, starting from zero. Financial survival would have been impossible if I had had to leave the field for several days to train new salespeople in the classroom. Conducting all the training in the field solved the problem. In between sales calls or at lunch, I used the time with my trainees to address how to handle the paperwork that comes with sales, such as how to fill out a contract and other such forms. The following chapter reveals the best field training and coaching practices.

No classroom simulation comes close to the genuine experience of a live sales presentation. No virtual reality can effectively re-create the dynamics of one salesperson observing another salesperson in the field, delivering a sales talk to a real prospect.

Additional advantages of field training include the following:

■ Killing two birds—selling and training—with one time management stone

- Increasing your personal selling time and, as a consequence, your personal income
- Eliminating the complaint/excuse about being "too busy" to sell because of the pressure to "take care of the organization"
- Sending the powerful message that you care enough to make sales calls with your team
- Demonstrating that you *really* believe in the value and salability of your product
- Establishing your hands-on leadership persona—you lead from the front
- Keeping one of the most competent sales reps in the field—you
- Maintaining the selling habit

Occasionally, most sales managers will experience a sudden decline in sales followed by a loss of manpower. Abruptly, the sales manager's override or bonus income shrinks below what it takes to maintain an established lifestyle. Sales managers who sell won't feel as acutely the decrease in personal income that occurs when others fail to deliver. They can increase their selling time more easily when the need arises. A sales manager who loses the personal selling habit finds it very difficult to "get back in the saddle."

I have seen promising sales management careers end in heartbreak and financial distress because a sales manager, even one who used to be a top-flight salesperson, could not overcome the fear of rejection and go back into the field.

If a sales manager stops selling, it doesn't take long for that manager's salespeople to draw the conclusion that one of the perks of sales management is to sell a lot less or even nothing at all. This poor example produces a ripple effect. Lower-level managers who earned their position by being competent sales reps think, "If my boss avoids the field, I guess I can skip a day or two, too." Thus, the consequence of this poor nonselling example is to take many of the best producers out of the field. The speed of the boss is the speed of the team.

Some sales management tasks cannot be done in the field while personally selling. Still, sales managers want to consider personal selling a primary activity. When developing their weekly schedule, effective sales managers first set their weekly selling time. Then, and only then, do they prioritize time for all the other sales management activities.

Sales managers take care of their organization by never being too busy to show team members how to make money in the field. Doing so sends the clear message to your sales professionals that they are important. Your trainees think, "Gee, the boss left the comfort of his office to be with me, to help me learn how to close more orders." Powerful stuff, that. Any wannabe sales manager can *talk* about selling methods, closing techniques, and market potential; the great sales managers *show* by *doing*.

QUESTIONS TO ASK YOURSELF

- What happens when you work in the field with your sales representatives? Is it good or bad?
- What do you consider the three main benefits of personal selling by the sales manager?
- Can you name three benefits of a sales manager *not* selling?
- Do you want to maintain your current amount of field selling time, or do you feel you would increase your effectiveness by taking more time to talk to customers?

Remember: The great sales managers never lose sight of the first Essential Activity: Sales managers *sell*.

Recommended books to help you maintain great sales skills:

- *The Sales Bible* by Jeffrey Gitomer
- *Low Profile Selling* by Tom Hopkins
- *How to Sell Anything to Anybody* by Joe Girard
- *Henry V* by William Shakespeare

CHAPTER 2
CHAMPION FIELD TRAINING

A platoon leader doesn't get his platoon to follow him by getting up and shouting and saying, "I am smarter. I am bigger. I am stronger. I am the leader." He gets men to go along with him because they want do it for him and they believe in him.

—Dwight D. Eisenhower, U.S. President

Nothing beats frontline field training, a technique that is as old as it is effective. Live field training with prospects is the best way to prepare employees for the real thing—because they are doing the real thing. The following example shows exactly what I mean:

> I became vice president of a multinational organization renowned for its hard-working sales managers. Each sales manager had a smart-looking office, a secretary, and a well-appointed training room—but only a few salespeople. Every two weeks the managers went through a recruiting cycle of hiring and training new people. The classroom training took five days because of the memorization required to learn the sales script. And since the sales recruits were not field-trained, their success rate was generally dismal. The sales managers were indeed working hard, but they were going broke, as they weren't making any money on their own sales or on override commissions from their salespeople.
>
> We took temporary drastic action. We eliminated all classroom training. Instead, sales managers were asked to make sure that all sales recruits observed seven in-the-field sales presentations. The results were instant and dramatic. Sales managers who had been on the brink of quitting started earning money on their personal sales. New sales recruits were inspired by what they saw. The trainees sat in on sales presentations often enough to learn how to sell the product. Soon, each sales manager had built a sales team. No sales manager had to "retire."

Field training—or, as some texts call it, "coaching"—must be both constant and variable as your sales associates move from sales recruit/trainee to rookie to veteran. The constant must be that managers work in the field with their sales partners at every stage; what varies is the type of coaching experience.

NEW RECRUITS

Let's start with your new sales recruits, who need to see and hear live sales practices in the field so that they can observe rather than be observed. New salespeople often need up to five or even as many as seven observed presentations before the odds swing to your favor that they will "make it."

Why five to seven observed sales presentations instead of just one or two? Let's walk through a little exercise to illustrate the point. We will replace the circumstance of a salesperson watching a live sales presentation with the alternative but similar situation of watching a movie.

The first time we fix our eyes on a movie screen, we just enjoy the experience. We put our brain in observation mode—we simply listen, watch, and escape. We don't analyze the actors' techniques, how the special effects work, or how the director contrives to carry us along for an emotional ride. We lose ourselves in the experience. The second time we watch the same movie, we notice dialogue and scenery that we missed the first time, and we anticipate some of the more dramatic scenes.

If we watch the movie a third time, we start to think a little like the director: We understand why some scenes were shot a certain way, or we surmise how the special effects director might have set up the scene. We have begun the shift from mere observation to a study-and-learn mode.

The new salesperson experiences this same metamorphosis. Sales recruits often admit to being impressed by their first observed sales presentation. A few may even wonder if they can ever be that good. However, by the third presentation, most sales trainees are *starting* to dissect the sales presentation and learn from the techniques being shown them. The salesperson-in-waiting begins to appreciate concepts like the need story and the automatic close.

Hopefully, by the fifth to seventh time your trainee has observed a live sales talk, he or she will have become a little bored and will be anxious, and may even demand, to deliver the next sales talk instead of observing. When the sales recruit says, "Send me in, coach!" you have successfully field-trained a new salesperson who has a bright future.

Let your sales trainee observe the presentations of different salespeople and managers. This variety offers several rewards. It will

■ *Make your recruits part of your sales family.* Two people working together start building a relationship. The new recruit feels less like a number and more like part of a team.

- *Assuage start-up fears your recruit may harbor.* Your recruit often wonders, "What is the *real* situation I have gotten myself into?" While you have faithfully and truthfully presented the work conditions, trust hasn't been earned yet. The members of your sales team perform a valuable trust-building function as part of field training.
- *Sharpen the field trainer's selling presentation.* There's nothing like an audience to generate a little more enthusiasm in the sales talk.
- *Reinforce companion selling.* The more you field-train, the more the habit of salespeople visiting prospects in tandem becomes the norm.
- *Increase the trainer's income.* The temptation to skip a selling day vanishes when your designated trainer is assigned a trainee to work with.
- *Develop managers faster.* An office culture built on the premise that "everyone field-trains" offers unlimited opportunities to teach good coaching habits. Everyone's a manager!
- *Build trust.* Asking your sales reps and junior managers to field-train sales recruits is a constant affirmation that you trust your people to put on a good show for the trainee.
- *Encourage a positive attitude.* Most of us are on our best behavior with new acquaintances. We put on our best, most positive face. The more often we do that, the more positive we become.

Do not assume that everyone understands her or his role in the field-training experience. Take five minutes to prepare your trainees for their first field observation episode. You will gain the utmost results from field training for both the trainee and the trainer if you coach your sales trainees before they enter the field as observers. Use this three-step preparation formula:

- Ask your trainees to be silent when they are observing a sales presentation.
- Instruct the trainee to watch the presentation as if it is a series of acts in a play—Act 1 is the warm-up, Act 2 is the need story, and so forth.
- Help the sales trainee anticipate how customers respond to the many probing, trial, and closing questions that will be asked.

After you've finished a training session, debrief the trainee promptly to reinforce what she or he just observed: For instance, ask questions like:

- "What did you learn from that presentation?"
- "Did you notice how many questions I asked?"

- "Did you see how I asked for the order by saying ____?"
- "How did the customer's attitude and body language change as I went through the need story?"

A missed sale often provides a better learning experience than a successful close, because the trainer has to go through the entire repertoire of closing techniques and overcoming objections.

ROOKIES AND THE TWO-DAY BLANK RULE

What about field training after the trainee has graduated to producer status? Consider this scenario: New salesperson A wrote an order today. New salesperson B has worked for two days without getting an order. You can bet $1,000 of my money on which salesperson is more likely to submit an order tomorrow. Which are you betting on? Each day that a salesperson works without submitting an order increases the likelihood of that salesperson's blanking the next day. A combination of cascading doubt and some continued technical sales presentation flaw can spiral any salesperson into a slump.

Once I recognized this phenomenon, I instituted the two-day blank rule, which has made me a small fortune. It works like this: If a new salesperson goes two complete working days without an order, that salesperson needs more field training the following day.

I used this system faithfully for a decade managing door-to-door crews. Your selling situation might be different. Maybe it will be three days or four presentations without an order before you *know* that the odds of continued failure have crept into the equation. Wherever the fault line lies, field training is a ready remedy. You *cannot* talk a salesperson out of a slump. Instead, set a standard for retraining in the field and stick to it.

COACHING THE VETERANS

Your veterans need field help as much as new recruits or rookies, but probably not as often. And certainly the method should be adjusted depending on how much experience they have and what specific problem they are facing. What is most important is everyone recognizes that frequent field coaching is part of your management philosophy. Your people then know that it's an honor to be selected to work with the boss for a day.

While new salespeople are usually best served by doing the observing, the veteran needs a combination of observing and being observed because the veteran needs a witness to his selling practices so that he can be told what he is doing right and what needs to be changed. Even Barry Bonds has a hitting coach to check his swing and stance. Let's review a few coaching guidelines when you are the observer:

- Everyone knows her role in the joint sales call. If you are the observer, will you jump in to close the order? If so, under what circumstances? What is the signal so that the transition is smooth and natural?

- Use the build–teach–build method of review after the sale. You start with a compliment to build up your staff member, then review the part of the selling process that needs improvement. Finally, you should find something else to compliment.

- After the sales call, start the discussion by asking your sales rep for his analysis. Practice your active listening skills. Self-criticism is easier to take than your criticism. You can direct the discussion with questions like "How would you evaluate our sales call?" or "Is there anything you would like to improve?"

- Different personality types require different approaches. Your debriefing style should take into account your salesperson's personality type, not yours.

- Make it clear that it is the technique that is at fault, not the person, who can learn a better technique.

- The quicker you provide the feedback, the better.

- Toward the end of the review, ask, "How will you handle this same situation the next time?"

- End all coaching sessions with a positive subject: the sales contest awards, the next training program, the new monthly selling special, and so on.

Regardless of your sales partners' career stage, the benefits of field training go beyond the improvement of selling skills. The time a manager and trainee spend together traveling to and from the appointment often exceeds the time spent on the presentation itself. That "getting to and from" time leverages the benefits of field training in a number of ways. You can

- *Augment your dream-building program.* Most sales managers hold clinics on goal setting. But a one-on-one personal goal-setting discussion packs more punch than a speech delivered to a room full of people. Take advantage of your informal time together to privately coach your people to reach for their life's dreams.

- *Solve personality conflicts.* Quality time to resolve the social and political issues that every sales office faces is hard to come by. Travel time affords the opportunity to let one of the protagonists air her grievances and gives you time to listen before you ask her to let it go.

- *Perk up closing clinics.* An in-depth analysis of your rep's closing techniques immediately after a sale usually brings about greater improvements than next-day reviews at the sales meeting.

When you act as a coach and provide constructive support through field training, you produce positive expectations and results. Your sales reps look forward to working with you because they expect their confidence, competency, and income to rise as a consequence. They know that your job is to make them the hero.

Over the years, I have participated in lively debates on *doing* versus *observing*: Is it better for sales managers to perform the selling activity while a sales associate observes and picks up good sales practices? Or should the sales manager spend more time observing the salesperson, followed by a debriefing session to correct faults? Which is best? However, at the core of the these debates were two fundamental agreements:

- Both observing and being observed have their place and their benefits.

- Most sales managers would increase sales and reduce turnover if they spent more time in the field using either method.

Effective field training or coaching drives sales like no other sales management activity. You build on your primary talent: your selling ability. You *know* how to sell. You may always be learning how to manage better, but field training is one thing you can be great at from the get-go.

QUESTIONS TO ASK YOURSELF

- What is your policy for field-training your new sales trainees and your veterans?
- How do your coaching techniques adjust as your sales partners gain experience?
- How clear is your policy to both yourself and your team members?
- Do your sales reps see working with you in the field as a perk?
- What is your system of debriefing after you observe your team member in the field?
- What would you like to improve in your field training practices?
- What would be the impact on your sales team if you worked in the field with your team one more day per week?

Suggested further reading on good coaching habits:

- *Sales Coaching: Making the Great Leap from Sales Manager to Sales Coach* by Linda Richardson
- *Selling to Managing* by Ronald Brown

SECOND ESSENTIAL ACTIVITY

PROSPECT

Prospecting acts as the linchpin for all that follows in this book. Unless you can show your sales professionals how to identify more prospects, you have little hope of inspiring your team to greatness—and no hope of building an empire. Prospecting is so important to successful selling that this book devotes five chapters to getting it right.

This second essential activity will help you accomplish two things:

- First, any thoughts that you cannot possibly expand your current sales force because "the market will not support more salespeople" will be banished forever.

- Second, this section will give you and your marketing support staff a complete range of prospecting tools to double, triple, or even quadruple the number of leads generated for your sales representatives.

CHAPTER 3

SEIZE ALL THE MARKET ALL THE TIME

One must change tactics every ten years if one wishes to maintain one's superiority.

—Napoleon Bonaparte, Emperor

The foundation for successful sales management is finding customers. The market is usually substantially larger than most sales managers imagine. If you recognize and *believe* that there are more prospects than your current sales force is reaching, you will be eager to recruit, train, and motivate ever more sales representatives.

Prospecting is finding qualified people who will give you or your salesperson the time—generally just 15 to 45 seconds—to deliver the first part of your appointment talk without brushing you off. After that initial successful contact, you have anywhere from two to four minutes to set the appointment for a sales talk. You are welcome to use a derivative of the following story to make your point that the market is always greater than is usually perceived. Your story will have a greater impact if you reveal the actual prospecting base of your territory. If you are not sure, visit your local chamber of commerce or library to obtain the data to make your "the market is huge" point. Googlers can surf to find the info. Now the story.

> The first time I talked about portable toilets and sandwiches, making the point that "there is more, much more to the market than meets the eye," was in 1993 in Taipei, Taiwan. Although sales were on the upswing, we feared that we might be exhausting the market, having just broken the 500-orders-a-month barrier. Then our marketing manager brought in some demographic data from the government showing that 1.2 million families in Taiwan had at least one child between the ages of zero and three. These parents represented our target market.
>
> I chose Bob Chu, a good selling manager and a bit of a skeptic, to help me drive home the magnitude of opportunity awaiting our sales force.
>
> "Bob," I said, "do you agree that the number of possible prospects is 1.2 million families?" Bob agreed.
>
> "Bob," I continued, "I have good news for you. Next Sunday, *all* 1.2 mil-

lion families have accepted my invitation to come to *your* home to listen to your sales demo. Each family has agreed to a private 45-minute sales presentation. By the way, you may want to call your wife and have her start making sandwiches now. Oh, and maybe order a few portable toilets.

"Now, Bob, if you have the stamina to talk to all 1.2 million families one by one, what percent can you sell?" Bob thought about it for a moment and said, "At least 10 percent." I went around the room and asked everyone the same question, with answers ranging from as low as 5 percent to as high as 33 percent. Finally, I said, "Does everyone agree that it's certain that we could sell at *least* 1 percent of those prospects?" Of course, everyone agreed—and then suddenly realized that this would more than double our current sales.

"So," I concluded, "what's the problem?" The managers suggested hiring more salespeople to use more prospecting methods to find more clients to contact. We did just that, and three years later, we broke the 20,000-order-a-year ceiling, a 300 percent increase.

"All the market all the time" is an idea that is simple, yet daunting.

Every company enjoys competence in at least one powerful method of prospecting or it wouldn't be in business. The issue is simple: You need to increase the number of methods of finding more customers in order to increase sales. Are you thinking, "Well, that's a brilliant analysis of the obvious"? As Sam Horn, author of *Tongue Fu,* says, "Just because something is common sense, doesn't mean it's common practice."

"All the market, all the time" presents an intimidating challenge. It requires sales managers to reach beyond their prospecting comfort zone to find and use additional lead-generating methods.

I have worked through this conversion process with more than 20 national sales forces in a dozen countries. The process is never easy to start because it requires a major change in mindset, but it's always worth the effort. Having a variety of prospecting approaches *always* produces more orders for the simple reason that no one approach can reach all the potential buyers of any product. Why would you want to limit yourself by sticking with one prospecting method? Why not go for it all?

Visualize two funnels jammed together over the open cover of a single Tupperware container. One funnel contains prospects; the other, sales representatives. When you mix the two, you get orders. The bigger the funnels, the more orders you get. It's that simple. Increasing sales is simply a matter of increasing the size of the two funnels that combine to produce orders: Hire more salespeople to sell to more prospects. Start with the "more prospects" funnel first. Focusing on prospects will give sales managers the confidence to hurdle the biggest obstacle they see to their success—that their sales force is close to optimizing the number of potential prospects. No more fear of "I can't hire any more salespeople. The current sales force has a hard time keeping busy as it is." This irrational "it's not my fault" fear stifles the sales manager's zeal to hire more salespeople.

A more varied and sophisticated prospecting commitment may require a new marketing perspective, a budgeting shuffle, more trained staff, and, most important, an open mind.

Rate your current and potential prospecting systems as either capital-intensive or labor-intensive. At the capital end of the scale, you have the company setting the appointments for your salespeople. The salesperson compensates the company for the appointment by either accepting a lower commission or paying a fee for each appointment. A notch down on the capital-intensive end of the spectrum are company-generated leads. While the salesperson still has to follow up on the lead, most of his time is still spent selling rather than prospecting.

At the opposite end of the scale is the labor-intensive system of going door to door, cold-call telephoning, and booth sales, because all or most of the prospecting is the responsibility of the salesperson.

As a rule, the more experienced and professional the sales force, the more likely it is that the prospecting systems will be capital-intensive. Younger, less-experienced sales forces tend to be more labor-intensive in their prospecting approaches. Since most companies using face-to-face sales have a sales force with a broad range of selling experience, using as much of the prospecting spectrum as possible makes good business sense.

Once a sales manager is competent in a minimum of 10 methods of prospecting, she can teach each salesperson at least three of those prospecting methods, depending on that salesperson's ability, personality type, career stage, and prejudices. The choice of prospecting tools is enormous.

I've listed many of these tools here and will go into them in more depth in the upcoming chapters.

Hail the Classics—Chapter 4

1. Door to door
2. Telephone appointment

Furnish Quality Company Leads—Chapter 5

1. National magazines
2. TV lead response
3. Direct-mail lead response
4. Third-party lead generation
5. Web-site lead generation

Generate Abundant Local Leads—Chapter 6

1. Party plan
2. Take-one boxes
3. Tear-off coupons
4. Business cards in the fish bowl
5. Handouts
6. Office marketing
7. Door hangers
8. Newspaper inserts
9. Local publications
10. Local third-party program
11. Bagging
12. Local mail-lead generation
13. Seminars
14. Referrals
15. Kiosks

Boost Exhibition Sales—Chapter 7

1. Exhibitions
2. Malls
3. National stores
4. Local stores
5. Three bites of the apple:
   ❏ Get a free-draw card

❏ Book an appointment

❏ Close the order on the spot

The classification of the various lead-generation programs can be argued and debated. The discerning reader might put the various marketing methods in a different order. Some lead-generation methods that are assigned to national headquarters in one company may be assigned to a regional or local authority in another. What matters is that you have access to the broadest possible range of prospecting methods.

A consequence of the mixed prospecting approach may be that each successive method of prospecting cuts into all of the previous methods of prospecting a little bit—an example of the law of diminishing returns. Some sales managers and companies have even used this law of diminishing returns as an excuse *not* to employ too many methods of prospecting, arguing that each new approach will be more expensive than the previous one, since many of the prospects approached with the newest method will already have been exposed (and unsuccessfully at that) to the other methods.

At first glance, this argument against adding more and different prospecting methods appears to be founded on common sense, but actually it has several flaws. First of all, it assumes that the most effective prospecting methods are already being used. This is not necessarily the case. Methods that were effective at some point in the company's history may have lost their potency. A prospecting system that is not being used may well turn out to be the most cost-effective choice. Testing new prospecting approaches protects a company's future.

The more prospecting methods you use, the more awareness of your company and its product you create in the marketplace. Prospecting builds brand recognition. Since the buying public prefers to buy merchandise from companies it recognizes, the more brand recognition you develop through various prospecting programs, the more likely it is that the prospect will be comfortable doing business with you and your company.

Some prospects need to be approached repeatedly, and in a variety of ways, before an appointment can be made or a sale concluded. Initial failure in converting a prospect to an order is often just part of the consciousness-raising process. Some prospects need more of this consciousness raising over a longer period of time than others. Circumstances can alter a prospect's needs or buying power. For example, a new job or a birth or death in the family can change a prospect's attitude the next time an approach is made.

Prospects come in a wide range of personalities and previous experiences. Some need to see live merchandise at a sales booth to feel comfortable about buying. Others prefer reading advertising copy in the comfort of their home. Some are enticed by the free gift rewarding a response. Then there are those who act on impulse, but whose impulsiveness may vary from day-to-day. Some prospects read magazines and newspapers, and mail in leads. Others also may read the ad copy, but can't be bothered to mail in a card. Lots of people visit malls and exhibitions when your company has a sales booth, but many more do not. So, you can see how unlikely it is that any one or two prospecting methods can access "all the market all the time."

The more ways you give a prospect to hear about your product or service, the better your chances of raising that prospect's subliminal need for it. This triggers the response that you or your salespeople hope to elicit, buying you those precious few seconds of time to earn permission to deliver the sales talk. In the next few chapters, we'll examine a wide range of prospecting methods and help you determine which is best for your bottom line.

QUESTIONS TO ASK YOURSELF

It just comes down to the question, "Do you want *all* the market *all* the time or just some of the market some of the time?" Before we move on to the following chapters and take a closer look at the various prospecting options you have, think about these questions:

- How many methods of prospecting are you using effectively now?
- What is the number of prospecting units in your market?
- What is the percentage of your market penetration each year?

Recommended books for those who want to delve into the marketing side of our business:

- *Principles of Marketing* by Philip Kotler and Gary Armstrong
- *Mastering Marketing,* a compendium from the *Financial Times*

CHAPTER 4

HAIL THE CLASSICS: DOOR TO DOOR AND TELEPHONE APPOINTMENT

I think I had a flair for [politics] but natural feelings are never enough. You've got to marry those natural feelings with really hard work—but the hard work comes more easily when you are doing things that you want to do.

—Margaret Thatcher, British Prime Minister

No matter how successful you or your company is in developing leads, including referrals, you cannot reach all the market without some cold calling. Some prospects just will not step forward and say, "Here I am."

There are plenty of ways to contact prospects other than cold calling, and we will review most of them in subsequent chapters. No matter how good these other methods are, however, the cold call will always have its place. Cold calling smoothes out the peaks and valleys of lead programs. Cold calling generates the lowest-cost orders. But prolonged cold calling can be daunting. By the time we migrate to sales management, we have learned that giving and observing sales presentations not only provides more joy than prospecting, but avoids burnout. The following early epiphany cut down on my cold calling while simultaneously increasing my selling time and getting the careers of new sales recruits off to a fast start.

> Here's how I learned a new definition of "bird dog." It was spring 1970, two years after the Vietnam Tet offensive and 6 months after I returned from my Peace Corps experience in Nigeria. I had jumped back into the encyclopedia business with Grolier, doing the door-to-door thing. I loved the selling; I hated the rejection.
>
> A competitor who had just gone under called me looking for a home for himself and his sales crew. Over lunch, Larry and I cut a deal. Then, while downing a piece of cherry pie, Larry casually asked, "Do you use the bird-dog system?"
>
> "What's that?" I replied.
>
> Larry volunteered that he too was tired of knocking on doors. So his training program for new people emphasized teaching them the door

opener plus the qualifying or introductory piece of the presentation. "Just enough," Larry explained, "so that the trainee can position me to deliver the presentation. I drop off two or three trainees in the field, park my car, and wait for one of them to fetch me to give a presentation to a waiting family."

Why hadn't I thought of this? I adopted the system on the spot. Where once I had thought 100 orders a year was an achievement, I was soon writing 300 orders a year. I'll always be grateful to Larry for showing me the way to simultaneously accelerate the training of new people and increase the number of presentations I could give to qualified prospects, all the while avoiding much of the rejection part of the business. What a deal!

DOOR TO DOOR

Face-to-face sales are enjoying a strong resurgence, as reported in a 2003 article by Jane Spenser in the *Wall Street Journal*:

> Dozens of companies, including AT&T Corp. and regional utilities, are unleashing armies of door-to-door sales representatives to pitch services such as phones, cable television, and natural gas. Comcast Corp. registered 40,000 customers last year with its door-to-door "win back" campaign that involved wooing customers from competition such as DirecTV.

Similarly, *Fortune* magazine featured Daryl Harms as "The Door-to-Door Billionaire" in its series "Eleven World-Class Entrepreneurs." Harms built his TV cable business by going "block to block, zeroing in on houses with the tallest antennas."

Recent "do not call" legislation has allowed millions of people to register their phone numbers to stop telemarketers. Many of these telemarketing companies are switching to face-to-face sales to move products and services. This is another reason the direct-sales industry will be growing by leaps and bounds in the years ahead.

Door-to-door selling was the preferred prospecting choice for so many companies for so many years that the direct-to-the-consumer full-commission sales industry was (and still is) often called "the door-to-door business," in much the same way that brand names like FedEx and Xerox have became verbs. Ironically, however, many door-to-door companies do not actually have any salespeople who go door to door.

The door-to-door method wore itself out with overuse. Aggravated home dwellers developed strong resistance to door-to-door salespeople. Cities and counties passed legislative restrictions on door-to-door selling. Astute sales managers responded by changing prospecting tactics. Those who did not change their door-knocking ways faded away. Ironically, this has meant that door-to-door has been relatively fallow over the past decade or so and thus is enjoying the resurgence noted earlier. A whole new generation has grown up since the era of too many salespeople using the same direct approach too many times in the same neighborhoods. The time is ripe to take advantage of this low-cost prospecting technique.

Here are five practical ways to get the most out of door-to-door selling:

1. *Card the neighborhood.* Maintain a card or Palm Pilot file on who lives at each address. Copy down the residents' names from the mailboxes or the list adjacent to the entry buzzer when canvassing apartments. Develop a code that gives you information quickly, such as "husband and wife only home together on weekends," "occupant has already been approached," and so forth. By doing so, you can rotate salespeople working the same housing without worrying about calling on the same person twice and also be the first to catch the much-prized new move-ins.

2. *Combine daytime appointments and nighttime orders.* Use the daytime, when people feel more comfortable talking to strangers, to set appointments and the evening to deliver the sales presentation. More working people than ever are home during the day. They may be self-employed, telecommuting, or working evening hours.

3. *Offer a free service gift.* Offer a free gift in exchange for an appointment. It is easier to make an appointment when the prospect is *guaranteed* to receive something *free*. For example:

- ❏ Home improvement—a free energy-efficiency check
- ❏ Water purifier—a free water analysis
- ❏ Educational products—a free child evaluation test
- ❏ Fitness center—a free seven-day trial

Tie in the gift with the product or service you are selling. Free tickets to a movie, a certificate to a restaurant, or some other enticing unrelated gift might sound like a good idea. But when you offer a gift with no tie-in to the product or service sold, you are guaranteed to get an appointment with people who have no interest in or need for your product.

4. *Use new salespeople to set appointments.* Teach new salespeople how to set appointments during their first week of training. New sales trainees can learn the short appointment talk more quickly than the much longer sales talk. The skills needed for setting appointments are more easily mastered than those needed for closing orders. Your new recruits are usually delighted to get a "training appointment fee" for setting appointments that result in an order. Not only do you create an effective low-cost appointment system, but you provide a learning exercise for your new salesperson. The training section in Chapter 10 provides more information about this sales trainee appointment.

5. *Hire door-to-door appointment setters.* The current (and increasing) resistance to phone selling, new legal hurdles, and telephone-call-filtering devices make door-to-door appointment setting at least worth a test.

An offshoot of door to door is "jumping in," which refers to a salesperson's approaching a prospect in a public place. The prospect is asked to participate in a questionnaire and/or to receive a free gift. This, in turn, will lead to an invitation to come to a nearby office or coffee shop for a sales presentation.

TELEPHONE APPOINTMENTS

Despite the popular and restrictive "do not call" legislation, there are still profitable and ethical ways to make the telephone work for you while adhering to the requirements and spirit of the law. For instance, charities are exempt, so you can tie the profits you make on your product to support of a worthwhile cause, which makes your selling a win for the customer, a win for you, and a win for the charity.

Many of the recommendations for cold-call telephoning also apply to following up leads. "Cold calling" refers to contacting a person who has not volunteered to be in your database by sending in a lead, filling out a free draw card at a sales booth, or some other method of previous contact. Your call comes out of the blue to someone whose name was either on a list you purchased, or in one of any number of directories, such as the Thomas registry.

The following suggestions will increase your telephone success rate:

■ *Read the script.* Reading from a script always outperforms winging it. *Always.*

■ *Host a telephone party.* Since cold-call telephoning is full of rejection, group calling ensures that everyone really calls rather than just thinks about it.

■ *Make your telephone parties fun; ring the bell.* Each time a person is successful, ring a bell, wave a flag, or send an electronic message if you have an electronic wall-mounted scoreboard.

■ *Keep track of the time your reps spend with each prospect.* You know the right amount of telephone time. Help your reps to quit wasting time with "suspects."

■ *Pick a prize.* Invite your salespeople to pick an envelope taped to the wall with a mystery prize each time an appointment is made. Maybe most of the envelopes have a dollar or a gift certificate for McDonald's, while a few envelopes contain a more expensive prize to generate a little excitement.

■ *Call Sunday night.* The best time to catch people you have missed on previous attempts is Sunday evening from six to nine. A once-a-month Sunday telephone party guarantees a sales boost. Since Sunday night is also a time sales reps do not relish working, try to tie in this seldom-used weekend time frame to a sales contest or some other event that encourages Sunday calling.

■ *Tape your reps' calls, with their knowledge.* Let them listen to their own appointment talks. Allow them to self-evaluate their calls first, before you review what they did right and what they can do to improve.

■ *Work with your reps.* Nothing motivates sales reps more than a sales manager who challenges the telephone.

■ *Offer a free gift.* Promise a free unconditional appointment gift tied to the product or service you are selling. For example, the cemetery industry provides a free estate plan review with an appointment. This freebie provides good value in exchange for an appointment.

■ *Use a smile machine.* Place a small stand-up mirror on each desk so that sales reps can check their smile meter. Voice quality improves with a smile.

■ *Supply snacks and drinks.* A little stomach bribe encourages attendance and sets a positive mood. Never miss an opportunity to show that you care.

Door-to-door and cold-call telephone appointments remain effective prospecting systems. Understanding the value of each "no" goes a long away to overcome the downside of cold calling. Every order has a value. Thus, every rejection also has a value, as it is the stepping-stone to the order.

Increasing sales through cold calling is simple: Double the number of contacts, and you double your income. Learn a more effective appointment approach, and you increase your income. As sales manager, you want to help your sales reps do both.

QUESTIONS TO ASK YOURSELF

- Are you getting the most out of these two relatively inexpensive prospecting techniques?
- How can your approach to cold calling be improved?
- What specific training or management actions can you take to increase your sales volume through improved cold calling?

Recommended reading to improve your telephone skills:

- *Cold Calling Techniques (That Really Work!)* by Stephan Schiffman
- *Telephone Sales Management and Motivation Made Easy* by Valerie Sloane
- *The Complete Guide to Telemarketing Management* by Joel Linchitz

CHAPTER 5
FURNISH QUALITY COMPANY LEADS

To improve is to change; to be perfect is to change often.
—Winston Churchill, British Prime Minister

"All the market all the time" suggests that the home office plays a significant role in the lead-generation process. Certain types of lead-generation systems, such as magazine lead generation, work best on a national or regional platform. National lead generation builds a brand name. This makes it easier to recruit salespeople and for those salespeople to generate local leads.

Branded products such as Electrolux, World Book, and Nextel can negotiate national advertising rates, third-party lead-response mail campaigns, and exhibit space within national chains.

Although this chapter is written somewhat from the perspective of a national company with a national sales force, the principles work just as well for a company with a single sales office in a single market. The following story reveals how critical it is to focus on supporting the salesperson by monitoring the *results* of the prospecting activity, not just the activity itself. It's not how many leads you generate; it's how many cost-effective orders those leads produce.

It was the mid-1980s. I had been invited to sit in on the budget and strategy meeting as a result of my success as national sales trainer for my organization. First up was a review of last year's lead-generation report, which revealed the cost per order from each lead source for the company, but not for the salesperson who bought the leads. After crunching the numbers on my handheld calculator, I tabulated the cost per order from each lead source for the salesperson. One summer lead program had produced lots of leads at a relatively low cost, but the conversion of those leads to orders was terrible.

The marketing director explained the logic behind the company's decision. "Think of the leads as a total mix. Summer is a tough time to generate the normal lead flow. But the average cost to the salesperson of all leads on an annual basis is profitable." Based on that thinking, the company concluded that it had to continue this program.

This didn't make sense to me. However, my persistence in pointing out the burdens of the summer lead program for the sales reps was rewarded by my being fired from the lead-planning committee. I made a vow to myself that I would change this practice if I were ever given the power to do so.

Fast-forward 15 years—same situation, different company. This time, however, I was the new president. The marketing manager echoed the sentiment I'd heard all those years ago: "We needed to reach the target of 125,000 leads a year. If the low lead-to-order conversion of some lead sources was expensive for the sales rep, it balanced out, since the overall closing rate of all the leads was satisfactory."

Remembering my vow, I said, "No more. We can put that money to better use." The marketing department used the money that was saved to experiment with new lead-generation programs. It discovered better lead sources at lower costs with higher conversion ratios. Two years later, it produced 350,000 solid leads for the company.

That experience taught me a valuable lesson: If you and your sales team brainstorm options, you can often come up with a more viable plan that benefits everyone involved.

Other characteristics of a good national lead program include a defined budget, no free leads, testing and measuring of lead-generation results, maximizing conversion of lead distribution, measurable standards for marketing bonuses, information sharing, TV advertising, and third-party lead generation.

Let's look at those characteristics a little more carefully.

SET A DEFINED BUDGET

Approximately 10 percent of the net sales price is a good barometer for establishing a marketing budget in the direct-to-the-consumer industry. This lead-generation tithing includes the contributions from both the company and the salesperson. If the sales personnel pay half the costs, then the net cost to the company is 5 percent.

CHARGE A REASONABLE RENTAL FEE FOR LEADS

Since the sales reps benefit the most from the leads, they should pay part of the cost of generating those leads. Providing free leads can have some negative consequences:

- Less incentive for sales representatives to generate their own leads
- Less money to generate more leads, as whatever the salesperson pays for a lead extends the company marketing budget
- Less inducement for sales managers to assign leads on a basis favoring the best closers

A good formula for deciding how much to charge salespeople on a per-lead basis is

- Calculate the closing rate for each category and/or source of leads. Do not commingle all leads into a single bucket.
- Determine how many leads the average salesperson must buy or rent in order to close an order from each category.
- Decide how much money a rep can afford to pay for each category of leads. A good rule of thumb is to keep the lead charge for any category of leads less than 25 percent of the commission earned.

ISSUE LEADS MORE THAN ONCE

This strategy increases lead conversion by 50 percent. I have done this with seven sales organizations in four countries with three product lines. The results are always the same: The number of leads converted to orders increases by *at least* 50 percent.

For most leads, the conversion time is 60 days or less from the time the lead is assigned to the salesperson to the time the order is submitted. However, I recommend that you give the first rep 90 days to convert the lead before reassigning the unconverted leads to someone else at a reduced cost to the sales reps.

Some 25 percent of all leads are not contacted at all by the end of 90 days! (If you doubt this, just have someone call 100 leads at random as a courtesy check and find out for yourself what the no-contact rate is for your sales group.)

After waiting another three months following the second assignment of leads, provide the unconverted leads for telephone group parties. This can be done more than once as long as you leave a decent time interval between reassignments so as not to irritate your prospecting base. Establish a "do not call again" system by having your reps flag a lead to be purged from your database when a prospect complains about being called too often.

USE LEADS FOR OTHER PURPOSES

Leads can also be used later in mail-order campaigns or be sold or traded to other companies. Make sure that your lead-response cards contain a sentence that customers can check if they do not want their names shared. Consumer legislation suggests that the best way to trade names is not to trade the name at all, but rather to trade access. Most consumer legislation allows you to contact people who have contacted you. So you may be able to include another company's promo piece in a mailing you generate in exchange for the other company's doing the same for you. Check your local laws before initiating any third-party access.

KEEP GOOD RECORDS

There are always more ways to generate leads than there is money available. Getting the most for your marketing dollar starts with good record keeping, and that means collecting the right information on the lead. You need more than a name, address, and phone number. Most people will tolerate two or three questions that help you identify whether the person is a suspect or a prospect. For instance, a home improvement lead should be asked if she is a renter or an owner. Asking the ages of children is important for most educational products and services.

A lead program for the preschool market provides a good example. Closing records showed that female sales reps had a slighter higher closing rate on all categories of leads. When those records were broken down into categories, however, we saw that with pregnant mom leads, the women closed twice as many leads as the men did. We stopped assigning those leads to the men, to everyone's benefit. The men were glad to get rid of those expensive leads (expensive because of their poor closing rate), the women received more leads that they could close, and the company benefited to the tune of more than $250,000 of extra annual sales.

A second case involved Internet lead assignment. Breakdown reports revealed that some sales associates and sales teams converted Internet leads at more than twice the average rate. For whatever reason, Internet-generated leads were different from most other leads. (Among other things, we happily discovered that most of the Internet leads came from prospects that we normally were not reaching.) Not surprisingly, we found that salespeople who regularly used computers were also more comfortable using their laptop version of the sales binder in sales presentations. Of course, the company tried to bring everyone up to speed on selling to Internet leads. Still, when our records clearly demonstrated that some people were consistently better with this category of leads, we adjusted our assignment of leads accordingly. Again, a win-win resulted: The increase in sales was over a million dollars a year, and we avoided punishing certain salespeople who dreaded receiving what for them was a lousy Internet lead.

ASSIGN LEADS BASED ON CLOSING ABILITY

The only criterion for assigning leads should be to maximize conversion. Reward your good converters by giving them more than their fair share of your precious lead assets. Train and encourage your poorer converters to develop their own low-cost leads and avoid the expense of buying company leads. Chapter 6 provides a dozen possibilities.

While assigning leads based exclusively on the lead-to-order conversion rate seems obvious, it's a practice that's not always followed. Sometimes a sales manager is tempted to try to jump-start new salespeople and other marginal converters by assigning them expensive—and limited—company leads. This does *not* help new recruits or marginal producers. Rather, such a practice will

- Reduce sales volume by taking those leads away from proven converters
- Make it more likely that the sales manager will later inherit lead charges from failed salespeople when they quit

TEST TEST TEST

There's no news here for anyone who has read anything on marketing—test what works and what doesn't. Some lead-generation money can almost always be better directed from the lowest quadrant of effectiveness to the highest quadrant. Know what your company is testing. Be at the forefront of lead-generation ideas to be tested and then measured by your marketing department.

IF IT DOESN'T GET LEADS, DON'T SPEND THE MONEY

Sponsoring events simply to promote "goodwill," paying for TV advertising to build brand recognition, or any other use of advertising money makes sense only if prospects have the opportunity to send in a lead card, call a toll-free number, or respond with an e-mail request. Recently I attended an arena football game where the home team enjoyed the sponsorship of several businesses. One such company, 24-Hour Fitness Center, capitalized on having its name displayed to the captive audience by making a smart marketing move. Throughout the game, fit and uniformed sales personal handed out to the fans invitations for a one-week free trial membership at the fitness centers.

Spending money on goodwill without a response mechanism only draws money from the lead-generation budget. This reduces the number of leads, which reduces the number of orders, which eventually reduces the number of salespeople you can support. The positive flip side of this coin suggests that money spent to generate leads also builds goodwill and brand awareness.

Consider five lead-generating programs that lend themselves to corporate headquarters oversight.

1. National Magazine Ads

Magazines are almost always the first and best choice for spending national lead-generation money. A prospect who sends in her name asking for information (and usually a related free gift) does so only after reading the ad copy. Respondents understand that it is likely that they will be contacted by a company representative as a consequence of submitting their name, address, e-mail address, and/or telephone number.

Targeted magazines focus on a defined audience. The explosion of special-interest magazines over the past two decades means that you can direct your magazine advertising to a particular audience. For example, you can advertise

- Exercise equipment in health magazines
- Early childhood education products in parent magazines
- Security protection systems in crime story magazines

2. TV Lead Response

Focus any lead-generation money spent on TV exposure on cable shows directed at audiences that fit the prospecting profile. Offer a toll-free response number. Many of the rules governing magazine advertising apply.

It is tempting to suspend good niche marketing rules and respond to the siren call of TV. Salespeople love to see their product on TV. Unless a toll-free number is included, however, any money spent on TV reduces the funds available for pure lead generation. How many leads are you willing to give up for the rush of seeing your product on TV?

The arguments for TV exposure are valid. TV advertising does build credibility and trust and give salespeople a morale boost. The problem remains, however, that most TV advertising simply costs too much unless you follow strict guidelines.

The late-night infomercials extolling the delights of various weight-control programs are a good example of more recent and positive development for the direct-sales industry. Weight control has more universal appeal than most direct-to-the-consumer products, because half the industrial world is overweight. A toll-free number to call for information or to order is always included.

PR on TV is a special case. Getting your product on TV *without paying for it* builds credibility like nothing else. In recent years I employed one person in each product line I managed whose job was to get free PR, mostly on TV. The PR person's job is threefold:

- First, spend time cultivating the key people in the media.
- Second, build relationships with satisfied customers. Produce videos recording customers' successful experiences with your product. Send

those videos to the media as part of your company's PR package. TV and other media will often use your media-pack content as is, because you made it easy for them to fill airtime or print space.

■ Third, sponsor newsworthy events. A great example of this was the Valentine poem contest Jessy created to promote our company's young adult home-study program. She audaciously solicited the mayor, who was in the middle of a reelection campaign. He submitted a poem. We notified the media. He got exposure as a loving husband as he read his poem for the six o'clock news, and we got more brand-building prime TV time than we ever dreamed of. He didn't win our contest, but he did win reelection.

3. Direct-Mail Response

The rising cost of postage and the public's growing disdain for junk mail makes direct mail a challenge. Still, with the right list, the right ad copy, and the right catchphrases on the envelope, you can generate high-quality leads on a cost-effective basis. Make sure your marketing department personnel have some experience and expertise in lead generation from direct mail.

4. Third-Party Lead Generation

Piggybacking or third-party lead generation allows you to insert your lead-generation flyer into the mailing pack of another company. Your company is the first party, the prospect on the receiving end of the mailing is the second party, and the company doing the mailing is the third party.

Credit card companies provide an inviting third-party opportunity. Visa and MasterCard want increased credit card usage. You have merchandise that customers can pay for with their credit card. Propose to the credit card's marketing department that you will offer its cardholders an *exclusive* offer and/or gift. The credit card company feels good about offering its customers a unique benefit while generating more credit card commissions.

Approach major chain stores with the same concept. For instance, stainless steel waterless cookware or exercise equipment flyers are a natural direct-mail tie-in with a health food store. A vacuum-cleaning flyer would work well with a home improvement outlet. Educational products are natural partners for bookstore or child-care center mailings.

The credit card company or other third party may ask for a piece of the action. Since this money is paid only on a results basis, a commission of up to 5 or 6 percent is about as high as you'd have to pay. But why pay at all? More often than not, what the third-party vendor really wants is more business from its customer base. So rather than too quickly agreeing to pay a commission to the third party, suggest alternatives such as the following:

1. *Buy from the third party.* When possible and practical, purchase your "buy today" closing premium from your third-party vendors as part of your strategy to insert flyers in the mailings of your selected third-party lead-generation partners. Maybe you can buy appointment gifts from the vendor.

2. *Be ready to lend a hand.* Some years ago, we had tried several times to arrange a joint mailing with one of the biggest department stores in the city. Even though the store rejected our offer, we kept up a friendly relationship. Then one day the store came to us with a problem. It had sponsored a big children's show, and ticket sales were way below expectations. Because the store knew that we sold children's products, it asked if we could help. We were happy to do so, and we worked out an agreement that benefited both parties. We bought several thousand of the show tickets at a good discount. We used the tickets as an appointment premium, and the store got a well-attended show. In addition, we received the okay to insert our lead-generating flyers with several of the store's subsequent billing statements. It pays to be gracious when you keep receiving no as an answer from a third party.

3. *Trade access.* Your company has a database of prospects and owners. Other vendors who target the same potential customer base would like to piggyback with you to gain access to those prospects. The key word is *access*. Privacy laws require that the third party mail your flyer to its customers and you in turn send its marketing pack to your customers. Customers still receive the marketing solicitation, while being assured that you have not given their information to another vendor.

Design your lead-swap proposal for a third-party tie-in from the perspective of the third party. Structure the partnership arrangement so that the third party gets more out of the deal than you do (*while*, of course, staying within your budget!).

5. Use Web-Site Lead Generation

In the face-to-face sales industry, the purpose of the Internet is to generate leads. Web sites are a lead-generating magazine ad in electronic form that offers some extra advantages.

The Web surpasses print media lead generation in a couple of aspects:

- Ad copy and appointment premiums can be tested in hours, instead of weeks or months.

- Sales representatives can contact the prospects much more quickly—like immediately.

Chapter 26, on the use of the Internet, has additional tips on Internet lead generation.

This chapter has focused on how the company can generate leads for its sales force. Now let's move on to the next chapter and review what sales associates can do for themselves.

QUESTIONS TO ASK YOURSELF

- How many of the five key company-managed lead systems are you using?
- What type of marketing records are you keeping so that you can select the best programs as market conditions change?
- Are leads being assigned based on the prime criterion of maximizing conversion to orders?
- What percentage of sales do you set aside to generate leads? Are your sales reps paying a fair price for leads?
- Can you increase your lead conversion by assigning the same leads in a managed sequence?
- Do you charge for leads based on the average of all leads, or do you determine the charges by category?
- What changes, if any, are you considering after reading this chapter?

Recommended books to help you spend your lead-generation dollars:

- *The New Marketing Era* by Paul Postma
- *Integrated Direct Marketing* by Ernan Roman

CHAPTER 6

GENERATE ABUNDANT LOCAL LEADS

If your ship doesn't come in, swim out to it.

—Jonathan Winters, Humorist

The previous chapter emphasized what the company or you as a sales manager can do to provide your sales associates with leads. This chapter focuses on what you can do to teach your sales partners to generate their own low-cost leads. You know the old proverb: "Give a rep a lead and he sells today; teach a rep how to find his own leads and he sells every day." Local marketing encourages sales managers to recruit aggressively without the twin fears of having to eat the unpaid lead charges of your new people and running out of leads to feed the existing sales force.

Seventy-five years ago, oil companies burned off gas from oil drilling before extracting the oil. The gas was considered a waste product. Now we know that gas is a valuable fuel. The following story illustrates how to turn another "waste product," the leftover free-draw cards from exhibits, into solid gold leads.

"What's this?" I asked, looking inside a large closet filled with boxes.

"Oh, that's all the free-draw cards people filled out at exhibitions," the sales manager said.

Tens of thousands of cards, going back at least two years, crammed the confined space. It was 1985. Only two days earlier, I had landed at London to start my new job as national sales trainer. Looking at all those boxes, I felt like a miner just off the boat in San Francisco in 1849, discovering gold the first day.

The free-draw cards had not been considered "real leads." I immediately recognized a chance to establish instant credibility with the sales managers, who knew me only as the new training guy.

"Give me a box," I said, "and let me see what I can do." In my office, I quietly read the free-draw appointment script supplied by headquarters; in two hours, I had set up five appointments. This gave me the courage to volunteer a demonstration the next day at 5 p.m., with four senior sales managers observing. Six appointments were made within two hours. We shared the leads. One of us got an order that night. We planned a national rollout soon after. The tone had been set to wean the sales force off the dependency on only two lead-generating systems, which had constrained growth for a decade.

Local prospecting methods are primarily low-cost, labor-intensive lead-generation techniques. Sales reps are able to produce an abundance of leads where they want them and when they need them. A number of happy consequences follow a robust local lead–generation commitment:

- Your new salespeople can enter our industry without going into debt buying or renting relatively expensive company leads.
- Your debt risks are reduced. Sales managers often guarantee the marketing debts of their salespeople in the event that a salesperson leaves the company before paying off her lead charges.
- You don't have to reduce the number of leads you give to your best performers in order to have enough leads to assign to your newcomers.
- Your lead-conversion rate improves. When new people are trained to generate their own leads from the get-go, your limited company leads can be assigned to your better-closing, more experienced reps.
- You can recruit a larger sales force than a sales manager who cannot generate local leads from a wide range of sources.
- Your current sales force will be more welcoming to newcomers, as the newcomers will not be competing for those precious company leads until they have earned their spurs.
- Your reps' neighborhood-generated leads reduce travel time. A happy consequence is more selling time.
- Veterans control their own fate. No longer are they dependent on the ups and downs of the company lead flow. While some veterans may initially resist the change from the comfort of total dependency on company-supplied leads, most come to see the advantages of a wider access to their market.

A sales manager with competence in at least 10 local lead–generation systems can, in turn, teach a broad range of prospecting tools so that each sales representative can choose the ones that best suit his or her personality, ability, and market situation. Your story to your sales team is, "I will expose you to 10 local lead–generating systems. You won't like them all. I ask you try them all. Then pick out the three that work best for you."

Now let's review these self-generating lead options.

1. PARTY PLAN

Some products, such as cookware, lend themselves ideally to group selling. Years ago in the U.S. Virgin Islands, my party-plan cookware team promoted Regal Ware by advertising, "Free $39 stainless steel vegetable cutter for hosting a healthy dinner." A prepaid postcard proclaiming this message was inserted into the free shopper magazine distributed through local retail outlets. This simple device helped keep three dinner-party sales reps busy for years in a small market.

Many direct-sales companies teach party-plan selling as the almost exclusive method of delivering a sales presentation. The effective and time-proven method of booking home parties is to ask friends and relatives to host a party. In turn, those attending the party are invited to host future parties in exchange for a gift and an enjoyable event. This works well unless somewhere along the line the chain breaks. When that happens, other local lead programs can be used to book party-plan events to start new chains, such as those that follow here.

2. TAKE-ONE BOXES

Anyone who has seen an American Express credit card application box at the cashier's counter of a restaurant understands the power and simplicity of the take-one box (TOB). You *take* the credit card application home, fill it out, and mail it back to the company.

Almost any direct-to-the-consumer product can generate high-quality leads with take-one boxes as long as you keep it simple. The size of the Amex box is about right. Emphasize the word *free* on top of the free lead card, followed by a picture of the gift you are offering for sending in the lead. Relate the gift to the product or service you are selling. You can place 10 to 20 take-one boxes in shops in an hour as long as your placement talk is less than 60 seconds.

The following statement is all you need to place TOBs: "Excuse me, I have a free gift and some valuable information for your customers. May I put this small, attractive take-one box here or there?" Never argue or give a long talk. One out of four or five shops will simply point to the place where you can put the TOB. Give a warm thank-you and move on to the next shop. You will want to check back on your TOBs about once a week for a month and then, depending on results, change to another location to get a fresh audience. Refill the TOBs where most of the brochures are gone; remove the ones where few or none of the brochures were taken. Start by placing TOBs with places you patronize, such as your local convenience store, beauty parlor, or dry cleaner. Don't overlook places like doctors' waiting rooms, hospitals, employee cafeterias, or reception areas in apartment buildings.

3. DROP-HERE BOXES

Companies like 24 Hour Fitness have a different approach to the take-one box:

- The ad copy is printed on a backboard attached to the back of a box.
- The box is approximately an eight-inch cube with a slot in the middle of the top.
- A pad of tear-off coupons is attached to the top of the box.
- The prospect is invited to fill out the coupon with her name and telephone number for a chance to win a six-month free membership at the gym, with a guarantee of winning a seven-day free membership.
- The prospect drops the coupon into the slot on top of the box.
- The salesperson picks up the filled-in coupons every few days.
- The sales counselor calls prospects, inviting them to come in and start using the seven-day free membership.

4. FISHBOWLS AND BUSINESS CARDS

A placard behind or next to a fishbowl invites people to drop in their business card for a free drawing or free gift.

5. HANDOUTS

Personally handing a flyer to a passerby is about as simple and direct as you can get. Think like a politician a week before the election. Candidates stand in front of schools and factories at peak times, when the foot traffic is heaviest. Concert locations, popular movie venues, and sports events are also ideal because people are often standing in line and are more likely to read your flyer on the spot. Pick up discarded flyers when you leave or you'll wear out your welcome at that location.

6. OFFICE MARKETING

It's easy to pass out lead-generating flyers in small and medium-sized businesses, as well as many government offices. Ask the receptionist if you can leave behind some information pamphlets with valuable information. If you get a no, say thank you and move on. If you get a yes, ask two questions. "How many people work here, so I can give you the correct number?" Then, depending on the size of the company and the level of security, instead of just handing the flyers to the receptionist, ask him or her, "Can I save you time by placing the free information brochures on the employees' desks or in their mailboxes?"

7. DOOR HANGERS

Apartments are ideal for door hangers. Make sure that the word *free* is printed in large red letters and that a postage-paid response card can be detached and mailed.

8. NEWSPAPER INSERTS

Newspaper inserts are usually a waste of money for most direct-to-the-consumer products, for the simple reason that you pay to reach *all* newspaper readers in a certain area, even though most of your industry's products are niche-oriented. Accordingly, the rate of return is usually a disappointment. Most of the time you are better off spending the money on some alternative prospecting activity.

Having made that disclaimer, let me explain why inserts in local and specialty publications sometimes make good sense. Inserting flyers in local publications can be effective if the local publication has special demographics and the cost is low. For instance, inserting flyers in the health store newsletter to generate cookware leads can be relatively cheap. (It may even cost you nothing if you do the stuffing yourself and give the shop a small gift.) The trick is to match your niche product with a niche audience at a reasonable cost.

9. LOCAL PUBLICATIONS

Local publications are almost always niche publications. Identify those publications that are distributed to your niche market. The per capita cost of reaching genuine prospects in niche or specialty publications is usually a fraction of the cost of reaching them through a daily newspaper. Keep in mind that the per capita cost may be lower even if the cost of reaching a reader of a niche publication or Web site is higher than that of reaching a reader of a mass media publication. What matters is the per capita cost of reaching a prospect with the interest and financial ability to purchase the product or service offered.

10. LOCAL THIRD-PARTY PROGRAMS

If generating third-party leads with major credit card companies or other national companies makes sense, it makes even more sense to create such associations locally. No matter what you are selling, there are companies that sell *other* products to the same prospects. Many of these vendors welcome the chance to defray some of their mailing or Web maintenance costs by cooperating with you. Your database is valuable to another vendor who has a similar prospecting profile, and vice versa. So why not trade database access? Just remember one important point: On the bottom of *all* leads, print a box for respondents to check if they do *not* want their name shared. Most people ignore the opportunity to do so, thus giving the vendor permission to exchange access to their name with other vendors.

11. BAGGING

Place your lead flyers in shopping bags at retail outlets. For example, you can place

- Educational products flyers at bookstores or children's clothing stores.
- Fire detection systems flyers at home improvement stores like the local version of Home Depot. (National chains are hard to work with; local stores tend to be more cooperative.)
- Exercise equipment flyers at vitamin supplement stores.
- Waterless stainless cookware product flyers at specialty foodstores.

Start your bagging program by approaching those vendors with whom you already have another marketing relationship.

12. LOCAL MAIL LEAD GENERATION

Generate leads from locally obtained mailing lists, such as those of local clubs, stores, companies, and similar affinity groups that escape the attention of a national marketing headquarters. These local mailing lists often outperform national lists because the affinity to your product is tighter and the mailing list tends to be more current. Some possibilities include

- Financial products through local service clubs
- Foreign-language products through travel agencies
- Home security systems through local insurance agencies offering home protection policies

13. SEMINARS

Invite prospects to a free lecture on a subject of concern or interest where your product is part of the solution to better living. Estate planners, plastic surgeons, and time-share enterprises use this method. Does your product lend itself to a one- or two-hour educational seminar where the list of attendees could later be solicited for a sale? You might offer an unconditional gift for attendance to sweeten the invitation.

14. REFERRALS

All sales personnel understand that referral business represents the ultimate in low-cost orders. A complete guide to generating referral business is given in Chapter 24 as part of the customer service segment of this book.

15. KIOSKS, COUNTERS, AND BOOTHS

This group of local lead–generation opportunities is reviewed as part of the next chapter, "Boost Exhibition Sales."

*   *   *

The possibilities for generating local leads can be both exciting and overwhelming. So many possibilities; so little time. Once you commit to an aggressive comprehensive local lead program, the following guidelines will help you take full advantage of your local lead–generation efforts:

■ *Promote rollouts.* Introduce a new prospecting tool with an introductory prospecting event. Offer awards based on the number of contacts or materials distributed to build enthusiasm.

■ *Conduct local marketing clinics.* Ongoing training exercises allow salespeople to build their prospecting competencies by practicing the various prospecting skills in the field. A typical clinic lasts four hours: one hour to explain and practice, two hours to perform the lead-generating activity, and a one-hour meet-back that allows everyone to report his successes.

■ *Supply prospecting materials.* Each lead-generation method requires its own set of materials. Chapter 25 suggests methods for getting the most out of your selling and prospecting tools.

■ *Schedule your program.* Rollouts and clinics work when they are part of your strategic planning schedule. Mark your calendar with rollouts and clinics well in advance.

■ *Hire a local marketing manager.* It is almost impossible for a sales manager to have enough time to manage a powerful, full-fledged local marketing program. A marketing manager can contact the malls and exhibitors to book booth space, negotiate third-party lead-generation campaigns, help conduct training, and handle the acquisition of prospecting tools such as free-draw cards, take-one boxes, and the like.

These 15 local lead–generation systems turbocharge prospecting, blowing away reluctance to keep expanding your sales force. No one method of prospecting can reach all your customers. No salesperson can simultaneously utilize all these methods. You need an ever-larger sales force to be trained in an ever-wider range of prospecting methods, making the next essential activity, recruiting, much more urgent.

QUESTIONS TO ASK YOURSELF

■ How many methods of prospecting are you using now?
■ What percentage of the market are you selling each year? Could you do more?
■ Would more prospecting methods increase sales?
■ Would more prospecting methods drive increased recruiting?
■ Which new techniques will you start to use first?
■ What is your three- to six-month plan to make all effective prospecting methods part of your sales team's selling competencies?

Additional reading material on prospecting methods emphasizing party-plan selling:

■ *Direct Sales* by Joyce M. Ross

CHAPTER 7
BOOST EXHIBITION SALES

Start by doing what is necessary, then what is possible, and suddenly you are doing the impossible.

—St. Francis of Assisi, Founder, Franciscan Order

There has been spectacular growth in sales booths, kiosks, and exhibition sales over the past 20 years. As a salesperson who started in the direct-to-the-consumer sales business, knocking on doors in all sorts of weather, I appreciated the day I went to work in a mall, where "the doors" came to me, as you can see in this story.

> Less than two months after I had arrived to head up this company's new sales division, new sales representatives Dan and Tom were working our first booth at a major department store. The product was a home study program, and our sales booth was located on the seventh floor, in front of the book section near the elevator. I dropped by around 7 p.m. after finishing up at the office.
> "No traffic," the pair complained.
> However, I had noticed a number of young prospects milling around downstairs in front of the department store. I took out a five-dollar bill and challenged them with, "If either of you can bring up a warm body to hear a presentation within five minutes, this bill is yours." Both qualified in less than three minutes. Dan got his first order that night, Tom the following night.

It took our face-to-face sales industry several years to understand that working a sales counter or booth was more than just having "the doors" come to the salesperson. Here is a summary of the differences and special opportunities of sales counter selling.

TECHNIQUES FOR BOOSTING EXHIBITION SALES

Deliver a Shorter and More Compact Sales Talk

Time is of the essence at the sales booth. Deliver a shorter and more suc-cinct sales talk than you would at an in-home presentation.

Expect a Lower Closing Percentage, but Higher Earnings per Day

Expect a lower closing percentage on your presentations than with in-home sales appointments, since you have less time to tell your story to prospects who may be only suspects. On the other hand, expect higher daily earnings at a good sales booth because you can deliver many more sales demonstrations and/or gather a ton of leads and appointments. Prospects are more disposed to chat with you at a sales booth than in a cold call at their door or on the phone.

Screen Quickly

Qualify genuine prospects during the first minute of the conversation. The sales pros quickly learn to stop working low-percentage prospects so that they can get back to the booth counter and start prospecting for a more qualified person to talk to. Your newer people need to be trained and fre-quently reminded not to waste time talking to suspects.

Get New Salespeople Started

New sales recruits can be trained to book appointments at a sales counter effectively in a day or two. You can place your new sales trainees at sales counters to book high-quality appointments even before they can deliver an effective sales presentation.

Show Off Live Merchandise

Your entire product can usually be fully displayed and demonstrated on lo-cation. In the home, you are often restricted to what you can hand-carry when showing the customer sample merchandise. For instance, it's difficult to bring an exercise chair, an entire ensemble of home improvement materials, or a complete set of home study books and videos on a home visit. Live merchandise displayed at an attractive sales kiosk converts more prospects to customers than just bringing your in-home sales kit to the booth.

Increase Your Credibility

Some prospects feel more comfortable buying in a public shopping location. Prospects often think (usually correctly) that you couldn't maintain a booth at a mall or show if you had consumer problems.

Enjoy Three Bites of the Apple

A sales booth provides the salesperson with three prospecting options, depending on the circumstances, the personality of the salesperson, and the time the prospect has available at the face-to-face booth visit.

- A free-draw card grants permission to call back later.
- An appointment for a certain time and date can be booked instantly.
- An order can be accepted on the spot.

In addition to booking sales booths at kiosks and exhibitions to sell orders on the spot, consider booking booths and counters in locations where no selling activity is allowed. Such a location can have numerous advantages:

- The number of locations expands exponentially because this practice eliminates the objections some shops have to their customers being subject to buying pressure from a salesperson working inside the store.
- The salesperson legitimately avoids giving price quotations at the counter because "the agreement with the store includes a prohibition on engaging in any sales activity."
- The cost of a no-sales-activity booth ranges from free to inexpensive.
- Chances improve to book high-traffic places, such as a grocery store or a factory cafeteria, where shoppers or workers are often too

busy to stop for a full sales presentation. It takes only four to seven minutes to book an appointment.

■ You can specify scheduling appointment-only locations during the store's busiest hours.

■ Appointment-only booths require less space, since the product is not demonstrated. This allows you to negotiate space at the entrances and exits.

■ Appointment-only booths are often perfect for new recruits. They can learn to obtain free-draw cards and/or set up appointments in their first days of training.

Now let's review the three bites of the apple.

■ *Free-draw cards.* No matter whether the booth is for selling or for booking appointments, the first step in the booth-selling process is always to request prospects to fill out the free-draw card to win the gift. As long as the gift is related to your product or service, you have a reasonable expectation that a person who agrees to fill out the free-draw card is a prospect. Think about this:

❏ A person wouldn't want to win something he or she did not want to own.

❏ The prospect who volunteers a phone number and address has given you permission to call later because you are no longer a stranger or a cold call.

Between 25 and 50 percent of booth orders ought to be derived from free-draw cards (FDCs) in the weeks following the sales booth activity. These delayed FDC orders are often the difference between making a profit on a booth and not making one.

■ *Booking appointments.* Use the following procedure at counters when prospects are too busy to sit for a sales talk or the agreement with the vendor does not allow selling.

❏ Prepare an appointment-only read-off binder, using bold print for the key phrases and smart-looking visuals.

❏ Set up appointments at the booth just like on the telephone by reading the script. Reading the script more than doubles the number of appointments when compared with reps ad libbing.

❏ Offer an attractive appointment gift to be delivered when you visit the prospect at home.

❏ Give the prospect three items to take home:

1. A brochure on your company's products or services

2. An appointment reminder with the time and date of the appointment, along with a picture of the gift to be presented

3. A cute magnet to place over the appointment reminder so that the prospect can place it on the fridge

❏ Call to verify the appointment. There will be about a 50 percent kick-out factor. It is a waste of time to drive to the prospect's home or business before verifying the appointment.

❏ Deliver your appointment gift upon entering the prospect's home or office unconditionally.

■ *Exhibition selling and closing premiums.* Exhibition selling is an exciting and growing sales opportunity. Maximum sales success at these shows is dependent on the "show offer." The best results demand a unique offer that is genuinely a good deal for the customer, who is being asked to buy an expensive item on impulse.

* * *

There is great drama at sales exhibition booths. Consumers are "just shopping." Still, attendance at these shows means that consumers are least open to the idea of maybe seeing something that they might want to own "some day." The eager salesperson warms to the challenge of making that "some day" be today—now, this instant. So, the dance begins, with a consumer agreeing to fill out the information card and/or agreeing to "just look" at the product.

The three-gift close has produced the best exhibition show results. It works like this:

Gift one. A reasonably priced gift is presented at the first trial close with little fanfare. Customers have been educated that there is always a gift for buying today at the show.

Gift two. This slightly better gift is held back until the second or third closing effort and is presented as a "reward" for the customer's hemming and hawing regarding a buying decision today. Again, most consumers expect that there might be a little something extra. A strong close is attempted at the presentation of gift two.

Gift three. This is the super gift. It works only if it is held back for at least 10 minutes into the close. The timing is as important as the value of the gift. The prospect is still resisting buying *today*. She definitely would like to have the product, or she would have left the booth a long time ago. The price is affordable, or the prospect would have departed. What remains is procrastination. "Am I doing the right thing? Maybe I should wait." The third gift is held back until *after* the salesperson has gone through all of his closes and can sense that the moment of truth is at hand. The prospect might say yes, and then again she might repeat, "Well I really need to think about this. Let me have your business card." *Now* is the time to present the third gift. The third gift needs to be powerful. The gift and the timing of the gift are designed to overwhelm all buying resistance.

I love going to these exhibitions just to watch salespeople in action. Midway through writing this book, I attended a consumer products exhibition at the Bleasdale Complex in Honolulu, Hawaii. I was treated to a professional cookware sales demonstration. What a masterful demonstration it was. I had sold stainless steel waterless cookware in the Caribbean during the 1970s, so I was anxious to see how this salesman matched up. I wished I had been as good!

The salesman demonstrated the cookware to an audience of 30 people seated on folding chairs in front of the demonstration area. The triple-gift-close netted him seven $1,200 orders on the spot!

At the end of his presentation, he gave the price of the various packages and stated that anyone buying today would also receive a vegetable cutter. This premium merited a five-minute display of how good this particular vegetable cutter was. Then he went through the first trial close.

As the audience studied the sales contracts he had just passed out, he reviewed the second gift, a set of kitchen knives. Again, we were treated to a five-minute demo. None of the audience had left the demo yet. Everyone continued to stare at the sales contract in his or her hand. I was sitting in the back, and I could tell that a few prospects might be ready to buy. The salesperson attempted a second trial close. "This was it" as far as the audience was concerned. Spouses looked at each other with the "what do you think" look. The salesman explained the shipping procedures and reviewed the benefits of buying a lifetime set of cookware, the money that would be saved, and the healthy meals that would be prepared. I could feel the tension building in the room. I wondered, "Is there more?"

I was not disappointed. Just as the audience was starting to fidget a bit, with maybe a few thinking of leaving, the salesman brought out an electric skillet with an oil core center. This was a $350 miracle skillet. The enthusiastic chef/salesman announced that since this was the company's fiftieth anniversary, everyone who bought *today* would receive this wonderful skillet *free*. Seven people bought. Actually, it was eight. I bought the skillet! I already had the cookware. It lasts a lifetime, so you only buy once.

HIRE AND TRAIN AT THE BOOTH

This is another opportunity to kill two key proverbial birds with a one-time activity stone. A booth is also a great place to conduct hiring interviews. The applicant certainly understands what the job is.

We conclude this chapter with four tips on booth management:

- Sales managers need to pay for the booths by some combination of headquarters's marketing budget, the sales manager's contribution, and the salesperson's contribution. Everyone (except for the newest recruits) benefiting from the sale contributes a proportionate share of the cost.

- While the home office marketing department can negotiate national or regional contracts for sales booths and counter stand locations with chain stores, it is often cheaper and faster to book local locations yourself.

- Inspect potential sales counter locations before you negotiate terms with the vendor. Plan to do so during the various time periods when you want to work that location.

- Consider hiring the marketing manager we discussed in the previous chapter to leverage your time and gain specialized expertise.

QUESTIONS TO ASK YOURSELF

- What percentage of your sales comes from exhibitions, kiosks, or sales counters? What are the possibilities?
- If you are selling at counters, are you getting the extra sales by making appointments and working your free-draw cards effectively?

■ Does it make sense to teach your new recruits how to use sales counters to make appointments at the end of the first week of training?

■ Does the design of your kiosks and exhibitions bring people to your sales counters?

■ Do you provide specialized training for closing at counters?

■ Do you have a special "triple-threat" set of closing premiums at your exhibitions?

Books primarily directed at business-to-business selling at trade shows that have great tips for our direct-sales industry:

■ *Over 88 Tips & Ideas to Supercharge Your Exhibit Sales* by Steve Miller and Charmel Bowden

■ *How to Get the Most out of Trade Shows* by Steve Miller

THIRD ESSENTIAL ACTIVITY

HIRE

Maybe I have been lucky. I have never felt that I had a recruiting problem. I have recruited salespeople in more than 20 countries selling many products. Job applicants who wanted to sell my product on full-commission compensation or on a provisional salary always came forward.

I hired my first salespeople when I was only 20 years old. Perhaps if I had started recruiting later in life, I might have analyzed the difficulties. It never occurred to me that recruiting was difficult. I was drilled, "Recruit every week." So I did. I formed the habit without giving it any thought. That habit has helped me build sales empires on four continents. That recruiting discipline allowed me to retire early in order to follow my passions for writing and traveling, and to own homes in both Hawaii and Florida.

"Sell every day, recruit every week" pulsated as my mantra. *Every* may not be literal. But constant, unrelenting personal selling and recruiting summarizes the job. Do that right, and everything else falls into place. Successful ongoing recruiting patterns hinge on habit, not on the success or failure of the most recent recruiting exercise, the time of year, or any other circumstance.

If you recruit only when all your sales representatives are "fully trained," you have the wrong mindset. If you recruit only when you need to hire a new salesperson, you are embracing the wrong approach. If you are afraid to recruit because you feel you just don't have the time, your priorities are out of whack. If you are afraid to recruit because some of your salespeople do not have enough leads to stay busy, you need better prospecting techniques, not fewer sales reps.

Hiring face-to-face commission sales representatives is neither easy nor difficult. It's just a process. Recruiting disappointments will always outnumber successes. It doesn't matter! The Direct Sales Association claims that more than 2,000,000 commission-based representatives sell face-to-face full-time in America. Another 9,000,000 people engage in some type of multilevel selling, such as Pre-Paid Legal, Amway, or Nu-Skin.

While most job seekers do not want to work as a commission salesperson or on a salary system that requires constant qualification criteria, *there will always be those who do*. Perhaps they prefer to have their results directly tied to their effort and talent, or perhaps they've seen what tremendous rewards can come from direct sales, or perhaps a "regular job" just never came along. The following two chapters on hiring will help you recruit and keep more than your fair share of the "those who do."

CHAPTER 8

EXPLOIT 17 POWERFUL, PROVEN RECRUITING TECHNIQUES

It's not a matter of life and death: It is more important than that.

—Vince Lombardi, NFL Coach

As sales manager, my recurring fear was that the one week that I did not recruit would be the very week that a potential superstar salesperson would be reading the "Help Wanted" section. I did not want to miss that opportunity. The following story illustrates one of the many simultaneous recruiting habits I exploited to build a sales empire. You just never know what will work on a particular day.

> He walked up to my sales counter, eyeing the red-lettered "Help Wanted" sign resting on its edge. "How does the job work?" he asked. Tim had moved to Guam a few months before. He had worked intermittently on a fishing boat catering to tourists, planning to learn the trade and then get his own boat. Tim told me that swabbing the deck and throwing chum into the water wasn't all he'd thought it would be.
>
> "Well," I replied, "if you've got the time, why don't you just watch me for a couple of hours?" Although I didn't get an order that day, Tim witnessed how congenial the selling environment was and how friendly people were, even in rejection. Tim went on to be the rookie of the year in 1988—not just in Guam, but in the entire United States. The habit of keeping that "Help Wanted" sign at the sales counter had paid off again.

That's just one example of a simple, low-cost, no-effort habit that produces steady results. In the following pages, you will find 17 proven hiring methods that you can use to fill your people inventory with outstanding sales performers.

1. NEWSPAPERS

When you write your recruiting ad copy, do so from the perspective of "What is the job seeker looking for?" The want-ad reader is hunting for job security, a ground-floor training opportunity, good income, management potential, and interesting work. Here are a few outstanding ad copy headlines guaranteed to captivate the job seeker.

■ *"More leads than current sales force can handle."* Job security in the direct-sales business means that salespeople have enough prospects. Proclaim that you have *too many* prospects; you just need more salespeople to contact this abundance. All too often, direct-sales applicants worry that they will be pressured to sell to friends and relatives. This presents a double anxiety. First, many people really do not want to try to sell a big-ticket item to people they know. Second, savvy job applicants understand that they will eventually run out of friends and relatives. Then what?

This book covers prospecting before it covers hiring. The abundance of leads provided by prospecting gives you ever more confidence to recruit a larger sales force aggressively. You have the practical lead-generation techniques to validate your claim that the market is far too large for your current sales force to handle.

■ *"National company expanding,"* *"new sales office opening,"* or *"new product requires manpower expansion."* Ground-floor opportunities appeal to the job seeker's constant hope that someday he or she will catch a successful product wave at the beginning and ride the crest to prosperity.

■ *"Full training offered"* or *"complete training program for qualified applicants."* Training assurances take away the "I am not qualified" fear.

■ *"Up to $500 a week to qualified applicants,"* *"salary of $2,000 a month plus performance bonuses,"* or *"three orders a week earns $1,400."* Promises of good income in your ad copy reflect your best effort to indicate earning potential. If your company has special perks, such as stock options at certain plateaus of achievement, don't be shy about proclaiming this good news. Companies that offer salaries or draws will (and should) emphasize the monthly income. If you are paying on a full-commission basis, consider quoting the average commission on an order in the context of weekly or monthly income potential. Think of the ad copy in the newspaper as a contract with the reader. What you put in that copy must be genuine and accurate. That is why "up to" a certain dollar amount and "to qualified applicants" are important phrases.

■ *"Management trainees required for expanding national company"* or *"90-day management training program offered to qualified applicants."* Management potential pulls in many job applicants who do not want "just a job as a salesperson."

Ambitious sales candidates covet a career that leads to management. In turn, ambitious sales managers hunt for potential managers and have a training program to develop managers in place.

■ *"Occasional overseas travel required"* or *"socials every Friday."* Is there something unique to or interesting about your workplace? Travel opportunities catch the eye of the job applicant. If sales trips are often to overseas destinations, include that information in your recruiting ad copy.

Writing recruiting ad copy is fun. Look at the phraseology of other sales companies when you are searching for a new catchphrase. Read an out-of-town newspaper for ideas; this allows you to borrow a phrase that will come across as unique and fresh in your market.

Catch readers' attention with smart-looking ads by using your imagination and some basic graphics. Black borders, white print on a black background, and 20-point **bold** headlines grab a reader's attention. If you feel you need help in designing an ad or if you want a wider choice of graphics, discuss the mechanics of ad writing and display advertising with your newspaper sales agent. He or she will be more than happy to coach you.

Keep an ad book. One section holds the ads you have already used, with the results noted under the ad. Another section contains ads from other companies that might act as a useful inspiration for form and content.

Maintain records of your newspaper recruiting. How much does it cost to recruit a producing salesperson? Which ads obtain the best results?

Weekly newspapers, such as entertainment and shopping guides, are cheap, effective alternatives to the dailies for your recruiting ads.

It is interesting to note that newspaper recruiting has become less important over the past few decades in recruiting a sales force. It is expensive. There are other alternatives. The remaining recruiting techniques may be more cost-effective for you than relying on newspaper recruiting.

2. CUSTOMERS

More than half of the sales force for the children's product division during my 11 years in Asia was what we called "users." The mothers owned the product. They loved the product. In addition to individual sales representatives and managers directly asking customers to consider selling the product, we sent out an annual recruiting letter modeled after the one I had used successfully with Encyclopedia Britannica years earlier. The 24 Fitness centers find some of their best sales counselors on the floor during workouts.

What does this tell us? Users or owners of a product bring heartfelt passion to selling that product because they are true believers in its benefits. Enthusiasm and sincerity make for a powerful sales presentation. (Asking satisfied owners to sell is not the same thing as selling the product to someone with the promise that he will "get his money back" by selling the product to his friends.)

3. PROSPECTS

One hot Saturday afternoon in the 1970s, I was canvassing door to door in Tutu, a new housing development in the hills of St. Thomas in the Virgin Islands. Dulce, a Hispanic single parent, really wanted to buy a set of the *New Book of Knowledge* for her daughter, but she simply did not have the money. I was struck by her lively personality, so I asked her whether she would consider selling the product. Surprised but flattered, she accepted and received training that very week. Dulce went on to specialize in selling to her affinity market for several years. You may not ask every person who doesn't buy to work for you, but you might want to develop the habit of being on the alert for questions from a prospect that suggest an interest in selling.

4. FRIENDS AND RELATIVES

One of my best friends, Beau, and I used to play backgammon once or twice a week. A schoolteacher by profession, Beau enjoyed his job—until he lost it. I not so casually asked him to come with me on a couple of sales calls. He knew I was making a good income, but he'd never thought of himself as a direct salesperson. Not only did he become a great salesperson, but he went on to be promoted to district manager within three years. During the 1960s, I recruited three of my fraternity brothers to sell encyclopedias. While none of them stuck to it for very long, they all made a little pocket change, and I picked up a few overrides on their orders. Win-win.

5. "HELP WANTED" SIGNS

Tim wasn't the only person who responded to my "Help Wanted" sign. Rose Marie passed by my sales counter just outside the military PX store one Saturday morning. The wife of an enlisted man, she was looking for a way to supplement her husband's income. Rose Marie soon was earning more money than if she had taken one of the typical military-dependent/wife jobs at minimum wage.

6. MAGAZINES

A company with a national sales force can advertise in national magazines. I once successfully recruited salespeople through *USA Today*, which reads more like a magazine than like a local newspaper. Local or regional magazines can be an excellent source of sales personnel as well.

Target the best media for your product, then write and place ads directed at their readership.

- The AARP magazine would be a natural venue for recruiting cemetery sales personnel, since most of the sales counselors in that industry are over 50 years of age.
- Use sports publications to recruit exercise equipment and health club sales reps.
- Home improvement magazines would be useful for recruiting home improvement sales personnel.

7. FLYER INSERTS

Having been newly promoted, Carol quickly started building her sales force with the concept of targeting neighborhood applicants. Instead of buying a small ad in the daily newspaper, she placed a colorful, information-packed, double-sided flyer inside her neighborhood's weekly shopper publications. She soon had a large pool of applicants to screen and hire. It worked so well that others soon copied her.

8. BULLETIN BOARDS

Talk about cheap: Sticking a recruiting poster on the various bulletin boards at supermarkets and community centers is about as low-cost as you can get. Carol, the flyer recruiter, also used this method as part of her "recruit the neighbors" program.

9. "BUMP INTO"

Nigeria, of all places, is the setting for my best example of being alert for "bump-into" recruiting.

Keith, an Englishman who was in the building contracting business, had bought a "bunch" of encyclopedias wholesale from a British publisher because he had heard about the high margins possible in direct sales. The problem was, Keith didn't know anything about the direct-selling business. Cartons of encyclopedias were sitting in a Lagos warehouse, just collecting dust.

I had just completed my Peace Corps service in Nigeria when I bumped into one of the few people who had bought a set of books from Keith. I tracked Keith down from information on the sales contract and cut a deal with him, and I was off and selling. In a few weeks I had sold five or six sets and had been paid as promised.

One evening soon after this, I struck up a conversation in a pub with another patron, Moses. As we chatted about our respective jobs, Moses asked enough questions about mine to let me know that he might be interested.

The next day I showed Moses an order. This was the type of job he was looking for. Within a few weeks, Moses had sold a few orders and had begun recruiting his friends. By the end of a month, we had almost 10 salespeople.

Eventually I left Nigeria. Two years later, when I set up my business in the Caribbean, Moses joined me for a year, selling encyclopedias. Was it luck that I bumped into Keith, who had the product, and Moses, who helped sell it? Or were those serendipitous events the result of a "keep alert for opportunity" habit?

Bob Baseman, former national sales director of Encyclopedia Britannica, always carried an "I like your style" business card to give to people he'd bump into that he would like to have drop by his office for an interview.

10. VENDORS

Tom, who cold-called me to sell advertising space in a local magazine, absolutely radiated enthusiasm. I did not buy advertising space, but I suggested that he ought to come in and talk to me about a pioneer sales management position with my new sales division. Three days later, Tom wrote his first order. Eventually, he built a sales team of 80 people.

11. JOB FAIRS

I attended my first job fair in England in 1985, when I was the national trainer for Encyclopedia Britannica. I had just learned how to administer the DISC personality tests, and I wanted to try them out. My assistant and I rented the smallest booth at the fair and offered passersby a free test. The two of us were kept very busy, as it seemed that everyone wanted to learn about his or her personality. The test revealed a lot about the person taking it: which newspaper he or she read, his or her favorite subjects in school, whether the person was neat or sloppy, and so forth. As we read off the results, we felt like fortune-tellers, except that we were simply interpreting the test. We became the hit of the fair. And we hired more than a dozen applicants, three or four of whom completed training and wrote an order.

A few years later in Taiwan, I created my own job fair. Our growing company needed some new administrative people, so I combined all the job descriptions, rented a room at a major hotel, placed the appropriate ads in the newspapers, and set up interview booths for the various departments that were hiring. Even though most of the people came to the fair seeking the administrative, salaried jobs—and we did fill all of these—we hired many more of the job seekers to enter sales training.

Job fairs are better than ever. Only last year I took a peek at the Honolulu job fair. Even though Hawaii had a only a 3 percent unemployment figure, thousands of job aspirants snaked around the entrance waiting to find a more fulfilling career. I was not disappointed to find direct-sales companies such as health clubs and health insurance companies busy interviewing eager people who wanted to improve their income.

12. COLLEGES AND UNIVERSITIES

I placed a cheap, four-line ad offering to pay "up to $35 a week" in the *Florida Gator*, the student newspaper at the University of Florida, where I attended school. In those days, $35 was half a commission. At the interview, I explained that if the person wrote just one order every two weeks, he or she could earn four times the prevailing minimum wage. I maintained a group of about a half dozen sales reps during my senior year. Ask yourself the obvious:

- Are college students still working their way through college?
- Would many college students prefer an alternative to working at the local fast-food eatery?
- Are college newspapers an inexpensive way to reach a huge pool of quick-learning, motivated salespeople?

English Now sold an English language program aimed at young adults in Japan. The best salespeople were also young adults. We targeted new college grads to expand our sales force. Recent college graduates in Japan wanted to work for the big-name, prestigious firms. However, not all job seekers got their first, or even their second, choice of employment. We didn't mind being their job of "last choice." We hired more than a hundred recent grads each year for several years, recruiting at campuses across the country.

13. COMPETITORS

Keep your eyes open for salespeople who might be unhappy with their company, their boss, or their job situation. You may meet these potential new salespeople when you are at your booth at an industry event or when you are attending outside sales or motivational training programs. Some companies award recruiting bonuses or temporary salaries to managers who recruit sales groups en masse. I never did that. Rather, I would pay double commission to all the sales reps for four weeks if the group consisted of at least five salespeople. Here were the conditions:

- The clock started ticking for the entire group when the first newly recruited ex-competitor wrote the first order. If one of the group lagged behind, perhaps bringing in her first order two weeks later, that person had only two weeks of double commission. The objective was to motivate everyone to get off to a fast start.
- The double commission was paid on the basic commission. It did not include management overrides or bonuses.
- The new salesperson had to turn in his old sales kit to get a new one. (No double kitting!)
- Each salesperson had to submit a current pay statement from her present company to verify that all the qualifying recruits were active and skilled sales representatives.

My former boss Herb continues to amaze me. He always seems to be finding what someone else might call a retread. Previously retired salespeople from our company and veteran competitors would call him. His reputation for being a fair and decent boss continues to be a recruiting strategy. Only last year a former colleague called from Sydney to find out if there was an opportunity. With Herb, there is *always* a special opportunity.

14. YOUR OWN STAFF

Set up a reward system to pay your administrative and sales personnel to recruit. Pay a small appearance fee for any applicant who shows up for the interview. Pay a fee when the first order is written. Then pay either a commission on the next 10 or so orders or a flat fee if the recruit reaches a certain sales volume. An annual awareness campaign pays great dividends. Compare the cost of this recruiting method with any other. You will like the numbers.

15. GOVERNMENT JOB CENTERS

Many government job centers now offer jobs in the direct-sales industries. It is worthwhile to check with your local unemployment office to find out if your company's pay package qualifies. I found my best job center recruit in London, England. John was only 20 at the time and a little rough around the edges, but he was a gamer. He became our youngest district manager within two years.

16. HEADHUNTERS

At one time headhunters would not consider recruiting for commission salespeople. This is no longer the case. Many recruiting agencies will work on a percentage of sales volume for a specified period of time. You have to troll the Yellow Pages or research online (try doing a search at Google.com) to find them.

17. THE INTERNET

I was working in Taiwan when the Internet "arrived." It did not take the eager, innovative Taiwanese long to see the advantages of using the Internet to recruit. It happened so quickly that soon managers were creating their own individual Web sites and using them to compete with other managers for recruits. Some of these sites were good; many were terrible. Seeing the need to standardize Web-site recruiting, the company created a first-class company Web site for all the managers to use. Applicants were shared among all the sales managers using an agreed-upon formula.

A good recruiting Web site is now standard for all empire-building sales companies. The right Web-site manager can build an attractive site, breaking through the surfing chaff so that the site pops up on the first Google.com page when job seekers type in key words.

WWW.Monster.com provides a great place to jump for an Internet alternative to recruiting. This site makes it easy.

✳   ✳   ✳

Once you adopt the mindset of building an empire, you will find using *all* the methods of recruiting to be both natural and necessary. Perhaps you can now better understand why I never thought recruiting was a problem. It is just a process—a constant, unrelenting process, to be sure, but one that is essential to the success of every sales manager.

QUESTIONS TO ASK YOURSELF

- How many of these 17 methods of recruiting have you used in the past three months?
- Do you have the records for the recruiting source of each of your sales reps?
- How much did it cost to find a sales rep using each method?
- Do some sales managers do better at certain types of recruiting than others?
- Is it worthwhile to find out how they are doing it?
- Do you have systems in place to use all the methods you want to use?

Recommended reading on hiring techniques:

- *Recruit & Sell* by Dr. Keith Laggos

CHAPTER 9
USE THE 10-STEP JOB-SELLING INTERVIEW

Your future depends on many things, but mostly it depends on you.

—Frank Tyger, Author

It doesn't matter who places the ad in the paper or distributes the recruiting inserts in the weekly shopper or places the "Help Wanted" sign on the sales counter; applicants will respond in equal numbers. It's what comes after you have an applicant's attention that makes the difference. What separates the great recruiters from the good or average recruiters is a determined mindset and an enthusiastic professionalism when conducting the recruiting interview. You bring the mindset; the rest you can learn. Hiring is more high-tech these days, but the basics remain the same. I still remember how I entered our wonderful industry as if it were only yesterday.

> "People slam doors in your face, dogs bark at you, and little ol' ladies chase you down the street with umbrellas. Could you withstand the mental anguish a job like this would impose on you?"
>
> Mr. Days had finally stopped talking. His eyes focused on mine. I had eight weeks to scramble together enough money to enter the University of Florida. My summer job of delivering telegrams on my Schwinn bike had been cut to weekend hours because they hired a guy with a motorcycle.
>
> "Yes," I replied, wondering if I should say more. The pause probably lasted only a few seconds, but it seemed like a lifetime. I needed the job.
>
> "Fine," Mr. Days replied. "Show up for training Monday."
>
> I sold just enough encyclopedias that summer to pay my school fees. Of course, the irony of the situation was that I had seen direct sales as merely temporary employment until a college degree qualified me for a real job. Little did I know that, at 18, I had begun my life's work.

The hiring interview is a mirror of the sales presentation. We sell jobs as opportunity. It makes sense, then, that our interview presentation should be as polished and persuasive as the presentation we use in selling our product. You want to create the right environment, provide instructive materials, ask the right questions, and show the applicant that you are a professional.

By doing so, you establish your credibility, and the more credibility you generate, the more likely it is that your applicant will trust your later claims and promises regarding your company, its products, and the career opportunity.

The method I've used for many years to conduct a successful interview is actually a two-part process: a four-step preparation for the interview followed by a ten-step interview.

PREPARATION FOR THE HIRING INTERVIEW

Review what needs to be done before you talk to the applicant. How well you prepare for the interview determines your hiring success rate as much as the actual interview itself. You want your applicant to be impressed with what she sees *before* you start the interview.

1. Set the Stage

Think of your waiting room and your interview room, the latter usually being your sales manager's office, as a stage set. You know the old saying, "You have only one chance to make a good first impression." Regardless of your office rental budget, your sales office can present a smart appearance. During my first days as district sales manager, I rented a small, unimpressive, but affordable office. My wife and I made a project of turning it into an inviting space. We applied a new coat of paint, put a few plants in the corners, and decked the walls with framed posters. We bought used, but good office furniture. Although modestly appointed, the office became a place where I enjoyed spending time.

In a well-turned-out office, pictures are hung straight, the magazines in the waiting room are current and neatly stacked, and the secretary's desk is clean and uncluttered. Peeling paint, scruffy furniture, and a carpet that needs vacuuming may send the applicant back out the door before you get a chance to make your case. Ideally, you have a recruiting film running to set the mood for your applicants as they wait their turn to be interviewed.

A clean waiting room, an entertaining video, a professional appearance—all those little things add up. Each day, when you walk into your office, stop a moment and ask, "How would I feel walking into this office if I were looking for a job?"

2. Application

Ask each job applicant to fill out two forms. *Print* your first form, the job application, on good-quality paper—an off-white or buff color suggests class. (Photocopying sends the wrong message.)

3. Personality Profile

Invite the applicant to complete a sales personality profile. This assessment not only gives you valuable information, but also upgrades the impression you make on the interviewee. If your company does not already offer a test, go to Google.com and type in "sales personality test." The last time I checked, there were 79,800 choices! My Web site, www.Malaghan.com, also offers a test, which you can download for free. Any aptitude appraisal is effective, as long as you use it intelligently in the interview. A suitable sales personality questionnaire with knowledgeable feedback establishes you as a credible personnel manager, not just some guy or gal trying to recruit a commission salesperson.

Most personality tests revolve around something called the DISC system: *D* for directive personality, *I* for influence personality, *S* for a stable personality, and *C* for a contemplative personality. Tony Alessandra is one of the leaders in this assessment field.

The Golden Rule is limiting in one sense, say Tony Alessandra and Mike O'Connor, who cowrote *People Smarts*, because it assumes that all human beings are alike. The authors propose instead a Platinum Rule, "Do unto others as they'd like done unto them," and concentrate on how to read people better so as to use the rule to succeed in business and industry. At the start they posit four behavioral styles: *directors* (D), who are forceful, competitive, decisive; socializers or *influencers* (I), who are outgoing, optimistic, gregarious; *stable relaters* (S), who are genial, stable, eager to please; and *contemplative thinkers* (C), who are self-controlled, cautious, analytical rather than emotional.

Their book, and others like it, continues with a checklist so readers can determine their own personality types and then advises learning to identify and adapt to the styles (or combinations of the styles) of others so as to advance, whether in peer groups, management, sales, or interactions with other businesses. The DISC system helps those who want to increase their sensitivity to others and their power to communicate.

4. The Tools

Would you try to sell your product or service with just a smile and a good rap talk? At the barest minimum, you use a sales binder and samples to support your sales presentation. The same is true for conducting a good hiring interview. Deliver the hiring talk with a smart-looking printed interview binder or visuals off your computer screen. The catchphrases and images keep you on track, as they reinforce the job-selling message.

Display the product in a way that best illustrates its advantages and is easily accessible to the applicant. Place a copy of your new sales recruit training outline on your desk. Keep a stack of leads on your desk so that the applicant can plainly see that you have "too many." Have a neat supply of prospecting tools on your interview table—magazine ads soliciting leads, take-one boxes, response flyers, and other lead-generating materials. Have your company brochure at the ready. Insert a full-disclosure explanation of your compensation system in the brochure. Make sure you are familiar with and adept at using your stage props.

THE INTERVIEW

You are organized. You have great tools. You are prepared. You are ready. It's time to start your 10-step job-selling presentation. At the end of each step of the interview, use a bridge question to engage the interviewee in the conversation and move on to the next step.

1. Warm Up the Applicant

Does this sound like the start of a sales talk? It should. The same warm mood you establish with potential customers works just as well for selling your prospects. The more the applicant relaxes, talking about sports or the family or his hometown, the easier it is for him to later focus on your message with a relaxed and open mind. *"Stephanie, I have your application here, but why don't you tell me a little about your work experience?"*

2. Review the Application

The best way to set the interviewee at ease is to ask a few questions related to the application. *"Alex, what did you like best about your last job?"* Again, this is just like the warm-up in the sales presentation.

3. Provide the Personality Profile Assessment

Point out the applicant's sales strengths, as revealed in the assessment. When done correctly, this builds up your credibility. *"Anita, do you feel you are the type of person who can be trained and who gets along easily with most people?"*

4. Sell Your Company and Your Product

Every company has a "founder's story." Get yours down to a well-honed, 60-second version, and make it pack a punch. Dramatize how your product helps people. Imagine that the job applicant is a sales prospect and sell your product. Once the interviewee covets ownership of your product, he is halfway to wanting to sell it. *"Ted, what do you like best about the product you just saw?"*

5. Sell the Prospecting System

At some point in the interview, your applicant will want to know, "How do I find customers?" Overcome the applicant's fear of prospecting by explaining your company's program for finding customers. Put those prospecting tools we talked about earlier to good use. Make it plain that your company has solved the problem of finding qualified prospects. *"Sheila, can you see that our salespeople have a steady and secure supply of qualified leads?"*

6. Sell the Training

The applicant now has a basic understanding of your product and how you find prospects. Still, the fear of failure may loom. Many applicants will wonder to themselves, "How am I going to learn all this?" Show them the training outline, assuring them you have a proven method of effective training. Clearly state that your time-tested training is designed for people without previous knowledge of the product or previous sales experience. Of course, if the person *does* have sales experience, adjust your hiring interview accordingly. I often said I was looking for people *without* sales experience because "they are easier to train." *"Tony, what do you think of our approach to training?"*

7. Sell the Management Opportunity

While most applicants for a sales job don't come into the interview with management in mind, you want them to leave the interview thinking that they are, or soon will be, manager trainees. You never know—the person sitting across your desk might well be thinking of the management prospects you could offer, and that's an opportunity you don't want to miss. Great sales managers are always looking for that next manager and have an active management development program to bring people into management early in their careers. *"Maria, what do you think of our company's management opportunities?"*

8. Sell the Income Opportunity

Never fudge on the pay. If you pay full commission, explain how it works and give the applicant a smart-looking handout explaining the system. If you pay a salary or a draw, then the explanation needs to fully disclose the qualifications. Don't be afraid that full disclosure will scare off the applicant. If you find that the job applicant is not prepared to work on a "results count" basis, that's fine. You don't want anyone on your sales team who thinks that great income opportunities come from showing up for work rather than from sales results. *"Jack, do you have any questions about our compensation plan?"*

9. Close

"Jane, choosing a job and a career is one of life's more important decisions. Since we've spoken for only about 15 minutes, it's difficult for me to adequately

judge your suitability for this opportunity in such a short time. And it must be hard for you to be sure if this business is right for you. However, at this point I feel very positive about your prospects for being successful in our company." Then I would move on to either 9A or 9B.

9A. Training Close

"What I would like to do is to invite you to attend our first day of training starting ____. This training is as much an extension of this interview process as it is initial training. You will learn the complete details of the benefits of our products, you will be provided with all the information on our various lead-generating programs, and you will observe a complete sales presentation. I will be judging your reactions during the day. You will be able to ask questions. At the end of the day, I will be in a better position to tell you if I think you can be truly successful in our industry, and you will know if this is the right job for you. *"Francis, does this make sense to you?"*

9B. Sales Demonstration Close

"What I would like to do is to invite you to accompany me or one of my best sales associates in the field while we visit a potential client, so that you can actually witness a complete product demonstration and see how a prospect reacts to the advantages and benefits of our product. Before and after the sales presentation, we can explain more details about our lead-generation system and training program. No doubt you will be thinking of other questions you wish you had asked during our interview. At the end of the sales presentation, we can talk about what you saw. I will then be in a better position to tell you if I think you can be truly successful in our industry, and you will know if this job is right for you. *"William, does this make sense to you?"*

10. Button Up

Conclude by handing the new hiree your company brochure with the compensation schedule. Confirm the time and date for either the start of training or the field observation exercise.

With this formula, you will consistently hire a steady stream of trainees. Think about your progress so far. You are convinced that you can be a selling sales manager providing an enthusiastic example of a love of selling. You are developing a host of prospecting tools to keep everyone productively busy, while at the same time demonstrating that you do not have enough salespeople to call all the prospects that could be called. You have a hiring system that fills your training room. Let's go on to the fourth Essential Activity—training.

QUESTIONS TO ASK YOURSELF

- How smart does your office look right now? If your boss called and said, "I'm dropping by in 15 minutes," would you have to scramble to tidy things up?
- Are you establishing a professional tone with top-quality job application forms and personality assessments?
- Do you have a complete set of smart-looking job-selling tools on your desk?
- Is your job interview as structured and professional as your sales talk?
- Do you close your job interview with a closing question confirming a start date or a follow-up interview time?

Most books on hiring interviews are designed for sales industries that have an elaborate process for hiring sales personnel who are paid regular salaries with bonuses. Still, there are several books with good material in them:

- *How to Hire & Develop Your Next Top Performer* by Herb Greenberg, Harold Weinstein, and Patrick Sweeney
- *Great Sales People Aren't Born, They're Hired* by Joseph Miller
- *People Smarts* and *Platinum Rule: The Four Basic Business Personalities and How They Can Lead You to Success* by Tony Alessandra, Ph.D., and Michael J. O'Connor, Ph.D.

FOURTH ESSENTIAL ACTIVITY

TRAIN

The best trainers have great charisma. Their presence fills a room. While these charismatic types will benefit from the information in the following chapters, this section speaks to the majority of us who were not born or blessed with a magnetic personality—those of us who have to work a little harder to hold an audience.

All worthwhile sales training focuses on a single mission: getting more orders. The methodology for accomplishing this mission becomes more sophisticated each year as our sales force continues to be smarter and brighter, helped along by the latest high-tech gadgetry. Our trainees watch MTV and Leno in the evening and get us in the morning. They compare, even if only subconsciously.

Excellence in training challenges us. Exit surveys show that failed salespeople cite "lack of training" almost as frequently as "my manager didn't support me" when disclosing the reasons they quit. Some sales managers dismiss such allegations as sour grapes from weak closers who have a poor attitude and a lousy work ethic. The more astute sales managers examine their training practices and strive to improve their effectiveness.

The training content for your sales associates changes at the different stages of their careers. Thus, our first three chapters look at sales trainees, new salespeople, and veterans. Then we proceed to three chapters on training and meeting techniques. The following is a quick overview:

- Chapter 10: Launching the new recruit to the point of his or her first order
- Chapter 11: Keeping new sales associates one more week
- Chapter 12: Rousing the veterans
- Chapter 13: Livening up your classroom techniques
- Chapter 14: Exploiting the power of off-site training
- Chapter 15: Conducting exciting sales meetings

We covered developing confident salespeople through field training in Chapter 2.

You might note the central theme, which is that training can and ought to be entertaining, interactive and, where appropriate, high-tech.

CHAPTER 10

LAUNCH THE NEW RECRUIT

All speech is vain and empty unless it be accompanied by action.

—Demosthenes, Orator/Philosopher

The purpose of each day's training of new sales recruits is to increase the likelihood that the trainees will return for the next day of training. No story better brings to life our fear that our best efforts to induce our new recruits to show up one more day will fall short than the launch of what would become a sales force of 1,000.

> I looked at Sam, our general manager, and said, "If all four of these newly recruited pioneer sales managers fail to sell at least one personal order this weekend, we will have to start all over."
>
> It had been five weeks since I arrived in Taiwan. After interviewing more than 20 applicants, we had selected four recruits to be our pioneer sales managers to sell an English study program to adults. We gave them a week of intense training, and then we were ready to go out into the field. We firmly believed that our first managers must be selling managers. I did not speak the language, so I would not be the one who wrote the first order.
>
> One of the four, Sophia, ate dinner that Friday night at her favorite noodle shop. She was so energized by her new job and the new product she was selling that she gave a spontaneous sales presentation at the restaurant. Three of the noodle shop workers, carried away by her infectious enthusiasm, became her first customers that weekend. Monday morning she had a story to tell. Inspired, the other three managers soon each had their first order. A $25-million-a-year business had been launched. I have often wondered what would have happened if Sophia had eaten at a different restaurant that night.

In the first-day introductory training, fulfill the promises made during your recruiting interview:

- Build credibility by reviewing your company's history and commitment to excellence.
- Show how your product or service satisfies an important customer need better than any other solution.

- Deliver a live presentation up to, but not including, the contract. "Show and tell" all your lead-generation systems.
- Give homework assignments, including passing out a few lead-generating flyers.
- End the day with an individual exit interview to resell the job.

Schedule subsequent days to include role-playing the sales talk, practicing appointment calls, and teaching more prospecting skills that will be used the day they are taught.

Most likely you already conduct a two- to five-day training exercise for new recruits. Your aim is to teach your recruits sufficient selling skills so that a reasonable percentage of them can find a prospect, set up an appointment, and deliver an enthusiastic presentation. Notice that there is no mention of teaching closing skills. That comes during the second and all remaining weeks of a salesperson's career.

The recruiting interview convinced your trainees to show up for training, but they may not be entirely sold on the idea of direct sales. More likely, your new sales recruits are still balancing the advantages of a flexible work schedule, personal growth, an interesting work environment, and greater income potential against their fears of income insecurity, worries about their inexperience, worries about how to find customers, and the greatest fear of all—fear of failure. You can be sure that at least a few of the trainee-applicants even debated whether to show up for the training. Many who do show up either just want to see what this sales thing is all about or are thinking, "Maybe I'll just do this until I find a 'real' job."

Most of us sales trainers have experienced a 50 percent or worse show-up rate on the second day of training at least once in our careers. We know how important it is to develop a convincing and compelling first-day training program. Conversely, we take pleasure in converting these skeptical Nervous Nellies into eager, expectant sales trainees who, in the space of a single day, come to believe that they just might be successful.

TRAIN IN SEVEN STEPS

Review the following proven seven-step winning formula for training new sales representatives.

1. Sell the Company

Use visual aids, such as attractive company brochures and/or a PowerPoint presentation, to establish credibility. Applicants want to know about the history of the company and the background of the individuals who lead it. Share the company founder's story of how one man or woman took an idea and converted it into a successful business. Show charts and graphs that illustrate the size and growth of the company. New companies can emphasize the ground-floor opportunity. Doesn't everyone wish he had been one of the first 100 employees of Microsoft?

2. Sell the Product or Service

Treat the trainees like potential customers. Go through an elaborate need story to prove that the product or service helps the customer. Appeal to the best of human nature by emphasizing how people have bettered their lives because a dedicated salesperson gave a good presentation. Dramatize how your company's salespeople are missionaries making the world a better place. Deliver a sales presentation only as far as the pre-close.

Do not cover closing or instructions on filling out a contract on this first day. Just drive home the message, "You are being trained to help people make good decisions so that they will have happier, healthier, more financially rewarding lives." You know you have done this right when the trainee says, "I'd like to have this product" and feels that prospects should own it for their own good. If possible, keep a sample of the product in the training room for trainees to look at and touch. A well-done video—20 minutes or even less in length—extolling your product or service makes a persuasive job-selling statement.

3. Sell the Market

Elaborate on what you told the sales applicants/trainees during the job interview: "There are more potential customers than the current sales force can handle." Show a map of your territory that clearly reveals the number of prospects. Then explain how many active salespeople you have. Let the trainees do the addition and division exercises with you on the whiteboard to prove your point.

4. Sell the Prospecting Approaches

Give details on how you find customers. Explain why your proven prospecting systems work so well. Assure your trainees that they can easily learn these proven prospecting methods. If you have a take-one box, a door-handle piece, or some other lead-generation tool, show how easy it is to distribute these lead-generating materials. Charge your recruits with a "start prospecting today!" message. Teach one method of prospecting the first day of training. Then give the trainees 10 to 20 lead-generating pieces, such as handouts or door-hangers, to distribute as homework that evening so that they can start obtaining leads immediately. End this session knowing that your sales trainees are confident that you have effective prospecting methods that are easily learned.

5. Sell Your Training System

Go through your entire training program curriculum. Reassure your trainees that everything they need to know in order to be successful will be covered. Back up your assertions with examples of successful salespeople who got off to a good start because they practiced what you taught.

As an example of your training materials, provide a scripted presentation outline to your trainees on the first day. Most companies teach a presentation outline that lists the key points of the sales talk, including scripted questions at each point to keep the prospect involved and answering in the affirmative. Here is one example without the questions, since each question to be answered yes must be developed specifically for each product or service.

- Warm up the customer to set her at ease before the selling process begins.
- Deliver the need story to raise the prospect's consciousness level so that she recognizes a problem that cries for remedy.
- Show how product features provide customer benefits that will solve these problems.
- Explain pricing and terms so that all the information needed to make a decision is clear.
- Summarize the need story, benefits, and pricing to ensure full understanding and tie it all together.

- Close. *Ask for the order! Now.*
- Sign the contract, referred to as "filling out the paperwork."
- Button up the order by once again reviewing and quickly reselling everything to set the customer at ease before your departure.

6. Sell the Opportunity

Reveal the entire compensation system to the applicants, including how *you* get paid. Full disclosure builds trust while emphasizing that your income is directly related to the success of the people you are training. Emphasize that what you are offering is much more than just a great compensation system. You are offering an intriguing array of possible opportunities: to move into management, to develop personal growth, and perhaps to enjoy interesting incentive travel while earning a much-higher-than-average income. Talk about your management development program. Drop a hint that you are ready to build a larger sales force and can do so only by spotting "a few good people" to move into management as soon as possible.

7. Review the Day

Give each trainee a five- to seven-minute private exit interview at the end of each day of training. This first day is most important in your relationship with that trainee, and this is your chance to end the session on a high note. Compliment the trainee's responses, demeanor, and attitude. Build up the trainee's confidence. Get a commitment to do the homework, including passing out a few lead-generation flyers. Dismiss each trainee separately to discourage the trainees from having their own meeting at Starbucks. All it takes is one cynic with a big mouth to undermine the good will, energy, and great expectations absorbed by the majority of your class. The individual review process reduces that risk. While you are giving the reviews, your field manager or a veteran salesperson can be delivering a practice sales presentation to keep the remaining trainees entertained while they wait their turn.

The sales manager usually conducts steps 1, 6, and 7 of new recruit training. As you develop competent people, delegate the other steps. Schedule your marketing manager, if you have one, to co-lead the discussion and practice session on prospecting methods, in tandem with either you or another sales manager who reports to you.

Here are a few other do's and don'ts on training new people:

- Do pay for the lunch.
- Do clean up the classroom each morning before the trainees arrive. You may be used to the junk and disarray, but the trainees are not.
- Do designate a "greeter" to meet the arriving trainees and give them something to do right away, with your greeter staying in the training room.
- Do use name tags until everyone knows everyone else.
- Do check the whiteboards each morning for erasers and magic markers that still have magic. For some reason, whenever I'm about to illustrate an important point, the markers either turn dry or completely disappear.

During the next two to four training days, follow up your initial training by doing the following.

Keep Prospecting

Don't just talk about it; do it. Each day, teach your trainees one new method of prospecting. Your speech might go like this: "Over the next month you will be exposed to seven to ten customer-finding methods. You may not like them all, and that's okay. Most successful sales reps use two or three methods at any one time. Right now, just try them all out as we teach them. Then, after you have had the experience of telephoning, working at a sales counter, passing out flyers, placing take-one boxes, and so on, you can choose which methods are most comfortable and effective for you. Today we are going to . . ." After your speech, teach one method that the trainees will do that evening after training. Give them something that they can do in 30 minutes or less.

Some trainees will quit regardless of how good your training is. However, if those trainees have distributed some marketing flyers, you may at least get a few leads back to pay for the training. More important, performing some kind of prospecting increases the trainee return rate because they want those leads they have worked to obtain. Win-win.

In my perfect world, the last day of training is Friday morning. Trainees are taught how to obtain appointments by working a sales counter at 9 a.m., and by noon they're booking appointments at the mall or supermarket as the weekend shoppers start arriving.

Assign Homework

Prospecting exercises lead the homework parade. Check out the following additional homework possibilities:

- *Practice writing sales contracts.* Teach the contract the second day and build a scenario of a model customer with regard to package and terms. Ask the trainees to fill in the blanks. Do this the third day with two contracts. Watch the mistakes made by the new sales reps on the contracts go down.
- *Practice the sales talk.* Give the trainee enough presentation materials to practice the sales talk at home in the evening.
- *Give a book to read.* If your company does not have a company storybook, then give the trainee something like Zig Ziglar's *See You at the Top* or Lisa Jimenez's *Conquer Fear*. Begin feeding the positive attitude.

All the classroom training in the world will be for naught if it is not accompanied by field training. That is covered in the first two chapters of the book.

MEASURE ENTRY-LEVEL TRAINING

How good is your entry-level training? You can find out. The results are likely to lead to improvements in your training, and thus to improvements in the number of trainees who become effective sales personnel. The most recent survey I conducted of more than 500 relatively new salespeople, spread among three sales groups in two countries, once again verified the case for good training. We directed the questionnaire to all new salespeople hired in a specific time frame and focused on just two training measurements:

   1. The number of live, in-the-field presentations witnessed by sales trainees

2. The number of classroom hours a trainee experienced before being allowed to deliver her first solo sales presentation to a real prospect

The measurements did not try to evaluate training quality, just the number of training hours in the classroom and number of field presentations observed. Simple.

The revelations were dramatic. Here is what we found:

- New salespeople who observed a minimum of three live sales presentations and also had at least 20 hours of classroom training had the highest degree of success.

- New salespeople who observed at least one presentation and had 10 to 20 hours of classroom training had a success rate that was less than half that of the first group.

- Those who witnessed no live sales demonstrations with a customer and had fewer than 10 hours of classroom training almost always failed.

This is one of the easiest surveys to conduct. The results will have a positive impact on how you train new people going forward.

QUESTIONS TO ASK YOURSELF

- What percentages of the recruits who enter your first day of training go on to submit an order? Do you keep records?
- How does your training compare with what we outlined?
- Are there any changes that you might want to make? What are they?
- Do you measure your results?
- Do you start your trainees prospecting from their first day? If not, what would be the expected results if you did?

Recommended books to help teach new sales personnel:

- *Selling for Dummies* by Tom Hopkins
- *Conquer Fear* by Lisa Jimenez
- *See You at the Top* by Zig Ziglar

CHAPTER 11
KEEP NEW SALES ASSOCIATES ONE MORE WEEK

Arriving at one goal is the starting point of another.

—John Dewey, Educator, Philosopher

Many Eastern philosophies espouse the idea of "living in the present." As it happens, that same philosophy works for retaining a successful sales force.

Teach new sales representatives enough selling skills to keep them selling for one more week. That's it. Focus on this week. What do your reps need to do and learn *this week* so that they will come back again next week? At the end of 90 days, every new salesperson will have either quit or joined the ranks of producing veterans.

Our business is very simple when we focus on the essentials. Salespeople quit when they think they cannot earn a commission or qualify for their salary. If they *think* they will be able to write an order soon, they will stay around to get that order. As sales managers, we must stoke the fires of expectations. We do this by daily teaching them selling skills and focusing their time on prospecting. Since my retirement, I still go back to Asia twice a year to conduct sales clinics for my former company. Last year I had a chance to ask Hiroko Chiba to remind me how she had gone from a team of six to almost a hundred full-time sales agents in three years. Here is her story.

> Keep them busy and expectant. For example, I have one new person who just won the top rookie award in the last contest. At the end of the first day of training, I gave her flyers to pass out in her neighborhood. At the end of her first week, I had her making appointments at counters. Every week she submits a schedule of how many take-one boxes she will put in stores, how many hours she will work the telephone, and what days she will schedule time at a sales booth.
>
> As manager, all I can really do is keep my team busy. That's what I can control. In addition, I can work in the field with them.

THREE THINGS RIGHT

Chiba-san's story reminded me of my own first team-building experience as a new field manager four decades ago. I was not very sophisticated, but I got three things right my first summer managing fellow college students.

First, as we rode in our classroom-on-wheels out into the field, we either read the book *Think and Grow Rich* by Napoleon Hill out loud to each other or practiced our sales talk.

Second, at the end of each day, I spent three to five minutes with each person behind the trunk of the car, privately reviewing the day's work and either congratulating success or discussing how the next time could be better.

Finally, and most important, I had a two-day intervention rule as outlined in Chapter 2. No orders for two days meant automatic field training.

Frequent Communication

Daily contact means daily results. Weekly contact means weekly results. You want daily results. Contact your sales reps daily. If you have a daily office meeting, you have a daily results strategy on autopilot. If your reps are not office-bound, then each one needs a daily phone call. (E-mail succeeds in disseminating information quickly; it fails miserably if you are trying to manage and motivate new sales partners.)

For at least the first three months, concentrate each day on five sales management objectives for your new sales representatives:

- Motivate your new sales reps. If this topic interests you, jump ahead to Chapter 20.

- Review *one prospecting technique*, as discussed in Part 2 of this book. Ask your salespeople, "What prospecting activity did you do today, and what will you do tomorrow?" Check on their bank of appointments.

- Debrief the most recent sales presentation.

- Cover at least one buying objection and practice the *rebuttal* that overcomes it.

- Teach one *closing* technique every day, such as building a good need story, using the automatic close process, or asking for a decision on a minor point. Keep your new people busy prospecting—

very busy. New salespeople don't quit because you work them too hard. They quit because they are not talking to enough prospects to earn a living.

Group Prospecting

Organize group prospecting events. Some new reps claim that they will prospect on their own. Don't bet on it. You are responsible for your team's time management. Time management means that your team spends enough time prospecting. It doesn't just happen by itself. Make it happen. Time-manage your sale associates to success.

- If you sell door to door, assign the new rep to work across the street from another salesperson—even if it's another new salesperson.
- If the telephone is effective for your business, then attendance at several telephone parties a week will produce the needed appointments.
- If it is booth prospecting that works for you, then schedule sales counter shifts with at least two people per shift, regardless of the size of the booth or the amount of traffic.

Enthusiasm Now, Closing Later

New salespeople are eager to learn the secrets of closing. However, first teach them a great need story and how to deliver an enthusiastic sales presentation laced with lots of positive questions to gain numerous little prospect commitments as the sales talk progresses.

Yes, teach new people your rebuttal scripts for objections like "I want to think it over" and "It costs too much." However, memorizing a host of rebuttals is no substitute for the more important—and more easily learned—good need story and peppering the sales talk with many little commitment questions.

If your salespeople can master these early basic presentation skills *with enthusiasm* and if you keep them busy prospecting, the following consequences occur:

- Your sales force turnover is reduced.
- Your sales volume increases.

- Your empire expands.
- Your reputation builds.

QUESTIONS TO ASK YOURSELF

- What is your system for helping your new people get started successfully?
- What is your policy if a new salesperson works for two days without submitting an order?
- Do you provide training and meetings designed specifically for your sales reps with less than three months' experience?
- How many hours a week do you expect your new salespeople to prospect?
- How do you manage their time to make sure it happens?
- What is the role of group prospecting in your team?
- How many of the five daily management activities for new people are you performing now?
- What changes might you consider to enhance your training for new salespeople?

Recommended books for this section:

- *Value-Added Sales Management* by Tom Reilly
- *Why Salespeople Fail* by Roy J. Hartmann

CHAPTER 12
ROUSE THE VETERANS

Enthusiasm can only be aroused by two things: first an ideal which takes the imagination by storm, and second, a definite, intelligible plan for carrying that ideal into practice.

—Arnold Toynbee, Nineteenth-Century Historian

Rousing veterans requires the employment of a combination of strategies: passionately teaching traditional, proven selling skills; improving their prospecting skills; and monitoring their time-management practices. You turbocharge your veterans when you pilot a steady migration of your best and brightest into management.

Recognizing and honing ambition are skills that I stumbled on early in the management game, as the following story highlights.

> My first summer as field manager, I recruited two Jims in June as colleges went on summer break. From the earliest days with my summer crew, I had talked up the management opportunity. Jim Bender and Jim Reading had just wanted a summer selling job, and here I was filling their heads with dreams of almost instant promotion. By mid-July, both Jims had been promoted to field manager and had developed their own crews for the duration of the summer. The lesson was embedded in me for all time: If I actively encouraged and developed salespeople into management, not only would I get more managers, but I would get them more quickly and keep sales reps in production longer. The example of bringing the two Jims into management early was never lost as I built my career based on quick promotions.

Training and inspiring your sales veterans are two sides of the same coin. You want to retain your sales vets longer. You want them to be more effective. Sales veterans are tough to train and inspire. They can run to cynicism. They have "been there, done that." Many of them need more help than they admit to needing. This and the next three chapters will provide you with the training tools to teach and motivate the most discriminating audience.

This chapter focuses on an assortment of sales-training objectives that form a confluence for the mother of all objectives: increased sales production. The training techniques used to reach these objectives will be covered in the following three "how to" chapters. Chapters 13 through 15 will arm you with effective coaching practices: *how* to provide exciting classroom training, *how* to use interesting locations for training, and *how* to conduct attention-grabbing sales meetings.

The word *training* suggests an emphasis on skills transference. As important and as critical as that is, sales-training exercises can be so much more. It is this "something more" that converts mundane training into a stimulating event that inspires an "I want to work harder, longer, and more effectively" attitude in your veterans.

The French writer and philosopher Voltaire introduced the phrase "in the best of all possible worlds." My question is, "In the best of all possible sales-training worlds, what is possible?" Consider the following comprehensive list of sales-training objectives, which includes, but goes beyond, technical selling skills.

■ *Talk up promotion opportunities.* Use all training exercises as reminders of future management potential.

■ *Promote bonding and team building.* Fashion training in such a way that the end result is a more closely knit team. Get out of the office. Use out-of-the-classroom training sites, such as parks, your home, or hotel conference rooms. Or rent a boat for half a day . . . anything to create a social mood to go along with the training objective.

■ *Integrate motivation.* The underpinning of all training is motivation. Bear in mind that the purpose of training is to get your "students" to *do* something that generates more sales. Sales reps are eager to attend sales and motivational seminars. They will pay money to learn how to make more money. If your sales personnel resist training, it means that they think attendance will "unmotivate" them and/or will take away field time—in other words, will cause them to lose money. If you want material on how to integrate motivation into training and *all* aspects of sales management, jump ahead to Chapter 20.

■ *Nurture initiative.* Do not tell your sales reps what to do. Give them the range of presentation and prospecting skills to choose from as circumstances dictate. The more respect you give your sales force and the more confidence you display in their ability to make the right decisions, the more loyalty you will create.

■ *Build self-confidence.* We all know that the hallmark of great closers is not just their technical techniques—it is the mental approach that they bring to the selling process. Lavishing praise is often more important than correcting mistakes.

■ *Increase retention.* Great training expectations mean that your sales team can hardly wait to attend your training because they *know* that they will leave the training session better salespeople. I never conducted a sales-training session where I was not very much aware that if I did not lift the spirits of the attendees, some might not return the following day.

■ *Have fun!* Let the sound of laughter and music resonate. This is not an assertion that all training is entertainment; it is a claim that training should be as entertaining as possible.

■ *Make your vets feel special.* "I have a problem and need your advice." Two of my mentors flattered me with this statement from time to time. How do you I think I felt? Training programs not only offer you a venue for publicly recognizing people in front of their peers, but also provide you with the opportunity to ask for and receive valuable help and advice.

■ *Promote change.* Start some of your training sessions with the statement, "The purpose of our training is to help you change something you are doing. If everything you were doing was perfect, training would not be necessary and thus would be a waste of both your and my time." Further, you might add, "In school, we took lessons. Our success was reflected by the grade we received on the test measuring how much we learned. Sales training is not merely an intellectual exercise, although I hope you will find it stimulating. It leads to action."

Certain types of training necessarily emphasize change: a new product, new rules for a sales contest, a new lead-generating technique, and so on. Beyond the obvious, however, all training is about change. Our mission is always to increase prospecting time and improve closing percentages. Our mission is to drive a constant process of going from where we are to where we want to be.

■ *Promote personal growth.* As Chapter 20, on motivation, reminds us, the pursuit of personal growth provides great motivation. Modern people have a tremendous thirst for knowledge. Stimulating and purposeful training is a perk for the brain. Most of us find joy in the learning process that goes beyond the practical considerations of increasing our income.

When you use the full complement of possibilities that training provides, you create an environment that attracts veterans to your training sessions and/or sales meetings. Now let's move on to the next three chapters to look at specific techniques you can use to maximize these possibilities.

QUESTIONS TO ASK YOURSELF

- What are your training objectives?
- How eagerly are your sales reps anticipating your next sales meeting or training session?
- How do you integrate all the possibilities of training into your training program?

Books you might find helpful in taking a different approach to your training:

- *Who Moved My Cheese?* by Spencer Johnson, M.D.
- *Life Is a Series of Presentations* by Tony Jeary

CHAPTER 13
LIVEN UP YOUR CLASSROOM TECHNIQUES

It's never too late. It's not impossible to teach people anything.

—Steve Allen, Humorist, Writer

Sales trainers are in the entertainment business. It is our ability to engage and hold an audience with a compelling message, delivered in the most memorable format possible and with the best stage props available, that moves listeners to do great things and to do them better than before. As sales trainers, we view training as "show time!" The following story dramatizes this, and maybe embellishes it just a bit, to make the point that all of us sales trainers are in show business.

> Great movies have been made about the lives of entertainers we admire. *The Jazz Singer*, *A Star Is Born*, *Coal Miner's Daughter* and, more recently, *Chicago*, all have depicted the nerve-wracking terror that comes with taking that first step onstage.
>
> You know the story line. It's just minutes until the fledging star must go on. The audience is expectant, demanding, and judgmental. Backstage, the performer anxiously makes last-minute adjustments to hair, makeup, and clothes; suddenly can't remember the words to sing or the chords to play; and may even seriously consider making a mad dash for the exit. Then the transformation takes place. As the entertainer's name is announced, we witness the adjustment in demeanor and bearing. The curtain goes up. The public persona takes precedence over the taut nerves. Our hero is transformed by the thrill of lights, the music, and the applause. *It's show time!*

EVEN TOM CRUISE HAS A COSTAR

No matter how dynamic a trainer you may be, the audience is better served by having at least two or three trainers conduct different segments. It's a smart idea, too, to rotate the trainers that conduct particular segments and provide a variety of leadership. For instance, when I first arrived in England in the mid-1980s as the national training director for Encyclopedia Britannica, my first assignment was to conduct the entire three-day basic training for all new sales hires. I was excited about my new assignment, and it showed in the trainees' responses to my efforts. However, training improved when I shared my time with the four London sales managers. Since most of the new salespeople would be assigned to one of the four, it helped to have the trainees meet their future boss early in the process. More important, each of the four sales managers seemed determined to be more effective and enthusiastic than the rest of us. The trainees kept getting a new voice. They had the impression that Encyclopedia Britannica was a large corporation with deep management talent. They were right. We had relatively very few dropouts in our new recruit training course.

Walk and Shout

Stroll around the room. Use vocal inflections to raise the volume and energy level. Occasional meandering obliges the trainees to keep moving their eyes and heads to keep up with you. It's harder for them to daydream when they are being stimulated by intermittent motion.

Notice the voice inflections of David Letterman, Jay Leno, Tom Brokaw, or Bill O'Reilly. Varying your oral intonation makes training more interesting and memorable. It helps keep your sales associates coming back, while improving the odds that they will remember the points you are trying to get across.

Exercise Keeps 'Em Awake

Ask group members, "Who has ever taken an aerobics class?" Almost always someone in the room will raise a hand, and with a little coaxing, that person will lead a two-minute exercise to oxygenate everyone's brain and get the blood flowing.

After lunch, I like to take a nap. So do most of the people in the training room. Unfortunately, we don't have that luxury. Instead of forcing down an extra cup of coffee at lunch to counteract afternoon drowsiness, you will find a little postmeal exercise to be an excellent antidote.

Another "start me up" exercise is to ask everyone to move the tables around. If you have started with a U-shaped configuration, change to a nor-mal, row-style classroom setup. Alternatively, the tables can be parallel with the back and front of the room or at a slight (20- to 30-degree) angle. Any form of physical movement serves as a mental stimulus.

Exploit Props and Visuals

Use an array of props for your stage set, also known as your training room. Thinking of yourself as an entertainer, with the trainees as your audience, makes a review of the various props and visuals easier to imagine and plan. The more stuff, the better. PowerPoint, overhead acetates, whiteboards and flip charts, various colored whiteboard pens, lots of writing materials, videos, wall posters, and special effects spark alertness and improve reten-tion.

The following are some helpful hints on the use of PowerPoint presen-tations:

- While they are a good and useful tool, PowerPoint presentations can also put people to sleep. Do not read PowerPoint or overhead acetate notes. You can never talk as fast as your audience can read.
- Feature an outline of the big points you want to cover and the catchphrases you want your trainees to remember. Displaying key phrases on the front white wall or screen keeps you and your audi-ence on track.
- Make an exception to the rule about displaying detailed notes on a screen when the group is working on an assignment during the training exercise. Then the one-page display on the screen should present all the information or rules that the group needs in order to complete the training exercise you have assigned.
- If you want your audience to have detailed notes, give them a handout.

Visuals consist of more than whiteboards and PowerPoints. They in-clude video clips, message posters adorning the walls, and physical objects. If your imagination ever needs inspiration, visit an elementary school class-room. All available wall space is used to reinforce a teaching message. As a result of attending the American Management Association course "Train the Trainer," I began handing out rubber duckies and small statues of the

American eagle at the start of my training sessions on "Ducks and Eagles." A former colleague of mine would use funnels of varying sizes to illustrate that building a sales team is a matter of pouring in a mixture of salespeople and prospects to get orders. The bigger the funnels, the more orders you will get. These props made a more dramatic point than just saying, "Direct sales is a numbers game."

A large demographic chart, clearly showing the enormous number of prospects available in the sales territory compared with the small percentage of orders already obtained, dramatically makes the point, "There are more orders out there just waiting to be written." This wall-hanging display gives the not-so-subtle reminder that the reason for today's training is to find and to sell more of those prospects.

Build in Interactivity

Maximize the amount of doing and talking time for your training participants. As most of us know, the sweetest sound is one's own voice. Strive to decrease your speaking time and increase the amount of doing and talking time for the participants in your training.

The more we train, the more we realize that the preexisting collective knowledge of our training group gives us a broad base to build upon if we but give them the chance. Rather than telling your group what the 10 most important characteristics of sales management are, you will get better results if you ask the trainees to volunteer the answers.

Try different formats for group interactivity. The most obvious is the one already alluded to, where the trainer stands in front of the whiteboard or flip chart with felt pen in hand, writing down the ideas of the participants. While this method is much better than just lecturing the group on what you know, even this interactive approach can eventually be ho-hum. Today's salespeople are brighter than ever. Their IQs, intellectual curiosity, and MTV attention span demand constantly changing stimuli. Here are some additional useful interactive formats.

The Debate

The next section of this book, on management development, encourages you to inform sales trainees as early as the initial hiring interview of the company's management opportunities. Some sales managers think it is better to wait until a salesperson has reached a certain level of orders before discussing management possibilities. I have railed about this delay for years. Eventually, I discovered that engaging sales managers in a debate arguing the pros and cons of this issue is more effective than relying on my "tell 'em early" speech.

It is easy to get volunteers to speak on both sides of an issue. The debate process more or less follows the debating society format, with three people to a "team." The first speaker for each side makes the case for his proposition, the second speaker makes the rebuttal arguments, and the final speaker summarizes the case for each side. Put people with a claim to debating experience in charge of the debate and/or have them act as advisors to one of the groups. Promote a trainee to the position of timer. The more people involved, the merrier. After a three- to five-minute preparation period, each speaker has one to three minutes to make her case.

For the record, following the "when to introduce the management opportunity" debate, most managers in the audience agree to the proposition that "the earlier, the better" approach is preferable.

Small-Group Breakouts

Divide your class into groups of three to five to discuss and report on a selected topic. For instance, one approach to generating new ideas for local lead-generating contests would be to ask each group to come up with five proposals. Another approach is to commission each team to design one to three mini-contests, complete with simple rules and prizes. Give each group seven to fifteen minutes to come up with its proposals. Then, a spokesperson for each team takes a few minutes to review the team's fantastic, stimulating recommendations with the other teams.

Use this type of small-team breakout brainstorming to encourage sales managers to commit to recruiting strategies other than placing ads in the newspapers. You could simply tell them alternative methods from your own experience or from Chapter 15 of this book. However, some of your training participants have heard these ideas before in some fashion. Wouldn't it be more effective to get the group to suggest recruiting alternatives? It is easier to ask people to go back to their offices on Monday and put their own plan into action than to ask them to adopt your plan or some other bigwig's.

Place trainees in groups with people with whom they normally do not work. The count-off system is easiest. If you want groups of four, then the first person is 1, the second person is 2, and so forth. All of the 1s gather in a particular spot and start working on the assignment, as do the 2s, 3s, and 4s. Keep changing the personnel makeup of the groups, so that by the end of training, almost everyone has had a chance to work with everyone else at least once in a small-group breakout.

Make sure that the seating arrangement makes it easy for the trainees to quickly organize into small groups. U-shaped seating does not work so well for planned breakout sessions. Desks or tables placed in rows with at least some walking space between them helps. Round tables are another alternative.

Keep an extra box of big, fat felt pens of various colors. Have enough flip charts for all the brainstorming stations.

Face-offs

"What is your best slump-breaking story?" While it might be nice for everyone to tell his story to the entire group, there simply is not enough time, nor are people's listening skills up to paying faithful attention to a five-minute story from each of 16 or so people. Effective story exchanges work well in groups of two or three. Other good face-off questions include

"What are your life's most important goals?"

"What is your best recruiting story that *doesn't* involve using a newspaper ad?"

"What was your biggest challenge in sales management, and how did you overcome it?"

Draw a Picture

Several years ago, I asked Larry Philbrook, an outside meeting facilitator, to help our sales managers and administration design a mission statement. The first thing he did was ask us to break into small groups and draw a picture of our company's mission as we now understood it. It was total chaos. Nobody knew quite what to do. However, little by little, each group got down to work and came up with a pictorial view of where the people in the group thought we were, which a spokesperson for the group explained. To say that there were divergent views would be an understatement. By the end of that first hour, each participant's imagination was ripened in a way that perhaps no other starting exercise could have accomplished. A very animated group then worked through the mission statement with an uncommon vigor.

Secret Ballots

"How many hours a week should a salesperson sit in front of a customer giving a sales presentation?" Posing this kind of question in a survey or on a ballot always sets off a lively discussion over what is reasonable and possible. This, in turn, leads to the awareness that a mere 20 percent increase in selling time dramatically increases discretionary income *more* than simply a corresponding 20 percent.

Other secret ballots could ask:

"How many sales presentations did you give last week, and of that number, how many times did someone else observe your live sales presentation?"

"How many times in the last three months did you conduct a recruiting program for new salespeople?"

"How often should you recruit new salespeople?"

"What percentage of orders should come from a salesperson's own lead-generation efforts?"

The list goes on and on. You can often use these secret ballots during training. Anytime you sense a lack of consensus or a divergent opinion on a subject or you want to know the group's mindset, conduct a quick vote. Secret ballots provide more accurate information than a show of hands or an open ballot, without embarrassing anybody. The purpose of training is to move sales practices from here to there. Often it helps if you know where "here" is.

Open Agenda

An adventurous training format for experienced sales personnel is the open agenda. It works like this:

- Management selects the general topic, for instance: "How can we increase sales by 20 percent in one year?"

- The training group sits in a circle, with plenty of sheets of paper and pens in the middle of the circle.

- Everyone is asked to write down one or more topics to be discussed during the training sessions.

- The trainer or facilitator uses a large sheet to list the gathered ideas under their appropriate categories.

- The group leader for each session is naturally the person who suggested the topic.

- Each session lasts for 60 to 90 minutes.

- Two to four sessions meet simultaneously throughout the day.

- Everyone freely selects the sessions to attend. Anyone may drop in on more than one session.

- People are asked to volunteer to be the scribe at each session and take notes.

There is no shortage of topics when the group sets the agenda. This type of exercise is an excellent tool for helping the entire sales organization move as one. The possibilities for this type of exercise include designing a new three-day training program for new sales recruits, creating a comprehensive plan to generate more local leads, revising the annual recruiting program, and coming up with stimulating sales contests with rules that reinforce strategic objectives. These sessions almost always generate a lot of recommendations for senior management as well. One idea that often comes out is a request for the administration to accompany salespeople in the field.

Follow-up is essential to the success of this type of exercise. Appoint chairpersons for the various action plans, such as sales-incentive contests, new face training, key-person training, lead generation, creating a new company Web site, and the like. A 90-day follow-up meeting provides accountability and ensures that a reasonable percentage of approved recommendations become reality.

Use Video and Video Feedback

Pocket-sized digital videocameras allow every trainer to be a movie director. Most trainers shoot a video of their sales representatives' simulated presentation. There is no greater critic than a salesperson watching her own sales demo on video. You might even tape yourself delivering a training program.

Taping a live presentation by your superstar salespeople with a real prospect in a real selling situation reveals best sales practices. How we simulate selling in the classroom is not exactly how we sell when we are talking to a real prospect. However, there is a right way and a wrong way to videotape live sales presentations. Let's start with the wrong way.

Some years ago, a sales manager had a friend send in a lead. The unsuspecting salesperson visited the "prospect" and was secretly filmed "selling" the order. The sales manager then surprised everyone, including the unsuspecting salesperson, by showing the filmed presentation at a national sales meeting. The superstar salesperson was not amused by the deception. A year or so later, the salesperson quit over another issue, although I always suspected that he was still smarting over the unauthorized filming. But he got even: He sued the company for the continued use of the sales demo film and demanded royalties! A modest settlement was made, and the secret film was laid to rest.

Now the right way. The basic idea—to film a real presentation by a superstar sales person—was right on. But if you want to use this tool, let your people know up front what you plan to do. Inform your sales force that over the next few months, a number of special leads will be issued to each one of them for a simulated prospect. The prospect will play hard to get, but eventually the salesperson's great closing techniques will prevail, and she will be paid on the order.

A hidden camera will record the sales talk, although the salesperson will not be aware of it at the time. After this announcement, make it clear that any salesperson who does not want to be filmed can decline to take part in the exercise without fear of repercussions. Then wait a couple of weeks and begin the filming. Finally, have the filmed salesperson sign a waiver agreement before you show the film.

The following is a list of other uses of videos in training:

- A standard company sales presentation to help new recruits.
- A welcome message from the president.
- The president's message introducing a new policy or product.
- Lead-generation marketing clinics featuring the salesperson who is renowned as the best lead generator using a particular method.

■ Closing and overcoming rebuttals role playing. Stage contests with your top sales associates at sales meetings. The audience votes on the best response, the winners get a prize, and all your sales force now has video access to the greatest rebuttals from the finest salespeople.

Ask yourself, "What are the most important selling and management practices that I want to teach, and who in my company has the reputation for being the best at a particular skill?" For instance, the best sales recruiter probably has a dynamic, well-structured, and reasonably short hiring interview. Certain sales managers seem to know how to produce orders from a booth better than others. So, why not ask the best to prepare a video on how they do it?

Encourage Role Playing

Salespeople can practice their sales talks, including handling rebuttals, with a listener. Wannabe and new sales managers may want to practice their recruiting interviews with their boss or another sales manager.

The trainee delivering the pretend presentation has a more interesting job than the person listening. Convert the passive listener into an engaged critic. Give the role-playing prospect a score sheet rating the performance of the practice sales talk, focusing on such criteria as enthusiasm, smiling, eye contact, body language, pronunciation, and voice inflection. In addition, you might ask the role-playing observer to list three good things that he noticed and only one area that might be improved.

Encourage Book Reading

More than once, I have seen how a reading assignment can launch a career habit of reading self-improvement books and magazines.

Think and Grow Rich, by Napoleon Hill; *How to Win Friends and Influence People*, by Dale Carnegie; *Jonathan Livingston Seagull*, by Richard Bach; and *See You at the Top*, by Zig Ziglar all remain great introductory classics for anyone who desires success in our industry—as well as in many other industries and life itself, for that matter. New classics include *Who Moved My Cheese*, by Spencer Johnson, M.D.; *Seven Habits of Highly Ef-*

fective People, by Stephen Covey; and Jack Welch's *Straight from the Gut.* Any book by Peter Drucker sends the reader on an exhilarating voyage to better management practices.

You may have your own favorite book that pushed your career along. Assigning your favorite self-help book provides everyone in your organization with a common, positive-reference anchor. An oral book report during the training program ensures that everyone actually does read the book. Oral book reports also help develop the public speaking skills that are so critical to sales management.

The audience plays a critic's role during the book report presentations, similar to the role of the listeners to the practice sales talk. Give the audience a book report evaluation sheet. You might use the Olympic-style approach, with 10 representing the highest rating and 1 the lowest. Consider evaluating the following public speaking and reporting skills:

■ *Voice.* How does the person delivering the book report use voice modulation, inflection, and pauses to keep the audience's attention?

■ *Eye contact.* How well does the speaker maintain eye contact with *everyone* in the room?

■ *Body language.* How does the speaker use gestures and other body language techniques, including moving around the room, to emphasize points and galvanize attention?

■ *Visual aids.* How professional-looking and effective are the visuals the person is using? It's a good policy to require the speaker in training to use at least one visual aid during her presentation.

■ *Content.* How well does the speaker summarize the author's main points in a way that relates to the sales job the audience has?

In addition, provide space on the evaluation form for the "judge" to write notes, which should be mostly positive, but also include helpful suggestions for improvement. This rating system not only keeps the audience busy rather than bored, but makes everyone conscious of what good delivery looks like.

If you want to add a little competitive spirit, add up all the points each speaker collectively receives from the audience and give modest prizes for the top three reports.

Return the evaluation forms to the speakers so that they can see the feedback. I leave it up to the judges whether they want to sign their names or make their assessment anonymously.

There are two basic approaches when assigning books to be read:

■ *Your book.* Assign one of your favorite books to provide a common perspective and shared vocabulary. Alternatively, you might provide a list of several favorites from which the trainees can choose.

■ *Their book.* Leave the choice up to the trainee as long as the selection meets a certain standard, such as a biography of a famous leader or a book with the word *leader* or *management* in the title.

Have you participated in a book club? The training part of your sales meetings takes an interesting turn if each week one person leads a discussion on one chapter of a sales or management book. Some sales managers lead a voluntary book-reading program on a different day from the sales meeting.

Make use of homework assignments to reinforce the book's main points. For instance, Jack Welch has some definite ideas on the role of passion in management success. A good question for participants to answer before training begins is, "How does Jack Welch's definition of *passion* relate to our company?"

Draw on Case Studies

Case studies lead to lively discussions, often bringing the participants to conclusions that lead to better management practices. Limit most case studies to a one-page scenario.

In writing a case study, you can be creative and have some fun. For instance, you might describe a situation that reveals one obvious problem, but after further review will expose other less evident dilemmas. Let's take the example of the following paragraph:

> Ann Baker is a dedicated new sales manager. She regularly reports to her office at 8:45 a.m. to prepare her day. She is the last to go home at night, usually leaving between 10 and 11 p.m. She conducts all the new face training from 10 a.m. to 2 p.m., Tuesday through Friday most weeks, and the weekly three-hour sales meeting on Mondays. Ann has a lot of paperwork she must attend to on a timely basis. She has found that talking to all salespeople takes up a lot of time. Her personal sales have dropped by more than 50 percent since she was promoted. Team sales are stagnant. Ann complains of fatigue.

This scenario provides a lot of room for discussion. Normally, the case study discussion group will come to the conclusion that Ann's setting the example of personal selling or observing her people selling is more important than talking about selling in the office. Digging a little deeper reveals issues of delegation and burnout. Who should be doing all that paperwork? Should Ann be conducting 100 percent of the training classes? You can discuss a lot of management practices from a single case study paragraph.

Ask your trainees to complete homework assignments before and after their training program. Here are a few examples of homework assignments *before* your training session commences:

- Submit a list of the three most important points of an article or book you assigned them to read. This increases the odds that the material will actually be read prior to training.
- Calculate the time and cost of generating a lead through various lead-generating programs.
- Name three people you should be spending more time with and three people you should spending less time with.
- "What is your most dramatic memory from your career with our company?"

Homework assignments *after* a training program are more action-based. After all, training is designed to either motivate the attendees to do something they were not doing before or get them doing what they have already been doing, only better and more often. The following are examples of after-the-training homework assignments:

- "Design a new prospecting activity contest" might follow a training program on either motivation or sales contests.
- "Create a one-page outline of your group leader's development program" is an excellent assignment following a management development program.
- "Name two new management activities you will delegate in the next 30 days" would follow a training session on delegation.
- "Name the number-one lifetime objective for your top five salespeople" could follow a training session on how to motivate your sales force.

No doubt your imagination can produce great homework assignments that are interesting, that focus your training group on the main points, and that ensure that something *happens* following training.

PROMOTE "SHOW AND DO" LEAD-GENERATING ACTIVITY

Try this five-step plan for conducting "show and do" marketing training activities:

1. *Prepare the materials.* No matter which lead-generation technique is being covered, make sure that all the items necessary for the entire group are ready and available in abundance.

2. *Teach (30 minutes).* Review the historical results of how many leads are generated by each hour of activity, followed by a demonstration of the method.

3. *Practice (30 minutes).* Supervise role-playing practice of the technique. Of course, if the lead-generating method is putting on door hangers, practice can be skipped.

4. *Do it (2 to 3 hours).* Lead your group into the field to position take-one boxes, place flyers with small businesses, knock on doors, or do whatever the activity is.

5. *Meet back (30 minutes).* Immediately after the activity, review what happened. A few folks will always have great stories that will inspire others (and themselves) to repeat the activity on their own before the next scheduled "show and do" marketing clinic.

QUESTIONS TO ASK YOURSELF

- Do you have a host of training ideas at the ready? Can you make your training more exciting?
- Can you get your training message across better?
- How many of this chapter's training techniques are you using now?
- Which ones can you add to your arsenal over the next 90 days?
- What type of homework assignments could you give before and after your training programs?

- How you will use videos in your training going forward?
- How can you better use PowerPoint and other visual aids?

Here are a number of books that can further help you deliver interesting programs:

- *The Sales Training Handbook* by Jeff Magee
- *The Big Book of Humorous Training Games* by Doni Tamblyn and Sharyn Weiss
- *The Trainer's Tool Kit* by Cy Charney and Kathy Conway
- *The Fun Factor* by Carolyn Greenwich

CHAPTER 14

EXPLOIT THE POWER OF OFF-SITE MEETINGS

I will study and get ready and some day my chance will come.

—Abraham Lincoln, U.S. President, 1861–1865

As you review all the possible objectives of training, the opportunities for dynamic, interesting training events expand. What also expands are the venues that are suitable or even necessary for vigorous training that stimulates veteran sales personnel. Sometimes a change of venue is a needed stimulus to send a message that something special is going to happen. You have three out-of-the-office opportunities:

- Innovative meeting venues
- Intensive training retreats
- Scholarships for third-party training

The following vignette exemplifies the possibilities of punctuating the importance of a sales meeting by stimulating the senses in an imaginative manner before and during the event.

Our annual Great Britain sales meeting promised to be an epochal event, as we had challenged ourselves to reverse a decade of flat sales. Prior annual sales meetings had been held at the Heathrow Airport Hotel, simply because it was convenient. This time we chose Stratford-on-Avon, the birthplace of Shakespeare, for what we hoped would be a "resurgence meeting." We launched a new commission system, introduced an overseas sales contest, and promoted new recruiting and lead-generating methods.

Taking a stroll around an airport hotel after the formal daytime agenda has concluded is rarely special or inspiring. In Stratford-on-Avon, it was impossible *not* to take a stroll. Small groups of salespeople meandered along the medieval village streets, shared a pint of brew at one of the Shakespearean-era pubs, or perched on the elevated cobblestones along the river's edge speculating on what all these positive changes would mean for their sales careers. Sales doubled over the next 18 months. The meeting provided an evocative bonding event, a common treasured memory that defined a new selling era.

Could we have done the same thing at the airport hotel? Maybe. Then again, maybe not.

You may not have castles, but no place on earth is completely devoid of interesting settings. Locations can be as fascinating as your imagination (and budget) allow. Let loose.

Motivate your sales associates by offering dynamic training retreats. If these are done right, your sales partners get charged up, ready to put *their* new plan into action. Market obstacles are seen in a new perspective. Each attendee designs his strategy for expanding the business.

One of my best advanced key-person training programs, centering on Stephen Covey's *Seven Habits of Highly Successful People*, took place in northern Thailand. Our sales managers were bused directly from the Chaing Mai airport to an elephant camp. Two by two, our managers climbed aboard their assigned four-legged transport. After a two-hour elephant ride through the jungle, the participants constructed "Tom Swift"— style river rafts from bamboo poles, giant inner tubes, and rigging. We then drifted downstream to our wilderness camp on our makeshift, leaky boats.

The next day, different teams led leadership seminars inspired by their assigned chapter of the Covey book. Between review sessions, the group braved the camp's assortment of obstacle courses and challenge activities, which required trust and teamwork between group members to complete successfully.

The second evening, the sales managers were given uncooked rice, water, vegetables, live chickens, and more bamboo poles and told to fix dinner. A few people had to be chicken terminators. The food may have not met gourmet standards, but the team building was phenomenal. What great memories that Spartan cookout provided.

Another time, we conducted survival training in Sabah, Malaysia, in the northern part of Borneo. The group was transported to the drop zone by helicopter and given 24 hours to find the base camp. Actually, we could have driven to the drop zone, but the helicopter gave the exercise the desired Rambo effect. Local guides traveled with the group to make sure everyone survived in good health. This time the assigned reading was *Who Moved My Cheese?* by Spencer Johnson, M.D.

We have planned whitewater rafting, bungee jumping, zip lines, rappelling, and other experiences that give participants a rush. While many of these exciting activities are well known, it is surprising how many sales associates knew about them only vicariously.

Most of these activities (except the elephant rides) can be done almost anywhere. Few communities have absolutely no interesting locations within two hours of the office. Outfitters are almost ubiquitous. Thanks to search engines like Google.com, any sales manager can discover a team-building experience that will create the memory and fun that sets her sales group apart from the others. This kind of creative leadership is all part of "building a persona," as outlined in Chapter 29. You can build themes around whitewater rafting, bungee jumping, and rappelling—all in the context of a training exercise designed to inspire personal-best results.

Let's move on to the specific objectives of productive off-site training.

■ *Nurture relationships.* Do you ever feel that you do not have sufficient time to build the type of relationships you want with your key sales partners? The immersion experience of off-site training gives you that time. You have a golden opportunity to discover what your team members are really thinking and feeling.

■ *Create bonding memories.* Adventure-based sales and management training creates lasting, shared, team-building memories. Associate your leadership with dramatic memories.

■ *Imprint the message.* Dramatic, evocative training reinforces the training mission by making an almost indelible impression. Not only do attendees remember spectacular feats through association, they remember your training objectives better.

■ *Reduce turnover.* Shared unique experiences build a sense of family. It is harder to quit your family than to quit "just a job."

■ *Forestall bickering.* Harmony and teamwork don't just happen. Constructive competition is not just a by-product of hopeful wishes. Team-building training events reduce dissension and conflict before the seemingly inevitable personality discords happen.

■ *Aid conflict resolution.* Sales teams can fall apart because of destructive personality conflicts. Sales decline. Promising careers end in acrimony. However, conflict resolution can sometimes be a by-product of your training event. For example, at one outbound event, two managers (one reporting to the other) who had barely spoken to each other for two years had a quiet "bury-the-hatchet" meeting after the discussion of the "Win-Win" chapter of the Covey book. This type of harmonious spin-off encounter has happened so often in my training programs that I have learned to anticipate it.

■ *Get everyone going in the same direction.* Extended training provides the time and platform to develop and sell the leader's vision.

■ *Promote a reputation for fun.* You have read and heard about great places to work. Providing this unusual getaway opportunity for your staff is one way to turn your organization into one of those great places.

■ *Facilitate and accelerate change.* Your team is more likely to embrace the changes you are promoting in a retreat setting. A captivating setting and a no-distractions time frame provide a stress-free environment that will allow you to set out your desired transformation objectives successfully.

You will note that many of the cited advantages of retreat-style training will also answer your question: "How do I motivate my people?"

A memory-building training adventure will be effective only if its prime purpose is to increase sales. Measure the success of your outbound retreat by the subsequent results.

ORGANIZING YOUR OWN RETREAT

There is no perfect formula for organizing memorable training events, but I have a few thoughts that you might consider when you are thinking about how to match your training objectives with the venue and time available.

■ Be 100 percent clear about your off-site training objectives. What is it that you want your team to accomplish following the training?

■ Combine an incentive travel program with a management development program. Arrive a day or two early. For the cost of the same airplane ticket, you can conduct leadership development seminars for a day or two before the other sales contest winners arrive.

■ Schedule the timing of training events and annual sales meetings to maximize sales. Some companies schedule training and meetings at the end or start of the fiscal year. This makes sense only if that timing is likely to increase sales more than any other schedule choice.

■ Offer light, high-energy food. Sugar-based snacks and heavy lunches guarantee snooziness.

■ Promote your off-site event. Hype it by putting up colorful posters around the office so that participants will be visually reminded about their upcoming destination.

■ Initiate a "beat the boss" contest. How do you motivate the people left behind who are not attending the meetings? It works like this: You, the boss, challenge your managers or key sales partners to meet or beat the average sales of the previous four weeks. If your left-behind team matches the four-week average, they win the bet. You pay 1-to-1 odds. However, you might give 2-to-1 odds for a 25 percent sales increase or 3-to-1 odds for a 50 percent sales increase. When you lose the bet, you win the sales war. Everybody loves to beat the boss!

Outside training does not mean only the training you provide. Offer your sales associates scholarships to attend outside training. Today we are blessed with Carnegie, the American Management Association, Tom Hopkins, Jeffrey Gitomer, and Brian Tracy, to name a few. Zig Ziglar still delivers his magic. Anthony Robbins enjoys well-deserved star power. Let your salespeople know that you value these programs by promoting attendance at them. Set the standards for winning full or partial scholarships to attend motivational and sales-training programs you believe in.

Today many renowned trainers offer tele-seminars. Check your favorite sales trainer's Web site for a time you and your sales associates can join the seminar. Sign up for free newsletters. You can go to my Web site, www.malaghan.net, for an extensive list of sales and sales management Web sites.

My 11 consecutive years of sales growth during the 1990s and beyond was due in large part to recurrent, off-site, attention-grabbing training events. I doubt if we could have expanded from $50 to $250 million in annual sales in a decade without them. Stimulating, outbound-type retreats supporting clear objectives are engines of sales growth.

QUESTIONS TO ASK YOURSELF

■ Have you conducted or attended a company retreat? What were the results?

■ Can you visualize how you could conduct a retreat that would bring your sales team to a new level?

- Where would you conduct that retreat?
- Look at the list of advantages given in the chapter and check off the ones that apply to your approach to sales management.
- What type of topic would you cover at a one- or two-day retreat? How would you organize it?
- What would be the response of your sales team if you offered a retreat in an interesting locale?
- How would you finance it?
- Would a focused retreat increase sales?

Recommended books to help foster "out-of-the-box" thinking on training:

- *Six Thinking Hats* by Edward de Bono
- *Straight from the Gut* by Jack Welch

CHAPTER 15
CONDUCT EXCITING SALES MEETINGS

A computer is talking to its owner: "I can be upgraded. Can you?"

—*The New Yorker* magazine cartoon

Face it: The word *meeting* does not usually connote excitement. The only time salespeople will be eager to attend your meetings will be when they know that the meetings will help them earn more money. Otherwise, they prefer to avoid meetings, believing that their time would be better spent selling. If fines must be levied to induce salespeople to show up for meetings, that indicates the sorry state of their expectations. Conversely, salespeople will pay their own money to attend an Anthony Robbins meeting, because they expect to earn far more money than the fees they must pay to attend the event. As you read the following anecdote, consider how you can turn your meeting nemesis into your strongest partner.

> "Robert is one pain in the you-know-what," explained sales manager Sally Carlson. "He is a star salesman, but he shows up late, always complains, and asks off-the-wall questions at my meetings."
>
> "Sally," I suggested, "why don't you put Robert in charge of your next meeting?"
>
> While putting the complainer in charge of the complaint does not always work, it did in this case. Not only did Robert show up on time, but he brought in a short video to view, had a printed agenda on everyone's desktop prior to the meeting, and conducted a vigorous session on competitors. Learning from the experience, Sally rotated the meeting chairmanship. She went on to become a district sales manager, with Robert in charge of one of her offices.

It is the sales manager's responsibility to conduct meetings that will increase the income of the attendees and do so in an interesting manner.

There are actually 60 recommendations for conducting time-efficient, productive meetings. These recommendations can be conveniently broken into the following five groups:

- Mindset
- Agenda
- Meeting preparation
- Starting the meeting
- Conducting the meeting

MINDSET

The mindset is the mental approach you bring to the meetings. What do you want to get out of those sales meetings? What is your strategy? What do you need to decide before you set the agenda?

1. *Is it your meeting or your team's meeting?* Make sure the meeting serves your "clients"—in other words, your sales force. It pays to be humble. The purpose of the sales meeting is to tell all your salespeople how great they are, not how good you are. How would you conduct your sales meetings if you were an outside consultant? How would you conduct your sales meetings if your sales force could vote on whether they wanted you back to conduct the next meeting?

2. *"If one of your sales members misses a meeting, will she miss anything?"* That's the question I asked myself as I reviewed my sales meeting agendas. We want our meeting content to be so compelling that anyone missing it will feel a great sense of loss.

3. *Plan for something to happen as a consequence of the meeting.* Issue a call to action. The prime purpose of all sales meetings is to get people to *do* something.

4. *Have a wish list.* Be clear about the purpose of each meeting. Establish your prime objectives. Your agenda follows your intent. Your meeting wish list embraces the critical-to-mission business objectives you are currently promoting.

5. *Revolve your meeting agenda around the five key selling competencies:*

- ❏ Prospecting skills
- ❏ Selling skills
- ❏ Product knowledge

❏ Communication skills

❏ Personal growth

Start with the question, "Which of the five selling competencies do I want to feature at my next sales meeting?"

6. *Schedule sales meetings just before the golden selling time* so that your sales meeting can be immediately followed by a selling or appointment activity.

7. *Stick to a routine.* Attendance and promptness are increased when the weekly sales meeting is at the same time every week.

AGENDA

Next comes your outline for the meeting, known as the agenda.

8. *Showcase your professionalism.* Prepare a proper agenda. You can conduct a sales meeting without an agenda, but you'll conduct a better meeting when you use one.

9. *Ask your team members to contribute to the agenda.* This simple act of respect and democracy ensures that the meeting is "their" meeting. Your agenda will be more dynamic when others contribute to it. Your appeal for agenda items not only reduces later off-the-wall surprises at your meetings, but gives you a valid reason to cut off such surprises if they suddenly occur.

10. *Delegate parts of the agenda.* Ask your sales team to conduct parts of your sales meetings. Involve as many people as possible. People listed on the agenda tend to show up at the meeting. Consider using the 50 percent rule: The sales manager makes sure that her time on stage is 50 percent or less of the total sales meeting time.

11. *Appoint a meeting chairman.* You might want to do what Sally did in the opening story of this chapter and appoint a chairman for some of your meetings. Your delegated sales associate prepares the agenda and conducts the meeting on your behalf.

12. *Limit* most *topics to 10 minutes or less.* The rapid pace reduces boredom. (Remember, you are competing with MTV.) It is better for your sales associates to complain, "I wish we had had more time for that topic" than "He talked too long" or "Oh, no, not that again!" This time limit allows for the one or two big matters that really do need more than 10 minutes.

13. *Schedule outside speakers.* You've heard the saying, "No man is a prophet in his own country." Giving your sales team an opportunity to hear other resources increases the likelihood that they'll perk up, pay attention, and listen with fresh ears. Arrange an exchange visit with other sales managers and/or invite a respected sales rep from another office to your sales meeting.

14. *Start your meetings with awards and recognition.* If you have an outside speaker, give that person the honor of giving the award or recognizing accomplishment.

15. *Schedule the occasional "dog and pony show."* This is what I called home office road shows. Twice a year, I tried to schedule visits to sales offices by teams of three or four headquarters managers from the collection, verification, customer service, marketing, accounting, and other administrative departments.

16. *Invite your customers to a meeting.* Happy customer stories are inspirational moments that stir salespeople to work with enthusiasm. Few moments are as electrifying as a customer reliving the sales call and championing your product or service. Satisfied customers validate careers.

17. *Evaluate your competitor's product.* A follow-up group discussion among your sales team on how your product is superior gets better results than if you just tell them.

18. *Use visual aids.* Use all the available tools to reinforce your message and keep the troops entertained during the process. A review of the visual aids section of Chapter 13 provides examples, such as PowerPoint, overhead projectors, and whiteboards.

19. *Invite Zig Ziglar or Jeffrey Gitomer to your meeting* via one of their videos. Show a clip from a movie that dramatizes a leadership point you want to make.

20. *Data matters.* Showing the results of a customer satisfaction survey is more compelling than saying, "After-sales service is important." Present statistics so that your "left-brainers" respect the fact that you're backing up your information with facts and measurable observations.

21. *Use case studies.* Just one or two paragraphs is all that is necessary.

MEETING PREPARATION

You've got your agenda set, but there are still a few things you can do *before* your meeting to ensure its success.

22. *Send out the agenda ahead of time,* although you should still hand out copies on the day of the meeting. An advance copy of the agenda says that you are prepared. A strong agenda with a good lead-off topic encourages attendance and promptness.

23. *Provide reasonable advance notice if the meeting time is changed or a special meeting is required.* Tolerance for absences and tardiness in such cases shows that you have a heart.

24. *A smart-looking meeting room sets the tone.* A sloppy appearance can sneak up on you. All you have to do is get used to the mess and have no one complain very loudly. When I have visited offices and asked local sales managers to clean up the room, they are often surprised twice—first, because I noticed something that they didn't think was noticeable, and second, at how nice the room looked after they finished tidying up.

25. *Get the seating right.* This is one of the reasons that the sales manager or his designate wants to set up the room prior to the meeting. Chairs and tables "arranged" in a helter-skelter fashion do not suggest a well-organized office.

26. *Use bribes to increase attendance.* Some of the bribes I have used over the years include occasionally giving a free company lead to everyone who shows up on time. The unpredictable and occasional extra contest point for promptness is another little bribe that gets the attention of eagles.

27. *Offer free coffee and doughnuts.* This perk, available 15 minutes prior to the meeting, is another one of those little bribes that encourage promptness. It's a cheap way to be a hero.

28. *Conduct private meetings to prepare your key sales personnel when a controversial or contentious subject is on the agenda.* It pays to take the time to disarm key players before the meeting. Conversely, letting your key people know some good news ahead of time is a sure-fire way of making them feel more important.

29. *Promote your sales meetings* the way Letterman, King, and Leno publicize their nightly telecasts. These talk-show hosts keep telling us how great the next show will be.

STARTING THE MEETING

It's start-up time. Review the following suggestions to open a lively, invigorating sales meeting.

30. *Get the mood right.* Start the music. The beat of Ricky Martin, Bruce Springsteen, or Beyoncé sets spirits soaring and elevates the mood of everyone in the room. Play the music during breaks.

31. *Be enthusiastic!* Every sales meeting is show time. If we want our sales team to be excited and optimistic, we must exude our own enthusiasm and optimism.

32. *Take off your sales manager's hat and replace it with a facilitator's hat.* Except for the time during which you are the speaker on a particular subject, your job is to think about all the rules for conducting a good meeting, not how to exercise your authority as the boss.

33. *Dress for success still works.* The best sales managers are usually among the best dressed.

34. *Start on time.* Attendees appreciate your honoring time commitments and keeping to a schedule. Do not let the latecomers dictate when the meeting starts. If you have a habit of starting 10 minutes late, why would anyone show up at the stated time?

35. *Aerobics is good.* This is especially true after a meeting break or if the meeting starts after lunch. A 90-second aerobic or stretching exercise starts the meeting positively.

36. *Tell your sales associates what you are going to cover at the start; summarize it at the end.* It's the old story: "Tell them what you are going to tell them, tell them, and then tell them what you told them."

37. *Keep the meeting moving.* At the start of the meeting, take your watch off your wrist and place it on top of the table next to the agenda. Ask permission from the audience to cut off folks who talk too long or who stray from the subject so that you can keep your promise to end the meeting on time. After a while, you will no longer need to announce this, as your group will get used to your "keep it moving" meeting pace.

CONDUCTING THE MEETING

Your meeting is off to a terrific start. Read on for thoughts on how to maintain that high standard throughout the meeting.

38. *Stick to your agenda.* Inevitably, you will encounter attempts to veer from the agenda. When that happens, just say, "That's an important subject, Ralph; however, if we are going to keep our commitment to end meetings on time, we need to cover that subject next week. I will also be happy to discuss that subject with you privately later today."

39. *Tell stories to make a point.* The Bible is full of parables that make a moral point by way of an interesting anecdote. (Who does not know the story of the prodigal son?) Here is my contribution of a story that makes a point. Have your sales representatives ever complained about the quality of leads? Try saying this: "This reminds me of the prison riot that resulted in taking hostages. The prisoners demanded TV time. The reporter asked, 'What were the main complaints?' 'Food,' replied the prisoners' spokesman. 'The food is so bad you can't eat it, and we are never allowed to go back for seconds.' "

40. *Reveal yourself.* Share personal stories; let your sales family own a bit of your soul. Your stories of how you overcame obstacles let your people understand your humanness while you make the point that persistence won the day.

41. *Try a little humor.* The best humor at sales meetings is self-deprecating humor. Let the audience know that you flunked your humility and listening classes. Humor and laughter help your meetings seem shorter. Build a repertoire of humorous stories.

42. *Keep a water glass handy for you and the other speakers.* This commonsense prop avoids dry mouth and a scratchy throat. Your sales force will appreciate small gestures like this; they let people know you care.

43. *Keep everyone involved.* Attendees who don't have a chance to speak will disengage. Don't just ask for volunteers when asking questions or seeking people for role playing. Ask the reserved members of your sales audience for their opinion and to join in the role playing.

44. *Ask for the group's help in answering questions.* Give your sales partners a chance to be the expert. You will probably be able to answer almost every question. However, other people in the sales group may be as skilled as you (or even better) on a particular subject and would be flattered if you stepped aside in their favor.

45. *Use names.* We all know that the best sound in any language is the resonance of our own name.

46. *Thank the complainers.* Part of my job as the senior sales executive was to visit sales offices. I always made time for Q&A, because I knew I'd be asked a tough question or two. In fact, that was one of the reasons I visited offices: It gave everyone a chance to have direct access to the boss, if only for a short time. When a question like, "Why do we have to pay so much money for sales materials?" came up, you could hear the silence. My standard and sincere response was, "Thank you for having the courage to ask that question." I would then look at the group and say, "Let's give Bill a round of applause for asking that question." After the applause I would add, "Bill, I am sure you are speaking for many people in this room today who share your frustration." Then I would get on with a response to this and other tricky questions, having defused the situation somewhat. The audience was more open to hearing my answer, and I faced a less hostile questioner, who may have asked the question to test me and even show off a bit.

47. *Vote early; vote often.* People love to vote. It engages the mind. However, you need to control the issue. You can't initiate a vote on something like, "How much do you want to increase commissions?" But you can let your salespeople vote on such issues as sales contest locations and some of the rules of those contests, which day of the week is best for the sales meeting, where to have the next monthly social, and which lead-generating activity should be featured at the next sales meeting.

48. *Do not let a few dominate the many.* Control the "time hog." (Remember the "keep it moving" pledge you made at the start of the meeting.) Defend your audience from the big talkers who attempt to take over discussions. Politely and firmly interrupt the droner after a brief period: "Thank you, Mary, you make a good point, but we really have to move on."

49. *Start a book-reading program.* Book readings can offer an entertaining aid to training. A short reading followed by a discussion of how the book can improve the audience's selling and management skills is another way to bring a "virtual" expert to your meeting while providing a discussion exercise in which everyone is engaged.

50. *Make decisions at meetings.* Meetings become more important when decisions are made with the advice and consultation of your sales associates. If a decision can be made, make it. Salespeople do not enjoy procrastination.

51. *Make sure that everyone is comfortable giving an opinion.* Part of the persona you cultivate is that you respect and appreciate all meeting input—even though sometimes you must impose a time limit. Know the difference between good-natured humor and ridicule, and make sure that people never feel the latter. People who are the objects of our jokes do not look forward to attending our meetings.

52. *Brainstorm problems.* A good agenda item is brainstorming a particular problem. Little things such as how to select members of the sales force for booth shift assignment or how to assign recycled leads are important to the team. These are good issues that clamor for transparency and fairness. Other brainstorming issues might include new prospecting or recruiting methods.

53. *Assign subcommittees to work on problems.* Many of the subjects listed under brainstorming or voting may well be best handled with a two-step process. Assign a small group of sales associates to meet during the week and come up with some recommendations for the larger group. This subcommittee approach also works well when sudden problems pop up at meetings. For example, if one of my salespeople complains during a meeting about a new credit policy, I may ask her to work with two other salespeople and a person from the administration to review the policy. This keeps the meeting on pace, while acknowledging the importance of the question.

54. *Convert to a lead-generation clinic.* Conduct a sales meeting dedicated almost exclusively to a prospecting technique. Use the clinic techniques outlined in Chapter 5.

55. *Produce videos.* A video addressing special topics, such as overcoming objections, through role playing by your star sales reps can be used again for training. Another benefit is that an audience that becomes part of the filming usually demonstrates increased attentiveness.

56. *Appoint a meeting critic.* If you are getting complaints about your meetings, ask someone (or one of those subcommittees) to evaluate the meeting on a variety of criteria, such as content, pace, and use of visuals. This is a good way to make the complainer part of the solution instead of part of the problem.

57. *Praise in public, criticize in private.* Though this is not a new concept, it always bears repeating. Not only does public criticism undermine the core purpose of the meeting (criticism does *not* motivate), but it undermines the loyalty of the person being criticized, while audience members are left wondering whether they will be the next victim.

58. *Ask attendees to write questions.* Large groups and new members of groups are sometimes reluctant to participate in Q&A. You may find that if you ask everyone to write down one or two questions, you will receive more questions from more people.

59. *End meetings on a hopeful note and with a call to action.* Send the attendees out with a vote of confidence, a hearty "I believe in you." Your wrap-up speech emphasizes what will *happen* in the coming days and weeks because of the sales meeting.

60. *End on time.* Once your habit of starting and ending on time is established, more people will show up at your meetings and be prompt about it.

*   *   *

It's our job to conduct meetings that our sales associates *want* to attend. Interesting, entertaining, sales-producing meetings don't just happen; attention-grabbing, income-producing meetings are a result of commitment followed by planning.

It's true, 60 meeting ideas is a bit much. But then again, conducting great meetings day after day is a bit much. Rather than focus on the number 60, think back to our beginning. Meetings can be broken into the five parts of meetings: the mindset with which you approach meetings, preparing the agenda, getting ready for your meeting, a good start to the meeting, and conducting the meeting. How can you improve in each area? Not surprisingly, the more you prepare, the better the meeting.

QUESTIONS TO ASK YOURSELF

- Are you satisfied with the content and excitement of your meetings?
- Do your people show up and show up on time?
- How can you make your meetings more interesting?
- Are you using visual aids and props?
- Are your sales associates eager to get to work after your sales meetings?
- Is there more you might do to include more of your sales partners in the preparation and conducting of your meetings?
- How well do you manage the pace of your meetings?
- Does every meeting end with a call to immediate action?
- Of the 60 ideas presented, what are the 6 most appealing new ideas that you want to start using immediately?

The following books provide even more details on conducting sales meetings:

- *How to Get the Most Out of Sales Meetings* by James Dance
- *Sales Meetings That Work* by Richard Cavalier

FIFTH ESSENTIAL ACTIVITY

REPLICATE YOURSELF

Empire builders have one important quality in common: They know that they can't do it all themselves. They understand that the secret of long-lasting success is replicating themselves, so they follow a blueprint that shows them how to build their empire by building strong leaders within their team. The following chapters focus on the strategies empire builders use to accelerate leadership development.

Some people are natural take-charge leaders; most people, however, are not. If you want to develop a sales empire, you can expand your leadership base by coaching other personality types, those who may be latent take-charge leaders if nurtured properly, on how to take the initiative. While you cannot convert all the members of your sales team into strong leaders, a vigorous development program will still increase the number of your sales personnel. And as "they" say, "It's a numbers game."

CHAPTER 16
START WITH THE FIRST STEP: THE GL

Trust men and they will be true to you; treat them greatly and they will show themselves great.

—Ralph Waldo Emerson, Author

Dynamic sales growth, delegation of duties, and management development all start with the first level of leadership, the group leader. Never was this so true and verified as when my first four pioneer hires in Taiwan in February 1992 were offered an empty office and a dream of starting a new business.

Dan, Sophia, Richard, and William all sat in front of me as I conducted a three-day training program on how to introduce our new product. Nobody had sold an order yet, but they were being paid a salary of $1,600 a month (plus commissions) for three months on the condition that they wrote at least two orders each month. Each was a pioneer sales manager without anyone reporting to him or her as yet.

My final instructions were simple. "First, you learn how to sell the product, and then you hire one or two people and show them how you sell the product." Within five years, those four individuals were managing a combined group of 300 salespeople producing more than $25 million a year.

First, let us define the term *group leader*. A group leader, or GL, is a person who

■ Writes personal orders
■ Directly supervises a team of two to seven people
■ Helps conduct classroom training
■ Actively recruits new salespeople
■ Wants to be promoted to sales manager

The job of the sales manager is to discover good salespeople who can become group leaders. The sales manager must positively *expose* a GL candidate to the management opportunity early and often, enthusiastically *build* the GL candidate's desire for the job, and patiently *teach* that GL candidate how to become a group leader through a combination of example and delegation.

Your personal commitment to your own success and growth precedes your search for new leaders. Let your group leaders feel the way you ooze commitment, success, and ambition. The successful sales manager creates an environment of leadership expectations. Your sales team *expects* that sales will increase. The members of the sales team *expect* frequent promotions.

The development of your expanding leadership team is built on trust. Potential leaders trust you because

- They admire your example.
- They believe in your fairness.
- They feel that you have confidence in them.
- They know that you have a plan for sales growth.

The development of group leaders is similar to the process for recruiting new salespeople. Once a person has demonstrated competent selling skills, it is time to recruit that person into management. Give everyone the opportunity—you might be surprised at who rises to the occasion.

The development of group leaders always means taking risks. Not everyone who tries out for the management team will make it. Your time and effort will be rewarded by the few great, enduring successes that are often the by-product of many patiently borne short-term failures. Failure is relative; not everyone who migrates to sales management is destined to lead an army, but many will shine with smaller groups.

RECRUITING GROUP LEADERS

Since the recruitment and development of group leaders is the starting point for management development (and thus sales growth), let's review the process of recruiting group leaders.

Ask!

Start your search for group leaders at the initial recruiting interview by adding the phrase, "A few successful sales candidates will also be selected for our 90-day (or six-month) management training program." Follow this up during the first day of basic sales training by explaining the selection process and training program for future leaders. Ask those who are qualified whether they might be interested in such a program.

As soon as a person has written a few orders, have a private "management counseling" session with her. Ask about her intentions. To those who respond favorably, explain your sales and management growth program. Impress upon her your need for new managers. Send the message that you have a positive vision for the future. You need bright new people to make it all possible.

No one I know has ever been insulted by being asked if he is interested in being trained for a leadership position. Therefore, *ask* about a person's interest in management early and often. The only qualifications are competence in personal selling and trainability. Do not wait until a salesperson feels ready. It's the job of the sales manager to get people ready. You get them ready by asking them to get ready. You promise to help them grow into the job.

Share!

Share your dreams and aspirations. Let your sales team know that you have bigger plans. Everyone likes to jump on board a winning organization. Let your sales team know that you are a winner.

Share your training and prospecting decisions. Doesn't everyone like to be part of the show? Doesn't everyone like to contribute to the betterment of his organization?

Share your plans for growth. Let everyone on the team, including the newest members, know your plans for expanding over the next three months, and over the next year as well. These plans are best made with the help of every level of your leadership group; they are common goals, arrived at as a group.

Share your attention. New leaders like to feel special. Ask for their advice. If you are good at explaining a problem, the answer will often be self-evident. Encourage the GLs to arrive at the right conclusion by themselves.

Romance!

Romance your eagles. If you want group leaders, court them. Take them to lunch. Give them a book on salesmanship or management. Tell them (again and again) that they have the potential to develop into outstanding leaders.

Romance your GLs at meetings. Give them high-profile assignments. Let them know that you are counting on their performance. Make them feel special.

Act!

Act early. Do not hesitate. One of the advantages of a "results count" compensation system is that it allows you to take promotion risks with limited or no financial liability.

Act often. Make a *habit* of talking about management opportunities. After a while, your sales force will think that migration to management is the natural way of things.

What happens when a salesperson agrees that she would like to become a manager? Let her know what will be expected of her. What she does is about to change. I have seen times when the only change is the title on the business card. You and the GL candidate must have a clear idea of what the job is and what the GL will *do* when she has been promoted.

LET GROUP LEADERS TRAIN

A GL is a person who directly supervises a team of two to seven people, continues to write personal orders, and helps to conduct training and meetings. The GL, or whatever title you give your basic building block of sales management, drives your expansion. Your GLs are what colleges are to the NFL and NBA and what the minor league system is to Major League Baseball. The GLs are your farm system for a champion sales organization.

The GL as Field Trainer

The GL starts his career with the "watch me" method. This means that the new recruits reporting to the GL learn how to prospect and how to sell by watching the GL in action. The effective GL must possess these two skills. The simplest way to pass them on to new recruits is to teach by example.

If the new GL does just two things, show the job and care about the people, that is enough to start a successful career in sales management.

The GL as a Classroom Trainer

Group leaders can help in classroom training by giving an enthusiastic practice sales talk. The new GL needs the practice, usually likes to show off a bit, enjoys the new role of teacher, and appreciates being recognized as a participating member of management.

Management development, and the delegation that drives this development, is an attitude. If your dream is to build a sales empire to the best of your ability, then you must develop the habit of developing new managers by "giving away your job" step by step. The next chapter, on delegation, goes through the mechanics of giving away your job.

QUESTIONS TO ASK YOURSELF

- At what career stage do you start to plant the seeds for your sales reps to think about a future in management?
- What is your system for cultivating an interest in management?
- Do you have a formal training program for novice managers?
- What is the job description for your first level of sales management?

Recommended books for new sales managers that can help you guide your newest managers:

- *Becoming a Manager: How New Managers Master the Challenges of Leadership* by Linda A. Hill
- *Just Promoted!* by Edward H. Betof
- *Becoming a Successful Manager* by Jack H. Grossman, Ph.D., and J. Robert Parkinson, Ph.D.

CHAPTER 17

DELEGATE

The art of choosing men is not nearly so difficult as the art of enabling those one has chosen to attain their full worth.

—Napoleon Bonaparte, Empire Builder

Delegation can be defined as authorizing others to carry out specific tasks under your general supervision. This skill is an integral part of your time-mastery strategy because it frees you to be more productive and creative. Luckily for me, as the following story reveals, I was forced to try delegation very early in my career because I had no other viable option. It was even luckier for my future that this early attempt worked.

> Necessity can be the mother of delegation. I managed a student sales office in my senior year at the University of Florida. I was also president of my fraternity and had a cabinet position in student government. Time was precious. I taught my student sales secretary to conduct the parts of sales training that were not directly related to sales, such as how to fill out a sales contract. Once a new student salesperson had written one order, I promoted him to assistant trainer on the condition that he would conduct training one day a week.
>
> By the end of the fall term, I had learned to delegate almost all my jobs. Several new salespeople quickly became student sales managers. Because of my willingness to delegate, our part-time office was competitive with other offices managed by full-time sales managers with full-time sales reps. My immediate motivation had been to leverage my time; I soon realized, however, I had discovered a lifelong method of accelerated management development. More than once I have wondered what type of life I would have had if I had tried to muddle though this early test by having given in to the philosophical trap, "If you want things done right, do them yourself."

Delegation is a powerful motivational tool. It improves employees' job security, increases their potential earning power, fulfills a need for self-improvement, provides them with a feeling of usefulness, and satisfies a yearning for power and recognition.

Delegation frees you to be more productive and creative. It forces you to become more organized because you must outline projects, assign responsibilities in bite-sized units, set deadlines, and check progress.

The best way to develop new sales managers continuously is to "show and tell" key people what you do so that they can do it. In other words, give away your job. It really is that simple. There was a time when I addressed delegation and management development as separate subjects, even though I stressed the importance of delegation as a tool for management development and emphasized that management development was a wonderful by-product of delegation. A new realization eventually dawned on me: Delegation and management development are so intertwined that they should be considered a single integrated discipline.

The advantages of delegation go beyond management development, just as the advantages of management development go beyond delegation. Delegation is also part and parcel of smart time management. Most managers who claim that it is impossible for them to get all their work done are simply telling the world that they either do not know how or refuse to delegate some of their work and/or the authority that should go with the delegated task.

DELEGATE EARLY; DELEGATE OFTEN

"When in my management career should I start delegating?" is an often-heard question during key-person training programs. The only reply possible is, "As soon as you have one person reporting to you."

One of the advantages of introducing your management development program during the hiring interview—and then reinforcing that commitment during the initial training period—is that it enables you to start delegating simple tasks early in your salespeople's careers.

It was not unusual for me to ask a person I had hired only a few weeks before to help me train new sales recruits. Naturally, that relatively new salesperson must have enjoyed some early success and possessed some natural enthusiasm. This early delegation served at least five purposes:

- It gave the new salesperson a chance to practice her appointment talk and sales presentation.
- It told the new salesperson that I was serious about early management training.

- It confirmed to the new salesperson, "I trust you."
- It freed up my time.
- It demonstrated to new sales recruits in their first training that early success was possible.

NEVER DO THINGS THAT YOU CAN DELEGATE

Try this: List all the activities that you and only you can do. Whatever is left is what you can delegate. Start by listing all the sales management activities you perform over a one-week period, such as hiring interviews, training, planning, conducting sales meetings, phoning your members at the end of the day, writing a training program, reviewing pay statements, and so on and so forth. Write it all down. Consider the following questions:

- How much time did you spend on each activity?
- Which of those activities can you teach others to do?
- If you trained all your key people to do all the tasks you *could* delegate, how would your schedule look?
- If you could train all those people *now*, would your sales team grow as a consequence?
- What do you wish you had more time for, and how much time would you have for it if others could do part of your current job?

You will be amazed at how much of what you do can be delegated. The more you delegate, the more time you can spend on those things that only *you* can do, such as field training your best and brightest.

When you examine the histories of great sales managers who have built large organizations, you discover that these empire builders realized who their key sales management partners were very early in their careers. Like you, they started as sales reps, then were promoted to group leader or some similar first-level management position. Those ambitious GLs who rose to the top dared to dream of recruiting a large sales force. Those special GLs shared their empire-building dream with their first sales team members. Those dreaming GLs persuaded their neophyte sales partners to help them hire and train others.

So, one of the first requirements of giving away your job is to know precisely what tasks you perform and how long it takes you to complete each one. Then you can start to plan your "give-away" program. The goal is simple: Delegate every job that can be delegated.

NEVER MAKE A DECISION THAT YOU CAN DELEGATE

One of the best perks of being the sales manager is that you are the person who gets to make the decisions. The daily schedule, the agenda for the sales meeting, how to spend your time—these prerogatives of management are what make management and leadership such a joy.

As you savor all this decision-making authority, consider this: More than likely, you aren't the only one who enjoys making decisions. The members of your sales team may want to have their say. Delegating a decision is more than asking for and listening to advice. It means letting another person decide an issue, plan a meeting, or supervise a local marketing clinic. It means that sometimes you ask your team to vote on a decision.

For instance, the choice of a leisure spot, whether it's as simple as deciding where to hold a TGIF party or as complicated as choosing the next sales contest destination, usually leaves one or two people unhappy. "Why not this place instead of that one?" someone will inevitably ask. This can be very frustrating. Try an alternative approach. Since the purpose of these events is to motivate the sales force, you'll get a lot more mileage from these leisure events if more salespeople are involved in planning them. Who better to choose the location than the people you are trying to motivate? More than that, you can avoid the claim that you always pick where you want to go, a point of view that will undermine the motivational purpose of the award or event.

Often, delegating the decision-making process on subjects such as the choice of which local marketing activity to promote at the next sales meeting, where to go for the next "safari" sales trip, or what goes on the agenda for the next week's sales meeting assumes that the particular event *will* happen. The how and where is what's delegated.

The "box" concept works with delegating decisions. Think of an assortment of boxes for a minute—some small, some big. When the authority you have or are delegated is limited, your decision box is small. As you gain successful experience, the authority box within which you operate is enlarged. Your sales staff must understand that the authority you delegate is not absolute. If the assignment is to prepare the agenda for the next sales meeting, it is understood that a certain format is to be followed, unless the person delegated to plan the agenda negotiates a change in the meeting format with you. As the person delegated to plan the agenda gains experience and demonstrates competence in conducting meetings, his box of responsibility gets bigger and bigger. New ideas are tried within the framework of the expanding authority box.

While the first and most obvious benefit of delegating decisions is the personal satisfaction that the delegatee will feel, a larger benefit is an actual improvement in decision making. Think of sales management as a fluid management challenge. Nothing ever stays the same. The more creative, innovative minds you can engage in setting sales meeting agendas, experimenting with prospecting ideas, and writing recruiting ads, the more likely it is that you—"you" meaning your entire sales force—will stumble on a better idea. Once that new, workable idea has been discovered, you own the idea forever. For the people you invited to help you in the process, the pride of being trusted lingers long after the assignment. Step by step, the members of your sales team gain the confidence to perform all the activities of a sales manager that only frequent practice provides. As a consequence, you find yourself in a position to be promoted.

Delegation also acts as a powerful motivational tool. Turnover in any business is a problem; in the direct sales business, it presents a particularly difficult challenge. You must continually spend a good portion of your time motivating your charges. While Chapter 20 reviews in depth how to use the 14 key motivational tools, let's take a sneak preview of how delegation satisfies some of those 14 motivational needs of salespeople and sales managers.

■ *Self-improvement.* It's human nature to seek personal growth and knowledge. (Remember Eve and the apple?) Delegating increasingly difficult assignments satisfies this desire.

■ *Job security.* Sales partners who are delegated important roles and trusted with decisions have stronger feelings of career commitment than those who are not afforded these privileges.

■ *Money.* An MIT (manager in training) has expectations of improving her income as a result of being delegated meaningful tasks that will lead to promotions.

■ *Power.* Genuine delegation grants the MIT power, authority, and prestige.

■ *Feelings of usefulness.* Delegation satisfies the need to contribute to the success of the group.

DELEGATE THE EIGHT ESSENTIAL ACTIVITIES

You know what you need to do *every day* to be successful. Let's review the activities involved in each of the functions of the sales manager and see how you can turn these activities into a delegation process and a management development program.

1. *Sell.* Assign new sales trainees to accompany your manager candidates in the field as observers.

2. *Prospect.* Ask your MITs to conduct a lead-generation technique exercise.

3. *Hire.* Invite your sales team to design a recruiting newspaper ad. Teach personal recruiting as early as the introductory sales training program. Group leaders and other MIT designates can observe the sales manager's interview. Soon, the MIT can give the recruiting interview with the sales manager observing.

4. *Train.* Break your training into small segments so that your sales associates can participate early and easily. Most salespeople and new managers are thrilled to be asked to deliver a simulated sales talk, critique a simulated sales talk given by new people, and conduct a seminar in some closing or prospecting technique.

5. *Replicate yourself.* Be ambitious. Make the commitment to go to the next level of management. Put a program in place to actively develop managers who can replace you.

6. *Motivate.* Encourage your sales associates to motivate others. When a group leader conducts a session on goal setting, she is often the main beneficiary of what is heard by the listeners.

7. *Manage.* Get everyone involved. Just as Henry Ford divided the manufacture of cars into small units so that he could easily train people to become competent in a single function, a sales manager can assign small segments of the management activities, such as kit checks, sales supply inventory, updating the leader board, and preparing the sales meeting agenda and distributing it to sales personnel.

8. *Lead.* Develop your GLs' confidence by asking them to lead a seminar on topics such as "new ways to find more customers" and/or to conduct an entire sales meeting. (Try taking a seat in the back of the room with your representatives.)

HOW TO DELEGATE

The following list provides some useful hints to help you delegate:

- Always be on the lookout for assignments to delegate. Every time you do something, ask yourself, "Who else could do this?"
- Be quick to praise and slow to criticize. Most people do the best they can most of the time.
- Be patient; understand the learning curve. Different people learn at different speeds.
- Use a report-back system so that your team knows that you will be reviewing the assigned tasks with them.
- Show interest in the results. This is a good time to practice those active listening skills.
- Outline the project to be delegated. This includes training outlines and other types of *written* instructions.
- Assign definite responsibilities. Be precise in your instructions.
- Identify the easiest tasks to delegate.
- Select candidates for the delegated tasks *early* in their careers.
- Assign one task to one person.
- Set deadlines. People need to know *when* the task should be completed.
- Inspect what you expect. Or as former president Ronald Reagan once said, "Trust, but verify."
- Assign work gradually.
- Delegate in advance; avoid last-minute crisis assignments.
- Let your team know that delegation is an honor.
- Rotate delegation tasks; keep everyone fresh.
- Identify tasks that you and only you should perform.

- Allow a person the freedom to carry out the assignment in his own way as long as he "stays within the box."
- Explain the benefits of the delegated tasks. Why is this assignment important? How is the assignment part of your management development program?
- Start today! Do not just think about delegating; *do it.*

It helps to look at delegation from the viewpoint of the person to whom the work is delegated. After all, delegation can be described as an implicit contract: A task is assigned and accepted. Each side has both responsibilities and expectations. As the delegator, you expect that the job will be done efficiently and effectively. The members of your sales group are entitled to certain expectations as well, including:

- Completely understanding what is expected of them when they are given an assignment
- Recognizing how their assignment fits into the overall success of the team's sales objectives
- Knowing that help is available when they have questions to be answered
- Receiving prompt feedback to let them know what they did well and what they need to improve upon
- Being actively encouraged to suggest new ideas for improving the assignment they are given

No management role is praised more in theory and applied less in practice than delegation. All managers praise it. So, if delegation is so good, why isn't everyone delegating? Let's examine some of the "yes, but" excuses that interfere with successful delegation.

   ■ *"I could do it better."* And you always will be able to do it better. The "I could do it better" attitude indicates a control-obsessed person. It is also a mark of impatience. A sales manager with this attitude really has a career choice: She can continue to "do it better," which will lead to disaffection on the part of the members of sales team, a higher rate of turnover, and eventual burnout, or she can let go of some of that control and develop valuable new managers.

   ■ *"Suppose the person makes a mistake?"* Anxiety is a powerful emotional impulse that can freeze action. Some managers may be so risk-averse that they have a difficult time assigning meaningful jobs to others. The fact is, people do make mistakes. Good training and careful instructions reduce, but do not eliminate, this risk. Remember to "trust, but verify." Which is more important: developing new sales managers or giving into anxiety?

■ *"I am not comfortable delegating."* Some people just hate to ask others to do something that they could do themselves. They do not like to impose. First of all, it is the *job* of the sales manager to assign tasks. Managers who do not delegate put severe limits on their ability to grow. The good news is that the more a manager delegates, the more comfortable he becomes with asking others to help. Remember, the person being asked to help is often pleased to be asked.

■ *"I will lose control."* That fear is a false one, since part of the delegation process includes your managers reporting back to you on their progress. So, no real control is lost; on the contrary, "control" is extended. I must warn, however, that managers who use words like *control* are likely to have more communication problems and more anxiety than managers who use words like *coach, guide,* and *teamwork.*

■ *"I don't have confidence in others' ability to do the job."* That is a problem of the manager, not of the person who could do the job. This attitude can be a severe handicap. Part of the motivation element of the sales manager's job is to build up the confidence of the individual members of the sales team. Sales managers with this "no confidence in others" complex need to make an extraordinary effort to delegate.

■ *"Delegation is not efficient; it takes longer to train someone than it does to just do it myself."* That may well be true the first time an assignment is delegated. However, you will often find that the enthusiasm most people bring to the assignment more than offsets the efficiency factor. The efficiency worries are misguided. In fact, *real* efficiency comes from having a cadre of trained salespeople who are competent in many tasks. The time it takes to teach someone the first time is a time-management investment that greatly increases efficiency later. Remember, you were in their shoes once, and someone took the time to delegate work to you so that you could learn.

Successful delegation motivates up-and-coming managers. It relieves the sales manager of some time-consuming duties. It builds the foundation for expansion.

Do you want more free time? Learn to delegate.

Do you want to reduce your dependence on personal orders? Learn to delegate.

Do you want increased loyalty from your team members? Learn to delegate.

Let me close this section on delegation by emphasizing the link between recruiting and delegation.

The more you recruit, the larger your talent pool will be.

The larger your talent pool, the more people you will discover you can delegate tasks to.

The more people you can delegate tasks to, the more eagles you will find to promote.

The more eagles you promote, the more successful you will become.

QUESTIONS TO ASK YOURSELF

- What is your policy on delegating?
- Do you make the same connection I do between delegation, management development, and sales growth?
- Going forward, what type of delegation approach will you be taking?
- What specific tasks can you delegate? Whom can you delegate them to?
- What type of tutorial will this delegation require?
- What will the impact on your sales growth over the next year be?

Additional books that help your focus on delegation:

- *The 3 Keys to Empowerment: Release the Power within People for Astonishing Results* by Ken Blanchard, John C. Carlos, and Alan Randolph
- *How to Delegate* by Robert Heller
- *If You Want It Done Right, You Don't Have to Do It Yourself!* by Donna M. Genett

CHAPTER 18

GROW THROUGH KEY-PERSON TRAINING

When you learn to live for others, they will live for you.

—Paramahansa Yogananda, Philosopher

The most enduring element of management development that you need to teach sales managers is how to be resourceful—how to think things through and reach a wise conclusion on their own. This Socratic-style facilitation starts the day you hire a salesperson. The following story encourages you not to wait as long as I did to convert your good instincts and management practices into a formalized training program.

For years, I used a system of training that created a steady stream of good sales managers. I had good classroom instincts, a bunch of notes, and a series of books I referred to—but, to be honest, I did not have a formal key-person training program, which I should have had.

When I was working with Joe Adams, president of Encyclopedia Britannica England, he dusted off a management training program he had used. I was the director of training at the time. Together, we put together a five-day training program that was broken into three parts over a three-month period. Just as for any university course, there were books to be read and homework assignments to be completed. The results were electrifying. The participants felt honored to be selected for this formal, fast-track program. Senior sales managers were delighted to be sales professors for parts of the program.

Promotions, which were based on sales volume and active producer criteria, accelerated rapidly as a consequence of this key-person development program. Sales managers successfully employing their newly acquired leadership skills, coupled with a tremendous rise in empire-building consciousness, created a buzz. This program, along with the introduction of local marketing and a new commission system, was one of the key reasons that we doubled the sales force and sales volume in less than two years.

The core idea worked so well that I introduced the same concept my first year as vice president of sales in Taiwan when Sales Manager Amos

Wong asked, "What's the company training program for managers?" The first graduating class of the "Keyman Training Program" was destined to provide the sales leadership in Taiwan and, later, Hong Kong for a decade.

Each company needs to design its own key-person training program for sales managers. However, I can share with you what I feel are the critical elements of a structured key-person sales management development course.

1. Divide the five- to six-day course into three one- or two-day segments, spread over a two- to three-month time frame. More than two consecutive days of training results not only in prolonged absence from the field, but also in learning overload. There is only so much that the human mind can absorb at one sitting. Ours is a "doing" business, not just an intellectual exercise in acquiring sound management principles. What MITs learn today they can practice tomorrow if they are not being taught too much at one time. At subsequent sessions, your MITs can report back on their successes or difficulties using the sales management practices covered in earlier sessions. Knowing that they must return and report increases the odds that they will practice what they learned.

2. Focus each session on a limited number of new management practices, to be immediately implemented when they return to their sales offices. Build each day around one or two of the eight essential activities that successful sales managers must do every day.

3. Key-person training programs will vary. You have the core management practices, which are a constant, and then you have situational campaigns, such as a special recruiting effort or a new sales campaign that you want to promote.

4. Assign leadership books to be read prior to each session. (You might consider making this book one of the assigned readings!) Assign book reports focusing on the following questions:

❑ How does this book *relate* to your job as sales manager?

❑ What was the message of this book to *you*?

❑ What are you going to *do* differently because you read this book?

5. View a movie portraying leadership. *Patton*, *Braveheart*, *Troy*, *Gone with the Wind*, and *Master and Commander* are captivating choices. My personal favorite is *Henry V* with Kenneth Branagh as Henry. Henry V commands from the front. He doesn't just talk about good fighting

(although the speech on St. Crispin's Day is the mother of all motivational speeches); he leads with sword in hand. The opening scene shows Henry building support for his sales—I mean military—campaign.

Here are a number of questions to ask at the end of the film:

❑ What do you admire about the leader(s) in the film?

❑ What did the leader(s) do right?

❑ What mistakes did the leader(s) make?

❑ What did the leader(s) do to inspire the troops?

❑ What did the leader(s) do that demotivated the troops?

❑ What type of sales manager would Scarlet O'Hara, Henry V, or George S. Patton have been?

It is fun to speculate on how Russell Crowe in *Master and Commander* or Mel Gibson in *Braveheart* would have recruited and trained an army of salespeople, conducted sales meetings, motivated high sales performance, and handled time management.

6. Never miss an opportunity to give a lead-generation commercial. Hang demographic maps on the classroom walls revealing the immense number of prospects that are available and the tiny percentage of market penetration to date. This demographic map emphasizes *why* you are conducting your key-person sales management development program. Your not-so-subliminal message reminds everyone that "our company has too few sales managers supervising too few salespeople trying to find the too many prospects who have escaped detection."

7. Review case studies of sales management experiences. Case studies are popular exercises in focusing sales managers on the practical side of managing a sales force. Case study discussions provide surprises. For instance, one paragraph in a case study might mention that some salespeople regularly show up late for the weekly sales meeting. This can prompt a lively debate on the merits of the tough approach, such as imposing fines on latecomers or absentees, locking the doors at the starting time, and so on, versus conducting sales meetings that are so exciting and meaningful that people are eager to attend.

8. Ask the administration to give its infomercial on credit policies, payroll administration, delivery, and customer service. Take credit policy as an example. Once sales managers have a better understanding of why certain customer information is needed on the credit application, they tend to be more compliant. As a happy consequence, this improved order submission process normally increases the percentage of submitted orders that are accepted. Never miss a chance to have administration and salespeople work with each other. Sometimes I think of this as a "de-fanging" benefit in the ongoing battle of "them versus us" between sales and administrative personnel. The investment in a combined dinner for key-person trainees and senior administrative personnel pays dividends for a long time.

9. Invite the most respected senior sales executive available to conduct some of the sessions. Select someone who possesses the qualities you want your staff to emulate and so can be a role model. Wannabe sales managers want to hear from the boss.

10. Assign practical homework at the end of the session, such as writing new recruiting ads or devising the rules for a new sales contest. Award a prize for the top three submissions.

11. End each session by having the manager trainers telling the group what they will *do* next week as a result of what they learned today.

Let me say a word to newly appointed sales managers at any level. After being appointed president of all sales and marketing in our Asian operation in August 1999, I learned that Japan was being added to my set of responsibilities. It was pure joy to conduct a six-day program with my senior sales management team in three separated two-day sessions. I got to know the managers; they got to know me. At the end of this program, we were all in sync on our management and leadership direction. We were one in objective and focus. The most satisfying moment came when I passed out graduation certificates to this cadre of great sales managers, who were destined to double sales in 30 months.

When I say that I conducted that program, I mean that I built on the knowledge that those participants brought with them. As a conductor, I was able to draw on the positive contributions of the entire sales management team, while still being able to sell my management and leadership approach to the group.

Management development is more than telling wannabe managers what to do and when to do it. The ultimate goal of sales management development is to give them confidence in their competence. You want sales managers who can stand on their own two feet. When the sales managers you have developed go beyond what you have taught them, you are then ready for the next career promotion in the ladder of sales management success.

QUESTIONS TO ASK YOURSELF

- What is your approach to management development?
- Do you have a sales management development program in place?
- Can you see yourself conducting a management development program for your key associates?
- What would be the impact on your sales force if you had a key-person training program?
- What would an outline of your five- or six-day sales management development program look like?
- What books would you assign for reading?
- Who would you ask to help conduct some of the sessions?
- Who would you choose to attend your course?
- Would a key-person training program increase sales? Would it make you more promotable?

The following books are recommended as reading assignments for your key-person trainees:

- *The 7 Habits of Highly Effective People* by Stephen Covey
- *Built to Last* by James C. Collins and Jerry I. Porras
- *See You at the Top* by Zig Ziglar
- *How to Win Friends and Influence People* by Dale Carnegie

SIXTH ESSENTIAL ACTIVITY

MOTIVATE

"How can I motivate my salespeople?" is the single question that is asked the most by sales managers. The next five chapters address this significant inquiry, providing potent techniques to fire up the members of your sales team to reach their full potential.

People fall into three different categories when it comes to motivation. There are the blessed few who are already self-starters and are self-motivated when you hire them. As a manager, all you need to do is treat these people right and *keep them talking about their dreams.*

The great majority of salespeople fall into the second group: those who have no clear goals, but who do have a vague concept that they would like to do a better job, make more money, and rise in their careers. You can be the stimulus that motivates your salespeople not only to fulfill their dreams, but to dare them to dream new goals that they had never thought possible or even previously imagined.

Finally, you have the last faction: the cynics. These are people who refuse to be motivated. Some of this unhappy minority even think that attempts at motivation are a "trick" to get them to work harder. There is little you can do for these people. Don't worry about them. Spend your time with the majority who do respond to your leadership and work to build better lives.

CHAPTER 19

VISUALIZE THE ALL-CONSUMING GOAL

If you want to be a big company tomorrow, start acting like it today.

—Peter F. Drucker

Motivating others is easy when you radiate confidence in your ability to reach compelling goals in both your personal and your business life. The idea is to have a goal so colossal that it inspires your entire sales team. No other 10 minutes of my life changed the lives of a group of sales managers I led (and thus my life as well) as dramatically as the following pledge, which ignited a sustained commitment to empire building.

> In September 1994, I addressed my leadership team and pledged that I would not retire until at least 10 people had become millionaires. In addition to that pledge, I put before them several sales volume goals that stretched their imagination, catapulting our various sales groups into a vortex of expectations. The foundations of these compelling sales goals were based on logic. The data clearly showed that the market potential existed. But it was the thunder of passion, the fervently expressed, undeniable belief that we would prevail that riveted their attention, created credibility, and inspired conviction. The goal was there for the taking.
>
> I concluded by earnestly stating, "You are exactly the right people at the right time to reach this goal."
>
> Was I able to keep that pledge? Yes—twice over.

The compelling-goal mindset is an integration of several interconnected ambitions. It's an amalgamation of your awe-inspiring business objective, your breathtaking personal resolutions, the embracing of your business goals by your team members, and the buy-in from your sales team to the business objectives and personal dreams.

Your example, enthusiasm, excitement, and positive attitude ignite the process. Everyone craves inspiration. Your job as sales manager is to respond to that yearning. You are a dream merchant.

"Some people see things as they are and ask, 'Why?' Others dream of things that never were and ask, 'Why not?' " Robert F. Kennedy used this inspiring concept as the theme of his campaign for the presidency in 1968. The innate power and inspiration of that ideal resonated with me, and I adopted it for my own life. Bobby Kennedy, like his brother, was assassinated, but the idea that dreams can come true lived on.

There is a great emotional war raging inside all of us. We all harbor daydreams in which we envision our success and happiness. Then those dreams collide with "reality" and remain just that—dreams. This chapter and the following two will help you overcome the doubts and obstacles so that you can win the "dreams come true" struggle.

The first step in motivating others is taking personal responsibility for your own life. People and circumstances can put obstacles in your path, but only you can decide whether to give in to those obstacles or to overcome them. Think of the people you admire. Write down four or five names. Then, next to each name, write down at least one obstacle that this person overcame. In many cases, we admire people who made it to the top because they did so through sheer force of personal will, defeating many difficulties along the way.

The second step consists of having a goal or set of goals worth getting excited about. Go back to your daydreams. What would you truly, passionately like to do, to own, to achieve? This is not the time to be tentative or timid. The people you admire thought big; they had great dreams. Few people are born extraordinary. It is the realization of his dreams that makes a person extraordinary.

No one is more ordinary than I. As a student, I was only slightly better than average, except for my love of reading. I struggled with math. I lived in a rented house with working-class parents who were alcoholics. There was no money and no scholarship for college. A month after graduating from high school, I got a job as a commission salesperson selling *Collier's Encyclopedia*. It changed my life.

I had little confidence that I could be a good, let alone a great, salesperson. But I did want to go to college. So I thought that if I worked harder than anyone else, I just might earn enough money during the summer to pay my tuition. I did. More than that, I learned that having a big, worthy goal would motivate me not only to work hard, but to learn how to work smart. I would not have worked so relentlessly in the humid heat of Florida that summer of 1961 for just "a little extra money." I had a big, compelling dream. I knew that at the end of the summer, I would enter either college or boot camp. I wanted college, and I knew it was up to me to make it happen. I was motivated.

Salespeople have a head start in realizing life's dreams because it is the nature of salespeople to have goals. We continually practice goal setting in ways that people in most occupations do not. For many people, their last great goal was to graduate from school. While graduation is a definite goal with a definite date, after receiving that diploma, many people just drift though life. They had a goal, and they achieved it. With no other goals in mind, they get a job, maybe get married, and maybe own a modest home and a car.

A salesperson and a sales manager have goals that reach beyond the ordinary. These people are driven by the vision of what they want to accomplish, or by the idea of owning what they most desire, or by the irrepressible desire to be the best and enjoy the satisfaction of their achievement. You never hear a successful salesperson or sales manager say, "It's so-and-so's (insert "father's, mother's, sibling's, spouse's, boss's, or dog's) fault that I am not accomplishing more." A person with a huge compelling goal never blames anyone else for her situation in life—that kind of person won't waste the time. A person with a huge compelling goal looks in the mirror and says, "I have a big dream. I am responsible for making that dream a reality. I will overcome all obstacles. I will stay the course until I realize my goal."

You can see why it is so important to have a *huge* compelling goal. Selling is not easy. Life is not easy. Failure, rejection, and disappointment are just waiting to sabotage you. A small goal is not going to carry you through these trials. Your huge compelling goal must get you excited, emotional, and driven.

When I was just a kid, I read *National Geographic* magazine at my uncle's home in a small town in Wisconsin. All those fascinating places were so far away, both in distance and in accessibility. It never occurred to me that I could actually *go* to *all* those places. It wasn't until my mid-twenties, when I set a goal of visiting a hundred countries during my lifetime, that those travel dreams started to come true. I'm up to 94 countries. The direct-sales business gave me the opportunity to realize that goal.

As a sales manager, you need to not only set a huge compelling goal for yourself, but inspire others to set their own huge compelling goals and understand how these personal goals can be achieved through reaching team sales goals.

The next chapter will review how to use the 14 key motivators to bring out the best in your sales team, and the chapter that follows it illustrates a nine-step goal-setting process that gives you and your sales partners the means to achieve specific goals.

The range of motivational opportunities spans the universe. In other words, it's limitless. Once you understand all the possibilities, you don't have to ask, "How do I motivate my salespeople?" You can create motivational excitement in your group by appealing to all the needs of the human psyche.

QUESTIONS TO ASK YOURSELF

- As you think of your sales team, into which of the three classifications of motivation (self-starters, no clear goals, cynics) would you place each member?
- How many are in the self-starter, self-motivated group?
- How many in the vague area?
- Do you have any antimotivation cynics?
- What are you doing to help those with vague concepts of goal setting?
- Do you have the type of compelling personal goals that set the example for your sales team?
- What is the great ambition of your life that is so compelling that it overwhelms all obstacles?

The suggested reading for the introductory chapter on motivation includes the enduring greatest classics:

- *Think and Grow Rich* by Napoleon Hill
- *The Power of Positive Thinking* by Norman Vincent Peale
- *The Magic of Thinking Big* by David Schwartz
- *How I Raised Myself from Failure to Success* by Frank Bettger
- *As a Man Thinketh* by James Allen

CHAPTER 20
MAKE THE MOST OF THE 14 GREATEST MOTIVATORS

In motivating people, you've got to engage their minds and their hearts. It is good business to have an employee feel part of the entire effort. . . . I motivate people, I hope, by example—and perhaps by excitement, by having provocative ideas to make others feel involved.

—Rupert Murdoch, Publisher

You cannot mass-produce motivation. Some business writers claim that motivation has a natural hierarchy. In reality, however, the sources of motivation vary. Not everyone is motivated by the same things. As a sales manager, you must use your judgment and experience to recognize the key motivators of each of the people under you. Different sparks light the fire of enthusiasm within different people. As you review the following vignette, think of how theater, drama, and imagery can sustain a personal dream in your managers that compels excellence and commitment in the workplace.

> It seems like only yesterday that David Smith, the founder of the company I was working for at the time, found out that Kenji Tanaka, one of his top sales managers, had a dream of building a house on the beach in his hometown of Matsumoto, Japan. David hired an architect to work with Tanaka on the design of that dream home. Then, at his own expense, David had a scale model made and sent to Tanaka's office. Every day, when Tanaka walked into his office, he saw his dream home prominently displayed inside a glass case. Two years later, I attended the Shinto house blessing of that beach home.

You may find David's gesture to be an extraordinary one, and it was. But it also paid off emotionally and monetarily for everyone involved.

The key to effectively motivating someone comes from learning about that person's dreams. When you get a person to talk about his dreams, with you as an active and interested listener, that person becomes more motivated—and self-motivated. Field training gives you a great opportunity to learn what motivates your salespeople. As you are chatting informally while traveling to a sales appointment, you might be surprised by how much you can find out with a simple question like, "What are your dreams?"

Right now, let's look at 14 key motivational factors and see how you can apply them to instill a desire to excel.

1. RECOGNITION

The more certain your selling eagles know they can count on you to recognize their best effort, the more likely they will be to make that effort. Most of us have an appetite for recognition that is never fully satisfied. Who has ever heard the complaint "My manager praises me too much"?

Sales contests are recognition platforms aimed at your strongest performers, who have the greatest urge to compete and win—and thus be recognized for their outstanding ability. That's why your sales contests are really aimed at the top 20 to 25 percent of your sales personnel, which produces 70 to 80 percent of sales volume. The highest-flying eagles respond exceedingly well to recognition.

However, recognition consists of far more than winning sales contests. Every level of sales management plays a role in recognition. The following list will give you some ideas on how to recognize your salespeople more often:

1. Ask for advice in both personal and public meetings.
2. Praise in public and criticize in private.
3. Say "thank you" and "please" at every opportunity.
4. Send frequent memos praising their performance.
5. Give a self-help book with a warm personal note written on the inside cover.
6. Send birthday cards.
7. Start sales meetings by recognizing top performers.
8. Coach any guest speakers to recognize the special achievement of your top producers.
9. Give credit for success to others; accept personal responsibility for failure.
10. Award small gifts for achievement.

11. Break into a smile when you first see your people.

12. Make "What's the good news?" your personal greeting.

Why not take a moment right now to write down what you can do to recognize others?

2. JOB SECURITY

Job security comes from having the confidence to do two things: find enough prospects and close enough sales.

Here are a few solid, positive actions that you can take to reduce job security worries in your sales team:

1. Teach 10 prospecting methods.

2. Field-train often.

3. Reinforce all the good news about the enormous number of prospects out there in the marketplace.

4. Remind everyone of her great earning potential.

5. Promote the new products that your company has under development.

6. Begin sales meetings and private conversations with the focus "Things are good, and they are going to get better."

7. Be proactive. Inoculate your salespeople against drifting into doubt by constantly talking enthusiastically about your shared glorious future.

3. SENSE OF BELONGING

Your sales associates want to feel that they are *part* of the group rather than being *apart* from the group. When they do, they stay longer.

One of my best bonding memories was the climbing of Mount Kinabalu in Sabah, Malaysia, where 19 of us made it to the top of the highest peak in Southeast Asia, over 12,000 feet high. All of us were amateurs. So we chose a mountain that had well-marked trails and no snow. As with other hikes I've taken over the years, two sales associates who were experienced trekkers planned the trip so that we all knew what to bring and what to expect. Years later, most of those 19 hikers were still with the company. And, as an indication of their fond memory of our shared accomplishment, they kept on display, in a prominent place in their offices, a picture of us reaching the peak together at sunrise.

In addition to the 19 sales partners who went to Malaysia, more than a hundred sales associates participated in various mini-bonding weekend practice hikes of four to six hours each. Many of the day hikers started to exercise more after having a tough time with a short practice hike—another benefit of the hike.

Salespeople are social animals. They tend to be friendly and outgoing, enjoying the company of others. A sales manager who builds a sense of family satisfies this sense of belonging. Conducting interactive sales meetings, planning company picnics, attending plays and sports events together, bringing in a birthday cake, going bowling as a group, putting on sports days, and engaging in other team activities all help create a desirable work environment. The benefits can be seen in a lower rate of turnover and fewer "people problems."

4. FRIENDLY WORK ENVIRONMENT

Your sales partners want a workplace that they can look forward to coming to each day.

Sometimes the boss thinks that the people reporting to him should accommodate and adapt to his personality. Strictly from a power hierarchy point of view, this presumption may be correct, but it's not very smart. The role of the sales manager is not to be lord and master of the sales force, but to motivate people to *want* to work. The more you accommodate your leadership style to the personality of each member of your sales team, the harder it will be for those people to choose not to work for you.

Demotivators—factors that make the workplace undesirable—include

- A sales manager with an unfriendly demeanor
- A salesperson whose behavior is disruptive
- Personality clashes between salespeople
- A strained relationship between the salesperson and her manager

When faced with these situations, those in charge may find it tempting to procrastinate in finding a solution, hoping that the problem will go away. It seldom does. A good sales manager takes a proactive approach by working through people problems one-on-one. Often simply orchestrating an opportunity for estranged salespeople to talk to each other or asking to talk with the disruptive salesperson privately will alleviate the problem.

Good motivation flourishes in a friendly work environment—and languishes in an unfriendly one.

5. POWER

The drive to lead, to decide, to make a dynamic difference is the stuff of sales legends.

While almost everyone relishes recognition, cherishes job security, and craves a sense of belonging, only a few have a strong need for power. However, those few are often high-impact players. Managed properly, they can become your eagles and managers.

Power-hungry sales associates can be the easiest or the most difficult to manage. If you try to overmanage power-driven people, they will resist you. An unpleasant series of power struggles is often the result. These people show up late, challenge you in public, and criticize you to your face or, worse, behind your back. On the other hand, if you publicly appreciate their contributions while grooming them for promotion, then you'll find yourself with strong allies. Let the power-hungry person know that you are her ticket to advancement.

6. MONEY

Money, in and of itself, is just paper. It is what money can buy that becomes the motivator.

Today, many discussions about motivation start off with the disclaimer, "Money is not the number one motivator for salespeople." Maybe that's so. Yet, even if money is only number two or three on a salesperson's motivational ladder, it is still a formidable force. And for some people, money *is* the prime motivator. Many people's feelings of self-worth stem directly from how much they make.

For others, having the financial freedom to buy the latest stuff ranks high. And any person who has just gone through a bankruptcy ordeal is very money-motivated. You *want* the members of your sales team to be motivated by money. Salespeople who are money-motivated will invest their time in becoming well trained so that they can work more effectively and ultimately become successful.

Your mission is to find out what your salespeople will do with the money they earn. Then, encourage each person to focus on his dreams. If it is a new car, go to the dealership with him and get the brochures. If it's to own a luxury home, visit an open house with him. This touch-and-feel reality exercise makes dreams real to your sales team and is an important first step in making them come true. Inspire your salespeople to discover, reveal, and reach their huge compelling goals. The next chapter will focus on this important dream-reaching process.

7. FREEDOM

Choice is the magic word that accentuates the freedom that is possible in our business.

Who does not wish to control her work environment? The freedom to define the extent of our own work ethic, to choose our prospecting emphasis, to select which customers to call on and when to call on them satisfies this urge to control our lives. We emphasize that benefit when we are hiring. Once the salesperson completes her initial training, it doesn't take long before she is captivated by the excitement of competing in sales contests, qualifying for the monthly bonus, and wanting to buy more new things. Thus, our motivated sales reps soon choose to exercise their freedom of choice by working harder and learning to be more effective.

On the other hand, some may use the flexibility our business grants them to live a more balanced life, even if it means bringing in a modest income. The wise sales manager recognizes, appreciates, and supports those who make this choice as well.

8. FEELINGS OF USEFULNESS

Most us share a need to feel that we matter, that we make a difference. We feel good about making a positive difference in the lives of others, as illustrated in this story:

The three women walked into the room, obviously nervous, their children holding their hands or clinging to their legs. They were mothers who had bought an English-language home study program for their toddlers. An audience of 40 salespeople, almost all strangers, sat up expectantly. The moms started slowly, a little embarrassed to be on the dais. Oh, but the stories they told once they'd warmed up and forgotten about their audience. Each told how her child was learning English and developing self-confidence. The moms told how they almost did not buy. They thanked their sales consultants for their persistence. Forty proud sales reps, goose bumps and all, leaned forward to catch every word. What a great job each sales rep knew he did at making a positive difference in the lives of his customers.

We all want to feel that there is some grand purpose to our life, that what we do makes a positive contribution. Your sales associates want to know that their work is significant to society, to their customers, to their company, and to you. It is your motivational duty to emphatically remind your sales associates that what they do matters.

The perceived image of a commission salesperson is not always positive. My dad once told me to get a "real job." Because salespeople must overcome this negative perception, you must strive to reassure your sales partners constantly of their importance. You never want to be the source of your salespeople's feeling worthless or having doubts; instead, you want them to know they can count on you to encourage them and remind them that they are making a difference.

Here are a few practices that you can employ to foster a sense of accomplishment:

- Share "good news" stories about how your product is helping people.
- Ask your sales associates to help you with training and other management functions.
- Seek your salespeople's opinion before making decisions.
- Let your sales partners know that you are counting on them.
- Tell your team members that they are important.

9. TRAINING AND SELF-IMPROVEMENT

"To be the best I can be." This is the most common answer given when people are asked, "What is it you want in your career?" or "What do you want to accomplish in your life?"

This universal answer shows why well-planned, enthusiastic training is so vital. Your job is to help satisfy this human need to constantly improve. Good training is a great motivator. While we sometimes think of sales training as just a means to increase company sales so that we can earn more money, we must not overlook the intellectual satisfaction that comes from good training. Your active promotion of self-improvement is, in itself, a motivation.

10. CONSISTENT LEADERSHIP

No one wants to work for a manager or a company where the manager's disposition and policies change frequently.

Are you the kind of manager whose people wonder, "What mood is the boss in today?" If so, you are undermining your effectiveness as a leader.

The most successful sales managers have a consistent style of management. They do not bounce from autocratic to coaching to persuasive to democratic and back to autocratic. Each of these forms of leadership can work—it's the switching back and forth between them that does not.

While flexibility is necessary for dynamic results, changing one particular policy frequently or reworking several policies at the same time is demotivating. For instance, if you find yourself changing the times and frequency of sales meetings often, it may mean that you have a tendency to be inconsistent. No matter what time you set for your sales meetings, someone will complain. Even a small gesture, such as picking a meeting time and sticking to it, will give your people a sense of stability and increase their confidence in you.

Consistency also means following company policy. Sales representatives find it disconcerting to receive company policy announcements, then have a sales manager say, "Never mind that. We do it differently here." A sales manager may be convinced that his approach is better than the company policy (and he may even be right), but the confusion that this "better" policy creates more than offsets the so-called benefits of those policies of the sales manager that conflict with company policy.

11. OPPORTUNITIES FOR PROMOTION

"If you want it, you can get it"—*it* being a chance for promotion.

Not everyone may want to be promoted, but until you learn otherwise, always assume that your team members do. Mention the possibilities at your hiring interview, during early training, and frequently thereafter.

Continue promoting the management training courses that you or your company conducts. Emphasize that management comes a step at a time. Remind everyone that you can reach your goals only if your sales associates succeed. No one will ever resent your saying to her, "You have management potential." If, while you are striving for promotion, you constantly coach the people under you to also qualify for promotion, you will have far fewer motivational problems than managers who are static.

12. FAIR TREATMENT

One of the quickest ways to demotivate a group is to play favorites.

Ricky was one of my best sales managers, a top producer with a dynamic personality. When he and three other managers secretly set up their own company and broke away, we lost half our sales force in a single day. Two days later, Frankie, one of the junior managers who had walked away, called me to arrange a secret meeting. Almost all of the good salespeople who had left showed up at the meeting. Frankie told the story of Betty, Ricky's girlfriend and "sales assistant." After Ricky conducted his first sales meeting at a posh hotel, Betty bragged that she had stolen the hotel towels, evidently with Ricky's approval. The salespeople were wondering whether, if Ricky condoned such a theft, they could trust all the sweet promises he had made them. Frankie, representing the salespeople from Ricky's breakaway group, said, "We want to come back," even though their disloyal manager had promised them more money and instant promotion. Grace, one of the other returnees, added, "You always treated us fairly; we trust you." It was a proud moment for the entire company and for me.

Every day you have a chance to make a "secret deal" that gives one person some advantage over others—or you can choose to be fair and impartial. Consistently motivate your team by adhering to equitable management principles in your lead distribution, your work assignment schedule for booths, and your selections for training programs.

13. A CHALLENGE

Work is more fun when it presents a challenge.

I have listened to the speeches of winners of sales contests for more than

40 years, and they boil down to one never-boring basic speech. The winner says, "I wanted so much to win this award, yet the challenge seemed almost impossible. But I kept trying; I didn't give up, and here I am. I did it!" These words never fail to inspire.

Create challenges that stretch the ability of each team member, while still making sure that everyone can feel a sense of victory if she tries hard enough. The challenge may be booking a quota of appointments, distributing a certain number of take-one boxes, or writing 10 orders in a month. Design challenges that give your sales team the opportunity to experience the exuberance of accomplishment.

Use inspiring stories. Those that tell of handicapped people who build businesses or orphans who become Olympic champions are great motivational legends. You can find them easily, have them at the ready, and use them to give your people a lift. I once offered a sales trip to South Africa as the reward for winning a sales contest. I had been inspired by Nelson Mandela's autobiography, which I had recently read in anticipation of the trip. A few weeks before the end of the contest, I held a sales meeting during which Adam, a struggling sales manager, recited all the problems he was having with recruiting new salespeople. I thought of the book I'd just read, and I could not resist relating the highlights of Nelson Mandela's odyssey. This man, imprisoned for almost three decades by his "white masters," never gave up. He was determined to prevail in changing the government of oppression while maintaining his composure and dignity. Sharing the inspiration of this story, the challenges Nelson Mandela successfully faced, put the sales managers' recruiting difficulties in a new perspective.

* * *

I have saved the best motivational tool for last: *You!* Your example, your enthusiasm, your excitement, and your positive attitude are the best motivators. The leader's attitude is contagious; if you are upbeat and optimistic, your salespeople will be, too.

Once you have established your own huge compelling goal, you can fill others with enthusiasm for doing the same. When you make your life a series of challenges, you can inspire others to follow your lead. You've got the idea. You know what to do. Your people will respond to that. Great motivators are those people who are motivated themselves. When you understand just how many different ways you can motivate people, you will never again ask, "How do I motivate the person who isn't working hard or who has a bad attitude?" You will know how to create positive morale and the incentive to give 100 percent by appealing to all the motivational needs of your sales partners.

QUESTIONS TO ASK YOURSELF

- How does your list of the great motivators compare with mine?
- What are the three greatest motivators?
- What 10 specific actions can you take to integrate motivational *practices* into the fabric of your leadership style and management policies?
- How important is your personal example as a motivator for your team?

Additional reading on motivation:

- *See You at the Top* by Zig Ziglar
- *Over the Top* by Zig Ziglar
- *Live a Thousand Years* by Giovanni Livera
- *7 Secrets to Successful Sales Management* by Jack D. Wilner
- *Sales Management* by Robert J. Calvin

CHAPTER 21
UTILIZE THE GOAL-SETTING PROCESS

Goals are dreams with deadlines.

—Dianna Scharf-Hunt, Author

Ask your sales associates about their dreams. They will often reveal what they want most, which means that you now know what drives them. As Zig Ziglar says, "You help them get what they want, they will help you get what you want." As you learn to help your sales associates learn the mechanical process of making dreams come true, you will be rewarded with far more than a high income, as the following memory suggests.

> "You made my dream come true." These were the first words out of the mouth of Sophia, one of my former protégés, whom I hadn't seen for quite a while. I was in town to conduct sales management workshops as part of my postretirement training commitment. Sophia had dropped by to say hello.
>
> "Do you remember asking me what my dream was when I opened up my first sales office 11 years ago?" she asked. I have a dream-session formula that I've used with many aspiring sales managers, but I had forgotten this one. I went into my intent active listening mode, hoping to find out what she was referring to. "I was 29 years old, and I told you that my dream was to buy a home and be able to retire when I was 40 to start a family."
>
> As she handed me her six-month-old baby, tangible proof of her successful attainment of that dream, we both had tears in our eyes.

As you probably know, real goals must be *written down* and accompanied by a plan to make them come true. I often conducted a brief but effective workshop on goal setting for my team members, using the following nine questions to help them determine, visualize, and then actualize their dreams:

1. What is the most important achievement in your life to date?

   What is the one shocking goal that you want to achieve in your life?

3. Visualize and draw a picture of your dream.
4. List five things that you will do to visualize your dream.
5. How much money do you need to realize your dream?
6. How much money must you save each year?
7. What must you do to earn that much money?
8. What is your definite date for reaching your goal?
9. When will you begin?

Let's review each of those nine steps as if you were actually conducting the workshop. For each step, I've included an actual script that you can use to help your team reach for the stars.

1. WHAT IS THE MOST IMPORTANT ACHIEVEMENT IN YOUR LIFE TO DATE?

Ask each person *not* to include getting married or having children. What you are looking for is an achievement that requires sustained commitment, such as graduating, buying a good home, getting a promotion, or helping his child reach a goal.

Tell Your Team

"What is the special achievement that still gives you goose bumps when you relive the moment?"

2. WHAT IS THE ONE SHOCKING GOAL THAT YOU WANT TO ACHIEVE IN YOUR LIFE?

Help your team members move from the mundane to the magnificent. Ask them to imagine a huge compelling goal, a target that excites the imagination.

The object of setting this goal is to provide a vision so powerful that it overwhelms the inevitable obstacles that challenge the will to persevere. The goal has to be potent enough to overcome the inclination to procrastinate, to waste time through poor time management practices, and to become distracted by trivia.

The purpose of the huge compelling goal is to powerfully alter your sales reps' work behavior, taking it to a new level of achievement. Owning a pre-owned Volkswagen, moving into a larger apartment, or enjoying a quick weekend getaway are worthy goals in the right context, but they are not the types of dreams that will change work behavior.

Tell Your Team

"*Compelling* and *huge* are the operative words. Everyone has a big dream, but all too often it is submerged. All of us, at one point or another in our lives, have daydreamed, 'What if?' We fantasized, we imagined, we let go of the ordinary boundaries that confine our dreams. Do it again, today. It may be the dream car, the million-dollar home, the three-month-long trip around the world . . . some dream so exciting that many people dismiss it as unrealistic.

"Today, write down the huge, compelling dream that excites your imagination and fires the passion within you."

3. VISUALIZE AND DRAW A PICTURE OF YOUR DREAM

Drawing a picture transforms your dream from the imagination and the printed word into a self-made visual aid. You do not have to be Picasso to draw a picture that represents a dream. A picture embeds the dream deeper and more strongly in our memory lodes.

Tell Your Team

"Have fun with your imagination and create a drawing of your dream. Visualize your home, your dream vacation, your retirement, your children's graduation from a prestigious university, or whatever will motivate you to achieve unprecedented excellence."

4. LIST FIVE THINGS THAT YOU WILL DO TO VISUALIZE YOUR DREAM

Most dreams do not come true. But they could. The number one reason for dreams failing to come true is the lack of follow-up. Conducting a dream session as an isolated event is *not* enough.

The traditional follow-up is to write down your dream, carry it on your person, and read it often to remind yourself of it. This is effective. I tried it after reading *Think and Grow Rich*. That book changed my life because it showed the possibilities of a richer life through belief, dedication, and imagination.

But it was not always enough. I succeeded and failed in fits and starts. I bought the Earl Nightingale tapes and others like them. They helped. Still, I couldn't quite *maintain* the winning success formula.

What was missing was the sustaining stoking of the fires. I was well into my forties before I finally found the formula that made all my dreams come true.

We have to conscientiously feed our dreams on an automatic basis to keep them alive. The great dreams cannot be accomplished in a day, a week, a month, or even a year. Sometimes it takes years of step-by-step mini-objectives to accomplish a worthy goal.

I learned to feed my dreams.

As revealed in Chapter 19, one of my dreams is to visit 100 countries. At one point I subscribed to 11 travel magazines. I have a bank of 36 file trays labeled by countries, like France or China; sections of continents, like the Balkans or Scandinavia; or type of travel, such as cruises, railroad, or adventure. It was and still is my dream bank. In addition, I own a library of more than a hundred travel books. Every time I pass by my travel cabinet, I think of all the places I have been and all the places I still want to go. More than 200 travel-related Web sites are saved on the "My Favorites" sector of my Microsoft Explorer. At the time of writing I am only six countries short of my dream of 100.

I also collected a library of sales and management books. Inspired by books written by Andy Grove and Jack Welch, I not only continued to learn how to build competence, but gathered information on the possibilities of building stronger, bigger sales organizations. Historical books about Alexander the Great, Caesar, and Cortés inspired me to build my own empire . . . of sales representatives. I retired with an army of 2,000 full-time sales reps reporting to sales managers, who in turn reported to me.

I always hated the rejection part of our profession. But my dream of the next trip (I always had a next trip planned) often kept me dialing for appointments, conducting the extra field training exercise, or forging ahead after a string of disappointments. I needed constant reminders that I sometimes had to do things I did not like in order to be able to do the things I loved.

Tell Your Team

"You can cultivate your ambition by feeding your dreams with a host of reminders of just what you are working for, of what it is that you want out of life. Win the struggle to have your fantasies of the huge compelling dream overwhelm the obstacles and life's trivia that try to lock you into mediocrity.

"List five things you will do to keep your dreams alive. If your goal is to own a Mercedes, visit a showroom. Pick up the brochures. Test-drive the car. Subscribe to a car magazine. If buying a dream home is the compelling goal, take a Sunday and visit open houses in your dream location. Put pictures of your dream home on the fridge or the vanity table."

5. HOW MUCH MONEY DO YOU NEED TO REALIZE YOUR DREAM?

It's truth and reality time. Exactly, precisely, how much money do you need in order to own what you want to own or do what you want to do? How much is that dream home? How much would you like to spend on travel? When do you want to retire, and what type of lifestyle do you want during retirement? What will college cost for the school you want your children to attend?

Tell Your Team

"Put some figures down for those huge compelling goals. It's not a goal unless you know how much it costs. Are your dreams and timetable realistic?

If you're making $30,000 a year and you plan to own a million-dollar home in 10 years, you have to either change your goal or change your income. Your goals must be doable. They have to be exciting enough to stretch you, but within the realm of possibility."

6. HOW MUCH MONEY MUST YOU SAVE EACH YEAR?

A good practice exercise is to plan a 10-year program to build a million-dollar liquid-asset estate. If the number of salespeople you manage increases each year, then your income will also increase. Obviously, if you spend *all* your money, you cannot become a millionaire unless you have a job that provides a million-dollar bonus in a single year. The good news about achieving success in sales management is that you can increase your personal consumption each year and also increase the *percentage* of income saved.

If you were then to go forward with your income and savings projection for another five years, you would make an amazing discovery: Your second million dollars comes very quickly. In the early days, it is a struggle to build your sales organization step by step. You save relatively little money in the first few years. But in each successive year you can save a larger percentage of your income, plus you have the money you already saved working for you. You have heard the expression, "The rich get richer." Now you know how they do it: They combine annual income with the compounded growth of the money they have previously saved.

This is a good time to review the "rule of 72," a rule of thumb that can help you compute how soon your money will double at a given interest rate. It's called the Rule of 72 because at an annual return of 10 percent, money doubles every 7.2 years, give or take a few days.

To use this simple rule, you just divide the annual interest rate into 72. For example, if you get 8 percent on an investment and that rate stays constant, your money will double in 72/8 or 9 years. A rate of 12 percent doubles your money in 6 years, and a rate of 18 percent doubles it in 4 years. This is often referred to as the "magic of compound interest."

You can also work backwards. Suppose you want to double your money in three years. Simply divide 72 by 3 and you will find that you need an annual return of 24 percent to reach your objective.

Tell Your Team

"Write down the amount of money you will save each year in one column. In the second column, write down how much money has accumulated. You want to start thinking what you will do with your cash. The stock market? Real estate? You might use 10 percent as your average annual rate of return for this exercise."

7. WHAT MUST YOU DO TO EARN THAT MUCH MONEY?

Most people realize that their goals require a *change* in their earnings, their spending, and their saving habits. Sales representatives and sales managers have a better chance than most people to make the necessary changes, because we have control over our work commitment and our ambition.

Tell Your Team

"A change in earnings requires a change in what you are doing. Prospecting methods, work habits, hiring more salespeople—something you *do* must change so that you can earn the money you need to realize your goals.

"What will you do differently going forward to produce the earnings you need?"

8. WHAT IS YOUR DEFINITE DATE FOR REACHING YOUR GOAL?

People who hope to reach their goal "someday" rarely get there. A target date is essential to achieving a goal.

Tell Your Team

"A goal without a deadline is not a goal. Set a specific date for reaching your huge compelling goal. To keep on track, set a series of subgoals along the way, each with a firm date by which that step is to be accomplished."

9. WHEN WILL YOU BEGIN?

A test to determine whether a goal is compelling enough is the decision to start now.

Tell Your Team

"Does your fervent desire to realize your dream overwhelm the human tendency to procrastinate? When will you begin to work toward your goal? 'Now' is the only acceptable answer if you are serious about making your dream come true."

*   *   *

Conduct this exercise at least once a year to help the members of your team make their dreams come true. Share with your team how using this formula is making your dreams come true. Your example will demonstrate the power of this exercise.

QUESTIONS TO ASK YOURSELF

- What type of goal-setting help do you provide for your sales associates now?
- How often do you conduct a formal dream or goal session with your sales associates? Is it structured?
- What is the number one life goal of each of your sales representatives?
- What have you done or are you doing to help each person to feed his dream?

Further reading on the mechanics of goal setting:

- *The Power of Focus* by Jack Canfield, Mark Victor Hansen, and Les Hewitt
- *Rich Dad, Poor Dad* by Robert T. Kiyosaki
- *The Richest Man in Babylon* by George S. Clason

CHAPTER 22
DESIGN WINNING SALES CONTESTS

There are no secrets to success. It is the result of preparation, hard work, learning from failure.

—Colin L. Powell, Secretary of State

The prime objective of a sales contest is to motivate the sales force to exceed what they would have done if the same money had simply been provided through a higher commission, awarded as a bonus, or retained by the company. The following story substantiates the idea that the extra time it takes to develop contest rules that maintain doubt until the end of the race is well worth the effort.

It was almost midnight on the night before the last day of a 17-week-long contest. The books would close at noon the following day. Based on orders turned in during the previous week, people thought they had a pretty good idea of who would win. But it was close. The rules of the contest had a number of handicap formulas that kept any one sales rep from running away with the victory. Up until the very last minute, no one knew for sure who would qualify for the award trips and who would be number one.

Two enterprising reps had a midnight brainstorm: They would target organizations that were open 24 hours a day. Minutes later, they started prospecting hospitals and police stations. They each sold three graveyard orders. One of the reps was able to qualify for the trip; the other took first place. The power of suspense validated our complicated handicap system and inspired these two sales reps to think outside the clock.

Sales contests are often thought of as separate and apart from the compensation system, even though the budget monies come from the same source, the rewards go to the same people, and the object of the expense is the same: maximizing sales production. It is easier to change the rules of the sales contest to influence behavior than it is to change the compensation system.

We will review two types of competition:

- Sales-revenue-driven contests, normally conducted by the home office over a period of time, usually three or more months.
- Prospecting activity and/or short-term sales contests on a local level—no longer than a month and usually much shorter.

COMPANYWIDE SALES CONTESTS

Let's start with a set of principles that will help you conduct revenue-generating sales contests that exceed your expectations:

1. Establish clear objectives other than increased sales volume.
2. Keep the outcome of the sales contest in doubt as long as possible—hopefully, until the last minute.
3. Use a handicap system to keep everyone in the race.
4. Offer *exciting* rewards.
5. Always have a contest in place.

Let's review these objectives in detail.

1. Establish Clear Objectives Other Than Increased Sales Volume

Prior to each contest, sales managers and leading sales reps should review the contest rules in the light of two primary factors:

First, how competitive is the current sales contest? Are there any changes that could be put in place that would make the next contest a little more spirited?

Second, what selling behavioral changes do you wish to promote? To put it another way, what are the current objectives of the company or special problems that need to be resolved?

This is the time to consider adding extra contest points for modifying selling behavior, such as meeting certain lead-conversion criteria, realizing a percentage of self-generated sales orders, taking orders where installment payments are made on auto-pay, or whatever it is that will make your sales force stronger.

2. Keep the Outcome of the Sales Contest in Doubt as Long as Possible—Hopefully, Until the Last Minute

When people can predict the winner, the contest rules are flawed. If the clear winners are already established after the first month or so, you'll end up with two undesirable outcomes:

1. The top salespeople will likely ease up and coast a bit when they realize that they have a big lead.

2. Those people who got off to a slow start will realize that the contest is pretty much over for them and will say to themselves things like, "I don't need a contest to motivate me to work" or "Why doesn't the company just pay everyone extra money for writing orders and not waste money on sales contests?"

The purpose of the sales contest is not simply to reward the best-performing salespeople with prizes and trips. Great sales contests help your high achievers attain maximum performance. They also give your average performers a chance to decide whether they want to make the effort to become eagles.

3. Use a Handicap System to Keep Everyone in the Race

In horse racing, extra weight is added to the saddles of the faster horses so that the people placing wagers at the pari-mutuel windows cannot easily predict the winners. Here are two handicap formulas for sales contests:

1. Subdivide contests into three or four stages.

2. Establish several competitive categories based on sales experience levels.

Subdivide

Split the contest into two to four stages of four to six weeks each. The winners of each stage receive contest points. The winner of the first stage may be awarded 20 points, and the second-place finisher 19, no matter how far behind she is in sales volume to the person who finished immediately above her in the rankings. This tends to keep the sales performers bunched up at the start of the final period of the contest. Baseball, football, and basketball leagues use a similar approach. They play most of the season to get into the play-offs. The play-offs are more exciting than the "regular" season—but you have to do well in the regular season to have a chance in the play-offs.

Categories

Place salespeople in various competitive categories depending on their career order. This means rookies and new salespeople have their own categories. If new people have to compete with veterans, not only will they have a difficult time winning, but they may also become discouraged and develop a "What's the use of working hard; I never win" mentality. The winning spirit developed while competing against peers nurtures and enhances the fighting spirit that characterizes eagles.

The same philosophy works for the sales managers' categories. However, rather than being based on career experience, sales managers' categories can be based on sales volume calculated during some previous agreed-upon period. Contest points can be awarded for percentage increases in sales over the previous contest period as well as for sales volume. When the winners are in doubt, the contestants have to try harder—which is, after all, the whole idea.

4. Offer Exciting Rewards

After more than four decades in sales management, I have found that nothing excites the best performers like travel to interesting locations. Right behind that are state-of-the-art electronic products, such as a 40-inch-wide flat-screen HDTV. You can use one or more of the many catalogue companies that offer prizes based on points. They work, but are the incentives exciting enough to motivate sales reps to work an extra weekend?

5. Always Have a Contest in Place

I am reminded of the story about a company's new CEO who asked one of his national sales managers, "Why are August and February projected to have lower sales than the other 10 months?" "Oh," responded the national sales manager, "those are the two months between sales contests." After the briefest of discussions, it was agreed that there would be no month off for the salespeople to "rest" between sales contests.

If sales contests increase sales production, there should always be a sales contest. If sales contests do not improve sales performance, either change the way the contests are managed or quit wasting the money. You know contests are effective when sales jump up during the last few weeks of the final contest period, as everyone makes the last push to win.

SALES OFFICE PROSPECTING EVENTS AND SHORT-TERM SALES CONTESTS

In addition to regular sales contests, short-term competitions, often directed toward increasing prospecting activity, instill fun and excitement into the daily work schedule. The following are a number of principles for good local sales contests that supplement company sales contests.

Spend Modestly

The emphasis of a local contest should not be on the size of the prize. Don't give away your income awarding big sales contest prizes. When a sales manager tries to give a big prize for a local contest, it is often a panic substitute for good sales management. At the local level, the excitement of the contest comes from the competitive spirit and the desire to win.

Emphasize Prospecting Activity

At the national level, sales contests need to be focused on orders because it is difficult to measure the prospecting activity of a single sales representative successfully. At the local level, the sales manager's emphasis is on prospecting, assuming that the company is already conducting a contest based on sales volume results.

Have Fun

Local contests should be fun. Bells ring when an appointment is made, red roses are sent to the spouse of the winner of a one-week contest, the losing team has to shine the shoes of the winning team, or the losing team eats corn flakes while buying the winning team steaks. Part of the fun of local contests is the brainstorming among sales managers and sales people to come up with wild and crazy ideas for mini-contests. It's all about having fun, stoking the competitive fires, and providing recognition for effort.

Short-Term Contest

One of my best mini-contests was "beat the boss." When I had to attend a meeting that took me out of the office for a few days, I would challenge the team to do better with the boss out of town. Managers and senior sales people could "bet" very small amounts of money that during the week I was gone, they would sell more than the average of the last four weeks. As an extra push, I would pay two-to-one if the sales results for the week I was gone were 25 percent higher than average.

* * *

Long-term or short-term, companywide or local, sales- or prospecting-based, all contests have the potential to increase sales far beyond the money spent to pay for the awards. Think about the Olympics. Track and field events create the most excitement. Six to eight of the world's best athletics begin at the starting block. At the sound of the gun, each athlete is motivated to be better than anyone else for the next few seconds. Every four years, new world records are set. What would happen if, instead of running *against* each other, all the runners simply ran the race by themselves? Each would be timed. At the end of these runs, the person who had the fastest time would be declared the winner. Would runners be as fast when running by themselves as they have been when running against each other? I think most of us would agree that it is the visible competition that drives the runners to be the absolute best they can be.

So it is with the best salespeople. The great sales contests nurture an Olympic excitement as the selling eagles attempt to fly ever higher in the competitive spirit of gold medal finalists.

QUESTIONS TO ASK YOURSELF

- How do you take advantage of companywide sales contests?
- Do you review the rules and coach your sales partners on how they can improve the odds that they will win?
- Do you tie in extra prospecting and recruiting events to the contest period?
- Do your review the prizes and current standings at your sales meetings?
- What types of contests do you manage?
- How much effort do you make to handicap the outcome?
- How often do you offer prizes for prospecting activity?
- What will you be doing differently to take advantage of the competitive spirit that sales contests generate?

Although there are no books dedicated to the types of sales contests favored by direct-sales companies, there are several books aimed at telemarketers with ideas that can be borrowed for any prospecting event:

- *Motivating with Sales Contests: The Complete Guide to Motivating Your Telephone Professionals with Contests That produce Record-Breaking Results* by David Worman
- *Fun and Gains: Motivate and Energize Staff with Workplace Games, Contests, and Activities* by Carolyn Greenwich

SEVENTH ESSENTIAL ACTIVITY

MANAGE

Peter Drucker says, "Leadership is doing the right things, while management is doing things right." The four chapters in this section are dedicated to four management activities:

1. Time management, which includes using the four-quadrant time grid, focusing your attention on your eagles, and activity scheduling
2. Customer service that leads to referrals and upgrades
3. Sales tools, including prospecting materials, closing premiums, and exhibition sales aids
4. The impact of electronics on the direct-sales industry, including the Internet, computers, laptop sales binders, and the host of software that make our lives more interesting and profitable.

CHAPTER 23
IMPROVE TIME MANAGEMENT

Everyone who's ever taken a shower has an idea. It's the person who gets out of the shower, dries off, and does something about it who makes a difference.

—Nolan Bushnell, Executive

The sales manager has the opportunity (and the obligation) to manage not only her own time, but also that of all the people in the organization. Perhaps the following story will remind you of why it is so important and so difficult to focus your time on your best and brightest.

"How can I help to motivate my poor producers?" This question came from a young man who had just completed a training session on time management for a group of new managers. At age 22, Caesar had all the makings of a bright star. He had made his reputation by selling five orders in five in-home presentations during a 23-hour marathon, in the course of which he drove more than 1,000 miles.

It was the wrong question, but one that I had heard often. For some reason, this time I had what proved to be an inspired answer. Not only did the group remember this story, but it spread throughout our organization and has been told and retold many times since. "The job, Caesar," I replied, "is to find ways to motivate your eagles to fly higher rather than trying to get your ducks off the ground." After that, I started passing out yellow rubber duckies and plaster molds of the proud American eagle during my time management sales clinics.

Sales managers who spend 90 percent of their people-management time with either their eagles or their new sales recruits maximize their effectiveness. They build empires.

Treat the rest of your sales force in a benign manner. You need to be nice and appreciative to your marginal producers; but if you expect to develop a big sales organization, you cannot afford to give them very much "couch time." You have to make conscious choices.

Make your sales management life relatively easy by

- Spending time with the right people
- Doing the right things
- Delegating

It's that easy. It's that hard.

One of the many advantages of a commission or a qualified salary-and-bonus system is that, in theory, it directs everyone to use each unit of time in the fashion that is most likely to increase sales volume. In practice, this seems hard to do. Why?

I am not certain of what the answer is, but I do have a list of suspects.

First, it is the nature of most salespeople, and certainly of almost all sales managers, to be friendly and talkative with everyone. But success in sales management demands that you beware of people who are high-maintenance time wasters. These are the marginal salespeople who are all talk and no action, who may have "good ideas," or want to complain about everything, or are simply compulsive talkers. Too often the sales manager's natural tendency is to be polite, a predisposition that sometimes interferes with the mission of managing a sales force. Part of the growing pains of most sales managers is learning how to say, "I would like to chat a little longer, but I have to _____." Frankly, when sales managers ask me how to handle these situations, I worry whether that manager has the strength of character to grow into a successful sales manager.

Second, most of us want to be considered fair. And we should be fair. Nevertheless, when fairness is misconstrued as a feeling that all salespeople deserve equal access to your time, you are, in fact, being unfair to the better producers. One of the rewards of being in the top 20 percent of sales producers is catching the boss's attention more often. That privileged access is earned and appropriate.

Third, there is that endearing human desire to "save" people. We see it with spouses who think that they can get their partners to stop drinking or gambling. Sales managers have gotten where they are because of years of success in converting prospects, their salespeople, and even their bosses to their point of view. I have even heard sales managers justify a slowdown or stoppage in recruiting new salespeople (and thus in the growth of their sales organization) by stating that they need to concentrate their management activity on their poorer-performing producers. It's no wonder that they often fail to see the futility of trying to "bring up" a marginally producing salesperson, regardless of a history of previous failed attempts. At some point, enough is enough.

Fourth is our ego. Most of us sales managers would like to be that first supermotivator who does not have to rely on the top 20 to 30 percent of his salespeople to produce 70 to 80 percent of the sales volume. Indeed, wouldn't it be nice if you could train and motivate everyone to be an equally high-producing salesperson? Making the right time-management choices to maximize sales success is one of the tougher tests for sales managers because it goes against our nature, which tells us to spend increasing amounts of time helping people to change their ways. Sometimes we just have to accept people as they are. Be grateful for the contributions of your reasonably competent, but less motivated and skilled, salespeople—and move on.

Think of your sales organization's growth objectives. What is the most likely source of new sales managers? Spend time with your eagles, not only for the purpose of challenging them to maintain or exceed their high level of sales, but also to guide them into management.

Despite all these various social pressures and human inclinations to spend their time on the wrong people, the triumphant sales managers develop the will and habit to concentrate their time on the eagles and the new salespeople. They know that they are more likely to find new eagles through constant recruiting than through trying to convert ducks into eagles.

Now let's move on to how you can leverage your time by focusing on what you do best, on what you do that makes a difference in sales management. If you can pursue activities that earn you more than $100 per hour, then avoid activities that produce less income. Hire competent staff. Use your daily planner to schedule yourself to perform those high-impact activities.

THE SALES SECRETARY/ADMINISTRATIVE ASSISTANT

Sales managers can drown in paperwork if they do not get help. "Help" often means a secretary or an administrative assistant. Paperwork can creep up on you. Think of yourself as a frog who is placed in a pan of cool water. If the pan is heated up slowly, the frog doesn't notice that he is being cooked and won't jump out of the pan. A manager trainee with one person to supervise doesn't need, and cannot afford, a secretary. A sales manager with a hundred people to supervise cannot function without administrative help. So when should a sales manager hire a secretary? The answer is simple: when the time you spend shuffling paper becomes a reason or an excuse not to execute a vital profitable function. For instance, when a sales manager says, "I don't have time to write personal orders," the time has come for her to hire at least a part-time secretary.

I have had sales managers tell me, "I can't afford to hire a secretary." Once you are managing 10 or more people, you cannot afford *not* to pay someone to handle your routine administrative tasks. This is a simple math problem. How much money do you earn per hour when you do each of the following?

- Write personal orders
- Recruit
- Train
- Motivate
- Handle paperwork
- Order supplies
- Place recruiting ads in newspapers
- Go to the post office
- Maintain your schedule calendar
- Organize your tax records
- Photocopy training materials

How much are you paid per hour for performing sales management activities, including writing personal orders? Now calculate how much per hour you will pay a secretary to handle your *nonmanagement* activities. Is there a difference?

THE MARKETING MANAGER

You are responsible for your team's prospecting efforts. The chapters on the second Essential Activity review a wide range of marketing activities that you can use to generate more leads. How much time do you have to book booth space, trade lists of names for a direct-mail program, or plan and conduct lead-generating activities like take-one boxes or passing out flyers at offices? A well-trained and enthusiastic marketing manager can generate far more sales volume than the cost of his salary and expenses.

Performing all the activities required for a robust marketing program while simultaneously executing all the other duties of a sales manager is a nearly impossible task. A marketing manager frees up your valuable time so that you can do those things that *only* the sales manager can do. Dynamic sales growth and the confidence to continue recruiting are dependent on an ever-increasing number of cheap, locally produced leads. Delegating this marketing task to your lead-generating manager frees you to perform your other tasks more efficiently.

A happy consequence of this use of delegating power is that a trained marketing manager can often do a better marketing job than the sales manager, because the marketing manager spends all of her time generating leads. (This is true as long as you do not try to assign personal or secretarial tasks to the marketing manager. That would be a poor use of delegation.)

SCHEDULING FOR SUCCESS

Well-organized, successful sales managers maintain a calendar going forward for at least 90 days. The larger your organization, the further forward you need to plan. The 90-day calendar is a simple, powerful tool that maximizes the effective use of your time and puts you in charge of your life. Instead of just doing things as they come up, or even scheduling a few events a month or so in advance, the 90-day calendar requires you to set aside days for personal selling activities (I used to set aside Fridays, Saturdays, and Sundays), recruiting, training, sales meetings, and management development activities. Include mini-breaks, anniversary dinners, school plays, and so forth in your scheduling.

The 90-day schedule attacks the procrastination problem. One benefit of your three-month daily planner is that it schedules the booking of prospecting events well in advance. Nothing is more discouraging than having to call around to all your booth location contacts at the last minute to book a sales counter location because "all of a sudden" you realize that not enough leads have come in this week.

Give your sales organization access to this calendar. At a glance, all your sales partners can see the important events scheduled over the next three months. Better yet, your maintaining this calendar sets an example that everyone will want to copy.

THE TIME GRID

A time grid can be made by simply drawing two lines. A vertical line is intersected in the middle by a horizontal line, forming four quadrants. The quadrants are labeled

- Urgent and important
- Not urgent and important
- Urgent and not important
- Not urgent and not important

Almost all your activities can be divided into those four categories. There are many similar types of time grids. This particular one was inspired by Stephen Covey's book, *Seven Habits of Highly Effective People.*

Spending most of your time in the upper right-hand quadrant, "not urgent and important," means that you plan your work in such a way that important tasks are completed *before* they become urgent. For instance, when a sales manager sets an example by having a "bank" of five to seven sales appointments booked by Monday morning, that means that the appointment setting was done in the "not urgent and important" quadrant. A sales manager who has no sales appointments booked by Monday morning will have to spend time in the "urgent and important" quadrant scrambling to set last-minute sales calls as a consequence of not having planned ahead.

"Urgent" means having to perform some last-minute activity to solve a problem that usually could have been better handled by simply planning ahead. In both the upper quadrants, the activity is equally important; what is different is the degree of professionalism involved in planning and anticipation. In a perfect world, there would no activity in the "urgent and important" quadrant because you would have performed all your important work before it become urgent.

"Urgent and important" activities are a consequence of either an unforeseen crisis or poor planning. If you have a sales booth at a kiosk in the mall and no one shows up, you have to drop what you are doing and get someone to that booth *now.* If this happens once, it is probably one of those emergencies that cannot be avoided. If it happens more than once, you have a management flaw.

Look at the two bottom quadrants, what I call time thieves. The lower left quadrant, "urgent and not important," consists of small, time-consuming, but hard to avoid tasks that interrupt the day. An example of "urgent and not important" activities is telephone calls: You need to answer the phone now, as the call could be important. Ideally, you ask your salespeople to call you only at a designated time during of the day. However, our business is a people business, and we would not enjoy the support and loyalty of our sales team if we enforced such a policy. A salesperson who drops by your home or office is urgent; the reason may not be important. Still, it is difficult to say, "I'm too busy to talk to you." Sometimes your salespeople need coaching time, even on unimportant matters. Your job is to *minimize* these urgent and not important activities. You have to choose who receives the larger chunks of your time.

Good time management means that you don't overschedule yourself so that you do have some time for some "urgent and not important" sales management activities. "Not urgent and not important" activities are the ones you want to try to eliminate. Five minutes at the coffee station talking about a sports event is friendly chitchat; thirty minutes is wasting time.

Consider two practical exercises to improve the use of your time:

1. *What you did*. List up to 24 activities that you performed in the past month, placing each one in the appropriate time quadrant reflecting how you performed that activity. This will give you a good idea of where you stand in personal time management. Next, fill out a second time grid with the same 24 activities. This time, either eliminate the activities or put them in the grid quadrants in which they *should* be.

2. *Ten most important activities*. List your ten most *important* sales management activities. Once you have that list, you'll find it is easier to schedule those activities so that they fall into the "not urgent and important" quadrant. Compare your "should do" list of your 10 most important sales management activities with the previous exercise showing what you *actually* did over the past four weeks. Place these activities in their proper quadrant.

As you fill the grids with the activities you are performing, ask yourself questions like

- "Am I waiting too long to plan for events?"
- "Am I performing functions that others could do?"
- "Am I performing functions that should not be done at all?"

Once you have completed the two exercises, ask yourself, "Am I satisfied with my time allocation?" If the answer is no, what will you do differently going forward?

If you perform this same exercise a month later, there should be a change in your list of 24 activities as you drop "not urgent and not important" activities and replace them with more important sales management functions.

Put this time management quadrant theory into practice in your time-management daily planner system. The purpose of your 90-day schedule is to move as many important functions, such as personal selling, recruiting, training, and sales meetings, into the upper right-hand "not urgent and important" quadrant. If you expand the upper right quadrant and shrink the upper left quadrant, your sales volume will increase because you are concentrating your time where it matters.

A SENSE OF URGENCY

"Do it yesterday" is not a bad motto for a sales manager. Procrastination is the bane of all management, but this is especially true of sales management. Prospecting is postponed until tomorrow to avoid rejection; settling a dispute between two salespeople is put off because it may be an unpleasant experience; a decision is avoided because you are not sure (and never will be) whether your decision is the risk-free right one. Ironically, if you approach your job with a sense of urgency, you will not have to spend a lot of time in the "urgent and important" quadrant. Sales managers who procrastinate spend a lot of panic time in that quadrant handling emergencies that could have been taken care of earlier in the "not urgent and important" quadrant.

Let's go back to the three examples of procrastination we just gave:

1. *Prospecting.* You will use your time more efficiently and do a better job when you perform your tasks as soon as you can. You know that telling yourself, "I'll book sales calls tomorrow" is just an excuse. If you plan to do it today, do it. Putting off prospecting will weigh you down with guilt feelings—a negative influence that saps your energy and resolve.

2. *Settling a dispute.* The longer you avoid dealing with a dispute, the more time you and your team will waste. You give away your valuable,

income-producing time to thinking and talking about the situation—as do the other people involved. At your first opportunity, call the two people in and find a way to solve the problem. The sooner you take care of disputes, the less important they tend to be. And by removing this distraction, you keep yourself and your time focused on productive tasks.

3. *Decision making.* No decision is risk-free. Rushing to make a decision can be disastrous. On the other hand, putting off making a decision can become a decision in itself. Your best course is to arm yourself with all the facts you can, make a sound and informed decision, then move on.

TIME MANAGEMENT FOR YOUR SALES TEAM

So far, we have addressed how the sales manager plans her own time. Now let's look at the sales manager's second time-management responsibility: How do you help your salespeople better utilize their time?

Most salespeople are engaged in face-to-face selling activity less than 10 hours a week. Check out your team's real selling hours with the following exercise.

Ask your salespeople to write down last week's selling activity, answering specific questions:

- How many presentations did they give to the decision maker? (Giving presentations to secretaries or spouses who cannot make a decision is not selling time.)
- How long was each presentation?

Their answers will show how many hours of *real* selling activity each of your sales associates engaged in—"selling" being defined as giving a sales presentation, face to face, to a bona fide prospect. It does *not* include prospecting time, driving time, attending a sales meeting, and so forth.

Champions engage in face-to-face selling 25 or more hours a week. They are focused. They are time-obsessive. Stay out of their way! These are your highest-flying super-eagles.

The easiest way for most salespeople to increase their sales production quickly is to convert more of their working time to *real* selling time. While you cannot directly influence the outcome of any single sales presentation unless you are with the salesperson, you can greatly influence both the selling skills (through training) and the time management of your sales force. Regardless of a salesperson's personality, enthusiasm, or competence, he will sell more by talking to more prospects.

Help your sales representatives increase their face-to-face selling time by three hours a week. That may not seem like much, but three more hours can be as much as 30 percent more selling time. Once they have increased their sales activity to this level, ratchet it up another two selling hours a week. Be prepared to help some marginal producers to move from *less than five* hours of genuine selling time to seven hours.

Here are some hints for helping your salespeople plan their time better:

1. *A 30-day schedule.* Sales management requires a 90-day-plus planning schedule. Salespeople need a 30-day schedule that is updated *daily*. This schedule includes booked sales appointments, sales meetings and training to attend, and, most important, time- and date-specific prospecting activities, such as kiosk shifts and blocks of time set aside for making telephone appointments or other forms of direct contact.

2. *Converting prospecting time to income.* If it takes three hours of prospecting to get a sales presentation, and three presentations to get an order, how many hours of prospecting does it take to get nine orders a month? This sounds like fourth-grade math, but few sales reps can give a specific answer to such a question. Conclude this math exercise by converting prospecting time into income. Every salesperson knows how much commission or bonus she earns on an order. As the sales manager, you want to convert this per-order income into an hourly "wage" that includes selling and prospecting time. If Amy's goal is nine orders a month:

   ❏ She knows that she needs to deliver 27 face-to-face presentations because her closing percentage is 33 percent.

   ❏ Since it takes three hours of prospecting to find a customer who is willing to listen to a presentation, Amy now knows that she needs to schedule 81 hours a month, or about 20 hours a week, for prospecting. So Amy's *real* goal is the prospecting activity.

   ❏ Further, Amy's presentation averages 90 minutes. Since it takes 27 presentations to obtain nine orders, that is another 40.5 hours of work. Add that to her prospecting time and we can see Amy's selling and prospecting hours total 121.5 hours a month.

❏ Amy earns an average of $400 per order, giving her an average monthly income of $3,600. Divide that by her 121.5 hours of selling time, and we can see Amy's wage is $29.63 per hour. So it helps Amy to know that she is earning about $30.00 an hour when she is dialing that phone for appointments, working that booth at the mall, or passing out flyers.

❏ Finally, at a goal-setting session, Amy can make the connections between an extra five hours a week for prospecting and reaching her life's objective.

3. *Group activities.* Avoidance of rejection is the number one reason that salespeople spend an insufficient amount of time prospecting. The salesperson's job can be lonely. Enthusiasm for prospecting can dwindle and die. You as the manager can combat that slow death by including group prospecting activities in your 90-day schedule. Group events such as telephone parties, take-one box clinics, and sales appointment booths at grocery stores are terrific examples of the sales manager's power to help her salespeople spend more time prospecting—and thus spend more time selling.

THE $50 RULE

The $50 rule says that you say yes when a person under you asks for financial support for some selling or recruiting activity that costs $50 or less. It doesn't have to be $50, of course—pick the amount that fits the situation. Junior managers may use a lower amount, while senior managers may have a higher amount. The amount may depend on the value of the product being sold. What's important is that you simply say yes to requests for a certain predetermined amount, be it $20, $100, or some other number that you can live with. This automatic consent will save you time. You do not want to spend time on "urgent and not important" tasks. Spending 30 minutes on analyzing the worth of a $50 request is a waste of time. Saying yes to requests for small amounts of money also means that you avoid being labeled as cheap. Everyone likes to get an instant yes once in a while. Be a hero and give it to your people.

TO-DO LIST

Carrying a to-do list on a printed form or on your PDA not only acts as a reminder that you need to do certain things, but also helps you choose your priorities so that you get your time quadrants right. When you look at your to-do list, you are more likely to do the most important thing on the list for the simple reason that you can see everything you need to do at a glance.

Time management is a combination of processes, discipline, and sometimes just plain will power. First, you develop a set of time management and planning practices. Next, you train yourself to follow those practices, turning them into habits. Finally, you motivate yourself to implement those processes to their maximum effect. That winning formula will guarantee sales growth through the better use of your time.

QUESTIONS TO ASK YOURSELF

- What type of forward schedule do you currently maintain?
- Does your schedule include three months of planned prospecting events?
- Can you think of three ways in which you can improve your time-allocation process?
- What can you do to increase your sales associates' selling time by three hours a week?

Additional books that can help you with time management:

- *The One Minute Manager* by Ken Blanchard and Spencer Johnson, M.D.
- *One Minute Sales Person, The Quickest Way to Sell People on Yourself, Your Services, Products, or Ideas—at Work and in Life* by Spencer Johnson, M.D.
- *10 Secrets of Time Management for Salespeople: Gain the Competitive Edge and Make Every Second Count* by Dave Kahle

CHAPTER 24
PROMOTE QUALITY CUSTOMER SERVICE AND UPGRADES

Take a chance! All life is a chance. The man who goes furthest is generally the one who is willing to do and dare.

—Dale Carnegie, Motivational Writer, Speaker

One of the easiest ways to make extra money is through after-sales service. It takes a lot of effort to sell an item to a stranger; it takes a fraction of that effort to sell it to a satisfied friend. This is a long way from the outdated attitude of "sell 'em and forget 'em."

The tin man is dead, may he rest in peace. Richard Dreyfus and Danny DeVito starred in the 1987 movie *The Tin Men*, a dark comedy "honoring" the worst sales practices of the home improvement business, and, by extension, the entire door-to-door sales industry. Arthur Miller's 1949 classic play *Death of a Salesman* was a reflection of the prototypical dysfunctional salesperson who chases impossible dreams while womanizing on road trips. Willie Loman and his son Biff were tragic characters. The story painted such a grim view of the life of a salesperson that it motivated me to think about finding a "real job" for years after I had entered the sales industry. It is my hope you will not have to experience the type of conversion that I underwent early in my career, as revealed in the following account.

> My private moment of truth concerning right and proper sales practices came in a meeting with Joe De La Cruz in San Juan, Puerto Rico. Joe was president of Caribe Grolier. "Mike," he said, "I know that you stateside guys don't sell books. You have been using that 'free advertising offer' pitch to get your foot in the door with clients. If I ever find out you've made a misleading statement in my territory, you'll never sell another order for me."
>
> I learned to sell books. I worked seven consecutive days without writing an order as I tried to adjust to a straight "tell 'em like it is" sales talk. Then, on my eighth selling day, I finally wrote two orders, and I went on to sell 300 orders the next year and for the next four subsequent years. I

had never sold more than 150 orders in a year when I used the "advertising campaign" pitch, which, as Joe had pointed out, was not completely honest. Instead of avoiding customers after a sale because I was embarrassed to see them face to face after beguiling them with a less-than-forthright sales presentation, I learned to build relationships and earn referral business.

My private conversion to a customer-centric sales strategy was mirrored throughout much of the direct-sales industry. Led by the Direct Sales Association (DSA), most of the direct-sales industry cleaned up its act during the 1970s. Certainly, there are still some companies and some salespeople who do not tell a straight story. The good news is that they are now a diminishing minority.

Today, astute sales managers have moved far beyond simply using ethical sales practices, as critical as those are, to build profitable long-term relationships with their first-time buyers. The goal now is to treat the customer's rising expectations with continued after-sales service that surpasses mere satisfaction.

The primary benefits of proactive customer service are

- We stay in business.
- We get more referrals.
- We can sell more upgrades.

STAY IN BUSINESS

The consumer today has great expectations regarding product quality and after-sales service. Today's buyer is far more sophisticated than the generation of consumers in the post-World War II era. Companies that "didn't get it," like Montgomery Ward, Studebaker, and Eastern Airlines, went out of business, while newcomers like Wal-Mart, Amway, 24 Hour Fitness, Ben & Jerry's Ice Cream, Starbucks, and Southwest Airlines became market-dominant brand names synonymous with customer service and good marketing. Prospects and buyers have greater expectations than ever before; great companies beat those expectations.

Recently I bought a new car. It was the first new car I'd bought in 12 years, as I had previously been provided with a company car. I bought a Lexus because of the car's reputation; I would do so again because of the professionalism of the selling situation. Not only was I spared the tired and untrue "I need to check with my manager to see if I can sell you this car below cost" selling approach, but I was happily subjected to a one-hour clinic on how to use all the gadgets—after I had paid for the car. A day later, I received an e-mail checking on my satisfaction with the car. If I had not been traveling, I would have received a phone call. A few days later, I received a two-page survey from Lexus, quizzing me on my experience buying the car. Two weeks later, I received an embossed card asking whether any of my friends had seen the car and were impressed. The card closed with a request for the names of such envious people.

The Lexus approach to selling and service reminded me of the changes our direct sales force had made during the early years in Taiwan. We started with the traditional "sell and forget" philosophy. However, a few of our early sales associates had sold vacuum cleaners for Electrolux in Taiwan, where, after making a sale, they were required to personally deliver the vacuum cleaner and make sure that the new owner could easily use all the features. Having been trained this way, these former Electrolux salespeople who had been recruited to sell our educational packages started an "open the box" after-the-sale service. Those particular sales representatives not only had fewer cancellations than most of the other salespeople, but also received easy referral orders.

The hallmarks of successful customer service include

- Having the salesperson either deliver the product to the customer or visit the customer shortly after the company delivers it to make sure that the client understands how to use the product.
- Building a customer Web site to cover FAQs and provide stories that motivate use of the product.
- Developing a follow-up contact system that includes a courtesy phone call to check on customer satisfaction and asking customers to fill out a survey evaluating their buying experience.
- Offering a users' club to your buyers. If you offer enough benefits, you can even charge a membership fee.
- Providing a warranty covering free replacement parts (other than consumables like a replacement bag for a vacuum cleaner or crayons in a child's product program) for an extended period of time. Think of how warranties have improved the auto business.

GET MORE REFERRAL BUSINESS

The idea of referrals must be as old as sales itself. The best way to garner referrals is to proactively take care of your customers. This yields two enduring benefits: Happy customers will willingly refer you to other prospects, and you can approach these original customers after they've enjoyed your product for a year or so and successfully sell them an item to add on to their initial purchase.

Satisfied customers respond well to mail-order offers. By the time I retired, the goal of my company was to sell the customer as much merchandise and services *after* the original sale as the amount of that first sale. When I left, that goal had not been reached, but each year we crept closer to that target as our after-sales service and post-sale offers continued to improve.

The system of obtaining referrals is rather simple:

- Ask
- Give a gift
- Conduct an annual campaign

Ask

Ask for referrals at different time intervals, starting from the moment of the sale. While a few new customers may give you a couple of names right off the bat, most of them need a little coaching. One good idea is to ask to look at their Christmas card list. More than half the people I asked for referrals did not give me any. No problem. If you make a *habit* of asking *everyone* for a referral, some customers will give you at least one. A few new buyers would even call their relatives or friends to book the appointment. While most referrals come at the point of sale, a follow-up phone call or visit after delivery will result in additional referrals. A follow-up call several months or even a year later will add a few more quality referrals. These delayed referrals often come as a result of a friend or relative seeing the product in the customer's home and asking about it.

Give a Gift

Offer a referral gift that complements the original purchase. Give the gift to your original customer for providing a referral who converts to an order. Give the same referral gift as an *extra* premium to the new customer who was referred. Win-win.

Conduct an Annual Campaign

Once a year, send your customers a unique referral offer, distinct from the standard referral offer, that has a 30- to 60-day time limit. Some of your clients will respond to this offer directly. More important, the mailed offer gives your salespeople an excuse to make an extra after-service call to their client base, during which they can not-so-casually mention the special referral program. This program gets all your salespeople contacting a huge percentage of your customer base. The number of prospecting contacts increases. You will get a spike in sales volume.

SELL MORE UPGRADES

Some years ago, while brainstorming how to deal with a sales slump, an innovator on our marketing staff suggested a companywide upgrade program. Christina noted two things. First, few customers bought all the products the company offered, even though we had a "super" package that allowed the customer to buy everything. Second, a few salespeople would go back to their customers a year or so later and "complete" the order. So why not test a campaign?

And so we did—successfully, as it turned out. Here's how we structured it:

1. First we reviewed all the purchases, looking for buying-opportunity patterns. Sure enough, most of the customers who did not buy the "super everything" product package fell into five clusters. Each of these five groups needed a particular add-on package to complete their program.

2. Next, we mailed a special promotional offer unique to each of the five groupings to our targeted clients. That offer included

❏ A special price

❏ A free gift premium

❏ A limited-time offer to qualify for the discount and the premium

3. Then we assigned the names of the targeted buyers to our sales force for follow-up.

4. We also assigned upgrade leads to the original sales rep when that was possible.

At the time, our sales force was averaging 300 orders a week. The upgrade campaign produced almost a thousand "extra" orders in a six-week period. The average size of the extra orders was only about half the size of the original order—but they were extra. Sales volume jumped. This same upgrade program was used later when the company introduced new items into the product mix.

An offshoot of this add-on program is the trade-in. For years, Britannica and World Book would offer $100 or so as a trade-in when buying a new set of encyclopedias. The traded-in sets of books were then donated to a school or library. Win-win-win.

After-sales customer service is not an expense. It is a profit center. For a modest investment in training the sales force to be attentive to postsales customer needs and providing the necessary home-office administration personnel, you build tremendous customer satisfaction and a continued profitable relationship with your client base.

There are company policies and referral-generating programs you can implement that will produce more referral business than ever before. However, it is what you do *before* you implement these referral and upgrade programs that determines their success. The requirement for a successful referral and upgrade program is a combination of professional selling practices and caring after-sales service, competently delivered. Customers expect more postsale service than ever before, and there's no reason not to give it to them. It's not only the right thing to do, it's the smart thing to do.

QUESTIONS TO ASK YOURSELF

- What type of organized referral program do you offer your clients?
- How well is your sales team coached to obtain referrals?
- Do you have an annual campaign, including a special offer, for referral orders?
- Do you track your customers' purchases?

- How often do you organize an upgrade campaign?
- What are you planning to do differently in order to obtain more referral and upgrade orders?

Additional books dedicated to customer service and referral business:

- *Delivering Knock Your Socks Off Service* by Ron Zemke and Kristin Anderson
- *Customer Satisfaction Is Worthless; Customer Loyalty Is Priceless* by Jeffrey Gitomer
- *76 Ways to Build a Straight Referral Business ASAP* by Lorna Riley
- *Endless Referrals* by Bob Burg

CHAPTER 25
DEVELOP SELLING AND PROSPECTING TOOLS

When you blame others, you give up your power to change.

—Anonymous

You and your company share responsibility for increasing the odds for the prospecting and selling success of your sales force. No matter how good a salesperson's closing ability may be, he can improve only if he has the right tools. While this chapter reviews some of the new high-tech sales tools, the following anecdote reminds us that old solutions like "inspect what you expect" remain effective management oversight options.

> It starts with something as simple as a "kit check." I remember, as a 20-year-old field manager, checking the sales materials each week at the back of the car as I picked up the lads (in those days it was *only* lads) after their door-knocking rounds. Since we were selling a set of books for hundreds of dollars, the salesperson's samples had to to reflect that value and be in perfect shape. Our sample volume was impressive: lots of color pictures, high-quality paper, and an attractive binding. Yet, some salespeople didn't get it. I would discover sample books with smudges and bent edges, which meant that the salesperson hadn't noticed, didn't care, or was too cheap to buy a replacement. Personal "junk" would be commingled with sales presentation materials inside sale kits.

My first week in the direct-sales business, I saw a marketing tool that I admired, but I didn't have the marketing sense to think, "Everyone ought to be doing this." As an 18-year-old sales novice, I was assigned to my first field manager. Bob enclosed his sample book in a custom-made leather cover. When he gave a presentation, he would slowly remove the sample book from its leather sheath and hold it like a chalice. While I admired this showmanship, it never occurred to me then to duplicate it. I just saw it as an interesting quirk—just like the thousands of people who ate at the first McDonald's without realizing the revolution that was at hand. It took someone who understood the marketing significance of a place like McDonald's (a fellow by the name of Ray Kroc) to make the revolution happen.

I recently did kit checks in Asia. The discoveries I made hadn't changed. The appearance of sales samples still ranged from smart to sloppy. I made it a habit to teach another generation of sales managers the importance of the kit check to make sure our customers always saw sharp-looking materials. I had also, by now, learned to learn from my observations when checking sales kits. For instance, some sales representatives had become newspaper clippers. They would read an interesting article that gave credibility to the need story. They would then cut out the article that supported their sales talk and add it their sales kit. This time, when observing an effective homemade sales tool, a lightbulb went off in my more attuned marketing head. Soon our marketing department was gathering such need-story support articles for distribution to *all* sales representatives.

The tools you provide for your salespeople do make a difference. The office appearance makes a difference. Oh, you can get by with a sloppy work environment and outmoded or tired sales tools. The closing ability of outstanding salespeople is still the largest single component of the sales talk. But, their sales presentation tools can either add to their closing strengths or detract from them.

Salespeople can prospect using their own devices; they do better when you offer professionally produced prospecting tools for at least 10 lead-generating techniques. When you control the quality of your selling tools and make sure that you provide the best selling and prospecting tools possible, you are more likely to find, develop, and *keep* great closers.

The three key selling tools that you want to give your people are sales presentation materials (known as kits), prospecting resources, and closing premiums.

SALES PRESENTATION MATERIALS

Because the transition to laptop sales binders is reviewed in the next chapter, we won't discuss it here. Let's consider selling presentation tools besides the sales binder.

The consumer normally uses two senses when buying a product: hearing and sight. Cookware salespeople are sometimes lucky enough to be able to use the senses of smell and taste. Exercise equipment salespeople can use the sense of touch. (And, I suppose, if the salesperson demonstrates the exercise equipment too vigorously, smell may not be an advantage.)

The strongest, most powerful sales presentations include a combination of tactile, visual, and auditory components. One of the reasons exhibitions are such a great selling venue is that the entire product can be displayed. Prospects can see, hear, touch, smell, and taste it, and even try it out.

To liven up your presentation—and make it more effective—ask yourself these questions: What can you do to involve your prospects in the sales presentation? How many of the five senses can you utilize?

SUPPLY AND CONTROL PROSPECTING MATERIALS

Often, the first impression that a prospect has of your company comes from the printed sales promotion piece. The promo material might be mailed to the prospect's home or be placed in a retail shop for customers to "take one." There are more than 20 prospecting methods; these devices are explained in great detail in Chapters 3 through 7. Empire-building sales managers need to be competent in at least 10 lead-generation techniques and provide the support materials for each technique to their team.

Telephone scripts are a good example of a powerful prospecting tool. Any sales operation that even partially relies on the telephone for setting up appointments, confirming appointments, or making sales needs a book of telephone scripts. A well-thought-out, tested telephone script *read* by the salesperson always outperforms the ad-lib approach.

New phraseology needs to be tested from time to time. If a particular phrase or word increases the call-to-appointment ratio, then the sales manager will want to add or substitute this new wording in the telephone script binder.

Be wary if you find that your sales force is distributing homemade marketing materials. A homemade sales piece means that at least one salesperson is not satisfied with the prospecting materials you and your company offer. Sometimes a salesperson feels that the home office cannot be trusted to handle the incoming inquiries from prospects. Such sales representatives want "their" prospects to contact them directly, not through the company bureaucracy. Find out what lies behind this "wake-up call" regarding your prospecting and sales materials.

Make it a habit to invite your top sales producers to work with your print and Web-site designers. If you include them in the process, they won't feel that it's necessary to produce their own materials.

DRAMATIC CLOSING PREMIUMS—HOW TO PICK THEM AND HOW TO USE THEM IN THE RIGHT SEQUENCE

Everyone in direct sales knows that the best closing device is the imminent ending of a good deal. The easiest and most dangerous closing tool is the discount. Discounting in the direct-sales business is chancey. Customers compare notes. People do not want to pay $1,500 for the same vacuum cleaner that their neighbor just got for $1,300. Nor does the public want to feel exploited when the "special price" is the permanent real price.

Bob Baseman of Encyclopedia Britannica understood this dilemma. In the early 1980s, when he was promoted to national sales director, he had instructions to make Britannica the cleanest direct-sales company ever. Bob imposed a zero-tolerance rule on sales-talk abuses. Simultaneously, Bob realized that salespeople still needed a closing tool that would give customers a reason to buy today.

Bob thought retail. Like you, he knew that he normally bought "good deals" when shopping. Stores would run specials. There were "White Sales," "Presidents' Day Sales," "After-Christmas Sales," "Anniversary Sales"—you know the routine. Car companies would offer special financing deals for a limited period.

So Bob introduced the monthly special offer. For instance, anyone buying in December could also buy the 54-volume Great Books for half price; in January, anyone who bought could use the Britannica research department 20 times per year instead of the normal 10 times per year for 10 years; in March, the three-volume replica of the first Britannica, published in 1768, was free; in April—you get the drift. Every month, the sales force had a special one-time offer that expired at the end of the month.

One of my own best examples of a great closing premium was a DVD player in the early days of DVDs. My former company in Taiwan sold an early education product aimed at toddlers that included VHS videos. We started offering the videos in the DVD format shortly after the technology had gained limited consumer acceptance. The problem was that in the first days of this DVD offer, few prospects had DVD players. DVD players were also relatively expensive. Our sales managers quickly volunteered that if we could find an inexpensive DVD player for our new customers, sales would jump.

We found a manufacturer who would make us a private-label DVD player for less than one-half the current retail price. The price for our sales package containing the DVD player was increased slightly over the regular price for our DVD offer. The salespeople not only agreed to forgo commissions and bonuses on the small DVD price increase, but also contributed some of their commission money to pay for the DVD player. The result was that if a customer purchased our early childhood education program during this limited time offer, he received a free DVD player. Salespeople got excited; the customers got excited. Sales soared.

*　*　*

In addition to these three key support tools, the following sales aids are part of your responsibility to help your sales force close more orders.

REBUTTAL BOOKS

Once new salespeople are able to deliver an enthusiastic presentation with a good need story, they have to work on their closing skills. Most professional closers agree that how you say it is more important than what you say. Still your choice of words and their sequence play a key role in converting prospects into customers—especially for new salespeople, since it takes longer to learn the "how" than the "what."

Therefore, maintain a rebuttal book that your salespeople can use to give winning replies to prospect responses such as "I want to think it over" and "It costs too much." Update the rebuttal book at least once a year.

LIBRARY

Provide an office library of books on salesmanship and sales management. Include audio versions of such books. The benefits of keeping this small library far outweigh the costs.

Additional selling support tools are reviewed in the following chapter, "Take Advantage of the Internet."

QUESTIONS TO ASK YOURSELF

■ How often do you perform a kit check to verify that your sales force is using approved sales materials that look smart?

■ Do you maintain a telephone and rebuttal script book? Should you? How often do you update it?

■ Do you have sharp-looking printed materials for each of your prospecting methods?

■ How often do you change the closing premiums?

■ Do your closing premiums create a sense of urgency, leading your prospects to want to make a decision today?

■ How often do you review your closing premiums with your sales partners?

■ Do you maintain a rebuttal book? If so, how often do you update it?

■ How many books and tapes are in your sales office's library? Are you satisfied with your library?

Books that can help you build better sales tools:

■ *The Sales Bible* by Jeffrey Gitomer
■ *Phrases That Sell* by Edward W. Werz and Sally Germain
■ *Words That Sell* by Richard Bayan
■ *Better Brochures, Catalogs and Mailing Pieces* by Jane Maas
■ *The Perfect Sales Piece* by Robert W. Bly

CHAPTER 26
TAKE ADVANTAGE OF THE INTERNET

There are always opportunities through which businessmen can profit handsomely if they will only recognize them.

—J. Paul Getty, Business Executive

Who can forget the overblown hype about how the Internet was going to make all retail businesses outmoded? Good-bye shopping malls and sales personnel! It's a new world, and it is all-electronic.

Thankfully, as the following narrative reveals, it sometimes pays to back an idea with modest means even if you are not sure about the outcome. This is just one example debunking the worry that the Internet would eliminate the direct-sales business as we know it. It's made it better!

> I will always appreciate Michael Collier. Mike was an English teacher in the customer support club for our English home study programs. In 1994, he boldly asked to give our senior management team a presentation on obtaining sales leads on the Internet. I wondered at the time what an English club support-staff guy was doing meddling in direct-sales marketing. However, we couldn't deny Mike's enthusiasm, and almost as a courtesy we reluctantly gave him 30 minutes to make his case. By the slimmest of skeptical margins, we approved a budget of $10,000 for six months to test his theory. That test changed our business forever. Within two years, 50 percent of our orders in that sales division were derived from Internet leads.

Fortunately, as this story dramatizes, a combination of my misgivings about the total revolution and my initial belief that the Internet was "just one more media place to obtain leads" resulted in my making the Internet my best new friend in the 1990s.

The Internet, huge increases in laptop memory, and software that is better than ever have brought about a revolution that builds upon the great, existing, so-called bricks-and-mortar foundation of the direct-sales industry. I am amazed at how the Internet and computers changed the businesses I managed in Asia from 1991 to 2002. When I first arrived, I had not even heard of the Internet, and I thought "the Web" was something to do with Charlotte and spiders. Yet by the time I left Asia, the Internet was responsible for 10 to 50 percent of sales, depending on the sales organization.

The Internet does not replace the direct-sales industry. Instead, it adds value to our business. It is a huge source of leads, it provides a tool for the delivery of a more dynamic sales presentation, it reduces buyer's remorse, and it improves sales training. As you review these and other Internet and computer opportunities, keep asking yourself, "How much of the potential use of these electronic advantages am I using?"

LEAD GENERATION

Prodded by Michael Collier, we began by thinking of the various Web sites as electronic magazines. Our company had generated leads in various target magazines for years. We kept records on the cost of leads and orders from each magazine. It wasn't much of a leap to do the same for Web sites.

Initially, we put our magazine ads on our Web site. Then we either paid or traded for advertising on other selected Web sites so that we could have our "ad links" displayed. We assigned the leads just like any other leads. We learned as we went along. The Internet ads took on more of an "Internet look." We found that we could give a sample English lesson from our home study product on our Web site. Initially, conversion rates for Internet leads were less than half the conversion rate of magazine leads. Gradually, however, some sales reps learned how to approach and sell these leads. Since our records revealed who was doing a good job with each category of lead, we could assign most of the Internet leads to sales reps who had those good conversion records. We discovered that lead generation online is cheaper and the results are quicker than almost any other type of lead sourcing. You can target your audience by placing ads only on Web sites that your client base will be looking at.

THE ELECTRONIC SALES BINDER

Laptops have given the direct salesperson a new, powerful sales presentation tool. The laptop's high-tech modern image gives the salesperson and his company greater credibility in an industry where credibility is often an issue.

Not only can the sales binder be replicated on the laptop screen, but many wonderful features can also be added. For instance, a computer can hold hundreds of pages of need-story material catalogued by prospect type. The same is true for endorsements or product information. The hard drive memory or DVD gives the salesperson the ability to tailor the presentation to the needs of the prospect. There is a potential danger here, though. Some salespeople will be tempted to show *everything* and bore the prospect to death. The benefits of choice, however, vastly outweigh the dangers of overdoing it.

Furthermore, all the pricing and payment terms can be kept at the ready in the computer. If your product is sold on an installment plan, the salesperson can more easily find a plan that is suitable for the client.

Remember the old adage that "one picture is worth a thousand words." Our sense of looking is stronger than our sense of listening. Thus, the visual sales presentation tools you provide for your sales force have a dramatic effect on sales. The laptop presentation has visual imagining capabilities that no printed binder can hope to match.

The easiest way to improve your sales binder is to watch your best salespeople in action. If you notice a good salesperson who either doesn't use the sales binder or adds pages, find out why. The best salespeople do not avoid using the company binder or add to it capriciously. Whatever changes they make are done to close more orders. Your pros will be eager to work with the design folks to build a more useful sales binder.

LEAVE-BEHIND BUTTON-UP

A leave-behind CD-ROM or DVD at the point of sale addresses the ancient problem of buyer's remorse. No doubt you already have some type of "button-up" procedure in which your sales representative reviews all the benefits and financial terms of the purchase as the last step in the presentation. At the end of the button-up, a "leave-behind" package is normally given to the new customer. The leave-behind package typically includes a copy of the contract and a pamphlet that reviews all those benefits once again. The real message of the leave-behind package is, *"Please* do not cancel."

Many parts of the sales presentation can be put on the CD-ROM. This not only reminds the buyer of why she made the purchase, but helps her to convince other members of the household or business who were not present during the sales presentation that this purchase was a good decision.

In addition, parts of some products can be "delivered" on the leave-behind CD-ROM or DVD. In my educational products business, we learned to put some learning material on the leave-behind CD-ROM that could be used immediately. Cookware companies could leave behind recipes; exercise equipment and fitness centers could deliver tips on good health habits; the cemetery industry could provide information on wills and other planning tools for the "final event."

ELECTRONIC TRAINING MANUALS

Today, most professional direct-sales companies have complete and smart-looking training manuals for all aspects of their business. This is a vast improvement over the old days, when many sales companies had only a sales script to memorize.

The best direct-sales companies have put or are putting their training materials online to ensure standardization, to allow for easy updates, and to include self-study tests that can be monitored. Every company can ensure that all of its sales personnel and sales managers are thoroughly familiar with all the basic skills needed to do the job. A good Web site won't make someone a great closer, but it will certainly promote consistency in training while improving closing and prospecting proficiency. You are effective without these electronic tools; you are more effective with them. They extend and expand your competence.

THE EXPANDED COMMUNICATOR

The use of e-mail allows frequent simultaneous communication with a larger group of people. There was no way I could have managed five direct-sales groups in three countries without the convenience and speed of e-mail. The number of people with whom I could communicate effectively on a daily basis increased dramatically over the decade of the 1990s.

The various electronic calendars, such as the one included in Microsoft

Outlook Express, not only make it easier for you to schedule activities, but also allow you to share your frequently updated schedule with all those who have with a need to know. In turn, others on your sales team can share their calendars with you. In an instant you can predict sales just by seeing how many sales presentations have been booked, and if the number of booked appointments is below target, you can do something about it.

SALES MEETINGS

Your sales meetings will be more dynamic with PowerPoint presentations. Complicated ideas can more readily be reduced to easy-to-understand graphs and pie charts. Review Chapter 15 for expanded possibilities.

INSTANT REPORTS

Sales and marketing reports can be available immediately. If something is askew, action can be directed toward a remedy almost in an instant. Chapters 3 through 7 show specifics.

BETTER WRITING

Your computer (I prefer the mobility of the laptop) is a marvelous thinking and writing aid. Microsoft Word can help you write letters, check spelling, and format documents. Furthermore, it's legible (unlike many people's handwriting.)

Microsoft Word allowed me to write, and rewrite, my ideas. I could disappear to a remote beach for a few days and tackle a complicated problem, breaking it down into bite-sized paragraphs. A clear definition of a problem is often half the solution. Sometimes, as I wrote about a thorny situation, solutions would magically jump into the Word document. I never had this experience with handwritten notes or the typewriter. Somehow, Word gave innovation and problem solving an entirely new dimension.

CUSTOMER SERVICE

The Internet is a boon to customer service. Chapter 24 reviews some of the options.

SALES BULLETINS AND PAY STATEMENTS

Today, sales bulletins are instant. I remember that in the "old days," the company would close the books on Thursday, print the weekly sales bulletin on Friday, and mail the results. If the mail service was prompt, we got our sales bulletins by Monday—the middle of the following Thursday-through-Wednesday sales week.

Compare that with today. Each company has a day of the week or month when all sales are final. Once the accounting department pushes the "books are closed" button, the information is dispatched to another database, where the results are configured, put into a sales bulletin, and published on the company Web site. Everyone can access sales contest results and recognition bulletins instantly. You or your secretary can print out a copy to post in the sales room.

It's the same for pay statements. Everyone can receive her pay statement electronically. Managers can review all pay statements for their sales group quickly.

The combination of the computer and the Internet is the most powerful new tool in the direct-sales business, just as it is for most businesses. You may well be taking advantage of these new electronic and Internet tools. If so, congratulations. You are a leader in your field. If not, you have an opportunity to ratchet up your success quotient.

QUESTIONS TO ASK YOURSELF

- How has your use of the Internet and the computer increased sales productivity in the past three years?
- Is your sales force using a laptop as the sales binder? If not, what would be the impact if they did?

■ What percentage of your leads are sourced from the Internet? What could you do to expand that source?

Additional reading on the impact computers and the Internet:

■ *Business @ the Speed of Thought* by Bill Gates

■ *The Internet for Dummies* by John R. Levine, Carol Baroudi, and Margaret Levine Young

■ *PC for Dummies,* 9th edition, by Dan Gookin

EIGHTH ESSENTIAL ACTIVITY

LEAD

Sales management leadership inspires salespeople to work hard—willingly. In *7 Secrets to Successful Sales Management,* Jack Wilner claims, "Leadership is the art of bringing out the best in the people you lead." No one is born with the power to inspire; it comes from the determined effort to cultivate and master a pantheon of skills. As Tony Robbins says, "Success leaves clues. If you know the combination, it does not matter who you are."

My first chapter in this section on leadership examines the 12 sales management demons, regularly reviewed in my workshops, that lurk in our dark recesses to defeat all our efforts to strive for excellence. We can do so much right for so many years and have it all tumble down in an instant because of some regretted personal failure. The antidote for each demon shows how to avoid these pitfalls.

After this "don't do that" chapter, we move on to the far more positive examination of the greatest sales leadership characteristics. They are not a great secret; you will no doubt recognize most of them. However, Chapter 28 gives you another opportunity to, as Stephen Covey advocates, "sharpen your saw"—to keep your leadership development awareness at the tip of your consciousness.

We close the book with a recipe for developing a charismatic personality. I know all too well that charisma can be cultivated. Following these techniques, *anyone* can learn how to exude charisma where and when it counts, leading your sales force to the next level of success.

Chapter 29 spells out the prime leadership attributes and emphasizes practices that you can *perform* to demonstrate winning leadership—"what it is" followed by "how to acquire it." When the attribute was already covered in a previous chapter, it is noted but is not repeated.

CHAPTER 27

AVOID THE 12 CAREER-WRECKING DEMONS

He who conquers others is strong; he who conquers himself is mighty.

—Lao-Tzu, Taoist Philosopher

"We have met the enemy and they is us." So said cartoon character Pogo when talking about American involvement in the Vietnam War in the 1970s. I have often thought of this statement when I watched myself or others sabotage success by doing something to diminish or even destroy outstanding sales performance.

All the other chapters in this book are designed to give you the tools to build a profitable direct-sales force. This chapter alone focuses on showing you how to *prevent* taking actions that undermine your commitment, ability, and reputation.

The 12 demons that you meet in this chapter undermine successful sales management. Rather than presenting a single anecdotal incident to begin this chapter, I'll use several stories to illustrate various demons.

Let's review the "dirty dozen" demons with a view that we can prevent some, defuse most, and work around the rest.

DEMON 1: BEING AN ARMCHAIR MANAGER

No sales manager ever earned his promotion sitting behind a desk. The most successful salespeople and junior field managers prefer a hands-on approach. Those with the ambition to earn their promotion to sales manager do not spend much time sitting on a chair, except to work the telephone to make appointments.

David was a dynamic salesperson who built his team by leading from the front. Eventually he hired Matt, a young man who, though neither sophisticated nor experienced in sales, knew enough to copy David's style. Matt worked hard, and his team grew by leaps and bounds. David became satisfied with living off the overrides. He started coming to the office late, leaving early, and ignoring personal selling. Matt's team kept growing; David's personal direct team kept shrinking. Matt maintained the necessary in-the-field work habits and within a year was responsible for more than 90 percent of David's combined sales. David could no longer do what he had once done so well. One weekend he quietly cleared out his desk.

Antidote to Demon 1

When you are promoted, keep doing those things that got you the promotion. Teach them to the people under you. Keep your focus on spending time in the field selling, watching people sell, and having people watch you sell. This is far more important than any activity you can perform while sitting behind your desk.

DEMON 2: "BUTTING" OVER ORDERS

A sales manager can never come out a winner in a "Whose order is it?" dispute against a salesperson. *Never.*

Barney had completed his initial basic sales training just one week prior to his working the encyclopedia sales booth at the mall. He couldn't believe his good luck when, on his first day, a prospect walked up and asked if she could look at the volumes on display. About 30 minutes later Barney had his first order—or so he thought. When Barney's sales manager, Ralph, reviewed the order, he thought he recognized the name of the customer. Sure enough, that same customer had sent in a lead a month before, and Ralph had delivered an in-home presentation without closing the order.

At first Ralph used his position to claim the order; later he backed down, but he still forced a split commission with Barney. Barney wrote a few more orders before quitting a few weeks later. But that incident followed Ralph like a bad order. By insisting on claiming the order, he forfeited the goodwill and trust of his team. Eventually most of the members of his team left, and he was never able to rebuild it successfully. So much was lost for the sake of a single order.

Ideally, every sales organization has a clear-cut policy on butting that prevents those no-win "Whose order is it?" disputes. We all know, however, that in real life such incidents do occur. It's bad enough when a sales manager must arbitrate a dispute between two salespeople on the same team or work with another sales manager to settle a claim between salespeople on different teams. But a sales manager who fights over a claim with a salesperson on her team (or on any other team, for that matter) creates an impossible situation. The righteousness of the claim is not the point. The sales manager loses simply by forcing the issue. Here's why.

First, no one likes to be bullied. Most of us have been programmed since childhood to resent anyone who uses a position of authority for personal gain, especially when it's at our expense. It is assumed that a sales manager who argues that he should prevail in the "Whose order is it?" dispute will win the argument by default, for the simple reason that the boss has clout.

Second, the sales manager's fight to win the butting argument undermines the assumed contract between a sales manager—who implicitly claims, "I will look after you"—and her salesperson—whose tacit response is, "I will give my best effort to sell." The sales manager who tries to win a butting dispute is often perceived as breaking the understood promise that a sales manager puts her people first. Trust is lost, maybe forever.

Third, arguments over client ownership waste a lot of time and create a counterproductive climate. It usually takes at least a week of negative energy to debate these cases, and typically the entire sales force becomes involved. The sales manager makes his case to the salespeople. The other claimant for the order counterattacks. People take sides. Working relationships become strained. Time that should be spent selling and prospecting is instead wasted on political infighting. And even when salespeople are engaging in sales-generating activities, they are less effective because there is a butting problem hanging over the team.

Even if the sales manager finally gives in to the salesperson's counterclaim, the bitter aftermath of the argument will linger for a long time. The debate becomes part of the folklore of that sales group, and the whole sordid event is dredged up from time to time to once again negatively affect the team. Veteran salespeople may even warn newcomers to be careful about their boss.

Antidote to Demon 2

It's only an order. Be a hero. Always give the salesperson (whether the person reports to you or to another manager) the disputed order.

DEMON 3: STINGINESS

No one likes stinginess. In a friend or coworker, it can be irritating; in a sales manager, it can be downright disastrous. Such behavior sends a variety of messages, none of them good. The sales manager is perceived not only as cheap, but as someone who doesn't value the sales force, which undercuts the message that the sales manager is a success model to be emulated.

Some years ago, a housewife turned sales manager had gone from managing zero producers to overseeing a team of more than 30. She continued to have a high rate of personal selling, and her example drove her team to have one of the highest order-per-producer ratios each month. However, when I talked to the people under her, they always brought up the fact that they had to pay for their own soft drinks and snacks at sales meetings. The sales manager would send her secretary down to the convenience store to buy sodas, doughnuts, and other such items, then charge the salespeople for whatever they consumed. This, and other petty types of stinginess, drove her team to distraction. Gradually, this fine team got so caught up in the issue that it faded away. I tried many times to talk the sales manager out of her tight-fisted folly, without success. Not long after, she "retired" to take care of her children.

This is an extreme example. The woman in question had deep problems that caused her to act against her own best interests in small money matters. She lost sight of the fact that a small investment in drinks, snacks, and other small treats for her team would result in an annuity of very large monthly commission checks.

Another case that turned out badly involved charging for photocopying in the sales office.

At first, the manager had no policy on photocopying, which encouraged the salespeople to abuse the privilege. Many of them would make hundreds of copies of their own marketing materials because it cost them nothing. To squash this practice, the sales manager went to the other extreme and instituted a policy of charging for all photocopies—even for a copy of an order. Even though the sales reps understood that they should pay for their own copying, they resented being charged for copies made on behalf of the company.

Many legitimate sales expenses can be charged to the salespeople, depending on the compensation arrangements. Normally, in the full-commission sector of the direct-sales business, sales reps are expected to contribute to training costs when an outside venue is used. Other typical expenses include sales booth shift fees, lead charges, and sales supplies. However, the sales manager must make the distinction between paying small petty costs, which he should pay for out of his pocket, and the bigger marketing or training cost items, where a fair arrangement with the salespeople should be worked out.

Antidote to Demon 3

Pay small expenses out of your pocket with a smile.

DEMON 4: SPENDING MONEY THAT YOU DO NOT HAVE

Rather than being stingy, more sales managers have the opposite problem: spending too much money, usually money that they do not have. An old sales adage makes an erroneous point: "The best way to motivate a salesperson is to keep that person in debt." While a great salesperson will work hard for a short time to dig his way out of debt, this false approach to sales does not represent good management. Debt is negative. Money in the bank is positive.

In the 1970s, I had several direct-sales distributorships in the Caribbean. I had reasonable sales volume. After seven years, my sales track record was good enough for me to be recruited as vice president of an international direct-sales company based in Japan. However, despite my record of good sales for seven years, I left the Caribbean in debt as a result of my aggressive expansion program. I had between 40 and 60 sales reps spread from the Bahamas to Trinidad, all of whom I continually visited from my base on the island of St. Thomas. I used credit cards to pay for airplanes and hotels, and although I racked up huge amounts of interest, I figured that the expansion would make it all worthwhile. I thought I was smarter than the banks, because they charged "only" 18 percent interest for credit cards. I was wrong, and it took me several years to pay off that debt.

Expansion is good, of course. Unfortunately, I did not wait to develop a territory fully before I moved on to the next island opportunity. If I had forced myself to use only cash to expand, I would have expanded more slowly, but, more important, I would have had a stronger and more profitable sales operation.

Yes, there are times when a sales manager should spend money as an investment to produce a future income stream; the opening of a new sales office and supporting a big marketing campaign are two good examples. However, if you wait until you have earned back your investment before starting another new project, you will give your expansion a firm foundation.

The sales industry has its share of compulsive spenders. The urge to buy the newest car or the latest designer bag can be alluring. Some sales managers claim that buying expensive items sets a good example for the people under them; it gives them a dream and shows that that dream is attainable. If you use cash to buy these luxury goods, and you can still save money, that may be true. But if you use credit cards to live an expensive lifestyle—without the funds to pay them off at the end of the month—you set the wrong type of example. Managers who get into debt often leave our industry as failures.

Antidote to Demon 4

Don't spend what you don't have.

DEMON 5: THINKING YOU FINALLY "KNOW IT ALL"

Success can lull us into feeling that we've finally arrived. We can get a bit smug about our stellar performance when our sales results exceed expectations.

The first night I arrived in Japan in October 1978, I had a meeting with the president, Herb Scheidel, whom I had worked for during my Florida book-selling years in the 1960s. Over dinner at a piano bar in Shibuya, he and I reminisced about our many years in sales management. I boasted that my assignment in Japan suited me well because I had so much experience and knew so much about the direct-sales industry. I was 35 years old, and I had 17 years of experience; if I didn't know it all, I thought I came very close.

However, 90 percent of what I know about the direct-sales industry today I learned *after* I informed my boss that I knew it all. Even in retirement, as I read other books on sales management and speak to sales managers in different industries, I know that the learning process is continuing.

Antidote to Demon 5

Attend courses, talk with colleagues, and read with an open mind. Keep trying out new ideas.

DEMON 6: NEGLECTING YOUR HEALTH

The job of a sales manager can be extremely demanding, both physically and mentally. The hours are long, and sales managers need to maintain a high level of energy consistently if they are to sell, motivate, and lead successfully.

During my last year in Asia, two middle-aged sales managers spent time in the hospital, suffering from fatigue. Both of these women had worked more than 20 straight days without a break. They hadn't felt that they had enough time to get some exercise. They just worked. I had failed to get the right message across.

Those sales managers who can't find the time to engage in some type of exercise for a half hour, three or four times a week, will be forced to find time to go to the doctor with colds, stomach problems, fatigue, stress, and other ailments. They will complain about being tired and/or lacking energy. Fit people who exercise regularly and do not smoke have a better chance of reaching their goals than people who are overweight, smoke, and do not exercise. That's just the way it is.

Antidote to Demon 6

Engage in some sort of physical exercise regularly and take at least one three-day weekend break a month.

DEMON 7: TAKING CREDIT FOR SUCCESS

A sales manager who says *I* often has a problem. It's much better to use *we* or the name of another salesperson when giving credit for sales success.

Some years ago, a senior sales executive took credit for a new supplementary product innovation. The added product helped the consumer use the primary product more easily and helped close more orders. Unfortunately, the person who took the credit had not actually done the work. But because the innovator who actually came up with the idea had moved thousands of miles away, this senior sales executive felt that he could get away with claiming the bragging rights.

He was not as safe as he thought, however. The word got back to the product developer that the sales manager had taken complete credit for the new product innovation without recognizing her contribution. She seethed with resentment that someone in a higher power position had stolen glory that legitimately belonged to her. The story eventually leaked out; not surprisingly, other similar stories also surfaced, and soon the negative folklore about this sales executive made the rounds throughout the company. A year later, that executive retired for "personal reasons."

There is irony to be found in this type of scenario. Such a person feels compelled to take credit for every success to win the approval of the "higher-ups." "See what *I* have done!" is his refrain. However, the effect of such bragging is often the opposite of what the braggart intended. Senior management often views such a manager with suspicion. Instead of being impressed by a braggart's claims, the higher-ups see glory hogging as a defect. They understand that one person's taking credit for a team's success is demoralizing to all the others who contributed.

Team members know how to retaliate when the boss takes credit for their idea or contribution. They may no longer cooperate in training or may stop giving suggestions on how to improve the business. A sales manager who gives in to the temptation of taking credit for the efforts of others will find it just about impossible to build effective teamwork.

Antidote to Demon 7

Make heroes. Look for ways to give credit to others. Your sales results are the only bragging you need to do.

DEMON 8: ALCOHOL ABUSE

While this topic could have been part of the section "Neglecting Your Health," I chose to make it separate to make sure that this destroyer of goals gets special treatment. We have all known people who have had alcohol problems. At a certain point, problems with alcohol go beyond being a bad habit and become a disease. I don't need to relate an anecdotal story here; we all have our own. However, I do have some comments I'd like to share.

If you have a problem with alcohol, please, get help. If one of the people under you has this problem, try to get the person to seek medical help. Do not waste your time trying to help this person build a sales team until the disease is being treated. A person who has a drinking problem simply cannot be relied upon. Spend your management development time with someone else—even if that someone else has less ability.

Antidote to Demon 8

If you have a personal problem with alcohol, seek help. Join AA or some other similar organization that can give you help if you simply ask for it. If one of your team members has such a problem, be a compassionate realist. Do not put this person in management until she has addressed the problem by seeking regular help. You can't cure the person; only the person can admit the problem and start treatment.

DEMON 9: HAVING AN AFFAIR WITH A COWORKER

Everyone loves a scandal, as evidenced by the popularity of publications and TV programs that specialize in gossipmongering. Nowhere is this truer than in the workplace. Office affairs are always a distraction. For instance, while the sales manager is conducting a class on overcoming objections, the rest of the group's attention is riveted on two people who are reported to be involved in an affair, eagerly watching for any telltale "signs" between them.

Some years ago, one of the best regional sales managers had an affair with his top producer. Both were married to other people at the time; the affair eventually destroyed both marriages. The scandal produced so much anger among other salespeople (especially the female staff, who, for the most part, were also married) that both of the people involved in the affair quit. Although they married each other, they did not live happily ever. The new marriage ended in divorce, and the senior sales manager never again managed a big sales organization.

No doubt everyone has a similar story. And that's the point. While two single people in the same sales office who fall in love can have a glorious ending, I have *never* heard of a good ending when a married sales manager has a relationship with someone else in the sales organization or on the sales support staff. Since many people view affairs by married people as a violation of trust, they transfer this violation of the marriage trust to the entire trust relationship they have with the boss. They wonder, "If this person is cheating on his spouse, how can he be trusted at all?" "If this person uses her position of power to date salespeople, how will I handle the pressure when I am approached?"

Antidote to Demon 9

If you are married, *never* become involved with anyone in your office, regardless of your problems at home. Never *ever* date a colleague who is married, regardless of his problems at home.

DEMON 10: LACK OF SELF-CONTROL

Strong emotions strongly displayed are one of the hallmarks of the successful sales manager. This visible characteristic helps motivate others to succeed and gives notice to the sales force of convictions firmly held.

This is my sad story, one that I hope you will take to heart. It was 1983. Sales were slow. My boss had told me that he would be patient, but one day he said something to the effect of, "You had better get sales up this month." Although it wasn't exactly a threat, the tone was sharp, which made me mad—boiling mad. After two days of inwardly fuming over the way I had been treated (the insult, of course, grew in magnitude with each mental replay), I decided to quit. To make sure everyone got the point, I copied my letter of resignation to enough people so that my normally forgiving boss would be forced into a position where he could not let me buy my bridge-burning resignation back. I walked out in a moment of triumphant self-righteousness.

My successor built a $50 million business over the next five years.

Giving in to anger often leads to losing self-control. When one person harbors resentment against another or takes a righteous stand on some perceived moral issue, two problems arise. The first is the holding onto the anger. This is ultimately self-defeating, because the negativity of the emotion eats away at the person and keeps her from resolving the issue. The second problem is the loss of self-control. Even though the injured party's point of view may be right, losing her temper often lets the person who caused the problem get away with his initial bad behavior, simply because many people view shouting, cursing, and other displays of anger as worse than the grievance itself.

Antidote to Demon 10

Forgive others, not because they deserve it, but because of the release and contentment it will bring you.

DEMON 11: COMPLAINING ABOUT THE BOSS

"It's my boss's fault." "My boss doesn't support me." If I had a dollar for every time I have heard this excuse for lack of success, I could have retired 10 years ago!

Carl was a great recruiter who wrote a ton of personal orders. But as a divisional sales manager, he had a few faults. He sometimes interfered with his junior managers' salespeople, and he could have spent more money to help the managers under him. One miffed undermanager named Jane overreacted to these minor problems. She started a campaign to get rid of Carl by complaining about him and spreading rumors about his personal life, some of them true. Jane got her wish when Carl finally quit and she was promoted to replace him. But he had the last laugh: a month later, he successfully recruited more than half of Jane's sales force to a competitor.

Years ago on the island of Guam, the Britannica sales manager responded to a "bad boss" complaint by simply stating, "Nobody likes their boss." While this statement is not 100 percent accurate, it does contain an element of truth. We all have within us a certain resentment of authority. We'd all like to do what *we* want to do, without having to solicit the approval or prior permission of our boss.

The responsibility of sales managers is to develop new managers, who, in turn, develop a team. Some new managers may receive more help from their boss than others. Regardless, the responsibility for the success or failure of any sales team belongs to that team's manager. Period. End of story. Any sales manager who blames a senior manager for her failure more than likely is one of those people who go through life proclaiming, "It's not my fault."

The road to success in sales management is paved with actions such as writing personal orders, recruiting good team members, motivating oneself and others, and managing local lead generation. Whenever I hear "It's my boss's fault," I wonder what would happen if instead of spending unproductive time complaining about the boss (which only serves to nourish a defeatist attitude), the manager would just get on with the job of sales management. I suspect his performance would improve.

Antidote to Demon 11

Accept 100 percent of the responsibility for your success or failure.

DEMON 12: MAKING "CONFIDENTIAL" DISPARAGING REMARKS

Any negative remark you make about another person has the potential for—and even the probability of—making its way back to the disparaged person, embellished and exaggerated by the people who have helped it along. There is no such thing as a confidential remark. If you say something about someone else, you should assume that that person will hear it.

Some years ago, I opened a new territory and moved several managers, as a group, to this new place. Both the senior and the junior manager prospered beyond their expectations. The junior manager could be difficult to deal with and sometimes made decisions that were contrary to the wishes of the senior manager. However, she was honest, she produced good sales volume, and she generally had a positive attitude. The senior manager,

Keith, confided to another manager, "I just can't trust Alice." Some time later, Alice heard about this remark. She seethed. She felt that she couldn't trust her boss. One thing led to another, and eventually Alice jumped ship and took most of her people with to a competitor, leaving Keith with less than half of his original sales force.

I often wondered how this situation would have played out if Keith had not confided his frustration in a private conversation with one Alice's peers. Part of success in sales management is getting the best out of difficult people without broadcasting the communication challenges.

We've all heard the children's rhyme, "Sticks and stones may break my bones, but words will never hurt me." This phrase is supposed to mean that words do not hurt people. Well, unfortunately, words *do* hurt people. People become distraught and angry when they learn that someone has spoken ill of them. Such feelings often lie at the root of the "communication problems" that sales managers have with salespeople, other sales managers, or their boss. We sales managers, who earn our living through the effective use of words, should know better than anyone the power of the spoken word.

Antidote to Demon 12

Do not say anything about anyone that you wouldn't say to that person directly.

* * *

The road to success is often as much about avoiding the potholes as it is about choosing the right course. Each of the demons in this chapter has brought down talented, hard-driving managers who did many things right. Many of these managers were charismatic. Most were hard working. All had many good leadership qualities. Yet, when they gave in to human nature's weaker side, they faltered. Some fought back and were given a second chance. Many joined the "what might have been" disappointments.

Success comes to those who avoid mistakes. My old friend and former boss, Herb Scheidel, has said that much of his early career success was the result of his being there. He was neither flashy nor spectacular, but he was consistent. Mature beyond his years, he avoided all the career-interrupting demons. He came to work early each day and did the work. He recruited faithfully. He managed his money well. He kept relations with the administration running smoothly. When there was a vacancy in the upper chain of command, a very young Herb was there. Inexperienced, perhaps, but there. He got the promotion and repeated the process. At age 23, he became district sales manager for three states.

At the end of the day, success often comes to those who master themselves, who exercise self-control over how they live, how they spend, how they treat others, and what they say. It has been my experience that most successful people go through painful growing periods as they learn the art of self-discipline. As with the other skills of sales management, self-control comes to those who make the effort to improve.

QUESTIONS TO ASK YOURSELF

- What one or two demons have held you back?
- What are you doing to address your demons in order to make sure that all your hard work to build a sales empire isn't sidetracked by a personal shortcoming?

Recommended books:

- *My Life* by Bill Clinton
- *Integrity Selling for the 21st Century* by Ron Willingham
- *What's Holding You Back?* by Sam Horn
- *Conquer Fear* by Lisa Jimenez
- *Alcoholics Anonymous* by Alcoholics Anonymous
- *The Decline and Fall of the Roman Empire* by Edward Gibbons

CHAPTER 28
BROADEN LEADERSHIP CHARACTERISTICS

Self-image sets the boundaries of individual accomplishment.

—Maxwell Maltz, Writer on Psycho-Cybernetics

The habits of good sales management don't just happen; they're acquired. That means that the best sales managers aren't born, they're made. If you are a proven, successful salesperson in your industry, if you have demonstrated the right personality and a strong work ethic, if you have overcome the fear of failure and rejection time and again, you have what it takes to be a sales manager. Our lead-off narrative confirms this happy truth one more time as I reveal how I selected a small group of ordinary salespeople who were willing to work extraordinarily hard to build an army of 1,000 sales representatives.

At one point in my career, I interviewed more than 30 people in selecting pioneer sales managers for a new territory. Four people made the initial cut; two more were quickly added. All of them were ambitious, had little or no sales management experience, and were under 30 years of age. I'm proud to say that together we built a multimillion-dollar-a-year business.

We all changed during this growth. The change was constant, as the organization grew from six salespeople to more than a thousand. We kept changing the sales contest rules and prospecting approaches. We would try something new, and, more often than not, it would fail. So we would try something else. However, each time the change we made turned out to be effective, we kept that policy, prospecting technique, hiring ad, or contest rule in effect for a long time.

The wonderful thing about change is that if it fails, you can drop it quickly. If it succeeds, you can continue it forever. One first-rate success wipes out the frustration of 10 small failures.

LEADERSHIP VERSUS MANAGEMENT

There are far more managers than leaders. Leadership is about choices, motivation, and change. Management is about organization and process. As we quoted management guru Peter Drucker in the introduction to the seventh Essential Activity, "Leadership is doing the right things, while managing is doing things right."

Consider the various functions of the job of a sales manager to see the contrast between leadership and management.

Leadership	Management
Making the decision to keep a 90-day schedule	Filling in the dates on your planning calendar with activities
Developing the habit of proactively solving disputes between two salespeople	The actual process of conflict resolution
Maintaining a policy of assigning leads based on who is most likely to convert those leads to orders	Making sure that your salespeople receive the leads on a timely basis
Motivating the people in your sales force to develop their own leads	Providing the necessary tools to help your people develop leads
Making the conscious decision to spend most of your management time with eagles and new people	Allocating your time so that it is to be consistent with your decision

You can be both a good manager and a bad leader. If you teach new sales recruits how to call company leads, that demonstrates good management, because you are teaching a skill. It could also be poor leadership, as it might be more important for new people to learn how to generate their own leads. If all of your reports to the home office are perfect, that's good management. If you are doing these reports personally and losing personal selling or recruiting time when you could assign the task to a secretary, that's poor leadership. If your sales meetings are well organized, that's good management. If you conduct the entire meeting by yourself, that's poor leadership.

Three Reasons for a Sales Manager's Success or Failure

The journey toward excellence travels an uneven highway. We all want to do better, but sometimes we have to do things that we do *not* want to do so that we can achieve success. Great sales managers develop the *habit* of doing things that they do not enjoy.

Every manager has three options in dealing with his responsibilities. Only one of these leads to success.

1. You know what to do, and you do it.
2. You do not know what to do, and thus you cannot do it.
3. You know what to do, and you don't do it.

How would you rate yourself? Which option best describes your choices as a sales manager?

Few of us are exclusively in one category. Of course, we strive to be in the first situation all the time. Sometimes we find ourselves in the second—not knowing what to do. That is easily cured. We can learn. (Studying this book is one way!) The third situation is the tough one. Most of us eventually learn what to do and then fail to *always* choose to do it. In his book *Seven Habits of Highly Effective People*, Stephen Covey makes the case that it's difficult but rewarding to make a habit of possibility number one. Effective leaders know what they have to do and make a habit of doing it.

TEN IMPORTANT CHARACTERISTICS OF THE MODERN SALES MANAGER

While there may be more than 10 characteristics of good sales managers, I wanted to create a list that would be easy to remember. So I have combined certain characteristics that, while not exactly identical, were close enough to group together.

Before you read the list, stop reading now, pause, and list the 10 most important sales management characteristics as you see them. Then review what I have listed. No doubt, we will have both a wide area of agreement and plenty of room for debate.

What is most critical, indeed essential, is for every sales manager and aspiring sales manager to recognize that the sales manager's inner qualities and values must come before technique. Ask yourself: "Who am I?" "Who do I want to become?" All the techniques of lead generation, recruiting, motivation, delegation, and management development must be built on a foundation of good character and good personal characteristics.

Most sales managers already have most of the characteristics of great sales management to some degree. It is the level of intensity of these sales management characteristics that determines the level of your commitment and your power of inspiration to get things done right.

Let's review those characteristics.

1. Change Leadership

Sales management is about constant change. Think for a moment about how much the job of both a salesperson and a sales manager revolves around *changing* for the better. The first starring role of a salesperson is to change a prospect's interest in the product into a decision to buy the product.

The sales manager's recruiting and training role routinely advocates change. In the recruiting interview, you change the applicant's image of the direct salesperson. Training new people often involves changing the sales trainee's perception of how the sales process really works

Dynamic change leaders are innovators. There always seems to be a buzz of activity around them. New product ideas, new prospecting methods, new training concepts continue to germinate. Innovation suggests a better, more interesting tomorrow. Innovators create excitement in the office. These leaders may be right-brained and blessed with imagination, voracious readers of professional publication, or cheerleaders for the innovators on the team. It does not matter where the source of innovation comes from as long as the leader is *never* satisfied with the status quo.

In his book *Good to Great*, Jim Collins hammers home the point that being "good" often stands in the way of being "great." Innovative change leaders rate themselves not against the competition or against other sales offices, but rather against their own high standards for what is possible. Their benchmark is their previous best record results.

Change—even successful change—often causes discomfort. I remember a meeting in which we reviewed proposed changes in our customer service policy. The changes were major. At the close of the meeting, Ron wondered aloud whether this policy was final. Then he asked, "When will the changes stop?" I probably ruined his day when I replied, "Never."

Change during a crisis is easier, because when the business is threatened, everyone is more willing to try something new. This was certainly the case with our children's educational product division in Japan in the late 1990s, when sales and manpower had dropped significantly. We sold fewer than 900 units during the entire month of August—less than half the monthly average of the previous year. Many changes were made in early September 1999 when I arrived as the new president, as we reinvented our early education products business. Thanks to the ideas and leadership of our sales managers, our business turned around.

Change in times of success can be just as important, as it can avoid a later crisis. Polly Sauer, who practically invented local marketing in direct sales in the 1980s, joined our company as marketing consultant when sales were already at a record level. The sales managers had started many local lead-generation programs that were producing results. However, the prospecting changes that Polly introduced made the system far more professional. She made a good thing better and even more successful. Sales jumped to still higher levels.

The old adage, "If it ain't broke, don't fix it," just doesn't apply in the modern business world.

2. Character—It Counts More than Ever

Merriam-Webster defines *character* as follows:

- One of the attributes or features that make up and distinguish an individual
- The complex of mental and ethical traits marking and often individualizing a person, group, or nation
- Moral excellence and firmness

Character is who you are. Your character is what you brought to your company. Character is the set of values that you believe in and *act upon* in all situations, not just when you think you will benefit from doing so.

There are ethical dilemmas in the sales industry. Do we tell the truth or misrepresent it to get an order? Do we talk to a prospect who has already told us that he is waiting for another salesperson from our company to follow up? Do we assign leads based on our publicly stated policy to maximize conversion, or do we do our friends a favor?

I remember, as a 20-year-old college student selling *Collier's Encyclopedia* during summer vacation, working with another field manager, Bill. Bill had a dynamic personality and had become a manager within six months of joining the company. In another six months, he became an office sales manager. I admired his energy, but I was disturbed by the way he fudged on ethics. He once bragged to me that he got two of his salespeople to write orders in his name so that he could qualify for his monthly manager's bonus. Another time, he showed me how to change the age of young prospects to 21 so that the order and credit application would be accepted.

While I couldn't go along his practices, I wondered if perhaps I was just young and naïve about the "real world." It turned out that I was not so naïve after all. Not only was Bill fired a year later because of tricky orders, but he never built a business. He stayed in the encyclopedia business for almost 20 years before dying of liver failure at the age of 39. Sadly, Bill died completely broke. Some companies kept giving Bill "one more chance" because he could produce orders. Shame on both Bill and those companies that continued to overlook his ethics in the pursuit of orders.

You do not have to go to this extreme to find examples. Every person can think of a situation in which she was disappointed in someone because a decision was not fair, a company rule was circumvented and then a lie was told to cover up, or a promise was made and not kept. You know how you felt when you either observed this action or were a victim of it. You probably vowed that you would never disappoint anyone through misrepresentation or manipulation.

Sometimes it's hard. You make a promise. Then, when you are supposed to make good on your promise, you find that keeping your commitment will be more painful than you anticipated. Maybe it will cost you more money than you thought. The money you save, the promise you break—these will cost you the respect of many people for a long time. Following right behind that loss of respect is diminished future income.

At the end of a sales contest, you may be tempted to give an order written by you or another salesperson to someone else to help him win a trip. Sure, maybe the person who wins the trip, with your unfair help, has a moment of appreciation. But can that person ever trust you to be fair in the future? Will that person wonder when it will be his turn to be the victim, instead of the benefactor, of your manipulations?

3. Passion, Positive Attitude, Enthusiasm, and Motivation

"Motivation," according to Tom Reilly in his book *Value-Added Sales Management*, "is the energy within the individual that excites, incites, and ignites behavior."

Passion that is muted isn't passion. Jack Welch, the former CEO and chairman of General Electric, claims in his book, *Jack: Straight from the Gut*, that he always looked for "passion" when evaluating GE management talent. Passion by its very nature is demonstrative and transparent. You know when others have it; others know when you have it.

While it is easy to have a great attitude when sales are soaring, the test of management comes when sales turn south or some plan goes awry. I call this the "unfair test."

The entire sales team looks to the sales manager in times of crisis. During the early hours of September 11, New Yorkers looked to Mayor Rudy Giuliani with fear and uncertainty. His staunch response conveyed the attitude that nothing could bring New York down. He spent more than 24 hours straight visiting the site of the destruction, encouraging rescue workers, talking to families with missing loved ones, and reassuring New Yorkers that their great city would heal.

Giuliani's attitude that New York would recover became contagious. He would have made a great sales manager. A bad sales week, a cancelled sales kiosk at the mall, a computer mix-up with the leads, a problem with the recruiting ad in the newspaper—none of these would have defeated or discouraged Giuliani. "It happens. So what?" would be his response, then he would take the approach of "Let's fix it and move on." That's a leader.

4. Love of Selling

The entire first chapter of this book focuses on one of the most important characteristics of outstanding sales leadership. I never lost the love of giving a sales presentation. I've given more than 10,000 sales presentations over my lifetime, yet each one was different. The excitement of reading the prospect's body language, the process of building up the prospect's desire to own what I was selling, and, finally, the challenge of closing the order never, ever got stale. Motivating my team members became easier when they could see that I loved the selling part of my job—as evidenced by my time in the field.

5. Ambition

The great sales managers want it all—and more. No matter what the current sales volume or the current size if the sales force is, they have the urge to do *better*. Sell *more*. *Now*.

Never apologize for wanting it all. In today's politically correct world, ambition is suspect. When someone like Martha Stewart indulges in material excess or Enron executives are caught fiddling the books, it is said that they were "too ambitious," as though this was a negative character trait that was responsible for their bad behavior. Ambition is a moral neutral. Mother Teresa was just as ambitious as Martha; it just took her to a different place.

Personal ambition is what makes our free-enterprise world work so well. The desire to do better, to own more, to be more secure, to be loved—all these contribute to the reasons why more people are living longer and living better than ever before. It's why your level of ambition will decide your career success. The more ambitious you are, the more you will do what is necessary to be successful on your own terms.

6. Persistence

Calvin Coolidge, who was president of a life insurance company before becoming President of the United States in 1923, said, "Nothing in the world can take the place of persistence. Talent will not; nothing is more common than unsuccessful men with talent. Genius will not; unrewarded genius is almost a proverb. Education will not; the world is full of educated derelicts. Persistence and determination alone are omnipotent."

Persistence is the characteristic that determines how well you pass (or even fail) the "unfair test." What happens when things don't go right?

Persistence is such a great, respected quality that two of the more popular and enduring catch phrases capture its essence. "When the going gets tough, the tough get going" and "If at first you don't succeed, try, try again."

The first phrase clearly recognizes that problems are tests of our mettle. Everyone is subject to misfortune, adversity, and unfair obstacles at some time. The phrase implies that many people stop in the face of adversity, while the tough-minded individual continues to forge ahead.

The second phrase is an instruction on what you must *do* in order to *be* persistent. It's simple, isn't it? Try again. While the mechanical process may be simple, the mental stress can be quite disheartening. If you tried and failed once, might you also fail on a second or third try? It is quite possible, even likely. However, the great sales managers do keep trying. Eventually there is a final try that wins the day.

7. Clear Sense of Direction

The best sales managers have the entire sales force working as a single, driven force to achieve a common purpose successfully. A clear business objective directs all your actions toward reaching specific goals. A popular business course, Management by Objectives, teaches management skills in this way. If you skipped the course, Yogi Berra summed it up nicely: "If you don't know where you are going, you might end up somewhere else."

A clear sense of direction is the gateway to two other leadership characteristics: decisiveness and inner toughness. Once you know where you want to lead your team, then the decision-making process gets a whole lot easier. You know what you want to do, and you have a plan for getting there. No temptation to procrastinate deters you. When you reach a fork in the road, you are confident that you'll make the right choice and do so resolutely.

As a successful, growing sales manager, you must make important decisions on how to keep yourself and others focused. Much like a parent whose decision may be unpopular with a child, you must make the tough choices and accept the consequences. Your clear sales-building purpose puts the steel in your backbone and toughens your resolve. Those who can make the difficult decisions when the need arises are the people who become successful sales managers.

8. Accepting of Responsibility for Failure; Sharing Credit for Success

Admired, effective leaders take complete responsibility for the results of their sales team. *Successful managers do not blame others for failure.*

Once you accept the fact that you, and you alone, are responsible for your results, you will focus on the solution instead of on allocating blame. You organize your team for success based on the situation you are dealt, not the situation you think you deserve. Some psychologists claim that maturity comes when you no longer blame your parents for your shortcomings. In sales management, maturity comes when you do not blame your boss, the company, the sales force, or the economy for the shortcomings of your sales team.

9. Empathy

Also known as "putting yourself in another person's shoes," empathy remains a good rule by which to live. You vicariously experience the feelings and thoughts of those around you. You feel the joy and the pain of your sales partners.

Active listening is the hallmark of empathy. Steven Sample, in his book *The Contrarian's Guide to Leadership*, claims, "Most people are terrible listeners because they think talking is more important than listening. But contrarian leaders know it is better to listen first and talk later."

In his book *Primal Leadership,* Daniel Goleman defines empathy as "sensing others' emotion, understanding their perspective, and taking active interest in their concerns."

Alexander the Great conquered much of the civilized world; his empire stretched from Greece to Western India. He finally stopped his conquest at the Indus River and decided to return to Persia and Greece by the unknown southern coastal route. It turned out to be a disastrous decision. The land was a barren wasteland, and water could be found nowhere.

One day, his loyal soldiers discovered a small plant that yielded enough water to fill half a soldier's helmet. Alexander's soldiers brought the water to him. But he did not drink it; instead, he turned the helmet upside down, letting the precious drops of water disappear into the harsh sand. If his soldiers could not drink water, neither would he.

10. Communication

Success comes only through other people; thus, getting the message across to the team is all-important. Our communication abilities present the picture that defines what people think we are. Ronald Reagan was called "The Great Communicator" because he was able to reach out and say the right words, with the right inflection, with obvious sincerity.

Communicators use all the available verbal and written tools they have at their command to promote common goals and the plans to make those goals happen. A team sales bulletin, a robust agenda at sales meetings, frequent telephone calls and e-mails to key people, quarterly planning meetings, and one-on-one sessions with eagles and new team members are all part of the communication matrix that is available to any sales manager, regardless of her charisma or speaking ability.

William "Skip" Miller's directive to sales managers in his book *Pro-active Sales Management* says, "It's the #1 job of the sales manager to create a culture." He goes on to claim, "There is a great deal of *leverage* to be had when the entire organization is focused on certain objectives and goals as the organization, and the goals and objectives must be established and communicated."

The great communicators develop the necessary social skills to congenially sell their vision. Their communication is constant, relentless, and focused.

The sales manager knows where he is going (or should!) and keeps selling the message to make sure that everyone is on board, moving forward in the same direction. Communication transforms a sales manager's private dream into a clear team vision of a better tomorrow.

*   *   *

Most people possess these 10 wonderful sales management characteristics to some degree; anyone can learn to enhance them. How does your list compare with mine? Did we disagree on a few? You are welcome to make your case for a better list by e-mailing me at mgm@malaghan.net or visiting my Web site at www.malaghan.net.

Find and define the 10 leadership characteristics that will embody a better you.

THE VISION THING

The sum of these characteristics is great. The development of them produces the so-called vision thing. Simply put, you have the vision thing if you can articulate a clear objective, your objective is exciting, and your people understand both the objective and *their* role in achieving it.

When I told 20 of my top sales managers in the fall of 1994 that it was my goal to retire only after I had helped 10 people in the room become millionaires, I had projected a vision that everyone understood, and everyone could see her place in that vision.

This vision thing has been an underpinning throughout this book in various guises: leadership, motivation, goal setting, and so forth. The combination of the 10 characteristics inspires others to do what they should do without your asking them to do it, and to be the best they can possibly be. The more you understand the vision thing, the more your sales volume will increase, the easier you will find it to breed new sales managers, the better and more credible motivator you will be, and the less frequent your sales team turnover will be.

The vision thing can be cultivated, and some techniques for doing so are included in the checklist in the following chapter, on developing personal charisma. The vision thing is a *conscious* process. When you are certain of your vision, your people will believe that you know where you are going and that you are capable of taking them with you.

Review your list of the 10 most important leadership characteristics with your management team as part of your key-person training program.

QUESTIONS TO ASK YOURSELF

- What are your three strongest leadership characteristics?
- What are the areas where you have the greatest opportunity for improvement?
- Who are your sports, political, and business heroes? Why?
- Think of the teachers, relatives, and friends you admire. What is about them that engenders your respect?

Recommended books that bring leadership alive:

- *Leadership Is an Art* by Max De Pree
- *Good to Great* by Jim Collins
- *Built to Last* by Jim Collins and Jerry Porras
- *Who Moved My Cheese?* by Spencer Johnson, M.D.
- *Theodore Rex* (Biography of Theodore Roosevelt) by Edmund Morris
- *Henry V* by William Shakespeare
- *Any* biography of Abraham Lincoln

CHAPTER 29

BUILD A CHARISMATIC PERSONA

I have found if you love life, life will love you back.
— Arthur Rubinstein, Conductor and Composer

Charisma—what it is, how to acquire it, and how to maintain it—is the focus of this last chapter.

Every boss projects an image. For sales managers, developing the right image is an important part of the job. Inevitably, your salespeople will form a collective opinion about you, but you needn't be a passive bystander at this exercise. In fact, the best leaders are conscious of this phenomenon and make an effort to shape their sales team's opinion of them. They do this by consistently operating with integrity, having high standards for themselves and their salespeople, and making it clear that they won't compromise on character issues. They also make the effort to *do* things, to develop the habits of "highly effective sales managers." This excerpt from my award-acceptance speech is an example of how sincerely sharing your innermost feelings with the people you lead continues to build your leadership persona.

> It had been 10 years since I had arrived in Taipei. I had started with vacant offices, no salespeople, and a few doubts, but a lot of hope. Today the crowd at our company's Chinese New Year party numbered 1,000 sales and administrative personnel. My wife, Tomoko, and I visited each of the 100 celebration tables, exchanging many a *compei* with a clink of our champagne glasses. (I had learned to feign a sip by that time!)
>
> We hugged many people. We thanked everyone (sometimes tearfully) for making our dreams come true. Some of the people in the crowd were grateful that they were one of the millionaires I had promised to create eight years earlier in Manila. I, too, had prospered beyond my wildest imagination. Just as I was about to give the short end-of-the-party speech, Herb, who had convinced me to come to Taiwan a decade ago, presented me with a Rolex watch in honor of my 10 years of service. The memories flooded back. I couldn't speak for a minute.

Finally, looking at the audience through misty eyes and putting the watch on my right wrist, I pledged, "This watch will always be on Taiwan time, to the end of my days, to remind me of the opportunity you have given me." It was an emotional and charismatic moment, because the sentiment was genuine. Today I still wear that watch—and, as always, it runs on Taiwan time.

It always surprised me when someone said, "You are charismatic." When a Tom Cruise or a Michael Jordan enters a room, he brings with him a magnetism that draws attention—that's charisma. Ronald Reagan standing on a podium facing the Berlin Wall, saying, "Mr. Gorbachev, tear down this wall" or Martin Luther King delivering his "I have a dream" speech—that's charisma. When I walked into a room full of strangers, no one noticed. Yet, when I used my persona to lead the people in my organizations, things would start to happen. Sales increased; expectations changed; goals were set, achieved, and surpassed. Looking back, I guess I did have a type of stealth charisma. It sorta snuck up on you.

Franklin D. Roosevelt was confined to a wheelchair and spoke softly. Ray Charles was blind. Yet they were undeniably charismatic. The point is, you don't have to be a Tony Robbins to influence and inspire people. *Anyone* can develop a magnetic, inspiring leadership style. It's a matter of ambition, commitment, and learned technique.

Cynics who think that learning to develop a persona sounds contrived or manipulative have missed the point. If you aspire to be a sales manager, you no doubt have already cultivated some leadership traits. Conscious understanding and purposeful development of those attributes will accelerate the maturation of your charisma. Exceptional sales management is not the natural outcome for a few people who have the gift of gab and enjoy telling people what to do. Our honorable "make things happen" profession rewards those who build on their strengths to develop a leadership persona and use it to increase sales through the efforts of others.

One effective way to consciously develop your leadership style is to read. Think of this as exercise for your leadership skills: Reading will keep them in shape. The following suggestions will enhance your reading skills:

- Be an active reader. Keep a yellow highlighter handy to draw attention to important points and a pen to write down "great thoughts" along the margin.
- Obvious subjects for your reading list include leadership, management, self-help, and motivation and inspiration. But stretching

your reading to embrace biographies of leaders from all fields—military, political, religious, and business leaders—and books on philosophy will serve you well.

■ Subscribe to magazines such as *Selling Power*, *Sales and Marketing*, and *Direct Sales Journal*. *Fortune* magazine almost always features stories on the world's best leaders.

■ Audio books convert driving and standing in line to dual-use activities.

Leadership charisma does *not* depend on your ability to be a great motivational speaker, although it obviously helps if you are. If that were required, few of us would ever inspire others. However, almost anyone can learn how to use a can-do attitude, the right words at the right time, and positive actions to lead their salespeople to success.

This chapter will demonstrate the techniques that produce a magnetic, inspiring, charismatic leader. By using a series of small actions, anyone can learn to master the art of dynamic leadership. It's all there for the taking.

Let's review the following list of characteristics that contribute to this magnetic quality called "charisma." Check to see which you already have and which you want to acquire. Some of the items may seem obvious. Yet I have observed thousands of sales managers ranging from poor to great, and I can tell you that the obvious doesn't seem so obvious in practice.

At the foundation of every great leader's success lies the respect of the people he leads. The more of these characteristics you can check off, the more respect you have earned. If you can check off most of these leadership characteristics, you are already a charismatic leader.

YOU LEAD BY EXAMPLE

You set the pace by your example. Leading by example is good in any business, but it is especially critical in managing salespeople, who start every pay period unemployed until they sell an order and who can quit at any time. What you *do* is more important than what you preach. Consider the example you set when you

■ Show enthusiasm for personal selling.

■ Observe selling presentations in the field.

- Relish being the first to try new prospecting methods.
- Are the first person in the office and the last to leave.
- Come to work dressed for success.
- Show respect for and courtesy to others by saying "please" and "thank you."
- Always tell the truth, especially when it's inconvenient.
- Say "I'm sorry" with conviction and sincerity when you make a mistake.

YOU MANAGE YOUR MONEY WELL

In our business, the sales manager who can manage her own money is the sales manager who will endure. The myth that spending more money than you have will keep you motivated is just that—a myth. Being broke or behind on your bills is a negative drain on your psyche and a big demotivator for your people. As a good money manager, you

- Pay your bills on time
- *Never* borrow money from the people under you or your peers.
- Avoid asking for advances from the company.
- Save money in the bank for a rainy day.

YOU ARE THE SLUMP BREAKER

A sales slump in your group or by one of your key people is just one of those unfair tests of sales management. How you respond to a slump tells everyone around you what kind of a leader you are. You proactively create some excitement and action with your group by

- Organizing prospecting parties.
- Conducting a three-hour, back-to-basics training program.
- Leading a role-playing contest.
- Planning something new, such as a field trip, a new prospecting technique, a new sales package, or a mini-contest.

- Doing something, doing more.
- Going into the field yourself and writing an order. (See the first characteristic.)

YOU WORK TO STAY FIT AND HEALTHY

It takes stamina to manage a sales force: to work long, hard hours and to do so with robust enthusiasm. Your sales team will either feed off your energy or starve for the lack of it. Your people look at you to catch a glimpse of what their life will be like a few years into the job. If you are not fit and healthy, your people will assume that working for you will lead them down the same path.

You can show them you lead a healthy lifestyle by

- Getting regular exercise, playing a sport, or going to the gym.
- Eating sensibly, including a hearty breakfast.
- Organizing a sports night to promote your sales partners' good health while simultaneously engaging in team building.
- Recharging your batteries by taking one long weekend break every month and scheduling several mini-vacations a year.
- Climbing at least four flights of stairs if your office location allows it.
- Promoting office golf and/or tennis tournaments.

YOU CREATE A SENSE OF URGENCY

Your most efficient weapon against the bane of all human progress—procrastination—is your ability to instill a sense of urgency in your sales team. The number one reason that salespeople don't earn more money is that they put off prospecting "until tomorrow." You generate a sense of urgency by

- Demonstrating the habit of "doing it now, not later."
- Always setting a completion date for tasks.

- Walking briskly and with purpose.
- Gathering facts quickly and making decisions promptly.
- Learning to hate personal procrastination.

YOU ACT PROACTIVELY

Proactivity in a sales manager translates into more of the sales manager's time being spent in the desirable time quadrant "not urgent and important."

Taking the initiative has its risks. You may fail. You may anger others who resent your acting on your own.

The former national sales manager of Encyclopedia Britannica, Bob Baseman, faced disaster in the 1970s when a three-month newspaper strike interrupted his recruiting in Detroit, Michigan. In those days, the *only* method used to recruit salespeople was through classified ads. Bob, who had built his reputation at Britannica by taking the initiative, used alternative recruiting methods. Not only did his efforts *increase* recruit response, but sales actually grew during the strike. He passed the "unfair test" in a big way.

Being proactive means that you

- Don't wait for someone else to solve the problem.
- Address problems before they reach the crisis stage.
- Accept responsibility for becoming part of the solution instead of being part of the problem by complaining or doing nothing.
- Anticipate problems and opportunities and introduce changes accordingly.
- Don't simply hope that problems go away, but jump in and start the solution process.

YOU ACT ASSERTIVELY

Some sales managers avoid being assertive; they are afraid that they might offend someone or draw attention to themselves. For people who want to succeed as sales managers, I have three words of advice: "Get over it." It is the job of a salesperson and a sales manager to be assertive. The sales talk is the very model of good assertiveness. We do everything we can, ethically, to get the customer to sign the order. We know that if we are too assertive, we'll alienate the customer and lose the order; if we are not assertive enough, the customer will "think it over."

It takes practice, but you can learn to walk the assertiveness line successfully by

- Making your case when you believe in something.
- Presenting a new, perhaps controversial idea for the company with confidence and professionalism.
- Standing up for a sales rep who has been wronged by a company decision.
- Calling your boss with your new idea.
- Putting an immediate end to any questionable practices by your salespeople.
- Testing new ideas.

YOU SPEAK WELL IN PUBLIC

Since all sales managers of a direct-sales force have spent years of selling, it is safe to say that we have mastered the art of speaking to strangers—which is not quite the same as speaking to an entire room full of strangers, better known as public speaking. While we may never be mistaken for Ronald Reagan or Martin Luther King, we can make the commitment to be the best speaker we are capable of becoming. Once you become a sales manager, public speaking obligations will soon follow. Unless you are already a compelling and captivating speaker, I recommend that you

- Attend the Dale Carnegie course.
- Join a Toastmaster's club to gain valuable public speaking experience and peer feedback.
- Use the speaking techniques suggested in Chapter 13.
- Attend speaking programs like those offered by Zig Ziglar, Tom Hopkins, or Tony Robbins.

YOU USE INNOVATION

You want your team to look to you as the problem solver. You know how to use innovation effectively, whether you're responding to changing conditions or just giving your salespeople something new to keep their enthusiasm and passion fresh. Try the following:

- *Steal*! Steal (or the more politically correct term, "borrow") ideas from any source.
- Conduct brainstorming sessions with your sales partners.
- Attend outside sales courses and speeches and take notes.
- Network with sales managers that you respect.
- Understand that it's okay for new ideas to fail because the good innovations can be used over and over while the bad ones are dropped quickly.

YOU ARE A CHANGE AGENT

In the previous chapter, we explained that effective leaders know how to use change in their never-ending quest for excellence. But random, irresponsible change can be disruptive, damaging, and downright disastrous. So, your first step is to ask, "What is it that I want to change, and why? What do I want the outcome to be?"

The most effective change agents are those sales managers who

- Believe that everything in the sales organization can be improved. They are not satisfied with the status quo.
- Engage in team exercises to review sales objectives and the changes that will be needed to reach them. You might review Chapters 14 and 15 for specific methods.
- Actively encourage their best salespeople to consider a transition to management.
- Help the members of your sales force change the way they allocate their time. Chapter 23 provides the details.
- Stand at the forefront of change when the company implements a new policy.

YOU ALWAYS APPEAR ENTHUSIASTIC

We started this book with an introduction around the theme "What's the good news?" because it shows the can-do attitude and commitment of the successful sales manager. When things get tough, the great leaders maintain this "good news" outlook—genuinely, because they know that every problem has a remedy.

When you consistently put in the time and effort to learn the skills of sales management, you build a confidence in yourself and your team that will get you past the rough patches. You can ask your team, "What's the good news?" without fear because, through your enthusiasm and your work ethic, you have created the valid expectation that tomorrow will always be better than today.

As Frank Bettger asserted in his classic book *How I Raised Myself from Failure to Success in Selling*: "If you want to feel enthusiastic, first you have to ACT enthusiastic." The more often you put on a show about your passion for your job and for the people around you, the more the show becomes your reality.

When my daughter was five, she once asked me if I was happy. When I replied, "Yes," she suggested, "Why don't you tell your face?" Let your people recognize passion in you. Here's how:

- Smile a lot.
- Walk into the office with an air of purpose.
- Say good and positive things about people—and mean them.
- Exude a love of life.
- Cultivate the use of positive words like *can, will,* and *do* and avoid their negative counterparts: *can't, won't,* and *don't.*
- Develop a personal, upbeat greeting, such as, "What's the good news?"
- When people ask you, "How are you doing?" respond with something like, "Fantastic and amazing."
- Empathize with a problem for a few seconds, then move on to the "What are we going to do about it?" phase immediately.
- See opportunities in problems.

It is your outward demeanor that lets everyone *know* that you have a resolute attitude. Remember the TV pictures of Giuliani after September 11?

You did not see a despondent, broken man, but rather a person with the energy, determination, and desire to respond positively in the face of disaster.

YOU POSSESS A PASSION TO GET THINGS RIGHT

One of the thrills of leadership comes from seeing a job done right. This reward doesn't depend on a lucky strike, but is a direct consequence of a sales manager's dedication to follow-through. Champion sales leaders never assume that "somehow it'll work out"; they make sure that it does.

Take a proactive approach to doing the job right by showing your sales team that you

- Pay attention to details.
- Follow the adage "Inspect what you expect," as coined by Joe Adams, former president of Encyclopedia Britannica, England.
- Create agendas for every sales meeting.
- Provide prospecting manuals for each technique.

YOU ACCEPT FULL RESPONSIBILITY

The sales business is a people business. Your reputation can make or break you. When you consistently accept responsibility for mishaps, keep your word, pay what you promised—in other words, do what you said you would do—you build a reputation for honesty and integrity. That's money in the bank for a sales manager.

You exhibit true leadership when you

- Admit it quickly when you make a mistake.
- Say "I'm sorry" with sincerity and conviction when you've hurt another person.
- Acknowledge "It's my fault" when business is not booming.
- Follow through on a promise.

YOU OPERATE WITH TRANSPARENCY

Transparency, in this context, means that you are fair, consistent, and predictable in how you lead your team. You make major decisions in conjunction with the people under you and your boss. You don't resort to special deals or hidden agendas when handing out leads, assigning time slots at selling events, or providing money for local lead-generation efforts.

Show your people that they can count on you by

- Assigning leads openly according to an established policy based on each person's closing ability.
- Teaming new recruits with junior managers following a standard practice that everyone understands.
- Sharing all sales reports with your entire sales team.

YOU ACT AS A DREAM MERCHANT

The successful commission or salary-draw-plus-bonus salesperson survives on dreams. The next order, the next big week, and the next promotion are all essential components of the daydreams that drive salespeople to try harder. Your job is to protect and nourish those dreams, to create the expectation that tomorrow will always be better than today, and to make this possible by giving them the tools to support that expectation. Refer to Chapters 19, 20, and 21 to review the steps in this process.

Keep the dream alive for your salespeople by

- Establishing and maintaining huge compelling goals in your own life.
- Sharing those dreams with your sales partners.
- Helping your team members create their own huge compelling goals.

YOU SHOW THAT YOU CARE

The relationship between a sales manager and a salesperson is nothing like the relationship between an administrator and a regular salaried employee.

The head of the engineering department at Ford doesn't constantly have to spend hours motivating people to show up for work. You do.

Most of us pledge, "I care," but salespeople tend to be skeptical of such promises. Nothing builds credibility and loyalty like *showing* that you care. A few ways you can do that are by

- Attending weddings and funerals.
- Visiting sales reps and their families in hospitals.
- Sending birthday, work anniversary, and Christmas cards. (If you really want to make a statement, send the ladies roses and the men a tie.)
- Learning the names of the salespeople's children, parents, spouses, and significant others and asking about them by name.
- Granting a person time off to solve a family crisis without laying on the guilt.
- Using body language and taking notes when listening to show that you care.
- Going into the field with your sales reps when they hit a rough spot. (You do not cop out by giving a "motivational talk" in lieu of going into the field.)

YOU DEVELOP A FAMILY

Salespeople tend to be social animals. Relationships, recognition, and a sense of belonging are more important to most salespeople than to the general populace. If you can create a sense of family in your sales organization, you will be rewarded with less turnover and fewer people problems. Practical family-building habits include

- Ordering pizza for the weekly telephone appointment party.
- Scheduling regular social activities with your team.
- Including spouses and significant others in many of your social events.
- Volunteering your home for the monthly team barbeque.
- Seeing to it that no one ever celebrates Thanksgiving alone.
- Organizing a comedy club night with your sales team.

YOU CHEER YOUR TEAM ON

In my 42 years of managing salespeople, no one ever complained that I said "thank you" too often. People never tire of hearing, "You're doing great. Keep up the good work!"

For salespeople, recognition often exceeds money as a motivator. Give the other person credit for success, even—in fact, particularly—when you might make the case that you were the greater cause of that success. Nothing pleases sales associates more than to be told by a third party, "I heard you came up with that good idea." They will work even harder to justify your high opinion and expectations of them.

Some ways in which you can cheer your team on are

- Giving credit to others whenever you can.
- Jotting congratulatory notes on pay statements.
- Sending e-mails acknowledging a special achievement with a cc to the upper chain of command.
- Beginning every meeting by recognizing a person or a team.

Refer to Chapter 20 for more opportunities to recognize your salespeople for their efforts.

YOU ARE A STORY TELLER

The Bible has remained a best-seller for two millennia not just for its great wisdom, but for its many wonderful stories. The Old Testament offers tales of unparalleled drama. In the New Testament, Jesus holds the attention of his listeners through his telling of entertaining parables.

You can use this same principle to make an indelible point to your salespeople. If you have not already done so, you want to:

- Develop a repertoire of stories that fit many occasions. (Of course, be careful not to tell the same story to the same audience too often!)
- Borrow stories from books you read, movies you watch, speeches you have heard, and anyone who ever told a story that you liked.

YOU KNOW HOW TO USE THE UNEXPECTED AND THE EXTRAORDINARY

When you exploit the drama of the unexpected, you build up your team, boost sales, and enhance your reputation as a leader. Extraordinary events create powerful shared memories that last forever and act to hold a group together. The sales partners who joined me in a variety of adventures, from bungee jumping to sleeping on the Great Wall of China to attending the play *Miss Saigon* on Broadway, have never forgotten these intoxicating bonding moments. The more indelible the memory, the stronger the team-building bond.

You may not have the budget that comes with managing a sales force of hundreds. However, almost every sales manager lives near someplace interesting that could provide a powerful bonding memory. Doing something out of the ordinary that most of your team would never do by themselves has a positive and dramatic effect. You will find this to be a fun and exciting way to confirm your reputation as a magnetic leader.

Some ideas on the unexpected and extraordinary things you might like to try include

- Announcing a sudden "double contest points" bonus during a certain week.
- Sending 100 red roses for a special achievement.
- Creating dramatic memories through activities like bungee jumping, white-water rafting, or scuba diving.
- Proclaiming a "beat the boss" contest. Issue a challenge to any two sales associates that you can submit more sales production in a three-day period than they can *combined*.
- Giving a lead rebate on old lead orders submitted within a short time frame.
- Declaring that you'll hold a drawing for two tickets to some special event for all those turning in an order *today*.

* * *

You now have more than a hundred specific actions to choose from to exemplify your leadership style. Demonstrating a combination of many leadership actions creates a powerful persona.

You can embody these traits as part and parcel of your ever-developing leadership persona. Make up your own list of actions that will create and sustain the self-image you want to project. Keep in mind that what you do must be genuine or your image will be that of a phony.

All the persona-building traits flow from a single source: If you love what you do, the people around you will often be inspired to do the same.

QUESTIONS TO ASK YOURSELF

- Were any of these persona-building activities beyond your competencies?
- How many of these practices are already part of your leadership practices?
- Which additional practices do you feel would help you develop your own unique charismatic leadership style?

Recommended books to help build your leader persona:

- *Jack: Straight from the Gut* by Jack Welch
- *Leadership Secrets of Attila the Hun* by Wess Roberts
- *The 21 Irrefutable Laws of Leadership* by John C. Maxwell
- *The Prince* by Niccolo Machiavelli
- *How to Win Friends and Influence People* by Dale Carnegie

INDEX

ABOUT THE AUTHOR

Michael G. Malaghan is qualified to write this book on sales management development for the simple reason that he did it—many times in many places. What he did was convert good salespeople into outstanding sales managers. Few leaders have come close to developing 1,000 sales managers over a lifetime. Mike has.

Mike started out as an 18-year-old door-to-door encyclopedia salesman working his way through college. He finished his career 41 years later as president of a company, leading five direct-sales organizations spread across Hong Kong, Taiwan, and Japan. Exactly how he developed sales managers rapidly so that he grew from 200 salespeople to 2,000 salespeople is the subject of Mike's book.

"Sales management development is not just motivation; rather, it is a set of skills systematically taught," according to this master of the eight Essential Activities successful sales managers must do every day.

You are invited to visit Mike's Web site at www.malaghan.com. He offers tele-seminars to support this book. Nothing would please him more than your sending him an e-mail asking him about his availability to accelerate the sales management development in your company.